# Routledge International Handbook of Internet Gambling

T0227540

Internet gambling is a rapidly growing phenomenon, which has profound social, psychological, economic, political, and policy implications. Until recently, Internet gambling has been understudied by the research community, but now a growing body of literature is emerging, on all aspects of Internet gambling and its attendant implications.

As jurisdictions around the world grapple to understand the best way to respond to Internet gambling from a commercial, regulatory, and social perspective, scholarly studies of Internet gambling are becoming an ever more crucial resource. The *Handbook of Internet Gambling* consolidates this emerging body of literature into a single reference volume. Its 20 chapters comprise groundbreaking contributions from the world's leading authorities in the commercial, clinical, political, and social aspects of Internet gambling.

It is sure to be a foundational resource for academics, students, regulators, politicians, policy makers, commercial providers, and health care professionals who have an interest in understanding the history, dynamics, and impacts of Internet gambling in a global context.

**Robert J. Williams** is a Professor in the Faculty of Health Sciences at the University of Lethbridge, Alberta, and a Coordinator for the Alberta Gambling Research Institute. Dr Williams teaches courses on gambling and provides frequent consultation to government, industry, the media, and public interest groups. He is one of the world's best-funded gambling researchers and a leading authority in the socioeconomic impacts of gambling, Internet gambling, prevention of problem gambling, the proportion of gambling revenue deriving from problem gamblers, the prevalence and nature of gambling in Aboriginal communities, the etiology of problem gambling, and best practices in the population assessment of gambling and problem gambling.

**Robert T. Wood** is an Associate Professor of Sociology, and Dean of the School of Graduate Studies at the University of Lethbridge, Alberta. Over the past decade, Dr Wood has been involved in a number of large-scale research projects, dealing with various socio-cultural aspects of problem gambling. He is known particularly for his studies on Internet gambling, the link between government gambling revenue and problem gamblers, and the prevention of problem gambling among teens.

**Jonathan Parke** is a Senior Lecturer at Salford Business School, University of Salford. Dr Parke has published over 30 peer-reviewed journal articles, book chapters, government reports, and other publications and has given over 40 conference papers and talks regarding Internet gambling, poker-playing, electronic gaming machines, and gambling-related risk.

# Routledge International Handbook of Internet Gambling

Edited by
Robert J. Williams, Robert T. Wood
and Jonathan Parke

LONDON AND NEW YORK

First published 2012 by Routledge

2 Park Square, Milton Park, Abingdon, Oxon OX14 4RN
711 Third Avenue, New York, NY 10017, USA

*Routledge is an imprint of the Taylor & Francis Group, an informa business*

First issued in paperback 2017

*British Library Cataloguing in Publication Data*
A catalogue record for this book is available from the British Library

*Library of Congress Cataloging in Publication Data*
Routledge international handbook of internet gambling / edited by Robert J. Williams,
Robert T. Wood, and Jonathan Parke. -- 1st ed.
p. cm.
Includes bibliographical references and index.
1. Internet gambling. I. Williams, Robert J. II. Wood, Robert T., 1972- III. Parke,
Jonathan. IV. Title: International handbook of internet gambling. V. Title: Handbook of
internet gambling.
GV1302.5.R678 2012
795.0285'4678--dc23

ISBN: 978-0-415-59443-1 (hbk)
ISBN: 978-1-138-11701-3 (pbk)

Typeset in Times New Roman
By Saxon Graphics Ltd, Derby

To our wives, Susan, Kristin, and Jane, who have provided the ongoing support needed for our academic efforts.

# Contents

# Illustrations

## Figures

## Tables

# Contributors

**Warwick Bartlett** is Chief Executive of Global Betting and Gaming Consultants, which he founded in 1998. He has been involved in the gambling industry since the 1960s and is chairman of the Association of British Bookmakers (ABB).

**Yale D. Belanger**, PhD, is Associate Professor of Native American Studies at the University of Lethbridge, Alberta, Canada. He is the author of *Gambling with the Future: The Evolution of Aboriginal Gaming in Canada* and *Ways of Knowing: An Introduction to Native Studies in Canada*, and the editor of *Aboriginal Self-Government in Canada: Current Trends and Issues* and *First Nations Gaming in Canada*.

**Bo J. Bernhard** is an Associate Professor of Sociology and Hotel Management at the University of Nevada, Las Vegas, where he also serves as Executive Director of the UNLV International Gaming Institute. A fifth-generation Las Vegan, Dr Bernhard has delivered lectures about gambling's sociological impacts on six continents.

**Phill Brear** was appointed Gibraltar's Gambling Commissioner in July 2011 following four years as Head of Gambling Regulation. He was Director of Operations with the British Gambling Commission from 2005 to 2007. Phill holds a first class Management degree from Manchester University, a diploma in Criminology from Cambridge University and the Queen's Police Medal.

**Jeffrey L. Derevensky**, PhD, is Professor and Director of Clinical Training in School/ Applied Child Psychology and a Professor in the Department of Psychiatry at McGill University. He is the co-director of the International Centre for Youth Gambling Problems and High Risk Behaviors and is a clinical consultant to numerous hospitals, school boards, government agencies, and corporations.

**Helen Doll** is a Senior Medical Statistician in the Health Services Research Unit, Department of Public Health, University of Oxford.

**William H. Dutton** is a Professor of Internet Studies at the Oxford Internet Institute, University of Oxford.

**David Forrest** is an economist who trained at the University of Western Ontario. He specializes in economic and econometric analysis of the sports and gambling sectors. He is

Professor of Economics in the University of Salford, UK, and Honorary Professor, Macau Polytechnic Institute.

**Sally Gainsbury** is a clinical psychologist and Post Doctoral Research Fellow in the Centre for Gambling Education and Research, Southern Cross University, Australia. Dr Gainsbury has been awarded over AUD$1.53 million in grants, published numerous papers and presented at international conferences. Her research has focused on Internet gambling, responsible gambling strategies, youth, and Internet-based treatment. Dr Gainsbury is the Associate Editor for *International Gambling Studies* and a reviewer for journals and research organizations.

**John Geddes** is a Senior Clinical Research Fellow and Professor of Epidemiological Psychiatry and Director of the Centre for Evidence-Based Mental Health, University of Oxford.

**Guy M. Goodwin** is W. A. Handley Professor of Psychiatry, Oxford University Department of Psychiatry.

**Mark D. Griffiths** is a Chartered Psychologist and Director of the International Gaming Research Unit at Nottingham Trent University, UK. He has published over 300 refereed research papers, three books, 65 book chapters, and over 1,000 other articles. He has won ten national and international awards for his research.

**George Häberling** is a Swiss attorney specializing in gambling, Anti Money Laundering compliance and commercial law. He is the author of Liechtenstein's new Gaming Act and regulations and is currently involved in various Swiss gambling legislation projects. www.haeberling-law.ch

**Keith Hawton** is a Professor of Psychiatry at Oxford University Department of Psychiatry and Director of the Centre for Suicide Research.

**Jakob Jonsson** is a clinical psychologist and PhD student with experience from the field of problem gambling since 1992. He works at Spelinstitutet, a private company specialized in problem and responsible gambling. Jakob is a member of the advisory board of Swedish Longitudinal Gambling Studies (SWELOGS) and the executive committee of the European Association for the Study of Gambling (EASG).

**Sytze F. Kingma** is Lecturer in the field of organizational space and technology at the department of Organization Sciences, VU University Amsterdam. Kingma has published widely on the topic of gambling and is the editor of *Global Gambling: Cultural Perspectives on Gambling Organizations* (Routledge, 2010).

**Richard A. LaBrie**, EdD, is an Instructor in Psychiatry at Harvard Medical School and Associate Director for Data Analysis at the Division on Addiction (DOA), Cambridge Health Alliance. Dr LaBrie's efforts at DOA include being Principal or Co-Principal Investigator of seven research projects and author of 28 peer-reviewed publications.

**Debi A. LaPlante**, PhD, is an Assistant Professor of Psychology at Harvard Medical School and Associate Director of the Division on Addiction, Cambridge Health Alliance. Dr LaPlante's research interests include epidemiological assessment of the natural history of addiction and the development of evidence-based early detection and intervention tools for addiction.

**Joanne Lloyd** is a Senior Postdoctoral Researcher at the Department of Psychiatry, Oxford University.

**John L. McMullan**, PhD, is a Professor of Sociology and Criminology at Saint Mary's University in Halifax, Nova Scotia, Canada. Professor McMullan is the author or co-author of eight books, twelve government reports, and over 60 academic articles on business crime; criminal organization; law enforcement; media; crime and justice; gambling and advertising; and gambling, crime, and social policy. He is a commissioner of the Law Reform Commission of Nova Scotia and a member of the executive board of the Nova Scotia Criminal Justice Association.

**Andrew Montgomery** is a Senior Agent with the Nevada Gaming Control Board. Born and raised in Washington DC, Andrew moved to Las Vegas and has spent his career in gaming regulation. He received a Masters of Business Administration and Masters of Hotel Administration from the University of Nevada, Las Vegas.

**Melody Morgan-Busher** has worked with the Internet gambling sector in various senior independent roles since this activity arrived in Europe in the late 1990s. She has enjoyed privileged access to over 100 Internet gambling operations of all sizes and types. She has a Masters in eBusiness and a first degree in Physics. Recently she has been engaged to provide condensed training to executives involved in Internet gambling.

**Sarah E. Nelson**, PhD, is an Assistant Professor of Psychology at Harvard Medical School and Associate Director of Research at the Division on Addiction, Cambridge Health Alliance. Dr Nelson's research interests include the development and distribution of gambling problems, driving under the influence (DUI), and other addictive behaviours.

**Adrian J. Parke** is a senior lecturer specializing in addiction disorders in the School of Psychology at the University of Lincoln, UK. Dr Parke is currently a member on the National Expert Panel for Electronic Gaming Machines (EGMs) in Britain, for the British Gambling Commission, and also provides academic research consultation for Internet gaming operators regarding responsible gambling strategies.

**Jonathan Parke** is a senior lecturer in Consumer Behaviour at Salford Business School, University of Salford, UK. Dr Parke has published over 30 peer-reviewed journal articles, book chapters, government reports and other publications and has given over 40 conference papers and talks regarding Internet gambling, gambling-related risk, self-regulation and sustainable practices in gambling provision. He also acts in a consultant capacity to regulators, industry and other stakeholders.

**Lorien Pilling** is a Director of Global Betting and Gaming Consultants. He has previously worked for William Hill and is a member of the Society for the Study of Gambling.

**Aunshul Rege**, PhD, is an Assistant Professor of Criminal Justice at Temple University in Philadelphia, USA. Her interests include cybercrime; environmental criminology and offender rationality; terrorism and security; surveillance and regulation; organized crime; and corporate crime. Her PhD research examined cybercrime and critical infrastructures.

**Jane L. Rigbye** is Head of Education Development at GamCare, UK, and currently combines her role with doctoral research with the International Gaming Research Unit at Nottingham Trent University. Her main research interests include gambling addiction in young people, barriers to treatment access, Internet gambling and online intervention.

**Robert D. Rogers** is a Professor of Cognitive Neuroscience at Oxford University Department of Psychiatry and Associate member of the Oxford Internet Institute.

**I. Nelson Rose**, JD Harvard Law School, is a Full Professor at Whittier Law School and Visiting Professor at the University of Macau and is recognized as one of the world's leading experts on gaming law. He is the author of *Gambling and the Law®*; co-author of *Internet Gaming Law* and *Gaming Law: Cases and Materials*; and co-editor-in-chief of the *Gaming Law Review and Economics*. His website: www.GamblingAndTheLaw.com.

**Howard J. Shaffer**, PhD, is an Associate Professor of Psychology at Harvard Medical School and Director of the Division on Addiction, Cambridge Health Alliance. Dr Shaffer's major interests include the social perception of addiction and disease, philosophy of science, addiction treatment outcome, and the natural history of addictive behaviours.

**Niko Suhonen**, PhD, is a researcher at the University of Eastern Finland. His skills and expertise include behavioural microeconomics and applied econometrics. His main research interests are individual decision making under risk and uncertainty. Currently, Suhonen is modelling bettors' risk preferences in pari-mutuel horse race betting.

**Leighton Vaughan Williams** is Professor of Economics and Finance and Director of the Betting Research Unit at Nottingham Business School, Nottingham Trent University, UK. He has acted for several years as a business consultant and as adviser to the UK Government on the taxation and regulation of betting and gaming.

**Robert J. Williams** is a Professor in the Faculty of Health Sciences at the University of Lethbridge, Alberta, Canada, and also a Coordinator for the Alberta Gambling Research Institute. Dr Williams teaches courses on gambling and provides frequent consultation to government, industry, the media, and public interest groups. He is one of the world's best-funded gambling researchers and a leading authority in the socioeconomic impacts of gambling, Internet gambling, prevention of problem gambling, and the prevalence and nature of gambling in Aboriginal communities.

**Richard Wood** is a psychologist who specializes in the study of both problematic and responsible gambling behaviour. He is a Director of GamRes Limited, an independent international research and consultancy company and www.GamTalk, an online support service for people with gambling issues.

**Robert T. Wood**, PhD, is an Associate Professor of Sociology and the Dean of Graduate Studies at the University of Lethbridge, Alberta, Canada. His current research interests focus primarily on the relationship between problem gambling and Internet gambling; the demographic provenance of government gambling revenues; and socio-historical shifts in official discourses and policies related to gambling.

**Natalia Zborowska** is a PhD candidate at the department of Organization Sciences, VU University Amsterdam. Natalia works on a project entitled 'The Europeanization of gambling organizations and the regulation of gambling in the European Union'. Her research interests include processes of technological innovation, governance and regulation of risk, and European Integration.

# Preface

'Internet gambling', 'online gambling', 'e-gaming', 'remote gambling', and 'interactive gambling' are interchangeable terms used to describe gambling that occurs via the Internet, interactive television, or mobile phone. It is distinguished from traditional gambling involving direct interaction at a land-based venue such as a lottery outlet, bingo hall, betting shop, horse race track, slots parlor, card room, or casino.

Internet gambling has burgeoned since its inception in 1995. All the traditional forms of gambling are now widely available online, 24 hours a day. Unfortunately, this rapid expansion and ready availability across jurisdictional boundaries has outpaced efforts of policy makers and academics to fully understand the Internet gambling phenomenon and its effects on society, thereby rendering it difficult to legislate and regulate Internet gambling in ways that are properly informed and that serve the greater good. Over the past several years, however, a growing body of academic literature pertaining to Internet gambling has emerged. As this literature grows both in terms of size and scope, and as policy makers, educators, and industry insiders are looking to the literature for guidance, it is of the highest importance to provide a single source where the most pertinent studies, conducted by the field's leading researchers, are compiled into a single reference volume. This is the overarching objective of the present book: to be a source of rigorously researched guidance on the economic, political, legal, methodological, and clinical ramifications of Internet gambling in contemporary society.

The book is divided into five parts. Part 1 contains a single chapter that provides the context for the rest of the volume by providing an overview of the history of Internet gambling; the current worldwide situation; and the major concerns with Internet gambling. Part 2: Commercial/Business Aspects speaks to the economic considerations relevant to online gambling, different business models, the industry players, and regulatory considerations. Part 3: Major Research Studies of Internet Gamblers presents an overview of the four major academic investigations that have been conducted on Internet gamblers. These studies shed light on the demographics, game play patterns, and problem gambling status of Internet gamblers and how Internet gamblers differ from non-Internet gamblers. Part 4: Clinical Aspects examines the evidence exploring the link between Internet gambling and harm as well as the potential for online player protection features and online support to mitigate effectively against this relationship. The final part, Legal and Policy Issues, provides more detail about the different legal frameworks and regulatory policies used in different jurisdictions around the world, the relationship between online gambling and crime, and the advantages and disadvantages of different policy approaches to Internet gambling.

# Part 1

# Introduction

# 1 History, current worldwide situation, and concerns with Internet gambling

*Robert J. Williams, Robert T. Wood, and Jonathan Parke*

## History of Internet gambling

When public and commercial use of the Internet began in the early and mid-1990s, it soon became apparent that this could also be a medium used for gambling. Two other developments helped set the stage. The first was the creation of gambling software by Microgaming in 1994/1995. The second was the development of encrypted communication protocols by CryptoLogic, in 1995, that allowed secure online monetary transactions. In 1995, a few sites (e.g., Gaming Club) began offering casino gambling games online without real money being wagered. Some sportsbooks (e.g., Intertops Casino, Sports Book, Ladbrokes) also created websites that listed their odds as well as toll-free numbers to phone to place bets. The first case of money actually being wagered over the Internet by the general public appears to be the online purchase of lottery tickets from the International Lottery in Liechtenstein for a manual drawing that occurred on October 7, 1995 (Romney, 1995).[1]

Rapid expansion followed, with most of the new online gambling sites being sport/race books and casinos basing their operations in Caribbean and Central American countries with permissive gambling legislation, low taxes/fees, and relatively lax enforcement. In January 1996, InterCasino, based in Antigua, became the first online casino to accept a wager online (4 Online Gambling.com, 2011; Business Wire, 2005). In 1996 and 1997, several other Caribbean islands (Netherland Antilles; Turks and Caicos; Dominican Republic; Grenada; St. Kitts and Nevis) and Central American countries (Costa Rica; Belize; Panama) began licensing, or at least hosting, online sports/race books and/or casinos. In the United Kingdom, Eurobet began offering online sports/race betting in 1996 (Eurobet, 2011). In Australia, Centrebet in the Northern Territory also began offering online sports betting in 1996, with three more sports/race books in operation by the end of 1997 (Senate Information Technologies Committee, 2000). A few more online lotteries emerged, when Finland granted a license to operate online lotteries to The National Lottery of Finland in 1996 (van der Gaast, 2001), and when the Coeur d'Alene tribe in Idaho began an online lottery in February 1997. The next couple of years saw other jurisdictions enter the game, most notably Gibraltar in 1998 and the Kahnawà:ke Mohawk Territory in Quebec in 1999.[2] By the end of 1996, it is estimated that about 15 online sites accepted wagers, increasing to over 200 by the end of 1997, 650 by the end of 1999, and 1,800 by the end of 2002 (Schwartz, 2006). Since 2006, the number of online gambling sites has fluctuated between 2,000 and 2,500. Revenues increased in a similar pattern. Hammer (2001) estimated that Internet gambling generated US$2.2 billion in 2000, compared to only $300 million several years earlier.

Most of the new Internet gambling sites, as well as most of the expansion in the early years, consisted of new companies not associated with any land-based gambling establishments. This was largely because established gambling providers did not want to do anything that might jeopardize their land-based licenses because of the grey legal status of Internet gambling.[3] There were some exceptions, such as some European countries that allowed their gambling monopoly to extend services online, existing UK-based sports/race books that went online (e.g., Eurobet in 1996; William Hill in 1998; Ladbrokes in 2000), and some existing Australian sports/race books and casinos that started legally adding online services in the late 1990s.[4] This has changed in recent years, as several countries now permit their established lottery operations and/or sports/race books to offer services over the Internet.

As indicated, the initial online gambling sites were *lotteries, sports/racing books, and online casinos*. The first Internet *bingo* site (QuadCard; www.ibingo.com) started offering cash prizes in 1998. The first Internet *poker* room (www.planetpoker.com) went online in 1998. A major expansion of online poker began in 2003, when the World Series of Poker became a popular televised show in the United States. Many of the entrants for the World Series qualified via online poker tournaments, and both the 2003 and 2004 champions were online poker players. In 2003, the estimated revenue from online poker was $365 million, which increased to approximately $2.4 billion in 2006 (Christiansen Capital Advisors, 2005). The first dedicated *backgammon* site for money (TrueMoneyGames) went online in 2001.

More recent additions to online gambling have been 'betting exchanges' and 'skill game sites'. Betting exchanges (e.g., 'BetFair' www.betfair.com being the largest, launched in June 2000) are sites that create a marketplace for bettors, whereby they post potential wagers on certain events (with accompanying odds and stake size), in the hope that someone will take them up on their offer(s). These wagers are primarily on sporting and horse racing events, but also include wagers on politics or reality television events, etc. Several of these sites have expanded to include person-to-person gambling on traditional casino games. Skill game sites (e.g., 'King' www.king.com being the largest, launched in 2004) offer a wide range of skill-oriented word games; puzzle games; strategy games (e.g., mahjong, chess); sports games (e.g., billiards, mini golf); card games (e.g., solitaire); arcade games (e.g., carnival shootout); trivia games; and video games. Most typically, players pay a fee to enter a tournament, with the winner(s) collecting the majority of the entrance fees. Sometimes the contest can be with another specific individual and sometimes it can be against your own previous 'high score'. Part of the expansion of skill game sites is rooted in the belief that these sites do not violate gambling prohibitions in jurisdictions that define gambling as 'games of chance'.[5]

There has always been a continuum between traditional gambling and investment/speculation in the financial markets.[6] This blurring has continued with some well established online gambling providers such as Bet365, Ladbrokes, Paddy Power, and William Hill adding *financial indices betting* (i.e., betting on the direction of the stock market, currencies, commodity prices, etc.) to their repertoire of online gambling options between 2007 and the present time. Although new to online gambling, betting on the direction of financial indices with an agency external to the stock exchange (where options and/or futures are not actually purchased and no transaction occurs on the exchange itself) is a very old form of gambling known as 'bucketeering'.[7]

## Other types of remote gambling

Gambling via a computer on the Internet is by far the most common form of remote gambling. However, there are two other methods of placing a 'remote' bet: via interactive television and via a telephone.

Interactive television (iTV) was first launched in the late 1990s in Hong Kong, Singapore, France, and England. This service allowed viewers to use their remote controls to select 'movies on demand', to vote for which program should be broadcast, or to vote for how a plot should unfold (Srivastava, 2002). However, iTV has now expanded to more countries and to more Internet-like services (i.e., interactive shopping, banking, customized weather reports, on-demand provision of sports scores, interactive music selection, video game playing, etc.). These expanded offerings have also included interactive gambling. TVG debuted in September 1999 in the United States. This service broadcasts live horse racing and permits betting via remote control, a web-enabled mobile device, or by phoning in. However, the primary penetration of iTV gambling has occurred in Europe, particularly the UK and France. For several years France and the UK have provided interactive bingo, lotteries, horse racing, and sports betting (Griffiths, 2006, *The Independent*, 2004). Currently however, iTV gambling still represents a fairly small percentage of the 'remote gambling' market. Even in the UK, which constitutes iTV's largest market, a much greater proportion of people gamble via the Internet. In June 2011, among UK adults who engaged in remote gambling in the previous four weeks (11.8 percent of the population), only 11 percent of these individuals reported doing so via the television, which is down from 24 percent of the 7.2 percent of remote gamblers in 2006 (Gambling Commission, 2011). Nonetheless, it seems certain that the opportunity for iTV gambling (as well as the raw number of people who use this option) will continue to increase, especially in Europe and Australia.[8]

Phoning in bets on sports or horse racing has been common in many jurisdictions for many years. However, this mode of gambling has accelerated with (a) the development of smartphones having Internet access, colour graphics, Java programming, the ability to run downloadable software, and (b) online gambling providers developing online gambling websites and software specific to mobile devices (Guardian.co.uk, 2011; Online.Casino.org, 2011). Here again, gambling via mobile phone tends to be only available in certain markets across the UK and Europe. Furthermore, even in these markets it is still less common than remote gambling via computer. However, unlike interactive television, it has kept its share of the expanding remote market: in 2006 approximately 31 percent of the 7.2 percent of remote gamblers in the UK gambled via mobile phone in the previous four weeks compared to 27 percent of the 11.8 percent remote gamblers in June 2011 (Gambling Commission, 2011).

## Current worldwide situation

In August 2011, there were 2,412 Internet gambling websites listed at www.online.casinocity. com,[9,10] Proportionately, 32.3 percent of these sites are online casinos, 24.5 percent are poker rooms, 18.3 percent are sports and race books, 16.7 percent are online bingos, 4.4 percent are lottery sites, 1.6 percent are skill game sites, 0.8 percent are betting exchanges, 0.8 percent are mahjong and rummy sites, and 0.6 percent are backgammon sites (Casino City, 2011).

The following individual sites are listed as the top 25 in terms of volume of online transactions: King.com, Betfair Sportsbook & Racebook, Party Poker, Game Duell, UK National Lottery, Bet365 Poker, 888 Casino, Rakuten Bank, WorldWinner, New York State Lottery, Party Casino, bwin Sportbook, Paddy Power Sportsbook, Bet365 Casino, Bet365 Sportsbook & Racebook, Mirror Scratchcards, Party Poker Italy, Racing Post Betting Site, Loterias y Apuestas del Estado, PokerStars, PMU.fr, EuroGrant, Yahoo Poker, SportingBet, and Pinnacle Sports (Casino City, 2011).

These 2,412 sites are owned by 665 different companies. The high number of sites relative to owners is primarily due to the larger owners creating multiple sites so as to create a larger presence on the web (often creating separate websites for different countries and for different types of online gambling). Some of these companies are publicly traded on stock exchanges, but most are privately owned. The top 25 online gambling companies in terms of volume of transactions are Betfair, Midasplayer.com, bwin, Bet365, Group 888, BetClic Everest Group, SportingBet, GameDuell, Tradonomi, Mansion Limited, REEL Malta, Unibet, William Hill, WHG Trading, Ladbrokes, Pinnacle Sports Worldwide, Europe Entertainment, Kolyma Corporation, Betsson AB, Imperial E-Club, MTG, Stan James, PKR, GVC Holdings, and Camelot Group (Casino City, 2011).

The 2,412 online sites operate in 74 different jurisdictions. Table 1.1 lists the top 25 jurisdictions by highest volume of online transactions and number of sites hosted (Casino City, 2011).

*Table 1.1* Top 25 online gambling jurisdictions in August 2011

| Jurisdiction | Volume of transactions (rank order) | Number of online gambling sites |
| --- | --- | --- |
| Gibraltar | 1 | 304 |
| Malta | 2 | 553 |
| United Kingdom | 3 | 119 |
| Tasmania | 4 | 2 |
| Cyprus | 5 | 62 |
| Alderney (British Channel Island) | 6 | 114 |
| United States | 7 | 29 |
| Isle of Man | 8 | 47 |
| Antigua and Barbuda | 9 | 68 |
| Netherland Antilles (Curacao) | 10 | 370 |
| Kahnawà:ke Mohawk Territory (Quebec) | 11 | 172 |
| Costa Rica | 12 | 204 |
| Italy | 13 | 69 |
| France | 14 | 26 |
| Japan | 15 | 2 |
| Spain | 16 | 3 |
| Switzerland | 17 | 2 |
| Virginia | 18 | 1 |
| New York | 19 | 1 |
| Australian Northern Territory | 20 | 11 |
| Macau | 21 | 2 |
| Austria | 22 | 11 |
| Ukraine | 23 | 2 |
| Finland | 24 | 7 |
| Western Australia | 25 | 3 |

Source: Casino City, 2011.

Many companies have developed their own gambling software. Many others use commercial software, with the most popular ones being from Microgaming (178 sites), Everleaf Gaming (156 sites), Electracade (155 sites), Playtech (152 sites), 888 (136 sites), GTECH G2 (133 sites), OpenBet (132 sites), and Net Entertainment (128 sites) (Casino City, 2011). Some sites require software downloads to play, while others allow playing on instant online software such as Java.

There are approximately 200 different online payment methods currently in use. Visa and MasterCard are the most popular methods and are accepted by about 87 percent of all sites. Other popular methods of payment are Neteller (accepted by 72 percent of sites), Moneybookers (accepted by 68 percent of sites), Bank Wire Transfer (accepted by 65 percent of sites), Maestro (debit card from MasterCard) (accepted by 45 percent of sites), Visa Electron (accepted by 37 percent of sites), and personal cheque (accepted by 23 percent of sites) (Casino City, 2011). Online casinos have been assigned an 'online gambling' merchant code by Visa and MasterCard. This electronic code is attached to every credit card transaction the company makes. Most US banks and financial institutions automatically reject all transactions with this code, so US players are generally unable to use credit cards with online casinos to make deposits. This limitation is partly responsible for the appearance of so many new non-credit card, non-US based, financial intermediaries in recent years.

Revenues are difficult to determine. However, Global Betting and Gaming Consultants (see Chapter 3) estimate that worldwide online gambling revenues were $11.7 billion in 2004, increasing to $29.3 billion in 2010. Online gambling revenue was estimated to account for 5.8 percent of the worldwide gambling market in 2007 and 7.5 percent in 2010 (see Chapter 3). There have been widely different estimates of the proportion of the market accounted for by different types of gambling. Consistent with these estimates, however, is the fact that sports and horse race betting, online casinos, and poker account for the large majority of the total share (RSeConsulting, 2006). Global Betting and Gaming Consultants (2009), estimate the specific portions in 2008 to be: 38 percent for sports/race books; 25 percent for casinos; 23 percent for poker; 7 percent for lotteries and skill game sites; and 7 percent for online bingo. Similarly, there are no reliable figures on market share of revenues by country. RSeConsulting (2006) estimates that 49 percent of Internet gamblers are from the Asia/Pacific region; 28–35 percent from the US, and 23 percent from Europe. Within Europe, there is some consensus that the UK comprises 50 percent of the market (Swiss Institute of Comparative Law, 2006).

A temporary slowing in the overall market occurred in 2007, due to the US prohibition of online gambling. However, long-term growth is still expected to be very positive as Internet use continues to expand, the quality of the Internet interface increases (e.g., live video-streaming, increased bandwidth), with increasing legalization of online gambling, and with increased public confidence and familiarity with Internet gambling. Internet gambling also has significant growth potential in that the large majority of adults in Western countries gamble, yet only a small fraction of these individuals have accessed the Internet to gamble. That being said, Internet gambling's relatively low market penetration after 16 years of existence (despite its convenience and offering better odds), is much lower than the penetration that occurred with other forms of gambling when they were first introduced. Hence, Internet gambling may end up filling a small market niche rather than replacing or supplementing land-based forms. To date, there is not much evidence of a negative impact on land-based revenues.

## Regulatory approach to Internet gambling in different jurisdictions[11]

In many countries, no clear legislation exists or applies to online gambling. In many cases, online gambling operators have taken advantage of this lack of clarity to set up operation in such jurisdictions (Balestra and Cabot, 2006; Rose and Owens, 2005). Currently, several countries prohibit most or all forms of online gambling. This includes Bermuda, Cambodia, China, Cuba, Germany, Greece, India, Malaysia, Romania, South Africa, and the Ukraine. In addition, many (predominantly Islamic) countries ban online gambling by virtue of their ban on all forms of gambling: Afghanistan, Algeria, Bangladesh, Bhutan, Indonesia, Iran, Jordan, Libya, Mali, Oman, Pakistan, Qatar, Saudi Arabia, Somalia, Sudan, Syria, United Arab Emirates, and Yemen (Online Casino Suite, 2011). At the other end are countries that have either completely legalized, or at least permit, all forms of online gambling. These include Antigua and Barbuda, Austria, Gibraltar, Liechtenstein, Netherland Antilles, Panama, the Philippines, Slovakia, and the UK.

A more common policy is to put some type of restriction on online gambling. For example, many countries allow certain forms of online gambling (most typically lotteries, instant lotteries, sports/race books) and make other forms illegal (most typically casino games): Australia, Belgium, Brazil, Canadian provinces, Chile, Czech Republic, Denmark, Finland, France, Hong Kong, Hungary, Iceland, Israel, Italy, Japan, Latvia, Lithuania, Luxembourg, Macau, the Netherlands, New Zealand, Norway, Poland, Portugal, Russia, Singapore, Slovenia, South Korea, Sweden, Switzerland, Taiwan, and the United States. Several countries prohibit residents from accessing online gambling outside the country (e.g., Austria, Belgium, Denmark, Estonia, France, Germany, Hong Kong, Hungary, Israel, Italy, Norway, Slovenia, South Korea, United States). Some countries restrict patronage of domestic online sites to residents only (e.g., Austria, Canadian provinces, Finland, the Philippines). A few countries permit online gambling, but prohibit their own residents from accessing these sites (e.g., Australia (online casinos), Malta, Papua New Guinea).

In jurisdictions where online gambling is permitted, there is wide divergence concerning how it is provided. Some jurisdictions allow private foreign commercial operators to provide online gambling services in a manner similar to other commercial products, although sometimes taxed at a much higher rate (e.g., Alderney, Antigua and Barbuda, Australia, Cyprus, Gibraltar, Ireland, Isle of Man, Italy, Kahnawà:ke Territory, Malta, Netherland Antilles). Some jurisdictions restrict the provision of all online gambling to one or two government-owned or government-controlled providers (Brazil, Canada, Denmark, Finland, Hungary, Iceland, Israel, Luxembourg, the Netherlands, Norway, Slovenia, South Korea, Sweden, Ukraine). A few countries restrict the provision of all online gambling to private monopolies (Austria, Hong Kong, Macau, Portugal, Singapore). Finally, some jurisdictions have a mixture of government-controlled monopolies (most typically providing online lotteries) and private commercial offerings (Belgium, France, Liechtenstein, Lithuania, New Zealand, the Philippines, Slovakia).

Current (July 2011) jurisdictional-specific regulations, in countries where this information is available, are as follows:

### North America

*Canada*

Canadian federal law only permits provincial governments to offer online gambling. The Atlantic Lottery Corporation (acting on behalf of the provinces of Prince Edward Island,

Nova Scotia, New Brunswick, and Newfoundland) began selling online lottery and sports betting tickets to citizens of the Atlantic Provinces in 2004. It added interactive instant games in 2005 and online bingo in 2007. In 2004 British Columbia began providing online sports betting, interactive instant games, and the online sale of land-based lottery tickets to British Columbia residents. It added online poker in 2009, and online bingo and casinos in 2010. In 2009 Ontario began selling online subscriptions to Ontario residents for the national lottery and will add other online services in 2012. In 2010 Quebec began offering online poker, casino table games, and online sports betting to Quebec residents.

Horse racing in Canada is regulated by the Canadian Pari-Mutuel Agency under the federal Department of Agriculture. In 2003, the federal agriculture minister made a rule change permitting horse racing bets to be placed, not just by telephone, but by 'any telecommunication device'. As a consequence, in January 2004, Woodbine Entertainment, a Toronto-based horse racing track operator, began accepting online bets from across Canada.

Certain Canadian Aboriginal groups have taken the position that they are sovereign nations able to enact their own gambling legislation. The Kahnawà:ke First Nation in Quebec began hosting online sites in 1999. In July 2007 it hosted more sites than any other jurisdiction ($n = 377$). Although the Quebec government consistently indicated that the Kahnawà:ke operation was illegal, no action was taken until 2007 when Cyber World Group, which administers online casinos located on the Kahnawà:ke reserve, pleaded guilty in Quebec to charges of illegal gambling and was ordered to pay a fine of $2 million (Online Casino Topic, 2007). As a consequence of this ruling, several online operators have moved their operations to other jurisdictions. Currently Kahnawà:ke is the fifth largest worldwide host of Internet gambling sites ($n = 172$).

## United States

The 2006 federal Unlawful Internet Gambling Enforcement Act (UIGEA) makes it illegal for all financial institutions to make fund transfers to online gambling sites. It is also illegal for Internet gambling providers to accept money transfers from potential US online gamblers. The UIGEA is not directed at individual bettors, and there have only been rare cases of prosecution of US citizens for placing an Internet bet (Rose and Owens, 2005).

The UIGEA exempts online within-state sales of lottery tickets (via terminals in retail outlets), between-state horse race betting, greyhound racing, and other types of within-state online gambling, as long as the individual state does not prohibit it (several states have explicitly prohibited Internet gambling).[12] Internet horse race wagering has been specifically legalized in the states of California, Nevada, Oregon, and South Dakota. It is unclear whether this legislation applies to 'skill games'. There are currently 14 online skill gambling sites operating within the United States that have opted to continue taking bets from other states that do not specifically prohibit online gambling (Casino City, 2011).

## Europe

### Austria

Austria licenses Austria-based companies to offer lottery services and sports betting via remote channels (Internet, mobile phones, and interactive television) as an extension of land-based operations. In addition, a monopoly has been granted to a private operator (Österreichische Lotterien Gesellschaft mbH in conjunction with Casinos Austria) to provide all forms of online gambling. Only Austrian residents are allowed to play at these sites. Austrian citizens are not permitted to gamble at foreign sites.

### Belgium

New legislation in 2011 allowed the licensing of online gambling to licensed land-based Belgium providers of these forms of gambling (i.e., casinos, sports betting, poker, horse racing). Online lotteries continue to be restricted to the state-owned La Loterie Nationale. Belgium citizens are not permitted to gamble at foreign sites. Furthermore, Belgium mandates financial and Internet service provider (ISP) blocking of foreign online sites.

### Cyprus

The Cypriot government provides licenses to online lotteries, betting exchanges, casino gaming, and sports betting. However, in late 2011 Cyprus will seek to enact a total ban on online gambling.

### Czech Republic

The only forms of online gambling currently allowed by domestic providers are online lotteries and sports betting. However, many foreign sites cater to Czech citizens.

### Denmark

The state monopoly (Danske Spil) provides online lotteries, instant games, sports betting, and bingo and is the only company legally allowed to do so. It has been providing services since 2002. In May 2011 Danish lawmakers agreed to amend the legislation to permit foreign online casino providers. Denmark mandates ISP blocking of non-licensed foreign sites.

### Estonia

In 2002 the national lottery started selling tickets over the Internet. Online gambling was legalized in 2010, but play (sports betting, bingo) must be limited to Estonian-licensed sites. Estonia mandates financial and ISP blocking of non-licensed foreign sites until 2011 at which point the market will be open to foreign operators.

### Finland

The state-owned company Veikkaus provides online sports betting and lotteries and the state-owned company Fintoto provides online horse race wagering. A third domestic company holds the license for slot machines and casino games, but the Act on Gaming does not permit such products to be offered via remote channels. Internet gambling is only provided to Finnish residents. However, Finnish gamblers are allowed to gamble on foreign online sites.

### France

France's state-owned gambling provider, the Française des Jeux, provides online lotteries, instant lotteries, poker, bingo, and horse/sports betting (beginning in 2003). Originally, foreign online operators were not permitted to either base their operations in France or to take bets from French citizens. However, after considerable pressure from the European Union, France started issuing licenses to foreign operators in 2010 (not lotteries, however, which continue to be provided by the Française des Jeux). France also has had interactive television gambling since 1999. France mandates financial and ISP blocking for non-licensed foreign sites.

## Germany

Prior to 2008, sports betting, horse race betting, and online lottery sales were permitted in Germany under a monopolistic regulatory regime that prohibits foreign operators. However, legislation in 2008 banned all forms of Internet gambling except for horse racing. Germany announced in April 2011 that it was going to permit online sports betting beginning in 2012. Germany has approved a controversial new measure that permits the implementation of software that searches out and blocks all illegal online activity (including online gambling).

## Greece

All Internet gambling in Greece is banned. However, to ensure compliance with European Union law, online gambling will be legalized and regulated in 2011.

## Hungary

Under current Hungarian law, only the state-owned gaming company Szerencsejáték can legally provide online gambling. It currently offers online lotteries and a sportsbook. As of 2006 Hungarian banks are prohibited from transferring payments to or from online gambling websites.

## Iceland

Iceland offers an online lottery and sports betting through a state-owned monopoly.

## Ireland

As in the United Kingdom, Ireland's bookmakers operate Internet-based services under the terms of their bookmaking licenses. Ireland began hosting online casinos and lotteries in 2003. The first online bookmaking sites were launched in 2004. Currently, sports betting, horse race betting, betting exchanges, poker, and skill games are offered online.

## Italy

Italy permits online sports betting, person-to-person betting, and online wagering on skill games (including poker) by both foreign and domestic operators. Instant online lottery games are provided by the domestic lottery provider. Italy requires ISPs to block foreign online providers without a domestic license.

*Latvia*

Online lottery and sports betting is available and has been legal since 2003. Although Latvians can gamble at foreign sites these sites must pay a 10 percent tax on profits they receive from Latvians.

*Liechtenstein*

A government-controlled monopoly provides online lotteries. Legislation in 2011 permitted the granting of online gambling licenses (for all forms of online gambling) to private operators.

*Lithuania*

In 2010 the state lottery company Olifeja was given the sole right to offer online gambling services in the country, and it currently provides online lotteries, bingo, and keno. Sports betting is provided by three of the country's largest sportsbooks.

*Luxembourg*

The current gambling laws do not directly address online gambling. Online gaming has been available in Luxembourg since 2007 in the form of traditional lotteries and instant games offered by the state-owned Loterie Nationale. Players can also participate in foreign online sites.

*Malta*

Malta began licensing online gambling sites in 2000. All forms of online gambling are permitted.

*The Netherlands*

Online lotteries are legal, and legally only provided by the one state-owned operator (De Lotto). In 2010 the Netherlands legalized online poker (partly because Dutch courts deemed it a game of skill). Recently the Dutch government indicated a desire to grant licenses for Internet gambling services and lift the current restrictions in 2012. The Netherlands mandates financial blocking of payments to foreign online gambling sites.

*Norway*

Online lotteries are provided by the state-owned and operated Norsk Tipping. Norsk Rikstoto provides online horse race betting. It is illegal for Norwegians to place bets with foreign online gambling companies and for these companies to accept bets from Norwegians. Norway mandates financial blocking of payments to foreign online gambling sites.

*Poland*

Online gambling is currently heavily restricted in Poland with operators required to pass several audits and pay significant fees and taxes to receive licensing. New amendments proposed in 2011 aim to ban online gambling with the exception of sports betting.

*Portugal*

A charity group, Santa Casa da Misericordia de Lisboa (SCML), has the exclusive license to provide an online lottery and sports betting as an extension of its land-based offerings.

*Romania*

Internet gambling is illegal. However, Romania is drafting legislation that would allow provision from domestic Romanian sites.

*Russian Federation*

A law passed in 2006 banned land-based casinos in all but four regions of Russia and banned all gambling over the Internet with the exception of sports betting.

*Slovakia*

Only domestic operators licensed by the Ministry of Finance are allowed to offer their online services in the country. Tipos, the state-run operator, offers online lottery, sports betting, bingo, keno, instant games, as well as online casino games including poker.

*Slovenia*

Slovenia allows online lotteries, instant games, and sports betting through its state-owned monopoly Sportna loterija. ISP blocking of foreign sites was mandated beginning in 2010.

*Spain*

Internet gambling has historically been an unregulated activity in Spain. However, in August 2010 Catalonia created its own legislation. In 2011 Spain passed legislation to license online gambling and in May 2011 the first license was granted to the country's largest land-based casino (to provide online casino games and poker).

*Sweden*

Sweden's state-owned gambling provider, Svenska Spel, is the exclusive provider of online lotteries, poker, bingo, and sports betting. Foreign providers are not permitted, although they will be allowed to apply for a sports betting license in the near future. However, it is not currently illegal to place bets at a foreign site.

*Switzerland*

The two state-run lottery companies and their owners, the cantons, provide online lotteries and sports betting (Villeneuve, 2011). All other forms of online gambling are unlawful. Swiss citizens are legally allowed to participate in foreign online gambling.

*Ukraine*

Ukraine allows its residents to play the state lottery online. All other forms of gambling, including online gambling, were prohibited in 2009.

*United Kingdom (UK)*

Prior to 2007, online sports betting, horse race betting, betting exchanges, and games of skill could be legally operated in the UK and played by UK residents. When the new Gambling Act came into force in 2007 it permitted all forms of privately operated Internet gambling to operate from UK soil, conditional upon regulation and licensing. A 15 percent Online Gaming Tax on profits is applied to all domestic online operators. The UK permits domestic operators to provide their services outside the UK and is the only European jurisdiction that permits foreign online providers without a UK license to provide online services to UK citizens. The UK also has had interactive/digital television gambling for several years whereby people can play bingo, the national lottery, or bet on horse racing or sports via their television remote control.

### Asia Pacific Region

*Australia*

Online gambling in Australia is regulated at the federal level by the Interactive Gambling Act of 2001. Online lotteries and the sale of lottery tickets over the Internet, as well as sports and race betting are viewed as extensions of land-based offerings and are licensed and regulated by the individual states and territories. Online keno games and instant win tickets/lotteries are prohibited. Companies are not allowed to offer online casino gambling and poker to Australian residents. Online sports/race betting currently operate in Tasmania, New South Wales, Victoria, Western Australia, the Australian Capital Territory, and the Northern Territory. In April 2008 interactive television betting was introduced in the state of Victoria. This has since been expanded to some other states.

*Cambodia*

It is illegal to participate in and/or to offer any form of online gambling.

*China*

It is illegal for Chinese companies to provide online gambling. It is also illegal for Chinese citizens to participate in online gambling. China also mandates ISP blocking of foreign and domestic online gambling sites.

HONG KONG (SPECIAL ADMINISTRATIVE REGION OF CHINA)

In 2002 the Hong Kong Legislative Council passed the Gambling (Amendment) Ordinance which banned Hong Kong residents from engaging in online gambling with operators outside Hong Kong. However, the Hong Kong Jockey Club – the legal private gambling monopoly – can, and does offer online lottery play, sports betting (soccer), and horse race betting to Hong Kong and non-Hong Kong residents.

MACAU (SPECIAL ADMINISTRATIVE REGION OF CHINA)

The government of Macau has authorized the Macau Jockey Club to offer horse race wagering over the Internet. It has also authorized the Sociedade de Loterias e Apostas Mutuas de Macau to offer online sports betting.

## *India*

Up until recently the Indian federal government did not specifically prohibit online gambling, although it is a banned offense under the Bombay Wager Act in the state of Maharashtra. However, the Indian government's new 2011 rules on objectionable web content tighten the law on online gambling and may leave operators open to criminal prosecution, according to legal experts. The state of Sikkim has permitted an online lottery since 2002. A couple of online rummy sites also exist in India.

## *Indonesia*

Online gambling is prohibited.

## *Israel*

The government-run online sports betting and lottery are the only forms of online gambling permitted. ISP and financial blocking is used to restrict access to foreign sites.

## *Japan*

Online sports/race betting as well as lotteries are the only legal forms of online gambling.

## *Malaysia*

Online gambling is prohibited. Financial blocking of online sites is mandated.

## *New Zealand*

Online horse racing and sports betting is offered exclusively by the New Zealand Racing Board (formerly known as the Totalisator Agency Board (TAB)). The state-owned lottery commission offered online lottery products in 2008. It is illegal to organize, manage, or promote any other source of online gambling in New Zealand. New Zealanders are not prohibited from wagering with offshore providers.

## *Papua New Guinea*

In 2007 Papua New Guinea passed the Gaming Control Bill which allows both land-based and online casinos. However, only foreigners are allowed to patronize online gambling sites based in a casino; entry fee and strict identity (ID) requirements are in place to keep New Guinea citizens from gambling.

## The Philippines

The Philippines permits both domestic and foreign operators to offer all forms of online gambling. The primary provider is the state-owned monopoly (Philippine Amusement and Gaming Corporation), which can only be used by Filipino players. On the other hand, sites licensed and hosted in the Cagayan Special Economic Zone are only open to foreign players.

## Singapore

The legality of online gambling in Singapore is somewhat unclear, but is generally thought to prohibit most forms of online gambling. Singapore Turf Club accepts bets online for horse racing. Singapore Pools accepts online bets on soccer and Grand Prix motor races.

## South Korea

Online sports betting through the Seoul Olympic Sports Promotion Foundation (SOSFO) is the only legal form of Internet gambling.

## Taiwan

Taiwan's sports lottery's products have been available online since 2008. Foreign online operators are not allowed to provide their services in Taiwan.

## Vietnam

The Pacific Lottery Corporation, a Canadian company, began providing a legal online lottery in Vietnam in 2008.

## South America

### Argentina

Argentina has licensed one online casino beginning in 2002 and an online sportsbook that went online in 2006. In 2008 Argentina banned all foreign gambling websites not paying Argentine taxes.

### Brazil

State governments are permitted under Brazilian law to allow lotteries to offer betting and gambling via the Internet. Several lotteries currently offer these online options.

### Chile

Both of Chile's lotteries offer their lottery products online; however, online casinos are prohibited. Online sports betting is also available.

### Venezuela

Venezuela hosts three online casinos and operates the Venezuelan national lottery online.

## *Africa*

### *Comoros*

Online casinos are offered by Comoros.

### *Mauritius*

Mauritius requires government licensure of online gaming operators and has offered such licenses since 1996.

### *South Africa*

South Africa legalized online gambling in 2008 and online sports betting was offered. However, in 2010 South Africa banned all forms of online gambling.

### *Swaziland*

Online gambling licenses were first issued in 1998. Online casinos and poker rooms are offered. However, customers can only be paid in rand currency.

## Concerns with Internet gambling

The final section of this chapter outlines the primary concerns about online gambling that need to be considered and/or addressed by governments and policy makers contemplating or currently engaged in providing online gambling. To be fair, some of these problems are attributable to the relative newness of the Internet gambling industry; the fact that most of the initial entrants into the industry were not well-established operators; and the fact that many of these new companies were locating in small jurisdictions with arguably more poorly developed and/or lax regulatory policies.[13] It is reasonable to expect that many of these problems will have lessened with the maturing of the industry, the entrance of well-established land-based operators, and the legalization and provision of Internet gambling by governments themselves in many larger countries. Thus, the final part of this section will re-examine the extent to which these problems are more historical rather than current.

### *Unfair, illegal, or irresponsible business practices*

There have been many cases where online sites have apparently not paid winnings, have cheated players with unfair games, or have absconded with player deposits (Games and Casino, 2011; McMullen and Rege, 2010). While this also occurs to some extent with land-based gambling, the ability for players or governments to seek recourse is often more limited, because of the foreign jurisdiction of some of these sites, and/or lax regulatory enforcement within some of these jurisdictions (Crowne-Mohammed and Andreacchi, 2009). Among a large sample of over 10,000 Internet casino and poker players from 96 countries, Parke and colleagues (see Chapter 8) found that over one-third claimed to have a dispute with an Internet casino or poker website, and the majority of respondents reported that operator responsiveness to player complaints needed to be improved. In the United States, security concerns (51 percent) and legitimacy (49 percent) were the main reasons for not playing online in an Ipsos Reid study of 2,167 US poker players (Ipsos Reid, 2005). Some 55 percent of US online gamblers believe that online casinos cheat players (American Gaming Association, 2006).

A related problem concerns the 'free play' sections of some of these sites that exist ostensibly to familiarize the person with the game and to improve their skill. However, they may have a more nefarious purpose, as some research has shown that the odds on some free play sites tend to favour the player rather than the casino (Sévigny, Cloutier, Pelletier, and Ladouceur, 2005).

### Unfair or illegal player practices

Interestingly, the American Gaming Association (2006) survey also found that 46 percent of online gamblers believed that *players* have also found ways to cheat. Here again, it is unclear how common an occurrence this is. For online gambling, there are several case reports of hackers having successfully altered online sites to pay wins (CBS News, 2008; McMullan and Perrier, 2007; McMullan and Rege, 2010; RseConsulting, 2006). Online poker appears to be particularly susceptible to deceptive player practices. One way of doing this is by means of collusion between online poker players playing at the same table (i.e., several of the players are actually in the same physical room using different computers). Another technique is employing automated computer programs using optimal play ('poker bots') against other players (e.g., Brunker, 2004; Dance, 2011).[14]

Industry representatives usually report their greatest problem to be individuals and criminal organizations demanding payments, and threatening otherwise to disrupt the site's online service prior to major sporting events, tournaments, etc. Reports indicate that online sites pay out millions of dollars in extortion money each year (Current Digest, 2006; Kshetri, 2005; RseConsulting, 2006; McMullan and Perrier, 2007; McMullan and Rege, 2007, 2010). The lack of clear legislation in many countries about these 'denial-of-service' attacks makes prosecution difficult.

An additional serious concern is money laundering. There are several ways in which this can be done either by the player or the site itself (RseConsulting, 2006; United States General Accounting Office, 2002). The magnitude of this problem is unknown, but it does exist and will continue to pose a problem, especially considering the lax regulatory structure of several jurisdictions where online gambling occurs (Hugel and Kelly, 2002; Mangion, 2010; Mills, 2001; McMullan and Rege, 2010).

### Internet gambling by prohibited groups

Online sites are typically required to bar certain people. These include employees of the site, people who have banned themselves from playing on the site, and underage gamblers (most sites ban individuals younger than 18).[15] The ability of online sites to effectively bar these groups depends on how rigorously they check ID and cross-reference new accounts against Internet Protocol (IP) addresses and banking details.

The primary concern has been with underage gambling, considering that Internet use tends to be highest among teenagers, and they commonly access the free play sections of online gambling sites (Derevensky and Gupta, 2007; Ipsos MORI, 2009; Messerlian, Byrne, and Derevensky, 2004; Mitka, 2001). There appears to be some reason for concern. The UK Gambling Commission determined that a third of all online casinos and bookmakers had deficiencies that could enable underage children to place bets (Drury, 2009). Indeed, a study in 2004, by NCH (Children's Charity), GamCare, and CitizenCard in the UK, found that a 16 year old with a debit card was able to place bets online on 30 out of 37 sites tested (NCH, 2004). Not surprisingly, then, a European survey found that 17 percent of visitors to online gambling sites were aged 17 or under (NetValue, 2002). A study in Nova Scotia, Canada, found that 6 percent of 15–17 year olds in the province reported playing poker online for money in 2006 (Gillis, 2006). Derevensky et al. (2006) found that 9 percent of a sample of Montreal, Quebec, high-school students reported having gambled for money on the Internet. In Alberta, 5 percent of students in grades 7 to 12 reported gambling online in 2005 (AADAC, 2007). Other studies in other jurisdictions have also consistently found that a small but significant percentage of adolescents gamble online in a comprehensive review of this issue (see Chapter 10).

### Problem gambling

There are several aspects of Internet gambling that may increase the risks for problem gambling. This is due to its greater convenience, 24-hour access, ability to play when intoxicated, the solitary nature of the play, the fact that gamblers are playing with 'electronic' cash, the ability to play multiple sites/games simultaneously, and because it is more difficult for *Internet* problem gamblers to avoid the temptation of online play (i.e., it is easier for a land-based problem gambler to avoid land-based casinos, racetracks, and bingo halls than it is for an online problem gambler to avoid using the Internet) (Griffiths, 1996, 1999, 2003; Griffiths and Parke, 2002; Griffiths and Wood, 2000; King, 1999; King and Barak, 1999; Parke, 2009; Schull, 2005; Shaffer, 1996; Wood, Williams, and Lawton, 2007).

Not surprisingly, then, research has found that the prevalence of problem gambling is three to four times higher among Internet gamblers compared to non-Internet gamblers (Gaming Intelligence Group, 2007; Griffiths and Barnes, 2008; Griffiths, Wood, and Parke, 2006; Ladd and Petry, 2002; Wood and Williams, 2007, 2009; and see Chapters 7 and 11). However, while there are good theoretical grounds to believe that Internet gambling has led to problem gambling, it is also quite possible that problem gamblers are simply gravitating to Internet gambling (i.e., adding it to their repertoire). To date, the directional nature of this association between problem gambling and Internet gambling is unclear, and cannot be disentangled except with longitudinal research. As will be described in greater detail later in this book (see Chapter 11), longitudinal research in Ontario has found that both directional routes occur, as well as simultaneous development of Internet gambling and problem gambling. Nonetheless, there is some evidence that Internet gambling leading to problem gambling tends to be a somewhat more common route than problem gambling leading to Internet gambling or simultaneous development of both.

Historically, it is also the case that relatively few online gambling sites made significant efforts to mitigate problem gambling. A 2004 study of 30 UK Internet gambling providers found that only seven made explicit reference to the risks of uncontrolled gambling (Smeaton and Griffiths, 2004). A review of 60 popular Internet poker, casino, and sports betting sites by Wiebe in 2006 revealed wide variations in the extent and types of player protection strategies. At one end, some sites simply provided a statement concerning age limits or a link to a Gamblers Anonymous site. At the other end, there were sites that provided self-exclusion options, an on-site counselor, and opportunities for setting time, money, and loss limits (Sychold, 2003; Wiebe, 2006).

## Recent developments in player protection and fair play

As stated earlier, some of these above-described issues may be historical rather than current. For example, while there will always be some online sites with unethical or unfair business practices, there is currently no need to access these sites when online gambling is now provided from many well-regulated domestically delivered government sites and/or private companies with well-established reputations who are certified by one of the many industry standard associations.

There has also been significant improvement in age verification systems, particularly in places such as the UK which now requires a robust age verification system as a condition of license (i.e., licensees are required to check the requisite sign-up information to open an account against various databases (usually involving a third party) to confirm that the customer is indeed aged 18 years or older). In a recent report on e-consumer protection, the UK-based Children's Charities' Coalition on Internet Safety (CHIS, 2010) identified the Internet gambling industry as an example of best practice in child protection for other e-commerce industries to emulate based on their strict enforcement and checks and relative success in minimizing access to 'under 18s'. A recent UK Gambling Commission mystery shopper exercise demonstrated that whereas 98 percent of land-based gambling venues had age verification weaknesses, this only occurred in a third of Internet gambling operations (see Chapter 10).

With regards to helping mitigate problem gambling, it has also been recognized that one of the important advantages of online gambling is that all activity is electronically recorded and linked to an identifiable individual. Thus, unlike land-based gambling, online gambling sites can provide the player with the opportunity to set time or spending limits (which many currently do). Most of these same sites also provide the opportunity for the person to bar himself/herself completely for a period of time, similar to the self-exclusion offered at land-based casinos. In addition, there has been considerable interest shown in using this player data to develop behavioural markers of risky play for the purposes of proactively alerting the player and/or implementing some type of automated restriction/intervention (Braverman and Shaffer, 2010; Broda et al., 2008; Shaffer et al., 2007).

Finally, there exists considerable momentum to create industry-wide standards. One prominent organization is the eCommerce and Online Gaming Regulation and Assurance (eCOGRA). This is a UK-based industry organization, launched in 2003, which certifies online sites as having prompt payments, safe storage of information, random games, honest advertising, and responsible gambling practices. Other similar organizations include the Remote Gambling Association (RGA), the European Gaming and Betting Association (EGBA), and the Interactive Gambling Council (IGC). In 2008, eCOGRA, RGA, EGBA, and IGC collectively developed an International Code of Conduct that set standards for Internet operators regarding measures to prevent underage gambling, the need to provide player protection tools, and mechanisms to promote fair play and resolve disputes. These principles have now been more formally adopted in the 2011 European Committee for Standardization Workshop Agreement (known as 'CWA 16259: 2011'). In addition, at the time of writing, the European Commission had launched a public consultation on the full range of issues related to both legal and illegal Internet gambling operations in Europe.

Thus, it is clear that some improvements have occurred with Internet gambling in the past 10 years. However, there is reason to be cautious about this apparent progress. For one, although well-established reputable sites registered in well-regulated jurisdictions now have a more dominant place in the marketplace, there is still an abundance of other sites without these characteristics. For another, player tracking and predictive analytics for risky play are currently being used by only a handful of operators (mostly state lotteries). In addition, the 'pre-commitment' constraints that many online sites now allow players to impose on their gambling behaviour tend to be voluntary, of short duration, and sometimes revocable. In general, voluntary, short, revocable constraints are probably of some benefit to non-problem gamblers (which may or may not translate into a decreased future incidence of problem gambling), but are likely to have more limited benefit to the compulsive and addictive behaviour of pathological gamblers (Williams, 2010).[16] However, even if longer-term irrevocable constraints were available, a significant disadvantage of online gambling is the ability of the player to circumvent these restrictions by directing his/her play to over 2,000 other sites (recognizing that problem gamblers are much more likely than non-problem gamblers to patronize non-domestic sites to begin with, e.g., see Chapter 7). It is very unlikely that there will ever be a system whereby constraints and/or banning at one site will be universally recognized and adopted at other sites. Despite the above-mentioned efforts to create industry-wide standards, it needs to be recognized that almost all these efforts have been restricted to Europe, and worldwide only a minority of sites and/or owners have sought and/or received eCOGRA certification or RGA membership.[17] Furthermore, the online gambling industry has expressed reluctance about cross-operator application of player-imposed restrictions because of privacy issues, cost, trust, and differing technology standards (Dragicevic, 2011). The reality is that effective preclusion of 'site jumping' minimally would need legislation requiring domestic Internet service providers to block foreign online gambling sites and for there to be active enforcement of this legislation (a policy option discussed in Chapter 20).

## Notes

1   In 1983 the first online stock market transaction was facilitated by E*Trade Financial (Stock-Trading-Warrior.com, 2011). However, online trading continued to be uncommon until the Internet became more widely accessible to the general public and some of the major companies began offering online trading (e.g., Charles Schwab in 1996).
2   Mauritius, Sweden, and Swaziland were other jurisdictions that began hosting sites.
3   Prosecution of some prominent online companies with connections to countries having clear online gambling prohibition reinforced this trend. In Canada this was best illustrated by the 1999 prosecution of Starnet Communications (Kyer and Hough, 2002).
4   In 1999 Lasseters in Alice Springs, Northern Territory (Australia), became the world's first land-based casino to go online.
5   Another type of online skill gaming that could be potentially construed as 'gambling' involves paying a subscription to join a role-playing skill site (e.g., Lineage2) where the accumulation of virtual money and property can be bought and sold in the real world (e.g., $2,500 virtual dollars = $1 real dollar). A second grey area of online gambling concerns role-playing sites (e.g., Second Life http://secondlife.com/) where your avatar may gamble with virtual money (having some value in the real-world marketplace) at a virtual casino.
6   Speculation/investment in financial markets technically meets the common definition of gambling, which is that a person is wagering something of material value on something with an unknown outcome in the hope of winning additional money or material goods. However, it has traditionally been differentiated from gambling by the fact that most stock market investment has a positive expected return (unlike most forms of gambling) and it has economic utility (e.g., purchasing stock in a company provides that company with funds to support its endeavours). However, this distinction is challenged by things such as 'day-trading', shorting stocks (betting that their share price will decrease), and placing bets on the movement of financial indices with an agency external to the financial markets.
7   Operation of a 'bucket shop' is still illegal in some Western jurisdictions.

8   In Australia, the state of Victoria introduced iTV gambling in April 2008 (Hogan, 2008). This was followed by New South Wales in October 2008, Queensland in April 2011, and South Australia in June 2011 (CalvinAyre.com, 2011).

9   This number does not include 73 additional sites that only provide betting on financial markets.

10  Online.casinocity.com is a US-based gambling portal that has been in operation since 1995. It is one of the world's most comprehensive and widely used online gambling portals, providing continually updated listing and access to the 2,412 available online sites, as well as ranking of their relative popularity based on monitoring and measuring the actual site usage of millions of online users. This portal also provides a comprehensive listing of online gaming jurisdictions, online gaming site owners, online gambling software, and online gambling news. It is important to recognize that it is not possible to independently verify online.casinocity.com's rankings. That being said, the present authors and others (e.g., McNeal, 2006) have found that their figures/rankings are similar to those provided by other sources and that their data have usually been accurate when independent verification has been possible.

11  The information in this section was gathered by the first author from considerable numbers of sources, too numerous to list. Certain online gambling portals were helpful starting points: www.casinocity.com, www.gamingzion.com, and www.onlinecasinosuite.com (World Gambling Review). Because the legal/regulatory situation is in constant flux, the information provided in this section should only be considered accurate as of July 2011.

12  The states of Illinois, Michigan, Indiana, Nevada, Oregon, South Dakota, Washington, and Louisiana have all passed legislation that specifically prohibits unauthorized forms of Internet gambling.

13  For example, the jurisdictions hosting the most sites in October 2006 were Costa Rica (382), Antigua and Barbuda (366), and the Kahnawà:ke Mohawk Territory (344). However, these jurisdictions have now slipped to fourth (Costa Rica, $n = 204$), fifth (Kahnawà:ke, $n = 172$), and ninth place (Antigua and Barbuda, $n = 68$).

14  Most (but not all) online gambling sites prohibit the use of poker bots and other automated software programs. However, it is very difficult to detect the presence of these non-human players.

15  Underage gambling is of particular concern to US legislators, as the legal age to gamble in most US states is 21.

16  The primary benefit to problem gamblers will be its ability to deter within-session 'chasing'.

17  In August 2011, eCOGRA listed 165 approved sites, only somewhat higher than the 116 listed in August 2007. Furthermore, only four of the top 50 online gambling sites identified by www.online.casinocity.com currently have eCOGRA certification (i.e., Party Poker, 888 Casino, Party Casino, bwin Sportbook). The RGA only has 30 member companies, with only 12 of the top 50 site owners identified by www.online.casinocity.com as having membership.

## References

4 Online Gambling.com (2011). 'Online casino industry development timeline'. Retrieved from http://www.4online-gambling.com/timeline.htm

AADAC (2007). 'Gambling among Alberta youth: The Alberta Youth Experience Survey 2005'. Retrieved from http://www.albertahealthservices.ca/2382.asp

American Gaming Association (2006). 'Gambling and the Internet'. *2006 AGA Survey of Casino Entertainment*. Author. Retrieved from http://www.americangaming.org/newsroom/press-releases/new-aga-survey-offers-depth-profile-us-internet-gamblers

Balestra, M., and Cabot, A. N. (2006). *The Internet gambling report (9th edition)*. Las Vegas: Trace Publications.

Braverman, J., and Shaffer, H. J. (2010). 'How do gamblers start gambling: identifying behavioural markers for high-risk Internet gambling'. *European Journal of Public Health*. doi:10.1093/eurpub/ckp232

Broda, A., LaPlante, D. A., Nelson, S. E., LaBrie, R. A., Bosworth, L. B., and Shaffer, H. J. (2008). 'Virtual harm reduction efforts for Internet gambling: effects of deposit limits on actual Internet sports gambling behavior'. *Harm Reduction Journal, 5*, 27.

Brunker, M. (2004). 'Are poker "bots" raking online pots?' *Internet roulette on msnbc. com.* Retrieved from http://www.msnbc.msn.com/id/6002298/

*Business Wire* (2005, December 16). 'Intertops.com celebrates 10 years online sports betting'. *Business Wire*. Retrieved from http://findarticles.com/p/articles/mi_m0EIN/is_2005_Dec_16/ai_n15949966

CalvinAyre.com (2011, June 10). 'Two Way officially launches TV betting service'. Retrieved July 28, 2011 from http://calvinayre.com/2011/06/10/business/two-way-officially-launches-tv-betting-service/

Casino City (2011). 'Online Casino City'. Retrieved from http://online.casinocity.com/

CBS News (2008, November 30). 'How online gamblers unmasked cheaters'. Retrieved from http://www.cbsnews.com/stories/2008/11/25/60minutes/main4633254.shtml

Children's Charities' Coalition on Internet Safety (CHIS) (2010). 'eConsumer protection: a response to a consultation by the Office of Fair Trading'. Retrieved July 25, 2011 from: http://www.chis.org.uk/2010/10/18/evidence-to-the-office-of-fair-trading-e-consumer-protection-

Christiansen Capital Advisors (2005). *eGaming Data Report*. New Gloucester, ME: Author. Retrieved from http://www.cca i.com

Crowne-Mohammed, E. A., and Andreacchi, R. (2009). 'The unavailability of common law remedies for victims of online gambling fraud'. *Gaming Law Review and Economics, 13*(4), 304–9.

*Current Digest of the Post Soviet Press* (2006). *Current Digest of the Post Soviet Press, 58*(40), 10.

Dance, G. (2011, March 13). 'Poker bots invade online gambling'. *New York Times*. Retrieved from http://www.nytimes.com/2011/03/14/science/14poker.html

Derevensky, J. L., and Gupta, R. (2007). 'Internet gambling amongst adolescents: a growing concern'. *International Journal of Mental Health and Addiction, 5*(2), 93–101.

Derevensky, J. L., Gupta, R., and McBride, J. (2006, August/September).' Internet gambling among youth: a cause for concern'. Presentation at the Global Remote and E-Gambling Research Institute Conference. Amsterdam, Netherlands.

Dragicevic, S. (2011). 'Time for change: the industry's approach to self-exclusion'. *World Online Gambling Law Report, 10*(7), 06–08.

Drury, I. (2009, January 13). 'Third of gambling websites let children place online bets'. *Mail Online.*

Eurobet (2011). 'Eurobet history'. Retrieved from http://help.eurobet.com/1/navigation/aboutus_frameset.html

Gambling Commission (2011*). Survey Data on Remote Gambling Participation*. July 2011.

Games and Casino (2011). 'Blacklisted casinos'. Retrieved from http://www.gamesandcasino.com/blacklist.htm

Gaming Intelligence Group (2007, October 5). *Results of Swedish Online Gambling Study Released.* Retrieved from http://www.responsiblegambling.org/articles/Results_of_Swedish_Online_Gambling_Study_released.pdf

Guardian.co.uk (2011, June 30). 'Gambling on smartphones takes off'. Retrieved July 29, 2011 from http://www.guardian.co.uk/business/2011/jun/30/gambling-on-smartphones-takes-off

Gillis, J. (2006, October 4). 'Youth gambling online: survey reveals most N.S. Internet gamblers are teens'. *Chronicle Herald*. Study conducted by D-Code Inc.

Global Betting and Gaming Consultants (2009). *Interactive Gambling Report*. September. http://www.gbgc.com/publications/internet-gambling-report

Griffiths, M. D. (1996). 'Gambling on the Internet: a brief note'. *Journal of Gambling Studies, 12*(4), 471–3.

— (1999). 'Gambling technologies: prospects for problem gambling'. *Journal of Gambling Studies, 15*(3), 265–83.

— (2003). 'Internet gambling: issues, concerns, and recommendations'. *CyberPsychology & Behavior, 6*(6), 557–68.

— (2006). 'Interactive television and gaming'. *World Online Gambling Law Report, 5*(2), 12–13.

Griffiths, M. D., and Barnes, A. (2008). 'Internet gambling: an online empirical study among student gamblers'. *International Journal of Mental Health and Addiction, 6,* 194–204.

Griffiths, M. D., and Parke, J. (2002). 'The social impact of Internet gambling'. *Social Science Computer Review, 20*(3), 312–20.

Griffiths, M. D., and Wood, R. T. A. (2000). 'Risk factors in adolescence: the case of gambling, videogame playing, and the Internet'. *Journal of Gambling Studies, 16*(2–3), 199–225.

Griffiths, M. D., Wood, R. T. A., and Parke, J. (2006, May). 'A psychosocial investigation of student online poker players'. Presentation at the 13th International Conference on Gambling. Lake Tahoe, Nevada.

Hammer, R. D. (2001). 'Does Internet gambling strengthen the U.S. economy? Don't bet on it'. *Federal Communications Law Journal, 54*(1), 103–28.

Hogan, J. (2008, June 4). 'Moves afoot to switch off TV gambling'. *The Age.* Retrieved from http://www.responsiblegambling.org/articles/Moves_afoot_to_switch_off_TV_gambling.pdf

Hugel, P., and Kelly, J. (2002). 'Internet gambling: credit cards and money laundering'. *Journal of Money Laundering Control, 6*(1), 57–65.

*The Independent* (2004, November 8). 'Gambling on TV? It's a sure thing'. http://www.independent.co.uk/news/media/gambling-on-tv-its-a-sure-thing-532400.html

Ipsos MORI, The National Lottery Commission. (2009). *British Survey of Children, the National Lottery, and Gambling 2008–2009.* Retrieved July 25, 2011 from: http://www.natlotcomm.gov.uk/assetsuploaded/documents/Children%20and%20gambling%20-FINAL%20VERSION%20140709.pdf

Ipsos Reid (2005). *Online poker in North America: a syndicated study.* Retrieved from www.ipsos-na.com.

King, S. A. (1999). 'Internet gambling and pornography: illustrative examples of the psychological consequences of communication anarchy'. *CyberPsychology & Behavior, 2*(3), 175–93.

King, S. A., and Barak, A. (1999). 'Compulsive Internet gambling: a new form of an old clinical pathology'. *CyberPsychology & Behavior, 2*(5), 441–56.

Kshetri, N. (2005). 'Hacking the odds'. *foreignpolicy.com.* http://www.foreignpolicy.com/story/cms.php?story_id = 2848

Kyer, C. I., and Hough, D. (2002). 'Is Internet gaming legal in Canada: a look at Starnet'. *Canadian Journal of Law & Technology, 1*(1). http://cjlt.dal.ca/vol1_no1/articles/01_01_KyeHou_gaming.pdf

Ladd, G. T., and Petry, N. M. (2002). 'Disordered gambling among university-based medical and dental patients: a focus on Internet gambling'. *Psychology of Addictive Behaviors, 16*(1), 76–9.

McMullan, J., and Perrier, D. (2007). 'The security of gambling and gambling with security: hacking, law enforcement and public policy'. *International Gambling Studies, 7*(1), 43–58.

McMullan, J., and Rege, A. (2007). 'Cyberextortion at online gambling sites: criminal organization and legal challenges'. *Gaming Law Review, 11*(6), 648–65.

— (2010, July). 'Online crime and Internet gambling'. *Journal of Gambling Issues, 24.*

McNeal, B. (2006). 'Website review: online Casino City'. *UNLV Gaming Research & Review Journal, 10*(1), 105.

Mangion, G. (2010). 'Perspective from Malta: money laundering and its relation to online gambling'. *Gaming Law Review and Economics, 14*(5), 363–70.

Messerlian, C., Byrne, A. M., and Derevensky, J. L. (2004). 'Gambling, youth and the Internet: should we be concerned?' *Canadian Child and Adolescent Psychiatry Review, 13*(1), 3–6.

Mills, J. (2001). 'Internet casinos: a sure bet for money laundering'. *Journal of Financial Crime, 8*(4), 365–83.

Mitka, M. (2001). 'Win or lose, Internet gambling stakes are high'. *JAMA: Journal of the American Medical Association 285*(8), 1005.

NCH (2004, July 27). 'Children as young as 11 can set up gambling accounts at the click of a button'. [press release by NCH, GamCare and CitizenCard]. Retrieved from http://www.gamcare.org.uk/news.php/27/press_release_underage_internet_gambling_study

NetValue (2002). *Europeans take a Gamble online.* [NetValue Survey, June 2002] Retrieved from http://www.egamingpro.com/description.php3?II=SSEuropeanonlinegambling&Lang=US&Menu =Enquete

Online.Casino.org (2011, July 19). 'Increase in gaming consumption among smartphone users'. Retrieved July 28, 2011 from http://www.onlinecasino.org/news/increase-gaming-consumption-among-smartphone-users

Online Casino Suite (2011). *Worldwide Gambling: international betting laws by country.* http:// onlinecasinosuite.com/website/

Online Casino Topic (2007, December 3). 'Cyber World Group of Golden Palace Casino charged 2 million dollars'. Retrieved from http://www.onlinecasinotopic.com/cyber-world-group-of-golden-palace-casino-charged-2-million-dollars-147.html

Parke, J. (2009). 'Consumer protection in Internet gambling: current issues and future directions'. Paper presented at the European Lotteries Conference on Social Responsibility, Barcelona, Spain.

Romney, J. (1995, October). 'Tiny Liechtenstein offers first-ever Internet lottery'. *The News and Observer Publishing Co.* Retrieved May 27, 2011 from http://technoculture.mira.net.au/ hypermail/0018.html

Rose, I. N., and Owens, M. D. (2005). *Internet Gaming Law.* Larchmont, NY: Mary Ann Liebert, Inc.

RSeConsulting (2006, October). *A Literature Review and Survey of Statistical Sources on Remote Gambling.* Final report.

Schull, N. D. (2005). 'Digital gambling: the coincidence of desire and design'. *Annals of the American Academy of Political and Social Science, 597*(1), 65–81.

Schwartz, D. G. (2006). *Roll the Bones: The History of Gambling.* New York: Gotham Books.

Senate Information Technologies Committee (2000). 'Netbets: a review of online gambling in Australia (Chapter 2: Online Gambling in Australia)'. *Report for the Select Committee on Information Technologies.* http://www.aph.gov.au/senate/committee/it_ctte/completed_inquiries/1999–02/ gambling/report/contents.htm

Sévigny, S., Cloutier, M., Pelletier, M., and Ladouceur, R. (2005). 'Internet gambling: misleading payout rates during the "demo" period'. *Computers in Human Behavior, 21,* 153–8.

Shaffer, H. J. (1996). 'Understanding the means and objects of addiction: technology, the Internet and gambling'. *Journal of Gambling Studies, 12*(4), 461–9.

Shaffer, H. J., LaPlante, D. A., LaBrie, R. A., and Nelson, S. E. (2007, December). 'Detecting at-risk Internet gambling'. *Brief Addiction Science Information Source (BASIS).*

Smeaton, M., and Griffiths, M. (2004). 'Internet gambling and social responsibility: an exploratory study'. *CyberPsychology & Behavior, 7*(1), 49–57.

Srivastava, H. O. (2002). *Interactive TV Technology and Markets.* Norwood, MA: Artech House

Stock-Trading-Warrior.com (2011). *The Meteoric History of Online Stock Trading:* http://www.stock-trading-warrior.com/History-of-Online-Stock-Trading.html

Swiss Institute of Comparative Law (2006). *Study of Gambling Services in the Internal Market of the European Union.* Final Report prepared for the European Commission.

Sychold, M. (2003, September). 'Problem gambling and player protection deficiencies on the Internet: international legal and regulatory solutions'. Presentation at the Discovery Conference, Toronto, ON. Retrieved from http://www.rgco.org/articles/martin_sychold_Discovery_2003.pdf

United States General Accounting Office (2002, December 3). 'Internet gambling: an overview of the issues'. *Government Reports.*

van der Gaast, R. (2001, September). 'Finland – Internet gaming update'. http://www.gamblinglicenses. com/PDF/Finland_internet_gaming_update_Sept_2001.pdf

Villeneuve, J-P. (2011). 'Gambling in Switzerland – actors and structures'. *Gaming Law Review and Economics, 15*(1–2), 27–37.

Wiebe, J. (2006). 'Internet gambling safeguards: What are online gaming sites doing to protect customers?' *Newslink,* Fall/Winter, 4–6. Published by the Responsible Gambling Council. Retrieved July 12, 2007 from http://www.responsiblegambling.org/articles/NewslinkFallWinter2006.pdf

Williams, R. J. (2010). *Pre-Commitment as a Strategy for Minimizing Gambling-Related Harm*. White Paper prepared for Unisys Australia Pty Limited and Responsible Gaming Networks (Victoria, Australia). July 8. Submission to Parliament of Australia Inquiry into Pre-Commitment Systems. http://hdl.handle.net/10133/1287.

Wood, R. T., and Williams, R. J. (2007). 'Problem gambling on the Internet: implications for Internet gambling policy in North America'. *New Media & Society, 9*(3), 520–42.

Wood, R. T., and Williams, R. J. (2009). *Internet Gambling: Prevalence, Patterns, Problems, and Policy Options.* Final Report prepared for the Ontario Problem Gambling Research Centre, Guelph, Ontario. Retrieved from http://hdl.handle.net/10133/693

Wood, R. T., Williams, R. J., and Lawton, P. (2007). 'Why do Internet gamblers prefer online versus land-based venues?' *Journal of Gambling Issues, 20* (June), 235–50. http://hdl.handle.net/10133/375

# Part 2

# Commercial/Business Aspects

# 2    Online gambling

## An economics perspective

*David Forrest*

## Introduction

A rich literature offers analysis of important issues within traditional land-based gambling industries. For example, economists have studied topics such as: the sensitivity of consumers to changes in take-out;[1] substitution between modes of gambling as relative prices/take-outs vary; cannibalization of existing by newly permitted forms of gambling; impact of gaming facilities on local economies and on local crime; and cyclical sensitivity of the demand for gambling products. In line with standard practice in modern economics, almost all such studies begin with predictions from economic theory, follow with econometric modelling of relevant primary or secondary data, and conclude with a discussion of the evidence and its implications for understanding behaviour or formulating policy.

It is striking that only a handful of published studies on remote gambling has emerged to parallel that on the older land-based industry. Likely this reflects not a lack of interest on the part of economists, but rather a paucity of data to which they can apply their econometric models. As Eadington (2004) notes, it is difficult to collect systematic information which measures the volume of online gambling globally (or taking place in any particular market) because suppliers are located in a wide variety of jurisdictions, often with light regulatory systems, and typically do not face a mandated requirement to report turnover data. Relying on consumer self-reports of their activities in online gambling is not an adequate substitute for these data, given the dubious legal status of the industry in many places, particularly the United States.

In the absence of a body of formal empirical evidence, this chapter is focused mainly on developing predictions from first principles and checking their consistency against broad trends which have accompanied the emergence of the Internet as a means of accessing consumer products in general, and gambling products in particular. Fortunately, trends to date have been consistent with theoretical predictions such that economics should be able to help us understand better what is happening now and what will likely happen in the future.

## The emergence and development of e-commerce

As in other industries, gamblers began to have the ability to make purchases via the Internet from the mid- to late 1990s on (the first online casino, licensed in Antigua, was launched in January 1996). Eventually, as access to the Internet became more widespread, this development was to induce major changes in the gambling landscape; but such changes were not of course unique to this industry. E-commerce has, for example, also changed the way people buy stocks and other financial products. And travel agents and record stores have all but disappeared from the high streets and shopping malls of Europe and North America (perhaps bookshops will follow and newspapers are certainly under pressure). It appears instructive, then, first to consider what are the general implications of e-commerce for pre-existing traditional industries and their consumers and then to ask whether gambling has particular characteristics that would be expected to make any effects more or less in magnitude than in the rest of the retailing and service economy.

Generally, the ongoing impact of the Internet might be expected to be similar to that of previous breakthroughs in transport and communications technology, from the railways and telephone on. Such changes create value in the economy by lowering the costs of supplying goods to consumers, thereby putting downward pressure on price. Because they also give access to more suppliers by consumers in any one location, and lower consumer search costs by making it easier for them to compare prices, they also increase the overall competitiveness of the business environment. This leads again to lower prices, this time through the dissipation of economic rents associated with market power in local economies. For each of these reasons, consumers are likely to capture a large part of the value created by the new technology because they will pay less for what they already purchase and will gain extra utility by purchasing additional units at the new, lower price. On the supply side, substantial losses in welfare may accrue to existing firms which had operated in previously monopolistic markets and now can no longer generate monopoly profit. But their loss is not a loss to the economy as a whole, because it represents only a transfer to another group, consumers.

Naturally, the size of such impacts from a new communications technology will vary on an industry-by-industry basis. Cost savings on the supply side may take many forms, depending on the industry. For example, sellers marketing books on the Internet save on provision of expensive premises in central locations. However, their ability to economize on inventory costs is also important: a small number of copies of a less popular title will be needed to be kept in the central warehouse of an Internet seller, so that any of the occasional orders from consumers can normally be met, but a collectively much larger number of copies would be needed if these occasional buyers could appear in any of a large network of bookshops around the country. Through such economies, available to Internet sellers, manufactured goods' prices to consumers will therefore be expected to fall as a result of the innovation that is represented by e-commerce. However, the size of the fall will be limited to the extent that there has been no direct impact from the new technology on the costs of the manufacturing process itself, which accounts for a significant part of the final price.

This line of thought points naturally towards services, rather than manufacturing, as being where most structural change will be expected to occur. This is consistent with Borenstein and Saloner (2001) who noted that early impacts from the Internet were strongest in industries where there was no physical product at all, citing, for example, the brokerage industry where investors were purchasing stocks on better terms than before, as online brokers eroded the markets of traditional stockbrokers. Similar trends occurred in insurance selling and travel agency services.

Gambling also offers no physical product; hence it may potentially have similar outcomes as those observed in financial and travel services. Outcomes could include revolutionary changes, such as the disappearance of bricks-and-mortar venues, but only when there are no barriers to entry in the Internet sector and where consumers regard the products of Internet and traditional firms as identical.

Where these assumptions hold, economic theory clearly predicts major change. Providers in a traditional market enjoy some degree of market power, because the size of the local market (for stockbroking, travel agency, gambling, whatever) is too small to support a sufficient number of firms for competitive conditions to be sustained. Let new technology now permit access to that local market by sellers from anywhere else in the world. If the marginal cost of supplying a customer is the same for new and old firms, any new entrant (local, national, or international) employing Internet selling will be able to undercut current local prices because these include a margin reflecting monopoly profit. New entrants will therefore offer cheaper service to capture market share and yet will still be able to earn some profit. The incumbents must then reduce their prices to sell anything (because consumers take the lower price if they perceive two products as identical). If there are no barriers to entry, new firms will be expected to continue to enter the market, driving down price further, in the end to the level of cost, extinguishing all economic profit for all suppliers, land-based and Internet alike. This is the new equilibrium, because no new entry will occur once economic profit is zero. In this new equilibrium, consumers purchase more of the product at a lower price, which is the social benefit of the change. It is indeterminate in this case how the market will finally be split between traditional and Internet providers.

However, it is important to recognize that this model does not allow for any cost savings enjoyed by Internet as compared to land-based suppliers. There are likely to be such savings because of lower rents on premises and lower labour costs (if orders by computer facilitate automation of the selling process). With this additional factor, there would still be economic profits for the Internet sector when price reaches the level at which the land-based incumbents are no longer making any surplus. Without barriers to entry in the Internet industry, new firms and competition will therefore drive price down even further until no land-based firm can make even zero economic profit at Internet sellers' level of costs. The land-based businesses will at that point have to exit the industry because they will be incurring actual economic losses – unless they can find cost savings (which some may be able to do if they had been taking their economic profits in the form of inefficiency and an easy life rather than in the form of money). Final predictions for such an industry are therefore that one will observe lower prices, higher total consumption, erosion of profits, and closures and/or efficiency gains among land-based suppliers.

The shift towards such a new equilibrium may start to occur quite quickly, even before penetration of the Internet among consumers has become very widespread, because prices in competitive markets are driven by marginal players, i.e. relatively few customers may have to gain access to the Internet for incumbents to feel pressure to lower prices to defend their market share. On the other hand, the changes may never work to their natural conclusion if the assumptions of the model are violated (regarding the lack of barriers to entry faced by firms and the perception of consumers that the offerings of the two types of supplier are identical). This may be the case in financial services where, for example, a barrier to entry may be presented by a regulatory agency, or local suppliers may be regarded by some customers as more trustworthy. In the latter case, some land-based incumbents may survive, even with higher costs than Internet providers, so long as there is a segment of the market willing to pay a sufficient premium to contract with those they judge less likely to defraud them. Thus, while the general expectation is that industries such as we have cited – insurance, broking, travel services, gambling – will change radically because of the Internet, these changes will vary in degree according to particular characteristics of the service in question.

## Particularities of gambling

In one sense, gambling is very like other financial services. For example a bookmaker is commonly characterized in the economics literature (Sauer, 1998) as simply selling a financial security where the pay-off happens to be state-contingent such that it pays the holder x or zero, depending on whether a named event occurs or not. Basic predictions concerning the impact of e-commerce should therefore be similar as for any financial services sector. But, in practice, gambling has several distinctive features relevant to the question of how extensively and in what form e-commerce will have its impact.

One assumption in the basic economic model is that consumers regard the product as the same whether supplied from the old (land) or the new (Internet) economy. Whether this reflects reality is likely to vary considerably both across individuals and across modes of gambling. Differences will be related to motives for gambling. For example, many sports bettors are driven mainly by the belief that their specialist knowledge will enable them to make money. They would have no reason to accept less favourable odds from land-based than from Internet bookmakers and therefore, if such customers predominated, it might be expected that either Internet commerce would eventually take over all of the market or land-based suppliers would have to adapt to accepting 'world' prices. On the other hand, many horse bettors and bingo and casino players are willing to pay for (lose money from) their hobby, not only because they find the game exciting, but also because the venue offers conviviality and social interaction. Such customers would regard Internet sites as a very poor substitute for land venues and, if such customers predominated, relatively little change might occur in these sectors. Bricks-and-mortar provision will survive even if it offers less value for money than the alternative because buyers, in effect, are willing to pay (a premium) for the attributes which only traditional suppliers offer. Internet bingo, casinos, and horse betting may generate new markets given the price and convenience, but the old market will not necessarily be cannibalized. There is analogy here with the survival of some cinemas when television arrived because, popular as the latter became, it could not replicate in the home the social experience of the public facility and was not therefore the perfect substitute assumed in the basic model above.

Of course, it may also be true that individual consumers have very different preferences from each other over the very attributes which distinguish land and Internet offerings of similar gambling products. Cotte and Latour (2009) interviewed samples of land and online casino players and found many of those who used land venues regarded the Internet as an inferior option because it lacked the exciting atmosphere and the social interaction with staff and with other players, which made visiting the casino an occasion (notwithstanding the attempts by gambling websites to provide equivalents such as sound effects and player chat rooms). On the other hand, online players positively preferred their participation in casino games not to be complicated by the pressures of a public setting. This mix of player preferences/motives permits coexistence of the old and new casino industries and prices need not necessarily converge (albeit that players who are not far from being indifferent between the two sectors will provide a price-sensitive group, which will limit the extent to which value for money can vary).

If pressed to express a view, I suspect that many commentators on gambling would guess that, across modes, betting may offer greater conformity than casino or bingo games with the environment assumed in the basic economic model of the impact of e-commerce. Other than in a few countries where betting shops offer a social context, wagering in person offers few advantages over betting on the Internet. For example, bets may simply be placed at a counter in a tobacconist as has been traditional in France, while in nearly all American states, off-track betting is illegal, though very widespread, and bets just have to be telephoned to the local 'underground bookmaker' (Strumpf, 2003). Such arrangements provide no additional amenities and therefore it appears reasonable to expect that betting is one mode where the assumption of perfect substitutability should hold. Most attention below will therefore be paid to testing the predictions of this model against experience in that sector.

The second particularity of gambling compared to other service industries is that, in a large majority of jurisdictions, providers have enjoyed often absolute monopoly power, either because gambling is illegal (the need for trust between buyer and seller deters the consumer from seeking alternative providers (Strumpf, 2003)), or because the state restricts the number of operator licences and/or the number of venues. In continental Europe, state-owned monopoly is the typical model; but, even elsewhere, the state often does still capture economic rents associated with the restrictions in supply through policies such as high gambling-specific taxes. Lack of a competitive market will usually permit high prices to be charged to consumers, which will result in less gambling activity compared with what they would otherwise choose. The scope for access to Internet extra-territorial supply to benefit consumers, partly at the expense of incumbent providers, therefore appears unusually high in the gambling sector compared with other, more competitive service industries. At the same time, the potential loss of economic rents accrued by government not only raises particular public policy (fiscal) issues, but also the possibility that the outcomes predicted by the basic economic model will be thwarted. Governments have a strong incentive to use their powers (which private owners in other industries do not possess) to follow protectionist policies designed to prevent consumers and new suppliers from finding each other and transacting (for example, governments can prohibit advertising by extra-territorial gambling companies or order blocking of their websites by Internet service providers). Several jurisdictions have followed this course and their policies provide a lively focus of contemporary legal and social debate on gambling on which economics may shed light.

A final distinctive aspect of gambling is that it is an activity which generates more controversy than most other industries on which e-commerce may have a potential impact. The basic economic model emphasizes that the new technology creates value for the economy, which manifests itself in a lower price and a higher level of consumption. Typically, such an outcome is taken by economists as enhancing social welfare but, in the case of gambling, there is a possibility that there will be a lowering of social welfare. This would arise if the benefit to recreational gamblers is more than offset by the harm to those whose play is dysfunctional. It is obvious that such an outcome is more likely if a disproportionate share of any increase in gambling activity is accounted for by current or potential problem or pathological gamblers. This is a further issue to be considered below.

## Betting:[2] impact on price and quantity

It was noted in the Introduction that there is a paucity of reliable data on the size of the global e-gambling sector and therefore of volumes of gambling as a whole. However, all estimates of aggregate betting volumes at sites for which information could be obtained show activity to be increasing. For example, recent estimates by H2 Gambling Capital (quoted in Remote Gambling Association, 2010) suggested that the annual amount bet globally in online betting grew from €16.3b in 2004 to €32.6b in 2008. Extrapolating rates of growth (always of course a somewhat speculative exercise) implied that the online market would further increase in size, to more than €50b by 2012.

This remarkable growth in the popularity of online betting does not appear, in every case, to have been at the expense of the volume of business transacted by traditional bookmakers. The United Kingdom is a relatively open market in that residents have an unambiguous right to place bets with extra-territorial suppliers. Despite the emergence of this new sector, the participation rate in sports betting with land bookmakers tripled between 1999 and 2010, according to the British Gambling Prevalence Survey, 2010 (Wardle et al., 2011). Increases in betting volume were noted in Vaughan Williams (2006) and are evident in particular for sports betting in recent Gambling Commission statistical reports, the latter showing also an increase in the number of retail outlets (Gambling Commission, 2010).[3]

That consumers in a relatively free market jurisdiction have been betting more over time in both new and old sectors suggests that bettors in both may simply have been responding to the stimulus of lower prices caused by greater competition as e-commerce became more widespread. H2 Gambling Capital data reveal a fall in the mean proportion of global online turnover retained by online bookmakers, from around 10 percent in 2004, to less than 9 percent in 2008, and with projection to below 8 percent by 2012 (Remote Gambling Association, 2010).

These are of course global averages across a variety of sports. They point to improving value for bettors over time as competition within the online sector itself becomes more intense and as traditional and established bookmakers come under pressure from extra-territorial supply (and from betting exchanges, discussed below). For a more specific illustration, on football (soccer), I obtained (from www.football-data.co.uk) closing odds offered by Ladbrokes, the largest British bookmaker, on football matches in the English Premier League (EPL) between seasons 2000–1 and 2010–11. Sampling of other bookmakers and other European leagues, from data archived on the same website, yielded very similar patterns.

Value for money from the perspective of bettors is conventionally assessed from odds data by using a figure called the over-round. Take, for example, an event with three possible outcomes, home win, draw, and away win. Suppose the bookmaker odds (in the format of decimal odds, the most common format for quoting odds in the football market) on a home win were 0.40. This means that 40 cents has to be staked on a home win if one euro is to be collected by the bettor in the event a home win occurs (the one euro collected would include both winnings, 60 cents, and return of the stake, 40 cents). The sum of the decimal odds on all three outcomes will normally be greater than one because, otherwise, there would be an opportunity for arbitrage: a bettor could bet on each of the three outcomes for a total stake below the one euro he would subsequently be entitled to collect. The margin by which the sum of the decimal odds (the over-round) exceeds one is a measure of the value for money offered to bettors. Let this margin be $m$. Assuming, hypothetically, that the bookmaker held equal liabilities on each event outcome, $m/(1-m)$ would then be the bookmaker's expected rate of return from the transaction. For the bettor, assuming that relative odds reflect true relative probabilities, then, $-m/(1+m)$ is the expected rate of return from betting randomly (to a payout of one euro) on any one of the outcomes of an event.

For example, Table 2.1 shows that the mean sum of the odds across the 380 matches in the EPL in 2000–1 was 1.1253. This is the over-round. The bookmaker commission is proxied (only proxied because it is assumed, but may not be true, that he has equal payout liabilities across outcomes) by $0.1253/1.1253 = 11.13$ percent. Similarly, the expected rate of return to a bettor who chooses randomly between home win, draw, and away win is $-11.13$ percent. Widely, 11.13 percent would be quoted as the bookmaker commission or, for bettors, the transaction cost of betting.

The data source presents odds for each EPL match since 2000–1. Internet betting was already available in 2000, so some erosion of over-round may have occurred earlier. Further, this was about the time when bookmakers began to take bets on individual matches (prior rules had restricted wagers to a combination of three games), allowing bookmakers, in effect, multiple commissions. The abandonment of this rule was itself explained by new Internet operators not enforcing a similar restriction and it implied greater real falls in commission than shown in the table.

*Table 2.1* Ladbrokes odds and over-round on English Premier League football matches

|  | Mean home odds | Mean away odds | Mean draw odds | Mean sum of odds | Implied commission (%) |
|---|---|---|---|---|---|
| 2000–1 | 0.5131 | 0.2952 | 0.3170 | 1.1253 | 11.13 |
| 2001–2 | 0.5091 | 0.2980 | 0.3167 | 1.1239 | 11.02 |
| 2002–3 | 0.5076 | 0.2962 | 0.3200 | 1.1238 | 11.02 |
| 2003–4 | 0.5017 | 0.2967 | 0.3251 | 1.1236 | 11.00 |
| 2004–5 | 0.5000 | 0.2968 | 0.3263 | 1.1229 | 10.94 |
| 2005–6 | 0.5001 | 0.2930 | 0.3296 | 1.1227 | 10.90 |
| 2006–7 | 0.4989 | 0.2947 | 0.3297 | 1.1232 | 10.97 |
| 2007–8 | 0.4974 | 0.2930 | 0.3315 | 1.1220 | 10.87 |
| 2008–9 | 0.4835 | 0.2862 | 0.3228 | 1.0926 | 8.48 |
| 2009–10 | 0.4842 | 0.2684 | 0.3223 | 1.0749 | 6.97 |
| 2010–11 | 0.4828 | 0.2731 | 0.3091 | 1.0650 | 6.10 |

Source: Calculated from www.football-data.co.uk

As access to the Internet became more widespread, one might have expected bookmaker commissions to be eroded. This happened in this very popular football betting market, as the table illustrates, though further research would be needed to establish why the fall in commission was concentrated in 2008–11. In any event, commissions were spectacularly lower in the final compared with the first season of the data, 6.10 percent compared with 11.13 percent.

Things were actually even better for the bettor than these figures suggest. Mean over-round varies little across providers but the relative odds on the three possible outcomes of a single match do display differences in some cases because, for example, odds setters at competing firms take different views on the prospects of the two teams. Before remote betting became accessible to nearly all, the customer could bet only on the basis of odds available at his local bookmaker. However, the new technology allows virtually costless comparison between odds quoted by a large number of international bookmakers (indeed comparison websites are available and just a click permits betting at the bookmaker offering the 'best odds' for the outcome one favours). The expected rate of return to random betting at an individual bookmaker is therefore no longer a true representation of the market conditions faced by the bettor who is alert to the possibilities of 'shopping around'. For EPL matches in 2010–11, I calculated the equivalent to over-round for each match by summing the 'best available' odds for home win, draw, and away win, 'best' defined across the list of bookmakers covered on the website (which includes only firms with an international reputation and a strong brand presence in the market). The mean over-round for the 380 matches was now 1.007, implying that random betting, but with the bettor always taking 'best odds', would have an expected return of –0.73 percent, i.e. quite close to break-even. This illustrates vividly how much better value has become available to the bettor across the period of Internet penetration.

An intriguing aside is that these changes in the last decade appear likely to have been a spur to professional betting. A successful professional bettor must rely on picking examples of 'mispricing' by odds setters such that, at 'true' probabilities, the expected rate of return is positive on some outcome on which a bet may be placed. High commissions provide a cushion which protects bookmakers from professional bettors with specialist ability or information. With the commission of 11.13 percent observed in 2000–1, an odds quote would have to deviate very far from the true relative probability of the event occurring before it would offer a positive expected return to bettors so skilled as to know true probabilities. As the effective commission approaches zero, as observed for 2010–11, even small errors can present (expected) profit opportunities, and less specialist knowledge than before is needed to beat the bookmaker. Consequently, the economist would predict that the more competitive market brought about by the new technology will have increased the number of professional bettors. This prediction is consistent with casual observation but is not formally testable because the requisite data are not available.

Returning to the more familiar notion of betting as entertainment, the gains to consumers from falls in bookmaker margins are likely to have been considerable. Changes in consumer welfare are typically evaluated by economists through employment of the concept of *consumer surplus*. The concept is based on representing the gain to a consumer from participation in any transaction as equal to the difference between what he would be willing to pay and what he actually has to pay. All but the most marginal consumer will enjoy positive consumer surplus. For example, I am offered the opportunity to place a one unit wager with an expected loss of 10 cents; but I enjoy the experience enough that I would still bet at any expected loss up to 15 cents, i.e. my 'willingness to pay' is 15 cents. If I am rational, I must anticipate 15 cents' worth of satisfaction from the bet (otherwise I would not be willing to pay that much) but, given I actually have to pay only 10 cents, I gain from the transaction: the value of my satisfaction exceeds the price. In this case, my gain or 'surplus' is measured as equivalent to 15–10 = 5 cents.[4] If the price of the product now drops because of competition, my surplus on that transaction increases by simply the fall in price. It is therefore easy to calculate the gain in the value of consumer surplus in respect of the amount of the product which is already being traded. But there will also be gains for those who buy the extra units sold when price falls and calculation of these gains requires an estimate of the extent to which the fall in price stimulates sales (the number of unit bets placed). The total increase in consumer surplus equals consumers' saving on what they buy already *plus* the consumer surplus on any new bets that are stimulated by the fall in commission rates.

The first element here represents a transfer from suppliers to consumers; but the second is a pure social gain which arises when consumers derive satisfaction from the units they previously did not buy because they were deterred by the monopoly price.

Let us be conservative. Consider only the fall in the commission rate at the single bookmaker shown in Table 2.1 (i.e. ignore further gains obtainable by shopping around). Commission fell from 11.13 percent to 6.10 percent. On every £1m of bets which bettors had been making initially, consumers will have saved £50,000. Let us continue to be conservative and assume that elasticity of demand for betting was –1 (i.e. the number of unit bets increased at the same proportionate rate as commission fell). That assumption allows us to estimate the consumer surplus on the additional bets as about £20,000. Therefore the overall gain in annual consumer surplus will have been about £70,000, £20,000 of which would be pure social gain, in a betting market where original annual turnover was £1m. Given the vast scale of aggregate betting markets in football, this would multiply up to a very large change in consumer welfare from increased competition and falling prices. This is consistent with findings, since the Australian Productivity Commission (1999), that the aggregate consumption benefit derived in gambling markets is very high, even when, as the Australian Productivity Commission recommended, some of the turnover (typically 30 percent) is discounted in the calculations to represent transactions made by problem gamblers whose willingness to pay is presumed not in fact to be based on rationality. If consumption benefit is high, any increase from better value odds will also be large. This consumption benefit accrues both to Internet bettors and to those who bet in the traditional way but who now get improved odds because of Internet competition.

While some of the benefit to consumers is offset by loss of monopoly profits, some of it, that associated with additional consumption, represents pure social gain. This element is greater, the more sensitive to value that bettors prove to be. In the extreme case where a jurisdiction had previously successfully prohibited betting, the entire consumer surplus generated when its residents use the new Internet betting comprises pure social gain. In economic analysis, such social gains comprise the new value the new technology creates for the economy.

## Efficiency gains

So far, social gains have not been defined to include savings to consumers when better value for money is offered on bets they were making already. These consumer benefits have been characterized simply as a transfer from the old providers to the existing customers. But this transfer is converted to a social gain if the improvement in value offered by existing providers is possible because those providers have responded to competition by achieving efficiency gains rather than just taking lower profits. Efficiency savings represent savings in resources and are counted therefore as social benefit. If efficiency gains are stimulated by competition, social benefit from the new technology will be enhanced as it will include some of the consumer gain counted above as merely a transfer.

It is typically difficult to observe efficiency gains within individual firms in any industry and hard therefore to verify whether productive efficiency indeed increases in a sector newly threatened by external competition. However, in the case of bookmaking, the setting of accurate odds is a key component of success in the industry and, since these odds are public, it can be tested whether the process of producing those odds became more efficient as competition intensified.

In Forrest, Goddard, and Simmons (2005), we assessed the accuracy of the odds at a number of British bookmakers in respect of a large sample of football matches. We compared the forecasting performance of odds with that of a very detailed statistical model for predicting football, developed from that first presented in Dobson and Goddard (2001). On standard performance metrics used in the forecasting literature, odds performed slightly worse than the model at the beginning of the Internet era but this was reversed as competition intensified. Compared with before, odds setters appeared better at processing public information as captured by the large number of variables in the statistical model and, further, appeared to employ more effectively any additional information they alone possessed. We concluded that this was a clear illustration of the potential of competition to concentrate minds and improve efficiency.

Naturally, British bookmakers[5] responded in other ways to the threat posed by new, remote providers. They established their own Internet presence; they lobbied successfully for tax concessions; and they diversified their product offering by installing very popular electronic roulette machines ('fixed odds betting terminals') in retail outlets. The number of betting shops in Britain remains comfortably above 8,000,[6] as it has since the 1980s, notwithstanding the free availability of an equivalent product online.

## The problem of problem gambling

The claim above is that e-gambling, as illustrated by the example of sports betting, has created value for society, and consumers have captured this value by enjoying more of the product at a lower price. This would likely be the conclusion had the industry under study been in any sector where e-commerce had made inroads.

Gambling is different, however, to the extent that public policy is seldom shaped by an emphasis on consumer interests. Eadington (1999) remarked that consumers of gambling services were treated as second-class citizens in that their interests were not counted in political debate. Indeed, extra consumption (the measure of social gain whenever an economist analyses a case where competition drives down price), is often characterized in the particular case of gambling as *harmful* rather than a 'good thing'.

Those who support measures to restrict competition because competition will stimulate consumption by lowering prices are often doing so to serve the interests of established providers. But that does not imply, of course, that their stated argument is necessarily fallacious. The legitimate point that underlies their argument is that, while the majority of gamblers play rationally, in the sense that they make an informed choice, a small number (but representing a much higher proportion of turnover) depart from rationality to the point of harming themselves and others by their consumption decisions. Any additional gambling activity may increase the extent of such harm. Evaluation of the social impact of e-gambling should therefore weigh the gains assessed to recreational consumers against any increase in harm from problem and pathological gambling.

Harm from gambling can take many forms. Sometimes, for example, it may be related to excessive devotion of time to gambling, to the detriment of employment, relationships, and even physical health. But it is excessive spending that is most emphasized in discussion of problem gambling, since this can lead to outcomes such as debt, bankruptcy, financially motivated crime, homelessness, domestic conflict, and suicide. A fair assumption appears to be, then, that harm is related closely to losses sustained in the gambling market. For this reason, a key question is whether the extra consumption of gambling in a more competitive market will lead to higher aggregate spending (player losses) by current and potential problem gamblers.

When competition drives down the price of any product, consumption invariably increases. But this does not necessarily lead to higher expenditure on the product. More units are purchased but the price paid for each one is lower. Since expenditure is the number of units *multiplied by* the price per unit, here the number of unit bets *multiplied by* the take-out, expenditure could in fact increase *or* decrease. It depends on whether the proportionate change in the number of units is greater than or less than the proportionate change in price. In the former case, demand is said by economists to be *elastic*, for example a 10 percent drop in price (take-out) induces a 20 percent increase in quantity (number of unit bets in this case). Then expenditure (player losses) goes up. In the latter case, demand is said by economists to be *inelastic*, for example a 10 percent drop in price (take-out) induces only a 5 percent increase in quantity (number of units bet in this case). Then expenditure (player losses) actually falls even though more bets are being placed.

In our context, it is clearly very relevant to know whether the demand for gambling services is in fact elastic or inelastic. In a report for the European Commission, the Swiss Institute of Comparative Law (2006) presented a survey of evidence in peer-reviewed journals on the elasticity of demand for gambling services. There was a clear consensus that players are generally highly sensitive to value for money. For example, it tabulates results from 15 articles evaluating elasticity of demand for either bookmaker or pari-mutuel betting; all but one of these found demand to be elastic, mostly strongly so. A study of casino slot machine gaming found elasticity varying over time but typically highly elastic. With this body of evidence in mind, it would have been reasonable to anticipate that, as the Internet drove down prices, including those levied at traditional outlets, the volume of gambling would increase by enough for consumer expenditure (player losses, gross gambling revenue (GGR), from the industry perspective) to be driven sharply upwards. And indeed this is what has transpired according to data cited above.

Therefore, if actual or potential problem gamblers respond to price similarly to the population as a whole, the evidence concerning elasticity would validate the proposition that greater price competition will lead to more social harm through greater financial losses associated with problem gambling (though this should still be weighed against gains to recreational gamblers). On the other hand, it cannot safely be assumed that elasticity is the same for actual and potential problem gamblers as in the market as a whole.

Alcohol is similar to gambling in that the commodity is sold to both 'responsible' and 'irresponsible' users. Manning, Blumberg, and Moulton (1995) were able to estimate elasticities for groups defined by different levels of alcohol use. Median drinkers exhibited elastic demand; but responsiveness to price declined with level of use and, for the heaviest 5 percent of drinkers (accounting for 36 percent of total consumption) elasticity was insignificantly different from zero, i.e. they were not at all sensitive to price.

Gambling, of course, has differences from alcohol, including perhaps less physical constraint on amount consumed. But, if the same pattern of elasticity held, there is the possibility that players who were problem gamblers would actually lose less money when offered better value for money and social harm would thereby decline rather than increase. A possible alternative scenario to this, for the most addicted to gambling, is that they would simply continue to spend all their disposable income on gambling and there would then be no change in their financial burden and its consequences (the case of *unit elasticity*, for example a 10 percent fall in take-out leads to a 10 percent increase in amount staked, with no change in player expenditure, i.e. losses).

All this is speculative because, to date, there have been no studies of demand elasticity specifically among problem gamblers and those at risk of problem gambling. This is clearly a line of research which could facilitate meaningful comparison between the positive impact of competition on the welfare of recreational gamblers and the *possibly* adverse effects (depending on elasticity) on the level of societal harm from problem gambling.

Of course, there are other dimensions than price that will be relevant to the issue of whether e-gambling has caused additional problem gambling harm (e.g. the style and pace of gambling offered might be different from that in land-based provision) and these are discussed in other chapters in this volume. But the price issue has taken on particular resonance in Europe. Several European states have come under pressure to open up their gambling markets to suppliers from other member states of the European Economic Area, following cases at the European Court of Justice concerning restrictions on trade in gambling services. Generally the Court has recognized that states have the right to impose restrictions on trade for reasons of customer protection or public order, but such limitations must be proportionate and consistent with other public policy.

In 2010, the gambling market in France was partially opened up when Loi 476/2010 made provision for licences to be issued for non-French operators to offer sports betting or poker from websites with an .fr suffix. But this was in the context of restrictions on payout ratios put in place by a decree ancillary to the legislation. In the case of sports betting, the maximum proportion of stakes that was permitted to be paid out as winnings was set by regulation at 85 percent and, with a tax levied in addition, bettors could receive only a 79 percent payback, reflected in significantly less favourable odds, i.e. higher over-round, than in other markets (MAG, 2011). Cynics might suspect that this ceiling on winnings was a means for protecting the economic interests of existing gambling providers in France, but the justification given was that it was for the protection of players who might suffer from compulsive gambling. This returns us to the question of elasticity of demand. Restrictions hurt recreational players unambiguously because they must accept less favourable odds or else gamble on unauthorized websites, but the financial losses sustained by problem gamblers as a result of their habit, and therefore the harm they do themselves, could be higher or lower depending on *their* elasticity. This is an empirical matter yet to be settled. Meanwhile, French recreational players could be losing heavily from the restriction for the sake of an unproven benefit of avoidance of social costs from problem gambling. Plainly there is scope for informative research here because what are effectively minimum price regulations have not previously been used as an instrument for addressing problem gambling issues in a competitive gaming market. The limitation of such regulation of course is that, if problem players are sensitive to price, it is in practice difficult to prevent them or any type of gambler gaining access to non-territorial websites offering lower take-out.

## Fiscal and other public policy issues

In all areas of e-commerce, the new ease with which new suppliers enter previously uncompetitive markets has eliminated economic rent formerly 'earned' by local suppliers as a result of their market power. The prospect of loss of economic rent in any context is likely to be met with a political response, but this is particularly the case for gambling where governments typically expropriate it for themselves through ownership or else taxation of gambling companies.

The unpalatable situation for governments on the emergence of e-gambling was that it would likely reduce the amount of surplus they could extract from the gambling industry. In one sense, this is a familiar story because the presence of an illegal sector has always been to some extent a constraint on the ability of the state to levy gambling taxes, and this is reflected in, for example, the history of gambling tax rates in the United States. Supply of remote gambling opportunities from other jurisdictions could be represented as just the development of another sort of illegal market akin to the old underground bookmakers and backstreet poker rooms. But it is more difficult to control the size of this new illegal market because it is foreign based and there are technological and social obstacles to preventing residents accessing it.

Many countries, for example the Netherlands, Germany, and the United States, have attempted to prevent their residents engaging in Internet gambling transactions with foreign suppliers. Instruments have included bans on advertising in mainstream media, requirements for Internet service providers to block access to foreign gambling websites and to remove such sites from search engine resources, and prohibition of processing of gambling-related transactions by domestic financial institutions. There are grounds for scepticism over the prospects for these sorts of measures to be successful for very long in protecting incumbent suppliers. Technology adapts to facilitate circumvention of restrictions. Advertising shifts to international social network and other websites. Word spreads on how individuals can still reach unauthorized websites. New financial products, such as e-wallets, are developed as alternatives to credit cards in wagering on foreign websites. Perhaps most important of all, there is a political constraint on how heavy-handed enforcement of all these measures can be because of a strong social consensus that the Internet should be free. As a result, states where legal modes of gambling represent an unattractive offer compared with what is available elsewhere will be liable to see their residents trade increasingly outside the jurisdiction. For example, MAG (2011) estimates that 75 percent of stakes on sports betting by French residents are placed on unauthorized websites. Thus states which seek to protect revenue by maintaining higher explicit or implicit gambling tax rates than in other markets may still face revenue decline because of diversion of trade to outside the jurisdiction.

The United Kingdom has long adopted a different model of regulating gambling than France and many other European states by assigning the supply of gambling services to a competitive private sector, albeit one with high market concentration. This led to a different threat to its tax revenue from e-gambling. The major operators responded to the possibilities of e-commerce (at the end of the 1990s) by moving offshore, to low-tax jurisdictions such as Gibraltar and those in the British Channel Islands. Their Internet operations could sell to the United Kingdom, and indeed international, markets, with all the advantage of brand names which enjoyed high recognition and trust, but with no need to offer the low payouts associated with high domestic gambling turnover taxes.

Of course, betting tax revenue did not go to zero when the major operators moved their online services offshore because the larger part of turnover was still derived from their retail branch networks. But tax had effectively been made optional and, given the threat to long-term revenue from more and more bettors gaining access to the Internet, betting tax was reformed quite quickly, a 6.75 percent on stakes replaced by a 15 percent tax on GGR. This amounted to a more than halving of the tax revenue claimed by government per one unit bet and the reform was sufficient to persuade the largest operators to move their Internet betting services back to the United Kingdom. The government lost revenue in the short term (Paton, Siegel, and Vaughan Williams, 2002) but subsequent growth in betting volumes in the mid-2000s, as consumers responded to enhanced betting value, was strong.[7]

This episode was an early example of what was to become a new global phenomenon, competition between jurisdictions to host gambling websites. As noted above, Internet gambling need not necessarily cannibalize the bricks-and-mortar industry (which may survive because it offers a different experience) but can still attract entirely new markets in terms of consumer spending. The size of the global market for all modes of online gambling was estimated as €10.7b (GGR) in 2008; the breakdown between modes was estimated as casino games 20 percent, bingo 8 percent, and poker 20 percent (Remote Gambling Association, 2010). This global e-gambling sector is effectively a new industry which is impressively large enough for many governments to have taken an interest in hosting.

Eadington (2004) notes that online casinos, given the structure of the games (and the ability of others to imitate innovations), offer little product differentiation, and there is ease of entry, such that the sector will have many of the characteristics of the economist's model of a perfectly competitive market. In such an environment, profit margins will be low and firms will struggle to supply a product which can generate a profit level above that of the long-run cost of capital.

In this context, firms will naturally be interested in where they should locate. Hosts can compete with each other to attract them by offering different fiscal and regulatory environments and standards of technological infrastructure. Fiscal inducements relate not only to gambling-specific taxes and licence fees but also to general corporate taxes. Firms will look to a low overall tax burden (not complicated too much by requirements on the degree to which operations have to be located in the jurisdiction). In this situation small jurisdictions have an advantage since the revenue potentially gained may be large enough, relative to the size of their overall economies, for them to be content to impose no gambling-specific or general business taxes at all and rely only on licence fees to collect an amount which covers infrastructure and regulatory costs. This explains the remarkable phenomenon that the Mohawk territory of Kahnawà:ke in Quebec, which has a population of only 8,000, is one of the leading locations for hosting top-100 online casino sites (Marshall, 2011). Similarly, relatively small territories, Malta and Gibraltar, dominate the Internet betting market in Europe, and American bettors have been serviced from places like Costa Rica.

Most of the jurisdictions specifically cited here offer environments with strong regulatory provision. Suppliers will look for the combination of cost levels and regulatory arrangements that will maximize profit. Cost levels will be driven low in terms of taxes and charges paid to host jurisdictions, but not to zero because the final consumers will prefer (be willing to pay more for) gambling in an appropriately regulated environment and this will be reflected in what gambling firms will be willing to pay to host jurisdictions.

Many customers will be interested in probity and require reassurance that they will not be cheated. However, their views on other aspects of player protection may be more ambiguous. Regulators in consumer countries often see an opportunity to take advantage of the technological possibilities by mandating inclusion of features designed to address problem gambling (pop-up warnings triggered by length or style of play are just one example); but players may be irritated by or resent paternalistic intrusion (see Chapter 13) and prefer websites licensed in jurisdictions with less proactive policies. Ultimately this will restrict the ability of regulators in consumer countries to impose their own preferences on degrees of player protection accorded to their own residents.[8]

In its Gambling Act (2005), the United Kingdom sought to attract new operators to use it as a location from which Internet gambling services could be offered. It established a rigorous regulatory framework and had the advantage that the domestic market, within which licence holders would be free to advertise, was the largest in Europe (European Commission, 2011). However, it has failed to attract any new international operators.[9] The idea behind the aspiration to be a centre for e-gambling was not necessarily wrong. There is a market for jurisdictional services. International consumers, and therefore the firms selling to them, might indeed be willing to pay, implicitly, for highly reputable regulatory services. But the Treasury set the tax rate to be applied, 15 percent of GGR, considerably in excess of that offered in rival jurisdictions and, given that there are other respected regulatory regimes, this proved to be well above the willingness to pay for the United Kingdom regulatory offer. This is another illustration that, in a global gambling market, governments will need to have more modest expectations about the share they can take from industry revenue.

## New gambling products

The bulk of the chapter has been focused on the impact of e-commerce on the price and quantity of existing gambling services, like sports betting and casino games, whether purchased in the old or new economy. But e-commerce has also spurred new products and new forms of market, which is likely to have led to further gains in consumer welfare (and perhaps new dangers as well in some cases). An example of a new product is the personalized photo album, readily supplied by online technology, but now imitated by photographic shops to protect their market share. An example of a new form of market is that the Internet made it feasible for airlines to fill unsold seats by online auctions. The most successful new forms of market have relied on the ability of widely separated buyers and sellers to be brought together on the Internet to trade in unusual products (such as certain collectables) where it may not have been even possible before for willing buyers to locate willing sellers. This is the phenomenon of e-Bay and person-to-person selling.

Parallel developments have been apparent in the gambling sector. In-play betting is a new product in the sense that it was previously feasible only for the highest-profile events. Internet technology allowed quoted odds to move rapidly as events unfolded in a sports event, for those odds to be communicated instantly to large numbers of bettors, and for these movements to be responded to by bettors before the moment was lost. This provided much more interest for bettors since wagering in-play is perceived as exciting and requiring special decision-taking skills (it also provides complementary activity to viewing an event on television).This is reflected in the fact that the substantial majority of money bet on football and tennis is now placed in-play rather than pre-event. This change in consumer behaviour was possible because the technology of online bookmakers and betting exchanges was readily adapted to in-play betting and, subsequently, traditional bookmakers have been induced to offer in-play as well to protect market share. Consumers therefore have a new product and this will be, for most users, a clear welfare gain, adopting, of course, the economist's principle of consumer sovereignty (the consumer's purchasing decision reflects what is best for him). However, research awaits to be done on whether the drama of in-play makes it a risky activity in terms of (irrational) problem gambling and there is also a concern among sports governing bodies that in-play betting presents new ways of manipulating sports events for betting gain, threatening the integrity of sport (Forrest, McHale, and McAuley, 2008).

Person-to-person selling has its counterpart in gambling in the betting exchange where the technology matches offers by participant to place or accept (lay) a bet that an event will happen. The exchange derives its income from charging commission on the transaction, the odds themselves being set by the offers from participants seeking to place or lay a bet. The commission rate is relatively low and the exchange has effectively removed a barrier on entry to bookmaking. Players in the market accept bets and therefore are effectively bookmakers, yet they do not have to invest in premises or marketing. As a result, odds are highly competitive and the growth of exchanges has been a further source of pressure on the margins of formal bookmakers.

The betting exchange is an example of a network good where the utility of one person's use of a service depends on how many other people use it. An exchange requires liquidity to be attractive, i.e. a good price can be obtained by a buyer only if he is put in touch with a number of possible sellers for a particular proposition (the more liquid the better). This makes it likely that, once one exchange becomes the market leader, those using other exchanges will transfer to it because of its liquidity advantage, and eventually, only one exchange survives. Thus there is an element of natural monopoly in the betting exchange and it is easily understood how Betfair has become so dominant in the jurisdictions it serves as to become synonymous with the very idea of a betting exchange.

Another example where it is network goods that emerge most strongly from e-commerce is poker. Poker now generates an estimated 20 percent of the global Internet gambling market (Remote Gambling Association, 2010) whereas it was a trivial element in land-based commercial gaming. This is clearly because playing poker requires opponents, and the Internet can provide opponents without the need to travel to a specialist venue, such as a casino. Liquidity is again important in web-based poker. This will put established, popular sites at an advantage compared with new entrants as sites with many active games provide short waiting times. This advantage to established sites provides a barrier to new entrants and thus, successful providers in this sector may be able to maintain economic profits (i.e. profits in excess of the cost of capital) in the long term.

The most obvious of all network goods is the lotto game, which comprises the largest gambling sector in Europe by GGR, and second only to casinos in the United States. A lotto game offers a low chance of winning a huge prize but because the game is pari-mutuel the prize becomes huge only by gathering together all the potential players' stakes in one place.

This makes lotto a natural monopoly, reflected in the fact it is also a statutory monopoly in nearly all jurisdictions. Incumbency this time favours the state sector.

Though many state monopolies have made it possible for their own residents to play online, lotteries generate minimal online activity relative to their importance in the land-based sector, accounting for less than 10 percent of global online GGR (Remote Gambling Association, 2010). The lack of competition permits very high take-outs (typically 40–60 percent) to be maintained to the disadvantage of consumers. This presents scope for price cuts by new entrants. However, immediate prospects of new entry appear weak in the case of high-prize games, particularly since pools available in many countries have been increased by operators combining to offer multi-state games, in America, Europe, Australia, and elsewhere. A new international lottery from a credible multinational enterprise is feasible but would be successful only with a high level of (risky) investment, the high cost arising not so much from substantial marketing expenses as from a need to top up prize funds from the operator's own resources (for as long as was necessary until there were sufficient players for the high prizes to be self-funded). However, payments of large prizes would be potentially easy to detect and block in jurisdictions that prohibited the sale of foreign lottery tickets. Hence, for a while longer, the lottery player appears likely to face high monopoly prices and will need to wait longer for the relief that other gamblers have obtained from the development of e-commerce and the erosion of monopoly power and monopoly profits.

## Notes

1   Take-out is the economist's concept of the price of gambling and is given by the expected value of the player's loss from a unit stake.
2   In discussion below, 'betting' refers to any wagering on horse and dog races, on other sports or on other events, such as the weather or television game shows. Following convention, the term 'sports betting' refers specifically to wagering on sports other than horse and dog racing. Thus sports betting is a segment of the wider betting industry. The distinction is often made in analysis of betting and parallels differences in legal status in many jurisdictions. For example, horse betting has long been a large sector in France but sports betting was illegal until 2010.
3   Such an outcome is less likely in jurisdictions with a highly restrictive policy on betting. For example, suppose there is a monopolist local supplier and Internet betting emerges internationally but is prohibited in this market. If price is maintained in the land-based outlets, there will be no stimulus to demand at the old provider but it may lose custom to the extent that, noting world prices are lower, some participants will find a way to circumvent the obstacles to using extra-jurisdictional supply.
4   Money here is being used as a numéraire to measure net satisfaction gained from the purchase. The 5 cents is therefore not a flow of money but a measure of consumer welfare.
5   Unlike many jurisdictions, betting in the United Kingdom had not been provided by a monopolist but there was an element of market power given that over half the market was served by three firms.
6   Indeed, it increased to over 8,900 by the end of 2010 (Gambling Commission, 2010).
7   Independent of implications for government revenue, there is a welfare case for easing or removing taxes on land-based providers of any product available tax-free in e-commerce (Goolsbee, 2001). A tax disadvantage for land providers will be an artificial inducement for substitution of Internet for land consumption to an extent beyond that which would reflect preferences over product characteristics in the two sectors. Here, bettors may prefer the betting shop environment but still accept lower satisfaction by trading on the Internet to avoid tax, a loss of consumer welfare.
8   On the other hand, 'white-listing' offers a weapon for consumer countries since recognition of licences granted in other jurisdictions allows advertising the product in mainstream media in those countries.
9   Indeed, in 2011, it lost an important business, Betfair, which moved its licence to Gibraltar. And, earlier, in 2009–10, Ladbrokes had relocated part of its online business offshore.

# References

Australian Productivity Commission (1999). *Australia's Gambling Industries* (Report no. 10). Canberra: AusInfo.

Borenstein, S., and Saloner, G. (2001). 'Economics and electronic commerce', *Journal of Economic Perspectives*, 15, 3–12.

Cotte, J., and Latour, K. A. (2009). 'Understanding online versus casino gambling', *Journal of Consumer Research*, 35, 742–58.

Dobson, S., and Goddard, J. (2001). *The Economics of Football*. Cambridge: Cambridge University Press.

Eadington, W. R. (1999). 'The economics of casino gambling', *Journal of Economic Perspectives*, 13, 173–92.

— (2004). 'The future of online gambling in the United States and elsewhere,' *Journal of Public Policy and Marketing*, 23, 214–19.

European Commission (2011). *Green Paper on On-line Gambling in the Internal Market*. Brussels: European Commission.

Forrest, D., Goddard, J., and Simmons, R. (2005). 'Odds-setters as forecasters: the case of English football', *International Journal of Forecasting*, 21, 551–64.

Forrest, D., McHale, I., and McAuley, K. (2008). 'Say it ain't so: betting related malpractice in sport', *International Journal of Sport Finance*, 3, 156–66.

Gambling Commission (2010). *Industry Statistics 2009/10*. Birmingham: Gambling Commission.

Goolsbee, A. (2001). 'The implications of electronic commerce for fiscal policy (and vice versa)', *Journal of Economic Perspectives*, 15, 13–23.

MAG (2011). *Jeux en Ligne in the French Market*. Rome: MAG Consulenti Associati.

Manning, W. G., Blumberg, L., and Moulton, L. H. (1995). 'The demand for alcohol: differential response to price', *Journal of Health Economics*, 14, 123–48.

Marshall, M. (2011). 'Online gaming in Kahnawà:ke', *Gaming Law Review and Economics*, 15, 335–41.

Paton, D., Siegel, D. S., and Vaughan Williams, L. (2002). 'A policy response to the e-commerce revolution: the case of betting taxation in the UK', *Economic Journal*, 112, F296–F314.

Remote Gambling Association (2010). *Sports Betting: Legal, Commercial and Integrity Issues*. London: Remote Gambling Association.

Sauer, R. D. (1998). 'The economics of wagering markets', *Journal of Economic Literature*, 36, 2021–64.

Strumpf, K. S. (2003). 'Illegal sports bookmakers'. *Working Paper*. University of North Carolina at Chapel Hill. February.

Swiss Institute of Comparative Law (2006). *Study of Gambling Services in the Internal Market of the European Union*. Lausane: Swiss Institute of Comparative Law.

Vaughan Williams, L. (2006). 'Betting the future online', *Significance*, 3, 10–12.

Wardle, H., Moody, A., Spence, S., Orford, J., Volberg, R., Jotangia, D., Griffiths, M., Hussey, D., and Dobbie, F. (2011). *British Gambling Prevalence Survey 2010*. London: The Stationery Office.

# 3  The Internet gambling industry

*Lorien Pilling and Warwick Bartlett*

The growth of the Internet gambling sector is closely linked to the development of Internet technology and e-commerce in general. As download speeds have quickened and the penetration of Broadband Internet technology in consumers' homes has increased, so the quality of e-gaming products has been improved. By comparison with the current games' graphics, speeds, and features, those early versions seem slow and basic. No doubt the same will be said of today's games in the next decade as technology moves on, particularly as three-dimensional graphics are incorporated into online casino and poker games.

There is a strong correlation between Broadband Internet penetration and the growth of Internet gambling. In 2009 global Broadband subscription stood at 7.0 per cent of the total population (ITU, 2010), while e-gaming's share of the total gambling market (including all products online and land-based) was 7.1 per cent, as measured by gross gaming yield (GGY) – the amount that customers lost to operators[1] (GBGC, 2010a). These low penetration rates suggest there is still substantial potential for growth in the e-gaming market over the next decade.

Given this correlation between Internet technology and e-gaming, it is not surprising that some of the most developed e-gaming markets have high levels of Broadband Internet usage in their general populations, for example: Denmark, Finland, Hong Kong, Singapore, Sweden, and the United Kingdom (UK).

In 2009 the Internet accounted for 90 per cent of global interactive gaming revenues, with the remainder being made up of revenues from mobile devices and interactive television (GBGC, 2010b). But the launch of new mobile devices such as Apple's iPhone and iPad, as well as the ongoing improvement in handset design and mobile Internet technology, means that mobile devices will take a greater share of the e-gaming market in the coming decade. Already in 2009 and 2010, a number of key Internet gambling brands have unveiled betting applications and games for the iPhone, such as Betfair, Ladbrokes, Paddy Power, and William Hill.

In May 2011 there were approximately 2,438 gambling websites offering a range of betting and gaming services, from sports betting through to lotteries (see Chapter 1). The market is very competitive, with operators working on tight margins, and various websites serve to increase competition by providing comparison services of the best odds and bonuses available.[2]

*Table 3.1* Interactive gambling's share (%) of total global gambling

| Year | 2007 | 2008 | 2009 | 2010 |
|---|---|---|---|---|
| Share (%) | 5.8 | 6.3 | 7.1 | 7.5 |

Source: GBGC, 2010a.

*Table 3.2* Global interactive gambling (GGY) (US$ billion), 2004–10

| Year | 2004 | 2005 | 2006 | 2007 | 2008 | 2009 | 2010 |
|------|------|------|------|------|------|------|------|
| GGY | 11.70 | 15.41 | 19.92 | 20.74 | 23.95 | 26.12 | 29.31 |

Source: GBGC, 2010b.

## Online gambling products

The main categories of online gambling products are:

- sports betting,
- casino games,
- poker,
- bingo,
- skill games,
- lotteries.

In 2009 the total interactive gambling market was estimated to be worth US$26.12 billion in GGY. This was an increase of 9 per cent from the $23.95 billion recorded in 2008. By 2011 Global Betting and Gaming Consultants (GBGC, 2010b) forecasts that the global interactive gambling market will have almost trebled in size from $11.70 billion in 2004.

In the last decade the e-gaming sector has shown strong growth in revenues every year except for 2007, when overall growth was 4 per cent and global Internet casino and poker revenues actually fell compared with 2006. The reason for this decline in revenues was action by the US government at the end of 2006 to prohibit financial transactions linked to Internet gambling and passing legislation that deemed Internet gambling to be unlawful. Many of the major Internet gambling firms that had been targeting customers in the United States ceased operating in the country almost overnight once the law was passed. This was particularly the case for companies such as PartyGaming, Sportingbet, and 888 Holdings, which are listed on the London Stock Markets and had the interests of their shareholders to consider (888 Holdings, 2006; PartyGaming, 2006; Sportingbet, 2006).

It is a measure of the resilience and entrepreneurialism of these companies that they were able to survive the loss of their main market and readjust their operations to develop their European businesses. Despite the new law and the withdrawal of most of the major e-gaming firms, Internet gambling still thrives in the United States and is served by privately owned companies licensed in jurisdictions outside the USA, such as Costa Rica, Kahnawà:ke (Canada), and the Isle of Man.

### *Sports betting*

Sports betting is the dominant online product in terms of gross win (same as GGY)[3] and accounted for 41 per cent of global e-gaming. This is partly because of the popularity of sports and the fact that betting on sports constantly challenges the customer's opinion against the odds set by the bookmaker. Online betting on horse racing and sports is regarded as more acceptable by governments than other forms of gambling, so is more widely permitted in certain markets. For example, monopoly operators such as the Japan Racing Association and Hong Kong Jockey Club have sizeable online betting operations.

The strong competition for customers between Internet sports betting firms has had the effect of driving down the gross win margins to which online sports books operate. Internet sports books aim for a gross win margin of between 7 and 10 per cent, while their land-based counterparts in the betting shops aim for 16 to 19 per cent. Sports betting also contains the most risk for the operator with the level of gross win being dependent on sports results. A run of winning favourites can have a detrimental impact on the gross win margin. If all the leading soccer teams win their matches over a single weekend, it can cause what is known as a 'wipe-out' for bookmakers.

The introduction of betting exchanges in the year 2000 revolutionised the sports betting model (Clarke, 2009). Betting exchanges use Internet technology to allow gamblers to bet directly with each other (peer-to-peer [P2P] betting), thus cutting out the need for traditional bookmakers. Betting exchanges also let the customers set their own odds and, unlike a traditional bookmaker which keeps its customers' losing bets, the betting exchange operator instead takes a commission for facilitating the betting process. The commission level is usually between 2 and 5 per cent of net winnings. This commission-based model is a much less risky business model because the betting exchange operator earns its commission regardless of the result of the sports event. The dominant operator in the betting exchange sector is Betfair,[4] although there are several others operating, including: WBX[5] and Betdaq.[6] Betfair, Betdaq, and WBX all hold licences from the UK Gambling Commission.

Betting exchanges have courted some controversy because it has been argued that they allow customers to act as unlicensed bookmakers by laying bets without being liable for the associated betting tax. It is also the case that individuals with insider knowledge or some ability actually to influence the outcome of a sporting event could potentially benefit from the relative anonymity of betting exchanges to place their bets.

Betfair was granted a licence by the Tasmanian government in 2005 but the state of Western Australia tried to implement a ban on citizens in the state from using Betfair in 2007. This ban was successfully appealed by the company, although Australian state governments are still opposed to the concept of betting exchanges. In Europe, the new French regulation concerning interactive gambling activities, which became operational in June 2010, also prohibits betting exchanges, as the government seeks to protect its domestic horse racing industry and the associated betting and tax revenues derived from the state-owned monopoly Pari Mutuel Urbain (PMU).

Betfair, however, has contributed to innovation and improvement within the Internet betting sector. The company was one of the pioneers of in-running betting (also called 'in-play' betting) which allows customers to continue betting after an event has started, particularly horse races. Typical in-play bets include: next goal scorer, number of goals scored in the first half, total corners, player to win the current set/game, runs scored in the next 'over'. Most sports books now offer numerous in-running markets on a range of sports such as football, golf, cricket, and tennis. This type of betting has become incredibly popular, with up to 70 per cent of bets on some games placed in-play. In-play betting really broke through as a product during the World Cup soccer tournament in South Africa in 2010 and has also been spurred by many sports books now broadcasting live sports events on their website (GBGC, 2010b). In-play betting tends to operate to a lower gross win margin than pre-match betting. In-play margins are in the range of 3 to 5 per cent of stakes, compared to 7 to 10 per cent for pre-match bets.

### Casino games

Online casino websites operate in much the same way as a land-based casino and offer many of the same casino games including: roulette, blackjack, baccarat, and slot machines. The games include a *house edge* which is the operator's gross win. Depending on the game, the operator's gross win margin can range from around 3 to 10 per cent. Betfair, however, does have a 'Zero Lounge Casino' which has removed the house edge from its games, e.g. its roulette wheel has no *zero*. This means that, based on optimal player strategy, the payout to customers is 100 per cent.

At the time of writing, the latest development in the online casino sector is *live dealer* casino games.[7] The improvements in Broadband Internet download speeds and Internet video streaming technology have enabled e-gaming firms to stream live casino games on their websites. Players watch a dealer deal a game live via a web-cam and place bets through the website. Games suitable for live dealer casinos include roulette, blackjack, baccarat, and Sic Bo. The appeal of live dealer casinos for players is that they remove the random number generator (RNG) of online casino games, which some cultures, particularly in Asia, do not trust. Other players, however, dislike live dealer casino because the games are slowed down too much. To ensure all players at the table have time to place their bets, there are defined betting periods before each spin or draw, which means that players do have to wait longer between bets than for RNG-based games.

### Poker and other skill games

Planet Poker claims the title of being the first Internet poker room to offer poker games for real money in 1998. This website was closely followed by competitor websites such as Paradise Poker and PokerRoom. The television series *Late Night Poker* aired its first series in the UK in 1999 and is credited with raising the profile, popularity, and image of the Texas hold'em poker game. The use of under the table cameras – now standard in poker broadcasts – made watching a game of poker on television more interesting because viewers could see each player's cards and assess the state of the game. The show also helped improve the image of poker, making it a more 'acceptable' game in mainstream entertainment.

The period between 2002 and 2004 was when online poker really exploded and established itself as a major Internet activity. There were several reasons for this boom in online poker. First, Internet technology was improving and better poker software made playing the game online easier and more attractive to players. New operators were entering the market, each spending money on marketing their own Internet poker room, but with the general effect of increasing the awareness of online poker in itself.

The importance of Chris Moneymaker winning the main event at the 2003 World Series of Poker (WSOP) in promoting Internet poker cannot be overestimated. As a story, it was a perfect marketing aid to the online poker industry. Moneymaker – even his surname is ideal – qualified for the World Series of Poker by winning an online satellite tournament hosted on the PokerStars website.[8] He paid just US$39 to play in this online tournament and turned it into $2.5 million by going on to win the main event at WSOP. It gave hope to the 'ordinary player' that they too might turn a small tournament fee into a life-changing prize.

In 2004 Greg Raymer also won the WSOP by qualifying for a place on the PokerStars website. These two winners helped boost PokerStars' popularity and it was becoming increasingly common for poker websites to offer seats at major land-based poker tournaments as prizes in their online games.

In the same year, 50 per cent of players at the Ladbrokes Poker Million qualified for their place in the tournament through the Ladbrokes.com poker room.

PartyGaming listed on the London Stock Exchange in June 2005, valued at GB£4.5 billion (US$8.7 billion). It seemed to mark the arrival of Internet poker both in the corporate and public arena. At the time, Party Poker was the largest poker website in the world, with a market share of around 48 per cent.

But a little over 12 months later, the Internet poker landscape was completely changed. The passing of the Unlawful Internet Gambling Enforcement Act (UIGEA) in the USA in October 2006 (US Congress, 2006) forced many poker websites to stop accepting customers from the USA. The move had a devastating effect on many websites because 85–90 per cent of their revenues had been generated by US players.

The balance of power now shifted to private operators who continued to take business from the USA, something that the publicly listed companies could not countenance. Those companies that continue to take revenues from the USA also are gaining an advantage in Europe too. This is because they can use their revenues from the USA to spend on marketing and business development in Europe's emerging markets such as Italy and France.

Online poker rooms generate revenues from their customers in two main ways. The first is by charging a percentage fee (*rake*) on each pot played in cash games. The amount of rake is determined by the size of the pot, the number of players, and the type of game being played. The rake tends to decrease as the limit on the table increases. It ranges from 1 to 5 per cent of the pot. The second is through tournament fees. To play in a poker tournament, the operator will charge each player a *buy-in* which is used to create a prize pool for the tournament winners and a tournament fee, which is the operator's revenue. The tournament fee ranges from 0 to 25 per cent of the buy-in amount.

As such, the business model is comparatively low risk, so long as a poker room can attract enough players (*liquidity*). The more people that an Internet poker room can attract to its website, the more games will be played and the more entrants it will get for its tournaments – both of which will generate revenues for the operators.

Liquidity is crucial for the success of an Internet poker room. When a player logs in to the website, they want to be able to find a poker game both of the type they want and at the limit level they wish to play at. If they cannot find a game quickly and easily, they will simply click to a competing website. Losing liquidity becomes a downward spiral for a poker room. As players drift away to competitors, the situation merely becomes worse for the operator because it is hosting fewer tables, meaning fewer players are able to find the kind of game they want.

Other skill games like backgammon, dominos, gin rummy, and skat operate on the same model. The operator will facilitate games and tournaments and in return will take a percentage of the stakes or tournament fees. However, to date none of the other games like backgammon or mahjong has experienced the same global popularity on the Internet as poker experienced, although they are popular in certain regions of the world like south-east Europe for backgammon and Asia for mahjong.

## *Bingo*

Bingo is still in its infancy on the Internet with many of the online operators launching their bingo websites only from 2006 onwards. Online bingo rooms use players' stakes to fund prize pools and take a percentage of the pool as their gross win. As well as the traditional 75-ball and 90-ball bingo games, bingo rooms also offer side games such as slots and instant win games. These can generate as much revenue as the main bingo game itself.

Online bingo is helping to extend the demographic appeal of Internet gambling because the game is being targeted primarily at women, as is shown by 888.com's bingo website which has the URL of 888ladies.com.[9] Internet bingo is also part of the trend in 2009/10 for social gaming, with players able to chat to each other in the bingo room and encouraged to create profiles for themselves on the site.

The growth of Internet bingo has undoubtedly been spurred by the introduction of smoking bans in many countries around Europe since 2000 (GBGC, 2007). Bingo players who are now unable to smoke while playing bingo in a bingo club have chosen to move online and play in their own home, where they can still smoke.

## *Lotteries*

Several national lotteries now allow their customers to buy lottery tickets online or via mobile phones for the main draw games. But some of the biggest lotteries – namely the state lotteries in the United States – are not currently permitted to offer ticket sales over the Internet.

The situation in 2011 is that a few state lotteries have wholeheartedly embraced the Internet as a sales channel, while the majority of lotteries are still developing their Internet strategies, if at all. Austrian Lotteries, for example, generated over 40 per cent of its total sales from online activity at its win2day.at website in 2009.[10] Win2day offers a full range of e-gaming products, not just lottery games. As well as buying their lottery tickets online, Austrian citizens also can play casino games, poker, and keno on the site. The Danish lottery Danske Spil[11] and Swedish lottery Svenska Spel[12] also have an extended range of online games alongside their traditional lottery games. Camelot, the operator of the UK national lottery, only offers online scratch cards and ticket sales through its website, but in 2009, 9.5 per cent of its total sales were through online and mobile sales channels.[13]

One reason for some state lotteries' reluctance to move online is that they are cautious about upsetting their established retail network of lottery agents. These agents work on a commission basis of lottery ticket sales and could lose income if more ticket sales were made online.

Private firms also offer a range of lottery-related products via the Internet. There are lottery agents who will purchase tickets for the major global lotteries on behalf of their customers, and who are based in a different country from that where the draw is being held. Bookmakers and other firms will also offer fixed-odds bets based on the results of the major lotteries around the world. In some of these bets customers can win smaller fixed amounts for matching one or two numbers drawn.[14] However, in general, it is difficult for a private company to generate sufficient player numbers to create a large enough Internet lottery jackpot in order to compete with the national lotteries which have formidable marketing and promotional resources at their disposal, as well as the benefit of a large retail network to create substantial jackpots.

## Regulation

In the early days of the e-gaming industry it tended to be primarily small island jurisdictions that would issue licences for Internet gambling, or those nations that already had a developed offshore financial services sector and saw Internet gambling as an extension to that business. In the mid- to late 1990s such jurisdictions included the likes of Antigua and Barbuda, Curaçao, Netherlands Antilles, and Costa Rica. As the decade ended, a growing number of jurisdictions implemented legislation to license Internet gambling operators in their borders. The common theme in the profile of these e-gaming jurisdictions was that they continued to be small island nations or jurisdictions that had a specific economic arrangement. For example:

- *Kahnawà:ke Mohawk Territory, Canada*: an Indian reserve in the Canadian province of Quebec. Since 1999 the Kahnawà:ke Gaming Commission has issued interactive gaming licences and, at the time of writing, is the only jurisdiction in North America that issues Internet gaming licences to private companies.
- *Isle of Man, UK:* a self-governing British Crown Dependency which has issued e-gaming licences since 2000. The Hilton Hotel on the island played host to the first Poker Million tournament in November 2000. The Isle of Man licenses the largest Internet poker operator in Rational Entertainment Enterprises Ltd (PokerStars) and since 2008 has been attracting some of the largest Asian sports betting firms as new licensees: Celton Manx (SBO Bet), Cube Ltd (188bet), and Welton Holdings Limited (Fun88).
- *Gibraltar, UK:* a British overseas territory located on the Iberian Peninsula which has a land border with Spain. It first offered licences in 1998. Gibraltar is home to some of the biggest brands in the European Internet gambling sector, including: Cassava Enterprises (888.com), bwin, Ladbrokes, PartyGaming, Victor Chandler, and William Hill.
- *Cagayan Special Economic Zone and Free Port, Philippines:* in 2003 the Interactive Gaming Act appointed First Cagayan Leisure and Resort Corporation as the master licensor in the zone with the brief to develop and regulate Internet gambling. It remains the only jurisdiction in Asia to issue Internet gambling licences (Pilling, 2009).
- *Malta:* an island nation in the Mediterranean and member of the European Union (EU). The island's EU status has made it attractive to e-gaming firms seeking to operate across borders into other EU member states. Malta is one of the leading jurisdictions as measured by the number of licensees on the island. It began issuing licences in 2001.
- Other offshore e-gaming jurisdictions include: *Alderney (Channel Islands), Northern Territory (Australia), Panama, Seychelles,* and *Swaziland.*

The 'offshore' status of many of the early Internet gambling jurisdictions was ideal for the operators and helped shape the business model for the sector. After an initial, annual licence fee many of these jurisdictions charged little or no gaming tax and, in addition, had low corporate and income tax.

Consumers benefited too. The low gaming tax meant that the e-gaming companies could offer better value to their customers in the form of higher payout percentages than their land-based counterparts. Land-based casinos, betting shops, and bingo halls had no option to move offshore and were trapped by the prevailing rate of gambling tax in their jurisdiction. They also had higher operating costs associated with maintaining a 'bricks-and-mortar' property and large numbers of employees, unlike the virtual casinos and poker rooms.

Until 2007 it was not possible to obtain a specific Internet gambling licence in a major mainland jurisdiction. This changed with the 2005 Gambling Act in Great Britain, which made specific provision for 'Remote Gambling' and licences for Internet gaming – casino, poker, and bingo. The tax rate for UK-licensed companies, however, was set at 15 per cent of gross profits, which was much higher than e-gaming firms were used to paying offshore. Consequently, very few firms applied for a licence in the UK. With the exodus of William Hill and Ladbrokes' sports betting operations to Gibraltar in 2009, Bet365 is one of the few major Internet sports books licensed in the UK (White, 2009). Most operators instead chose to remain offshore in one of the 'white-listed' jurisdictions approved by the UK government. The jurisdictions are: Malta (and any European Economic Area [EEA] state), Gibraltar, Antigua and Barbuda, Isle of Man, Alderney, and Tasmania.

In 2006/7 Italy too was developing legislation that would enable companies to take an e-gaming licence in Italy itself. It was a fairly tortuous regulatory process which lasted almost four years. Early on in the process one of the key events was the publication by the Italian authorities of a 'black list' of foreign gambling websites that Italian customers would be blocked from accessing. This blocking began in February 2006. Later the same year a licence tender process was held for both land-based and remote licences as the Italian government of Romano Prodi sought new sources of revenue to finance its budget.

The new regulations were subject to great scrutiny by the European Commission, which suggested some amendments to the proposed regulation in April 2008. Under the revised regulation, a gambling company that is licensed and based in another EU jurisdiction can apply to the Italian regulator (AAMS) for a licence provided they can demonstrate a turnover of €1.5m over the previous two years. An alternative option is to provide AAMS with a bank guarantee for the same amount. An operator's gaming servers can be located outside Italy as long as they are within the EU and are linked to the central AAMS system which validates bets and ensures the taxes are paid on Italian gambling activity.

Other EU member states have been looking at Italy's regulatory model and adapting it to their own laws. France introduced similar regulation in 2010 in time for the World Cup and Spain too is reported to be planning its own Italian-inspired Internet gambling regulation.

Many of the leading EU member states regard Internet gambling as a threat to their tax base and local vested interests. Several countries have state-owned gambling operations or state-granted gambling monopolies which are used to raise government revenues. Naturally they are keen to protect these revenues.

Legal battles between governments and Internet companies have been running almost since the industry was born and have been escalated to the European Court of Justice (ECJ). One of the key cases in Europe was Case C243/01 upon which the ECJ ruled in November 2003 and is more commonly known as the *Gambelli* case. The case concerned Mr Piergiorgio Gambelli and other plaintiffs who operated in Italy on behalf of betting firm Stanley International Betting Ltd. Stanley International took bets from retail agents in Italy which were transferred using the Internet to Stanley's headquarters in the UK. At the heart of the case was the argument that there is freedom of establishment and freedom to provide services across borders within the EU, as set out in Articles 43 and 49 of the EC Treaty.

This argument has continued to be debated since then (see Case C338/04 [2007] Placanica) in Italy and other EU member states. Between 2006 and 2008 the European Commission had infringement proceedings under way against 10 EU states, requesting information on the countries' gambling legislation to determine whether the restrictions were compatible with the EC Treaty.

Governments, too, have argued amongst themselves over Internet gambling services. In March 2003 the government of Antigua and Barbuda initiated a case (WT/DS285 *United States – Measures Affecting the Cross-Border Supply of Gambling and Betting Services*) against the United States at the World Trade Organization (WTO) concerning the US stance of prohibiting cross-border remote gambling services. Antigua argued that the restrictive policy breached international trade treaties.

Antigua had several rulings go in its favour in the case but has yet to gain any compensation and by 2011 the USA had not altered its gambling policy to make it compliant (Mendel, 2007).

## Challenges and influences on Internet gambling

As the Internet gambling industry enters the next decade of its development, it will be influenced by a number of factors that will define how the industry will mature and what business models will succeed.

### Existing competition

The Internet gambling market is already extremely competitive. There are already more than 2,300 websites worldwide offering gambling services and they are available at just a few clicks of the customers' mouse. However, within each sector of the market there are currently a handful of major operators that dominate, and then a mass of smaller operators. In online sports betting, for example, companies such as Bet365, Betfair, bwin, SBOBet, and William Hill are key operators. Fulltilt and PokerStars are the dominant brands in Internet poker rooms.

Two features that all the different sectors of e-gaming have in common are that they operate on very tight margins and have to work extremely hard to attract new customers and retain existing ones. Internet sports books aim for a gross win margin of between 8 and 10 per cent, but sports results can mean that margins can fluctuate greatly quarter on quarter. For example, the pre-match betting margin for Maltese-licensed Unibet in the four quarters of 2009 was: 11.3 per cent, 6.3 per cent, 6.0 per cent, and 11.9 per cent.

Internet poker rooms typically take between 1 and 5 per cent of the amount in the pot as commission or rake.

The e-gaming industry is one of the few consumer sectors that have adopted a strategy of buying its customers. All e-gaming companies offer generous sign-up bonuses to new customers and will offer incentives to dormant accounts to try to reactivate them to bet. In the online poker sector in particular there has been something of an arms race with the level of bonuses being offered reaching unsustainable levels. Some poker rooms will offer a bonus to the value of more than 100 per cent on a new player's first deposit of funds in their account. It is a measure of how competitive the market is. All these incentives, however, mean that customers have very little loyalty to gaming brands and will happily switch to another site simply to take advantage of another bonus. A new customer may choose one brand over another simply because of the free bet or bonus that is being offered.

Aside from the bonuses being offered, there is often very little difference between the websites of rival e-gaming companies. The layout of the websites looks similar and they will be offering a similar array of gambling products, in many cases powered by the same software. There is certainly an argument that all that differentiates rival companies is their corporate colours, brand, and marketing activities.

### New entrants

Although the sector is already very competitive, new entrants are still keen to come into the market. In many cases these new entrants have no existing connection with the gambling industry. They have included magazine publishers, television broadcasters, and airlines.

One common feature of these new entrants is that revenues have been falling in their main activity because advertising revenues were falling or business models changing, especially during the recession of 2008/9. In the UK in particular, gambling is much more high profile than it has been, with more advertising, sports sponsorship, and poker being broadcast on television. There is the perception that it is an easy business from which to make money. This perception is not an accurate one, but there is some encouragement for new companies entering the Internet gambling arena. First, customers have no particular brand loyalty, so will be receptive to new entrants and, for customers, the cost of switching between operators is low.

The barrier of entry in the e-gaming market is relatively low too. To launch a gambling website does not require a great deal of capital. Funds are required to purchase a gambling licence and software, but it does not have to be a large sum. In the UK the application fee for a remote gambling licence costs approximately GB£15,000, depending on the gambling services that are offered and the gross gambling yield of the company. The annual fee for an Internet gambling company generating less than GB£5.5 million in gross gambling yield is also in the region of GB£15,000.

There is a level of Internet gambling software to suit every budget, although the quality will, of course, vary. There is also the option for companies to develop their own software in-house rather than buying it from an existing supplier.

So the barriers to getting into the Internet gambling industry are relatively low, but the barriers to making a success of a new e-gaming business are high and becoming higher. The existing market is already very competitive and a substantial marketing budget is required to attract players. Established companies have the benefit of extensive customer behaviour data to plan marketing and customer relationship management. Regulatory costs involved in being able to operate in multiple European markets are rising too.

Finally, new companies coming into gambling from other sectors are often more risk-averse than they realise. This is particularly the case when it comes to sports betting where they cannot cope with the uncertainty of fluctuations in margin and periods of bad runs of results. For this reason many new entrants consider either pari-mutuel (pool betting) or lottery models which are less risky. But these models have high failure rates because they need large numbers of players to participate in order to generate sufficient prize pools and are not as attractive to gamblers as the higher payout fixed-odds models.

### *Suppliers*

There are a number of key suppliers that can exert an influence on the direction of Internet gambling: telecommunications providers, payment providers and banks, gambling software suppliers, marketing affiliates, and media suppliers.

In many offshore jurisdictions there is a limited supply of data centres and telecommunications providers and, as a result, they exert significant influence because it is not always easy for a gaming operator to switch to a rival supplier.

The ability to move money quickly and easily between the customer and operator is crucial to a successful e-gaming business. Its importance can be measured by the fact that governments focus on payment transactions when trying to prohibit Internet gambling. The US Unlawful Internet Gambling Enforcement Act 2006 (UIGEA) is a classic example. Norway's Payment Act was passed in February 2010 and came into force in June 2010 (Parker, 2010b). It too has made it illegal to process payments for Internet gambling where the gambling operator does not hold a Norwegian licence.

Banks too have an uneasy relationship with e-gaming. However, because of the difficulties posed by banks, a number of firms such as Counting House,[15] Glue Pay,[16] and Neteller[17] have been set up to help facilitate payments from restricted or difficult jurisdictions.

The leading gaming software firms like Microgaming and Playtech hold significant bargaining power and can afford to be selective as to which operators to license their games software. Typically this will depend on the size of the customer, its brand and reputation, its existing database of clients, and the size of its marketing budget. The more the gaming operator can bring to the deal, the greater negotiating power they have with the software firm. In the Internet poker sector, several firms have tried and failed to write their own software and the most common practice is to join an existing network to benefit from pooled liquidity of players. Playtech's ipoker, Boss Media's International Poker Network (IPN), Entraction, and Ongame are some of the leading poker networks.

Advertising and marketing are very important aspects of the Internet gambling business, so media and marketing affiliates are key suppliers to the industry. In the UK print, television, and Internet media are generally accepting of gambling adverts, but that is not the case around Europe. In July 2010, for example, the ECJ upheld Sweden's ban on advertising in the country's media for online gambling that is not licensed in Sweden (Parker, 2010a). Finland brought in a similar advertising ban in 2010.

From late 2008 the search engine Google began allowing search campaigns from Internet gambling operators licensed in the UK or Alderney, Gibraltar, and the Isle of Man. These campaigns, however, were only allowed to target the UK. Since December 2009, the social networking website Facebook has had a policy of not carrying gambling advertising, but fan pages are allowed, as are free-to-play gambling-style applications.

So there are still some restrictions on advertising Internet gambling, but the Internet also allows a number of ways around these obstacles. Affiliate websites that drive customers to the gambling sites have been a very effective mechanism for recruiting players. A good affiliate site with high volumes of traffic can hold significant influence with the e-gaming operators because they are an important source of new players. Affiliates usually work on a revenue share of players' losses or, less commonly, a fixed fee per player recruited by the affiliate.

### Customers

As already stated, the gambler is in a very strong position within Internet gambling. E-gaming firms are desperate to sign them up and will offer generous bonuses to attract them. Customers are not particularly loyal and can easily switch websites and find the same games and bets elsewhere. As a result, marketing is a hugely important activity for e-gaming.

Across the sector it is not unusual for operators to spend the equivalent of 25 per cent of their revenues on marketing activities. The leading firms are spending many tens of millions of dollars each year competing with each other for customers.

### Substitutes

There is always competition from new products in the e-gaming sector and games are always evolving and being improved. But there is little long-term advantage in many of these products; the early entrants have a short period of benefit, but if something proves popular it is easy for other firms to add that game to their website.

Betfair's betting exchange model was perhaps the most revolutionary substitute product to launch in Internet gambling and that was in 2000. Betfair predicted the death of the traditional bookmaker when it was launched, which has not come to pass. But it has certainly shaken up the bookmakers and had an effect on the betting margins on horse racing in the UK.

### Role of government

Perhaps the greatest force that influences the e-gaming market in Europe is government. It has been the case for the last decade and will continue to be so in the next decade. Governments have an uneasy relationship with the Internet and the loss of their control and power it brings. Many governments are also not in favour of gambling in general, unless it is run under their own monopoly.

Governments around the world have adopted different approaches to Internet gambling. Some have so far chosen to ignore it, or state that existing legislation for traditional, land-based gambling covers all the new developments in Internet gambling too. Other governments have actively chosen to prohibit Internet gambling, such as the United States and Portugal, or restrict Internet gambling to state-run monopolies, such as Hong Kong and Finland.

Since 2006 there has been some slow movement towards the regulation of Internet gambling in a number of the major economies of the European Union, such as Italy and France. Government is a very powerful influence on Internet gambling and its decisions on prohibition of products, tax rates, and licensing requirements will determine the future shape of the Internet gambling market in Europe and around the world.

## Notes

1   Gross gaming yield (GGY) definition: stakes minus customer winnings. It is the amount that customers lose to a gambling operator. It is also known as gross win or revenues.
2   http://www.oddschecker.com/
3   Gross win definition: stakes minus customer winnings. It is the amount that customers lose to a gambling operator. It is also known as gross gambling yield (GGY).
4   http://www.betfair.com/
5   http://www.wbx.com/
6   http://www.betdaq.com
7   http://www.vclivecasino.com/
8   http://www.pokerstars.com/
9   http://www.888ladies.com/
10  http://www.win2day.at/gaming/
11  http://www.danskespil.dk/
12  http://svenskaspel.se
13  http://www.national-lottery.co.uk/
14  https://www.mylotto24.co.uk/; http://sports.williamhill.com/bet/en-gb/lotto
15  http://www.countinghouseltd.com/
16  http://www.gluepay.com/
17  https://www.neteller.com/

## References

888 Holdings PLC (2006, October 2). *US Legislation*, statement to London Stock Exchange.
Clarke, J. (2009). 'Andrew Black: punter who revolutionised gambling'. *Moneyweek*. Retrieved September 6, 2010, from http://www.moneyweek.com/news-and-charts/entrepreneurs-my-first-million-andrew-black-betfair-44933.aspx
Global Betting and Gaming Consultants (GBGC) (2007). *Fewer Chips Without Fire? The Smoking Bans Go Global*, UK.
— (2010a). *Global Gambling Report, 5th edn*, Isle of Man.
— (2010b). *Interactive Gambling Report*, Isle of Man.
ITU (2010). Internet and Broadband usage statistics. *International Telecommunication Union*. Retrieved September 3, 2010, from http://www.itu.int/ITU-D/ict/statistics/index.html
Mendel, M. (2007). 'The sideshow that became a vital trade issue'. *Casino & Gaming International*, *4*, 81–4.
Parker, J. (2010a). 'Boost to monopolies as ECJ backs Swedish laws'. *EGaming Review*. Retrieved August 26, 2010, from http://www.egrmagazine.com/news/575372/boost-to-monopolies-as-ecj-backs-swedish-laws.thtml
— (2010b). 'Norway online gambling payments ban signed into law'. *EGaming Review*. Retrieved August 25, 2010, from http://www.egrmagazine.com/news/516917/norway-online-gambling-payments-ban-signed-into-law.thtml

PartyGaming PLC (2006, October 2). *Port Security Act,* statement to London Stock Exchange.

Pilling, L. (2009). 'Diamond mines or money pits – developments in Asian gambling markets'. *Newsletter of the Society for the Study of Gambling, 43,* 22–7.

Sportingbet PLC (2006, October 13). *Disposal of US Operations,* statement to London Stock Exchange.

US Congress (2006). 'Unlawful Internet Gambling Enforcement Act' (UIGEA), *Security and Accountability For Every Port Act 2006* (SAFE Port Act), HR 4954, US.

White, G. (2009). 'William Hill set to lead the field offshore'. *The Telegraph*. Retrieved September 6, 2010, from http://www.telegraph.co.uk/finance/newsbysector/retailandconsumer/5961456/William-Hill-set-to-lead-the-field-offshore.html

# 4 Business models for Internet gambling

*Melody Morgan-Busher*

## Introduction

Internet gambling has been seen as a 'money machine' by some entrepreneurs and investors; Steve Budin faxed the message 'I just saw an Internet machine that can turn air into money!' after seeing an early online casino demonstrated (Budin, 2007). Budin's offshore telephone sportsbook ran from Central America until 1998 when he was arrested by the American authorities and the business was shut down. When closed, his offshore betting business was reported as generating $20m gross profits before expenses ($10m net). His business was poised to move online and was anticipating further significant growth. This old story illustrates both the opportunities and challenges of Internet gambling as a business. The market seems certain, yet the legal status of the industry is confused at best.

The American Unlawful Internet Gambling Enforcement Act (UIGEA) knocked the industry hard in late 2006 and altered the landscape, yet a Merrill Lynch report from a decade ago which predicted global Internet gambling revenue rising beyond $100,000,000,000 per annum (Hartman, 2006) by 2015 is *still* showing up in business plans and investor relations documents. Another hiatus occurred in this sector in late April 2011, when fresh enforcement actions in the USA were launched against several large operators. The lack of clear law, hard data, and a dearth of academic review all add to the mystery of this sector.

Despite the present global recession, many publicly traded Internet gambling companies continue to post profits. A useful table of public financial data for a range of operators was compiled and published by KPMG in 2010 and is freely available online.[1] Some start-up operators have grown into international corporate players within a decade and a few have become household names. This is an impressive commercial achievement by any measure.

Yet, despite the opportunities, Internet gambling operators can fail and even some well-established brands are in decline. Plausible reasons for financial failure in this sector include the following:

- *Poor Internet connectivity.* Operators may lose market share if players suffer slow games or outages due to bandwidth issues – especially if other operators offer similar services.
- *Cash-flow issues following adverse sporting outcomes or jackpot wins.* Operators may need to pay out large wins on sports event results offered with high or compound odds. Jackpots may also pay out large sums and – if truly random – may do so earlier than budgeted.
- *Launch problems.* Marketing campaigns begin several months ahead of 'Go Live' so late-onset technical or regulatory issues that hinder services can compromise both launch and brand.

- *Lack of market share.* A threshold 'critical mass' is required for most operators to be profitable. Most business plans project a rapid growth in player numbers due to marketing promotions, but few allow adequately for attrition as players move on to the next new offer.
- *Marketing errors.* Major overheads for most operators include payouts to players and partners (bonuses and affiliate schemes) designed to attract signups and stimulate activity. Traditional broadcast advertising (e.g. press and TV) is expensive and difficult to evaluate. Wasted marketing budget cannot be recovered.
- *Weak financial planning/financial control.* Given the difficulty of assessing player liabilities or predicting revenue/costs, operators can unwittingly fall into a negative equity position relying by default on player deposits to provide liquidity.
- *Poor customer service.* Operators who treat players badly (slow payouts or poor games) are likely to lose their reputation and so deter registrations.
- *Technical or operational failure.* Operators usually offer service *24x7*, but usage may spike during sporting events or certain hours. Peak demand can overload capacity and lead to timeouts or even a server crash. Failure may disrupt the database causing loss of player trust.
- *Fraud by players or staff.* Cheating by players or staff who abuse privileged access can skim funds and damage the brand if publicised.
- *Dispute with a vital supplier.* Disagreement with a key supplier may prove terminal if unresolved. Often an operator cannot replace a partner without cooperation so a commercial dispute in this sector is akin to an acrimonious divorce.
- *Legal or regulatory costs.* Internet gambling operators work with lower margins than traditional gambling businesses, but are treated as 'cash cows' by many governments.
- *Hostile external economic conditions.* The impact of the recession on the habits of players is beyond the control of any individual operator, but may reduce the total online market.
- *Hurtful exchange rate movements.* When the operator incurs its costs in one currency but makes its revenue in another, the relative value of these currencies may significantly impact profitability and is a cost the operator must absorb (often registered weeks after it is incurred).
- *Competition from unlicensed operators.* It is relatively common for an unlicensed operator to trade without prosecution regardless of the law, avoiding compliance costs and taxation. Some 85 per cent of the European market for Internet gambling was allegedly with unlicensed operators in 2011.
- *Inability to pass credit card and similar payments.* The VISA/MasterCard consortium applies its own screening and security standards. An operator breaching these standards may be severely fined by the consortium and/or barred from accessing the Visa/MasterCard payment network.
- *Leakage of key data, loss of critical staff, or breakdown of control system.* Even without staff turnover, commercially valuable data and know-how is at risk through *ICT* vulnerabilities.
- *Blackmail and extortion.* Smear campaign attempts are common in this industry. Some are genuine grievances; others are fostered up by competitors or organised criminals. Hackers are known to have threatened *denial of service* attacks unless paid off.
- *Asset freeze.* If an operator has concentrated its funds/the player funds in a single place, any legal pressure that causes its bank to freeze liquid assets is likely to cripple the business and cause a cash-flow crisis.

- *Inconsistent management.* As all Internet gambling operations, except the Board-level management, can be outsourced, the boundaries of an Internet gambling business are fluid. Services and suppliers are frequently included or discontinued according to performance. Executives often change also. Business strategy, morale, and reputation may suffer.

## Internet gambling operations: definitions and overview

As Internet gambling is distinguished from other online games by being offered 'with prizes', a control system is required to ensure financial sustainability and to allow relevant audit. Some operators do offer 'Internet gambling with prizes' free of charge as a promotion for related activities; this arrangement occurred in France as a means of bypassing restrictive gambling laws.[2]

The term 'operator' indicates a business which earns its revenue selling Internet gambling. Operators may trade business-to-consumer (*B2C*) serving 'players' directly and B2C operators own their 'player database'. Alternatively an operator may be a business-to-business (*B2B*) 'service provider' that provides the Internet gambling-related technical infrastructure and/or skills to other B2C operators.

The gross gambling revenue (*GGR*) is defined as 'turnover' – 'winnings' for a given period where turnover is the total stakes placed by players and winnings is the amount due to

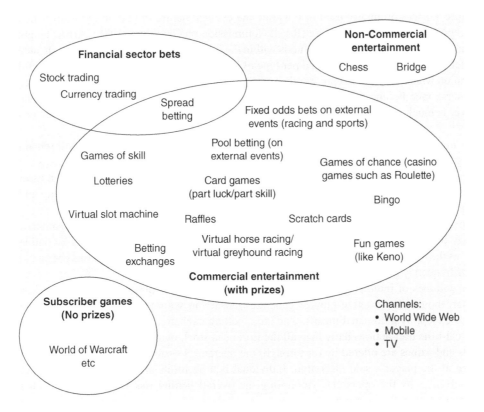

*Figure 4.1* Internet gambling modes and median, 2000–10

players for successful bets. However, operators often speak of *gross margin* instead, which is GGR – commissions paid. Commissions that are paid to partner operators (such as service providers or intermediaries) are often calculated according to turnover or GGR generated – known as a 'revenue share'.

Most Internet gambling is offered on a 'pay first, play later' basis for historic and logistic reasons. This was a necessary precaution in the early days when micropayments were difficult and the enforcement of debts at a distance dubious. It is a simple policy favourable to operators which is widely accepted.

Players' funds are recorded in online 'player accounts' or *virtual wallets* visible to the individual player only when logged in. The balance of the player account is increased by the operator to reflect wins or promotional bonuses earned. Stakes are deducted when a bet is struck and winnings (if any) are credited when the event result is known (which may be days or even months later).

Staff dealing with player support or fraud screening will be able to view the balances, bets, and transactions of any player through the operators' *back end* website. There are occasions when a gamble may need to be reversed by the system or manually by staff. Such actions should generate audit trails in the control system.

When a player's online balance is exhausted, no more stakes can be placed. The balance should never be negative. Players are not generally allowed to register more than one account.

Most player accounts are accessed by a simple login and password. Better security measures are available from some operators – particularly those handling high-value customers.

Figure 4.2 was originally used to illustrate the cyclical nature of gambling turnover in a 1978 report on *Gambling in Britain* (Royal Commission on Gambling, 1978). Arrow length indicated the speed of circulation of funds within the betting system; the loop width indicated the relative volume of funds engaged per type of betting; this diagram still serves as a useful illustration where the inputs represent the various Internet gambling 'products' (which range from horse race betting to poker games). The model is meant to convey the concept that turnover is much greater than player expenditure as most stakes use funds won on previous bets.

It is important to appreciate that player funds deposited for Internet gambling will remain in the gambling system until withdrawn or lost to the operator. Gradually player deposits are converted from being a liability (a debt that may need to be repaid) into revenue (an asset owned by the business). This conversion of deposits to revenue relies on player activity and on wins remaining on deposit.

The speed of re-cycling of funds (stake/play/re-stake) depends on both game and gambler, but may be only a few seconds in some automated forms of Internet gambling like online 'slots' as the betting process is almost 'frictionless'. The stakes are often small (maybe cents) in high-frequency games.

The volumes of internal gambling transactions generated per player can be huge; taken together, thousands of active players generate transaction volumes that are impossible to monitor except by automated means. One large betting exchange operator claims to handle more real-time transactions daily than all the European stock markets put together.

Bets and games are offered by (or through) the operator's system and may be accepted or ignored at the player's sole discretion. Individual betting limits are usually set per player (themselves or by the operator). Monitoring the overall betting risk is a basic automated function to protect the operator.

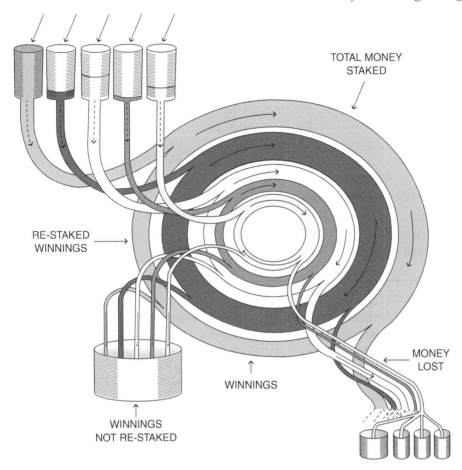

*Figure 4.2* The 'Hydrodynamic Model' of gambling
Source: Adapted from the Royal Commission on Gambling, 1978.

## Betting margins

All gamblers expect a reasonable chance of winning; the relevant ratio of money staked compared to funds credited as winnings is known as the 'payback ratio' which can be anywhere between 0 per cent (all bets lost and all stakes are forfeit to operator) to well over 100 per cent (i.e. players make money from the game at the expense of the operator). Payback ratios are calculated on the grossed-up stakes and total wins for a period (not for one player) over a large number of games.

The gross margin earned by an operator per game is approximately the reciprocal of the payback ratio and both vary by type of game (product). When the payback ratio is 95 per cent, the approximate gross margin for the operator of providing that game is 5 per cent. If the operator is contractually obliged to share half his revenue with a business partner then the margin actually retained by the operator may be about 2.5 per cent of turnover.

Table 4.1 shows an indicative 'likely margin' per 'game type' based on typical payback ratios. The operational risk (op. risk) varies according to game type. Sports/fixed odds gambling relates to events beyond the relevant operators' control that may have large value

*Table 4.1* Internet gambling mode according to estimated GGR and operational risk

| Game type | Likely margin | Op. risk | Duration (range) |
| --- | --- | --- | --- |
| Sports/fixed odds | c.10% | High | Seconds–years |
| Pools/pari mutuel | c.10% | Low | Days–weeks |
| Betting exchanges | c.5% | Low | Instant–months |
| Virtual races/games | c.10% | Medium | Minutes–months |
| Financial betting/FX | Varies with markets | High | Days–months |
| Casino/slots | 2–7% | Medium | Seconds |
| Solo card games | c.5% | Low | Seconds–minutes |
| Bingo | c.30% | Medium | Minutes |
| Backgammon/chess | c.2% commission | Low | Minutes–hours |
| Poker ring games | 5% customised | Low | Minutes–days |
| Lotteries/scratchcards | Up to 45% or more | Low | Instant–months |
| Mobile phone apps | 1–5% | Low | Seconds |
| Tournaments | c.50% | Low | Hours–days |

bets and defy prediction; these are 'high risk'. Casino and slots show as 'medium risk' since all prizes are paid by the operator; any abuse of the software or the data that favours players is a cost to the business so protective alarms are built in. Poker games and lotteries are generally 'low risk' because the operator merely brokers bets between players and does not fund winnings. The duration of the game is defined here as the time elapsed between striking a bet and its settlement. Prizes, commissions, and rules are set and declared in advance of game play to ensure fairness.

The likely margin of fixed odds is based on the bookmaker's prediction of outcomes. A bookmaker expects to pay out some players at each event, but will keep the stakes of the rest. The odds offered should ensure that what is being earned is more than what is being paid out. The Internet bookmaker is greatly assisted by having software to show his current betting position, the odds of other bookmakers, and betting trends. Online bookmakers offer better odds than traditional bookmakers as their margin is less.

In poker and other peer-to-peer or player-to-player (*P2P*) multiplayer games, the margin arises from the commission charged on gambles brokered between players which are managed by the operator through their software. This commission is often called 'rake' and is usually charged per new hand played. In games of chance (casino, slots, lotteries, scratchcards), the margin arises from the difference between the value of prizes and the statistical chance of their being won. This payout ratio may be varied by the operator by changing the game logic or amending the prize paid per result. Prizes due are stored in a fixed 'payout table' referenced by the software. Spread betting and foreign exchange trading (FX) lie on the border between gambling and financial services where the prize is proportional to the accuracy of the bet. These may require different licensing and control frameworks unless offered as 'fixed odds'.

## Player profiles and product type

Research by operators has shown typical sportsbook gamblers spend less than €200 per month with a single operator whilst 'high rollers' routinely lose over €5,000 per month. Big budget gamblers are monitored by operators in case they may be problem gamblers or possess better information than the in-house odds setter. Limits are applied to large-value bets by default unless the gambler has been granted very important player (*VIP*) status.

Many operators avoid the high-risk, high-return option of high rollers preferring amateur gamblers who provide a steady stream of revenue at low risk (this policy will be dictated to the bookmakers by management). Other operators actively seek VIP clients through selective marketing and exclusive offers. Operators with a mix of ordinary and VIP players may find that the revenue of a single VIP player is worth 100+ others.

In poker, operator research has shown that most amateur players spend less than €50 per month on their hobby and contribute very little revenue individually. More involved poker players' turnover may be more than €500 per month and generate the bulk of the operator's revenue; however, good players generally stake funds won from less-skilled players. Poker is thus a 'food chain' where all the funds entered into the gambling cycle gravitate into the hands of successful players. Until poker funds are withdrawn from play, all the money risked in poker is earning commission for the operator at rates of around 5 per cent (commonly known as the 'rake') per round.

The popularity of poker a few years ago has suffered due to an excess of 'sharks' scaring away the 'fish' because 'newbie' (i.e. new) players are unhappy losing on a regular basis. Many operators now try to protect inexperienced poker players who are the lifeblood of the business. Profitable players are those who play for fun, return to play often, and recommend the game to friends.

To feed the system and spur growth, poker operators often offer poker training online and games which can be played for free. Poker is offered as 'ring games' (where players sit around a virtual poker table and play for a shared pot) or 'tournaments' where the final winner is decided by a knockout contest over many rounds. Rakeback discounts are offered to generate loyalty amongst poker players – the most generous will pay good poker players to visit the tables of the operator. Celebrity players are also often engaged to generate player interest. Chat is offered to stimulate an online community feeling.

The commission rate (margin) charged in betting exchanges is usually around 5 per cent. Player-specific discounts may be made by the operator each month subject to the terms and conditions (*T&Cs*) agreed. High-volume customers are often other bookmakers who may use software to link up automated hedging accounts.[3]

Casino games are not generally considered to be skill games and are mostly available on demand. These games are so automated that there is relatively little operator monitoring. The stakes are usually low (often < €1) so players may spend hours in the casino without losing much money. Of players who use an online casino, about 20 per cent will make a profit each month due to the high payout rates provided. Of the 80 per cent of casino players who lose, some spend over €1,000 per month. A few VIP players may generate over half the casino revenue. Some online casinos specialise in offering only 'high stakes' games that appeal to these 'big spenders' (who are screened for problem gambling).

The margins on lotteries and scratchcards vary widely; these often offer very poor odds to players (odds of millions to 1 to win!). Players cannot assess the actual payout ratio without knowing how many tickets are sold or if prizes are awarded to unsold/unclaimed tickets. Some online lotteries address this by opting for independent verification of their gaming data and all prize awards. The margin on lotteries and scratchcards is very favourable to the operator and this market is dominated by national monopolies. Lottery players are a distinct market segment from other online gamblers.

The margins for bingo operations are above average at around 30 per cent of turnover, implying a relatively 'elastic' market as players are not price sensitive if the service provides the features they expect (chat, variety, ease of use, good payout handling, etc.) and matches or exceeds the offline experience.

## Prizes and settlement of wins

Prizes for ordinary games and bets are due as per the terms and rules accepted by players when the bet is struck (any subsequent changes to the terms are not relevant to a confirmed bet). Tournaments or jackpots (large prizes) are offered for some 'games of chance' to stimulate repeat play and customer loyalty. Tournaments may require 'buy-in' with points earned by frequent play and offer a nice reward. Jackpots collect a small levy per game and may be 'seeded' by the operator at a minimum prize value. Most jackpots rise without limit until paid out when triggered by a random event. Prize settlements relating to games of chance and 'skill games' are generally fully automated.

A sportsbook event may be sold at differing odds over time so the settlement of bets requires each bet to be referenced individually by the system. Shift work is often required of bookmakers as the large financial risks related to settling fixed odds bets requires human oversight. Supervision can be conducted remotely, but bookmakers need high-speed access to the relevant sports broadcasts and automated control systems. Delay of event settlement deprives players of their funds so inhibits new betting and can damage player loyalty.

Bookmakers are linked to specialist service providers (such as SIS[4]), which provide event schedules, results, and images via data feeds sent in a pre-set format as the sports events happen. Market odds are also bought from specialists, like Betradar.[5] Automated interfaces can update event listings and results (tens to thousands of events may be offered on a sportsbook website).

## Payments to and from the operator

The most popular way for players to deposit funds to date has been by credit or debit card transaction. The consortium headed by Visa and MasterCard require their merchants to pass through a vetting procedure (conducted by the *Acquiring Bank*) after which a merchant account code (*MAC*) is assigned. The MAC for a casino is 7994 and for betting is 7995. This coding is used by credit card companies to monitor, and even to bar, payments related to Internet gambling deposits.

Alternative payment methods are growing in popularity for Internet gambling as they are often cheaper options. The Neteller payment service was once the method of choice for players based in the USA until the company was effectively closed down for several months by the authorities there. Neteller was regulated by the British Financial Services Authority (*FSA*) and continues as a strong competitor to PayPal serving e-commerce merchants. Other regulated e-wallets that are widely used for Internet gambling payments are MoneyBookers, Paysafe, etc. – these identify the player and the source of funds, and record payments that are gambling related. Anonymous payment methods (such as Paypoint, UKash, pre-paid credit cards) are available; tracing the origin of such funds seems impossible. There are a host of non-European e-wallet and e-money systems in use online – some of which are effectively unregulated anywhere.

The utility and convenience of alternative payment systems means that for many players they now rival the traditional, highly regulated payment methods in trust and popularity.

A player balance is generally a mix of funds which can be withdrawn immediately and funds which may be staked, but not withdrawn unless they are risked a set number of times as stakes in games or bets. Restrictions on withdrawals are applied automatically by the operator and defined in its terms and conditions (T&C).

Fraud screening is a continuous activity and is compulsory before a major withdrawal can be authorised; gamblers may be challenged to prove their identity or age at withdrawal. Activity and gambling history are reviewed and any abnormal patterns (such as addictive behaviour or a sudden rash of wins) may be investigated by the operator's staff. Operators also need to guard against losses due to credit card 'chargebacks' – transactions where the player cancels the payments alleging error or abuse – because these are costly in staff time and fines, and can lead to barring of the operator from the credit card payment system.

If declared in the T&Cs at registration, an inactive gamblers' account balance may be charged a regular fee as a sort of maintenance charge to eliminate minor balances and encourage activity. Paying interest on gamblers' deposits to attract funds is not permitted unless the operator holds a 'deposit-taking banking licence', but Internet gambling may offer loyalty schemes that give credits.

It is worth noting that opportunities to earn interest or speculate with the gambling deposits/wins held as client funds exist. Such activities lie outside the scope of this chapter since they are never declared as a component of the Internet gambling business model and are usually prohibited.

## Relevance of intangible assets to Internet gambling

A prime asset of any Internet gambling operator is its list of loyal customers. The more accurate the database and the more active and affluent the players in it, the better the business. Such intangible asset value is only measured when an operator is bought privately or sold to the public via a stock market. A player database may be legitimately sold or shared – and it may also be stolen or spoiled. Transfer of personal player data is generally approved by players at registration when they accept the T&Cs offered. Player deposits can also be 'assigned' (the transfer of beneficial ownership) subject to the T&Cs. The player database owned by an Internet gambling operator may claim millions of registered customers. However, many player accounts are disused. Accounts may be spurious or exploratory also. Some operators retain inactive player records indefinitely for marketing or compliance reasons. Dormant accounts are often used to promote new gambling offers, since people who register once are far easier to attract. The player database is a major intangible asset.

Operators may own unique software (for offering or managing Internet gambling). Such software can be protected by copyright and may be sold, leased, licensed, or loaned to partners. The value of software is difficult to quantify as it devalues rapidly if not maintained. Internet gambling operators may specialise, by offering a particular competence or service. Operators aim to create recognised brands through beautiful website graphics or original game design; these intangible assets may be copyrighted, trademarked, or patented. 'Domain names' are also valuable intangible assets especially when memorable, known, and well ranked in Internet search engines. Despite registering intellectual property rights (*IPR*), court action is rare in this industry even where there is clear infringement. However IPR protection enables an operator to prove their rights allowing them to commoditise these. Valuing intangible assets is a very relevant skill in this sector.

The tangible assets of an Internet gambling operator are usually minimal – comprising information technology (IT) hardware, office furniture, and vehicles. Such inventory items rapidly depreciate so may be leased rather than owned. The value of an Internet gambling operator is vested almost completely in its intangible assets.

Despite instability, the last decade has seen many successful 'floatations' (properly known as Initial Public Offerings or IPOs) for Internet gambling operators on stock markets in America, Britain, Canada, Germany, Sweden, etc. which demonstrate confidence in the sustainability of Internet gambling. When an operator is publicly listed, it becomes subject to additional auditing and reporting requirements. Many Internet gambling operators opt to sell their shares on stock markets which specialise in trading higher-risk equities (stocks) – such as the Alternative Investment Market (AIM) in Britain or NASDAQ in America – as these markets apply lighter governance rules and provide lower guarantees to those buying shares.

## Internet gambling 'licensing'

'Licensing' is used to indicate both legal sanction to operate in or from a jurisdiction and a commercial agreement between a software supplier and a third party. Both forms of licence will be documented, subject to conditions, and may expire or be revoked.

A jurisdictional licence is said to be 'a privilege and not a right'. Licensing authorities generally offer neither appeal nor compensation to operators whose application or licence is refused, debated, or delayed (regardless of reason) giving rise to 'regulatory risk'. An unintended consequence of heavy regulation is it may attract only the 'big boys' (too-big-to-fail operators) or the 'cowboys' (reckless operators). Unmitigated regulatory risk will deter 'new boys' (innovative start-ups) and limit investment by 'good boys' (operators with formal risk management). Arbitrary regulation discourages communication between licensee and the licensing body, isolating regulatory staff from developments.

Commercial licensing allows an operator to run third-party software in order to establish or enhance their Internet gambling business. It is common for operators to combine the services and software of multiple suppliers into a mix that appeals to their particular market. Any dispute arising from a commercial licensing agreement is a civil matter and may be taken to court in the jurisdiction named in the contract. However, most disputes are settled out of court with non-disclosure terms attached so that settlement terms stay out of the public domain.

## Segmentation of services and markets

Internet gambling services can be divided into the following broad types:

- *Single-user services*, such as casino, slots, and virtual races; the risk of the bet is always carried by the operator – who controls the offer, rules, funds, and calculates all prizes/fees. This type of game is automated and provided 'on demand'. Designed to be emotionally appealing, such games are short-lived. The result, determined by a Random Number Generator (*RNG*) embedded in the gaming system, is known immediately.
- *Multi-user services* include sports betting, pool betting, bingo games, lotteries, and scratchcards where the operator aims to involve many gamblers in a single event. If linked to a declared schedule, the users will have to wait to know if they have won. Results of external events are unpredictable and the operator must ensure that the costs of all possible outcomes are covered financially through 'event risk management'. The degree of automation in such games varies – sports betting demands expert monitoring facilitated by the capture and collation of information online.
- *Player-to-player services* include poker rooms and betting exchanges where the operator does not carry any gaming risk. Funds are transferred from those whose bet was lost to

the winner(s); the operator levies a fee for acting as 'honest broker' and for providing an attractive online environment where players can meet and gamble.

Gambling services offered online can also be differentiated by:

- *Delivery channel – PC/mobile phone/kiosk/TV.* The nature of the channel will impose technical and operational limitations. It will also define how emotionally and socially engaging the game is.
- *Gambling product – sports/casino/poker/other.* Most gamblers prefer one or other of these products. Cross-selling between products is possible for a minority – to fill in time or provide new challenges, but the motivation to bet differs between fulfil, thrill, skill, and maybe plain kill.
- *Game type.* Poker/blackjack are alternative forms of card games which fall within the same product group, but offer different styles of entertainment.
- *Game rules.* European roulette v. American roulette or Texas hold'em v. seven card stud are refinements within a game type. These differences can impact the number of available players and also the chance of winning.
- *Game timeframe – instant/live/simulated on-demand/deferred/long term.* The immediacy of a game may be a factor in the entertainment value it offers. The trend is that casual players seek colourful, easy and quick games whereas more serious players seek more challenging and longer-timeframe games.
- *Customer demographics.* The audiovisual context of the game may be tailored to a target age – twenties/thirties/forties/fifties/retired. It may also be designed to appeal to a particular gender.
- *Customer economics.* Some operators serve only wealthy, referred players.
- *Customer skill.* Some operators may exclude inexperienced or professional gamblers; other operators recruit players from an area regardless of their skill level.
- *Payment methods supported – credit card/e-wallet/e-money.* The convenience and familiarity of deposit and withdrawal methods is a major factor for most players. Many payment systems are localised and the operator must match the payment patterns of its target market.
- *Market – jurisdiction/language/culture.* Regulatory and marketing issues may constrain an operator to work within a single nation. The staff or financial resources of an operator may limit them to a few particular markets or sub-markets. The specialisation of an operator may determine that they only cover certain game types or target certain markets (e.g. ex-USSR).

Players are commonly segmented by:

- *preferences* (nationality declared, product used, currency deposited, location);
- *promotion* (responded to bonus offer or marketing campaign);
- *referral* (affiliate, friend, agent, etc.);
- *financial status* (spend/bet/deposit/withdrawal to date).

The data available to Internet gambling operators facilitates detailed profiling of active gamblers.

## Operator roles and responsibilities

The B2C operator is always responsible at law for the commercial relationship with players and named when a player deposits funds. However, it is common to find that B2C operators delegate operations to a B2B platform (or payment processing to a *Payment Aggregator*) acting as their agent. Various models are outlined below to help recognise how responsibilities may be divided.

### *Proprietary B2C*

The simplest organisational structure for a B2C Internet gambling operator is when all software and skills are kept in-house. This requires competence to design and deliver quality gambling software. It also requires the ICT skills to set up and manage complex technical infrastructure. Technical self-sufficiency avoids the cost of revenue share agreements and allows tactics to be updated almost instantly. However, all development and security risks are carried alone so the service can prove uncompetitive or vulnerable to attack.

### *Hosted B2C*

A popular organisational structure for a start-up B2C Internet gambling operator involves working with an existing B2B platform. The contract terms are generally dictated by the B2B operator. Typically a sliding scale of fees applies (rates improve as B2C turnover rises) and often a minimum marketing spend specified. There may also be one-off charges for setting up the operator and also a significant deposit payable to the platform. More details on hosted operations are given below.

### *B2C Reseller*

Internet gambling operators are often cautious of scaling up too quickly or spreading their resources too thinly so may appoint 'intermediaries' to reduce their marketing and support costs when venturing into non-core markets. Sharing the risk of growth is achieved by partnering with resellers/intermediaries in the target market to reduce the cost of failure.

Cloned websites known as 'skins' are often used to enter new markets (different imagery or language, but same games, same odds, same prizes, same rules, and so on). The skin website updates and customer care may be managed by the intermediary, but the prime operator remains liable for handling funds/payments and licensing relationships (with or without assistance from a B2B platform). A typical revenue share deal for a 'White Label skin' is about 50 per cent of traffic relayed through the skin website.

The main cost that the skin reseller/intermediary operator must bear is the marketing. The skin operator may have specialist knowledge relevant to 'localising' the service. Alternatively the skin operator may have an existing customer base, brand, or significant budget to invest in launching its operation.

Other resellers who cultivate customer relationships amongst those inclined to enjoy Internet gambling are often classed as 'affiliates'. A customer may follow a recommended link provided by the affiliate without realising that their referral was a commercial transaction. Examples of this include a football team supporters' club website with links to a sponsoring Internet gambling operator. Fans of the club may visit the operator's website to use a bonus voucher or to find coverage of a specific game.

Affiliates are passive resellers as they do not manage clients, merely influence them. Affiliates can earn a one-time fee for each person referred who is converted into a 'real money player'; this is due upon the first deposit by the player. Alternatively affiliates may opt to earn 'lifetime fees' which can be up to 50 per cent (normally 30–40 per cent) of the net income generated by players they have referred. This becomes very lucrative for affiliates if their marketing strategy succeeds in referring active players.

Agents are resellers with land-based betting shops or other sales outlets through which bets are resold. When transferring bets, agents must always identify the origin of the gamble or game. The agent is merely bringing the bet within reach of a player (who may not have Internet access). There is debate over the legality of this model in some European jurisdictions.

As outlined above, B2C reselling arrangements vary, but the concept is always the same – the reseller markets and supports one or more Internet gambling operators in return for a share of the revenue generated. Resellers focus on the market preferences and provide useful feedback.

Some affiliate networks have grown into multi-level marketing (*MLM*) where specialist operators recruit affiliates to promote online casinos. MLM affiliates earn brokerage fees from the process rather than dealing directly with either operators or players. As a result of the volume, benefits, and risks of Affiliate Management, specialised software has now evolved to manage affiliate relationships – such as 'Netrefer', for example.

### B2B platform hosting standalone operators

Platform service providers may offer template solutions to their client B2C operators. The result is that there will be a common 'look and feel' between B2C operators using the same platform, but each will be differentiated by its website content, its T&Cs, and the mix of games offered. The individual games may also be mildly customised (different payout ratios, variations in rules).

The platform runs the hardware and software required by each B2C operator. Today, clients of a B2B platform are usually only logically distinct so even the bandwidth and backups of the B2B may be shared between multiple clients. The motivation for B2C operators to take a cloned software solution is simplicity and reliability. The drawback is that the B2C operator has little influence over the design or quality of the software used and must trust the platform not to leak or abuse the confidential data held on behalf of the operator. The range of services provided by the B2B platform varies widely and the share of the revenue kept by the platform is adjusted to suit. Platform fees vary between 10 and 50 per cent of GGR.

A *back end* website will be configured for the B2C operator to control and report on their operations with user accounts for the B2C operator's staff. The back end varies in design and style according to the platform's sophistication; some back end websites provide 'click-through' screens with powerful query tools and reporting; other back end systems are slow and difficult to use. The stability and scope of the back end control system is easily overlooked yet the reliability of management decisions, of compliance, and of commercial success for an online gambling operator is directly related to the quality of the back end website (unseen by players and by most regulators).

Figure 4.3 is intended to convey the concept that B2C operators may be satellites linked to a single B2B operator that takes care of their technical needs. Each B2C operator may then rely on a number of affiliates to link to their players. Where the B2B platform handles payments for its B2C clients, the aggregation of payment processing can result in greatly reduced transaction costs since the platform can negotiate better than an individual, small operator. Note that the various B2C operators may be in direct competition with each other yet sharing a single host platform.

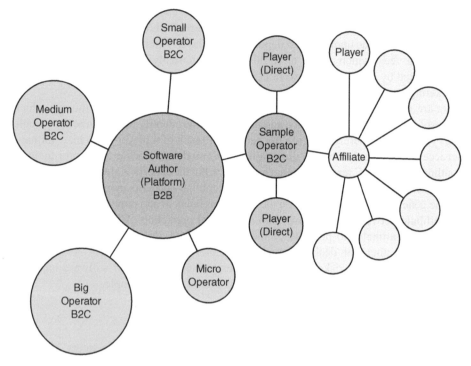

*Figure 4.3* Relationship between one platform and multiple operators

### B2B platform hosting networked operators

Some platform service providers specialise in linking clients together into a cooperative network that allows the registered players of each B2C operator to meet with the players of the rest. This business model is very relevant to online poker. The main benefit is a wider range of active games available 24x7. B2C operators also benefit from shared liquidity (more money in play to attract players) and from better fraud screening. Such B2B platforms often impose strict 'rakeback' limits to avoid conflict between competitors that share the same P2P network.

### Unhosted B2B services

Successful proprietary B2C operators may choose to license their software to other operators in new markets without 'hosting' their clients. A fixed fee/royalty or bill for any customisation may be charged and/or a revenue share. Territorial limits may be specified and further assignment of the software by the licensee prohibited.

Internet gambling software development is challenging as the software must be fast, scalable, reliable, serve all popular browser clients and work over most network conditions. Website content must combine action, innovation, and excitement yet inspire trust. Internet gambling software requires all the features of Internet banking and e-commerce plus most of the tricks of modern media. Constant updates to logic, graphics, and text are required. Some specialist software providers exist to service B2B or B2C operators. Not being involved in live gambling, such software authors are generally exempt from jurisdictional licensing controls and free of gambling embargos – see Cryptologic Inc. which has traded continuously on the NASDAQ since 2000.

There are many boutique software businesses specialising in the integration or optimisation of Internet gambling operations. Some specialists sell market intelligence to Internet gambling operators. Other dedicated businesses perform 'market making' to stimulate gambling by seeding games.

A summary of the main types of operation and the key points of differentiation are presented in Table 4.2.

*Table 4.2* Summary of operator types and key points of differentiation

| *Summary table* | *Points of differentiation* |
|---|---|
| Proprietary B2C operator | Exclusive rights to software developed or bought |
| | Player database privacy managed in-house |
| | Able to amend system at will |
| | Requires in-house skills to manage or perform technical tasks |
| Hosted B2C operator | Dependent on platform for key processes and reputation |
| | System changes at discretion of platform (and often at cost) |
| | B2C operator does not need to employ technical staff |
| Reseller B2C operator | Manage marketing, but delegate most operational tasks |
| | B2C operator does not need to employ (m)any technical staff |
| | Risk of 'platform lock-in' as player database is held hostage |
| B2B platform hosting standalone B2C | Platform does not deal directly with players (unless customer care is included in their service package) |
| | Platform usually services multiple B2C client operators – each of which is completely segregated from the rest |
| | Platform must employ technical specialists |
| B2B platform hosting networked B2C | Platform deals directly with players for fraud screening |
| | Platform services multiple B2C client operators – each of which is known to the rest and integrated into the network |
| | Platform must employ technical specialists |
| Unhosted B2B services operator | Software authors provide gaming and/or control system code without involvement in live gaming/gambling activity |
| | Market makers use automated interfaces to place bets and stimulate interest in games |
| | Information service providers sell real-time data in pre-set format that can be automatically uploaded by B2C operators |
| | *Note:* When not a party to any gambling, the business needs no licence (even if its revenue is gambling-dependent) |

## Overview of costs

Telecommunications bandwidth quality and prices vary according to location; lowest prices are found in North America/Caribbean or on mainland Europe. Bandwidth consumption reflects the type of gambling supported (poker requires high-capacity, quality bandwidth; lottery games require little bandwidth and are fault tolerant). As an indication, some medium-sized Maltese operators spent over €1,000,000 per annum on webhosting and bandwidth alone in 2011.

Marketing costs vary according to the methods preferred – 'scattergun' media advertising has been replaced by targeted promotions via affiliates, mobile phone messaging, and social networking sites. One operator reported spending nearly €20,000,000 on advertising in their 2005 accounts during a major marketing push to establish their brand. Sponsorship of sports events has also been used for promotion.

Further analysis of costs and choices is given below.

### Capital or fixed costs

These are mostly incurred prior to earning revenue:

*   *Software* can be shareware, in-house, developed by third parties, bought off-the-shelf, or leased – or unofficially reverse-engineered or pirated for gaming and control functions. Software may be paid for by revenue share. Dedicated software is also required to manage technical operations and risks.
*   *Hardware* can be bought, shared, or leased; costs may be minimised through 'virtualisation' (splitting one physical server into multiple virtual servers) or 'cloud computing' (whereby flexible server capacity is obtained over the Internet from third parties such as Amazon) if permitted and practical. The hardware includes dedicated servers, office computers, and communication devices. Server costs may be outsourced to a B2B platform.
*   *Costs for hosting and connecting web servers* (and fallback server sites/extra domains). A range of IP addresses and domain names are required which may be costly to acquire.
*   *Share capital and third party bonds.* Given the high risk of the sector, most business partners will insist on a deposit. A regulated operator may be required to have fully paid-up share capital above a threshold, e.g. a minimum equity of €100,000 is mandated for any independent Malta-based online sportsbook.
*   *Direct costs associated with obtaining a licence or complying with regulatory requirements.* Most licensing jurisdictions charge the applicants a one-off fee to cover 'due diligence' checks. There may be related costs to incorporating a company in the relevant jurisdiction and for opening a 'merchant account' to receive credit card payments. It is often necessary to engage consultants to navigate the licensing process and document the operator's control system.
*   *Staff recruitment.* Salaries in this sector are higher than average and some roles may be mandated by regulators as a condition of licensing, e.g. a local 'key official' may be required. Recruitment may involve 'finder fees' paid to suitable agencies.

### Main operating expenses (Opex)

These are normally incurred during or after the launch:

- *Promotions and marketing.* The major cost of operations is attracting players to choose the services offered through ongoing marketing and customer retention campaigns.
- *Telecommunications/bandwidth.* Standalone operators must pay for the traffic received by player-facing *front end* and staff-facing back end servers. Traffic rises with growth, but can also escalate for unprofitable reasons (such as players browsing for information without betting).
- *Payouts.* Some days or seasons are bad for operators if the players win more often than chance implies likely. Reserves are required to keep the business trading through a bad season or to help tide a casino operator over large prize wins.
- *Information security.* Outages can kill customer loyalty and put an operator out of business. Proactive IT protection is achieved through dedicated engineers, external consultancy, and skilled in-house fraud prevention teams.
- *Ongoing taxation and/or licensing fees.* The choice of jurisdiction for establishment will impact the taxation and licensing fees due (see Table 4.3).
- *Costs of financing.* Some operators launch using bank loans, but many are financed by their shareholders who may specify a repayment schedule with interest.
- *Innovation and service enhancement.* Most operators need to continually update their services and website to gain and maintain market share.
- *Intellectual property rights payments.* Access to a well-known brand may be crucial to market share, but an expensive overhead.
- *Salaries and fees.* Good personnel are liable to be poached so demand high salaries with perks/travel as common extras.

Note that the last three in this list are optional/atypical as they depend on the level of automation and outsourcing applicable.

### Jurisdictional licence and gaming tax

A European licence used to be considered valid across the internal market based on the single market principles. Recently, a 'walled garden' approach has been imposed under which operators may be required to seek a licence in each EU market they serve. The cost of a French Internet gambling licence alone has been quoted as €8,700,000 so this trend appears prohibitively expensive for pan-European operations.

In addition to the direct cost of licensing, the political status of a jurisdiction and factors such as government stability, local culture, and the attitude of the regulator can impact cost-based considerations since they influence the exposure to regulatory risk and need of reserves.

It is difficult to compare the prime jurisdictions that license Internet gambling targeted at European players. Some indication is given in Table 4.3 based on publicly available information collected in early 2011.

## Accounting considerations and risk factors

There are many financial factors to balance in Internet gambling. Strong internal controls are indicated yet most control system software is subject to frequent updates and limited user testing. Some operators extract daily transactions into a data warehouse to enable powerful offline queries to extract intelligence from their data. A simpler approach is a daily updated 'dashboard' display of 'critical success factors' achieved with spreadsheet software and manual data entry showing metrics such as:

Table 4.3 Licence fees and tax rate comparison, 2011 (approximate)

| | Alderney British Crown Dependency | Curaçao Dutch Caribbean | Gibraltar British Overseas Territory | Isle of Man British Crown Dependency | Malta EU Member State | United Kingdom EU Member State |
|---|---|---|---|---|---|---|
| Licence classes | 6 (B2C, B2B, Core, Foreign, Hosting, Temporary) | 2 (Sub-licences only available) | 1 | 2 (Full, sub-licence) | 4 (Games of Chance, Matchbook, P2P, B2B) with variations | 8 (covering specific game types) |
| Application fee | £10,000 | uncertain | zero | £1,000 | €5,000 (€2,300 application + €2,700 certification) | £651–£63,671 to suit scale/scope |
| Annual fee | £10,000–£140,000 | $12,000–$67,200 | £2,000 | £35,000 | €7,000 | £1,594–£144,000 to suit scale/scope |
| Gaming tax | 0% | 0% | 1% of turnover/gross margin. Minimum £85,000 p.a. but capped | 1.5% of gross margin | €7,000 p.a. – games of chance, 0.5% gross margin on matchbook; 5% of yield on P2P, €5,000 p.a. for B2B platform | 15% on gross margin |
| Profit tax | 10% | <= 2% | <= 2% | 0% | 5% | 20–28% |
| VAT? | No VAT | No VAT | No VAT | No output VAT, but input VAT applicable | No output VAT, but input VAT applies | No output VAT, but input VAT applies |
| Compliance costs | Significant | Low | Significant | Significant | Significant | Significant |

Notes
A useful summary can be found online entitled *Green Paper on On-line Gambling in the Internal Market*. This Green Paper (published March 2011) requested feedback from interested parties and provided some well-presented (but not entirely accurate) information on the Internet gambling sector.
For more information on the Green Paper, Staff Working Paper, and summary of responses see the following:
ec.europa.eu/internal_market/consultations/docs/2011/online_gambling/com2011_128_en.pdf
ec.europa.eu/internal_market/consultations/docs/2011/online_gambling/sec2011_321_en.pdf
ec.europa.eu/yourvoice/consultations/2011/index_en.htm – see July 31 2011 entry

- numbers of new player registrations;
- gross deposits;
- gross withdrawals;
- gross revenue;
- gross wins;
- largest prize won.

All are reported per day, week, or month as required. Structured Query Language (*SQL*) queries may be used to extract this data too.

Many operators interface their proprietary gaming system(s) to official ledgers (as seen by their external auditor) via a spreadsheet export/import routine. Accounting adjustments made in the ledgers are usually not reflected back into the live gaming system unless the two systems are fully integrated.

Reconciliations between the online player balances and the related client funds held at bank are rare because of the continual flux of player funds due to 24x7 gambling activity. External auditor checks may include test bets, but anomalous transactions can go undetected if beyond the scope of the audit.

Good accounting policies help top management make informed decisions. Well-run operators produce financial statements quarterly or monthly to assist them steer the business. The quality of the control system software, accounting procedures, and data held will strongly determine the accuracy of management reports and forecasts. The best control systems will incorporate data retrieved from third-party data sources relevant to the business as is indicated in Figure 4.4.

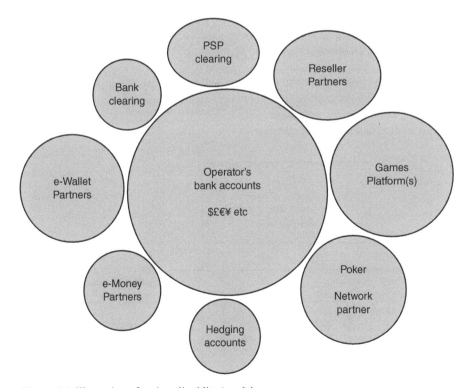

*Figure 4.4* Illustration of various liquidity 'pools'

## Deductions by platforms or partners

The supply chain for Internet gambling involves many parties who are generally paid by 'revenue share' to motivate effort and to minimise the main fixed overheads. The commercial terms agreed between operators and platforms are jealously guarded secrets subject to significant negotiation. Large, strongly branded operators can obtain better terms than start-ups.

## Strategies and business models

Budgets required to establish an Internet gambling business depend on the operator's resources in terms of brand, skills, customer relationships, and staff. Broad categories of licensed Internet gambling operators established in the European region are:

- *New start-up* – offering an innovative service or addressing a neglected/niche market.
- *Land-based spin-off* – benefiting from established reputation/clientele/liquidity/ knowledge.
- *Consolidation* – joint venture/merger/buyout of Internet gambling operator(s).
- *Alternate* – established operator seeks a/another licence to spread 'regulatory risk'.
- *Re-branding or re-location* – established operator opts to change style or operating base.

The strategies discussed in this section are only those relevant to a transparent, accountable, licit business that intends to trade for many years. Illicit business models are not covered but do represent competition that must be anticipated.

Most new operators are launched by businesses engaged in the information, communications and entertainment services (*ICE*) arena as there are shared skills. When seeking funding, licensing, or partnership, an operator's business plan will need to explain:

- critical assumptions made relating to the current and future business environment;
- established customer relationships relevant to the market selected;
- unique selling point or niche advantage;
- market(s) targeted and marketing strategies;

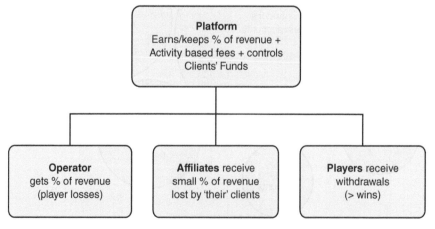

*Figure 4.5* Logical division of funds for B2B and B2C hierarchy

- opportunities and points of differentiation from the competition;
- organisational structure (chain of command) and control strategy employed (usually two organisation charts are relevant – the external ownership hierarchy and the internal structure showing departments, roles, and responsibilities);
- key positions and personnel;
- financial forecasts;
- sources of funding and ultimate beneficial ownership (those who receive profits).

The success of operators may well correlate with the clarity of their business plan and marketing strategy. It is common in this sector for the business model to evolve within a few years as the operator recognises new opportunities and realigns its services. This should not be seen as a fault.

The personality-driven management style pervades Internet gambling (and regulation), which contrasts with the mandatory Investment Committee procedures and risk-management policies required of hedge funds and other licensed financial institutions that are similarly exposed to high-value transaction fraud and sudden market shifts.

The main choices facing an Internet gambling start-up are whether to be:

- *platform-based* (spreads software research and development (*R&D*) costs; simplest and quickest option);
- *standalone* (avoids platform or software development costs; leverages in-house assets);
- *collaborative* (pick'n'mix of own systems/controls with outsourcing/hosting solutions).

### Platform-based start-up

A start-up business can reduce launch costs to almost nil if able to agree terms with a suitable platform. However, platforms prefer known brands or established operators. The start-up business must sell itself to the platform and may be forced to accept poor commercial terms as a result – at least initially. Most contracts are 'rolling agreements' that continue by default so some escape or review clauses are worth adding in. A 'right of audit' clause must be included to allow the start-up business to review settlements.

Using a platform constrains the operator to choose from an existing range of games, but guarantees ongoing support and development. Most platforms provide the initial website 'customisation' to apply the start-up operator's look and feel. Some also provide integration services enabling real-time communication between the platform's proprietary software and other games or payment options used by the operator, so improving the player experience.

Platforms may bundle non-technical activities – such as customer support, marketing, and payment processing – with their service. Other suppliers simply lease basic software to the client who has to engage the appropriate technical and operational staff plus acquire the relevant hosting environment.

The choice of going for a fully hosted service or managing operations in-house will depend on the skills, experience, and budget available in the start-up business. The costs payable to the platform reflect its degree of involvement and the amount of risk it accepts – higher fees for more services.

Another benefit of partnering with a platform is access to merchant accounts and relative ease of licensing if the platform is pre-approved. A platform with a strong reputation may also help with the branding of the new start-up which has to win affiliate and player trust.

### Standalone start-up

Standalone start-up implies authoring or purchasing all the software required to provide Internet gambling services. This requires major investment. The need for accounting, security, resilience, and record management adds complexity to even the simplest gaming operation. Licensing requirements may impose extra functionality (e.g. responsible gambling measures). Player management is a significant commitment in both programming and support terms. The days of working from the garage to turn a great idea into a profitable online game are probably over. Even pirating existing gaming software (always a risk for operators) cannot produce a sound gaming system.

The cost of software development can be reduced by offshoring programming, but this requires expert project management at a level of system design and documentation not often seen in this sector. Large land-based gambling businesses may have the resources to develop a new proprietary system.

Since the UIGEA and the recession, an increasing number of mergers between two or more independent operators have been seen whereby market share, know-how, and resources are pooled; however, the brand of one or both would usually be retained (see for example the merger of PartyGaming and bwin).

### Collaborative start-up

If a minor operator is struggling, it may join forces with selected competitors either through a joint venture or as a commercial client. This model is very common where an operator has a particular strength (such as sportsbook), but feels in need of add-on games to round out its service. Typically such an operator would run its own control system software and then integrate various third-party software games via bespoke interfaces. A summary of collaborative operator strategy is given in Figure 4.6.

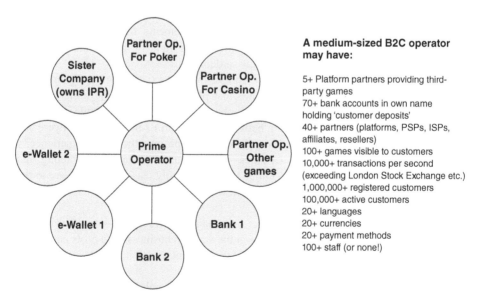

**A medium-sized B2C operator may have:**

5+ Platform partners providing third-party games
70+ bank accounts in own name holding 'customer deposits'
40+ partners (platforms, PSPs, ISPs, affiliates, resellers)
100+ games visible to customers
10,000+ transactions per second (exceeding London Stock Exchange etc.)
1,000,000+ registered customers
100,000+ active customers
20+ languages
20+ currencies
20+ payment methods
100+ staff (or none!)

*Figure 4.6* Collaborative operator strategy

# Conclusion

Consolidation of Internet gambling operators into conglomerates with improved commercial power, marketing pull, and political leverage appears inevitable; however, this future overlooks the poor history of corporate mergers where there are divergent cultures, distinct ICT systems, and incompatible internal controls. Operator takeovers, where player lists and liquidity are assimilated, but some gaming software is discarded, are anticipated to be the most commercially successful.

A counter-trend is emerging as Internet gambling operators diversify into fresh markets (such as the ex-USSR) to try out new brands. By splitting their business interests across separate entities, operators may reduce their exposure in any single market or jurisdiction (and protect their brands).

Operational risk rises with complexity and Internet gambling may rely on a variety of unstable, linked business models. As the supply chain extends and software layers multiply, the strength of the governance applied to monitor operations needs to be intensified. However, investment in testing and internal auditing cannot be expected within a sector subject to very high levels of market and regulatory risk. Neither can mature controls be expected in a business environment where 'speed to market' is more important to market share than 'quality'.

The sector would welcome harmonised regulation to reduce regulatory risk and justify marketing strategies that can capitalise on the licensing investment. Most players remain confused by the European licensing situation and a licence from an EU member state brings little direct benefit in terms of player perception, regardless of cost.

Harmonised regulation across Europe could facilitate an 'end-to-end' review of core processes located within the region and the provision of better financial data to investors and regulators. New approaches to auditing seem overdue for Internet gambling – and e-commerce generally; these ought to measure the flow of funds continuously rather than reporting a momentary, historical snapshot that may be neither representative nor reliable.

Whatever else happens, the growth of this sector appears assured although individual operators will continue to fail when their systems or control capacity is overloaded. It seems likely that operators who succeed will gradually coalesce. Some predict that land-based operators will reintegrate with online gambling operators to preserve their business. Convergence between Internet gambling operators and mainstream telecommunications and media operators is likely if the sector becomes recognised and respectable.

The greatest competition faced by regulated European Internet gambling operators today comes from elusive unlicensed 'outlaws' who will continue to take market share until appropriate enforcement and public awareness are improved. Understanding the business models of the sector is an essential step towards this end.

# Notes

1  www.kpmg.com/GI/en/IssuesAndInsights/ArticlesPublications/Documents/Online-Gaming-A-Gamble-or-a-Sure-Bet.pdf (see particularly the financial information on pages 14 and 15).
2  http://www.FreeSportsBet.com – offers free sports bets (unregulated) and earns advertising income.
3  In such cases, the 'player' may be a legal person (a business) and not a 'natural person' (a human).
4  For more information see: www.satelliteinfo.co.uk/
5  For more information see: www.betradar.com

## References

Budin, S. (2007). *Bets, Drugs, and Rock & Roll: The Rise and Fall of the World's First Offshore Sports Gambling Empire*. New York: Skyhorse Publishing.

Burnett, A. (2011). 'Bet the World' report. Merrill Lynch publication.

Royal Commission on Gambling. (1978). *Final Report Cmnd 7200*. London: Her Majesty's Stationery Office.

## Glossary and acronyms

**24×7**   service provided all day, every day.

**Acquiring Bank**   regulated financial institution that has a relationship with the credit card consortium (headed by Visa and MasterCard) through which it is delegated to open and maintain bank accounts for merchants that are allowed to take credit card payments. The acquiring bank is responsible for conducting due diligence checks and will usually inspect the memorandum of association to assess the nature of the business.

**B2B**   Business-to-Business operator which earns its income from selling services to other operators in this sector.

**B2C**   Business-to-Consumer operator which earns its income from selling games or betting opportunities to consumers (players).

**Back End**   website seen by staff of operator and used to manage operations.

**Denial of Service**   a denial of service attack is an attempt to overwhelm an online service provider so as to disrupt their normal service.

**Front End**   website seen by customers of operator (players) and used to play games/place bets.

**FSA**   Financial Services Authority (regulator for the banking industry in Great Britain during the period covered, 2000–10).

**GGR**   Gross Gambling Revenue which is the income of the operator before any deductions. It is either (stakes less wins) for fixed odds betting or the fees charged to players for providing the gambling opportunity (for player-to-player games).

**Gross Margin**   (also called gross profit margin or gross profit rate) is the difference between revenue and cost before accounting for certain other costs. Generally, it is calculated as the selling price of an item, less the cost of goods sold (production or acquisition costs, essentially).

**ICE**   Information, Communications and Entertainment industries (software, gaming, media, etc.).

**ICT**   Information and Communications Technologies. A term equivalent to IT (information technology) or IS (information systems) that specifically includes the networking and Internet elements that must be considered and controlled.

**IPR**   Intellectual Property Rights such as patent, trademark or copyright privileges which can be asserted, leased, or sold on.

**MAC**   Merchant Account Code assigned by the Visa/MasterCard credit card system to indicate the nature of the merchant's business.

**MLM**   Multi-Level Marketing which involves a tiered approach to driving traffic to the operator via a network of affiliates.

**P2P**   Peer-to-Peer or Player-to-Player transactions.

**Payment Aggregator**   a payment service provider which will accept monies from customers on behalf of clients; the payment aggregator adds value because of the established infrastructure and relationships made available (which are difficult for small or new operators to achieve alone).

**PSP** Payment Service Provider who manages online fund movements with multiple third parties.

**R&D** Research and Development.

**RNG** Random Number Generator (a software or hardware device that produces a continuous high-speed stream of numbers that can be used to determine the result of games, the sequence of cards dealt, etc.). A certified RNG is one that has been bench-tested by a specialist testing laboratory to ensure that the output is unpredictable. (*Note:* Pseudo-random RNGs may be predictable if the seed value and time of initiation are known).

**SQL** Structured Query Language, which is a generic database programming language with a widely used syntax. There are many proprietary versions available, but the key commands are standardised.

**T&Cs** Terms and Conditions (the unilateral contract offered via the operator's website which must be accepted by every registered player).

**VIP** Very Important Player.

# 5   Regulation and reputation

## The Gibraltar approach

*Natalia Zborowska, Sytze F. Kingma,
and Phill Brear*

## Introduction

The rise of Internet gambling transformed not only the traditional ways of providing gambling, but also the established approaches to gambling regulation. With the prohibition of Internet gambling in the USA in 2006, the major Internet gambling operators concentrated their businesses on Europe. However, the competition from private Internet operators was being resisted by the majority of European Union (EU) member states. Despite numerous decisions by the European Court of Justice (ECJ), which appeared to support Treaty provisions for the free movement of services, the 2004 proposal of the Commission to include gambling into the Services Directive[1] and a number of the infringement procedures,[2] the national monopolies and protected markets continued to maintain and defend their position.

Risks associated with the industry, such as problem gambling or money laundering, have been used as the main argument for constraining the market. With the transformation of gambling into a transnational activity the nature of risks associated with this industry has also transformed: gambling risks have also become transnationalized. Therefore, in order to challenge existing rules and regulations, the Internet gambling industry must demonstrate its ability to manage the risks associated with its services. Risk management, however, does not pertain only to the risk of excessive gambling and crime. A significant feature of the risk relates also to organizational legitimacy. Contesting the perception of the public and policy makers by devising self-regulatory standards or managing 'reputational risk' (Power, 2007), is one of the strategies of Internet gambling operators to legitimize the industry. As argued by Levi-Faur (2005) efficient markets do not exist outside the state and the society in which they operate, and they require efficient regulatory frameworks which not only facilitate transactions and enhance trust, but also 'mitigate negative externalities' through the regulation of risk (p. 14). The few European jurisdictions that have decided to license and regulate Internet gambling, therefore, play a vital role in this process, with Gibraltar being one of the key players.

There are a number of reasons for choosing Gibraltar as a case study. First, alongside the United Kingdom and Malta, it was one of the first three territories within the EU to facilitate the establishment and development of Internet gambling by allowing private providers to operate from their territories and supply Internet gambling beyond those territories. It is also the EU territory with the longest relationship with the Internet gambling industry. Gibraltar argues to be the 'unique' Internet gambling jurisdiction: only licensing operators with a proven track record, requiring high technical standards as part of the licensing process, and with a commitment of management, staff, and IT infrastructure within the jurisdiction. The operators licensed in Gibraltar are undoubtedly the market leaders in terms of scale of online operations, and 7 out of 20 of them are publicly listed companies.

This chapter examines the ways in which Gibraltar regulates this newly emerging industry. It offers insights into the development of Internet gambling services in Gibraltar, the stability of which is dependent on the reputation of the territory and the industry. The transnationalization of gambling, as well as the significance of the reputation and trust for both the industry and the territory require a combination of both private and state regulatory efforts. We therefore concentrate on the ways in which the Internet operators based in Gibraltar and the state actors 'co-create' the new regulations. It is argued that by legalizing and regulating Internet gambling, Gibraltar encourages the technological and the regulatory innovations necessary for the operation of Internet gambling. We address in particular the paradox between on the one hand the legitimization of the Internet gambling industry, and with this the production of transnational risks, and on the other hand the development of sound Internet gambling regulation in order to reduce these risks. Whilst the state together with the industry becomes a risk producer, it is at the same time a risk taker and risk regulator.

In the next section we make the theoretical connection between offshore gambling and risk regulation, in particular the notions of 'transnational risk' (Beck, 1999) and reputational risk (Power, 2007). Subsequently the development of Gibraltar into an 'Internet gambling hub' will be outlined. This is followed by an analysis of the public–private 'co-creation' of regulatory standards for Internet gambling in Gibraltar. We conclude with an analysis of Gibraltar's role in the shaping of EU gambling regulation.

## Internet gambling and risk regulation

Thus far, scientific and political debates regarding the regulation of Internet gambling have focused primarily on the responses of the European institutions and the member states to the cross-border reach of Internet gambling, as well as the litigation and lobbying to which Internet gambling companies resort in order to promote their interests (Kingma, 2008; Della Sala, 2010). Such views, however, overlook the role played by the jurisdictions that accommodate, license, and regulate Internet gambling companies. The widespread common understanding of the phenomenon of Internet gambling, and its regulation and control, is in line with what Reed (2004) calls 'The Cyberspace fallacy':

> The Cyberspace fallacy states that the Internet is a new jurisdiction, in which none of the existing rules and regulations apply. This jurisdiction has no physical existence: it is a virtual space which expands and contracts as the different networks and computers, which collectively make up Internet, connect to and disconnect from each other.... The world-wide accessibility of the Internet means that no one legal jurisdiction has de jure or de facto control of these activities. From all this, it is concluded that no jurisdiction has any control.
> (p. 1)

However, as several authors have argued, there is a real and material side of the virtual world of the Internet which is of crucial importance for understanding the phenomenon of the Internet itself (Castells 2001; Woolgar, 2002; Shields, 2003). While Internet gambling organizations may have a global reach, and may be flexible, networked, and virtual, they nevertheless always have a material existence somewhere, and are linked in many ways to local services, communities, and regulations. In order to avoid the cyberspace fallacy mentioned by Reed (2004), we will draw attention to the regulatory frameworks of the jurisdictions in which Internet gambling companies are located or have their licences.

Since 1994 when Antigua and Barbuda issued the first licence for an offshore remote gambling company, small offshore states have played an important role in the development of the industry. Not only do they accommodate the Internet gambling operators, they also challenge the existing onshore rules and legislations either themselves or via the industry. After the USA outlawed Internet gambling in 2006, Antigua formally challenged the ban via the World Trade Organization (WTO).

Although the origins of contemporary offshore economies have been linked with the creation of offshore financial centres, the developments of the Internet and telecommunications contributed greatly to the development of new offshore sectors such as Internet sex or Internet gambling (Palan, 2003). Prevented from establishing their businesses in onshore territories due to high tax rates or the absence or restrictions of legislative provisions and licensing systems, with few exceptions, gambling companies based themselves offshore to provide their services over the Internet. As argued by Palan (1998), the development of the offshore economy is promoting the development of juridical spaces 'in which economic activities can develop more or less without hindrance' (p. 64). By offering 'residence' via a licence acquisition many offshore tax havens, such as the Netherlands Antilles (Curaçao), Antigua and Barbuda, and Costa Rica, attracted hundreds of Internet gambling companies to their territories, offering a material basis for the advancement of the industry.

The expansion of the offshore economy and fierce competition between jurisdictions led, however, towards a 'race to the bottom' or regulatory laxity, which began in the 1980s (Palan, 2003). This contributed to growing concerns over the illicit nature of some offshore businesses, and major institutional bodies such as the Organisation for Economic Co-operation and Development (OECD), the International Monetary Fund (IMF), and the EU have expressed their concerns over the growth and nature of many offshore centres and transactions (Cobb, 2001; Palan, Murphy, and Chavagneux, 2010). Criticism from those institutions and the 'onshore' world resulted in the restructuring of many offshore economies. Offshore places began to reshape and promote themselves as reputable jurisdictions, which regulate, control, and supervise their services and products (Cobb, 2001).

We refer in particular to Hudson (1998) who provides strong arguments for understanding the origins and the development of offshore financial centres and their regulatory standards. By using the concept of 'place' developed by Massey (1993), Hudson argues that offshore centres are socially constructed places shaped by local and extra-local actors who are involved in regulatory bargaining, which is a process in which affected stakeholders negotiate and collaborate with governments in order to develop policies and regulations. Therefore, in order to understand the construction of offshore centres we must examine the positions of the governments and corporations and 'the ways they relate to each other in the process of regulatory bargaining' (Hudson, 1998: 918). Furthermore, trust is argued to be central to the social construction of places: '[S]ocial construction generates agreement on what place is' (ibid.: 917); such agreement, however, depends on and reproduces trust. We suggest that trust relates to the idea of reputational risk discussed by Power (2007). We argue that reputational risk and reputation management are crucial for understanding the development of Gibraltar into the leading Internet gambling jurisdiction.

It has previously been argued that together with the legalization and liberalization of gambling markets, in which gambling becomes normalized as a consumer good, the regulatory focus shifts from a rule-based mode towards a risk-based mode of regulation (Kingma, 2004; Cosgrave, 2006). In the risk-based mode regulation focuses on the side effects and unintended consequences of commercial gambling, rather than on constraining the settings for gambling consumption and prescriptions for the operation of gambling services. In the field of gambling, a rule-based approach might refer to a monopoly situation in which the operator is severely constrained; a risk-based mode might refer to exploitation based on free market forces which are only tempered in view of the risks relating to problem gambling and crime. An increasing awareness of, and regulatory focus on, side effects such as problem gambling and crime renders gambling part of the 'risk society' as defined by Beck (1992). Since Internet gambling may be characterized by the reduction of immediate controls and material constraints on the consumption of gambling services, the regulatory significance of gambling risks only increases.

To a certain extent the risk society already implies a 'world risk society' (Beck, 1999). With the transnationalization of gambling and the export of gambling risks to consumers based in jurisdictions other than those from which the gambling services are offered, the need for new modes of gambling regulation increases. The emergence of new issues triggers the emergence of new governance spaces with new networks of actors mobilizing to be involved and gain control, often challenging and undermining existing regimes and state control (Djelic and Sahlin-Andersson, 2006). Multiple actors such as non-governmental organizations (NGOs), civil society groups, or professional associations are increasingly involved in framing, shaping, and producing new rules and regulations in areas as diverse as finance, pollution, and education (ibid.). Furthermore, as argued by Power (2007), stimulated by scandals and catastrophic events, 'governance is being reinvented in terms of capabilities for effective risk management' (p. viii). Risk management has become central to the new kind of regulation, where correction of externalities becomes an integral part of modern regulation.

Both the state actors and the industry are acting in an environment of uncertainty, where failure is possible and the legitimacy and reputation of the participants are at stake. Modern states have recently become explicit about risk management and are increasingly adopting concepts and standards from the private sector (Power, 2004). By adopting risk-management practices the state attempts to improve its ability to control risks. States are increasingly preoccupied not only with the minimization of negative externalities through regulation, but also with the management of public expectations and perceptions towards the state's ability to manage risk.

To minimize the undesirable side effects of activities and manage risks posed to the reputation of the state, regulatory agencies are created, which in turn employ risk-based 'responsive' approaches to regulation (Power, 2004). In the risk regime of regulation, self-regulation at the organizational level of gambling operators is as important as state regulation (Kingma, 2004). According to Power (2007), the rising significance of risk management represents a new phase of corporate governance. In this new phase internal control becomes as important, and sometimes takes precedence over, external control and regulations. Self-regulation and compliance to normative rules of organizational conduct become the new standard to which external control agencies develop a complementary role. The work of external control agencies, which becomes relevant in case of failure of internal controls, is defined in terms of meta-control or 'the control of control'.

An approach which is described as 'enforced self-regulation', which combines state and corporate regulatory efforts (Hutter, 2006), often relies on the internal controls and self-organization of regulatees. Accordingly, private sectors and professional services are becoming co-creators of risk management and regulation. The government broadly outlines standards which the private sector is expected to meet. The private sector develops risk-management systems and rules to secure and monitor compliance, as well as the procedures that deal with non-compliance. The role of the regulatory officials is to oversee this process. The expertise of private actors in technically complex areas is one of the reasons why regulators increasingly rely on private actors to shape policy (Heritier and Eckert, 2008). Risk-based regulation can be used as a part of the regulators' own reputation risk-management process (Power, 2004). Therefore, at the local level state and private actor networks work together to create a place-specific regulatory model which is ultimately affecting the perception of a jurisdiction as a safe and reputable place to operate from, and contributes to an increase in the client network via direct and indirect marketing strategies (Cobb, 2001).

With regard to reputational risk management, it is important to emphasize that the reputation of the offshore centre, Gibraltar, and the Internet gambling industry are intertwined: Gibraltar needs to be perceived as a reputable jurisdiction to ensure economic stability of the territory, which is partially reliant on the Internet gambling industry. Therefore Gibraltar must find a regulatory balance between controlling the industry and allowing for its development. The Internet gambling sector is counting on the reputational advantages of being licensed and regulated in a reputable jurisdiction with a tight regulatory regime in order to legitimize itself. Moreover, being licensed by an EU member state empowers the Gibraltar industry to challenge existing regimes and pursue their interests on the European level in order to gain access to the European-wide market. Regulation of the industry by Gibraltar not only enhances legitimacy and trust, but also has political implications. It has enabled the argument for Treaty enforcement with regard to the free movement of services, promoted the current revision of gambling legislation in a number of the EU member states, stimulated action towards the development of an EU Directive by the European Commission, and provided a 'collaboration' agenda for subsets of each six-month Presidency for a number of years.

## Gibraltar as an Internet gambling hub

When in 2000 the OECD identified Gibraltar as one of the 35 jurisdictions that met the technical criteria for being a tax haven, the government of Gibraltar decided to readapt their strategy for economic development. The government made a commitment to improve the transparency of its tax and regulatory systems. The steps taken by Gibraltar have included the abolition of the tax-exempt company scheme,[3] the signing of 18 Tax Information Exchange Agreements, and tax system reform which reduced company tax from 22 to 10 percent for all companies, and therefore ended the distinction between onshore and offshore business.

The perception and reputation of Gibraltar is, therefore, of paramount importance to the Gibraltar government. The Chief Minister commented in an interview: 'our international reputation is about the only economic resource that we have at the core of all our economic policies'.[4] This concern not only relates to Internet gambling but builds upon policies that were developed for the regulation and overhaul of the finance and shipping sectors. The concern over reputation was partly developed in response to outside pressures from international organizations such as the OECD. At the same time the influence of the local authorities should not be underestimated. In 1996 the Chief Minister Peter Caruana and his administration committed to the transformation of Gibraltar's reputation and its economy. Their efforts have been acknowledged by much of the local population, international organizations, and the businesses based in Gibraltar. A Gibraltar lawyer commented on this fact as follows:

> It could be argued that the last [2007] elections the Chief Minister has won because of how well he has done with this [Internet gambling] and the other. Bringing the reputation of Gibraltar to a high standard, 12, 14 years ago Gibraltar was not considered a reputable jurisdiction. Now it is, widely it is.[5]

Also, the businesses based in Gibraltar, including Internet gambling companies, are not relocating from the territory despite the fact that from 2011 the tax rate is significantly higher after tax reform. Having paid 1 percent gambling duty with a ceiling of €500,000 per year, from 2011, Internet gambling providers will be exposed to 10 percent company tax. Their decision to stay in Gibraltar underlines the importance of the territory's reputation as the leading Internet gambling jurisdiction and the robustness of its regulatory system, as well as the relations between the local authorities and the industry.

The development of Gibraltar into an Internet gambling hub took place in three phases. The foundations of Gibraltar's Internet gambling industry were established as early as 1989, when Gibraltar issued its first 'offshore gambling licence' to a local bookmaker to cater for betting by non-resident customers. After the reopening of the Spain–Gibraltar border in 1985, British nationals residing in Spain could finally visit Gibraltar and Gibraltar's betting shops. High street betting shops so popular in Britain were not present in Spain, so the reopening of the border enabled them to bet again. However, the Gibraltar betting entrepreneur had to compete with the well-known and established British bookmakers, who were also taking bets over the phone. The offshore gambling licence which allowed the taking of bets from customers residing outside of Gibraltar with only 1 percent betting tax gave a competitive advantage at a time when betting with the UK-based operators meant paying 9 percent tax.

The second phase started in 1993 when the British betting company Ladbrokes opened their telephone betting operation in Gibraltar. In this phase the development of higher volume offshore betting began, providing the local government with considerable income and a boost for employment in the territory through betting management and call centres. In 1996 Victor Chandler International, another British bookmaker, was also granted a Gibraltar betting licence. Until 1999 the impact upon the United Kingdom betting market was constrained by a voluntary code between the offshore-based operators which agreed not to accept bets from British customers (HM Treasury, 1999). The code was breached by Victor Chandler International in May 1999, which started actively servicing UK customers. The violation was triggered by the decision of the Irish government to cut betting tax from nearly 10 to 5 percent. This was seen as a huge threat to Victor Chandler International, which feared losing UK clients to Irish betting operators (Doward, 2000). Other bookmakers followed the lead of Victor Chandler International. Initially servicing customers mostly from the Far East, in 1999 Ladbrokes started offering betting services to British customers over the phone or fax without 9 percent betting duty; it was employing 250 people in Gibraltar. An attractive tax regime, and the same currency and language appealed to other well-known bookmaking companies and other British operators such as Stan James also gained a licence and moved their operations to Gibraltar, creating over 500 jobs. Typically, the bookmakers offered nil deductions over the Internet and only 3 percent over the telephone (HM Treasury, 2000).

The actions of Gibraltar and of the bookmakers, causing an exodus of the major British bookmakers to Gibraltar, was met with criticism by the British Treasury which accused the bookmakers of exploiting a loophole in the advertising ban by promoting 'tax-free' offshore betting in the United Kingdom using teletext services (HM Treasury, 1999). By that time the benefits of the betting industry were recognized by Gibraltar, and Gibraltar authorities were eager to guard their 'right to have their own taxation and powers' (Panorama, 1999). Gibraltar obtained this right in 1969 with the formation of the Gibraltar House of Assembly and the 1969 Constitution (Garcia, 2002). But the Gibraltar government was cautious about the industry's growth and the potential damage which the gambling industry could cause to the image and reputation of the jurisdiction. For this reason, Gibraltar capped the number of licences to seven, making Gibraltar licences the most desirable ones. The last, seventh licence, was obtained by Simon Bold, the founder and main shareholder of Liverpool-based Mawdsley Bookmakers. In 1999 Simon Bold moved to Gibraltar founding Simon Bold (Gibraltar) Ltd, operating telephone and Internet betting. Simon Bold was subsequently acquired in 2001 by betandwin.com for the price of around €2 million in shares and cash (Klein, 2001). The acquisition of Simon Bold and the Gibraltar licence was seen by the Austrian betting company bwin as a gateway to international markets. It was the first Gibraltar licence not to be obtained by a well-known British bookmaker, which was diversifying its own means of offering betting to include phone and Internet.

Bwin was established in 1997 in Austria as an Internet bookmaker without prior experience in operating betting shops. The company grew rapidly and within three years, bwin completed the most successful initial public offering in the history of the Austrian Stock Exchange, raising capital of €55 million (www.bwin.ag).

In 2001 the British government removed betting duty and replaced it with a lower-cost 'Gross Profits Tax' in order to 'stop the boom in offshore tax-free gambling which costs the exchequer millions of pounds a year', thus making Gibraltar betting licences less attractive (BBC News, 2001). Some British operators moved their telephone betting services back to the UK. For example, Ladbrokes took this step, reducing their Gibraltar workforce from 250 to 25 in late 2001.[6]

During this time the third phase took shape. In this phase the dot com boom took Internet gambling to a new level. The industry diversified and as well as telephone and Internet sports betting, it had started offering Internet poker, casino games, bingo, lottery, and betting exchanges, turning over hundreds of millions of dollars per year. Moreover, the long-lasting disputes over the legality of Internet gambling supported by the 1961 Wire Act[7] in the USA, and the subsequent passing of the Unlawful Internet Gambling Enforcement Act (UIGEA) in 2006, contributed to the suspension of real-money operations by many Internet gambling providers. All Gibraltar operators suspended their services in the USA. This meant that the European market became the main market for Internet gambling. Being located in a European jurisdiction was vital if the operators wanted to argue for EU-wide regulation. As the co-CEO of bwin explained during an interview:

> In 1999 there were few places that you could go to – Gibraltar, Isle of Man and the Caribbean. We thought, well, if we do it, we have to stay in Europe. We cannot argue a European case being in Antigua, so we had to join either the Isle of Man or Gibraltar.[8]

The demand for the European licence grew and apart from the betting licence, in 1998 Gibraltar introduced a parallel casino licence which permitted a variety of gaming products to be provided through the Internet. Ladbrokes were among the first to set up their Internet casino gaming operation in Gibraltar. In this phase of development, in order to control the industry and minimize the reputational risk, the Gibraltar government continued its strategy of controlled growth for the gambling industry despite the absence of economic pressures from the UK government that had applied in respect of betting taxes. Standards initially set by the established British bookmakers had to be maintained and, as explained by the Chief Minister, Gibraltar was looking for:

> partners in looking after the jurisdictional reputation and we were looking for companies that would attach as much importance to their corporate reputations as we did for our jurisdiction reputation. And because we felt that that would give us a sort of partnership of the willing and would make the regulatory system easier to deliver...[9]

A further reason for Gibraltar's careful and restrictive approach to Internet gambling was the government's desire to maintain the diversity of the Gibraltar economy. The Gibraltar government is not willing to rely on a single business sector for the stability of the economy. Although they actively limited the number of licences, nearly 10 percent of the Gibraltar workforce was employed by the gambling industry in 2010. The benefits from Internet gambling companies are not limited to gaming tax and employment opportunities, they also create upward demand on the Gibraltar telecommunication infrastructure, employees pay their income tax in Gibraltar, rent offices and accommodation, and create demand for legal, banking, and other services.

As underlined by the Chief Minister, due to the relatively small size of the Gibraltar economy, Gibraltar does not require a large number of gambling companies in order to have a significant impact on the local economy. By careful selection of their gambling operators, Gibraltar opted for quality rather than quantity, and brought together parties for the co-creation of a regulatory regime, comprising a small number of 'reputational risk-sensitive' operators, with a government prepared to allow them to operate within that risk framework.

Currently, as of March 2011, 20 operators are licensed in Gibraltar. They hold a total of 35 licences: 21 for gaming, 13 for betting, and one for spread betting in financial products.[10] An overview of the companies present in Gibraltar in 2011 as well as their gambling activities is presented in Table 5.1.

The Gibraltar Internet gambling operators are represented by the Gibraltar Betting and Gaming Association (GBGA), which was formed in 2003. All operators licensed in Gibraltar are members of this association. The chairman of the association is the Gibraltar bookmaker who was granted the first offshore betting licence in Gibraltar. He currently works for PartyGaming. The GBGA acts as interlocutor between the industry and the government, which work together not only on regulatory issues, but also on solving local problems that the industry encounters, such as infrastructure development, the price and reliability of telecommunications, and the labour market. Apart from everyday issues the industry also works closely together on maintaining the good name of the operators and the jurisdiction.

In the case of Gibraltar, 'cooperation' also means physical proximity. The scarcity of space has always been a defining condition for any organizational practice in Gibraltar. This scarcity not only implies business constraints but also serves as an enabling condition because close proximity means more opportunities for synergy between businesses and face-to-face cooperation. Up until the 1990s, when the military presence was starting to diminish, only 20 percent of the territory was accessible to civilians. New office and housing space had to be found promptly in order to accommodate the demand from the services sector. Land reclamation allowed for some expansion of the territory and multiple modern office and housing estates have been constructed within a decade. The Europort building complex, which was built in the early 1990s, has accommodated eight Internet gambling companies and their 400 employees as well as the gambling regulator. Literally across the road in the Eurotowers, two more gambling companies have their offices and a few cafés and restaurants where employees go for their morning coffee, lunch, or dinner. Within a 10-minute walk you can reach Watergardens, another modern complex, where a further four gambling companies are situated. The rest are scattered around the town, but all of them are within walking distance of each other and the regulator. Such proximity and the unavoidable informal contacts it creates between management, staff, technicians, regulator, and the wider public should not be underestimated in terms of enhanced communication links and quality and speed of information sharing.

*Table 5.1* Operators licensed in Gibraltar

|  | Licensed operators | Gambling activity |
|---|---|---|
| 1 | Ladbrokes (International) Ltd | Betting |
|  |  | Gaming |
|  | Ladbrokes Sportsbook LP | Betting |
| 2 | Victor Chandler (International) Ltd | Betting |
|  |  | Gaming |
| 3 | Eurobet (Gibraltar) Ltd | Gaming |
| 4 | Stan James (Gibraltar) Ltd | Betting |
|  |  | Gaming |
| 5 | Bwin International Ltd | Betting |
|  |  | Gaming |
|  | (Ongame Network Ltd) | Gaming |
| 6 | Tower Rock Limited (Carmen Media Group Ltd) | Gaming |
| 7 | St Minver Ltd | Gaming |
| 8 | 32 Red Plc | Gaming |
|  |  | Betting |
| 9 | Digibet Ltd | Betting |
|  |  | Gaming |
| 10 | Cassava Enterprises (Gibraltar) Ltd (888.com Plc) | Betting |
|  |  | Gaming |
| 11 | Mansion (Gibraltar) Ltd | Gaming |
| 12 | Partygaming Plc (PGB Ltd) | Betting |
|  | (ElectraWorks Ltd) | Gaming |
| 13 | Prospreads Limited (formerly FuturesBetting.com Ltd) | Financial spread betting |
| 14 | Partouche Interactive (Gibraltar) Ltd | Gaming |
| 15 | WHG (International) Ltd (formerly William Hill (Gibraltar) Ltd) | Gaming |
|  | WHG (International) Ltd | Betting |
|  | WHG Trading Limited | Gaming |
|  | WHG Trading Limited | Betting |
| 16 | Hillside (Gibraltar) Ltd (Bet365 Group Ltd) | Gaming |
| 17 | Petfre (Gibraltar) Ltd (Betfred) | Betting |
|  |  | Gaming |
| 18 | Gamesys (Gibraltar) Ltd (formerly Entertaining Play Limited) | Gaming |
| 19 | Probability (Gibraltar) Ltd | Gaming |
| 20 | Betfair | Betting exchange |

Source: Adapted from Government of Gibraltar, Information Services (www.gibraltar.gov.gi) and GRA (2009/10).

## The Gibraltar regulation approach

Gambling regulation in Gibraltar builds on the general approach to regulation which Gibraltar has adopted during recent years. The initial decision to license a small number of well-known and established risk-sensitive operators could be seen as a way of safeguarding the reputation of the territory. Unlike other jurisdictions that are interested in attracting as much business as possible to their territories, Gibraltar has not accepted 'brass plate' licensing of Internet gambling companies. Brass plating permits gaming servers to be located within the territory but management and control to rest elsewhere in the world. As such, they are beyond the statutory powers of the licensing government and regulator, which instead rely on an agreement to accept 'extra-territorial' supervision by the travelling regulator and return to the licensing jurisdiction on an occasional basis. Paradoxically, it is not uncommon for brass plate licence holders to be unlicensed in the state where their management and control are exercised, with a head office and company direction and supporting activities acted out without direct regulatory constraints but notionally to the written rules of the licensing jurisdiction. This dissociation of management control from technical operations has more in common with the early uncontrolled offshore enterprises and is largely compensated for by rule-based regulation as opposed to the risk-based approach, with the out-of-state parties provided with and required to demonstrate detailed application of systems and procedures.

Gibraltar's public position is that of 'home to the world's leading online gambling operators' (GRA, 2009/10), and 'something of an online gambling capital' (Atkinson, 2006). However, Gibraltar does not actively seek to attract Internet gambling providers to the territory. On the contrary, on their website, the Gibraltar government openly 'warns' the potential applicants that 'Licences are generally difficult to obtain'.[11]

In order to maintain the position of a reputable jurisdiction, which remains vulnerable to process failures due to error, slippage in standards, or simply being overtaken by new malicious attacks, the Internet gambling industry is supervised and controlled by the government. As previously touched on, this control starts with a strict licensing process that does not accept applications until the interested party is able to satisfy the government of its reputational foundations. A solid background and an unquestionable business plan constitute the first of the requirements. Also, the operators must meet the government policy of developing and maintaining a substantial presence in Gibraltar. Companies must maintain legal and physical offices in Gibraltar, establish management positions and a number of employees (Gibraltar Licensing Authority, 2011). The diversity of the operators' antecedents and operating structures means that some of the companies maintain their headquarters and support centres in other jurisdictions with equivalent or proportionate regulatory or corporate governance regimes. They are allowed to operate from Gibraltar on the basis that they locate key management and operational personnel and equipment there. Other companies have their headquarters based in Gibraltar, but support, or non-licensable functions elsewhere. This is a reflection of the globalization of the product and the markets, with low-cost states providing low-risk activities (call centres, IT development) and higher-risk, licence-triggering, or control activities at the centre.

Another important aspect of the licensing process is due diligence, in particular the checks on key personnel and technology. For all the managerial positions in Gibraltar a series of checks are conducted in order to establish whether people behind the operation are 'fit and proper'. Background probity checks, as well as establishing whether they have sufficient knowledge and experience to hold and properly conduct respective positions is coupled with detailed financial and criminal checks. Gibraltar law enforcement agencies work together with financial intelligence agencies that provide them with information on criminal records and international intelligence reports. Any changes in key personnel must be submitted for approval.

The technology that underpins the operation must also be approved in terms of its architecture, location, and content. This task is shared between independent test houses, which have also been approved for competence and checked for integrity, and the regulator or his authorized nominees. Five test houses[12] based in the UK, Australia, and Canada have thus far been approved for this purpose. The role of test houses is to analyse software and equipment against manufacturers' specifications and legislative and regulatory requirements.[13] All operators must be able to demonstrate that their games and systems meet relevant standards within a dynamic, complex, and highly competitive industry.

The introduction of the new Gibraltar Gambling Act in 2005 could be considered as the consolidation of Gibraltar's regulatory approach to Internet gambling. The 2005 Gambling Act came into operation in October 2006, repealing the 1958 Gaming Act. It avoided detailed prescription and sought instead to provide a new regulatory framework for Gibraltar's gambling industry. For the first time a specific provision was made for Internet gambling, covering the principles of technical and professional competence, player protection, and the integrity of gambling products. The purpose of the Act was to 'modernise Gibraltar's legislation and to create a statutory licensing and regulatory framework to suit Gibraltar's status as "home to the world's leading online gambling operators"' (GRA 2009/10: 71).

The Act also created a new body, the Gambling Commissioner, with supervisory responsibilities then being divided between the Licensing Authority and the Commissioner. The Licensing Authority is designated as the Minister responsible for gambling. At present the Chief Minister, who is also the Finance Minister, carries out this function. Unusually, the government takes direct responsibility for its policy decisions. The Licensing Authority carries out its functions through the Gambling Division of the Ministry of Finance, and is responsible for evaluating applications, determining and amending licences, and imposing terms and conditions on licencees.[14] The direct and close involvement of the head of government demonstrates that Internet gambling is regarded as a key industry in Gibraltar.

The Gambling Commissioner, which is currently designated to the Gibraltar Regulatory Authority (GRA), is responsible for ensuring that the holders of licences conduct their undertakings in accordance with the terms of their licences and provisions made by the Act (ibid.). Amongst the legislative provisions is that they should do so 'in such a manner as to maintain the good reputation of Gibraltar' (Government of Gibraltar, 2005). We observe here, that in Gibraltar the concern for reputation is instituted by law.

The Gibraltar Gambling Act introduces a minimum age for participation in gambling. It also makes specific provisions for responsible gambling and for money laundering. Although the Act broadly indicates the requirements relating to, for instance, the minimum age for gambling, the specific methods to achieve those requirements are left to industry self-regulation, overseen by the Gambling Commissioner. The Act states: 'A licence holder shall take all reasonable steps to prevent any person from participating in the gambling activities provided by the licence holder unless he is at least of the minimum permitted age' (section 37. [1]). Moreover, the Act obliges Internet gambling operators to establish and maintain effective systems of internal controls and procedures in order to monitor their activities. This is a clear case of enforced self-regulation. It also indicates a reliance on the industry standards and procedures to achieve desired regulatory outcomes. Regulation must remain flexible in order to be able to provide for the constantly evolving industry and the methods and practices available to it to meet regulatory obligations. Therefore, broad guidelines are provided and the industry is empowered to implement procedures which will enable them to satisfy those guidelines. Although further specifications and somewhat more detailed guidelines were introduced by the Code of Practice for the Gambling Industry in 2009, the regulator remains consistent in this broad approach to regulating the industry:

> It is the Gambling Commissioner's preference to keep the scale of formal requirements to a necessary minimum, and deal with as much guidance as possible by way of the more flexible and speedy codes of practice, as opposed to seeking statutory Regulations.
>
> (GRA, 2009)

In section 5.3 of the Generic Code of Practice, which develops the principles of the Gambling Act, the regulatory expectations on 'self-exclusion systems', which offer customers the option of excluding themselves from an operator's gambling services, the Code of Practice explicitly recognizes the self-regulatory standards devised by industry associations:

> Subject to the Gambling Commissioner's further advice, self exclusion systems modeled on mainstream industry bodies' advice, and recognised by the Commissioner, such as GamCare, eCogra and RGA, will be regarded as effective systems for the purposes of this requirement.

In section 7.3, the Code of Practice further specifies the areas which the industry should include into their internal controls and operating procedures required by the Gambling Act. They include:

> corporate structure and reporting; internal and external audit arrangements; accounting and financial control standards; customer and transaction controls (including fraud and security arrangements); business continuity/disaster recovery plans; anti money laundering arrangements; age verification procedures; problem gambling and self exclusion policies; customer complaints arrangements; system testing and security arrangements; and web content and customer control measures to ensure that sites do not contain or access inappropriate material.

The aforementioned provisions clearly indicate that the Internet gambling industry is expected to effectively self-regulate and institute structures and procedures required by law, or run the risk of having less flexible and dynamic arrangements imposed on it.

Heavy reliance on the regulatory capacity of the regulatees, and their responses to the legal requirements constitute, however, one of the weaknesses of the enforced self-regulation approach (Hutter, 2001). The effectiveness of self-regulation ultimately depends on the 'control of control', i.e. the extent to which self-regulation is actually monitored and maintained.

In Gibraltar the regulator works in close cooperation and consultation with the Licensing Authority and the industry. The industry was consulted to provide their input with regard to the 2005 Gambling Act. The Code of Practice and the 2010 Anti Money Laundering Arrangements are also the result of public–private cooperation between the regulator and the industry. The industry is currently involved in developing the Remote Technical and Operating Standards. The industry is invited to respond to the proposed documents, but importantly, the regulator and the industry frequently meet face to face during the GBGA meetings and individual encounters. This process of consultation not only allows for the content of the legislation to be established, but it is also a vital learning and knowledge-sharing experience. During the process both parties learn and discuss their respective priorities, expectations, and concerns. Exchanges take place at short notice and the regulator is able to meet personally with the key personnel of the companies and the employees. The physical proximity coupled with the requirement of physical presence of personnel in Gibraltar, therefore, contributes to the uniqueness of the territory and its gambling regulatory regime.

Regulatory engagement with operators is achieved through a range of more structured, but complementary processes. Customer complaint monitoring and investigation provide the most significant indications of non-compliance with the regulatory standards. The nature of customer complaints captures the diversity of the engaged population. While complaints may centre on the misunderstanding of rules, they extend to customers' discovery of second- and third-tier 'bugs' in software, i.e. a coding error that requires a prior or two prior events to occur before it can be triggered, or even 'non rational' events to be selected by the player to trigger the 'error'. Such is the focus of many players' attention to the performance of games, even for trivial sums, that coding errors are quickly identified and invariably exploited, with the deviation from truly random outcomes stimulating anomalous play and payout patterns.

Substantive complaints invariably involve an examination of the operator's adherence to compliance policies and the decision making of staff. They trigger visits to an operator's premises, examination of records, and direct explanations of events. Complainants may be quick to point out real and imagined compliance failures by operators to support their claims. Complaints can be managed promptly, as physical proximity and the number of operators allows the regulator to act without delay. The proximity as well as the requirement to maintain a substantial presence in Gibraltar again also allows the regulator to visit licensees and examine their equipment and operations to ensure compliance with Gibraltar's regulatory model.

The regulator also employs intelligence mechanisms to monitor the activities and conduct of the operators. This includes information from foreign authorities and regulators as well as checks performed via Internet search tools, gambling-related forums, and blogs. Reports and self-reports from the industry constitute another control mechanism employed by the regulator:

- Regulatory Returns Reports provide statistical information about the operators' activities. This includes information about responsible gambling, complaints, and operational data.
- Licence holders' incident reports are also requested on an ad hoc basis with respect to specific compliance breaches and failures and the regulator expects the industry to report any substantive breach, threat, or contravention of Gibraltar's regulatory model.

Moreover, in an industry where reputation holds so much importance, best practices executed by one operator are frequently observed and adopted by others, whereas bad practices and behaviour are often flagged by customers or competitors. The small location, employees changing companies, and friends and family members working for competitors, means that operators gain an insight into what their competitors are doing. The high value of Gibraltar's gambling licence for the industry means that the operators are willing to comply with conditions and rules imposed on them by Gibraltar's authorities. The co-creation of those rules also commits the industry to compliance.

The robust regulatory regime as well as monitoring mechanisms might be vital for the industry in its attempts to expand the European market, where Gibraltar as well as the Internet gambling industry has to 'convince' the public and policy makers that they are reliable, reputable, and heavily regulated. The Internet gambling industry has to demonstrate that it is committed to managing the transnational gambling risks such as underage gambling, problem gambling, money laundering, and match-fixing.

## Conclusion

In this chapter we have analysed the development of Gibraltar into the world's primary Internet gambling jurisdiction. We argued that offshore jurisdictions play a crucial role in the development of Internet gambling, and that for Gibraltar reputation is a major asset and concern. Internet gambling companies perceive Gibraltar as a legal and reputational gateway to the EU market. There is growing evidence that the USA has the same perspective with a series of US/Gibraltar joint ventures reported in industry media and Gibraltar remaining unblemished by the 'Black Friday' indictments of April 2011. This has turned Gibraltar into a producer and manager of 'transnational' gambling risks related to underage gambling, problem gambling, and fraud. In order to address these risks and maintain a good reputation Gibraltar recognizes that a solid regulatory framework for the Internet gambling industry is a vital interest. In this conclusion we would like to draw attention to three major points.

First, for Internet gambling, a regulatory framework and a solid reputation are not self-evident features of offshore jurisdictions, but should rather be viewed as active policy achievements. In this respect the Gibraltar regulatory framework for Internet gambling is consistent with the regulatory approach developed for the financial sector. The Gibraltar authorities, however, did not want to make the economy over-reliant on a single sector. At the same time developments in global telecommunications provided new opportunities for the gambling industry to offer their services remotely and expand their markets. By offering competitive taxation levels and an adaptive regulatory regime Gibraltar attracted a number of British bookmakers to the territory wishing to take advantage of taxation and regulation differentials between Gibraltar and the UK.

Second, the settlement of Internet gambling companies and the application of gambling regulations did not immediately constitute Gibraltar as an Internet 'gambling hub' but rather meant the beginning of a transitional phase in which Gibraltar developed new regulatory standards and procedures under direct supervision of the Chief Minister. The development of the Internet gambling business and regulation involved a differentiated network of actors who gradually 'enrolled' in the policy-making and regulatory process, notably the Chief Minister, the GRA, the Gambling Commissioner, the Internet gambling companies, and the GBGA. In the process of public–private 'co-creation' of regulatory standards, gambling practices were modified and new regulatory standards emerged. This process included the development of specialized artifacts such as the 2005 Gambling Act, the Codes of Practice, and more mundane aspects such as the Europort complex which accommodates the regulator and many operators. The strategy of controlled growth was crucial because it made the licences a scarce and precious resource to the operators. We have drawn special attention to the role of reputation management which was explicitly referred to in the Gibraltar Gambling Act. Reputation should therefore not be regarded as a mere side effect of gambling operations but as an effect which, in terms of reputational risk (Power, 2007), now forms an integral part of the regulation of Internet gambling.

Third, the Gibraltar regulatory approach to gambling involved the introduction of a specific balance between state authorities and regulators on the one hand and Internet gambling organizations on the other. The Gibraltar approach is not only characterized by close cooperation and the co-creation of regulatory standards, but also by the model of enforced self-regulation. This model means that governments establish broad standards and oversee the process of industry compliance with the standards. However, it is the companies themselves who further specify the rules and develop risk-management systems and systems of compliance and monitoring of that compliance. In this model regulation becomes dependent upon the commitments and capacity of the industry, and the ability of the state to find and maintain an optimal monitoring role. For the Internet gambling industry, being based and regulated in Gibraltar is vital to the pursuit of their argument for the open European market.

## Notes

1   Directive 2006/123/EC on services in the internal market was designed in order to establish free market for services in the EU by simplifying national procedures and removing barriers to provision of cross-border services. It was adopted by the European Parliament and the Council on 12 December 2006.
2   EU member states are responsible for the implementation and compliance with EU law. If a member state fails to comply, the European Commission can open an infringement procedure against that state. Initially, the Commission itself attempts to bring the infringement to an end. However, if the member state does not conform voluntarily it may refer the case to the ECJ. Infringement procedure follows several formal stages.
3   An Exempt Company was a non-resident company that was exempt from corporation tax on the profits of the company and instead paid a fixed annual duty between £225 and £300 to the Gibraltar government.
4   Interview with Chief Minister Peter Caruana, October 2010.
5   Interview with Gibraltar lawyer, November 2008.
6   Interview with respondent 4.
7   The Wire Act prohibits interstate telephone betting but pre-dates the Internet and has not been amended to include it.
8   Interview with co-CEO of bwin, January 2009.
9   Interview with Chief Minister Peter Caruana, November 2010.
10   Government of Gibraltar, Information Services.
11   http://www.gibraltar.gov.gi/internet-gaming
12   The test houses are: Technical Systems Testing (TST); eCommerce and Online Gaming Regulation and Assurance (eCOGRA); iTech Labs Australia (iTech); Gaming Associates Pty Ltd; Gaming Laboratories International Europe B.V.
13   www.gamingassociates.com
14   Email communication with N. Macias, Assistant Gambling Supervisor, December 2008.

## References

Atkinson, S. (2006, August 14). 'Gibraltar proves a winning bet'. Retrieved from http://news.bbc. co.uk/1/hi/business/4776021.stm
BBC News. (2001, October 6). 'Punters rush for tax-free betting'. *BBC News*. Retrieved from http://news.bbc.co.uk/1/hi/business/1580478.stm
Beck, U. (1992). *Risk society: Towards a new modernity*. London: Sage.
— (1999). *World risk society*. Cambridge: Polity Press.
Castells, M. (2001). *The Internet galaxy*. Oxford: Oxford University Press.
Cobb, S. C. (2001). 'Globalization in a small island context: Creating and marketing competitive advantage for offshore financial services'. *Geografiska Annaler. Series B, Human Geography, 83*(4), 161–74.
Cosgrave, J. (2006). 'Governing the gambling citizen: The state, consumption, and risk'. In J. F. Cosgrave, and T. R. Klassen (eds), *Gambling in 21st century Canada: Citizens, consumers, and the state* (46–69). Montreal: McGill-Queens University Press.

Della Sala, V. (2010). 'Stakes and states: Gambling and the single market'. *Journal of European Public Policy, 17*(7), 1024–38.

Djelic, M. L., and Sahlin-Andersson, K. (eds) (2006). *Transnational governance: Institutional dynamics of regulation.* Cambridge: Cambridge University Press.

Doward, J. (2000). 'A rock and a cheap flutter'. Retrieved from http://www.guardian.co.uk/technology/2000/sep/24/business.theobserver

Garcia, J. (2002). *Gibraltar. The making of a people.* Gibraltar: Panorama Publishing.

Gibraltar Licensing Authority. (2011). *Internet gaming.* http://www.gibraltar.gov.gi/internet-gaming.

Government of Gibraltar. (2005). 'Gambling Act 2005'. Gibraltar. Act No. 2005–72.

GRA. (2009). *Code of practice for the gambling industry – The generic code.* Gibraltar: Gibraltar Regulatory Authority.

— (2009/10). *Annual report.* Gibraltar: Gibraltar Regulatory Authority.

Heritier, A., and Eckert, S. (2008). 'New modes of governance in the shadow of hierarchy: Self-regulation by industry in Europe'. *Journal of Public Policy, 28*(01), 113–38.

HM Treasury. (1999). 'Government to take action on offshore bookies'. Retrieved from http://www.hm-treasury.gov.uk/pbr_pn_ce2.htm.

— (2000). 'CE1 reform of betting duty'. Retrieved from http://www.hm-treasury.gov.uk/bud_bud00_pressbetting.htm

Hudson, A. C. (1998). 'Placing trust, trusting place: On the social construction of offshore financial centres'. *Political Geography, 17*(8), 915–37.

Hutter, B. M. (2001). 'Is enforced self-regulation a form of risk taking?: The case of railway health and safety'. *International Journal of the Sociology of Law, 29*(4), 379–400.

— (2006). 'The role of non-State actors in regulation'. Discussion Papers. Retrieved from http://eprints.lse.ac.uk/36118/1/Disspaper37.pdf

Kingma, S. F. (2004). 'Gambling and the risk society: The liberalisation and legitimation crisis of gambling in the Netherlands'. *International Gambling Studies, 4*(1), 47–67.

— (2008). 'The liberalization and (re)regulation of Dutch gambling markets: National consequences of the changing European context'. *Regulation & Governance, 2*(4), 445–58.

Klein, K. (2001). 'betandwin.com acquires 100% holding in Simon Bold (Gibraltar) Ltd'. bwin press release. Retrieved from http://reports.huginonline.com/826059/91206.pdf

Levi-Faur, D. (2005). 'The global diffusion of regulatory capitalism'. *Annals of the American Academy of Political and Social Science, 598*(1), 12–32.

Massey, D. (1993) 'Power-geometry and a progressive sense of place'. In J. Bird, B. Curtis, T. Putnam, and L. Tickner (eds), *Mapping the futures: Local cultures, global change* (59–69). London: Routledge.

Palan, R. (1998). 'The emergence of an offshore economy'. *Futures, 30*(1), 63–73.

— (2003). *The offshore world: Sovereign markets, virtual places and nomad millionaires.* Ithaca, NY: Cornell University Press.

Palan, R., Murphy, R., and Chavagneux, C. (2010). *Tax havens: How globalization really works.* Ithaca, NY: Cornell University Press.

Panorama. (1999, September 13). 'Britain warns Gibraltar over betting'. Retrieved from http://www.panorama.gi/archive/990913.html

Power, M. (2004). *The risk management of everything. Rethinking the politics of uncertainty.* London: Demos.

— (2007). *Organized uncertainty. Designing a world of risk management.* Oxford: Oxford University Press.

Reed, C. (2004). *Internet law: Texts and materials.* Cambridge: Cambridge University Press.

Shields, R. (2003). *The virtual.* London: Routledge.

Woolgar, S. (ed.) (2002). *Virtual society? Technology, cyberbole, reality.* Oxford: Oxford University Press.

# Part 3

# Major Research Studies of Internet Gamblers

# 6 The Casino City study

## A large-scale international study of online gamblers

*Robert T. Wood and Robert J. Williams*

Beginning in the early to mid-1990s, as Internet access expanded into workplaces and private residences, gamblers were introduced to a new realm of Internet-based gambling opportunities. Each of the traditional forms of gambling, widely available in land-based venues, soon appeared in electronic format over the Internet, and have since been easily accessible to any person with an Internet connection and means of electronically transferring money. Virtually mediated casino table games, slot machines, poker, bingos, lotteries, sports wagering, horse race betting, and skill games are all now readily accessible, with new forms of gambling and new sites being added each year. Indeed, as of May 2011, there were 2,430 Internet gambling websites in operation (Casino City, 2011), with recent international Internet gambling prevalence rates ranging from 0.4 percent in Iceland to 14.0 percent in the United Kingdom (see American Gaming Association [AGA], 2008; Gambling Commission, 2010; Jonsson and Rönnberg, 2009; Motivaction International, 2005; National Centre for Social Research, 2011; Olason and Gretarsson, 2009; Sandven, 2007; Wood and Williams, 2009).

While the worldwide rate of Internet gambling is relatively low, it is likely to increase as more jurisdictions opt to regulate and legalize Internet gambling, and as citizens are exposed in greater numbers to Internet gambling as a legitimate and easily accessible gambling option. Unfortunately, however, in most jurisdictions, the expansion of Internet gambling is outpacing the creation of effective regulatory policies. Consequently, we find ourselves in a situation where we have insufficient knowledge of Internet gambling, including the characteristics and game preferences of Internet gamblers, the social and psychological dynamics of Internet gambling behaviour, and the potential link between Internet gambling and problem gambling. Moreover, and more importantly, we have limited knowledge of the extent to which Internet gamblers systematically differ from their land-based counterparts.

In light of these persisting substantive gaps in the academic literature, this chapter presents crucial comparative results from the Casino City study, which was conducted by the present authors (see Wood and Williams, 2009). In particular, drawing upon survey data from 1,954 international Internet gamblers and 5,967 land-based gamblers, this chapter addresses a number of important and under-researched questions about Internet gamblers:

1 What are the comparative demographic and health characteristics of Internet versus land-based gamblers?
2 What are the game-play patterns of Internet gamblers?
3 What are the perceived advantages and disadvantages of gambling online, versus gambling in a land-based venue?
4 What are the comparative gambling expenditures of Internet versus land-based gamblers?

5    What is the comparative rate of problem gambling among Internet versus land-based gamblers?
6    What characteristics are predictive of someone being an Internet gambler?
7    What characteristics are predictive of someone being a problem, versus non-problem, Internet gambler?

Having addressed these questions, this chapter concludes with a detailed discussion of how the present findings conform or diverge from those observed in previous studies. Thus, as opposed to beginning this chapter with a traditional review of literature, we instead incorporate the review of literature into our discussion of findings, in order to facilitate a direct comparison between our own findings and those of past researchers.

## Methodology

### *Obtaining a small representative sample of Canadian Internet gamblers*

A number of studies of the characteristics of Internet gamblers have been conducted over the past several years (see Wood and Williams, 2009; Williams and Wood, 2007 for a review). Unfortunately, almost all of them have relied on convenience samples, whereby Internet gamblers self-select themselves into an online study. Researchers in these past studies acknowledge that the ability to generalize their conclusions is severely limited by non-random sampling techniques, but correctly point out that the low prevalence rate of Internet gambling makes it prohibitively costly to derive a large random sample of Internet gamblers from the general population. The Casino City study makes substantial progress towards overcoming past limitations of sampling and representativeness, by using a two-phased approach to data collection, and a weighted approach to data analysis.

Our first phase of data collection involved conducting a computer-assisted random digit dial telephone survey of 8,498 Canadians. The household member was randomly selected, the majority of the phoning occurred in the evening and on weekends, and most refusals were contacted again at a later time and asked to reconsider doing the survey. The 'Canadian Telephone Survey' was kept short to increase the chances the person would participate (average of 12.7 minutes), and the survey was conducted either in English or French, depending on the respondent's preference. There were exhaustive attempts to contact the person (up to 48 attempts). Phone calls were spread over an 18-month period, from January 2006 to June 2007, to mitigate any seasonal fluctuations in gambling behaviour and to maximize the chances of contacting the person.

Of the 8,498 adults surveyed, 6,010 were gamblers, including 179 Internet gamblers (299 if including Internet stock market gambling). An overall response rate of 45.6 percent to the telephone survey was achieved using calculations recommended by the Council of American Survey Research Organizations (CASRO, 1982), which essentially is the number of completions divided by the estimated number of eligible respondents. To ensure that the sample was a representative sample of Canadian adults, the data was weighted by: (a) *provincial size*, to ensure that each province's representation in the final data set was proportionate to its population in 2006/7; (b) *household size*, to correct for the under-sampling of individuals from large households and the oversampling of people from small households; and (c) *age by gender*, to ensure that the sample approximated the prevalence of each age by gender grouping in the 2006 Canadian census, thereby correcting for the under-sampling of males and younger people that typically occurs in telephone surveys.

*Obtaining large international samples of land-based and Internet gamblers*

In light of our pilot-study success in recruiting Internet gamblers from online gambling-related websites (see Wood and Williams, 2007a), we decided to recruit participants at a prominent gambling web portal, www.casinocity.com.[1] Casino City is currently one of the most popular online gambling portals (if not the most popular), receiving more than half a million visits per month (personal communication, May 2008, Andrea Mullaney, Casino City). Casino City provides directories and information for both Internet and land-based gambling opportunities, and we therefore felt that drawing a sample from such a website would enable us to draw important statistical comparisons between Internet gamblers and those who gamble only in land-based venues.

We purchased advertising space on www.casinocity.com, and placed banner links on the portal from June 15 through December 15, 2007. In total, we purchased 2 million impressions, meaning our banner links were shown 2 million times over the six-month time span. The banner links contained the logo of the university where the authors are employed, along with professionally designed graphics and captions that would appeal to gamblers. Clicking the link directed participants to a homepage for an online questionnaire ('International Online Survey'). At the questionnaire homepage, participants were able to choose from seven languages (English, French, German, Italian, Spanish, Mandarin, and Japanese). These particular languages were chosen as they are the most common languages offered on online gambling sites. Translations of the questionnaire were all done by professional translating services. Having selected a language, participants were then presented with an informed consent preamble, which outlined the purpose of the study, and which reminded potential participants about the voluntary nature of their participation. No personally identifying information was collected about participants, and all participants were assured of complete anonymity in any subsequent research reports or publications. In order to minimize repeat responses, a *cookie* was built into the survey, such that those who attempted to repeat the survey were politely denied access and reminded that they had already completed the survey once before.[2]

Using this method, 12,521 people completed one or more sections of the online survey. Within this group there were 7,921 people who provided comprehensive information about their gambling behaviour, 1,954 of whom were Internet gamblers (2,241 including Internet stock market gambling). People from 105 different countries participated, with the primary countries being: United States (76.3 percent); Canada (9.6 percent); and the United Kingdom (3.3 percent).

## Questionnaire

The Canadian Telephone Survey and the International Online Survey contained the following sections, using the same question wording:

- *Gambling behaviour.* Respondents were asked about their preferred type of gambling, the frequency of their gambling, and their patterns of financial expenditure.
- *Definition of gambling.* Respondents were asked about a variety of activities, some of which might be considered traditional forms of gambling, and others which might be commonly understood as risk taking. Our goal was to gauge common perceptions of the conceptual parameters of which activities do (or do not) qualify as gambling behaviour.
- *Gambling attitudes scale.* These questions assessed people's beliefs about the harms versus benefits of gambling, the morality of gambling, and appropriate policy concerning legalization of gambling.

- *Gambling fallacies scale.* This battery of questions consists of 10 items designed to test resistance to common gambling fallacies, such as believing in the ability to manipulate the outcome of a random event.
- *Problem gambling.* Problem gambling was assessed using the short 9-item version of the Canadian Problem Gambling Index (CPGI).
- *Demographic characteristics.* Respondents were asked about their age, gender, ethnicity, employment status, education, and socioeconomic status as indicated by income and debt.
- *Perceived advantages and disadvantages of Internet gambling.* Respondents were asked to identify, from a list of fixed choices, any perceived advantages or disadvantages associated with gambling online, versus gambling in a land-based venue.

## *Weighting*

In order to correct for the self-selected bias of the international online sample, a weighting factor was calculated that matched the characteristics of the subsample of the 171 Canadian Internet gamblers from the International Online Survey, to the characteristics of the more representative sample of 179 Canadian Internet gamblers from the Canadian Telephone Survey.[3]

Statistically, the main differences between the two samples were: average score on the Canadian Problem Gambling Index, net monthly gambling win/loss, and age (see Table 6.1). Weightings for each of these three variables were calculated and used, singly and in combination, to determine which combination produced the best match between the online and telephone samples. Once the weighting factor was determined, it was then applied to the entire online sample to make this much larger and richer data set much more representative (see Table 6.2). It is this latter, weighted data set from which the findings of the present study are derived.

*Table 6.1* Demographic characteristics and gambling behaviour of Canadian Internet gamblers from both the telephone and online surveys (unweighted)

|  | *Canadians from phone survey* | *Canadians from online survey* |
|---|---|---|
| % Male | 82.4% | 84.8% |
| Age | 35.53 | 42.01 |
| Educational level[1] | 6.48 | 6.51 |
| Household income[2] | 7.46 | 6.62 |
| Gambling attitude score | 0.67 | 0.78 |
| Gambling fallacies score | 6.91 | 7.63 |
| # Gambling types played | 4.70 | 4.27 |
| Net win/loss monthly average | −$541.09 | −$107.63 |
| Net win/loss monthly median | −$89.00 | −$109.00 |
| CPGI total | 1.62 | 3.13 |

Notes
1  Ranging from 1 = no schooling to 9 = professional degree (law, medicine, dentistry) or graduate degree (Masters, PhD).
2  Household income category, ranging from 1 = < $20,000 to 12 = > $150,000.
CPGI = Canadian Problem Gambling Index.

*Table 6.2* Demographic characteristics and gambling behaviour of Canadian Internet gamblers from both the telephone and online surveys (after weighting)

|  | *Canadian phone survey* | *International online survey* |
|---|---|---|
| % Male | 82.4% | 85.9% |
| Age | 35.53 | 43.87 |
| Educational level[1] | 6.48 | 6.50 |
| Household income[2] | 7.46 | 6.84 |
| Gambling attitude score | 0.67 | 0.87 |
| Gambling fallacies score | 6.91 | 7.51 |
| # Gambling types played | 4.70 | 4.19 |
| Net win/loss monthly average | −$541.09 | −$166.55 |
| Net win/loss monthly median | −$89.00 | −$90.00 |
| CPGI total | 1.62 | 1.62 |

Notes
1  Ranging from 1 = no schooling to 9 = professional degree (law, medicine, dentistry) or graduate degree (Masters, PhD).
2  Household income category, ranging from 1 = < $20,000 to 12 = > $150,000.
CPGI = Canadian Problem Gambling Index.

## Results

### *Demographic and health characteristics*

The demographic characteristics of our International sample are presented in Table 6.3. In terms of gender distribution, online gamblers were far more likely to be male when compared to land-based gamblers. Internet gamblers were also, on average, younger (45.7 years) than their land-based gambling counterparts (51.2 years). An important policy concern is the extent to which underage gamblers access Internet gambling venues (see Derevensky and Gupta, 2007; Derevensky, Gupta, and McBride, 2006). The present study found that only 0.4 percent of Internet gamblers were under 18, a rate even lower than that observed among non-Internet gamblers (0.9 percent).[4] Internet gamblers were also less likely to be married (53.2 percent), more likely to be employed full-time (62.7 percent), more likely to be a student (4.4 percent), and reported higher average household income (US$60,100). The household debt of Internet gamblers is not substantially different from that of non-Internet gamblers.

When asked about lifestyle and health, the Internet gamblers in our study reported higher rates of tobacco, alcohol, and street drug use, compared to their non-Internet counterparts (see Table 6.3). Internet gamblers also reported a somewhat higher rate of substance abuse or dependence (13 percent), as well as a higher rate of addictions in other areas (10.4 percent). Both Internet and non-Internet gamblers were relatively similar in terms of mental health problems and the presence of a significant physical disability or chronic health problem.

*Table 6.3* Comparative demographic characteristics of Internet and non-Internet gamblers

| | Internet gamblers (%) | Non-Internet gamblers (%) |
|---|---|---|
| *Gender* | | |
| Male | 78.0 | 58.0 |
| *Age* | | |
| < 18 | 0.4 | 0.9 |
| 18–19 | 1.7 | 0.8 |
| 20–29 | 15.9 | 8.6 |
| 30–39 | 17.2 | 10.7 |
| 40–49 | 22.5 | 19.5 |
| 50–59 | 23.6 | 29.6 |
| 60–69 | 14.5 | 19.9 |
| 70–79 | 3.6 | 8.0 |
| 80+ | 0.7 | 1.8 |
| Average | 45.7 | 51.2 |
| *Marital Status* | | |
| Married | 53.2 | 61.9 |
| Living with partner | 13.3 | 8.6 |
| Widowed | 2.1 | 3.7 |
| Divorced or separated | 11.8 | 11.6 |
| Never married | 19.6 | 14.2 |
| *Education* | | |
| Less than high school | 4.3 | 5.5 |
| Completed high school | 18.2 | 19.7 |
| Some technical school/college/university | 28.4 | 26.9 |
| Completed technical school | 8.0 | 8.1 |
| Completed college/university | 30.2 | 27.8 |
| Professional or graduate degree | 11.0 | 11.9 |
| *Employment* | | |
| Employed full-time | 62.7 | 58.0 |
| Employed part-time | 7.0 | 6.3 |
| Homemaker | 3.4 | 3.9 |
| Unemployed and seeking work | 2.4 | 4.7 |
| Retired | 16.6 | 22.6 |
| Student | 4.4 | 1.8 |
| Disability/Leave/Strike | 3.5 | 2.6 |
| *Household Income* | | |
| Less than US$29,999 | 21.5 | 20.8 |

| | Internet gamblers (%) | Non-Internet gamblers (%) |
|---|---|---|
| US$30,000–49,999 | 19.0 | 21.5 |
| US$50,000–69,999 | 16.3 | 19.1 |
| US$70,000–89,999 | 14.3 | 13.5 |
| US$90,000–119,999 | 13.2 | 12.8 |
| US$120,000–149,999 | 7.3 | 4.9 |
| More than US$150,000 | 8.3 | 7.5 |
| Average | US$60,100 | US$57,600 |
| *Household Debt* | | |
| Less than US$1,000 | 32.3 | 32.4 |
| Median | US$10,000 | US$14,000 |
| Average | US$76,728 | US$66,948 |
| *Substance Use* | | |
| Past month tobacco use | 44.3 | 33.1 |
| Past month alcohol use | 72.9 | 66.4 |
| Past month other drug use | 11.7 | 5.5 |
| *Addictions* | | |
| History of substance abuse or dependence | 13.0 | 11.5 |
| History of other addictions | 10.4 | 6.7 |
| *Health* | | |
| Past year serious mental health problem | 10.3 | 10.6 |
| Physical disability or chronic health problem that limits activity | 14.9 | 15.0 |

### Game-play patterns of Internet gamblers

Table 6.4 indicates that Internet gamblers are involved in a wide array of land-based gambling, in addition to Internet gambling. Indeed, they report involvement with an average of 4.1 different gambling formats, versus an average of only 2.6 for non-Internet gamblers. Moreover, Internet gamblers have higher yearly and weekly involvement in almost every kind of gambling. The proportionate differences are especially pronounced for sports betting, betting on horse or dog races, and betting on games of skill, such as poker.

Table 6.5 indicates the percentage of Internet gamblers that engage in each type of online gambling, as well as the gender distribution of the patronage. As the table illustrates, games of skill are by far the most popular type of game, with poker yielding the highest rates of participation, at 54.1 percent. Moreover, certain types of online gambling are clearly preferred by one gender over another. Sports betting, horse/dog race betting, and games of skill are overwhelmingly preferred by males, whereas online bingo is preferred by females.

We asked Internet and non-Internet gamblers to report their typical monthly gambling expenditures for each commonly available gambling type (in the equivalent of US dollars).[5] The average overall expenditures were much higher among Internet gamblers, when compared to the non-Internet gamblers (see Table 6.6). Internet gamblers reported an average

*Table 6.4* Involvement in various forms of gambling among Internet and non-Internet gamblers

| | Any past year involvement | | Weekly involvement in past year | |
|---|---|---|---|---|
| | Internet gamblers (%) | Non-Internet gamblers (%) | Internet gamblers (%) | Non-Internet gamblers (%) |
| Lotteries | 69.9 | 70.8 | 24.2 | 19.9 |
| Instant win | 60.7 | 57.4 | 13.7 | 10.2 |
| Games of skill (e.g., poker) against other Individuals | 59.3 | 28.6 | 41.8 | 5.9 |
| Electronic gaming machines | 53.2 | 49.5 | 10.7 | 4.8 |
| Casino table games | 46.9 | 21.4 | 5.9 | 1.7 |
| Sports betting | 41.6 | 13.6 | 16.3 | 2.7 |
| Horse and dog racing | 26.2 | 9.3 | 6.3 | 0.9 |
| Bingo | 15.7 | 8.4 | 3.9 | 0.6 |
| *Average number of games played* | 4.1 | 2.6 | 4.1 | 2.6 |

*Table 6.5* Types of games played over the Internet among Internet gamblers

| | Internet gamblers (%) | % of patronage that is male | % of patronage that is female |
|---|---|---|---|
| Games of skill (e.g., poker) | 64.0 | 84.0 | 16.0 |
| Casinos | 26.4 | 67.6 | 32.3 |
| Sports betting | 23.2 | 92.7 | 7.3 |
| Horse and dog racing | 12.7 | 92.5 | 7.5 |
| Lotteries | 11.1 | 63.7 | 36.3 |
| Bingo | 7.4 | 39.1 | 60.9 |

*Table 6.6* Comparative net monthly gambling expenditure of Internet and non-Internet gamblers (for gamblers who engage in that type)

| | Internet gamblers | Non-Internet gamblers |
|---|---|---|
| Casino table games | –$113.56 | –$120.53 |
| Electronic gaming machines | –$94.37 | –$70.55 |
| Sports betting | –$39.47 | –$14.45 |
| Horse and dog racing | –$35.71 | –$24.69 |
| Games of skill (includes poker) | –$35.21 | +$9.13 |
| Bingo | –$30.57 | –$20.78 |
| Lottery ticket purchases | –$28.05 | –$13.48 |
| Instant win tickets | –$13.22 | –$8.17 |
| *Total expenditure average* | –$195.14 | –$70.93 |
| *Total expenditure median* | –$80.00 | –$19.26 |

net monthly expenditure of –US$195.14, and non-Internet gamblers report an average net expenditure of –US$70.93. The median net monthly expenditure for the International Internet gamblers was –US$80.00, which is more than four times the median expenditure of –US$19.26 reported by their non-Internet counterparts. Additionally, looking at expenditures by game type, we see that Internet gamblers report higher mean expenditures for every form of gambling, with the exception of casino table games.

### *Motivations for gambling on the Internet*

The extent to which gamblers perceive Internet venues as offering advantages over land-based gambling may have implications for crafting future policies on Internet gambling. When asked about the advantages of gambling online, versus gambling in land-based venues, Internet gamblers identified 24-hour availability (56.5 percent), and not having to drive or leave the house (50.8 percent), as the two most popular advantages proffered by Internet gambling (see Table 6.7). The least popular advantage was the perception of higher payout rates, which was identified by only 7.6 percent of Internet gamblers.

When asked about the disadvantages of gambling online, Internet gamblers most frequently identified issues related to fairness and security (see Table 6.8). Indeed, having been identified by 36.1 percent of Internet gamblers, the most commonly identified disadvantage was the difficulty in verifying the fairness of games. The next most commonly identified disadvantage (25.4 percent) was worry about monetary deposits being safe and having wins paid out in a timely fashion. The issue which seemed to concern Internet gamblers the least was the difficulty in excluding underage gamblers, with only 9.0 percent identifying this as an issue.

*Table 6.7* Perceived advantages of gambling at Internet versus land-based venues

|  | *Internet gamblers (%)* |
| --- | --- |
| 24-hour availability/convenience | 56.5 |
| Don't have to drive/leave the house | 50.8 |
| More physically comfortable | 23.3 |
| Lower secondary costs (travel, food, drinks) | 23.1 |
| No crowds | 22.5 |
| Greater privacy/anonymity | 22.3 |
| No unpleasant people | 20.5 |
| Better game experience | 18.4 |
| Less smoke | 16.9 |
| Less noise | 16.5 |
| Land-based gambling unavailable or illegal | 14.0 |
| Able to smoke | 12.5 |
| Higher payout rates | 7.6 |
| Other | 4.3 |

*Table 6.8* Perceived disadvantages of gambling at Internet versus land-based venues

|  | Internet gamblers (%) |
|---|---|
| Difficulty verifying fairness of games | 36.1 |
| Worry about monetary deposits being safe/having wins paid out in timely fashion | 25.4 |
| Lack of face-to-face contact makes betting more difficult | 25.3 |
| Illegality | 18.9 |
| Poorer social atmosphere (no crowds, too isolating) | 18.5 |
| Easier to spend more money | 18.5 |
| Poorer game experience | 17.5 |
| Too convenient | 16.3 |
| Poorer physical atmosphere (lacks the lights and noise of a real casino, etc.) | 15.9 |
| Have to use credit cards rather than cash | 13.0 |
| More addictive | 11.7 |
| Difficulty excluding underage gamblers | 9.0 |
| Other | 2.8 |

### Problem gambling among Internet gamblers

Using the criteria of the Canadian Problem Gambling Index, a total of 16.6 percent of Internet gamblers were either moderate (CPGI score of 3–7) or severe (CPGI score of 8+) problem gamblers, compared to a rate of 5.7 percent among non-Internet gamblers (see Table 6.9). Only 39.9 percent of Internet gamblers were classified as non-problem gamblers, which is less than half the rate of 82.1 percent observed among their non-Internet gambling counterparts.

We were interested in assessing the extent to which Internet problem gamblers sought treatment for problems, as well as the viability of future Internet-based treatment initiatives (see Table 6.10). Only a small proportion of Internet problem gamblers (9.4 percent) reported ever seeking help for a gambling problem. Those who had sought help most commonly reported either Gamblers Anonymous or some other counselling service as the source of help. Interestingly, only 29.8 percent indicated that they would be most comfortable seeking some sort of Internet-based counselling service.

*Table 6.9* Rates of problem gambling among Internet and non-Internet gamblers

|  | Internet gamblers (%) | Non-Internet gamblers (%) |
|---|---|---|
| Non-problem gambler | 39.9 | 82.1 |
| At-risk gambler | 43.4 | 12.3 |
| Moderate problem gambler | 12.8 | 4.0 |
| Severe problem gambler | 3.8 | 1.7 |
| *Average CPGI score* | 1.80 | 0.52 |

*Table 6.10* Help seeking for problem gambling among Internet and non-Internet problem gamblers

|  | Internet gamblers (%) | Non-Internet gamblers (%) |
|---|---|---|
| *Ever sought help for problems?* | | |
| Yes | 9.4 | 5.0 |
| No | 90.6 | 95.0 |
| *Where did you seek help from?* | | |
| Gamblers Anonymous | 21.4 | 75.0 |
| Counselling service | 17.9 | 0 |
| Friends | 10.7 | 25.0 |
| Psychologist | 10.7 | 0 |
| Psychiatrist | 10.7 | 0 |
| Family doctor | 7.1 | 0 |
| Family | 7.1 | 0 |
| Pastor/minister/priest | 7.1 | 0 |
| Telephone help/hot line | 7.1 | 0 |
| *If you were to seek help where would you be most comfortable seeking it from?* | | |
| Face-to-face counselling | 70.2 | 65.4 |
| Internet counselling | 29.8 | 34.6 |

### *Characteristics statistically differentiating Internet from non-Internet gamblers*

The cross-tabulations and descriptive statistics in the previous section, while instructive, do not indicate the *relative importance* of differentiating variables, or the extent to which the association of some variables to Internet gambling may be an artifact of their correlation with other variables that are primarily responsible for the relationship. Simultaneous analysis of all relevant variables, using multivariate logistic regression, helps disentangle these effects.

Hence, an SPSS (Statistical Package for the Social Sciences) logistic regression investigated characteristics differentiating Internet from non-Internet gamblers (see Table 6.11). The predictor variables were gender; age; marital status; level of education; employment status; household income; household debt; ethnic origin; country of residence; use of tobacco; use of alcohol; use of illicit drugs; presence of a physical disability; having a significant mental health problem; number of gambling formats engaged in; net win/loss on all gambling in a typical month; CPGI score; history of substance abuse; history of other addictions; family history of problem gambling; gambling attitudes; and gambling fallacies. The skewness of certain variables (CPGI score; number of gambling formats engaged in; household debt) was reduced with inverse transformations. The significant negative skewness and positive kurtosis of the net win/loss variable could not be corrected. However, six outliers with standard scores greater than +5.0 in the net win/loss variable were winsorized. Missing values for all continuous variables were replaced with the series mean. Missing values for most categorical variables were replaced with the mode. Entry of the variables into the equation was simultaneous. Data from 8,174 people were available for analysis, including 2,254 Internet gamblers[6] and 5,919 non-Internet gamblers. Each Internet gambler received a weighting to ensure they had equivalent overall importance to non-Internet gamblers in the calculations used to identify characteristics that maximally differentiated the two groups.

A test of the full model, with 22 predictors, against a constant-only model was statistically significant, $\chi^2$ (50) = 3366.54, $p < .0001$, indicating that the 22 predictors, as a set, reliably distinguished between Internet gamblers and non-Internet gamblers. The variance accounted for was moderate, with Nagelkerke $R$ squared = 34.7 percent. Overall prediction success was 73.3 percent, with 71.9 percent of non-Internet gamblers correctly classified and 74.7 percent of Internet gamblers correctly classified. Table 6.11 shows regression coefficients, Wald statistics, and odds ratios for each of the 22 predictors, with the predictors ordered from strongest to weakest. According to the Wald criterion, the top three predictors ($p < .001$) of someone being an Internet gambler are: 1) gambling on a greater number of gambling formats; 2) having a higher CPGI score; and 3) being of the male gender.

*Table 6.11* Logistic regression of characteristics differentiating Internet from non-Internet gamblers

| | B | Wald | Significance | Odds ratio |
|---|---|---|---|---|
| # Gambling formats | −7.064 | 948.029 | .000 | .001 |
| CPGI score | −1.579 | 422.154 | .000 | .206 |
| Gender | .920 | 241.346 | .000 | 2.508 |
| Country | | 186.323 | .000 | |
| *Hungary* | 3.984 | 49.984 | .000 | 53.731 |
| *United Kingdom* | .954 | 48.136 | .000 | 2.597 |
| *Italy* | 1.854 | 34.926 | .000 | 6.388 |
| *Canada* | .434 | 26.944 | .000 | 1.543 |
| *Switzerland* | 1.431 | 10.389 | .001 | 4.183 |
| *Costa Rica* | 2.798 | 10.120 | .001 | 16.419 |
| *Germany* | 6.441 | 9.770 | .002 | 627.018 |
| *The Netherlands* | .907 | 4.206 | .040 | 2.477 |
| *The Philippines* | .973 | 4.050 | .044 | 2.645 |
| *New Zealand* | .845 | 3.671 | .055 | 2.327 |
| *Finland* | 7.327 | 1.609 | .205 | 1521.266 |
| *Australia* | .372 | 1.254 | .263 | 1.451 |
| *Ireland* | .210 | .264 | .607 | 1.234 |
| *France* | .226 | .227 | .634 | 1.254 |
| *Romania* | .142 | .058 | .810 | 1.153 |
| *South Africa* | .044 | .010 | .922 | 1.045 |
| *Sweden* | 21.573 | .000 | .997 | 234000 |
| *Norway* | 19.945 | .000 | .998 | 459100 |
| *Other* | .454 | 17.230 | .000 | 1.575 |
| Tobacco use | .581 | 92.493 | .000 | 1.787 |
| Gambling fallacies | .138 | 81.520 | .000 | 1.148 |
| Employment status | | 56.287 | .000 | |
| *Unemployed* | −.865 | 35.393 | .000 | .421 |

|  | *B* | *Wald* | *Significance* | *Odds ratio* |
|---|---|---|---|---|
| Homemaker | .388 | 7.983 | .005 | 1.474 |
| Sick leave, maternity leave, etc. | .385 | 5.384 | .020 | 1.470 |
| Employed part-time | .223 | 4.695 | .030 | 1.250 |
| Retired | .082 | 1.174 | .279 | 1.085 |
| Student | −.158 | .796 | .372 | .854 |
| Age | −.018 | 55.690 | .000 | .982 |
| Gambling attitudes | .106 | 52.078 | .000 | 1.112 |
| Gambling expenditure | .000 | 50.733 | .000 | 1.000 |
| Ethnic origins |  | 40.151 | .000 |  |
| Asian | −.514 | 39.470 | .000 | .598 |
| European | −.499 | 6.805 | .009 | .607 |
| Aboriginal, Inuit or Métis | −.273 | 1.508 | .220 | .761 |
| Marital status |  | 32.195 | .000 |  |
| Never married | .415 | 25.448 | .000 | 1.514 |
| Living with a partner | .288 | 10.955 | .001 | 1.333 |
| Divorced or Separated | .176 | 4.414 | .036 | 1.193 |
| Widowed | .026 | .030 | .863 | 1.026 |
| Alcohol use | −.363 | 31.610 | .000 | .696 |
| Illicit drug use | .532 | 22.026 | .000 | 1.702 |
| Household income | .038 | 17.765 | .000 | 1.039 |
| Household debt | .000 | 7.691 | .006 | 1.000 |
| Physical disability | .460 | 6.821 | .005 | 1.285 |
| Mental health problems | −.251 | 5.373 | .020 | .778 |
| History of other addictions | .162 | 1.820 | .177 | 1.176 |
| History of substance abuse | −.100 | 1.079 | .299 | .905 |
| Educational achievement | .002 | .019 | .892 | 1.002 |
| Family history of problem | −.006 | .002 | .964 | .994 |

### Characteristics statistically differentiating Internet problem from non-problem gamblers

A final analysis looked at the characteristics that differentiated Internet problem gamblers from Internet non-problem gamblers (see Table 6.12). All variables used in the previous analyses were used in the present analysis with the exception of CPGI score. Data cleaning procedures were also identical. Entry of the variables into the equation was simultaneous. Data from 1,445 people were available for analysis, including 240 Internet problem gamblers and 1,206 non-problem Internet gamblers. Each problem Internet gambler received a weighting to ensure they had equivalent overall importance in the calculations used to identify characteristics that maximally differentiated the two groups.

A test of the full model with all 21 predictors, against a constant-only model, was statistically significant, $\chi^2$ (49) = 763.79, $p < .0001$, indicating that the 21 predictors, as a set, reliably distinguished between Internet problem gamblers and Internet non-problem gamblers. The variance accounted for was moderate, with Nagelkerke $R$ squared = 36.5 percent. Overall prediction success was 74.7 percent, with 77.9 percent of Internet problem gamblers correctly classified and 70.9 percent of Internet non-problem gamblers correctly classified. Table 6.12 shows regression coefficients, Wald statistics, and odds ratios for each of the 21 predictors with the predictors ordered from strongest to weakest. According to the Wald criterion, the top three variables that significantly predicted ($p < .001$) someone being an Internet problem gambler are: (1) gambling on a greater number of gambling formats; (2) reporting a higher gambling expenditure; and (3) mental health problems.

*Table 6.12* Logistic regression of characteristics differentiating problem Internet gamblers from non-problem Internet gamblers

| | B | Wald | Significance | Odds ratio |
|---|---|---|---|---|
| # Gambling types | −5.116 | 69.579 | .000 | .006 |
| Gambling expenditure | .000 | 52.084 | .000 | .999 |
| Mental health problems | 1.152 | 47.664 | .000 | 3.164 |
| Country | | 45.660 | .001 | 1.333 |
| *United Kingdom* | .735 | 13.991 | .000 | .851 |
| *South Africa* | 2.108 | 6.892 | .009 | 5.881 |
| *Sweden* | −1.299 | 5.905 | .015 | 1.974 |
| *Canada* | .287 | 3.251 | .071 | 2.085 |
| *Germany* | .696 | 2.136 | .144 | .985 |
| *Romania* | 1.772 | 1.942 | .164 | 1.949 |
| *Australia* | .680 | 1.676 | .195 | .596 |
| *France* | −1.830 | 1.385 | .239 | 8.233 |
| *The Netherlands* | −1.154 | .794 | .373 | .000 |
| *Hungary* | −.517 | .662 | .416 | .315 |
| *Finland* | −.385 | .562 | .453 | 2.006 |
| *The Philippines* | −.503 | .550 | .458 | .393 |
| *Norway* | −.935 | .460 | .498 | .160 |
| *Italy* | −.161 | .210 | .647 | .680 |
| *New Zealand* | −.262 | .099 | .753 | .000 |
| *Ireland* | −.016 | .001 | .980 | .273 |
| *Costa Rica* | −20.607 | .000 | .999 | .770 |
| *Switzerland* | −19.919 | .000 | .999 | .605 |
| *Other* | .667 | 7.919 | .005 | .925 |
| Family history of problem | 1.204 | 35.737 | .000 | 3.334 |
| Household income | −.105 | 33.639 | .000 | .900 |
| Marital status | | 29.962 | .000 | |

|  | B | Wald | Significance | Odds ratio |
|---|---|---|---|---|
| *Never married* | .617 | 15.328 | .000 | 1.853 |
| *Divorced or separated* | −.324 | 3.744 | .053 | .723 |
| *Living with a partner* | −.218 | 1.691 | .193 | .804 |
| *Widowed* | .149 | .144 | .704 | 1.161 |
| Ethnic origins |  | 27.487 | .000 |  |
| *Asian* | 1.246 | 13.429 | .000 | 3.477 |
| *Aboriginal, Inuit or Métis* | .971 | 9.313 | .002 | 2.640 |
| *European* | −.069 | .216 | .642 | .934 |
| Gambling fallacies | −.123 | 16.012 | .000 | .885 |
| Employment status |  | 14.245 | .027 |  |
| *Retired* | −.390 | 4.940 | .026 | .677 |
| *Unemployed* | .695 | 3.877 | .049 | 2.003 |
| *Homemaker* | −.538 | 2.794 | .095 | .584 |
| *Sick leave, maternity leave* | −.500 | 2.959 | .085 | .606 |
| *Employed part-time* | −.190 | .825 | .364 | .827 |
| *Student* | .006 | .000 | .983 | 1.006 |
| Gambling attitudes | −.111 | 13.471 | .000 | .895 |
| History of other addictions | .564 | 11.758 | .001 | 1.757 |
| Household debt | .000 | 7.755 | .005 | 1.000 |
| Age | −.012 | 5.868 | .015 | .988 |
| Physical disability | −.257 | 2.355 | .125 | .774 |
| History of substance abuse | −.171 | 1.117 | .291 | .843 |
| Educational achievement | −.022 | .393 | .531 | .978 |
| Tobacco use | .061 | .340 | .560 | 1.063 |
| Gender | −.078 | .302 | .583 | .925 |
| Illicit drug use | −.064 | .162 | .687 | .938 |
| Alcohol use | −.007 | .003 | .955 | .993 |

## Discussion

### Demographic characteristics

Internet gamblers are distinguished by many demographic features. Although they are predominately male (78.0 percent), certain types of online gambling are preferred by one gender over another. The patronage of online sports betting, horse/dog race betting, and games of skill is overwhelmingly male, whereas the patronage of online bingo is predominantly female. Marital status and employment status of Internet gamblers tends to reflect the distributions found in the general adult population, with most people being married or living common-law and most being employed full-time. Being divorced/separated or living common-law was the marital status most predictive of being an Internet gambler. Being employed is also significantly associated. Most of the Internet gamblers in our sample are of European ancestry (80.8 percent). However, being of non-European ancestry significantly predicts Internet gambling. All age groups are represented among Internet gamblers, but there is no age group that is markedly overrepresented (average age of Internet gamblers is 45.7 years). Nonetheless, younger age was a significant predictor of Internet gambling in this data set. Internet gamblers have high past month rates of substance use (44.3 percent for tobacco and 11.7 percent for illicit drugs). Any type of substance use is a significant predictor of a person being an Internet gambler. Average household income for Internet gamblers is US$60,100 and average household debt is US$76,728. Household income significantly predicted Internet gambling status, but debt did not. On average, Internet gamblers are slightly better educated than the average person, with 41.2 percent having completed college or university. Educational attainment was not predictive of Internet gambling, however. Internet gamblers reported levels of physical disabilities and chronic health problems (14.9 percent) and mental health problems (10.3 percent) that were not significantly different from non-Internet gamblers.

The demographic characteristics found in the present study are consistent with previous research. Almost all studies have found Internet gambling to be more common among males. The UK Gambling Commission's ongoing survey of remote gambling has consistently found males to have about twice the rate of online gambling participation compared to females (Gambling Commission, 2010). In a sample of US online casino players, poker players, and sports bettors ($n = 522$), the American Gaming Association (AGA, 2006) found that 68 percent were male. In another undifferentiated and self-selected sample of all types of worldwide online gamblers ($n = 1,920$), Wood and Williams (2007a) found 68 percent of the sample to be male. Among a sample of 473 British university students, 85 percent of the Internet gamblers were male (Griffiths and Barnes, 2007).

The gender preferences for specific game type, found in the present study, are also consistent with findings from other studies. Woolley (2003) found 85–90 percent male patronage for an Australian TAB company (sports and horse race betting). LaBrie, LaPlante, Nelson, Schumann, and Shaffer (2007) examined the demographic characteristics of everyone opening an account with a European online sportsbook (bwin Interactive Entertainment AG[7]) in February 2005 ($n = 40,499$) and found 92 percent to be male. Males outnumbered females, 10 to 1, in a large-scale study of online poker in Sweden (Gaming Intelligence Group, 2007). In contrast, a more equal gender ratio has been found for online casinos. McMillen and Woolley (2003) report that the percentage of males at one well-established Internet casino was only 50 percent. Similarly, in a worldwide self-selected sample of 10,865 online casino and/or poker gamblers from 96 countries, 58 percent were male (with a majority of casino players being female) (eCOGRA, 2007).

Previous studies consistently find that Internet gamblers tend to be young. For example, high rates of online gambling on college campuses are reported by Brown (2006), Griffiths and Barnes (2007), Helstron, Bryan, and Hutchison (2007), and Petry and Weinstock (2007). Here again, the average age of online gamblers appears to be partially a function of game type and perhaps country. Woolley (2003) found that 35–54 was the most common age group among the sports and horse race bettors in his studies. LaBrie et al. (2007) found the average age of European sports bettors to be 31 ($SD = 10$). The eCommerce and Online Gaming Regulation and Assurance (eCOGRA, 2007) study found the most common age group for online poker players to be 26–35, but the average age of online casino players to be 46–55. In undifferentiated samples of online gamblers, the average age was 34 in the Wood and Williams (2007a) study, and mid-thirties in the AGA study (AGA, 2006). A survey of European online gaming companies found that 63 percent of their patrons were ages 18–35

(Swiss Institute of Comparative Law, 2006). Online poker players in Sweden are predominantly in their twenties (Gaming Intelligence Group, 2007).

The present study's findings about socioeconomic status are also supported by prior research. Socioeconomic status of online sports and horse race bettors was found to be higher than the Australian average in the studies by Woolley (2003), with a notable percentage of people belonging to professional or managerial occupations (whose jobs rely upon familiarity with and competent use of the Internet). The AGA (2006) study found that 61 percent of their sample had at least a college degree; 41 percent earned more than $75,000 a year; and almost all of them used the Internet for other activities. Wood and Williams (2007a) found that 60 percent of their sample had at least some post-secondary education, and 65 percent reported being comfortable conducting business and purchasing transactions over the Internet.

### Game-play patterns

In terms of game-play patterns, perhaps the most important finding is that virtually all Internet gamblers also gamble on several land-based gambling formats, with 4.1 being the average number of formats among our Internet gambling sample. The number of gambling formats engaged in is more powerful than any other variable (including the demographic ones) for predicting Internet gambling. Furthermore, Internet gamblers engage in *all* types of gambling more frequently than their land-based counterparts, and also report higher average gambling expenditures. Internationally, the average net monthly gambling expenditure is US$195.14 for Internet gamblers, compared to US$70.93 for non-Internet gamblers. Hence, what all of this seems to indicate is that Internet gambling is primarily used as an additional form of gambling, added to the repertoire of people who appear to be already heavily involved in gambling.[8]

### Motivations

In terms of motivations for gambling online, Internet gamblers overwhelmingly identified the 24-hour availability and convenience of Internet gambling to be its main advantage. Secondary advantages, mentioned by a smaller percentage, include a better game experience; more physically comfortable; lack of crowds; anonymity; better payout rates; less smoke; and being able to smoke.

These findings about motivation to gamble online are largely consistent with prior research. Among a small sample of British university online gamblers, the primary reasons given for gambling online were: ease of access (84 percent), flexibility of use (75 percent), 24-hour availability (66 percent), because friends do (67 percent), large gambling choice (57 percent), advertising (40 percent), anonymity (25 percent), access to demo games (21 percent), and because family members did (14 percent) (Griffiths and Barnes, 2007). In the AGA (2006) study, the main reasons respondents reported for betting online were convenience (48 percent); fun/exciting/entertaining (24 percent); more comfortable, don't have to drive (24 percent); able to win money (9 percent); and enjoy the anonymity and privacy (6 percent). To relieve boredom and for excitement were the most common reasons cited by youth (age 12–24) in the Derevensky et al. (2006) study. In the Wood, Williams, and Lawton (2007) study, the primary reasons respondents gave for gambling on the Internet were: (1) the relative convenience, comfort, and ease of Internet gambling; (2) an aversion to the atmosphere and clientele of land-based venues; (3) a preference for the pace and nature of online game-play; and (4) the potential for higher wins and lower overall expenditures when gambling online. In the eCOGRA (2007) study, the most important things that people wanted from Internet casino websites were: good bonuses (76 percent), a variety of games (62 percent), good deposit methods (57 percent), and a site with a solid reputation (57 percent). Fun and entertainment tended to rank above the profit motive as reasons for play. Convenience was a major factor cited by Wood and Griffiths (2008) in a qualitative study of Swedish poker players.

### Problem gambling

Among our sample of Internet gamblers, the two most significant predictors of being a problem versus non-problem Internet gambler were participating in a greater number of gambling formats, and reporting a higher net financial expenditure on gambling. The prevalence of problem gambling is three to four times higher among Internet gamblers in our study, compared to non-Internet gamblers. Having problems with gambling is, in fact, one of the characteristics that best predicts that someone is an Internet gambler. Among our sample, 16.6 percent were either moderate or severe problem gamblers, versus a rate of 5.7 percent among land-based gamblers. This finding is very consistent with findings from other studies. In an online study of 422 self-selected online university poker players, 18 percent of the sample was classified as problem gamblers using the Diagnostic and Statistical Manual of Mental Disorders (DSM-IV; American Psychiatric Association, 2000) criteria (Griffiths, Wood, and Parke, 2006). Internet gamblers were also significantly more likely to be problem gamblers in another study of university students by Griffiths and Barnes (2007). In a study of disordered gambling among university students, Ladd and Petry (2002) found that the mean South Oaks Gambling Screen (SOGS) score (7.8) among university Internet gamblers was over four times higher than the mean SOGS score (1.8) for non-Internet gamblers. A 2005 study of 12,717 Dutch Internet users between 18 and 55 years old found that 14 percent of online gamblers were 'at risk' of problem behaviour, but none actually evidenced problematic behaviour (Motivaction International, 2005).[9] Among a self-selected online sample of 1,920 Internet gamblers, Wood and Williams (2007a) found 23 percent to be moderate problem gamblers on the CPGI, and another 20 percent were found to be severe problem gamblers. In a 2006 study of 16,500 Swedish poker players, 27 percent were classified as potential problem gamblers (Gaming Intelligence Group, 2007). A similar study of 3,000 Swedish online poker players by Jonsson (2008) found 23 percent of players were either moderate or severe problem gamblers as measured by the CPGI.

From a policy perspective, it is important to understand the role that Internet gambling plays in the development of problem gambling. There are several aspects of Internet gambling that may increase the risks for problem gambling. These include the much greater convenience and ease of access; the relative comfort of playing at home; the greater anonymity; the solitary nature of the play; the immersive nature of the interface; the fact that gamblers are playing with 'electronic' cash; the ability to play multiple sites/games simultaneously; and the ability of online gamblers to play under the acute influence of drugs or alcohol[10] (Griffiths, 1996, 1999, 2003; Griffiths and Parke, 2002; Griffiths and Wood, 2000; King, 1999; King and Barak, 1999; LaRose, Mastro, and Eastin, 2001; Schull, 2005; Shaffer, 1996; Wood, Williams, and Lawton, 2007). In the present study, roughly half of Internet problem gamblers reported there was a specific type of gambling that contributed to their problems more than others, with slot machines (23.8 percent); poker (21.7 percent); and Internet gambling (11.3 percent) being the most commonly reported. Hence, the implication is that while Internet gambling is an important contributing factor to gambling problems in a portion of problem gamblers, it does not appear to be the main cause of problem gambling for most of them.[11]

This is consistent with the evidence that Internet gamblers are likely heavy gamblers to begin with, who have simply added Internet gambling to their repertoire.

Roughly 9 percent of Internet problem gamblers had sought help for their problems and they had sought help from a wide variety of sources. Interestingly, the large majority of Internet problem gamblers would be more comfortable seeking help from a face-to-face counselling service rather than from an Internet-based counselling service (perhaps because accessing the Internet for help also puts them at risk for online gambling). Some researchers had posited that Internet gamblers might be particularly receptive to Internet-based counselling or other online interventions (Horton, Harrigan, Horbay, and Turner, 2001; Monaghan, 2009; Wood and Williams, 2007a).[12] However, the present results suggest that while online services can serve as a useful adjunct to land-based treatment, it is not likely to be a panacea for this particular population.

## Conclusion

Internet gambling is a relative newcomer to the world of gambling opportunities, but the number and variety of Internet gambling venues, as well as the ease of access to those venues, has progressed with incredible speed since the late 1990s. This speed of progression has left most jurisdictions in a situation of cultural lag; a term which sociologists commonly use to refer to conditions where a society experiences a gap between developments in technology and the moral/legal institutions intended to shape and regulate such developments. In other words, the phenomenon of Internet gambling developed with such velocity, that it outpaced the ability of both the research and policy-making communities to understand the nature of the phenomenon and to determine the most appropriate ways of regulating it. Thankfully, recent studies are shedding much-needed light onto the nature and dynamics of Internet gambling, and we believe that the Casino City study makes a notable contribution to the broader goal of understanding.

As the research community generates increasingly valid data about the characteristics of Internet gamblers, their gambling patterns, and their propensity for problem gambling, an empirical foundation is being laid upon which governments and policy makers can decide how to best proceed. Ultimately, all jurisdictions will have to confront the reality of Internet gambling, and will be tasked with designing appropriate policies along a continuum anchored by complete prohibition on the one end, and complete non-regulation, on the other. Thus, we conclude this chapter with an appeal for subsequent policy-oriented research, rooted in validated facts about Internet gamblers and the nature of Internet gambling. In particular, future policy will benefit from empirical research on:

- responsible and irresponsible Internet gambling business practices;
- the relationship between Internet gambling and problem gambling;
- the source and nature of Internet gambling revenue, with a particular focus on revenue generated for governments;
- the viability of Internet-based prevention and treatment programs; and
- the social and economic costs of government-sponsored Internet gambling.

In pursuing these issues, researchers must overcome a range of methodological dilemmas associated with the study of Internet gamblers, and we hope that the Casino City study will assist in that respect. The primary methodological difficulty for researchers is the recruitment of samples of Internet gamblers that are both large and representative. Indeed, given the low prevalence rate of Internet gambling in the general population, it is difficult to generate a large and representative sample using typical randomization techniques, such as random digit dialing. To achieve a sample size of only 500 Internet gamblers, for example, approximately 25,000 adults in the general population (at least in the Canadian context), would need to agree to a telephone interview. The costs associated with such a project would far exceed the levels of research funding that are normally available to the academic researcher. It is indeed easy to generate a large yet self-selected sample of Internet gamblers, via recruitment efforts at Internet gambling-related websites. It is not possible, however, in the absence of corroborating information, to generalize from such samples to the broader population. We maintain that the two-tiered sampling protocol, used in the Casino City study, represents a reasonable and relatively valid compromise. Thus, we encourage other researchers to adopt a similar approach; that is, recruiting a large self-selected online sample, in conjunction with a small yet representative sample, which would then be used for the purpose of weighting. Such an approach is certainly not immune to methodological critique, but it is nonetheless superior to using convenience samples, however large they may be, as the sole foundation for research.

In addition to making important methodological contributions to the academic literature, the Casino City study raises questions of a broader philosophical nature. In particular, the consistent finding of an association between Internet gambling and problem gambling (confirmed in the present study) raises questions about the legitimacy of government expansion into Internet gambling. Indeed, governments in many jurisdictions, including Canada, are making serious and meaningful efforts to expand into the business of Internet gambling, and are doing so without an adequate appreciation of the associated personal and societal risks (Gainsbury and Wood, 2010). While we hope that the Casino City study can be used as a partial foundation for responsible and well-considered policies, this study speaks to the broader need to assess the extent to which government-sponsored gambling is properly aligned with the essence of democratic government in our society, which is to ensure the greater good and to serve the needs and interests of citizens.

## Acknowledgment

This chapter is an expanded and revised version of a previously published article: Wood, Robert T. and Robert J. Williams (2011). 'A comparative profile of the Internet gambler: Demographic characteristics, game-play patterns, and problem gambling status'. *New Media & Society*, *13*(7), 1123–41.

## Notes

1   Gambling web portals provide listings of available gambling venues/sites in different jurisdictions.
2   It is, of course, possible for people to remove cookies from their computer hard drive. However, our pilot study of online research methodology enabled us to identify repeat responders, and we found that only 38 respondents, out of 1,844, or 2.1 percent, were 'repeat customers' (Wood and Williams, 2007a). Thus, we are confident that repeat responders pose only a small and insignificant contribution to the data set.
3   This does require the assumption that the sampling biases of online Canadian Internet gamblers are similar to the sampling biases of online Internet gamblers from other countries. While we believe this is a reasonable assumption (both theoretically, and based on the data), it is a difficult one to unambiguously prove. Nonetheless, this procedure still represents a substantial methodological improvement over not weighting the data at all (which has been done in all other online surveys collected in this manner).

4   Investigation of underage gambling was not done with the Canadian Telephone Survey because of ethical and logistical issues (i.e., need to obtain parental permission to survey underage youth over the phone).

5   Based on our findings in a past study of the optimal way of wording gambling expenditure questions (see Wood and Williams, 2007b), we asked respondents to report how much money they 'spend on gambling in a typical month', emphasizing that 'spend' refers to net loss/win.

6   This was the available number of Internet gamblers after data were weighted. Prior to weighting, only 1,954 were available.

7   An Austrian sportsbook registered in Gibraltar. Transactions in Euros only.

8   Although this is the most plausible scenario, it must be remembered that because this is correlational data, the directional relationship cannot be unambiguously determined (i.e., it is possible that engagement in Internet gambling led to engagement in multiple forms of land-based gambling).

9   It is not clear how 'at-risk' and 'problem behaviours' were defined.

10  Substance use while gambling has a direct link to excessive and disinhibited play (Baron and Dickerson, 1999; Ellery, Stewart, and Loba, 2005; Kyngdon and Dickerson, 1999).

11  Of course, it must be recognized that this data simply reflect problem gamblers' *perceptions* of what forms were most problematic.

12  Online counselling is currently being offered in the UK. Supported by the Responsibility in Gambling Trust, GamAid provides 'instant, real-time, one-to-one professional guidance for remote gamblers whose gambling activities are out of control or for those who wish to better understand the concepts of responsible gaming' (Wood and Griffiths, 2006). Early findings indicate that while only 1 percent of online gamblers accessed the link button from participating gambling websites, women in particular found the service to be helpful.

## REFERENCES

American Gaming Association (AGA) (2006). 'Gambling and the Internet'. *2006 AGA Survey of Casino Entertainment*. Retrieved December 21, 2010 from http://www.americangaming.org/assets/files/2006_Survey_for_Web.pdf

—— (2008). 'State of the states: The AGA survey of casino entertainment 2008'. Retrieved December 21, 2010 from http://www.americangaming.org/assets/files/aga_2008_sos.pdf

American Psychiatric Association (2000). *DSM IV-TR: Diagnostic and Statistical Manual of Mental Disorders – Text Revision* (fourth edn). Washington, DC: American Psychiatric Association.

Baron, E., and Dickerson, M.G. (1999). 'Alcohol consumption and self-control of gambling behaviour'. *Journal of Gambling Studies, 15*, 3–15.

Brown, S. J. (2006). 'The surge in online gambling on college campuses'. *New Directions for Student Services, 113*, 53–61.

Casino City (2011). *Online Casino City*. Retrieved from http://online.casinocity.com

Council of American Survey Research Organizations (CASRO) (1982). *On the Definition of Response Rates*. Port Jefferson, NY: CASRO.

Derevensky, J. L., and Gupta, R. (2007). 'Internet gambling amongst adolescents: A growing concern'. *International Journal of Mental Health and Addiction, 5*(2), 93–101.

Derevensky, J. L., Gupta, R., and McBride, J. (2006, August/September). 'Internet gambling among youth: A cause for concern'. Paper presented at the Global Remote and E-Gambling Research Institute Conference, Amsterdam, Netherlands.

eCommerce and Online Gaming Regulation and Assurance (eCOGRA) (2007). *An Exploratory Investigation into the Attitudes and Behaviours of Internet Casino and Poker Players*. Retrieved July 13, 2007 from http://www.ecogra.org/Downloads/eCOGRA_Global_Online_Gambler_Report.pdf

Ellery, M., Stewart, S. H., and Loba, P. (2005). 'Alcohol's effects on video lottery terminal (VLT) play among probable pathological and non-pathological gamblers'. *Journal of Gambling Studies, 21*(3), 299–324.

Gainsbury, S., and Wood, R. T. (2010, April). 'Is legalized gambling in North America inevitable? An international perspective'. Presentation at the Ontario Responsible Gambling Council, Discovery Conference. Retrieved from http://www.responsiblegambling.org/articles/Sally_Gainsbury.pdf

Gambling Commission (2010). *Survey Data on Remote Gambling Participation*. Retrieved December 21, 2010 from http://www.gamblingcommission.gov.uk/Client/detail.asp?ContentId=184

Gaming Intelligence Group (2007). *Results of Swedish Online Gambling Study Released*. Retrieved October 5, 2007 from http://www.responsiblegambling.org/articles/Results_of_Swedish_Online_Gambling_Study_released.pdf

Griffiths, M. (1996). 'Gambling on the Internet: A brief note'. *Journal of Gambling Studies, 12*(4), 471–3.

— (1999). 'Gambling technologies: Prospects for problem gambling'. *Journal of Gambling Studies, 15*(3), 265–83.

— (2003). 'Internet gambling: Issues, concerns, and recommendations'. *CyberPsychology & Behavior, 6*(6), 557–68.

Griffiths, M., and Barnes, A. (2007). 'Internet gambling: An online empirical study among student gamblers'. *International Journal of Mental Health and Addiction, 6*, 194–204. doi:10.1007/s11469-007-9083-7

Griffiths, M. D., and Parke, J. (2002). 'The social impact of Internet gambling'. *Social Science Computer Review, 20*(3), 312–20.

Griffiths, M., and Wood, R. T. A. (2000). 'Risk factors in adolescence: The case of gambling, videogame playing, and the Internet'. *Journal of Gambling Studies, 16*(2–3), 199–225.

Griffiths, M., Wood, R. T. A., and Parke, J. (2006). 'A psychosocial investigation of student online poker players'. Paper presented at the 13th International Conference on Gambling. Lake Tahoe, Nevada.

Helstron, A. W., Bryan, A., and Hutchison, K. E. (2007). 'Internet gambling among college students'. *International Pediatrics, 22*(2), 66–9.

Horton, K. D., Harrigan, K. A., Horbay, R., and Turner, N (2001). *The Effectiveness of Interactive Problem Gambling Awareness and Prevention Programs*. Ontario Substance Abuse Bureau, Ministry of Health and Long Term Care.

Jonsson, J. (2008). 'Responsible gaming and gambling problems among 3000 Swedish Internet poker players'. Presentation at the 7th European Association for the Study of Gambling Conference. Retrieved December 21, 2010 from http://www.assissa.eu/easg/thursday/1400-ses3/jonsson_jakob.pdf

Jonsson, J., and Rönnberg, S. (2009). 'Sweden'. In G. Meyer, T. Hayer, and M. Griffiths (eds), *Problem Gambling in Europe* (299–316). New York: Springer.

King, S. A. (1999). 'Internet gambling and pornography: Illustrative examples of the psychological consequences of communication anarchy'. *CyberPsychology and Behavior, 2*(3), 175–93.

King, S. A., and Barak, A. (1999). 'Compulsive Internet gambling: A new form of an old clinical pathology'. *CyberPsychology & Behavior, 2*(5), 441–56.

Kyngdon, A., and Dickerson, M. (1999). 'An experimental study of the effect of prior alcohol consumption on a simulated gambling activity'. *Addiction, 94*(5), 697–707.

LaBrie, R. A., LaPlante, D. A., Nelson, S. E., Schumann, A., and Shaffer, H. J. (2007). 'Assessing the playing field: A prospective longitudinal study of Internet sports gambling behavior'. *Journal of Gambling Studies, 23*(3), 347–62.

Ladd, G. T., and Petry, N. M. (2002). 'Disordered gambling among university-based medical and dental patients: A focus on Internet gambling'. *Psychology of Addictive Behaviors, 16*(1), 76–9.

LaRose, R., Mastro, D., and Eastin, M. S. (2001). 'Understanding Internet usage: A social cognitive approach to uses and gratifications'. *Social Science Computer Review, 19*(4), 395–413.

McMillen, J., and Woolley, R. (2003). 'Australian online gambling policy: A lost opportunity?' Presentation at the Pacific Conference on I-Gaming, Alice Springs.

Monaghan, S. (2009). 'Responsible gambling strategies for Internet gambling: The theoretical and empirical base of using pop-up messages to encourage self-awareness'. *Computers in Human Behavior, 25*, 202–7.

Motivaction International (2005). 'Netherland's participation in paid interactive Internet gaming'. Retrieved from http://www.toezichtkansspelen.nl/information.html

National Centre for Social Research (2011). *British Gambling Prevalence Survey 2010.* National Centre for Social Research. Report prepared for the UK Gambling Commission.

Olason, D. T., and Gretarsson, S. J. (2009). 'Iceland'. In G. Meyer, T. Hayer, and M. Griffiths (eds), *Problem Gambling in Europe* (137–52). New York: Springer.

Petry, N. M., and Weinstock, J. (2007). 'Internet gambling is common in college students and associated with poor mental health'. *American Journal on Addictions, 16*, 325–30.

Sandven, U. H. (2007, May). 'The present situation in Norway'. Presentation at the 6th Nordic Conference on Gambling and Policy Issues, Copenhagen. Retrieved December 21, 2010 from http://www.snsus.org/pdf/20070521/unn_hovda_sandveen-snsus_2007.pdf

Schull, N. D. (2005). 'Digital gambling: The coincidence of desire and design'. *Annals of the American Academy of Political and Social Science, 597*(1), 65–81.

Shaffer, H. J. (1996). 'Understanding the means and objects of addiction: Technology, the Internet and gambling'. *Journal of Gambling Studies, 12*(4), 461–9.

Swiss Institute of Comparative Law (2006). *Study of Gambling Services in the Internal Market of the European Union.* Final report prepared for the European Commission.

Williams, R. J., and Wood, R. T. (2007). *Internet Gambling: A Comprehensive Review and Synthesis of the Literature.* Final report prepared for the Ontario Problem Gambling Research Centre.

Wood, R. T. A., and Griffiths, M. D. (2006). 'The GamAid Pilot Evaluation Study'. Presentation at the Global Remote and E-Gambling Research Institute Conference. August 31–September 1. Amsterdam, Netherlands.

— (2008). 'Why Swedish people play online poker and factors that can increase or decrease trust in poker websites: A qualitative investigation', *Journal of Gambling Issues.* Retrieved from http://www.camh.net/egambling/issue21/pdfs/06wood.pdf.

Wood, R. T. and Williams, R. J. (2007a). 'Problem gambling on the Internet: Implications for Internet gambling policy in North America'. *New Media & Society, 9*(3), 520–42.

— (2007b). 'How much money do you spend on gambling? The comparative validity of question wordings used to assess gambling expenditure'. *International Journal of Social Research Methodology: Theory & Practice, 10*(1), 63–77.

— (2009). *Internet Gambling: Prevalence, Patterns, Problems, and Policy Options.* Final report prepared for the Ontario Problem Gambling Research Centre.

Wood, R. T., Williams, R. J., and Lawton, P. (2007). 'Why do Internet gamblers prefer online versus land-based venues? Some preliminary findings and implications'. *Journal of Gambling Issues, 20 (June)*, 235–50.

Woolley, R. (2003). 'Mapping Internet gambling: Emerging modes of online participation in wagering and sports betting'. *International Gambling Studies, 3*(1), 3–21.

# 7 Internet poker in Sweden in 2007

*Jakob Jonsson*

As a clinical psychologist specializing in problem gambling, I met my first Internet poker player seeking treatment in 2003. He and subsequent others had many similarities with other problem gamblers playing other games, but there were also differences. Their erroneous gambling beliefs were poker-specific and some had actually been very successful players. This new group of problem gamblers sparked an interest to know more about online poker players. This chapter presents highlights from my contribution to the Swedish government evaluation of the introduction of Internet poker at Svenska Spel (a state-owned gambling operator).

In March 2006, Svenska Spel launched poker at www.svenskaspel.se. There had been a great deal of debate in connection with the authorization of Internet poker. The main idea behind authorization was to redirect Swedish poker players from foreign sites to a socially safer domestic site. Two of the reviewing authorities, the Swedish National Institute of Public Health (SNIPH) and the Gaming Board, had opposed the application. SNIPH emphasized that Internet poker for various reasons may be a dangerous form of gambling where players run a greater risk of developing problems. SNIPH also stated, however, that there is very little scientific knowledge about Internet poker and its connections with gambling problems. The Gaming Board argued that authorization increased Svenska Spel's competitiveness more than it provided social protection. It would be in opposition to European Union (EU) legislation.

Nonetheless, Svenska Spel was provided with temporary authorization to offer Internet poker. The authorization contained a number of conditions to ensure social protection. These included: that only people above the age of 18 were allowed to play, that everyone must set limits in regard to time and money, that a player shall have the possibility to exclude himself from playing, and there would be limits in regards to marketing. A final condition was that there needed to be scientific evaluation of this initiative. To attract people to the new site, it was given a Swedish character and Svenska Spel extracted a very low commission (*rake*) from the poker play.

## Why is Internet poker considered to be a dangerous game and what do we know about how responsible gaming measures work?

A review by Jonsson (2005) identified very few studies regarding Internet poker and gambling problems, and very little systematic knowledge about the effects of earlier Swedish gaming policy, such as the introduction of new games and responsible gaming programs. However, it was clear that Internet poker contained all or most of the risk factors for problem gambling that research has thus far identified. Thus, one argument for an introduction of a legal Swedish

Internet poker site was that it would offer a responsible gaming program that would be more comprehensive than on most foreign sites.

What argued against an introduction was that the overall participation in online poker might increase and result in more gambling problems. An additional consideration was that customers at a Swedish legal Internet poker site might not be loyal customers. Unlike a player self-excluded at a physical casino, a person who is self-excluded from one poker site can go to another. From a responsible gaming viewpoint, the ideal situation would be that the Internet poker players were loyal to Svenska Spel and that the site 'brought home' players who had previously played at other sites.

## What do we currently know about Internet poker gaming in Sweden and gambling problems associated with it?

In the first measurement of a longitudinal representative Swedish gambling study (SWELOGS) in 2008–9, 8,167 Swedes in the age range 16–84 answered questions on gambling behaviour and gambling problems. Respondents not reached by telephone received a postal questionnaire. Approximately 10 percent had played poker (both online and land-based) during the past year, 16.8 percent of the men and 4 percent of the women. In the age range 18–24 years, as many as 45 percent of the men and 7 percent of the women had played poker during the past year. Of the poker players aged 16–84, 22.5 percent had low risk, 7.4 percent moderate risk, and 1.9 percent had problematic gambling according to the Canadian Problem Gambling Index (CPGI) (Ferris and Wynne, 2001). The highest prevalence of gambling problems among poker players was found in males 18–24 years old, with 12.5 percent showing moderate risk and 2.8 percent problematic gambling (Statens folkhälsoinstitut, 2010a).

A nationwide telephone survey about Swedish Internet poker players and gambling problems ($n = 16,500$) was carried out by Tryggvesson (2007). Approximately 1.9 percent of the population 16 years old and above had played Internet poker in the past 30 days, representing between 126,000 and 157,000 Swedes. Of the Internet poker players, 26.8 percent stated they had at least one gambling-related problem according to Fors,[1] a three-question survey used in SNIPH's national health survey. Of those that only played at Svenska Spel, 12.7 percent had at least one problem response on Fors compared to 31.2 percent if a person played on another site, or 32.3 percent if a person played at both at Svenska Spel and another site. As a comparison, when Fors was used in the Swedish National Agency for Public Health's annual public health survey, only 2 percent of women and 5 percent of the men have had at least one problem response on Fors (Wadman, Boström, and Karlsson, 2007).

Another indication of the connection between Internet poker and gambling problems is the number of Internet poker players identifying Internet poker as a problem game when they call the national support lines for gambling addiction. In the second half of 2004, when Internet poker was registered as a problem game to differentiate it from other Internet games, 5 percent of those who called stated that Internet poker was a problem for them (Nyman and Creutzer, 2008). However, by 2006, Internet poker was the second most common problem game referred to, identified by 29.5 percent of callers (Nyman and Creutzer, 2008). By 2007 it was the most common problem game, identified by 29.9 percent of callers (Nyman, 2009). During 2008 and 2009, Internet poker was back at second place with around 24 percent reporting it as their problem game (Enmark, 2009; Statens folkhälsoinstitut, 2010b).

Thus, while it is clear that there is a strong association between Internet poker and problem gambling, we do not know whether Internet gambling is contributing to problem gambling or whether problem gamblers are attracted to Internet poker. In addition, we do not know to what extent Svenska Spel's Internet poker constitutes a 'safer alternative' to other poker sites. We also do not know the extent to which players are 'brought home' to Svenska Spel from other sites, or players leave Svenska Spel for other sites.

## Aims

1   To study the prevalence of gambling problems among Swedish Internet poker players.
2   To provide a picture of who has left Svenska Spel's poker site and who has moved to playing there.
3   To describe the use and efficiency of responsible gaming measures at Svenska Spel regarding Internet poker.

## Method

This chapter is based on two surveys:

*Study 1:* Swedish Internet poker players' gaming, reason for choice of poker site and degree of gambling problems (Online Panel survey).

*Study 2:* Use and efficiency of responsible gaming measures among Internet poker players at Svenska Spel (Svenska Spel survey).

### Study 1

This was an online panel web survey carried out via Norstats AB's online panel between December 4 and December 15, 2007. Everyone in their web panel between the ages of 18 and 75 (62,362 Swedes) was asked whether they had played Internet poker during the past three months. Those that answered yes to this question could then continue and respond to the web survey. The web panel survey was open until there were a total of 2,000 responses. A total of 2,002 complete surveys were obtained. The first question was answered by 28,798 persons, representing a response rate of 46.2 percent.

The survey contained questions about current and previous Internet poker playing and the reasons why a person played at Svenska Spel or another site. Those playing at Svenska Spel were asked what they thought about setting limits for their gaming. In addition, two different gambling problem scales were administered, Fors and PGSI poker modified,[2] as well as questions regarding whether they had sought help for gambling problems. The data was subsequently weighted by gender and age in order to be representative of Swedish Internet poker players. The reference dataset was Svenska Spel's with 20,800 responses from telephone surveys from the last 12 months.[3]

### Study 2 (Svenska Spel Survey)

A random selection was made of 3,000 of Svenska Spel's customers who had played poker at svenskaspel.se at least once during the period September–November 2007. Due to non-current e-mail addresses, the survey reached only 2,575. Of these, 1,049 responded, of which 18 declined to participate (response rate of 40 percent). The self-administered online survey was carried out between December 17, 2007, and January 13, 2008, and contained similar questions to Study 1. The participants in the survey were found to be representative for Svenska Spel's customers with regard to gender and age, thus no post-hoc weighting was required.

## Results

### *Who are the Swedish Internet poker players?*

The Online Panel survey found that the average Internet poker player is male (88 percent) and roughly 32 years old. Two-thirds are either blue-collar workers (33 percent) or salaried employees (34 percent), whereas 6 percent are small business owners, and 15 percent are students. The remaining 12 percent include those seeking employment, disabled people, and those on sick leave, as well as retirees and persons on parental leave.

### *Self-reported gambling behaviour among Swedish Internet poker players*

On average, Internet poker players actively play on two poker sites. Roughly half (54.2 percent) play online poker at least once a week. More than half of Internet poker players (55.6 percent) play at least two hours during a typical gaming session. One-fourth of Internet poker players are frequent players who play at least once a week and play at least two hours during a typical gaming session. If instead one looks at the stated frequency in regard to any gambling for money, 8.8 percent report that they gamble daily or almost daily, an additional 42.1 percent state that they gamble every week, 28.4 percent every month, and 17.3 percent more seldom. Thus, it is clear that Internet poker players are a relatively gaming-intensive group compared with the rest of the population. In the Swedish population survey from 2008–9, only 44 percent had gambled once a month or more frequently (Statens folkhälsoinstitut, 2010a).

### *Gambling problems among Swedish Internet poker players in relation to gaming sites*

As illustrated in Table 7.1, the percentage of Internet poker players from the Online Panel survey that have severe problem gambling on the PGSI is 8.2 percent, with another 14.8 percent having moderate risk gambling habits. In comparison, approximately 0.3 percent of the Swedish population between the ages of 16–84 had problematic gambling habits and 1.9 percent moderate risk gambling habits in the population survey carried out 2008–9. And among the poker players in this study, 1.9 percent had problematic gambling and 7.4 percent moderate risk gambling (Statens folkhälsoinstitut, 2010a). However, it is important to note that the former result is from an online panel, and the latter result is from a telephone interview supplemented by postal questionnaires. Work conducted by Williams and Volberg (in preparation) has shown that survey modality significantly impacts obtained rates of problem gambling, with online panel rates being significantly higher than 'true' rates.

### *Demographic predictors of problem gambling*

Table 7.1 illustrates that problem gambling did not differ significantly as a function of gender. Among both women and men the percentage with problematic gambling was 8.3 percent, the percentage with moderate risk gambling was 14.5 percent for women and 14.9 percent for men (Chi Square (2df) = .04). Age was a much stronger predictor of problem gambling

*Table 7.1* Results of the Online Panel survey

| | | N | Problematic gambling (PGSI 8–27) (%) | Moderate risk (PGSI 3–7) (%) |
|---|---|---|---|---|
| All Internet poker players | | 2,002 | 8.2 | 14.8 |
| | Men | 1,756 | 8.3 | 14.9 |
| | Women | 242 | 8.3 | 14.5 |
| | Age 18–27 | 748 | 12.7 | 16.0 |
| | Age 28–40 | 894 | 5.3 | 14.5 |
| | Age 41+ | 357 | 6.7 | 13.2 |
| | Employed | 1,457 | 6.1 | 13.4 |
| | Students | 308 | 15.9 | 19.5 |
| | Other | 234 | 12.0 | 17.9 |
| Svenska Spel's Internet poker customers | | 1,062 | 5.5 | 14.0 |
| Current poker site for Svenska Spel's Internet poker players | Svenska Spel patrons only | 567 | 2.6 | 8.8 |
| | Other poker site(s) only | 938 | 11. 4 | 15.9 |
| | Both Svenska Spel & other sites | 495 | 8.7 | 19.8 |

status, with the youngest age group (18–27 years), having the highest percentage of problematic and moderate risk gambling habits: 12.7 percent and 16.0 percent respectively. As can be seen, rates of problem gambling were significantly lower in the older age groups (Chi Square (2df) = 34.8, $p < .001$). There were also significant differences in the percentage with problematic and moderate risk gambling habits as a function of employment status. The employed group has the lowest percentage of problematic and moderate risk gambling habits, 6.1 percent and 13.4 percent respectively. Students had the highest percentage with problems, with 15.9 percent having problematic gambling habits and 19.5 percent with moderate risk gambling habits. The 'other' group (such as those on disability, on parental leave, and retirees) also had a high percentage of problems: 12.0 percent with problematic gambling habits and 17.9 percent with moderate risk gambling habits (Chi Square (4df) = 51.7, $p < .001$).

### Gambling problems as a function of site patronization

The Svenska Spel survey found that 2.8 percent of online poker players had problematic gambling and another 16.1 percent had moderate risk gambling. By comparison, the Online Panel survey found that among Svenska Spel's customers (regardless of whether they also played at another site or not), 5.5 percent had problematic gambling habits and 14 percent had moderate risk gambling habits. For the Online Panel survey, the difference compared with the total population of Internet poker players is stronger if you look at the group that only played Internet poker at Svenska Spel. Of this latter group, only 2.6 percent had problematic gambling habits and 8.8 percent had moderate risk gambling habits. Of the players that played at both Svenska Spel and another site, 8.7 percent had problematic gambling habits and 19.8 percent had moderate risk gambling habits. The highest percentage of players with problematic gambling habits (11.4 percent) was found in the group that only played at one site, which was not Svenska Spel, with another 15.9 percent having moderate risk gambling habits. Overall, the differences in the percentage of gambling problems as a function of site patronization was statistically significant (Chi Square (4df) = 69.8, $p < .001$).

Two percent of everyone in the Online Panel survey had sought help during the past 12 months due to problems with their Internet poker gambling. However, of those with problematic gambling habits, 21.7 percent had sought help.

## *Multiple regression analysis of what predicts problem gambling*

Above, we have analysed how gender, age, occupation, and gaming site patronization are each related to problematic gambling habits among Internet poker players. To control for the correlation of these variables amongst each other, a multiple regression analysis was used to establish their relative importance in predicting total PGSI-score in the Online Panel dataset. Using simultaneous variable entry, $R$ was found to be significantly different from zero: $F$ (7, 1992) = 19.93, $p < 0.001$. However, the percentage of variance accounted for was quite small, at 6.5 percent. As illustrated in Table 7.2, the best predictor of problem gambling score was being a high frequency player (defined as playing at least once a week with at least two hours per session). Patronization of a non-Svenska Spel site was also significantly predictive, as was being a student, and being in the 'Other employment' group, and being of younger age. Gender and playing at Svenska Spel were not significant predictors. It is of special interest that playing at Svenska Spel's poker site does not increase the risk for problems, but neither does it reduce the risk (the weak negative connection is far from significant).

The results should be interpreted with caution. Causal connections are not proven, and the fact that the predictors only explain 6.2 percent of the variance indicates that factors not taken into consideration by the model have a very large influence on problem gambling (e.g., co-morbid substance abuse, mental health problems, etc.).

*Table 7.2* Multiple regression prediction of PGSI score from the Online Panel survey

| Model | *Unstandardized coefficients* | | *Standardized coefficients* | | |
|---|---|---|---|---|---|
| | *B* | *Std. error* | *Beta* | *t* | *Sig.* |
| 1   (Constant) | 2.160 | .523 | | 4.125 | .000 |
| Sex | −.121 | .265 | −.010 | −.455 | .649 |
| Age | −.033 | .010 | −.082 | −3.459 | .001 |
| Svenska Spel patron | −.090 | .218 | −.011 | −.414 | .679 |
| Other site patron | .983 | .243 | .112 | 4.043 | .000 |
| Student | 1.173 | .260 | .107 | 4.514 | .000 |
| Other employment | 1.177 | .272 | .096 | 4.321 | .000 |
| High frequency play | 1.053 | .204 | .115 | 5.159 | .000 |

Note: 'Employed' was used as the reference group for Student and 'Other employment status'.

### Debut site and redirection

Svenska Spel had approximately 105,000 active Internet poker customers from October to December 2007 according to its register. From the Online Panel survey, 53 percent stated that they had played at Svenska Spel in the past three months (28 percent played at Svenska Spel only, 25 percent at Svenska Spel and other companies, 27 percent at other companies only). Thus, it can be estimated that the total number of Swedish online poker players is 105,000/0.53, roughly 200,000 people (see Figure 7.1).

Using the same projections from the Online Panel survey, of the 200,000 active Internet poker players, an estimated 55,000 play only with Svenska Spel, 50,000 play at both Svenska Spel and at least one other company, and 95,000 play only with other companies.

On examining how the players moved from the site they initially started playing at ('debut site') to where they currently play, results from the Online Panel survey showed that Svenska Spel, wholly or partially, has redirected 55,000 players to its site. However, 35,000 players who started playing Internet poker at Svenska Spel reported that they have fully or partially gone over to playing at another site.

Figure 7.2 shows where those who started playing Internet poker at Svenska Spel are now active. Of these, 51.9 percent have remained totally loyal to Svenska Spel and do not play Internet poker at any other site. However, 22.6 percent play Internet poker at both Svenska Spel and at least one other site and 25.5 percent no longer play at Svenska Spel. What Figure 7.2 also shows is that individuals who began with Svenska Spel and did not play at any other site for the first three months have considerably higher rates of subsequent loyalty.

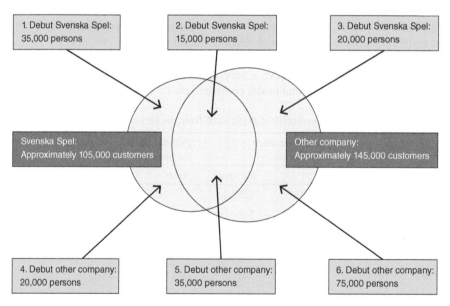

*Figure 7.1* Current gaming site patronization of Swedish Internet poker players as a function of initial site patronization ('debut site')

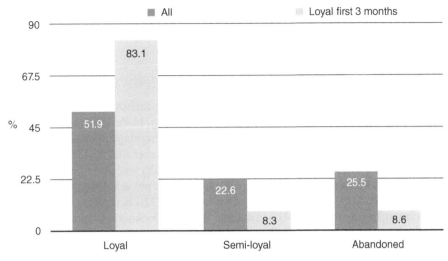

*Figure 7.2* Current patronization of the Svenska Spel Internet poker site by players who began Internet poker play at Svenska Spel

Note: All *n* = 721; Loyal first 3 months *n* = 424

### Demographic differences as a function of site patronage

Here, we shall address the question as to whether site patronage differs in regard to distribution of age, gender, and occupation. Regarding occupation, the following categories are used; blue-collar workers, salaried employees, self-employed, students, and other. The category 'other' includes those seeking employment, those on disability pension, retirees, and those on parental leave. Table 7.3 shows that people who only patronized Svenska Spel were more

*Table 7.3* Gaming site patronization and demographic features (*n* = 2,000)

|  |  | Only Svenska Spel | Both Svenska Spel and other sites | Only other site |
|---|---|---|---|---|
| *n* |  | 567 | 495 | 938 |
| Sex |  |  |  |  |
|  | Men | 85.9% | 91.1% | 87.3% |
|  | Women | 14.1% | 8.9% | 12.7% |
| Age |  |  |  |  |
|  | Mean | 34.5 years | 32.4 years | 30.9 years |
|  | 18–27 | 29.6% | 34.2% | 43.7% |
|  | 28–40 | 46.9% | 48.4% | 41.6% |
|  | 41– | 23.5% | 17.4% | 14.7% |
| Primary occupation |  |  |  |  |
|  | Blue-collar worker | 33.5% | 30.7% | 33.7% |
|  | Salaried employee | 41.1% | 37.2% | 28.3% |
|  | Self-employed | 5.5% | 5.9% | 6.1% |
|  | Student | 10.1% | 13.9% | 19.3% |
|  | Other | 9.9% | 12.3% | 12.6% |

likely to be female (Chi Square (2df) = 7.23, $p < .05$), to be somewhat older (Chi Square (4df) = 39.86, $p < .001$), and to have a lower percentage of students and people in the other employment category (Chi Square (8df) = 43.0, $p < .001$).

### Gambling behaviour as a function of site patronage

As illustrated in Table 7.4, the groups differ significantly from each other both in regard to time and frequency playing poker and total frequency of gambling. In the group that plays at both Svenska Spel and other sites, there is a significantly higher percentage (68.0 percent) who play at least two hours per session, than those who only play at another site (56.4 percent) and those who only play at Svenska Spel (43.4 percent) (Chi Square (2df) = 65.3, $p < .001$). In addition, this group has a larger percentage of people who play Internet poker at least once a week (56.8 percent) compared to people who only play at Svenska Spel (32.1 percent) or just at other sites (31.4 percent) (Chi Square (2df) = 99.6, $p < .001$). When just looking at frequent players (those who play at least two hours a week) the group that plays at both Svenska Spel and other sites also has the highest percentage of people who play at least two hours on a weekly basis (41.3 percent) compared with only 15.7 percent among people who only play at Svenska Spel and 22.0 percent who only play at other sites (Chi Square (2df) = 100.9, $p < .001$).[4] Finally, with regard to total gambling frequency, once again the group that played at both Svenska Spel and another site had the highest percentage that plays daily or almost daily (20.4 percent) compared with the other groups (Chi Square (4df) = 98.1, $p < .001$).

### Use of responsible gaming measures and their effectiveness

The final comparison is an examination of the extent to which responsible gambling tools are used as well as their self-reported effectiveness. From a responsible gaming perspective, if players are stopped by limits that they themselves set but then go on to another gaming site, this is reflective of an ineffective limit.

*Table 7.4* Self-reported frequency and time spent gambling as a function of site patronage

|  |  | Only Svenska Spel | Both Svenska Spel and other sites | Only other site |
| --- | --- | --- | --- | --- |
| *n* |  | 567 | 495 | 938 |
| Time poker |  |  |  |  |
|  | < 2 hr per session | 56.6% | 32.0% | 43.6% |
|  | ≥ 2 hr per session | 43.4% | 68.0% | 56.4% |
| Frequency poker |  |  |  |  |
|  | < once per week | 67.9% | 43.2% | 68.6% |
|  | ≥ once per week | 32.1% | 56.8% | 31.4% |
| Frequent poker players |  |  |  |  |
|  | < 2 hr/once/week | 84.3% | 58.7% | 78.0% |
|  | ≥ 2 hr/once/week | 15.7% | 41.3% | 22.0% |
| Frequency all gambling |  |  |  |  |
|  | Daily/almost daily | 10.2% | 20.4% | 8.8% |
|  | Every week | 47.3% | 48.1% | 35.9% |
|  | Less often | 42.5% | 31.5% | 55.3% |

*Time and money limits*

As seen in Table 7.5, in total, 59.1 percent of the total sample set reasonable limits for 'time'. In this context, a 'reasonable limit' was defined as a limit that they planned to gamble within (set by 31.2 percent) or a limit they judged to be slightly higher than they planned to gamble within (set by 27.9 percent). A total of 40.9 percent reported setting 'a high limit in order to avoid being blocked' (e.g., for example, it is possible to set the time limit to 24-hours a day). A larger percentage, 66.7 percent set reasonable 'amount' limits, with 42.0 percent setting a limit that was in accordance with what they planned to play for and 24.7 percent setting a somewhat higher limit.

In terms of effectiveness, 44.8 percent reported they had been stopped from playing, due to these limits. Of these individuals, 62.6 percent reported they had not played poker on the Internet (on another site) since they had been stopped, and 67.7 percent did not alter their limits. Of those who had been stopped by the limits, 41.6 percent reported they had been stopped once, 21.2 percent twice, 9.1 percent three times, and 5 percent four times. Almost one-fourth, 23.4 percent, had been stopped five times or more.

Table 7.5 also illustrates that a somewhat larger percentage of those who only play poker at Svenska Spel set reasonable time limits compared to other groups. The difference is statistically significant (Chi Square (2df) = 19.8, $p < .001$). The same pattern can be observed for monetary limits (71.9 percent set reasonable monetary limits for exclusive Svenska Spel customers versus 59.7 percent for customers who patronized various sites). Here again the difference between the groups is statistically significant (Chi Square (2df) = 16.7, $p < .001$). Furthermore, a much higher percentage of exclusive Svenska Spel customers (78 percent versus 37.5 percent) did not play poker at another site when they were stopped by the limits (Chi Square (1df) = 76.2, $p < .001$). To some extent this difference is expected since the group of exclusive Svenska Spel customers is defined by playing at Svenska Spel only during the last three months. There was no significant difference in the percentage of people who did not change their limits after having reached them as a function of whether they were Svenska Spel customers or whether they patronized several sites (68.2 percent versus 67.0 percent respectively).

*Table 7.5* Use and effectiveness of responsible gambling tools

| *Responsible gaming measures* | *All (n = 1,031) (%)* | *Only Svenska Spel (n = 623) (%)* | *Svenska Spel plus other sites (n = 405) (%)* | *Risk players (PGSI 3+) (n = 271) (%)* | *Non-risk players (PGSI 0–2) (n = 753) (%)* |
|---|---|---|---|---|---|
| Reasonable time limits set | 59.1 | 64.1 | 51.2 | 53.5 | 61.0 |
| Reasonable monetary limits set | 66.7 | 71.9 | 59.7 | 63.8 | 68.1 |
| Ceased playing when limits reached | 62.6 | 78.0 | 37.5 | 49.7 | 69.4 |
| Did not change limits when limits reached | 67.7 | 68.2 | 67.0 | 70.8 | 66.1 |
| Blocked poker account | 5.4 | 3.9 | 7.7 | 11.1 | 3.3 |
| Ceased playing after blocking account | 76.4 | 91.7 | 64.5 | 70.0 | 84.0 |
| Use of self-test | 16.4 | 13.7 | 20.5 | 24.4 | 13.5 |
| Reduced gambling as a result of self-test | 43.8 | 33.0 | 50.0 | 33.0 | 75.0 |

Note: Reasonable limits = people set limits that they planned to play for, or slightly more.

For the moderate risk and problem gamblers, 25.5 percent set the time limits for how long they planned to play, and 28.0 percent somewhat higher (total reasonable limit setting of 53.5 percent). For the group of non-risk players, the corresponding figures were 33.2 percent and 27.8 percent respectively (total reasonable limit setting of 61.0 percent). The difference between the groups is statistically significant (Chi Square (1df) = 6.5, $p < .05$). Concerning monetary limits, the difference between the groups was not statistically significant, with 40.2 percent of the risk players setting a limit that was in accordance with what they planned to play for and 23.6 percent setting a somewhat higher limit. Corresponding figures for the group of non-risk players was 42.9 percent and 25.2 percent.

A total of 59.4 percent of the moderate risk and problem gamblers reported they had been stopped by the limits at some point, compared with 40.0 percent of the group of non-risk players, with this difference being statistically significant (Chi Square (1df) = 30.4, $p < .001$). In terms of the effectiveness of these limits, for the moderate risk and problem gamblers, 49.7 percent reported not playing poker at another site when they were stopped by the limits compared to 69.4 percent for the group of non-risk players. The difference between the groups is statistically significant (Chi Square (1df) = 17.5, $p < .001$). However, there was no significant difference in the percentage of moderate risk and problem gamblers who retained their limits after reaching them (i.e., did not change them) compared to the recreational/non-risk players (70.8 percent versus 66.1 percent).

In summary, it would appear that reasonable time and monetary limits are set by most players, especially exclusive Svenska Spel players and non-problem gamblers. For those individuals who set reasonable limits, most of these individuals abide by these limits (i.e., do not actively try to circumvent them by playing elsewhere or changing the limits), although here again, this abidance is more characteristic of exclusive Svenska Spel players and non-problem gamblers.

## Blocked accounts

Blocking access to one's poker account is another, even more potent responsible gaming measure that Svenska Spel customers can employ. However, as seen in Table 7.5, only 5.4 percent of people reported using this strategy. Use of this strategy varied significantly as a function of site patronage, with only 3.9 percent of Svenska Spel customers using this compared to 7.7 percent of people who used multiple sites (Chi Square (1df) = 6.99, $p < .001$). Use of this strategy also varied significantly as a function of risk status, with 11.1 percent of moderate risk and problem gamblers blocking their poker account at some point compared to only 3.3 percent of recreational gamblers (Chi Square (2df) = 16.7, $p < .001$).

The effectiveness of this strategy was fairly high, with 76.4 percent of people reporting that they did not subsequently play poker at any other place during the time they had blocked their poker account. Here again, this varied as a function of patronage, with a significantly higher percentage of Svenska Spel customers not gambling elsewhere compared to people who patronized multiple sites (91.7 percent versus 64.5 percent; Chi Square (1df) = 5.52, $p < .05$). Effectiveness also varied as a function of risk status, with 70 percent of the moderate and problem gamblers not gambling elsewhere compared to 84 percent of non-problem gamblers. The difference between these groups was not statistically significant, partly due to small sample sizes (Chi Square (1df) = 1.48, $p > .05$).

To summarize, account blocking is an infrequently used responsible gambling measure most often used by moderate risk and problem gamblers and by people who patronize multiple sites. When employed, however, the large majority of people do not play poker during the period their account is blocked, with this being especially true for Svenska Spel customers and non-problem gamblers.

*Self-test*

Svenska Spel has a self-test where players can receive objective feedback on their gambling habits, with people receiving a yellow or red light being alerted to the fact they should start to think about and review their gambling habits. People receiving a red light, for example, are encouraged to contact a helpline for problem gamblers.

A total of 16.4 percent reported they had taken the self-test at least once, with 6.0 percent reporting they received red, 13.1 percent receiving yellow, 38.7 percent receiving a green light, and 42.2 percent not remembering the result of the test. Of those receiving a yellow or red light, 43.8 percent stated that they had reduced their gambling as a result of the test results. Of those that did not remember their result, 14 percent reported they had reduced their gambling due to the results.

In the group that only played at Svenska Spel, 13.7 percent had taken the self-test compared to 20.5 percent in the group that also played at another site. The difference between the groups was statistically significant (Chi Square (1df) = 8.40, $p < .01$). In the group of risk players, 24.4 percent had taken the self-test, compared to 13.5 percent in the group of non-risk players. The difference between the groups is also statistically significant (Chi Square (1df) = 17.0, $p < .001$). Interestingly, when receiving a yellow or red light from the self-test, a much greater percentage of non-problem gamblers had a subsequent decrease in their gambling behaviour (75 percent) compared to the moderate risk and problem gamblers (33.3 percent), suggesting a greater potential for these 'alerts' to influence the behaviour of non-problem rather than problem gamblers.

### Opinions regarding Svenska Spel's responsible gaming measures

As illustrated in Table 7.6, the majority of Svenska Spel's customers reported appreciating the site's responsible gaming measures. People were also asked if they thought that Svenska Spel's tools provided sufficient opportunity to keep poker playing under control. A majority, 83.3 percent, thought they were totally sufficient, 5.9 percent believed they were insufficient, and 10.8 percent did not know or did not answer the question.

*Table 7.6* Opinions about different responsible gaming measures ($n = 1,031$)

| Measure (%) | Very good (%) | Good (%) | Neither good nor bad (%) | Bad (%) | Very bad (%) |
|---|---|---|---|---|---|
| Time limits | 28.3 | 35.0 | 29.6 | 4.6 | 2.0 |
| Monetary limits | 42.4 | 36.6 | 17.1 | 2.3 | 1.6 |

## Discussion

The main justification behind the authorization of Internet poker at Svenska Spel was to redirect Swedish poker players from foreign sites to a domestic site with better player protection. There is good reason for seeking this redirection to a safer site in light of the fact that (a) online poker is one of the most cited 'problem games' on the Swedish helpline, and

(b) the Online Panel survey established that 23 percent of Swedish online poker players have either moderate risk or problem gambling.

The present study estimates that creation of a domestically available Internet poker site resulted in 28 percent of existing Swedish online poker players patronizing the new Svenska Spel poker site exclusively, another 25 percent patronizing Svenska Spel in addition to other sites, and 47 percent continuing to patronize only foreign sites. There is a high degree of player mobility as well, with approximately one-fourth of active players that began playing poker at Svenska Spel currently being active players only at other sites. Thus, the goal to redirect players to a potentially safer domestic site has only been partially successful.

Svenska Spel does, in fact, provide better player protection than many other sites by virtue of the fact that (a) it has several responsible gambling tools available to patrons, and (b) setting limits is mandatory (although these limits can be unreasonably high). Furthermore, there are indications that these responsible gambling measures have some effectiveness compared to other sites, as evidenced by (a) the lower rates of problem gamblers at this site, (b) the higher utilization rates of responsible gambling measures at Svenska Spel, and (c) the somewhat greater effectiveness of these measures for exclusive Svenska Spel customers.

However, what is not known is whether more responsible gamblers naturally gravitate to the Svenska Spel site or whether the Svenska Spel site creates more responsible gamblers. In addition, the prevalence of Internet poker has probably increased as a result of the Svenska Spel site, as 30 percent of the 200,000 active poker players in 2007 reported that their initial foray into Internet poker was on the Svenska Spel site. (Although, it could be argued that some of these players would have started playing poker anyway.)

### *Limitations*

*Are Internet poker players from the Online Panel study representative of Swedish Internet poker players?*

This can be questioned, since the response rate was only approximately 47 percent and no analysis of the characteristics of refusals has been done. On the other hand, the data have been weighted in regard to gender and age in order to be representative of Swedish Internet poker players. Furthermore, results in this survey are in general agreement with the outcome of Tryggvesson's survey (Tryggvesson, 2007). The Internet poker players in this survey come from an online panel that was stratified according to basic demographic characteristics to match the Swedish population (e.g., age, gender, education). However, it is important to note that unpublished work by Williams and Volberg (in preparation) has found that online panelists have significantly higher rates of pathology compared to the general population

*To what extent are the participants in Study 2 representative of Svenska Spel's active Internet poker customers?*

It was not possible to carry out an analysis of the characteristics of refusals (60 percent), which calls into question whether the results are representative. However, the selection is random among Svenska Spel's active Internet poker players, and approximately 1 percent of those customers participated in the survey. The correspondence with Svenska Spel's data for active Internet poker players also demonstrates that the selection is representative in regard to gender and age. This suggests that the survey is valid for the population of active Internet poker players at Svenska Spel.

# Notes

1   The three Fors questions are: During the last 12 months, how many times have you – tried to decrease your gambling? – felt restless and irritated if not being able to gamble? – lied about your gambling? Answering fomat never/1–2 times/3 times or more.
2   The Problem Gambling Severity Index (PGSI) was modified to cover poker gambling only. For example: Thinking about the past 12 months, have you bet more on poker than you could really afford to lose?
3   Svenska Spel continously surveys the Swedish population with 400 respondents every week.
4   One possible source of error in the comparison is that the group 'Both Svenska Spel and other sites', have not been asked about their total Internet poker gaming, but rather frequency and time questions regarding gaming at Svenska Spel and 'other sites', respectively. Instead of trying to summarize the frequency and time, their highest value has been used. For example, if an individual plays 1–3 times a week at Svenska Spel and once a month at another site, then that individual has received a value of at least once a week. This method can overestimate the time the group normally devotes to poker and underestimate the frequency. In regard to frequency for all types of gaming, everyone was asked the same question.

# References

Enmark, B. (2009). *Årsrapport stödlinjen 2008.* Annual report helpline 2008. Retrieved from http://www.fhi.se/Publikationer/Alla-publikationer/Arsrapport-Stodlinjen-2008

Ferris, J., and Wynne, H. (2001). 'The Canadian Problem Gambling Index: User Manual'. *Report to the Canadian Inter-Provincial Task Force on Problem Gambling.*

Jonsson, J. (2005). *Nätpoker. Det vetenskapliga kunskapsläget och en diskussion kring vilken betydelse en introduktion av en svensk legal nätpokersite skulle få avseende totalkonsumtion och spelproblem.* [Scientific review and a discussion on the effects of an introduction of a Swedish legal poker site regarding total consumption and gambling problems.] Östersund: Statens folkhälsoinstitut.

Nyman, A. (2009) *Rapport från Stöd-och hjälplinjen för spelare och anhöriga 2007.* [Helpline annual report 2007.] http://www.fhi.se/Publikationer/Alla-publikationer/Rapport-fran-Stod – och-hjalplin jen-for-spelare-och-anhoriga

Nyman, A., and Creutzer, M. (2008). *Nationella stödlinjen 2002–2006.* [The national helpline 2002–6.] http://www.fhi.se/Publikationer/Alla-publikationer/Nationella-stodlinjen-2002–2006

Statens folkhälsoinstitut (2010a). *Spel om pengar och spelproblem i Sverige 2008/2009. Huvudresultat från SWELOGS befolkningsstudie.* [Gambling and gambling problems in Sweden 2008/2009. Main results from SWELOGS epidemiological study – *R 2010:23*] http://www.fhi.se/Publikationer/Alla-publikationer/Spel-om-pengar-och-spelproblem-i-Sverige-20082009-Huvudresultat-fran-SWELOGS-befolkningsstudie

— (2010b). *Årsrapport stödlinjen 2009* [Annual report helpline 2009] http://www.fhi.se/Publikationer/Alla-publikationer/Arsrapport-Stodlinjen-2009

Tryggvesson, K. (2007) *Nätpokerspelandet i Sverige – omfattning, utveckling och karaktär 2006.* SoRAD – *Forskningsrapport nr 43.* [Internet poker gaming in Sweden – scope, development and character 2006. SoRAD – *Research Report no. 43.*] Stockholm: Stockholms universitet.

Wadman, C., Boström, G., and Karlsson, A.S. (2007). *Hälsa på lika villkor – resultaten från nationella folkhälsoenkäten 2006.* Statens Folkhälsoinstitut rapport nr A-2007-01. [Health on equal terms – results from the national public health survey 2006. Swedish National Agency for Public Health report no. A-2007-01.].

Williams, R.J., and Volberg, R.A. (2009). 'Impact of survey description, administration format, and exclusionary criteria on population prevalence rates of problem gambling'. *International Gambling Studies, 9*(2), 101–17.

Williams, R.J., and Volberg, R.A. (in preparation). 'Relative representativeness and validity of online panels compared to telephone surveys for the assessment of gambling and problem gambling'.

# 8 The eCOGRA global online gambler report

*Jonathan Parke, Adrian J. Parke,*
*Jane L. Rigbye, Niko Suhonen,*
*and Leighton Vaughan Williams*

## Introduction

Elsewhere in this book the scale and growth of Internet gambling is discussed, alongside predictions that its popularity will continue. For example, Global Betting and Gaming Consultants (see Chapter 3) discuss its trajectory, estimating that worldwide Internet gambling revenues tripled between 2004 and 2010. Such growth is impressive given the immense regulatory uncertainty surrounding the industry. Yet during this period there seemed to be a lag in associated research, the extent of which was disproportionately low. In late 2006, in response to, and in anticipation of, such growth, eCOGRA (eCommerce and Online Gaming Regulation and Assurance) sought to learn more about player behaviour, preferences, and attitudes and wanted to give players an opportunity to communicate their views, concerns, and approvals by commissioning the global online gambler report.

At the time of this research there was a paucity of academic research on Internet gambling. The academic research in existence prior to 2006 consisted primarily of speculation and commentary (e.g. Griffiths, 1996, 1999, 2003a, 2003b; Griffiths and Parke, 2002; Griffiths, Parke, Wood, and Parke, 2006; King, 1999; King and Barak, 1999; Laffey, 2005; Shaffer 1996; Smeaton and Griffiths, 2004) each playing an important role in provoking debate, and setting the research agenda, particularly in the absence of available data and research opportunity. There was also a handful of empirical studies (e.g. Griffiths, 2001; Ialomiteanu and Adlaf, 2002; Ladd and Petry, 2002; Woolley, 2003) although these primarily had a health-related focus. Such a focus of attention still remains today. Around 95 percent of the 70 or so studies on Internet gambling have problem gambling (and its mediation), or policy as their primary focus.

Consequently, a substantial knowledge gap existed (and arguably still exists five years on) regarding questions of who, what, where, how, and why in relation to consumer participation in Internet gambling. In addition to helping to fill this gap, this research initiative also sought to generate knowledge regarding consumer attitudes on trust, cheating, and disputes. Thus, the objectives of this study were broad and exploratory. Specifically, objectives included exploring the following areas of interest:

1  Internet poker and casino behaviour, including who gambles, in what way, why, and with what consequences;
2  fair, honest, and responsible provision of Internet gambling with a particular focus on neglected areas including trust, disputes, and customer service; and
3  idiosyncratic and peripheral factors to Internet gambling such as cognitive aspects of play (e.g. belief in luck and understanding of probability), perceptions of skill and other potentially interesting attitudes, preferences, and behaviour identified a priori.

This research did not cover any of the following specific topics: offline or 'land-based' gambling; other forms of remote gambling (e.g. interactive TV, mobile); Internet gambling other than casino and poker (e.g. Internet sports betting, Internet lottery, Internet bingo, Internet instant win games, etc.); problem gambling behaviour and its treatment; or detailed aspects of player strategy.

Data were collected using both qualitative (focus groups) and quantitative (survey) techniques. The rest of this chapter will consider some of the key findings from both studies[1] preceded by a brief account of the research methods employed. Despite these data being collected in 2006, the relative importance and current implications of these findings are also discussed.

## Study 1 – Internet survey

### *Methodological approach*

A total of 85 questions, including closed and open-ended questions, were used to collect data on demographic, behavioural, and cognitive variables; attitudes towards player protection; and the positive and negative aspects of Internet gambling. Data for the quantitative investigation were collected using Internet Mediated Research (IMR) via an Internet data collection tool from August until December 2006. This was a self-selected sample whereby Internet gamblers could choose to participate by clicking a link that was brought to their attention either by e-mail from their Internet gambling operator or through a portal (i.e. web community or information website).

Those targeted were individuals who had gambled at Internet casino sites, Internet poker sites, or both within the last three months. Overall, data from 10,838 participants (58 percent male, 42 percent female) were analysed following the removal of data from 25 participants who were under the age of 18. A brief summary of key participant information is included in Table 8.1. This survey was one of the first to be carried out with the extensive cooperation of the Internet gambling industry. Gaming and betting operators representing over 100 online

*Table 8.1* Demographic characteristics of sample

|  |  | Casino (n = 7,342) | Poker (n = 5,461) |
|---|---|---|---|
| *Gender* | Males (%) | 45.2 | 74.5 |
|  | Females (%) | 54.8 | 25.5 |
| *Age* | under 18 | 0.1 | 0.2 |
|  | 18–25 (%) | 5.4 | 12 |
|  | 26–35 (%) | 19 | 26.9 |
|  | 36–45 (%) | 26.4 | 25.4 |
|  | 46–55 (%) | 29.5 | 20.8 |
|  | 56–65 (%) | 15.4 | 11 |
|  | Over 65 (%) | 4.2 | 3.7 |
| *Country of residence* | USA (%) | 68.1 | 55.3 |
|  | Canada (%) | 7.8 | 9.1 |
|  | UK (%) | 5.9 | 13.2 |
|  | Australia (%) | 1.8 | 2.3 |
|  | Other (%) | 16.4 | 20.1 |

gambling sites, reputable portals (i.e. information and news sites), and the media brought this survey to the attention of players in over 100 different countries. Financial information was collected and is presented in US dollars.

## Results

### General Internet gambling behaviour

INTERNET GAMBLING PREFERENCES

The most popular modes of Internet gambling included Internet slots ($n = 6,086$, 56.8 percent) and Internet poker ($n = 4,786$, 47 percent). As presented in Table 8.2, men and women differed in the extent to which they participated in modes of Internet gambling. Women were more likely to play games of chance such as slots and bingo, whereas men were more likely to play games of skill such as poker and sports betting.

INTERNET GAMBLING ENVIRONMENT

Some 89.7 percent of respondents claim that they gamble online most frequently at home, followed by playing at work (8.3 percent). All 'other' locations included at other peoples' houses, and public places such as universities, Internet cafés, libraries, and hotels. These combined represent the remaining 2 percent of the respondents. Significantly more women (9.1 percent of female respondents) reported playing at work than men (7.6 percent of male respondents), $x^2 = 32.4$, df $= 4$, p. $< 0.001$.

TIME OF PLAY

The majority of respondents reported playing in the evening ($n = 7,352$, 68.8 percent), with over half playing late at night ($n = 5,451$, 50.9 percent). Both men and women gave similar responses, with the most notable difference being that more than a third of women play in the morning compared to a quarter of men (see Table 8.3).

*Table 8.2* Participation rates and gender differences in modes of Internet gambling ($n = 10,719$)

|  | Women (%) | Men (%) | $x^2$ (df) |
|---|---|---|---|
| Video slots | 84.1 | 37.0 | 2,359.7 (1) |
| Video poker | 31.3 | 21.4 | 134.7 (1) |
| Sports betting and horse racing | 2.5 | 11.9 | 314.5(1) |
| Poker | 22.1 | 61.0 | 1,599.5 (1) |
| Blackjack | 14.0 | 20.7 | 81.3 (1) |
| Roulette | 5.1 | 8.8 | 54.8 (1) |
| Lottery | 10.3 | 7.4 | 28.1 (1) |
| Bingo | 21.1 | 5.8 | 568.6 (1) |
| Other games (e.g. backgammon, mahjong) | 8.2 | 4.1 | 81.9 (1) |

Note: All associations with gender are significant to at least p. $< .01$ level.

*Table 8.3* Time of play (*n* = 10,719)

|  | Women (%) | Men (%) | $x^2$ (df) |
|---|---|---|---|
| Morning | 37.6 | 25.9 | 168.8 (1)* |
| Lunchtime | 16.8 | 15 | 6.1 (1)* |
| Afternoon | 31.9 | 29.7 | 6.3 (1)* |
| Evening | 66.8 | 69.9 | 11.8 (1)** |
| Late night | 52.9 | 49.3 | 13.4 (1)** |

Notes: **p. < .01 level. *p. < .05 level.

## Internet poker

Internet poker players, based on modal class, were most likely to: be male (74.5 percent); aged 26–35 (26.9 percent); play two to three times per week (26.8 percent); have visited only one poker site in the preceding three months (24.1 percent); have played for two to three years (23.6 percent); play for between one and two hours per session (33.3 percent); play one table at a time (64 percent), and play at big blind levels (equivalent to minimum bets per hand of poker) of $0.50 to $2.00 (61.2 percent). Table 8.4 gives a complete summary of frequencies for these variables.

GENERAL PLAYER BEHAVIOUR AND GENDER DIFFERENCES

Men were more likely to play Internet poker (71 percent compared to 33 percent of women), $x^2$ = 1,412, df = 1, p. < 0.001. Men were also more likely to play more frequently, $x^2$ = 437.47, df = 7, p. < 0.001, as demonstrated in Table 8.5. Men (81.8 percent compared to 53.5 percent of women) were more likely to play either 2–3 times per day, daily, or 2–3 times per week. Men also reported playing for longer periods of time, $x^2$ = 221.85, df = 8, p. < 0.001. Women were more likely to play for less than an hour when compared to men. There were fewer differences between men and women over very long periods of time (over eight hours of play per session) as demonstrated in Table 8.5.

Men reported playing with a larger percentage of their bankroll[2] at any one table, $x^2$ = 79.99, df = 6, p. < 0.001. Most notably, females (20.1 percent of women compared to 10.8 percent of men) were more likely to play with less than 2 percent of their bankroll and males (54.6 percent of men compared to 44.6 percent of women) were more likely to play with between 6 and 40 percent of their bankroll. There were no significant differences between men and women playing more than 40 percent of their bankroll. Men were more likely to play at higher stakes (big blinds) tables than women, $x^2$ = 64.13, df = 10, p. < 0.001. Whilst women were most likely to play at either $0.20 or $0.50 blind levels, men were most likely to play $1.00, $2.00, $4, and $5 levels. In the higher stakes games, gender differences were considerably smaller. Whilst the 64 percent of respondents stated that they usually play at just one table, men were also more likely to play at more poker tables simultaneously, $x^2$ = 44.55, df = 6, p. < 0.001.

Table 8.4 Key player demographics and behaviours at a glance – Internet poker

| Gender (n = 5,415) | Female | Male |
|---|---|---|
| % | 25.5 | 74.5 |

| Age (n = 5,450) | 18–25 | 26–35 | 36–45 | 46–55 | 56–65 | over 65 |
|---|---|---|---|---|---|---|
| % | 12.1 | 26.9 | 25.5 | 20.8 | 11.0 | 3.7 |

| Number of poker websites played in the preceding 3 months (n = 5,028) | 1 | 2 | 3 | 4 | 5 | 6 | more than 6 |
|---|---|---|---|---|---|---|---|
| % | 24.1 | 24.0 | 20.1 | 11.3 | 6.1 | 2.2 | 12.2 |

| Frequency of sessions (n = 5,067) | 2–3 times a day | daily | 2–3 times a week | weekly | 2–3 times a month | monthly | 2–3 times a year | Annually |
|---|---|---|---|---|---|---|---|---|
| % | 25.6 | 22.3 | 26.8 | 7.0 | 7.3 | 6.8 | 3.2 | 1.0 |

| Started playing online (n = 5,059) | less than 3 months ago | 3–6 months ago | 6–12 months ago | 12–18 months ago | 18–24 months ago | 2–3 years ago | 4–5 years ago | more than 5 years ago |
|---|---|---|---|---|---|---|---|---|
| % | 5.4 | 8.7 | 16.5 | 16.6 | 15.8 | 23.6 | 8.1 | 5.2 |

| Average length of session (n = 5,051) | less than 15 minutes | 15–30 minutes | 30–60 minutes | 1–2 hours | 2–4 hours | 4–6 hours | 6–8 hours | 8–12 hours | more than 12 hours |
|---|---|---|---|---|---|---|---|---|---|
| % | 1.4 | 4.8 | 13.6 | 33.3 | 30.9 | 10.3 | 3.4 | 1.2 | 1.1 |

| Tables played simultaneously (n = 5,052) | 1 | 2 | 3 | 4 | 5 | 6 | more than 6 |
|---|---|---|---|---|---|---|---|
| % | 64 | 23.5 | 6.3 | 4.0 | 0.6 | 0.4 | 1.2 |

| Preferred stake levels (n = 4,534) | $0.20 | $0.50 | $1.00 | $2 | $4 | $5 | $10 | $20 | $50 | $100–200 |
|---|---|---|---|---|---|---|---|---|---|---|
| % | 17.8 | 24.0 | 16.5 | 20.8 | 7.8 | 7.3 | 2.8 | 1.1 | .8 | 1.2 |

*Table 8.5* Duration of sessions according to gender (% total frequency within gender)

|  | <15 mins | 15–30 mins | 30–60 mins | 1–2 hrs | 2–4 hrs | 4–6 hrs | 6–8 hrs | > 8 hrs |
|---|---|---|---|---|---|---|---|---|
| Male | 0.9 | 2.9 | 12.1 | 34.7 | 32.9 | 10.7 | 3.5 | 2.3 |
| Female | 3.4 | 10.7 | 18.1 | 29.4 | 24.1 | 9.1 | 3.1 | 2.2 |

### Internet casino

According to modal class, Internet casino gamblers were most likely to be female (54.8 percent); aged between 46 and 55 years (29.5 percent); play two to three times per week (37 percent); have visited more than six Internet casino sites in the preceding three months (25 percent); have played for two to three years (22.4 percent), on average play one to two hours per session (30.3 percent), and wager between $30 and $60 per session (18.1 percent). Table 8.6 gives a complete summary of frequencies for these variables.

#### WHAT PLAYERS WANT FROM AN INTERNET CASINO

The most important factors in determining choice of casino website were 'bonuses'[3] (with 77 percent endorsement from respondents); 'game variety' (62.1 percent); 'deposit method' (i.e. that it was easy and secure, 56.8 percent); 'has solid reputation' (56.8 percent); and 'promptness of payouts' (54.4 percent). The least important factors were 'financial statements'[4] (12.9 percent); 'sound effects' (10 percent); 'licensing deals', e.g. Hollywood-themed games (4.7 percent); and 'music' (4.5 percent).

#### FACTORS PREDICTING PREFERENCES FOR MODE OF INTERNET GAMBLING

Table 8.7 shows the findings from a logit equation detailing the impact of each independent variable on the likelihood of playing at Internet casinos only, Internet poker only, or playing both Internet poker and Internet casino.[5] Being female, older, or resident in Japan was positively related to playing only Internet casino games. Men, younger players, students, weekend players, or residents of Canada, the UK, Germany, or the Republic of Ireland were more likely to only play Internet poker. Men, younger players, and Danish residents were more likely to play both.

### Player protection, fair play, and disputes

#### RESPONSIBLE GAMBLING FEATURES

Across five responsible gambling features (limits on spending and time, self-exclusion, regular financial statements, and responsible gambling information) 51–75 percent of players reported that they would find these at least 'quite useful' (see Table 8.8). Participants were more likely to endorse the utility of responsible gambling strategies if they reported chasing losses, were under the age of 35, played casinos rather than poker, or were female.

Table 8.6 Key player demographics and behaviours at a glance – Internet casino

**Gender (n = 7,000)**

| Female | Male |
|---|---|
| 54.8 | 45.2 |

%

**Age (n = 7,337)**

| 18–25 | 26–35 | 36–45 | 46–55 | 56–65 | over 65 |
|---|---|---|---|---|---|
| 5.4 | 19.0 | 26.4 | 29.5 | 15.4 | 4.2 |

%

**Number of casino websites played in the preceding 3 months (n = 6,853)**

| 1 | 2 | 3 | 4 | 5 | 6 | more than 6 |
|---|---|---|---|---|---|---|
| 14.5 | 15.7 | 19.1 | 13.5 | 8.0 | 4.2 | 25.0 |

%

**Frequency of sessions (n = 6,906)**

| 2–3 times a day | daily | 2–3 times a week | weekly | 2–3 times a month | monthly | 2–3 times a year | Annually |
|---|---|---|---|---|---|---|---|
| 13.8 | 14.7 | 37.0 | 10.2 | 13.5 | 6.4 | 3.4 | .9 |

%

**Started playing online (n = 6,896)**

| less than 3 months ago | 3–6 months ago | 6–12 months ago | 12–18 months ago | 18–24 months ago | 2–3 years ago | 4–5 years ago | more than 5 years ago |
|---|---|---|---|---|---|---|---|
| 6.7 | 8.6 | 12.8 | 10.0 | 9.5 | 22.4 | 15.2 | 14.8 |

%

**Average length of session (n = 6,888)**

| less than 15 minutes | 15–30 minutes | 30–60 minutes | 1–2 hours | 2–4 hours | 4–6 hours | 6–8 hours | 8–12 hours | more than 12 hours |
|---|---|---|---|---|---|---|---|---|
| 1.4 | 7.0 | 18.3 | 30.3 | 26.5 | 10.1 | 3.4 | 1.4 | 1.5 |

%

**Average wagered per session (n = 6,772)**

| less than $10 | $10–$30 | $30–$60 | $60–$100 | $100–$200 | $200–$500 | $500–$1,000 | $1,000–$2,000 | $2,000–$5,000 | more than $5,000 |
|---|---|---|---|---|---|---|---|---|---|
| 12.0 | 16.5 | 18.1 | 17.8 | 15.3 | 10.5 | 4.7 | 2.4 | 1.7 | 1.1 |

%

*Table 8.7* Logit regression results – consumer preferences of mode of Internet gambling (marginal effects)

| Independent variable | dy/dx Plays casino only | Plays poker only | Plays poker and casino |
|---|---|---|---|
| Gender (1 = female) | 0.37* | −0.34* | −0.03* |
| Age | 0.06* | −0.04* | −0.03* |
| Unemployed | −0.03 | 0 | 0.03 |
| Student | −0.19* | 0.16* | 0.02 |
| Full-time parent | −0.04 | 0 | 0.04 |
| Retired | −0.05* | 0.03 | 0.02 |
| Weekend | −0.08* | 0.08* | 0 |
| Work | 0.02 | −0.04 | 0.02 |
| United States | −0.04* | 0.01 | 0.03 |
| Australia | −0.08 | 0.06 | 0.02 |
| Canada | −0.10* | 0.09* | 0.01 |
| China | −0.17 | −0.05 | 0.22 |
| UK | −0.17* | 0.20* | −0.03 |
| Germany | −0.01 | 0.14* | −0.13* |
| Japan | 0.37* | −0.16* | −0.21* |
| The Netherlands | 0.02 | −0.05 | 0.02 |
| Norway | −0.01 | −0.09 | 0.1 |
| Sweden | −0.11 | 0.12 | −0.01 |
| Denmark | −0.27* | 0.12 | 0.15* |
| Rep. Ireland | −0.23* | 0.45* | −0.22* |
| New Zealand | 0.05 | −0.03 | −0.02 |

Notes

dy/dx is for discrete change of dummy variable from 0 to 1.

* Denotes significance at the 0.01 level. It is also worth noting that results relating to country of residence should be treated with caution because of the small number of observations for some countries (e.g. Japan, $n = 15$).

*Table 8.8* Players' perception of the value of responsible gambling features

| Feature | Not at all useful (%) | Not very useful (%) | Quite useful (%) | Very useful (%) | Extremely useful (%) |
|---|---|---|---|---|---|
| Self-set spending limits ($n = 8,587$) | 11.2 | 18.4 | 40.1 | 18.1 | 12.2 |
| Self-set time limits ($n = 8,463$) | 18.9 | 30.9 | 32 | 11.7 | 6.6 |
| Self-exclusion ($n = 8,200$) | 16.4 | 26.2 | 34.8 | 12.7 | 9.9 |
| Regular financial statements ($n = 8,391$) | 9.1 | 15.7 | 42 | 20.2 | 12.9 |
| Self-assessment test ($n = 8,272$) | 14.3 | 23.3 | 38.2 | 15.4 | 8.8 |

More than a third of respondents claimed to have had a dispute at some point with an operator. Although there were no differences between men and women ($x^2 = .06$, df = 8, p. = .79), Internet casino players were more likely to have had a dispute (38.7 percent) compared to Internet poker players (29.7 percent), $x^2 = 64.9$, df = 1, p. < .0001. Just under half the respondents in this survey who reported having had a dispute said it had been resolved. The most common problems reported by players were experiencing an Internet disconnection or software malfunction during play (with only 10 percent and 19 percent respectively never experiencing these problems). Overall, only half of respondents felt that online gambling software was fair and random, and over a third of respondents thought there was an 'on/off switch that could turn the software in favour of the operator'. The need for raising awareness about regulation was emphasized by the fact that the most common response from players when asked how well they thought the industry was regulated was that they did not know.

Despite the lack of awareness among players regarding regulation, the majority of players consider third-party reports,[6] endorsements, and general vigilance regarding unfair play to be important. For example, 88 percent and 91 percent of respondents, respectively, rated reputable third-party reports on payout percentages and the randomness of software as at least 'somewhat important' to their overall confidence in outcome determination. Furthermore, 87 percent of players reported that, in an attempt to minimize the impact of cheating, they play on the 'biggest named' sites and watch out for any 'unusual behaviour'. Finally, when asked about the level of customer service offered in the Internet gambling industry, it was rated better than that of other industries (with 38.6 percent rating it as better compared to 13.6 percent rating it as worse).

## Top 10 'best things' about Internet gambling

This section was created based on answers from the open-ended question 'what is the best thing about gambling online' to which there were 6,654 respondents. Answers were thematically categorized and ranked according to frequency as detailed in Table 8.9. The majority of respondents (*n* = 3,925) reported that convenience and accessibility were the best things about Internet gambling. These respondents felt that having continual access, with no need to travel to Internet casinos or poker rooms and being able to commence or terminate

*Table 8.9* Top 10 'best things' about Internet gambling (*n* = 6,654)

| Rank | Reason | Responses |
|------|--------|-----------|
| 1 | Convenience and accessibility | 3,925 |
| 2 | Fun and excitement | 1,075 |
| 3 | Winning and financial reward | 893 |
| 4 | Anonymity and privacy | 427 |
| 5 | Relaxation | 329 |
| 6 | Better value and lower stakes | 186 |
| 7 | Relieves boredom | 157 |
| 8 | Speed | 153 |
| 9 | No need for staff | 148 |
| 10 | Variety (*games; blinds; players*) | 144 |

play in whatever way the players deem appropriate (with exceptions, e.g. poker tournaments) was the best thing about gambling online. Other aspects related to convenience and accessibility not making the top 10 included 'doing other things simultaneously' ($n = 112$), including smoking; consuming alcohol; playing in bed; playing while doing housework; playing while listening to your own preferred choice of music, etc. It was also reported that the Internet provides access to players who have or live with someone who has a disability or illness ($n = 52$).

Other popular draws of Internet gambling that were reported included 'fun and excitement' ($n = 1,075$) followed by 'winning and financial reward' ($n = 893$). It is interesting to note that winning ranks third behind 'convenience and accessibility' but more notably behind 'fun and excitement' (other motivational factors). Anonymity and privacy ($n = 427$) applied to: newer players concerned about learning how to play; avoiding crowds; not being judged or evaluated; and freedom to express themselves as they wish (e.g. swap gender; pray; laugh). This factor is also related to other reported benefits not making the top 10 including 'personal safety' ($n = 68$); 'lack of intimidation' ($n = 12$), and the fact that some 'tells and body language may be hidden' when playing poker ($n = 9$). Females were particularly attracted to the privacy and anonymity that the Internet affords.

Overall 'better value and availability of lower stakes' ($n = 186$) included the availability of lower stakes or free play, the absence of travel costs or tipping the dealer, and overall smaller margins (i.e. a higher return to player). There were also other positive aspects reported by players which did not make it into the top 10. Bonuses ($n = 111$) were considered to be an important benefit of Internet gambling, particularly as they were considered to be more generous online and with greater availability. Internet gambling was also favoured because it does not have a 'smoky environment' ($n = 102$); offers more 'social interaction' ($n = 76$); and allows players (new players in particular) greater opportunity to improve their game ($n = 39$) either through play-for-free, low stakes, or the general volume of practice one can get (particularly at skill games such as poker).

## Top 10 'worst things' about Internet gambling

This section was created based on answers from the open-ended question 'what is the worst thing about gambling online' to which there were 6,346 respondents (see Table 8.10). The most popular response ($n = 1,668$) was 'losing and negative financial implications'. This factor is also related to other perceived losses of playing online not making the top 10, such as 'not winning enough' ($n = 268$), 'electronic cash' (i.e. the value of money spent is devalued in a virtual environment, $n = 92$), and 'bad beats' (i.e. losing in statistically unlikely situations, $n = 76$).

The most common complaint related to 'payment issues' was the length of time taken to receive winning payouts and the ability to make a 'reverse withdrawal' (i.e. gambling with funds after making a request to withdraw it from the account). 'Cheating and low levels of trust' in the site or other players ($n = 646$) included issues surrounding whether the games were truly random, and whether pokerbots were being used. Despite topping the best things list, 'convenience and accessibility' ($n = 530$) were reported to present problems namely by facilitating players to spend more time and/or money than they can afford. 'Barriers to playing' ($n = 350$) was also identified as a drawback including legal issues such as prohibition or regulatory ambiguity.

*Table 8.10* Top 10 'worst things' about Internet gambling (*n* = 6,346)

| Rank | Reason | Responses |
| --- | --- | --- |
| 1 | Losing and negative financial implications | 1,668 |
| 2 | Payment issues (problems withdrawing or depositing money) | 1,075 |
| 3 | Concern regarding addiction and vulnerable populations | 781 |
| 4 | Cheating and low levels of trust | 646 |
| 5 | Convenience and accessibility | 530 |
| 6 | Barriers to playing (e.g. legal restrictions and ambiguities) | 350 |
| 7 | Technological problems (disconnection; spam; pop-ups; complex software) | 345 |
| 8 | Nothing (love it) | 295 |
| 9 | Other irritating people (ignorance; racism; use of bad language; slow players) | 159 |
| 10 | Poor customer service | 132 |

There were other negative aspects recorded by players which did not make it into the top 10. Losing time while playing or staying up late (*n* = 102) was a common response, as was Internet gambling lacking atmosphere or not being as engaging as gambling at a land-based casino (*n* = 86). Other aspects raised were lack of or misleading bonuses (*n* = 78), concern over security of personal information (*n* = 73), or the lack of regulation of Internet gambling (*n* = 64).

## Study 2 – focus groups

### Methodological approach

Fifteen focus groups were conducted across five countries: Canada, the USA, the UK, Sweden, and Germany. In total 94 participants took part. All focus groups were conducted in English language, and were audio recorded and transcribed verbatim. Of the 94 participants to take part in the focus groups, 12 were female and the remaining 82 were male. The mean age of each focus group ranged from 27 to 37 years.

Table 8.11 provides further participant details. Given the hard-to-reach nature of this particular population, and the limited resources available, a non-probability sampling approach was used.

*Table 8.11* Focus group composition – age, gender, and location

| Location | Total number of participants | Gender | Mean age | Age range |
| --- | --- | --- | --- | --- |
| Canada | 18 | 1 female, 17 males | 37.5 | 21–60 |
| Germany | 17 | 7 females, 10 males | 28.1 | 20–45 |
| Sweden | 25 | 4 females, 21 males | 32.8 | 17–60 |
| UK | 23 | 23 males | 27.2 | 18–43 |
| USA | 11 | 11 males | 31.6 | 19–56 |

**Results and discussion**

The main themes generated from the data have been summarized into brief sections below relating to motivation, consumer preferences, and their views on player protection. The findings reported here are abridged; therefore the most salient themes only are described below.

*Motivation*

The majority of participants cited their primary motivation for gambling on the Internet as 'entertainment' and generally viewed it as a leisure activity. One unexpected and interesting conclusion to be drawn was that Internet gamblers reported being willing to accept losses over the long term.

> 'For me its entertainment, because if I lost even over time I would still put money in. If I wouldn't get money out, I'll still be playing.' (Male, Canada)

While money was seen as important in creating excitement, it was generally accepted that generating long-term profit was unlikely. Although obviously preferred, profitable Internet poker play[7] was not critical to continued patronage at Internet poker sites. Participants reported that they were simply paying for their entertainment, with a chance that they might win some money back as a factor which added to the excitement. Many players felt that if they were not gambling on the Internet, they would likely be taking part in other recreational activities that they would have to pay for, with no chance of a return on their money. However, money was considered to be an important secondary motivator. Participants explained that without the possibility of winning money, Internet gambling would not hold the same entertainment value or cause the same level of excitement.

> 'playing for fun takes the fun out of it.' (Male, Canada)

*Site selection factors*

The most common determining factors in site choice were being 'large', 'well known', or recommended by friends. Such sites were often considered to be attached to a land-based sports book, or to have a strong presence in terms of advertising and endorsement.

> 'I just moved from the High Street,…then the Ladbrokes website, and I started gambling with their casinos…it's like a brand name.' (Male, UK)

Reliability of the website and its software was another salient factor described by participants. Players wanted minimal software 'glitches' or 'faults' especially during high stakes play, or at a time that may be construed as affecting the gambling outcome.

*Bonuses*

In contrast to the survey findings, the majority of focus group participants reported that this did not affect where they chose to play. However, there was a minority of players who said that they opened a number of accounts with different sites in order to take advantage of the best bonuses (some referring to themselves as 'bonus-hunters').

'I don't know if I've ever made a deposit without a bonus associated – either a sign up bonus or a deposit bonus.' (Male, Canada)

It was interesting to note that these players were most likely to have experienced disputes with websites, although this may be explained by the fact that they were likely to have used more sites than other participants exhibiting less interest in bonus acquisition.

### Portals

Contrary to survey findings, the majority of players in the focus groups reported either ignorance or indifference towards Internet gambling 'portals' (i.e. web communities, information sites, or forums dedicated to gambling and its various modes). Players that did use them were more likely to play Internet poker professionally or be self-proclaimed bonus-hunters at casinos. Based on focus group data, it may be important that portals be seen as 'independent' rather than working with, or being sponsored by, an Internet gambling operator.

'I think a lot of those sites, they have their own agenda in what room they want to promote.' (Male, USA)

A forum sponsored by a particular site may run the risk of being considered to provide partial information, reviews, and advice. Even if players' views are inaccurate, this needs to be made clear to avoid any ambiguity and reassure at least some portal users.

### Cheating

When discussing 'player-led' cheating, some participants' expressed the view that this is likely to be in the form of collusion or 'add-ons' (additional hardware or software used to improve performance – usually in relation to poker). There were mixed views regarding just how threatening this may be as some thought that an over-reliance on such a small amount of information may cause some players to overestimate their advantage while playing and neglect other available information. Most players reported that they did in fact trust the larger, more reputable sites and claim that 'operator-led' cheating was unlikely and not something that would normally cause concern.

'if you're found to be cheating then every single player would just go and no-one would ever trust them again, the whole industry would collapse, online gambling would probably collapse.' (Male, UK)

### Responsible gambling

The overwhelming majority of participants felt that the Internet gambling websites should only have limited accountability in ensuring players gambled responsibly. Participants reported that the responsibility should ultimately rest with the player. Some participants felt that excessive regulation may only frustrate players who may ultimately feel that their liberties have been infringed. This may be particularly true of players who have lost money, and then subsequently be informed that they have reached their limit and may no longer continue gambling. It could be the case that in such scenarios, players feel they are being prevented from winning their money back. Based on data collected in these focus groups, players preferred a 'light touch' approach whereby they may have the option to receive information or use responsible gambling features as a personal choice but not as a mandatory requirement. The possibility of a conflict of interest was raised, with some participants thinking it was not possible for operators to maximize commercial performance and social performance simultaneously. In contrast, other players expressed a different view, suggesting that honesty, transparency, and responsible provision would attract new players and retain existing players, improving long-term sustainability and increasing market share. An interesting concern expressed by some of the more experienced Internet poker players was that more effective player protection and responsible gambling features may limit spending among other weaker poker players, thereby 'cutting off their food chain':

> 'The players who have gambling problems are primarily the same as the one's who consistently make me money to help me pay my way through college. Responsible gambling is a good idea in theory, but if that theory became reality it would personally cost me a lot of money. Therefore I am unsure of my position on responsible online gambling.' (Male, USA)

*Preferences*

Interestingly, the characteristics of Internet gambling that participants tended to value most were often those that caused most concern – convenience and accessibility. On the one hand players placed enormous value on convenience, but some also felt that accessibility and convenience could lead to excessive involvement in terms of time and money. Anonymity and privacy were also considered to be a 'double-edged sword'; while players tended to enjoy the fact that the Internet allowed them to maintain their privacy, they disliked the lack of social interaction. This was particularly true of Internet poker players who enjoyed being able to express their own emotions about particular hands or events during the game to themselves, but disliked that they could not see other players' reactions (i.e. read non-verbal cues or 'tells') or receive social reinforcement from the rest of the table if they won.

**Conclusions**

Some of the findings of the focus group study highlight the important contribution that qualitative research can make in understanding the subtleties that often exist within this complex social behaviour. For example, financial motivation is often difficult to conceptualize and capture with an operational definition. Findings from the focus groups have helped delineate two different aspects of the relationship between money and Internet gambling motivation. The motivation to generate interest, distraction, or excitement, for which monetary risk is important, and for some, essential, is very different from the motivation to generate income or profit. This distinction is important and suggests that 'money' should not be grouped together as one dimension, or as one question in a survey. This also provides some support for the claim by industry executives that, for most consumers, Internet gambling is a bona fide leisure activity (to which some refer, in the Internet gambling industry, as 'moneytainment'). It was also interesting to note that the difficult philosophical and ethical questions associated with player protection is further complicated by the finding that for some players, for some modes of gambling (e.g. poker), preventing one player from losing money is preventing some players from winning money. Such subtle issues raise difficult questions about the merits of intervention and protection, and its real impact on consumer experience and appeal. As with any qualitative research the information derived is subjective and cannot be generalized to all Internet gamblers. However, information gathered from firsthand accounts does help develop a more detailed, nuanced understanding of the concerns, attitudes, and behaviours of Internet gamblers from a variety of jurisdictions.

## Discussion

Internet casino and Internet poker players responding to this survey represented a wide range of ages, backgrounds, levels of experience, and levels of involvement. Although this self-selected sample is not a representative sample, it does capture behaviours, attitudes and preferences of players across a full spectrum of important variables. Nevertheless, it would be incorrect to suggest that these demographic and behavioural data represent definitive profiles of Internet casino or poker players. There are, however, important conclusions to be drawn from these data that will contribute to a better overall understanding of Internet gambling behaviour. While there is not enough scope in this chapter to discuss all the key findings in detail, what follows is an overview of the more noteworthy issues and their implications.

### Internet gambling behaviour

A significant finding is that the vast majority of Internet gamblers have played with more than one gambling website in the three months preceding the survey, with 25 percent and 12 percent of Internet casino and poker players, respectively, reporting that they have played with at least six different operators in the preceding three months. This adds useful context to findings from Internet gambling research using player-tracked, account-based data. For example, pioneering research from the bwin.party Division on Addictions Research Collaborative concluded that the vast majority of their cohort had only a moderate level of involvement in each of the three main modes of Internet gambling: poker, casino, and sports betting (LaBrie, LaPlante, Nelson, Schumann, and Shaffer, 2007; LaBrie, Kaplan, LaPlante, Nelson, and Shaffer, 2008; LaPlante, Kleschinsky, LaBrie, Nelson, and Shaffer, 2009). Critically then, whether we are considering €3–4 of net expenditure per week for the whole sample, or substantially higher levels of net expenditure for the 'most involved' subgroups, it needs to be remembered that this represents only a portion of overall levels of money and time being spent. These net expenditure figures represent only one mode of gambling (e.g. poker) with only one Internet gambling provider (i.e. bwin). A critical question then is, 'how large a portion does this represent?'

The finding that Internet gamblers engage in a larger number of gambling activities is widespread (LaPlante, Nelson, LaBrie, and Shaffer, 2009; Vaughan Williams, Page, Parke, and Rigbye, 2008; Wood and Williams, 2009, 2011; and see Chapter 6). In one survey among adolescents, Internet gamblers reported engaging, on average, in around seven different types of gambling activities, the highest of any other type of gambling (Welte, Barnes, Tidwell, and Hoffman, 2009). So overall net expenditure on Internet gambling per individual could be considerably higher, if some of these players have numerous accounts, for numerous modes of gambling. Even then, for most players this will not necessarily equate to excessively large sums of money or long periods of time. But it is essential that this distinction and qualification is made when considering the implications of research using player-tracked, account-based data. Future research should build on this line of enquiry and examine the interaction between number of accounts held, reasons for combined use, account-switching behaviour, and correlates to such behaviour (e.g. problem gambling, gambling mode, and levels of involvement).

Gender characteristics in this study were only partially consistent with findings from other studies reporting that between 68 and 85 percent of Internet gamblers were male (Griffiths and Barnes, 2007; Wood and Williams, 2007, 2011; and see Chapter 6). Findings from this study indicated that only 58 percent of Internet gamblers were male. Specifically, 75 percent of poker players were men, and 55 percent of Internet casino players were women. The finding that Internet poker participation is predominantly male is well supported in the literature with figures ranging from 84 to 86 percent of Internet poker players being male (Hopley and Nicki, 2010; LaPlante et al., 2009; Wood, Griffiths, and Parke, 2007; Wood and Williams, 2011; and see Chapter 6). However, evidence on the relationship between gender and Internet casino participation is less well established. For example, some studies have concluded that Internet casino participation is heavily dominated by men. LaBrie et al. (2008) reported that 93 percent of their sample of Internet casino players was male. Other studies have found greater gender equivalence in participation levels. Woolley (2003), for example, found that women accounted for 50 percent of all members at one 'well-established' Internet casino. Wood and Williams (2011; and see Chapter 6) reported that two-thirds of Internet casino players were male.

A possible reason for the wide variation in these reported rates of gendered participation at Internet casinos relates to how games are conceptualized and organized for the purposes of commerce or research. *Internet casino* is a broad term which can account for several different types of games which can vary considerably in their design and structure. While the relationship between gender and mode of Internet gambling remains somewhat unclear, there is a growing body of literature highlighting why women may be more attracted to the Internet as a medium. Evidence from this research, and from other studies (e.g. Corney and Davis, 2010) have identified specific features such as privacy, anonymity, security, and a combination of attributes that make it a good place to learn and experiment (e.g. low stakes, free play, etc.). As a result of these factors, traditional gender stereotypes in gambling could be beginning to erode away after 30 years of inertia. Recent dissipation of gender differences has also been noted elsewhere (Corney and Davis, 2010; LaPlante, Nelson, LaBrie, and Shaffer, 2006).

### *Player protection, fair play, and disputes*

Gamblers as consumers may be suspicious given the nature of the products and services that they buy. This problem is heightened when gambling takes place online, as there is less evidence of the authenticity and fairness of gambling outcomes. Therefore, it should not be surprising that over a third of players have disputed at least one outcome or event in relation to Internet gambling. This may even occur in situations where the supply of the game and the transaction of money is fair and legitimate. For example, figures published by eCOGRA in 2007, showed that only 58 percent of disputes directed to them by players within a certain time frame were indeed valid. In many ways, this makes the gambling industry unique and perhaps more challenging than other industries. For example, with many other consumer transactions, objective judgments can be made post-purchase regarding the quality of the product which has been bought. This is not the case with Internet gambling.

There are two manifest challenges from these findings. First, players' concerns need to be addressed in a real way through developing and maintaining high industry standards in player protection and fair play. Second, and perhaps more crucially, better explanation, greater transparency, and more efficient communication is needed to provide players with information in order to be better informed, make better decisions (in terms of site selection and decision making during game play), and minimize mistrust and disputes, particularly in cases without any basis. The Internet gambling industry is trying to deal with disputes, many of which may be unfounded; for this reason greater clarity and improved communication can only improve the situation for all stakeholders.

Players reported a preference for responsible gambling features that facilitated their decision making rather than restricted their play. For example, financial statements were the most strongly endorsed tool, with time limits being rated as the least preferred option. Data from the focus groups confirmed this sentiment, with most participants preferring a light touch approach to player protection and suggesting that responsible gambling features should not be overly restrictive 'within-session' (i.e. when engaged in play, players would not want a time limit to prematurely terminate their session particularly if they were enjoying themselves or trying to win back losses). These findings reinforce those from other studies examining player preferences on player protection (Griffiths, Wood, and Parke, 2009). Obviously player preferences may not necessarily be correlated with actual effectiveness as a harm minimization technique. In other words, simply because some players do not want restrictive player protection features affecting their gambling, such restrictive intervention may still have an overall positive impact on their gambling experience, and on the social consequences more generally. We suggest that further research is carried out to explore the interface between player preferences, engagement of responsible gambling tools, and their overall effectiveness in preventing and reducing harm. There is also room for experimentation, at either the operational or regulatory level, to optimize the most efficient method of provision and enforcement. For example, operators and/or regulators could mandate that customers make regular decisions regarding limit-setting, but the size and nature of these limits remain at the player's discretion. There are of course numerous possibilities for optimization to meet players' preferences while minimizing risk and harm. Clearly, such research will be critical for long-term sustainability of the gambling industry, for which the cooperation and goodwill of the industry will be vital for its implementation and success.

### Internet as a medium – the pros and cons

A range of advantages and disadvantages of Internet gambling were identified by over 9,000 participants in the survey. Many of the advantages reported here have been identified in other research: for example, convenience and accessibility, avoiding the negative characteristics of offline venues, privacy and anonymity, better value, fun and excitement, variety, speed, optimal conditions for learning how to play, providing for players who are disabled or geographically immobile, and permitting players to multi-task when playing (Corney and Davis, 2010; Cotte and Latour, 2009; Griffiths and Barnes, 2007; Griffiths, Parke, Wood, and Rigbye, 2009; Wood and Williams, 2011; and see Chapter 6; Wood, Williams, and Lawton, 2007). Many of these had also been reiterated during the focus group study. These findings provide further confirmation that there are numerous advantages to using the Internet as a medium through which to gamble, and offer tangible justification for its growth and popularity.

Less well documented are the potential disadvantages of using the Internet as a medium. Some of the reported downsides were arguably predictable (e.g. losing money, losing time, cheating, etc.). However, financial loss, the most common concern, clearly applies to offline gambling as well. Based on the current research, it is unclear to what extent participants think this varies according to gambling medium. However, concerns about withdrawing and depositing money, technical problems such as disconnections and software malfunctions, and a potentially disinhibiting environment that may foster 'bad behaviour' clearly are medium-specific issues. These, and various other concerns, represent a new set of problems for gamblers that never existed before Internet gambling. While many of these issues may simply be teething pains that one would find with the introduction of other new forms of consumption or e-commerce, these findings lend weight to the call by Shaffer, Peller, LaPlante, Nelson, and LaBrie (2010) to treat Internet gambling as distinct from land-based gambling, particularly when making clinical, commercial, or policy decisions, until more research is done.

### *Limitations*

The findings from this research should be interpreted with caution given the inherent limitations, the most obvious of which is that self-selected samples (like the one used here), where participants make a decision whether or not to participate in a survey, are unlikely to be fully representative of all Internet gamblers. There are two reasons for this. First, those willing to take the time to respond to a survey may not be the same types of player as those who are unwilling. Second, not all players will have had an equal chance of being made aware of the survey. Specifically, in addition to players being e-mailed the survey link, it was also promoted on various portals. Players visiting portals may be more involved or more skilful than an average player (Hopley and Nicki, 2010). It should also be noted that these data refer only to casino and poker modes of Internet gambling. It could be true that perspectives on fair play may be different among sports bettors where outcome determination is more transparent and therefore less likely to invoke suspicion among players (e.g. a televised sporting event that players can see for themselves rather than a random number generator that they may neither understand or personally verify).

As noted previously, the data were collected in late 2006. Thus it is likely that behaviours, preferences, and attitudes will have changed since then. In the interim, operators and regulators have been working together to develop codes of conduct encouraging sites to adopt various player protection and responsible gambling protocols (e.g. the CEN Workshop Agreement 'CWA 16259: 2011'), and therefore player attitudes and experiences may have improved as a result of a better regulatory environment.

## Conclusion

Drawing useful and valid conclusions from data collected in 2006 is not a straightforward task given the fast-paced nature of an industry driven and defined by technological advancement. Nevertheless, while we invite cautious consideration of the data, we consider these findings to be useful for a variety of reasons. First, this survey contains information about Internet gambling behaviours, attitudes, and preferences some of which have not been replicated elsewhere. While the extent of the validity of these findings may be challenged given our methodological approach and/or when the data were collected, we feel that these findings make a significant contribution to our understanding of Internet gambling. At the very least, they serve as a benchmark to examine differences in findings from similar research using more recent datasets or findings from research using different methodologies. Second, some modest findings from this broad exploratory investigation can give considerable context to other research initiatives using different research methods with different objectives (e.g. research using player-tracked data).

## Acknowledgments

Thanks are extended to eCOGRA,[8] and Andrew Beveridge (CEO) for commissioning this research program at a time when stakeholders were in desperate need to understand more about this phenomenon. We would also like to thank 888.com, Microgaming, and bwin for their commitment in recruiting participants from their database of customers. Participants were also made aware of the survey through the cooperation of various reputable gaming portals including: Casino City; Casino Gold Pages; Casino Man; Casinomeister; Compatible Poker; Casino Winners Club; Gambling Online Magazine; Gambling Mountain; Games and Casino; Gone Gambling; Guide to the Best Casinos; Online Casino Conditions; Online Casino Reviewer; Betsage; Online Poker Rules; Practical Gambling; Refresh Poker; and Reviewed Casinos and we would like to extend our thanks for their involvement too. We would also like to acknowledge Dr Richard Wood, of GamRes Ltd, for coordinating focus groups in Germany and Sweden.

## Notes

1   Findings in relation to player protection, cognitive variables, and the focus group study are covered in more detail in academic papers currently under academic peer review or in preparation.

2   Bankroll refers to amount of funds ring-fenced for gambling. 'Good bankroll management', particularly in poker, is argued to involve risking a small proportion of such funds at any one poker table or on any one bet (Vorhaus, 2003; Angelo, 2007), especially in order to prolong the leisure value of the bankroll.

3   'Bonuses' are monetary or gift incentives for joining or playing at a site and are usually subject to various conditions and restrictions to prevent abuse.

4   'Financial statements' or account histories offer a summary of player transactions that should provide useful information such as deposits, withdrawals, and net expenditure.

5   Statistical note (and see Table 8.7): to predict the three combinations of gambling mode preferences, we used a multinomial logit response model. The individual choice between gaming modes is 'discrete', and choice is multinomial in the sense that gamblers can choose between several alternatives. In practice this means that we have an *unordered* response variable with more than two categories. These kinds of models are usually called multinomial models (logit and probit) in which the dependent variable is composed of a polytomous category having multiple choices. In this case, we wanted to model the potential influence of explanatory variables such as age, gender, country, and occupation. The model gives the probability that mode is chosen conditional on a set of explanatory variables. More precisely, we consider the case in which the dependent variable is a multinomial outcome equal to one if a gambler participates in 'Internet casino only' or in 'Internet poker only' or 'Internet poker and casino'. The main aim of this analysis is to identify the characteristics of individuals who exhibit such mode preferences. Note that in general, the interpretation of coefficient parameters is not as straightforward as in a linear model. Thus, it is important to calculate and present the marginal effects to all options that tell us the impact of a change in an independent variable on the dependent variable. The marginal effects are calculated with all interval or continuous variables set equal at the means of the independent variables and all dummy variables set equal to zero. For example, if the marginal effect of age is 0.06, this implies that increase in age by one unit (interval) on average increases the probability of an Internet casino only preference by 6 percent. Respectively, if the marginal effect of gender is 0.37, this implies that being female increases this probability by about 37 percent.

6   'Third-party reports' relate to independent verification and testing of the fairness and randomness of Internet gambling software.

7   Profitable long-term play is generally the focus of Internet poker play rather than Internet casino play.

8   eCOGRA (eCommerce and Online Gaming Regulation and Assurance) is the independent standards authority for the online gambling industry and is committed to protecting online casino and poker players around the world. The non-profit organization addresses important issues to

players: fast payouts, fair gaming, responsive and efficient service, and responsible operator conduct. For more information see www.ecogra.org.

# References

Angelo, T. (2007). *Elements of Poker*. Author.

Corney, R., and Davis, J. (2010). 'The attractions and risks of Internet gambling for women: A qualitative study'. *Journal of Gambling Issues, 24*. Retrieved from http://jgi.camh.net/doi/pdf/10.4309/jgi.2010.24.8

Cotte, J., and Latour, K. A. (2009). 'Blackjack in the kitchen: Understanding online versus casino gambling'. *Journal of Consumer Research, 35*(5), 742–58.

Griffiths, M. D. (1996). 'Gambling on the Internet: A brief note'. *Journal of Gambling Studies, 12*(4), 471–3.

— (1999). 'Gambling technologies: Prospects for problem gambling'. *Journal of Gambling Studies, 15*(3), 265–83.

— (2001). 'Internet gambling: Preliminary results of the first UK prevalence study'. *Journal of Gambling Issues, 5*. Retrieved from http://www.camh.net/egambling/issue5/research/griffiths_article.html

— (2003a). 'Internet abuse in the workplace: Issues and concerns for employers and employment counsellors'. *Journal of Employment Counselling, 40*(2), 87–96.

— (2003b). 'Internet gambling: Issues, concerns, and recommendations'. *CyberPsychology & Behavior, 6*(6), 557–68.

Griffiths, M., and Barnes, A. (2007). 'Internet gambling: An online empirical study among student gamblers'. *International Journal of Mental Health and Addiction, 6*(2), 194–204.

Griffiths, M., and Parke, J. (2002). 'The social impact of Internet gambling'. *Social Science Computer Review, 20*(3), 312–20.

Griffiths, M., Parke, A., Wood, R. T., and Parke, J. (2006). 'Internet gambling: An overview of psychosocial impacts'. *UNLV Gaming Research & Review Journal, 10*(1), 27–39.

Griffiths, M., Parke, J., Wood, R. T., and Rigbye, J. L. (2009). 'Online poker gambling in university students: Further findings from an online survey'. *International Journal of Mental Health and Addiction, 8*(1), 82–9.

Griffiths, M.D., Wood, R. T. A., and Parke, J. (2009). 'Social responsibility tools in online gambling: A survey of attitudes and behaviour among Internet gamblers'. *CyberPsychology & Behavior, 12*, 413–21.

Hopley, A. B., and Nicki, R. M. (2010). 'Predictive factors of excessive online poker playing'. *Cyberpsychology, Behaviour and Social Networking, 13*(4), 379–85.

Ialomiteanu, A., and Adlaf, E. (2002). 'Internet gambling among Ontario adults'. *Journal of Gambling Issues, 5*. Retrieved from http://www.camh.net/egambling/issue5/research/ialomiteanu_adlaf_article.html

King, S. A. (1999). 'Internet gambling and pornography: Illustrative examples of the psychological consequences of communication anarchy'. *CyberPsychology & Behavior, 2*(3), 175–93.

King, S. A., and Barak, A. (1999). 'Compulsive Internet gambling: A new form of an old clinical pathology'. *CyberPsychology & Behavior, 2*(5), 441–56.

LaBrie, R. A., Kaplan, S. A., LaPlante, D. A., Nelson, S. E., and Shaffer, H. J. (2008). 'Inside the virtual casino: A prospective longitudinal study of Internet casino gambling'. *European Journal of Public Health, 18*(4), 410–16.

LaBrie, R. A., LaPlante, D. A., Nelson, S. E., Schumann, A., and Shaffer, H. J. (2007). 'Assessing the playing field: A prospective longitudinal study of Internet sports gambling behavior'. *Journal of Gambling Studies, 23*(3), 347–62.

Ladd, G. T., and Petry, N. M. (2002). 'Disordered gambling among university-based medical and dental patients: A focus on Internet gambling'. *Psychology of Addictive Behaviors, 16*(1), 76–9.

Laffey, D. (2005). 'Entrepreneurship and innovation in the UK betting industry: The rise of person-to-person betting'. *European Management Journal, 23*(3), 351–9.

LaPlante, D. A., Kleschinsky, J. H., LaBrie, R. A., Nelson, S. E., and Shaffer, H. J. (2009). 'Sitting at the virtual poker table: A prospective epidemiological study of actual Internet poker gambling behavior'. *Computers in Human Behavior, 25*(3), 711–17.

LaPlante, D. A., Nelson, S. E., LaBrie, R. A., and Shaffer, H. J. (2006). 'Men and women playing games: Gender and gambling preferences of Iowa gambling treatment program participants'. *Journal of Gambling Studies, 22*(1), 65–80.

LaPlante, D. A., Nelson, S. E., LaBrie, R. A., and Shaffer, H. J. (2009). 'Disordered gambling, type of gambling and gambling involvement in the British Gambling Prevalence Survey 2007'. *European Journal of Public Health.* Advance online publication. doi:10.1093/eurpub/ckp177.

Shaffer, H. J. (1996). 'Understanding the means and objects of addiction: Technology, the Internet and gambling'. *Journal of Gambling Studies, 12*(4), 461–9.

Shaffer, H. J., Peller, A. J., LaPlante, D. A., Nelson, S. E., and LaBrie, R. A. (2010). 'Toward a paradigm shift in Internet gambling research: From opinion and self-report to actual behavior'. *Addiction Research & Theory, 18*(3), 270–83.

Smeaton, M., and Griffiths, M. (2004). 'Internet gambling and social responsibility: An exploratory study'. *CyberPsychology & Behavior, 7*(1), 49–57.

Vaughan Williams, L., Page, L., Parke, J., and Rigbye, J. L. (2008). *A Secondary Analysis of the British Gambling Prevalence Survey 2007.* Report prepared for the Gambling Commission, Great Britain.

Vorhaus, J. (2003). *Killer Poker Online: Crushing the Internet Game.* New York: Lyle Stuart.

Welte, J. W., Barnes, G. M., Tidwell, M. O., and Hoffman, J. H. (2009). 'The association of form of gambling with problem gambling among American youth'. *Psychology of Addictive Behaviours, 23*, 105–12.

Wood, R. T., and Williams, R. J. (2007). 'Problem gambling on the Internet: Implications for Internet gambling policy in North America'. *New Media & Society, 9*(3), 520–42.

— (2009). *Internet Gambling: Prevalence, Patterns, Problems, and Policy Options.* Final Report prepared for the Ontario Problem Gambling Research Centre, Guelph, Ontario. Retrieved January 5, 2009, from http://hdl.handle.net/10133/693

— (2011). 'A comparative profile of the Internet gambler: Demographic characteristics, game play patterns, and problem gambling status'. *New Media & Society.* Retrieved July 27, 2011, from http://nms.sagepub.com/content/early/2011/04/29/1461444810397650.full.pdf+html

Wood, R. T., Griffiths, M., and Parke, J. (2007). 'Acquisition, development, and maintenance of online poker playing in a student sample'. *CyberPsychology & Behavior, 10*(3), 354–61.

Wood, R. T., Williams, R. J., and Lawton, P. (2007). 'Why do Internet gamblers prefer online versus land-based venues?' *Journal of Gambling Issues*, 20 (June), 235–50. Retrieved from http://hdl.handle.net/10133/375

Woolley, R. (2003). 'Mapping Internet gambling: Emerging modes of online participation in wagering and sports betting'. *International Gambling Studies, 3*(1), 3–21.

# 9 The *bwin.party* Division on Addiction Research Collaborative

## Challenges for the 'normal science' of Internet gambling

*Debi A. LaPlante, Sarah E. Nelson,*
*Richard A. LaBrie, and Howard J. Shaffer*

## Introduction

According to Kuhn (1970), science develops through a series of identifiable but unpredictable phases: pre-paradigmatic, normal science, and revolutionary science. These phases apply across the spectrum of scientific inquiry, and are not limited to the most grand (e.g., the Copernican revolution) of scientific domains. These phases also apply to more narrow areas of interest, such as addictive behaviour, generally, and gambling, specifically (Gambino and Shaffer, 1979; Shaffer, 1986; Shaffer and Gambino, 1979). During a pre-paradigm phase, researchers debate models, theories, and methods. This period is characterized by conflicting ideas and dissent among researchers. When a field adopts a shared perspective about its central matters (i.e., a paradigm), an era of 'normal science' commences. During normal science, a central paradigm guides research theory and methods, while simultaneously blinding people to alternative viewpoints.

The science of Internet gambling, arguably, is in a period of 'normal science'. We qualify this statement with 'arguably' because distinguishing pre-paradigm science from the challenges that emerge during normal science is difficult. Both phases evidence periods of dissent among researchers, though normal science is less tumultuous. For the purposes of this discussion, we take the position that most researchers conducting scientific inquiries related to Internet gambling use common methods (i.e., the methodological trend is the use of self-reported behaviour) and share a common understanding of the likely impact of Internet gambling on individuals (i.e., the conceptual view is that objects stimulate addiction, and Internet gambling inherently is dangerous).

As is true for all scientific fields, during periods of normal science, researchers conduct their studies to solve important puzzles associated with a common paradigm. However, occasionally such puzzle-solving research yields information that is inconsistent with the prevailing methodological and conceptual paradigm. Such anomalies challenge paradigm-related consensus and require either resolution into the existing paradigm, or the commencement of a period of 'revolutionary science'. Such revolutions ultimately define a new methodological and conceptual paradigm and lead to a new period of normal science. The purpose of this chapter is to describe briefly some Internet gambling-related empirical challenges that an academic/industry partnership (i.e., the *bwin.party* Division on Addiction Research Collaborative) has created for the current period of normal science.

## Pre-paradigmatic science and speculation

The Internet was and continues to be one of the most important technological advances in history. In addition to economic, political, regulatory, and other attention, the Internet deserves scientific attention. Although not a direct source of information, the Internet comprises a growing host of computer links that provide a route by which computer users access information stored on remote computers. Via its web-like links, the Internet has opened the door to the development of a new social system that has widespread ramifications for existing social systems. The Internet already has changed several primary societal systems such as business interactions, the entertainment industry, marketing, and interpersonal communication. Its biggest impact, perhaps, is on information sharing. Individuals now have access to larger and more diverse amounts of information than ever before, and systems designed to prevent access to specific information are failing.

The abundance of easily accessible content is both a boon and a bane for the Internet linkage system. Users can access information that ranges from helpful (e.g., health-related resources) to harmful (e.g., child pornography). Furthermore, the linkage system itself, because of the speed and ease of information acquisition, has the potential to both (1) increase efficiency and knowledge, and (2) encourage short attention spans and wasted time. Although professional commentary focusing on the Internet and its many influences is extensive, empirical research noticeably is lacking and well-designed empirical research is scant. Consequently, it is difficult to say with confidence what specific impacts the Internet has on its users.

As use of the Internet expands to reach more and diverse population segments, the social system it generates evolves and gains strength. Some people even have compared Internet use to a developing culture, claiming that: 'Based on the information we have, we believe that computing is more than a set of skills. It is embedded in a social system consisting of shared values and norms, a special vocabulary and humor, status and prestige ordering, and differentiation of members from nonmembers. In short, it is a culture' (Kiesler and Sproull, 1985: 453). Although local cultures undoubtedly colour how individuals view and use the Internet, it follows that the Internet itself is allowing for the creation of a global culture of information sharing and communication that crosses geopolitical borders and boundaries.

Nonetheless, the reach of this new 'culture' is unknown. In addition to differences in access based on socio-economic status, aspects of the Internet's social system might make it more attractive to people with certain attributes rather than others. For example, in a survey of multiple college campuses across the Midwestern United States, Jones, Johnson-Yale, Millermaier, and Pérez (2009) found that 50 percent of men reported spending three or more hours online daily, compared to 33 percent of women. Another study found that students at a public university spent more time online than private university students, and that male college students at that public university tended to spend more time online (i.e., on average 6.89 hours/week) than women at that university (i.e., 3.93 hours/week). The researchers did not observe such a difference at the small private university (i.e., 2.9 hours/week and 2.19 hours/week, spent by male and female students, respectively) (Davis, Smith, Rodrigue, and Pulvers, 1999). Finally, a US Department of Education report found no gender usage differences among K-12 students, suggesting this gap might be generational (DeBell and Chapman, 2006). Hence, even among those who have easy access to the Internet, use varies widely and changes quickly.

For some, the notion of a global culture that crosses geopolitical boundaries is utopian; others have been alarmed at the unchecked rapid expansion of Internet-related technology. There are aspects of Internet-accessible information that potentially could contribute to dysfunctional Internet use. For example, interactive features of websites, distinct from face-to-face interactions, could generate a new experience of excitement. Chat rooms provide easy access to people who behave dysfunctionally but might appear normal – chatting with people who consistently shop compulsively, for instance, might influence perceptions of social norms, leading one to believe that shopping excessively is normal and common (LaRose, 2001). Similarly, direct email from websites might generate urges for potentially problematic behaviour at times when the urges normally might not occur (e.g., at work, late at night, etc.). Direct email might represent a new type of 'trigger' for unwanted, yet desired, behaviour. As we suggested earlier, the architecture of the Internet also might be conducive to problematic use. Specifically, the Internet allows for rapid transitions between sites that have linked content. The breadth of information and the rapid and varied access to this information create a range of risky consequences. For example, although difficulty in obtaining information or engaging in an activity traditionally might have promoted some discretion, easy access to information might promote unsystematic exploration, impulsive behaviour, and unanticipated urges to explore.

The potential risks associated with the Internet combined with an ever-increasing participation in the Internet have led a number of researchers to speculate about Internet addiction. There currently is no gold standard by which to distinguish Internet-addicted individuals from those who are frequent users of the Internet. Further, it remains to be determined whether people actually can get addicted to the Internet at all. For example, do individuals develop problems with their Internet experience (e.g., novelty, sensation seeking) or the content that becomes accessible via the Internet (e.g., gambling or pornography: Shaffer, Hall, and Vander Bilt, 2000)?

## The 'normal science' of Internet gambling

Like the Internet, researchers have raised concerns about Internet gambling and its consequences for the public health (Mitka, 2001). For instance, King and Barak noted, 'Internet gambling is characterized by unique factors that make it potentially addictive in a manner that is different from the way in which traditional gambling can be addictive' (King and Barak, 1999: 452). More recently, Kindt said, 'The ability to put a gambling or casino app on a smart phone would be a recipe for economic disaster. That would truly be a killer app, because the number of personal bankruptcies and people addicted to gambling would just absolutely soar' (Samuel, 2010). Concerns about Internet gambling, in part, are due to the observation that offline gambling is associated with a number of adverse physiological and psychosocial outcomes, such as co-occurring addictive behaviour, poor psychosocial functioning, and more (Korn and Shaffer, 1999).

Another reason for public health concern is that Internet gambling is one of the fastest growing gambling-related industries (Christian Capital Advisers, 2006; Horn, 2002). Although some contend its worldwide growth is smaller than land-based gambling (Miller, 2006), the industry is expected to continue to grow (Christian Capital Advisers, 2006). This is a concern because exposure to potentially harmful elements might contribute to poor public health (Shaffer, LaBrie, and LaPlante, 2004). As the Internet newly exposes more people to gambling, society's risk for developing gambling-related disorders might increase. Internet gambling represents a relatively new opportunity for exposure to gambling opportunities, and therefore, at least a temporary, pre-adaptation, risk for elevated gambling participation and gambling-related problems (LaPlante, Schumann, LaBrie, and Shaffer, 2008; LaPlante and Shaffer, 2007; Shaffer, LaBrie et al., 2004).

In addition, it has been argued that Internet gambling lacks a number of important fail-safes, such as the ability to protect underage and problem gamblers, and the potential for unprincipled marketing techniques, such as embedding (i.e., gaming sites using keywords like 'compulsive gambling' for search engines) and serial pop-ups (Griffiths and Parke, 2002). Similarly, observers have said that Internet gambling can do little to prevent gambling while intoxicated or gambling at work (Griffiths, 1999). Twenty-four-hour easy access to gambling also might provide an outlet for urges that otherwise would go unfulfilled.

As LaPlante and Braverman (2010) reviewed, estimates of Internet gambling prevalence among the general population do not support the notion that Internet gambling currently is widespread. For example, major published general population prevalence studies show that few people report experience with Internet gambling. Specifically, the British Gambling Prevalence Survey (BGPS) reported that between September 2006 and March 2007 about 6 percent of participants reported gambling via the Internet during the past year (Griffiths, Wardle, Orford, Sproston, and Erens, 2009; LaPlante, Nelson, LaBrie, and Shaffer, 2009). A United States (US) study reported that about 2 percent of a nationally representative sample of individuals 14–21 years old who participated in a survey between August 2005 and January 2007 reported gambling via the Internet during the past year (Welte, Barnes, Tidwell, and Hoffman, 2009). Another US study of the general adult population, that took place between February 2001 and April 2003, found that 1 percent of gamblers reported Internet gambling (Kessler et al., 2008).

With respect to gambling-related problems, general population surveys have indicated that individuals who report participating in Internet gambling are at increased risk for gambling-related problems. For example, the BGPS suggested that only 0.3 percent of the full population met the Diagnostic and Statistical Manual of Mental Disorders (DSM-IV; American Psychiatric Association, 2000) criteria for past-year pathological gambling, but about 5 percent of individuals who reported gambling via the Internet during the past year met these diagnostic criteria (Griffiths et al., 2009; LaPlante, Nelson et al., 2009). Similarly, a Canadian study reporting data from population-based surveys conducted in Canada between 2001 and 2005 reported elevated rates of problems among individuals who preferred Internet gambling compared with other types of gambling (Holtgraves, 2009). A Norwegian survey conducted between January and March 2007 observed that 0.3 percent of the general population met criteria for past-year pathological gambling; those who met these criteria ranked Internet gambling as one of the top two most important gambling types (Bakken, Gotestam, Grawe, Wenzel, and Oren, 2009). A US study found that whereas 1 percent of gamblers reported Internet gambling, 7.5 percent of individuals who had gambling-related problems reported Internet gambling (Kessler et al., 2008).

Finally, research related to Internet gambling among special populations has produced widely varying results. This variability is most evident, perhaps, among studies involving college student samples. In our sample, 97.4 percent of college students from a 2001 US survey of a nationally representative sample reported never having gambled using the Internet (LaBrie, Shaffer, LaPlante, and Wechsler, 2003). More recent studies reporting findings from convenience samples indicate higher rates of participation (i.e., 10 percent and 23 percent, Kerber, 2005; Petry and Weinstock, 2007). Using convenience samples, studies of medical treatment seekers similarly have shown moderate lifetime involvement with Internet gambling (i.e., 8.1 percent and 6.9 percent), but high rates of gambling-related problems among individuals who report such lifetime experience (Ladd and Petry, 2002; Petry, 2006). Other convenience samples, such as samples of gamblers recruited through online sites associated with gambling websites, or other means, often report even higher rates of gambling-related problems for their samples (e.g., Matthews, Farnsworth, and Griffiths, 2009; McBride and Derevensky, 2009; Wood, Griffiths, and Parke, 2007; Wood and Williams, 2007).

Unfortunately, most of the early research focusing on the prevalence of Internet gambling and disordered Internet gambling is not necessarily representative of the population at large or the subgroups of the general population to which they should generalize. Furthermore, the empirical data collected were self-reported: the guiding methodological approach for this period is the use of recalled data. Though relatively valid for basic prevalence estimates, self-report data are vulnerable to a variety of biases that limit their usefulness for inferring causality or temporal sequence, including faulty memory, self-deception, other deception (e.g., impression management), and simple reporting errors. Nonetheless, these studies ushered in the current period of 'normal science' for Internet gambling research. The guiding conceptual view for this period includes the assumption that Internet gambling is an especially dangerous form of gambling predominantly characterized by excess.

## Challenges for the normal science of Internet gambling: the *bwin.party* Division on Addiction Research Collaborative

Public awareness of tobacco industry and pharmaceutical industry data tampering and/or suppression likely has contributed to a general uneasiness about industry and academia working together. Although industry and academic goals often are unique and disparate, these objectives do not discount a productive and informative working relationship. For such a relationship to be successful, several safeguards are necessary. The relationship must assure academic freedom to maintain scientific independence. Also, industry partners must recognize that the commitment to utilizing science as a guide to best business practices is not one that typically will yield short-term accomplishments, as defined by industry interests. Such short-term goal products might more likely emerge from consultancy relationships, but not scientific partners. This means that, at a very basic level, the pace of science is very different from the pace of industry. Although the pace of science often is slower than the pace of development that industry typically employs, the long-term public health benefits of a science-based approach outweigh those gleaned from short-term approaches.

Manfred Bodner, who was the co-founder of *betandwin.com* before the company became *bwin* (today it is *bwin.party*), initiated a meeting with the faculty and staff of the Division on Addiction to discuss his interest in establishing a scientific foundation upon which he could build *bwin*'s corporate social responsibility policies and practices. The Division faculty initially was reluctant to meet because of conventional views suggesting Internet gambling was a risky and adverse technology. Based upon his experience and expertise in e-commerce, Bodner proposed to Division faculty a research collaborative that would examine the actual gambling behaviour of *bwin* subscribers. From there, together we developed a goal for this scientific activity: to develop algorithms that could identify patterns of disordered gambling. We recognized that the Internet should provide a safer context within which to gamble or conduct other e-commerce because the behaviour of consumers could be carefully monitored and any aberrations from patterns of normal behaviour could be technologically identified. During this initial meeting, we agreed that once we could reliably identify patterns of disordered gambling, we should be able to prevent the progression to more adverse states by identifying patterns that were associated with the transformation from recreational to disordered gambling.

Ultimately, this Boston meeting yielded a research collaborative between *bwin* and the Division on Addiction that has broad and sweeping goals. These objectives include (1) developing evidence-based algorithms that reliably identify disordered Internet gambling and (2) identifying patterns of Internet gambling behaviour that predict the development of disordered gambling. The ultimate objective that emerged from the Boston meeting and the early days of this collaboration was to identify predictors of gambling disorders and develop interventions that successfully could interrupt the transition from gambling to disordered gambling.

Cooperation from the Internet gambling industry is essential to establish a meaningful and comprehensive understanding of Internet gambling-related problems. Worldwide, we are not aware of any researchers who have published research related to the link between actual Internet gambling behaviour and clinical difficulties (i.e., studied the association between specific Internet gambling patterns and psychopathology). The absence of research about this link creates a critical and large gap in society's understanding of Internet gambling. None of the early Internet gambling research can illuminate whether specific patterns of Internet gambling behaviour are particularly problematic and/or represent clinically defined levels of a gambling-related disorder. As mentioned previously, limitations of sampling representativeness and self-report preclude such an achievement. Realizing this goal requires cooperation between the Internet gambling industry and academia. Such cooperation provides the opportunity for objective interpretation of comprehensive population-level records of Internet gambling behaviour matched to traditional assessments of gambling-related disorder.

## Empirical challenges for normal science: a new epidemiology of Internet gambling

A primary goal of our scientific activity has been to develop research questions (e.g., what are the distribution and determinants of actual Internet gambling?) and publish peer-reviewed scholarly and scientific papers that make use of the retrieved electronic records of *bwin* subscriber gambling activity. To accomplish this goal, we initially focused on the preparation of three epidemiological descriptions of the main betting activities at *bwin* (i.e., sports betting, casino gaming, and poker playing). These analyses resulted in three publications (LaBrie, Kaplan, LaPlante, Nelson, and Shaffer, 2008; LaBrie, LaPlante, Nelson, Schumann, and Shaffer, 2007; LaPlante, Kleschinsky, LaBrie, Nelson, and Shaffer, 2009). During 2007, the Division on Addiction published the first epidemiological analyses of actual Internet sports gambling behaviour (LaBrie et al., 2007). This study's findings, enabled by a methodological shift from data recall (i.e., self-report) to retrieval (i.e., comprehensive records of actual Internet gambling activity), provided the first critical challenges to the prevailing 'normal science' of Internet gambling.

### *The nature of online sportsbook gambling (LaBrie et al., 2007)*

The first published account of actual Internet gambling subscriber activity included an analysis of eight months of the fixed odds bets on the outcome of sporting contests and live action bets on the outcome of events within sporting contests for 40,499 Internet sports gambling service subscribers. The sample includes all individuals who subscribed to *bwin* from February 1 through February 27, 2005, with the following exclusions: (1) individuals who did not first bet with their own money until less than one month before the end of the study period (2 percent) and (2) individuals who never bet on sporting events (< 3 percent).

*Cohort characteristics*

The information we had available included a few demographic characteristics. The overwhelming majority of subscribers were males in their early thirties. Most of the cohort reported that they were from Germany, Greece, Poland, Spain, or Turkey. Other prevalent countries included France, Austria, Denmark, Italy, and Switzerland. People from 75 other countries accounted for 4 percent of the cohort.

*Cohort gambling behaviour*

Fixed odds betting events are relatively slow cycling propositions on the outcomes of games, whereas live action betting provides the opportunity for quick-paced betting on events within games, such as who will get the next corner kick. In the analytic sample, 15,705 bet on fixed odds only, 780 on live action only, and 24,014 bet on both types. Our analyses determined that the actual betting behaviour of our sample of Internet gambling subscribers was very different from what conventional wisdom related to Internet gambling would suggest. For instance, during the eight-month study, the median behaviour of the members of our sample was to complete less than 40 fixed odds bets and less than 20 live action bets. Members of our sample tended to be active bettors for about half (i.e., four months) of the study period. We determined that all the betting variability we observed was skewed heavily toward smaller values, indicating that whereas the majority of our sample gambled moderately, some of the sample exhibited relatively more extreme betting behaviour. Table 9.1 displays the median betting activity for our sample on a variety of variables.

Notably, we observed somewhat rational betting behaviour among the full sample. For instance, individuals seemed to moderate their gambling based on their losses. As percent lost increased, duration, number of bets, bets per day, euros per bet, and total wagers all decreased. Losing seemed to discourage ongoing gambling. At the population level, individuals did not seem to chase their losses. Alternative explanations are that financial limitations, caused by losing, precluded ongoing gambling online or that those cases with only one or two bets disproportionately influence the percent loss (i.e., participants who made few bets might tend to have large percent losses with limited involvement).

*Table 9.1* Median gambling behaviour of fixed odds and live action bettors

| Measure | Fixed odds (n = 39,719) | Live action (n = 24,794) |
|---|---|---|
| Duration (in days, out of 240 possible days) | 116 | 40 |
| Frequency (%) | 23 | 27 |
| Number of bets | 36 | 15 |
| Bets/day | 2.5 | 2.8 |
| Euros/bet | 4 | 4 |
| Total wagered (Euros) | 148 | 61 |
| Net loss (euros) | 33 | 9 |
| % Lost | 29 | 18 |

Notes
Duration = interval in days between first and last bet; Frequency = percent of days within duration when a bet was placed; Net loss = total wagers minus total winnings; % Lost = net loss divided by total wagered. The fixed odds and live action groups were not independent.

*Heavily involved bettors*

The preponderance of public statements claiming that Internet gambling would yield unmanageably high levels of betting activity in any sample of Internet gamblers led us to suspect that we would observe such activity among our sample. So, our observation of modest population-level gambling activity generated some concern for the possibility that we had generated an incomplete or biased description of Internet gambling activity among our sample (perhaps due to a preponderance of fan betting). To test this assumption we examined centile plots of each of our variables of interest to determine whether some of our sample evidenced discontinuously high values. We determined that we could reasonably isolate groups of 'top 1 percent bettors', who 'spent' the most money and made the most bets. These groups of individuals do not directly translate into groups of individuals who have gambling-related problems, but are of scientific interest for establishing a complete epidemiological description of gamblers at potentially greater risk for disordered behaviour. As expected, many of the values for these groups were more extreme than the rest of the sample; however, the top 1 percent subgroups shared important features that characterized the complete sample as behaving rationally. Compulsive or immoderate gambling would anticipate a positive relationship between amount wagered and percent lost. However, the top 1 percent of the sample on amount wagered evidenced lower percent losses than the rest of the sample and the other top 1 percent groups. This is an example of how more extremely involved bettors share characteristics of the full sample, such as moderation of gambling following losses. Table 9.2 displays the median gambling activity for three top 1 percent groups on a variety of variables to illustrate the extent of gambling involvement among some *bwin* participants.

### The nature of online casino gambling (LaBrie et al., 2008)

Our second published account of actual Internet gambling subscriber activity analysed two years of casino games betting activity among 4,222 subscribers who opened a betting account during February 2005 and played casino games. The population of subscribers from which we created our sample included 48,114 people; however, only 8,472 ever played a casino game. To provide an epidemiology of those subscribers who were engaged casino players,

*Table 9.2* Median gambling behaviour of top 1 percent groups by betting activity

| Measure | Top 1% on net loss | | Top 1% on total wagered | | Top 1% on number of bets | |
|---|---|---|---|---|---|---|
| | *Fixed odds* | *Live action* | *Fixed odds* | *Live action* | *Fixed odds* | *Live action* |
| Duration (240 possible days) | 215 | 213 | 217 | 209 | 220 | 217 |
| Frequency (%) | 42 | 49 | 48 | 56 | 57 | 65 |
| Number of bets | 423 | 973 | 423 | 1,034 | 2,371 | 2,150 |
| Bets/day | 5.4 | 11.3 | 4.7 | 10.7 | 26.4 | 18.5 |
| Euros/bet | 23 | 34 | 44 | 53 | 1 | 6 |
| Total wagered (euros) | 10,259 | 29,144 | 16,784 | 44,111 | 4,144 | 15,743 |
| Net loss (euros) | 2,645 | 3,052 | 1,544 | 1,973 | 740 | 1,111 |
| % Lost | 29 | 12 | 9 | 4 | 18 | 7 |

Notes
Fixed odds *n* = 397; Live action *n* = 247.

we eliminated those who played fewer than four days during the two-year study period, those who did not play casino games until the last month of the study period, and those who only played casino games with promotional money, rather than their own.

Many researchers have argued that the structure of casino-type games makes these games especially likely to stimulate, or at least be associated with, excessive gambling behaviour (Griffiths, 1993; LaPlante, Nelson et al., 2009; Welte et al., 2009). Consequently, we expected that our epidemiological analyses of casino games gambling would reveal much greater betting activity, compared with our epidemiological analyses of sportsbook gambling. Because the casino games analyses include data representing two years of betting and the sportsbook analyses only the first eight months of betting data, some measures (i.e., Duration) are dissimilar.

*Cohort characteristics*

As with the sportsbook cohort, we determined that our sample of casino games bettors were mainly males in their early thirties. Most of the cohort hailed from Germany, Austria, Greece, Spain, France, Denmark, Italy, Turkey, and Poland. The remaining 10 percent of the sample originated from 37 different countries.

*Cohort gambling behaviour*

We analysed 14.8 million bets, which amounted to 114.7 million euros risked, and losses of 3.5 million euros. We determined that casino game betting was less active than we anticipated. For instance, during the two-year study, individuals typically bet on casino games for 18 days of their active period; that is, 7 percent of the days from their first casino bet to their last recorded casino bet (i.e., 261 days for participants with median durations). On each of those days, we estimated that subscribers lost about 6.5 euros. Like the sportsbook sample, we observed that losses moderated gambling behaviour (i.e., losses were associated with reductions in gambling activity). Bad luck appeared to be a disincentive for gambling. Interestingly, we also observed that gambling duration and gambling frequency had a negative relationship. This relationship suggests two styles of play existed for the sample: playing on more days during a shorter total play period, or playing less frequently, but for a longer time. Table 9.3 displays the median gambling behaviour of casino games bettors.

*Table 9.3* Median gambling behaviour of casino games bettors (*n* = 4,222)

| Measure | Median |
| --- | --- |
| Duration (in days, out of 720 possible days) | 261 |
| Frequency (%) | 7 |
| Number of bets | 532 |
| Bets per day | 49 |
| Euros per bet | 4 |
| Total wagered (euros) | 2,603 |
| Net loss (euros) | 117 |
| % Lost | 5.5 |

Notes
Duration = interval in days between first and last bet; Frequency = percent of days within duration when a bet was placed; Net loss = total wagers minus total winnings; % Lost = net loss divided by total wagered.

*Heavily involved bettors*

The betting activity variables we examined were markedly skewed toward smaller values. This suggested that whereas the majority of our sample gambled moderately, some of the sample exhibited more extreme betting behaviour. We determined by examining centile plots of our variables of interest that we reliably could isolate a group of 'top 5 percent' bettors, who 'spent' the most money: those who were highest on the total wagered variable. Evidence of discontinuity occurred at the 95th centile, rather than 99th, as it did for the sportsbook sample. These extreme bettors generated lower percent losses than the full sample. However, they bet more during their active period (i.e., about 106 versus 18 days); on each of those days, subscribers lost about 63 euros. Table 9.4 displays the median gambling activity for the top 5 percent group on a variety of variables.

## The nature of online poker gambling (LaPlante et al., 2009)

Our third published account of actual Internet gambling subscriber activity analysed two years of the daily records of poker play by session. During this study period, *bwin* poker players bought and cashed chips at the beginning and end of each session. The available *bwin* records of activity did not include information about the specific hands of poker. Our information included values in euros for chips purchased and chips cashed (if any) for each session for 3,445 individuals who subscribed to *bwin*.com during February 2005 and played poker with more than a passing interest. We excluded individuals who bet on fewer than four poker sessions, and those who did not begin gambling on poker until the last month of the study period. As with the other samples, we did this to ensure that our sample did not provide inaccurately low estimates of poker gambling because of the inclusion of individuals who only played poker with minimal interest. Because poker gambling, like sportsbook gambling, is a chance game that attempts to incorporate a measure of skill, we anticipated that the epidemiology of poker gambling would resemble what we observed for sportsbook gambling records.

*Cohort characteristics*

People who played poker were mostly male and in their late twenties. The majority of poker players were from Denmark, Germany, France, Austria, and Spain. Other countries with meaningful representation included Turkey, Italy, Greece, Poland, Norway, Switzerland, Sweden, and Portugal. The remaining 33 countries accounted for 4.2 percent of our sample.

*Table 9.4* Median gambling behaviour of top 5 percent group of casino games bettors ($n = 212$)

| Measure | Median |
| --- | --- |
| Duration (in days, out of 720 possible days) | 529 |
| Frequency (%) | 20 |
| Number of bets | 10,465 |
| Bets per day | 188 |
| Euros per bet | 25 |
| Total wagered (euros) | 233,195 |
| Net loss (euros | 6,698 |
| % Lost | 2.5 |

Notes
Duration = interval in days between first and last bet; Net Loss = total wagers minus total winnings; % Lost = net loss divided by total wagered.

*Cohort gambling behaviour*

Poker betting was slightly more active than sportsbook or casino games betting. Specifically, poker bettors had an active duration of more than six months, and during that time, played poker about one session every three days. People who played poker for a longer time tended to play fewer sessions, and individuals who lost larger proportions of their wagers tended to have shorter durations of involvement and played fewer poker sessions when they were involved. Table 9.5 displays the poker activity of the sample for a variety of variables.

*Heavily Involved Bettors*

We again observed that our variables of interest were heavily skewed toward smaller values, indicating that although the majority of the sample was in line with the general sample description, a portion of the sample were more extreme in their poker activity. We determined by examining centile plots of our variables of interest that we reliably could isolate a group of 'top 5 percent' bettors, who 'spent' the most money: those who were highest on total wagered. Evidence of discontinuity occurred at the 95th centile, as it did for the casino games sample. In contrast to the full sample, these players were active for about 18.5 months and participated in about 1.5 sessions per day during their active period. Their wagering was at least 75 times more than the full sample, but the percent lost they experienced was lower. Table 9.6 displays the median poker betting behaviour of this top 5 percent group, defined by the total they wagered.

*Table 9.5* Median gambling behaviour of poker bettors (*n* = 3,445)

| Measure | Median |
| --- | --- |
| Duration (in days, out of 720 possible days) | 196 |
| Total sessions | 60 |
| Sessions/day | 0.6 |
| Euros/session | 13 |
| Total wagered (euros) | 807 |
| Net loss (euros) | 106 |
| % Lost | 20 |

Notes
Duration = interval in days between first and last bet; Net loss = total wagers minus total winnings; % Lost = net loss divided by total wagered.

*Table 9.6* Median gambling behaviour of top 5 percent group of poker bettors (*n* = 173)

| Measure | Median |
| --- | --- |
| Duration (in days, out of 720 possible days) | 565 |
| Total sessions | 818 |
| Sessions/day | 1.6 |
| Euros/session | 89 |
| Total wagered (euros) | 55,012 |
| Net loss (euros) | 1,941 |
| % Lost | 3 |

Notes
Duration = interval in days between first and last bet; Net loss = total wagers minus total winnings; % Lost = net loss divided by total wagered.

### Building on the foundation of actual Internet gambling

To date, these studies provide the first and only epidemiological descriptions of actual Internet gambling behaviour. By showing moderate levels of gambling-related activity, this body of research diverges significantly from what the prevailing conceptual paradigm was suggesting about Internet gambling. Nevertheless, these studies are not without limitations, and a full discussion is available in the original articles. To illustrate, future work can advance this area in two very important ways. First, a multi-company dataset would allow researchers to determine the frequency and impact of actual multi-site Internet gambling. The aforementioned studies are restricted to a single website, and therefore cross-site activity, as well as the generalizability beyond that website, is unknown. Second, to date, researchers have not been able to link independent clinical outcomes with actual Internet gambling behaviour. Consequently, although we might hypothesize that groups, such as the gamblers at the extreme end of distributions (e.g., heavily involved bettors), might be likely to contain a large number of individuals who have gambling-related problems, at this time, it is impossible to draw this conclusion with any certainty. Nevertheless, the need to identify people who already have gambling-related problems, or who are at risk for the development of such problems, is a priority and such information is essential to do so. A first step toward the identification of developing gambling problems among Internet gamblers is empirically to locate behavioural markers of potential gambling-related problems. As we discuss in the next section, preliminary research of the *bwin.party* Division on Addiction Research Collaborative has begun to establish the possibility of accomplishing this goal.

## The Potential of a new normal science: behavioural markers for Internet gambling disorder

The Internet holds the potential to help as well as harm. The very aspects of the Internet that raise concern (e.g., tracking of individual behaviour, 24/7 accessibility) also can be leveraged to prevent and reduce potential harms. In addition to advancing science related to Internet gambling, creating evidence-based responsible gambling resources, and educating the public about gambling and gambling-related problems, one of the overarching goals of the Collaborative is the development of *evidence-based* predictive algorithms for the detection of both the future development of gambling-related problems, and the identification of individuals who already have gambling-related problems. To date, we have published three papers about actual predictive markers of potential gambling-related problems (Braverman and Shaffer, 2010; LaBrie and Shaffer, 2011; Xuan and Shaffer, 2009); as this chapter goes to press, these represent the only papers on this topic of which we are aware.

Nevertheless, as we editorialized in the *Brief Addiction Science Information Source* (Shaffer, LaPlante, LaBrie, and Nelson, 2007), land-based and online gaming companies are racing to create algorithms that will identify people who are at risk for developing problematic gambling behaviour. Unfortunately, supporters of this effort are nowhere near the finish line for that race; perhaps worse, the competitors are quite possibly off-track.

There is so little available empirical information about Internet gambling behaviour and characteristics of problematic Internet gambling that early efforts to develop psychometrically accurate algorithms are at high risk for error. For example, researchers cannot say with the confidence that derives from empirical evidence that any of the leading candidates for identifying land-based characteristics of problematic gambling behaviour also apply to online gambling behaviour. The nature of Internet gambling is sufficiently distinct from land-based opportunities to suggest that although some factors might generalize fairly well, others will not, and still others unique to Internet gambling remain to be determined. We do not know yet if there are unique risk factors associated with Internet gambling.

Public information about land-based identification algorithms is limited. In one exception, the Saskatchewan Gaming Corporation (SGC) published information in a peer-reviewed journal about their algorithm-guided identification system (iCare) to identify at-risk gamblers (Davies, 2007); they also presented related peer-reviewed findings at international conferences. Though their system is preliminary, an evidence-based research plan that integrates algorithm development with diagnostic interviews of SGC patrons has guided its initial development. This approach gives SGC some confidence that its multivariable identification algorithm maintains at least a minimum level of clinical useful specificity and sensitivity.

Unlike the SGC, the development strategy for online identification algorithms, such as PlayScan, is not publicly available. Unless the development of PlayScan followed procedures similar to those used by SGC, the sensitivity (i.e., likelihood of accurate identification of individuals who have a problem), specificity (i.e., likelihood of accurate identification of individuals who do not have a problem), and positive predictive value (i.e., the likelihood that an individual estimated to have a problem, actually has a problem) of its identification of 'problem gambling' is uncertain. We are concerned that adapting problematic gambling characteristics gleaned from land-based research and/or relying on professional or conventional wisdom about problematic gambling characteristics is unlikely to result in behavioural profiles that can withstand traditional scientific scrutiny.

The risks and hazards associated with prematurely bringing an identification algorithm to the Internet market are considerable. A product without acceptable specificity, sensitivity, and predictive accuracy places a company and its consumers at unnecessary risk. To illustrate, problematic gambling behaviour is a low base-rate phenomenon. This means that an algorithm can claim a success rate of 90 percent due to its specificity (i.e., likelihood of accurately identifying individuals who do not have gambling problems), but yield minimal to no sensitivity (i.e., likelihood of accurately identifying individuals who do have problems). Finally, the algorithm must have predictive value. Absent predictive accuracy, the best that an algorithm can offer is a transient identification that might not be accurate the next day or beyond. The likelihood of sensitivity errors (i.e., falsely identifying someone who has a problem as being problem-free) and the absence of predictive power place companies at great risk for litigation and players at risk for ongoing harm that can be avoided with careful and systematic research and planning.

The best next steps in the development of responsible gambling for Internet gambling companies are to identify the actual public health risks associated with online gambling and to develop a comprehensive profile of characteristics that empirically can distinguish problematic Internet gambling behaviour from recreational Internet gambling at the earliest possible moment. Until the next investigative steps are accomplished, identification algorithms for online gaming consumers will be of dubious value.

In the following discussion, we review the first publications to identify behavioural markers of potential gambling-related problems experienced by actual Internet gambling subscribers. These papers represent three types of predictive markers: markers proximal to a gambling-related event, markers distal from a gambling-related event, and general markers of a gambling-related event.

### Proximal markers (Xuan and Shaffer, 2009)

The first published account of behavioural markers of Internet gambling-related problems focused on the gambling patterns that occur immediately before *bwin.party* Internet gamblers end their gambling. Specifically, we examined behavioural patterns associated with account closing for self-reported reasons related to gambling-related problems. Cases of interest included individuals who wagered on live action betting events at least three times and reported that they closed their accounts for reasons related to gambling-related problems. Although conventional wisdom holds that chasing losses (i.e., increasing stakes and/or betting on propositions with longer odds to recoup losses) would be a primary marker of disordered gambling behaviour, our analysis of these data provided mixed support for chasing as a marker. Analyses of monetary loss revealed that, compared to matched controls, cases experienced increasing losses per bet during their final betting days and also increased their stakes per bet; controls did not increase their stakes or losses in the same time period. Contrary to conventional expectations, cases played odds that are more conservative during their final betting days; controls did not change their odds at the end of their sampling period. Finally, both cases and controls decreased the number of bets per active betting day during their final betting days or, in the case of controls, the last betting days in the sampling period. So, near the end of their gambling, cases entered into a losing betting pattern, during which they reduced their betting activity and increased their stakes on shorter odds, rather than longer odds. Though the increased stakes per bet is suggestive of chasing, the rest of the pattern is inconsistent with what the chasing hypothesis suggests. If chasing were prevalent among those who closed their accounts due to gambling-related problems, their behaviour during the losing betting pattern should have included increased betting activity and increased stakes on longer odds propositions.

### Distal markers (Braverman and Shaffer, 2010)

The second published account of behavioural markers of Internet gambling-related problems focused on the predictive value of early Internet gambling patterns for encountering gambling-related problems. We examined behavioural markers of a sample ($n = 530$) of account closers who reported a reason for closing their account with *bwin* derived from the population of gamblers who subscribed to *bwin* during February 2005. We excluded from our analyses individuals who had less than two active betting days during their first month as a registered *bwin* subscriber. Account closers in the analytic sample consisted of 176 who reported closing their account for gambling-related problems, 98 who reported closing their account because they were unsatisfied with the service they received, and 256 who reported they closed their account because they had no interest in gambling.

Using information about betting behaviour during first 30 days after they started betting, betting frequency (i.e., total number of active betting days), intensity (i.e., total wagers/ frequency), variability (i.e., standard deviation of wagers), and trajectory (i.e., slope of wagers), we clustered the account closers and determined a four-cluster solution was stable and reliable. The first identified cluster consisted of 15 individuals who had relatively high activity and high variability during their first 30 days. The second cluster included 22 individuals who had low first 30-day activity. Individuals who were in the third cluster ($n = 115$) evidenced high activity, but low variability in their wagering. Finally, the fourth cluster of 378 individuals evidenced relatively moderate betting during their first 30 days. These clusters related to the reasons that individuals reported when they closed their accounts: 73

percent of cluster 1 closed for gambling-related problems; 45 percent of cluster 2; 29 percent of cluster 3; and, 32 percent of cluster 4. These findings suggest that high activity and high variability of wagering during one's first 30 days of activity at *bwin* is a marker for later closing one's account due to gambling-related problems.

### Generalized markers (LaBrie and Shaffer, 2011)

The third published account of behavioural markers of Internet gambling-related problems focused on whether it is possible to distinguish subgroups of gamblers with problems based upon how Internet gamblers play during their active subscription period. We began with a sample ($n = 679$) of account closers who closed their account with *bwin* within 24 months of subscribing in February 2005. Some 215 reported closing their account for gambling-related problems, 113 closed their accounts because they were unsatisfied with their service, and 351 reported no more interest in gambling. We assessed whether we could identify a distinct core group of individuals who closed their accounts for gambling-related problems and shared common, exaggerated gambling behaviours. To accomplish this, we conducted a series of discriminant function analyses. These analyses identified groups of gambling-related problem account closers who we could and could not discriminate from other account closers. Overall, gambling-related problem account closers differed from other account closers on their duration of involvement with *bwin* and total winnings. We could correctly discriminate about 50 percent of gambling-related problem account closers (i.e., distinctive) from those account closers who were no longer interested in *bwin*. We then compared those we could discriminate with those we could not discriminate to determine how their gambling behaviour differed. This subsequent stepwise discriminant function analysis revealed that when we compared distinctive gambling-related problem account closers with the non-distinctive gambling-related problem account closers, using frequency of wagering, bets per day, duration of subscription, and total number of wagers, we could accurately classify 93 percent of the distinctive group and 91 percent of the non-distinctive group. Distinctive closers bet with greater frequency, made more bets per day, spent more euros on each bet, and had more active betting days.

### The way forward for the science of early detection

The identification of behavioural sets of markers for potential gambling-related problems shows the promise of this area for the classification of risk associated with the development of gambling-related problems. However, to move this area of work forward, researchers must use actual gambling data to identify empirically additional behavioural markers; then, scientists will need to engage in an investigative process that will narrow down and integrate the various markers to an efficacious predictive model. It also is important to expand upon the variety of clinical outcomes that the predictive algorithms target. The aforementioned studies relied on a clinical proxy outcome (i.e., closing one's account for reasons related to gambling-related problems), and the results associated with other clinical measures could be divergent. Ultimately, once researchers publish reliable and valid predictive algorithms, the difficult task of creating appropriate evidence-based intervention can begin.

## Concluding Thoughts

The *bwin.party* Division on Addiction Research Collaborative epidemiological and behavioural marker studies reveal findings that stand in marked contrast to the contemporary popular assumptions about Internet gambling behaviour. For instance, population-level betting activity seemed comparatively modest to what conventional wisdom would predict. To date, the reasons for this deviation are unclear. However, the competing evidence might result from several sources: methodological aspects (i.e., data reflecting self-report versus retrieval of actual behaviour); inappropriate extrapolation from land-based studies; and/or site-specific idiosyncrasies. The source articles discuss other possibilities, as well. Alternatively, it might be that the paradigm and its derivative conceptual and methodological perspectives currently guiding this period of normal science related to Internet gambling require revision. If that is the case, then we are destined for a period of revolutionary science that will define a new paradigm for the next period of normal science. Therefore, these studies champion a clarion call to researchers and policy makers for more research that uses actual Internet gambling data.

The Collaborative encourages scientists around the world to contribute to the growing knowledge base related to actual Internet gambling. To facilitate such contributions, the Collaborative makes such data freely available to anyone through the web-based *Transparency Project* data archive (www.thetransparencyproject.org). The *Transparency Project* is the world's first free publicly accessible data archive for privately funded addiction-related datasets, such as those obtained from *bwin.party*. Likewise, we encourage other scientists to archive their databases publicly. It is our belief that such engagement will speed the process of advancing scientific discovery and improving the public's health. These goals should supersede all others.

The technological advances offered by Internet technology can usher in a new era of transparency for government, industry, and science. Perhaps this will translate into a methodological paradigm shift that ultimately will guide scientists for years to come. Minimally, such data sharing will facilitate scientific investigations that can pursue whether the Collaborative's empirical challenges should provoke revolutionary science, or not.

At the start of this chapter, we argued that the study of Internet gambling is in a period of normal science. Some people might question how a paradigm emerged considering the limited scientific evidence available, compared to other better-developed scientific fields. As is common for relatively new fields of study, the race to be first to comment on an issue, as a means of establishing authority and expertise, can yield stage-setting hypotheses that have limited resemblance to reality. Although early conjecture can create much-needed attention for new fields, speculation also often creates a non-empirical conceptual trajectory that is difficult, at best, to correct. For example, most early papers related to Internet gambling speculated that it is uniquely dangerous. This position has gained widespread acceptance. This kind of bias shapes study construction to yield findings that are consistent with the original theoretical model and derivative hypotheses (Bakan, 1967; Kuhn, 1970).

Another consequence of early misinformation is the misdirection of prevention and intervention efforts. Because of the amount of individualized gambling-related information collected, web-based gambling companies can intervene in ways not possible for land-based gambling. Specifically, using advanced algorithms, companies can operate automated risk-detection systems that provide early warning messaging to site subscribers who are at risk for the development of gambling-related problems. However, if such algorithms rest on faulty assumptions, their potential for false positives and false negatives is great.

The difficulty of breaking established conceptual and empirical trajectories is a result of the intellectual and scientific inertia associated with the need to fill a nascent field's vacuums with predictions, models, and explanations. The grip of such trajectories is likely to be particularly strong for fields that have significant public health concerns, but underdeveloped public response options. Taking a cautious path likely will protect more people than taking a radical course. This is the case for Internet gambling because so much remains unknown, so few regulations are well defined, and the public widely accepts gambling, in general, to pose a public health risk. However, taking an extremely conservative path risks backlash. This possibility suggests that empirically guided decision making can lead to an optimal balance between caution and personal liberty.

Finally, it is important to note that the isolation of a single type of gambling as inherently addictive is inconsistent with contemporary models of addiction (Shaffer, LaPlante et al., 2004; Shaffer, LaPlante, and Nelson, in press). Such models indicate that the object of addiction does not drive the development of addiction. Instead, addiction emerges because of a complicated interaction between individuals, their environment, and the objects with which they interact. Consequently, what might eventually emerge as a primary object of obsession and/or addiction for one person might be completely uninteresting to another. Empirical studies of gambling-related involvement support the proposition that specific objects play a minor role in the development of addictive behaviour (LaPlante, Nelson et al., 2009). If objects themselves were inherently addictive, such inter-individual variance would not occur. It's just not that simple.

Just as researchers and clinicians are beginning to accept new models of addiction that allow for the inclusion of non-substance expressions of addiction, we hope that researchers and clinicians also will begin to embrace the need to consider carefully the ongoing challenges to the prevailing paradigm. For Internet gambling, this means extending beyond self-report mechanisms of data collection to include the retrieval and examination of dynamic records of actual behaviour and recognizing that the path to addiction is multi-factorial.

## Acknowledgments

The Division on Addiction receives support from the following organizations: *bwin.party* Digital Entertainment; National Institute of Mental Health; National Institute on Alcohol Abuse and Alcoholism; Saint Francis House; the Century Council; Massachusetts Council on Compulsive Gambling.

## References

American Psychiatric Association. (2000). *DSM IV-TR: Diagnostic and statistical manual of mental disorders – Text revision* (4th edn). Washington, DC: American Psychiatric Association.

Bakan, D. (1967). *On method: Toward a reconstruction of psychological investigation* (1st edn). San Francisco: Jossey-Bass.

Bakken, I. J., Gotestam, K. G., Grawe, R. W., Wenzel, H. G., and Oren, A. (2009). 'Gambling behavior and gambling problems in Norway 2007'. *Scandinavian Journal of Psychology, 50*(4), 333–9.

Braverman, J., and Shaffer, H. J. (2010). 'How do gamblers start gambling: Identifying behavioural markers for high-risk Internet gambling'. *European Journal of Public Health,* advance access, 1 – 6.

Christian Capital Advisers, I. (2006). 'Global Internet gambling revenue estimates and projections [2001–10, $M, US]'. Retrieved from http://www.cca-i.com/Primary%20Navigation/Online%20 Data%20Store/internet_gambling_data.htm

Davies, B. (2007). 'iCare: Integrating responsible gaming into casino operation'. *International Journal of Mental Health and Addiction, 5*(4), 307–10.

Davis, S. F., Smith, B. G., Rodrigue, K., and Pulvers, K. (1999). 'An examination of Internet usage on two college campuses'. *College Student Journal, 33*(2), 257–60.

DeBell, M., and Chapman, C. (2006). *Computer and Internet use by students in 2003 (NCES 2006– 065)*. Washington, DC: National Center for Education Statistics.

Gambino, B., and Shaffer, H. J. (1979). 'The concept of paradigm and the treatment of addiction'. *Professional Psychology, 10*, 207–23.

Griffiths, M. D. (1993). 'Fruit machine gambling: The importance of structural characteristics'. *Journal of Gambling Studies, 9*(2), 101–20.

— (1999). 'Gambling technologies: Prospects for problem gambling'. *Journal of Gambling Studies, 15*(3), 265–83.

Griffiths, M. D., and Parke, J. (2002). 'The social impact of Internet gambling'. *Social Science Computer Review, 20*(3), 312–20.

Griffiths, M. D., Wardle, H., Orford, J., Sproston, K., and Erens, B. (2009). 'Sociodemographic correlates of Internet gambling: Findings from the 2007 British Gambling Prevalence Survey'. *CyberPsychology & Behavior, 12*(2), 199–202.

Holtgraves, T. (2009). 'Gambling, gambling activities, and problem gambling'. *Psychology of Addictive Behaviors, 23*(2), 295–302.

Horn, J. (2002). 'Point and bet. Internet gambling's explosive growth has made it the Web's killer app. Now critics are trying to pull the plug'. *Newsweek, 140*(18), 50–2.

Jones, S., Johnson-Yale, C., Millermaier, S., and Pérez, F. S. (2009). 'U.S. college students' Internet use: Race, gender and digital divides'. *Journal of Computer-Mediated Communication, 14*, 244–64.

Kerber, C. S. (2005). 'Problem and pathological gambling among college athletes'. *Annals of Clinical Psychiatry, 17*(4), 243–7.

Kessler, R. C., Hwang, I., LaBrie, R. A., Petukhova, M., Sampson, N. A., Winters, K. C., et al. (2008). 'DSM-IV pathological gambling in the National Comorbidity Survey Replication'. *Psychological Medicine 38*(9), 1351–60.

Kiesler, S., and Sproull, L. (1985). 'Pool halls, chips, and war games: Women in the culture of computing'. *Psychology of Women Quarterly, 9*(4), 451–62.

King, S. A., and Barak, A. (1999). 'Compulsive Internet gambling: A new form of an old clinical pathology'. *CyberPsychology & Behavior, 2*(5), 441–56.

Korn, D. A., and Shaffer, H. J. (1999). 'Gambling and the health of the public: Adopting a public health perspective'. *Journal of Gambling Studies, 15*(4), 289–365.

Kuhn, T. S. (1970). *The structure of scientific revolutions* (2nd edn). Chicago: University of Chicago Press.

LaBrie, R. A., and Shaffer, H. J. (2011). 'Identifying behavioral markers of disordered Internet sports gambling'. *Addiction Research & Theory, 19*(1), 56–65. doi:10.3109/16066359.2010.512106.

LaBrie, R. A., Kaplan, S. A., LaPlante, D. A., Nelson, S. E., and Shaffer, H. J. (2008). 'Inside the virtual casino: A prospective longitudinal study of Internet casino gambling'. *European Journal of Public Health, 18*(4), 410–16.

LaBrie, R. A., LaPlante, D. A., Nelson, S. E., Schumann, A., and Shaffer, H. J. (2007). 'Assessing the playing field: A prospective longitudinal study of Internet sports gambling behavior'. *Journal of Gambling Studies, 23*(3), 347–62.

LaBrie, R. A., Shaffer, H. J., LaPlante, D. A., and Wechsler, H. (2003). 'Correlates of college student gambling in the United States'. *Journal of American College Health, 52*(2), 53–62.

Ladd, G. T., and Petry, N. M. (2002). 'Disordered gambling among university-based medical and dental patients: A focus on Internet gambling'. *Psychology of Addictive Behaviors, 16*(1), 76–9.

LaPlante, D. A., and Braverman, J. (2010). 'El juego en internet: Situacion actual y propuestas para la prevencion y la intervencion'. In E. Echeburua, E. Becona, and F. Labrador (eds), *Avances en la clinica y el tratamiento del juego patologico*. Madrid: Ediciones Piramide.

LaPlante, D. A., and Shaffer, H. J. (2007). 'Understanding the influence of gambling opportunities: Expanding exposure models to include adaptation'. *American Journal of Orthopsychiatry, 77*(4), 616–23.

LaPlante, D. A., Kleschinsky, J. H., LaBrie, R. A., Nelson, S. E., and Shaffer, H. J. (2009). 'Sitting at the virtual poker table: A prospective epidemiological study of actual Internet poker gambling behavior'. *Computers in Human Behavior, 25*(3), 711–17.

LaPlante, D. A., Nelson, S. E., LaBrie, R. A., and Shaffer, H. J. (2009). 'Disordered gambling, type of gambling and gambling involvement in the British Gambling Prevalence Survey 2007'. *European Journal of Public Health*. Advance online publication. doi:10.1093/eurpub/ckp177.

LaPlante, D. A., Schumann, A., LaBrie, R. A., and Shaffer, H. J. (2008). 'Population trends in Internet sports gambling'. *Computers in Human Behavior, 24*(5), 2399–414.

LaRose, R. (2001). 'On the negative effects of e-commerce: A sociocognitive exploration of unregulated on-line buying'. *Journal of Computer-Mediated Communication, 6*(3), N.P.

McBride, J., and Derevensky, J. (2009). 'Internet gambling behavior in a sample of online gamblers'. *International Journal of Mental Health and Addiction, 7*(1), 149–67.

Matthews, N., Farnsworth, B., and Griffiths, M. D. (2009). 'A pilot study of problem gambling among student online gamblers: Mood states as predictors of problematic behavior'. *CyberPsychology & Behavior, 12*(6), 741–5.

Miller, R. (2006). 'The need for self regulations and alternative dispute resolution to moderate consumer perceptions of perceived risk with Internet gambling'. *UNLV Gaming Research & Review Journal, 10*(1), 51–8.

Mitka, M. (2001). 'Win or lose, Internet gambling stakes are high'. *Journal of the American Medical Association, 285*(8), 1005.

Petry, N. M. (2006). 'Internet gambling: An emerging concern in family practice medicine?' *Family Practice, 23*, 421–6.

Petry, N. M., and Weinstock, J. (2007). 'Internet gambling is common in college students and associated with poor mental health'. *American Journal on Addictions, 16*(5), 325–30.

Samuel, S. (2010, December 11). 'Conservatives warn against online gambling bill'. *Christian Post*. Retrieved December 14, 2010, from http://www.christianpost.com/article/20101211/conservatives-warn-against-online-gambling-bill/

Shaffer, H. J. (1986). 'Conceptual crises and the addictions: A philosophy of science perspective'. *Journal of Substance Abuse Treatment, 3*, 285–96.

Shaffer, H. J., and Gambino, B. (1979). 'Addiction paradigms II: Theory, research, and practice'. *Journal of Psychedelic Drugs, 11*, 299–304.

Shaffer, H. J., Hall, M. N., and Vander Bilt, J. (2000). '"Computer addiction": A critical consideration'. *American Journal of Orthopsychiatry, 70*(2), 162–8.

Shaffer, H. J., LaBrie, R. A., and LaPlante, D. (2004). 'Laying the foundation for quantifying regional exposure to social phenomena: Considering the case of legalized gambling as a public health toxin'. *Psychology of Addictive Behaviors, 18*(1), 40–8.

Shaffer, H. J., LaPlante, D. A., LaBrie, R. A., Kidman, R. C., Donato, A. N., and Stanton, M. V. (2004). 'Toward a syndrome model of addiction: Multiple expressions, common etiology'. *Harvard Review of Psychiatry, 12*, 367–74.

Shaffer, H. J., LaPlante, D. A., LaBrie, R. A., and Nelson, S. E. (2007). 'Op-Ed/Editorials: Detecting at-risk Internet behavior'. *The Brief Addiction Science Information Source (BASIS)*. Retrieved December 13, 2010, from http://www.basisonline.org/2007/12/index.html

Shaffer, H. J., LaPlante, D. A., and Nelson, S. E. (eds). (in press). *The American Psychological Association Addiction Syndrome Handbook*. Washington, DC: American Psychological Association Press.

Welte, J. W., Barnes, G. M., Tidwell, M.-C. O., and Hoffman, J. H. (2009). 'The association of form of gambling with problem gambling among American youth'. *Psychology of Addictive Behaviors, 23*(1), 105–12.

Wood, R. T. A., and Williams, R. J. (2007). 'Problem gambling on the Internet: Implications for Internet gambling policy in North America'. *New Media & Society, 9*(3), 520–42.

Wood, R. T. A., Griffiths, M. D., and Parke, J. (2007). 'Acquisition, development, and maintenance of online poker playing in a student sample'. *CyberPsychology & Behavior, 10*(3), 354–61.

Xuan, Z., and Shaffer, H. J. (2009). 'How do gamblers end gambling: Longitudinal analysis of Internet gambling behaviors prior to account closure due to gambling related problems'. *Journal of Gambling Studies, 25*(2), 239–52.

# Part 4
# Clinical Aspects

# 10  Online gambling among youth

## Cause for concern?

*Mark D. Griffiths, Jeffrey L. Derevensky,*
*and Jonathan Parke*

## Introduction

Internet gambling continues to grow at an unprecedented rate. While there still remains economic uncertainly and legal impediments, the number of countries regulating and/or operating sites continues to increase rapidly. The widespread social acceptance of gambling in general and the adoption of technological advances associated with the Internet itself likely has been an important contributing factor in its growth and popularity. Yet, Internet gambling in general, and in particular how it impacts young people, remains a relatively under-researched area. While our current knowledge remains in its infancy and the prevalence rates remain relatively low (Griffiths, 2010), researchers and clinicians are predicting greater involvement among youth as more countries legalize, license, or operate this form of gambling and alternative methods of payment are developed. This chapter provides a review of the relevant literature relating to online gambling among youth. The chapter comprises four sections: (a) the empirical studies on adolescent Internet gambling, (b) online gambling-like experiences during adolescence, (c) adolescent gambling via social networking sites, and (d) adolescent gambling via online penny auction sites. Age verification in relation to prevention and regulation are examined. A cautionary note is important when examining the research in this chapter. The studies presented vary in terms of the methodological procedures used to collect data, cultural and geographical differences, and the year the data were collected, all of which likely influence their results.

## Background

There is little doubt that youth gambling prevalence rates in most jurisdictions have increased as availability, accessibility, and social acceptance have risen (Volberg, Gupta, Griffiths, Olason, and Delfabbro, 2010). Gambling has become normalized and widely accepted. As such, it should come as no great surprise that it is viewed as a popular form of entertainment for adolescents and adults alike. Studies on youth gambling in more traditional, non-online, settings generally reveal that the predominant reasons for engaging in this behaviour are for entertainment and enjoyment, excitement, and to make money (Derevensky, 2008). While questions as to the effectiveness of legal statutes prohibiting underage gambling from accessing government-regulated forms of gambling (e.g., lottery playing, casinos, electronic gambling machines) have been raised, procedures are in fact in place to limit their accessibility. As well, there is ample evidence that youth are engaged in both regulated and non-regulated forms of gambling.

Gambling via Internet gambling sites takes many different forms, whether wagering on traditional forms of gambling (e.g., sports events, casino-style games, poker, bingo, lotteries, skill-based activities, betting exchanges, etc.) or non-traditional activities (e.g., the outcome of a political race, spelling bee contest, hot dog eating contest, nomination of supreme court judges, winners of reality shows, personal academic performance, celebrity marriages, whether celebrities will become incarcerated and locations of where they will adopt a child, etc.). An examination of the activities found on Internet gambling sites reveals significant diversity, to appeal to any age group, gender, and cultural group.

Internet gambling, while similar in many ways to land-based forms of gambling, has notable features that make it highly appealing. Motivations for engaging in online gambling include convenience, availability, ease of access, multiple games, entertainment, enjoyment, excitement, anonymity, and privacy (American Gaming Association, 2006; Griffiths and Barnes, 2008; Griffiths and Parke, 2002; McBride and Derevensky, 2009, 2010; Wood, Griffiths, and Parke, 2007). Other less frequently reported reasons include an aversion to the clientele and atmosphere of land-based venues and the ability to assume opposite sex roles (Griffiths, 2003; Wood et al., 2007). A disturbing trend amongst youth seems to suggest that Internet gambling is now perceived to be a functional way to relieve boredom (Derevensky and Gupta, 2007; McBride and Derevensky, 2009).

Given online gambling's popularity, are youth particularly vulnerable to Internet gambling? An early national Internet gambling prevalence survey of 2,098 people in the UK by Griffiths (2001) (including 119 adolescents; aged 15 to 19 years) suggested that at that time no teenagers reported gambling on the Internet; however, 4 percent of teenagers indicated they would like to try online gambling. There is little doubt that this generation of youth have spent most of their lives embracing the Internet for multiple reasons (e.g., education, purchasing items, acquiring information, playing games, etc.). Gambling may be viewed as just one extension of its use.

There is a growing body of adult research suggesting that Internet gambling may be problematic. Such findings have been found in nationally representative adult surveys (e.g., Griffiths, Wardle, Orford, Sproston, and Erens, 2009, 2010) and those of young adults (McBride and Derevensky, 2009), with children and adolescents commonly thought to be more susceptible and vulnerable in terms of developing a gambling problem (Derevensky, 2008; Meyer, Hayer, and Griffiths, 2009). The question remains *will Internet gambling result in increased problem gambling prevalence rates?* This is a serious concern among treatment providers, legislators, regulators, and public health officials.

## Empirical studies on adolescent Internet gambling

While virtually all Internet gambling sites have some age restrictions, the enforcement of these restrictions is highly variable. An early study in the UK found that a 16-year-old was able to place bets online on 81 percent (30 out of 37) sites tested, and a European survey reported that 17 percent of visitors to online gambling sites were under the age of 18 (NCH, 2004; NetValue, 2002). Among a sample of online gamblers, there was widespread belief that underage players are gambling online and several participants in their focus groups reported noticing fellow gamblers soliciting help for their homework via chat boxes (Cotte and Latour, 2009). Early studies of online gambling have suggested that in spite of legal or social responsibility prohibitions many online gambling sites failed to provide stringent age checks and/or age verification procedures (e.g., Smeaton and Griffiths, 2004). There are further suggestions that while the current situation has improved considerably as a result of regulatory provisions of Internet gambling sites, age verification procedures are often limited at best, with many not having any verification procedures in place. As such, online gambling by underage minors remains of significant concern. Furthermore, it has been noted that the distinction between gambling and video gaming is becoming ever more blurred and that gaming convergence is widespread (Griffiths, 2008a, 2008b; de Freitas and Griffiths, 2008; King, Delfabbro, and Griffiths, 2010). For example, many gaming sites incorporate similar technology to video games, have similar graphic features, and offer rewards in the form of 'tokens' or 'credits' where gamblers can exchange tokens or credits for a monetary prize.

Given the concern among policy makers and clinicians it is surprising that there have only been a limited number of studies examining youth Internet gambling. The following review focuses on studies examining the impact of Internet gambling on adolescents and young adults.

## Empirical studies of online gambling among youth

Brunelle and her colleagues (Brunelle, Gendron, Leclerc, Cousineau, and Dufour, 2008; Brunelle, Gendron, Dufour, Leclerc, and Cousineau, 2009) carried out a study comparing the profiles of young non-gamblers, gamblers, and Internet gamblers in relation to severity of substances use (Germain, Guyon, Landry et al., 2007), impulsivity and risk taking among Quebec adolescents. They surveyed 1,876 high-school students (46 percent male; 54 percent female), aged 14 to 18 years (mean = 15.4 years), and reported that 93.5 percent of adolescents (95 percent male; 92 percent female) reported having gambled in the previous 12 months, with 8 percent (13 percent males; 3 percent females) having gambled on the Internet during the same time period. They also reported that 35 percent of youth (49 percent males; 21 percent females) had played the 'free play'/'demo' mode on Internet gambling sites. Males were significantly more likely than females to gamble in general, gamble on the Internet, and play the 'free play' modes on Internet gambling sites. Using the Diagnostic and Statistical Manual of Mental Disorders (DSM-IV-J), 3 percent of their participants were found to be problem gamblers. They also found significantly more problem gamblers among those individuals gambling on the Internet (11 percent) compared to those who did not gamble on the Internet (1.57 percent), with no gender differences found for any type of problem gambling. Further findings revealed that nearly 7 percent of the participants had a substance use problem and that those with problematic substance use were also more likely to be Internet gamblers (4 percent non-gamblers; 8 percent gamblers; 18 percent Internet gamblers) (see Table 10.1). In relation to impulsivity, Internet gamblers and non-Internet gamblers had

*Table 10.1* Substance use by gamblers, Internet gamblers, and non-gamblers ($n = 1,876$)

| Type of substance use | Non-gambler (%) | Gambler (%) | Lifetime Internet gambler (%) |
| --- | --- | --- | --- |
| Alcohol** | 76.9 | 91.3 | 96.3 |
| Tobacco** | 26.3 | 42.6 | 51.5 |
| Cannabis** | 26.8 | 40.6 | 55.1 |
| Hallucinogens** | 5.4 | 10.0 | 12.5 |
| Speed | 6.3 | 13.1 | 19.9 |
| Cocaine** | 1.0 | 3.8 | 5.9 |
| Solvents | 0.2 | 1.0 | 1.5 |
| Heroin* | 0.6 | 1.0 | 3.7 |

Notes
Comparison between gamblers and non-gamblers: * $p < 0.05$; ** $p < 0.001$.
Source: Adapted from Brunelle, Gendron, et al., 2009.

significantly higher scores on measures of impulsivity and risk taking than non-gamblers. As expected, problem gamblers also had significantly higher scores on impulsivity and risk taking than non-problem gamblers.

Using the same data set, Brunelle, Cousineau, Dufour, Gendron, and Leclerc (2009) examined some of the contextual elements surrounding Internet gambling among adolescents. They examined the types of Internet games, Internet gambling initiation contexts, and Internet gambling contexts in general (e.g., when, where, with whom, how long, etc.). Of the 137 Internet gamblers, only 0.8 percent had regularly played for money at an online casino while 1.9 percent had regularly played for money on online poker sites (see Table 10.2). However, the 'play for free' modes were played more regularly in both online casinos (8.9 percent) and online poker (13.8 percent) (see Table 10.2). The results revealed that 37 percent of online gambling was done primarily with friends, 34 percent with an immediate family member, 23 percent with other family members, 2 percent alone, and 4 percent with others.

Brunelle, Cousineau et al. (2009) in a qualitative examination interviewed 37 adolescent online gamblers and reported that the primary types of online gambling carried out were poker, blackjack, electronic gambling (slot) machines, bingo, and sports betting. While most of the gambling was done either at home or in school, the vast majority was played in the evening so it is unlikely that playing at school was highly prevalent. Those who played for more than two hours at a time were most likely to engage in this behaviour on their own whereas playing socially with others was more likely to be done for much less time per session. Most online gamblers found the atmosphere exciting and pleasant (rather than stressful or serious). Brunelle and her colleagues concluded that (a) poker was the most popular form of online gambling, (b) adolescent online gamblers were more likely to be problem gamblers compared with those who did not gamble online, (c) most initiation of online gambling took place with family members, (d) most adolescent online gamblers began by playing in the 'free play' mode, and (e) for many adolescents, online gambling was a way to make money, occupied them when they had nothing else to do, and allowed them to socialize.

Olason and his colleagues (Olason, 2009; Olason, Kristjansdottir, Einarsdottir et al., 2011) reported two studies examining gambling behaviour among Icelandic adolescents that included questions relating to Internet gambling. The first in-class study comprised 1,513 adolescents aged 16 to 18 years (730 males; 783 females). The second school-based study comprised 1,537 adolescents aged 13 to 18 years (768 males; 747 females). The surveys included questions relating to gambling on Icelandic Internet websites (lotto, sports pools, sports betting) and on foreign websites (poker, casino games, sports betting, and 'free play' modes). In addition to assessing their gambling behaviour, students completed the DSM-IV-MR-J (Fisher, 2000), a gambling screen assessing severity of gambling and gambling-related problems.

*Table 10.2* Types of Internet games played in the last 12 months (*n* = 137)

|  | Never (%) | Once (%) | Occasionally (%) | Regularly (%) |
| --- | --- | --- | --- | --- |
| Internet casino (for money) | 95.4 | 2.3 | 1.5 | 0.8 |
| Internet casino ('free play' mode) | 75.2 | 8.5 | 7.4 | 8.9 |
| Internet poker (for money) | 94.7 | 1.7 | 1.7 | 1.9 |
| Internet poker ('free play' mode) | 71.9 | 8.0 | 8.0 | 13.8 |

Source: Adapted from Brunelle, Cousineau et al., 2009.

In relation to participation, Olason (2009) reported that in the first study, 62 percent of the participants had gambled, 11 percent were regular gamblers, 20 percent had gambled on the Internet, and just under 4 percent were regular Internet gamblers. In the second study, 57 percent of the participants had gambled, 8 percent were regular gamblers, 24 percent had gambled on the Internet, and just over 4 percent were regular Internet gamblers. Table 10.3 outlines in more detail the findings in relation to Internet gambling. In both studies, males were significantly more likely than females to gamble on the Internet (32 percent boys vs. 9 percent girls in study I; 37 percent boys vs. 11.5 percent girls in study II). The results in relation to problem gambling revealed a prevalence rate of 3 percent problem gambling in the first study and 2.2 percent in the second study. However, among those who had gambled on the Internet, the problem gambling prevalence rates were significantly higher, 10.1 percent and 7.5 percent respectively. The results also revealed that 11.5 percent of the adolescents had used their own personal credit card, 23.1 percent had used their personal debit card, 15.4 percent had used a parents' credit card while 50 percent had used another method of payment (e.g., brother's credit card, loans from friends, electronic cash, PayPal, Neteller, bonus money, etc.).

In the UK, Griffiths and Wood (2007) surveyed 8,017 young people between 12 and 15 years of age about their Internet gambling behaviour. Like the studies by Olason and his colleagues, their survey included the DSM-IV-MR-J screen to identify problematic gambling behaviour. The study examined remote gambling in relation to use of the National Lottery products online. Adolescents were asked *'Have you ever played any National Lottery game on the Internet?'* Those who reported having gambled on the Internet were also asked *'Which, if any, of the following games have you played in the past seven days?'* Students were presented with the following options: (1) instant win games for money, (2) free instant win games, (3) lotto, and (4) one of the other lottery draw games. Those who had experience of gambling online were also asked how they accessed and played the National Lottery games on the Internet. The following options were presented: (1) the system let me register, (2) I played along with my parents, (3) another adult let me play, (4) I used my parent's/guardian's online National Lottery account with their permission, (5) I used my parent's/guardian's online National Lottery account without their permission, and (6) played free games.

*Table 10.3* Types of games played on the Internet by Icelandic adolescents

| | Study I: regular gamblers (n = 1,513) (%) | Study I: total gamblers (n = 1,513) (%) | Study II: regular gamblers (n = 1,537) (%) | Study II: total gamblers (n = 1,537) (%) |
|---|---|---|---|---|
| *Icelandic websites* | | | | |
| Lotto | 0.6 | 2.4 | 0.5 | 8.7 |
| Sports pools | 0.7 | 3.4 | 0.9 | 8.5 |
| Sports betting | 0.8 | 2.9 | 1.2 | 6.2 |
| *Foreign websites* | | | | |
| Online poker | 0.6 | 1.9 | 1.8 | 6.5 |
| Casino games | 2.2 | 15.8 | 1.8 | 12.3 |
| Sports betting | – | – | 0.5 | 1.9 |
| 'Free play' modes | 3.3 | 28 | – | – |

Source: Adapted from Olason, 2009.

The results revealed that approximately one in twelve young people (8 percent), age 12 to 15 years, reported having played a National Lottery game via the Internet. Boys were more likely than girls to endorse playing the National Lottery games via the Internet (10 percent vs. 6 percent), as were young people who were Asian and Black. Not surprisingly, young people identified as 'problem gamblers' on the DSM-IV-MR-J were more likely than 'social gamblers' to have played a National Lottery game on the Internet (37 percent compared with 9 percent). Of those who had gambled on the Internet, a quarter of the adolescents revealed they had played free instant win games (24 percent), nearly one in five had played instant win games for money (19 percent) or the Lotto (18 percent), and 10 percent had played another draw. Problem gamblers were more likely to have played every game in the past week, compared with social gamblers who were less likely to remember what games they had played during the same time period. Young people with parents who approve of their gambling were more likely to have played online instant win games for money (35 percent vs. 19 percent), Lotto (40 percent vs. 15 percent), or other draw games (22 percent vs. 6 percent). Not surprisingly, their results clearly suggest that youth with parental consent were more likely to gamble online.

Griffiths and Wood (2007) also noted that of youth who gambled online, 29 percent reported playing free games, 18 percent reported that the system let them register, 16 percent played along with their parents, 10 percent used their parent's online National Lottery account with their permission, and 7 percent used their parents' account without permission. However, it should be noted that one-third of online players reported they 'couldn't remember' (35 percent) the method used for payment. Overall, among all young people (and not just players), 2 percent played National Lottery games online with their parents and 2 percent have played independently without their parents. Those who have played independently are most likely to have played free games, with just 0.3 percent of young people having played National Lottery games on their own for money. More recently, Ipsos MORI (2009) in a survey of 8,598 students, aged 11–15 years, from 201 schools reported that overall, 1 percent of youth gambled on the Internet for money in the past seven days.

In the USA, Welte, Barnes, Tidwell, and Hoffman (2009), assessed the relationship between specific types of gambling and the extent of problem gambling reported by American adolescents and young adults using data from the National Survey of Youth and Gambling, comprising 2,274 youth age 14–21 years. They found that 2 percent of respondents (3 percent males; 0 percent females) reported gambling online in the past 12 months, with respondents having gambled online an average of 48 days per year. This represented the percentage of any form of gambling reported in the survey. They also noted that 65 percent of respondents who gambled on the Internet reported having at least one symptom on the South Oaks Gambling Screen Revised for Adolescents (SOGS-RA; Winters, Stinchfield, and Fulkerson, 1993), which again was the highest of the 15 forms of gambling being considered. Statistical analyses revealed that when participation in other forms of gambling was controlled, the link between Internet gambling and problem gambling among youth was no longer significant. In other words, they concluded that young Internet gamblers were likely to experience more problem gambling symptoms by virtue of gambling on multiple gambling activities as opposed to the properties of Internet gambling itself. Indeed, this was supported in part by the data, with Internet gamblers engaging with an average of 6.9 different types of gambling within the last 12 months, the highest level of gambling versatility reported by players of any of the 15 gambling activities. A more recent report by the Annenberg Foundation suggests that despite efforts by the US government to impose restrictions on Internet gambling, college-age youth are accessing online gambling sites at a growing rate. Based upon the latest

National Annenberg Survey of Youth, monthly use of Internet gambling sites dramatically increased from 4.4 percent to 16.0 percent between 2008 and 2010 (Romer, 2010). Projecting onto the national sample, the results suggest that more than 400,000 males between age 18 and 22 gamble on Internet gambling sites at least weekly. Rates among adolescent males are considerably lower but they report a significant number (estimated to be approximately 530,000 adolescents) access gambling sites monthly. While card playing is the predominant online gambling activity, it is suggested that youth are engaged in multiple forms of online gambling. While the overall rate of increase in Internet gambling was not as pronounced for females, the rates tripled for female adolescents (0.5 percent in 2008 to 1.5 percent in 2010) and increased by over 4 percent for young female adults (0.0 percent in 2008 to 4.4 percent in 2010).

An early study by Byrne (2004; Messerlian, Byrne, and Derevensky, 2004) in Canada of 2,087 adolescents and young adults (43 percent males; 57 percent females) found that more individuals under the age of 18 than 18 to 24 year olds played 'free play' games on Internet gambling sites (43 percent vs. 33 percent for males; 42 percent vs. 29 percent for females). The most popular form of 'free play' activity for both groups was card playing (poker and blackjack), with less frequent gamblers (i.e., those gambling less than once per month) playing slot machines or other forms of online gambling machines.

Over the past year, almost one in twenty (4.6 percent) of the participants (7.8 percent males; 2.3 percent females) had gambled online with their own money. When examined by age, those under 18 years were more likely to be male (8.6 percent; over 18 years 6.8 percent) than female (3.2 percent; over 18 years 1.3 percent). The two most popular forms of Internet gambling for youth were card playing (online poker) and sports betting, similar to the recent results reported by Romer (2010). For those who gambled online for money, Byrne reported that many did so with a family member (i.e., parent or older sibling). Among Internet gamblers, the prevalence rate of problem gambling was almost 19 percent. Although very high, similar rates of problem gambling prevalence among self-selected samples have been reported by other research studies on youth gambling (e.g., Griffiths and Barnes, 2008; Griffiths, Parke, Wood, and Rigbye, 2010; Matthews, Farnsworth, and Griffiths, 2009; Wood, Griffiths, and Parke, 2007). Byrne reported no significant gender differences but did note that the younger the person gambling online, the more likely they were to exhibit problem gambling.

Meerkamper (2010), in a recent survey of 569 Canadian youth (age 15–18 years) reported 8 percent had gambled online with their own money. They were also asked where they had acquired their money to gamble online and the most popular responses included personal savings (63 percent), previous winnings (30 percent), PayPal account (16 percent), loans from friends or family members (16 percent), their personal credit card (7 percent), or their parents' credit card (5 percent).

In addition to the studies of Byrne and Meerkamper, there have also been some smaller more locally based studies done in various parts of Canada. For instance, Meerkamper (2006) reported that more than one in twenty teenagers in Nova Scotia aged 15–17 years reported playing online poker for money. Poulin and Elliot (2007) reported that in the past year, 4.2 percent of adolescents had gambled for money online in Atlantic Canada, and in Montreal, almost one in ten teenagers (9 percent) gambled online for money (Derevensky and Gupta, 2007). A summary of the main findings of all the major surveys concerning online gambling can be found in Table 10.4. This table also demonstrates that males are significantly more likely to gamble online compared to females.

*Table 10.4* Summary of main findings of studies investigating online gambling in youth

| Researcher (year) | Country | Age (number) | Prevalence of online gambling; gender differences | Problem gambling |
|---|---|---|---|---|
| Byrne (2004) | Canada | 16–24 years (n = 2,087) | 4.6% past year; 7.8% male/2.3% female | Prevalence rate of problem gambling in Internet gamblers was almost 19% |
| Griffiths & Wood (2007) | UK | 12–15 years (n = 8,017) | 8% past year; 10% male/6% female | Problem gamblers more likely than social gamblers to gamble on the Internet (37% vs. 9%) |
| Welte et al. (2009) | USA | 14–21 years (n = 2,274) | 2% past year; 3% male/0% female | Internet gamblers were likely to experience more problem gambling symptoms by virtue of gambling on more forms of gambling, as opposed to the properties of Internet gambling itself |
| Olason (2009) | Iceland | 16–18 years (n = 1,513) | 20% ever; 4% regularly; 32% male/9% female | Problem gambling among gamblers was 3%. Among Internet gamblers it was significantly higher at 10.1% |
| Olason et al. (2011) | Iceland | 13–18 years (n = 1,537) | 24% ever; 4% regularly; 37% male/11.5% female | Problem gambling among gamblers was 2.2%. Among Internet gamblers it was significantly higher at 7.5% |
| Ipsos MORI (2009) | UK | 11–15 years (n = 8,598) | 1% past week | [Not reported] |
| Brunelle, Cousineau et al. (2009) | Canada | 14–18 years (n = 1,876) | 8% past year; 13% male/3% female | Significantly more Internet gamblers (11%) were likely to be problem gamblers than those who did not gamble on the Internet (1.5%) |
| Meerkamper (2010) | Canada | 15–21 years (n = 1,000) | 8% past year | [Not reported] |

## Online gambling-like experiences in adolescence

Over the last decade, there have been a number of published reports examining gambling-like experiences engaged in by adolescents including instant win games in children's snacks like crisps and chocolate (Griffiths, 1997) and money-free gambling that could include 'free play', 'practice', and 'demo' games on Internet gambling sites (Griffiths and Wood, 2007). North American studies have reported that anywhere between 25 and 50 percent of teenagers have played 'free play' games via Internet gambling sites (Byrne, 2004; Derevensky and Gupta, 2007; McBride and Derevensky, 2010; Poulin and Elliot, 2007; Brunelle, Cousineau et al., 2009). In the study by Griffiths and Wood (2007), outlined earlier, of the 8 percent of youth who had gambled online, a quarter of respondents said they had played free instant win games (24 percent).

Ipsos MORI (2009) reported that 28 percent of their sample of youth (n = 8,598) in the UK had participated in money-free gambling of some sort in the week preceding the survey. As depicted in Figure 10.1, just over a quarter of adolescents had played in 'money-free mode' in the week preceding the survey, with opportunities on the social networking sites four or five times more popular than those presented on actual gambling sites. Using statistical modelling to further examine the same data, Forrest, McHale, and Parke (2009) reported that gambling in money-free mode was the single most important predictor of whether the child had gambled for money and one of the most important predictors of problem gambling. However, it should be noted that this relationship is correlational and not necessarily causal. The possibility and extent to which money-free gambling is responsible for real gambling participation and gambling-related risk and harm could only be confirmed using longitudinal data. Ipsos MORI also found that those children who reported: being male; having a black or white ethnic background; earning or receiving £30 in the last week; and having parents who were gamblers were all significantly more likely to have gambled in money-free mode in the specified time period.

Meerkamper (2010) recently reported that 33 percent of 388 underage minors (15–18 years) had gambled online using the 'free play' modes and/or via online social networking sites. He suggested the reasons for playing online free (gambling) games were to relieve boredom (59 percent), fun (49 percent), excitement (thrill) (15 percent), because their friends play (14 percent), and because it was perceived to be a good way to improve their skills before they start to play with real money. A significant minority (22 percent) also reported they played because it was on a social networking site (e.g., Facebook). The survey also asked what the adolescents had learned from playing online for free. The most popular responses were that they learned how to manage risk (24 percent), learned how to play better (18 percent), had increased confidence by playing (10 percent), and it had prepared them for playing online with money. It was also reported that 8 percent of these youth had been invited to gamble for real money while playing in the free play mode.

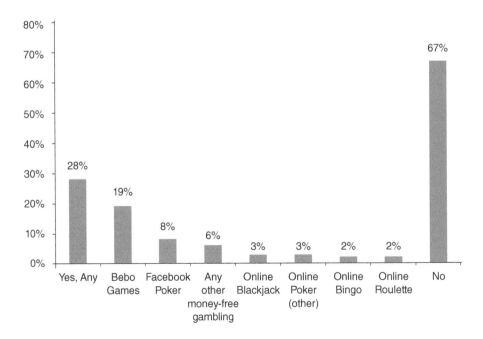

*Figure 10.1* Money-free gambling in the last seven days

Source: Adapted from Ipsos MORI, 2009

Some clinical researchers have asserted that youth gambling in money-free mode may be a cause for significant concern (e.g., Derevensky, 2008; Derevensky and Gupta, 2007; Griffiths, 2003; Griffiths and Wood, 2007; Messerlian et al., 2004; Mitka, 2001). It has been alleged that such opportunities encourage teenagers to practise before 'graduating' to playing for money games at online casinos (Kelley, Todosichuk, and Azmier, 2001) and that a 'precautionary principle' should be applied which prevents adolescents from being exposed to gambling-like experiences (Hyder and Juul, 2008). However, the specific impact of money-free play remains unclear. Despite the strong correlation of money-free play with both gambling participation and problem gambling (Forrest, McHale, and Parke, 2009; McBride and Derevensky, 2009), there is currently no conclusive evidence to suggest that money-free play causes individuals to start gambling for actual money or to be more at risk of experiencing gambling-related harm, although there is a growing body of correlational evidence.

The use of 'free play' sites is not the only type of online gambling-like experience in which adolescents can now engage. Griffiths, King, and Delfabbro (2009) identified other types of gambling-like experiences including gambling via social networking sites and gambling via online penny auction sites.

## Adolescent gambling via social networking sites

Across the world, the social networking phenomenon has spread rapidly. Despite the fact that the minimum age for most major social networking sites is usually 13 years (and 14 years on MySpace), a study by the Office of Communications (2008) in the UK reported that just over a quarter (27 percent) of 8 to 11 year olds who are aware of social networking sites said that they had a profile on a social networking site. A recent report by Meerkamper (2010) revealed that poker groups were the number one favourite site among Facebook users. The most popular social networking site used by children was Bebo (63 percent).

Recently, Downs (2008) noted that content-generated risks from this new leisure activity have not been investigated in any detail, yet young people using these sites are able to easily gain access to gambling activities. Downs claimed that the potential of social networking sites to 'normalize' gambling behaviours may change the social understandings of the role of gambling among young people. For example, while socially responsible gambling emphasizes that money spent gambling may not offer a return other than the pleasure gained from the game, the social networking utilities can present gambling as a viable route for the acquisition of scarce virtual goods. According to Downs's pilot research, there were 25 poker applications on Bebo (and over 500 separate poker groups) and in excess of 100 poker applications on Facebook (and over 1,000 separate poker groups). These poker sites featured some with real prizes, some with cash-play options, and all easily downloadable by underage minors along with many free trial games. The largest of these poker groups had in excess of several thousand members and in one group surveyed, 15 percent of those in the group declared they were under the age of 18 years. Furthermore, gambling applications typically contain sidebar advertisements and hyperlinks to actual gambling sites.

Downs also reported a type of pseudo-gambling among 'Fluff Friends' that has over 100,000 active users per month. In this social networking forum, users (typically young girls) create 'Fluff' Art. To do this they have to earn *munny* (*sic*) – a type of virtual money through pet racing. Pet racing costs one point per race and winnings can be up to 4,000 points. While there is no actual money exchanged, young children are learning the mechanics of gambling and Downs asserts there are serious questions about whether gambling with virtual money encourages positive attitudes towards gambling in young people. For instance, does gambling with virtual money lead to an increased prevalence of actual gambling? She also asks to what extent are gambling-related groups on social networking sites being used by minors under 18 years and whether membership within such groups facilitates access to commercial gambling sites. It also seems only natural for youth to question whether they should game on Internet sites if they were winning 'play money' (Sevigny, Cloutier, Pelletier, and Ladouceur, 2005).

## Adolescent gambling via online penny auction sites

Another gambling-like activity is participation in online penny auctions such as Madbid, Swoopo, Bid Boogie, Rapid Bargain and Budson (Griffiths, 2008c). In order to participate in an online penny auction, the person needs to place a bid in an ongoing auction. Bids can only be made in one penny (or one euro cent) increments. They can do this by (a) placing a bid by sending a text message from their mobile phone (at £1.50 or €1.50 a bid plus operator's costs) or (b) placing a bid through the creation of an online account where the person purchases a 'bundle' of bids (at 75 pence/75 cents to £1.40/€1.40 a bid depending on how big a bundle they buy in advance). To bid by text message, a person sends a message with the code for the specific product that they want to bid on. There is no limit to how many bids can be submitted on the same auction product. There is also no limit on how many different products can be bid on at any one time.

For example, here is an example of a real winning bid outlined by Griffiths (2008c). A PlayStation videogame console (retail price of £310) was won in a penny auction for £8.34. To the winner of the auction, this was won at a hugely discounted price. However, what this really means is that there were 834 separate bids for this item, all costing up to £1.50 per bid (depending whether it was done online or via mobile phone). Looking at the 'bid history', most of the final 50 bids were made by just two individuals who, at a minimum, spent at least £30 in those final bids trying to secure the item. Although one person won the console, the other person spent a considerable amount of money and received nothing in return. Griffiths (2008c) has argued that this is Internet gambling under another name. Anyone with a mobile phone (e.g., the vast majority of teenagers) can participate in such an activity and it could be argued that many of the items in the auctions appeal particularly to teenage audiences (video game consoles, MP3 players, laptops, etc.). To what extent this very new form of online activity with gambling-like experiences is impacting youth is as yet undetermined, but this is one area where further research is needed.

## Conclusions

While there is some variation in participation rates reported in the studies considered in this review, the limited number of surveys reveal that a small but significant minority of adolescents can and do gamble on the Internet. Several of the studies reported a past-year Internet gambling prevalence rate of approximately 4 percent (Byrne, 2004; Meerkamper, 2006; Poulin and Elliot, 2007), while some reported a lower figure (2 percent) (Welte et al., 2009) and others report the rate as being considerably higher (e.g., 8 percent, Gendron, Brunelle, Leclerc, Dufour, and Cousineau, 2009, Meerkamper, 2010; 9 percent, Derevensky and Gupta, 2007; and 20–24 percent, Olason, 2009, Olason et al., 2010). Interestingly, lower rates of participation were found for the United States (although recent research by Romer (2010) with a limited number of adolescents and young adults suggests large increases) and English-speaking Canadian provinces, with higher rates being reported in Quebec and Europe.

It was also found that adolescent Internet gamblers were significantly more likely to be problem gamblers (e.g. Gendron et al., 2009; McBride and Derevensky, 2009; Olason et al., 2010). It may be the case that problem gamblers are more susceptible and/or vulnerable to gambling online and the fact that it is easily accessible with few verifications in place for underage gambling is a cause for concern. To make matters worse, there appears to be little concern among parents about youth gambling (Campbell, Derevensky, Meerkamper and Cutajar, 2011). However, it may also be that adolescent problem gamblers gravitate to the Internet, adding it as an additional mode of gambling to their general repertoire of gambling behaviours as suggested by Wood and Williams (2009). Consistent with findings reported in this review, Wood and Williams reported a higher rate of problem gambling among Internet gamblers compared to non-Internet gamblers. Importantly, they noted that since other modes of gambling (other than Internet) were reported by participants as the main cause of their gambling problems, it was most likely that Internet gamblers were already heavy gamblers to begin with and that this was simply a new venue to play to complement their existing gambling activities. This is also consistent with initial conclusions by Welte and his colleagues (2009) and McBride and Derevensky (2009) who suggested the increased risk to be the consequence of wide-ranging participation in gambling activities rather than being a direct causal link between Internet gambling and problem gambling.

Given the complexity of the available evidence, the role of Internet gambling in creating adolescent problem gamblers should be treated with caution. However, it is clear that research that can help to identify the impact of Internet gambling on either creating or facilitating gambling-related harm among adolescents should be made a research priority. The incidence of youth engaging in free play gambling sites is also a serious concern. As Derevensky (2008) noted, this may be a training program for future gamblers. There is also clinical evidence that youth are prone to stealing their parents' credit cards to engage in this behaviour. Such research should consider the potentially different roles that Internet gambling may play in creating new forms of harm and in exacerbating existing forms of harm.

Another interesting theme to emerge was that friends and family were reported to play an important role in the online gambling experience among adolescents. For example, Brunelle, Cousineau et al. (2009) reported that only 2 percent of Internet gambling was done with the adolescent playing alone. The fact that 57 percent of gambling was done with a family member and 37 percent done with friends emphasizes the social acceptability and nature of Internet gambling among adolescents; an activity that has been traditionally noted as being an asocial activity. Similar findings were also reported by Griffiths and Wood (2007) and Campbell and Derevensky (in press). These figures appear to be significantly different to trends among adults with one study reporting that 59 percent of adult respondents indicated that they always gambled alone (Valentine and Hughes, 2008). There are two potential implications of these findings. First, future research must explore the nature and the specific impact of the social processes in adolescent Internet gambling. The role of family may be particularly important in this regard. Second, parents clearly need to be educated about gambling (and its potential problems) in the same way as other potentially addictive behaviours (e.g., drinking, smoking, drug taking, etc.). Such findings are corroborated by both adolescent and parent studies.

With respect to regulation, there seem to be significant developments in trying to prevent underage individuals gambling online with clear licensing conditions and codes of practice being recommended, implemented, and regular compliance checks being performed for a number of sites (e.g., see guidelines by the Global Gambling Guidance Group [G4; http://www.gx4.com/], or eCommerce Online Gaming Regulation and Assurance [eCOGRA; http://www.

ecogra.org/]). However, with at least one in three regulated sites still permitting easy access to underage players, it is clear that there is still much work to do. Some operations must tighten their age verification systems by using more sophisticated cross-referencing options and stricter criteria, even at the risk of losing customers. As well, even though there is some evidence, at least in the United Kingdom, that access to gambling online may prove more difficult relative to securing offline access, underage Internet gamblers may only need to get through the hurdles once. In other words, once an adolescent has managed to get through age verification systems and register, they can gamble again repeatedly. This differs from offline facilities where adolescents would have to deceive the 'gatekeepers' on each separate visit.

It should be emphasized that regulatory performance and compliance is only one aspect of preventing underage Internet gambling. It seems that with only 23 percent of underage Internet gamblers using their own debit cards to register and pay for their gambling, most are being assisted in some way with their payment (i.e., using friends, family or sponsored credit cards,[1] prepaid credit cards). In one survey, 17 percent of those that had played the lottery on the Internet had accessed their parents' accounts (either with or without their permission) (Griffiths and Wood, 2007). This places a significant level of responsibility with older friends and family members, either in terms of refusing assistance in accessing actual gambling opportunities or in closely monitoring the use of credit cards for which they have ultimate responsibility.

There appear to be two challenges in relation to parents preventing underage Internet gambling. First, parents must have the appropriate knowledge, attitudes, awareness, and intentions to prevent underage gambling. While parents may have the ability to prevent underage online gambling, they may permit or assist their child as a result of viewing such behaviour as a harmless and/or fun activity. Second, even if parents are motivated to prevent underage Internet gambling, they must be prepared to monitor their child's Internet usage, and where made available, spending on credit and debit cards and other types of accounts should be monitored. Educating parents should be one of the key components of any strategy aimed at preventing or minimizing underage Internet gambling. Innovative anti-gambling software has been developed and in some jurisdictions has been offered without cost (e.g., the BetStopper program in Nova Scotia).

The issue of payment is perhaps one of the most important areas for further research. More work is needed to explore the relationship between underage payment mechanisms and the development of problem gambling. Derevensky (2010), reporting results from a study of youth, age 17–20, noted that 44 percent used a personal credit card, 6 percent used a family member's credit card with permission, 4 percent used a family member's credit card without permission, 26 percent used a debit card, 6 percent used personal cheques, and 27 percent used a wire or bank transfer to pay for their Internet wagering. What if an adolescent is gambling using someone else's credit or debit card and they are not winning or losing their own money, will this have the same implications for developing or facilitating problem gambling? Factors which have been linked to the development and facilitation of problem gambling (e.g., the big win; chasing; arousal) could be argued to be dependent on the extent to which a gambler is winning or losing their own money.

Finally, there is evidence to suggest that 'money-free' gambling plays a critically important role for adolescents in conceptualizing and experiencing Internet gambling. Over one in three adolescents have been reported to gamble in money-free mode (Byrne, 2004; Gendron et al., 2009), with Ipsos MORI (2009) reporting that 28 percent of 11–15 year olds in a recent UK sample had done so within the last week. It is argued that it is through money-free gambling (using social networking sites or 'demo' modes of real gambling sites) that children are being introduced to the principles and excitement of gambling without experiencing the consequences of losing actual money. Early research has shown it is significantly more commonplace to win while 'gambling' on the first few goes on a 'demo' or 'free play' game (Sevigny et al., 2005), although this is not the case for all games (e.g., UK National Lottery games). The same study also reported that it was commonplace for gamblers to have extended winning streaks during prolonged periods while playing in the 'demo' modes. However, there have been significant regulatory developments in recent years with improved codes of practice requiring that age verification also applies to 'demo modes' and that such modes should be an accurate representation of the actual playing experience including the probability of winning and the rate of return to the player (e.g., see British Gambling Commission, 2007).

Based upon the available literature, it may be important to distinguish between the different types of money-free gambling being made available – namely social networking modes and 'demo' or 'free play' modes. Initial considerations suggest that these may be different both in nature and in impact. For example, as Downs (2008) argues, players gambling in social networking modes may experience a different type and level of reinforcement than those gambling in 'demo' mode. On some social networking sites, the accumulation of 'play money' or 'points' may have implications for buying virtual goods or services or being eligible for certain privileges. This may increase the value and meaning of the gambling event to the individual. Second, when considering the 'flow' and intention of individuals accessing such sites, it could be argued that individuals accessing money-free gambling through social networking sites may be more likely to be induced or persuaded to play given that these website visitors' primary intention may have been social interaction (i.e., the primary function of the website) in contrast to those playing in 'demo' mode where gambling is the primary function of the website. Interestingly, four or five times more children report playing money-free gambling on social networking sites compared to 'demo' or 'free play' modes on gambling websites. It is suggested that the nature and impact of various forms of money-free gambling should be the subject of further research and empirical investigation.

Some experts claim that *'the exposure of children to gambling-like activities, games of chance with fake money, and play with materials of potential financial value should be seen as risks that need to be controlled'* (Hyder and Juul, 2008: 203). However, to date, such individuals have failed to give an adequate explanation for the underlying reasons. No evidence or speculation are provided regarding the process by which gambling-like experiences may increase risk as opposed to moderating the risk or having no effect on potential risk.

The rise and challenges of Internet gambling cannot be seen in isolation, particularly as there is ever-increasing social acceptance and multimedia integration between the Internet, mobile phones, and interactive television. Furthermore, young people are very proficient in using and accessing these media tools and are likely to be increasingly exposed to remote gambling opportunities. These young people with expertise in this technology, their perceived invulnerability, and belief that they are more intelligent than their adult counterparts, will therefore require education and guidance to enable them to cope with the challenges of convenience gambling in all its guises. Parents, teachers, health professionals, and other practitioners also need to be made aware of the same information.

## Acknowledgment

Parts of this chapter were originally published in: Griffiths, M. D. and Parke, J. (2010). 'Adolescent gambling on the Internet: A review'. *International Journal of Adolescent Medicine and Health*, 22, 59–75.

## Note

1   Credit cards are not normally available to customers under 18 years of age unless they are guaranteed by an adult or the adult is the primary card holder.

## References

American Gaming Association (2006). 'State of the States 2006'. *The American Gaming Association survey of casino entertainment*. Retrieved from http://www.americangaming.org/survey/2006/reference/ref.html.

Brunelle, N., Cousineau, M-M., Dufour, M., Gendron, A., and Leclerc, D. (2009, March). 'A look at the contextual elements surrounding Internet gambling among adolescents'. Paper presented at the 8th Annual Conference of Alberta Gaming Research Institute, Banff Center, Alberta.

Brunelle, N., Gendron, A., Leclerc, D., Cousineau, M-M., and Dufour, M. (2008, November). 'Gambling, Internet gambling and substance use among Quebec youth'. Poster paper presented at the 9th Annual NCRG Conference on Gambling and Addiction, Las Vegas, Nevada.

Brunelle, N., Gendron, A., Dufour, M., Leclerc, D., and Cousineau, M-M. (2009, February). 'Gambling among youth in relation with alcohol and drug use, delinquency and psychological distress'. Paper presented at the International Center for Youth Gambling Problems and High-Risk Behaviour, McGill University, Canada.

Byrne, A. (2004). 'An exploratory study of Internet gambling among youth'. Unpublished Master's thesis. McGill University, Montreal.

Campbell, C., Derevensky, J., Meerkamper, E. and Cutajar, J. (2011). 'Parents' perceptions of adolescent gambling: A Canadian national study'. <http://youthgambling.mcgill.ca/en/PDF/Publications/2011/Parents_perceptions.pdf> *Journal of Gambling Issues*, *25*, 36–53.

Cotte, J., and Latour, K. (2009). 'Blackjack in the kitchen: Understanding inline versus casino gambling'. *Journal of Consumer Research, 35*, 742–58.

de Freitas, S., and Griffiths, M. D. (2008). 'The convergence of gaming practices with other media forms: What potential for learning?' A review of the literature. *Learning, Media and Technology*, *33*, 11–20.

Derevensky, J. (2008). 'Gambling behaviours and adolescent substance use disorders'. In Y. Kaminer, and O. G. Buckstein (eds). *Adolescent substance abuse: Psychiatric comorbidity and high risk behaviours* (403–33). New York: Haworth Press.

— (2010, March). 'Internet gambling: The tip of the iceberg'. Paper presented at the New York Council on Problem Gambling annual convention. Albany, New York.

Derevensky, J. and Gupta, R. (2007). 'Internet gambling amongst adolescents: A growing concern'. *International Journal of Mental Health and Addiction, 5*, 93–101.

Downs, C. (2008, September). 'The Facebook phenomenon: Social networking and gambling'. Paper presented at the Gambling and Social Responsibility Forum Conference, Manchester Metropolitan University, Manchester.

Fisher, S. (2000). 'Developing the DSM-IV-MR-J criteria to identify adolescent problem gambling in non-clinical populations'. *Journal of Gambling Studies, 16*(2/3), 253–74.

Forrest, D. K, McHale, I., and Parke, J. (2009). 'Appendix 5: Full report of statistical regression analysis'. In Ipsos MORI, *British survey of children, the National Lottery and gambling 2008–9: Report of a quantitative survey*. London: National Lottery Commission.

Gambling Commission (2007). 'Remote gambling and software technical standards'. (Technical Standards Paper). Retrieved July 30, 2009 from http://www.gamblingcommission.gov.uk/UploadDocs/publications/Document/Remote%20Gambling%20and%20Software%20Technical%20Standards.pdf

Gendron, A., Brunelle, N., Leclerc, D., Dufour, M., and Cousineau, M-M. (2009, March). 'Comparison of the profiles of young non-gamblers, gamblers and Internet gamblers relative to psychological distress, severity of substances use and impulsiveness/risk taking'. Poster presented at the 8th Annual Conference of Alberta Gaming Research Institute, Banff Center, Alberta.

Germain, M., Guyon, L., Landry, M., Tremblay, J., Brunelle, N., and Bergeron, J. (2007). *DEP-ADO. Detection of alcohol and drug prevention in adolescents (Version 3.2).* Recherche et intervention sur les substances psychoactives – Quebec (RISQ).

Griffiths, M. D. (1997). 'Instant-win promotions: Part of the gambling environment?' *Education and Health, 15,* 62–3.

— (2001). 'Internet gambling: Preliminary results of the first UK prevalence study', *Journal of Gambling Issues, 5.* Retrieved October 7, 2010 from http://www.camh.net/egambling/issue5/research/griffiths_article.html

— (2003). 'Internet gambling: Issues, concerns and recommendations'. *CyberPsychology and Behavior, 6,* 557–68.

— (2008a). 'Digital impact, crossover technologies and gambling practices'. *Casino and Gaming International, 4*(3), 37–42.

— (2008b). 'Convergence of gambling and computer game playing: Implications'. *E-Commerce, Law and Policy, 10*(2), 12–13.

— (2008c). 'Online "penny auction" sites: Regulation needed'. *E-Finance & Payments Law & Policy, 2*(12), 14–16.

— (2010). 'Gambling addiction on the Internet'. In K. Young, and C. Nabuco de Abreu (eds), *Internet addiction: A handbook for evaluation and treatment.* New York: Wiley, 191–211.

Griffiths, M. D., and Barnes, A. (2008). 'Internet gambling: An online empirical study among student gamblers'. *International Journal of Mental Health and Addiction, 6,* 194–204.

Griffiths, M. D., and Parke, J. (2002). 'The social impact of Internet gambling'. *Social Science Computer Review, 20,* 312–20.

Griffiths, M. D., and Wood, R. T. A. (2007). 'Adolescent Internet gambling: Preliminary results of a national survey'. *Education and Health, 25,* 23–7.

Griffiths, M. D., King, D., and Delfabbro, P. (2009). 'Adolescent gambling-like experiences: Are they a cause for concern?' *Education and Health, 27,* 27–30.

Griffiths, M. D., Parke, J., Wood, R. T. A., and Rigbye, J. (2010). 'Online poker gambling in university students: Further findings from an online survey'. *International Journal of Mental Health and Addiction, 8,* 82–9.

Griffiths, M. D., Wardle, J., Orford, J., Sproston, K., and Erens, B. (2009). 'Socio-demographic correlates of Internet gambling: findings from the 2007 British Gambling Prevalence Survey'. *CyberPsychology and Behaviour, 12,* 199–202.

— (2010). 'Internet gambling, health, smoking and alcohol use: Findings from the 2007 British Gambling Prevalence Survey'. *International Journal of Mental Health and Addiction.* doi:10.1007/s11469-009-9246-9.

Hyder, A. A., and Juul, N. H. (2008). 'Games, gambling, and children: Applying the precautionary principle for child health'. *Journal of Child Adolescent Psychiatric Nursing, 21,* 202–4.

Ipsos MORI, The National Lottery Commission (2009). *British survey of children, the National Lottery, and gambling 2008–2009.* London: National Lottery Commision. Retrieved from: http://www.natlotcomm.gov.uk/assetsuploaded/documents/Children%20and%20gambling%20-FINAL%20VERSION%20140709.pdf

Kelley, R., Todosichuk, P., and Azmier, J. J. (2001). *Gambling@home: Internet gambling in Canada.* (Gambling in Canada Research Report No. 15). Calgary, AB: Canada West Foundation.

King, D. L., Delfabbro, P. H., and Griffiths, M. D. (2010). 'The convergence of gambling and digital media: Implications for gambling in young people'. *Journal of Gambling Studies, 26,* 175–87.

Matthews, N., Farnsworth, W. F., and Griffiths, M. D. (2009). 'A pilot study of problem gambling among student online gamblers: Mood states as predictors of problematic behaviour'. *CyberPsychology & behavior, 12*(6), 741–5.

Meyer, G., Hayer, T., and Griffiths, M. D. (eds). (2009). *Problem gambling in Europe – Challenges, prevention and interventions.* New York: Springer.

McBride, J., and Derevensky, J. (2009). 'Internet gambling behaviour in a sample of online gamblers'. *International Journal of Mental Health and Addiction, 7,* 149–67.

— (2010). 'Internet gambling among college students'. Unpublished manuscript, McGill University, Montreal Canada.

Meerkamper, E. (2006). *Decoding risk: Gambling attitudes and behaviours amongst youth in Nova Scotia.* Report prepared for the Nova Scotia Gaming Corporation.

— (2010, October). 'Youth gambling 2.0: Understanding youth gambling, emerging technologies, and social platforms'. Paper presented at the Nova Scotia Gaming Corporation 6th Annual Responsible Gambling Conference, Halifax, Nova Scotia.

Messerlian, C., Byrne, A. M., and Derevensky, J. L. (2004). 'Gambling, youth and the Internet: Should we be concerned?' *Canadian Child and Adolescent Psychiatry Review, 13*(1), 3–6.

Mitka, M. (2001). 'Win or lose, Internet gambling stakes are high'. *Journal of the American Medical Association, 285*(8), 1005.

NCH (2004). *Children as young as 11 can set up gambling accounts at the click of a button.* July 27 press release by NCH, GamCare and CitizenCard. Available at http://www.nch.org.uk/information/index.php?i=77&r=288.

NetValue (2002). *Europeans take a gamble online.* NetValue Survey, June. Available at http://www.nua.ie/surveys/analysis/weekly_editorial/archives/issue1no307.html.

Office of Communications (2008). 'Social networking: A quantitative and qualitative research report into attitudes, behaviours and use'. Retrieved June 17, 2009 from www.ofcom.org.uk

Olason, D. (2009, April). 'Internet gambling and problem gambling among 13–18 year adolescents in Iceland'. Paper presented at the 7th SNSUS Conference (The Big Picture: Gambling in Perspective), Helsinki, Finland.

Olason, D. T., Kristjansdottir, E., Einarsdottir, H., Bjarnason, G., and Derevensky, J. L. (2011). 'Internet gambling and problem gambling among 13 to 18 year old adolescents in Iceland'. <http://youthgambling.mcgill.ca/en/PDF/Publications/2011/Internet_gambling_problem_gambling.pdf> *International Journal of Mental Health and Addiction, 9*, 257–63.

Poulin, C., and Elliot, D. (2007). *Student drug use survey in the Atlantic Provinces: Atlantic Technical Report.* Halifax: Dalhousie University, Community Health and Epidemiology.

Romer, D. (2010). *Internet gambling among male and female youth ages 18 to 24.* Report from the Annenberg Public Policy Center, University of Pennsylvania.

Sevigny, S., Cloutier, M., Pelletier, M., and Ladouceur, R. (2005). 'Internet gambling: Misleading payout rates during the "demo" period'. *Computers in Human Behaviour, 21*, 153–8.

Smeaton, M., and Griffiths, M. D. (2004). 'Internet gambling and social responsibility: An exploratory study'. *CyberPsychology and Behavior, 7*, 49–57.

Valentine, G., and Hughes, K. (2008). *New forms of gambling participation: Problem Internet gambling and the role of the family.* Report prepared for the Responsibility in Gambling Trust.

Volberg, R. A., Gupta, R., Griffiths, M. D., Olason, D. T., and Delfabbro, P. (2010). 'An international perspective on youth gambling studies'. *International Journal of Adolescent Medicine and Health, 22*, 3–38.

Welte, J. W., Barnes, G. M., Tidwell, M. O., and Hoffman, J. H. (2009). 'The association of form of gambling with problem gambling among American youth'. *Psychology of Addictive Behaviours, 23*, 105–12.

Winters, K. C., Stinchfield, R. D., and Fulkerson, J. (1993). 'Toward the development of an adolescent gambling problem severity scale'. *Journal of Gambling Studies, 9*, 63–84.

Wood, R., and Williams, R. (2009). *Internet gambling: Prevalence, patterns, problems, and policy options.* Guelph, Ontario: Ontario Problem Gambling Research Centre.

Wood, R. T. A., Griffiths, M. D., and Parke, J. (2007). 'The acquisition, development, and maintenance of online poker playing in a student sample'. *CyberPsychology and Behavior, 10*, 354–61.

# 11 The relationship between Internet gambling and problem gambling

*Robert T. Wood, Robert J. Williams,*
*and Jonathan Parke*

## Introduction

It is a well-established fact that a small proportion of adults who gamble, in all jurisdictions and across all gaming formats, are properly classified as problem gamblers. Indeed, despite the common rhetoric espousing the importance of 'responsible gambling' and despite the efforts in most jurisdictions to implement 'responsible gambling' features to various gambling platforms, it seems a near impossibility to achieve a situation where government-sponsored gambling and the complete amelioration of problem gambling can coexist. To be sure, rates of problem gambling in most jurisdictions are relatively low, with standardized rates across international jurisdictions ranging from a low of 0.5 percent to a high of 7.6 percent (Williams, Volberg, and Stevens, 2012). Nonetheless, while policy makers may find comfort and affirmation in the fact that overall problem gambling rates are low, it is clear that not all gambling formats enjoy the same relationship with problem gambling, and that some types of gambling may be inherently more risky or dangerous. Internet gambling is potentially one such form, with studies repeatedly demonstrating that Internet gamblers, relative to non-Internet gamblers, are much more likely to experience gambling problems. However, while the existence of an association between Internet and problem gambling has been well documented, there remains much ambiguity about the direction and temporality of the relationship, as well as the particular causes of this relationship. In other words, it remains unclear the extent to which problem gambling is facilitated by the Internet gambling experience, or whether problem gamblers (who are often highly versatile gamblers) disproportionately gravitate towards the Internet as one more format in their broader gambling repertoire. Moreover, it remains unclear the extent to which Internet gambling is an *inherently* more risky form of gambling, or whether other variables associated with Internet gambling are the primary causes.

In order to shed light upon these issues, this chapter is devoted to presenting and critically evaluating the academic evidence on the relationship between Internet gambling and problem gambling. To that end, we review the existing literature which identifies the presence of such a relationship, as well as recent research that raises critical questions about the extent to which Internet gambling is inherently more harmful or risky than other formats. In response to the cumulative methodological limitations of the research literature, we conclude with an appeal for additional longitudinal research, which is sensitive to the diachronic and situational complexities of the Internet gambling experience.

## An association exists between Internet gambling and problem gambling

The research community first speculated about the potential relationship between Internet gambling and problem gambling in the several years after the initial appearance of the

Internet gambling phenomenon (Azmier, 2000; Griffiths, 1996; Hammer, 2001; Shaffer, 1996; Smith, and Wynne, 2002; Wiebe, Single, and Falkowski-Ham, 2001). Earlier studies, however, largely relied upon small, non-random, cross-sectional samples of Internet gamblers. Ladd and Petry (2002), for example, conducted a study of Internet gambling among 389 university health clinic patients, all of whom had gambled at least once in their lifetime, but only 31 of whom had ever gambled on the Internet. Compared to the non-Internet gamblers in this sample, these 31 Internet gamblers were three to four times more likely to be classified as level two or level three gamblers according to the South Oaks Gambling Screen (SOGS) criteria. While the Ladd and Petry study, among others, is credited as pioneering in its identification of a relationship between Internet and problem gambling, it yields little insight into the temporal direction of the relationship, and the small self-selected sample makes it difficult to determine the strength of the relationship or to generalize to the broader population of gamblers.

Subsequent studies replicated the finding of disproportionate rates of problem gambling among Internet gamblers, using generally larger samples (although still self-selected in nature), often recruited online. In an online study of 422 self-selected online university poker players, 18 percent of the sample was classified as problem gamblers using the Diagnostic and Statistical Manual of Mental Disorders (DSM-IV; American Psychiatric Association, 2000) criteria (Griffiths, Wood, and Parke, 2006). Internet gamblers were also significantly more likely to be problem gamblers in another study of university students by Griffiths and Barnes (2008). Among a sample of 1,920 Internet gamblers recruited from an online gambling portal, Wood and Williams (2007) found 23 percent to be moderate problem gamblers on the Canadian Problem Gambling Index (CPGI; using 3–7 criterion), and an additional 20 percent were found to be severe problem gamblers (using an 8+ criterion). Using similar methodology, McBride and Derevensky (2009) observed a problem gambling prevalence rate of 23.3 percent among a self-selected sample of 563 Internet gamblers.

The proportion of Internet users who opt to participate in online surveys is very low. Consequently, it is quite possible that surveys concerning online gambling may disproportionately attract heavy and/or problem gamblers. Random sampling of members of 'online panels' helps to correct this bias to some extent (Göritz, 2007; Göritz, Reinhold, and Batinic, 2002; cf. Williams and Volberg, 2011). Using this methodology, a 2005 study of 12,717 Dutch Internet users found that 14 percent of the sample gamblers were potential problem gamblers (Motivaction International, 2005). Similarly, a Swedish online panel study of 3,000 online poker players in 2007 found that 23 percent of players were either moderate or severe problem gamblers as measured by the CPGI (see Chapter 7).

The Casino City study (see Chapter 6) used random digit dialing to survey a representative sample of 8,498 Canadians. The characteristics of the 179 Internet gamblers within this sample were used to weight a much larger survey of international Internet gamblers recruited from an online gambling portal (*n* = 7,921, including 1,954 Internet gamblers). Because both samples included Internet as well as land-based gamblers, a direct comparison could be made between the two populations. This particular study found that Internet gamblers were about three times more likely than their land-based counterparts to be classified as problem gamblers.

The most unambiguous evidence showing that Internet gambling is associated with a higher rate of problem gambling comes from jurisdiction-wide population surveys using either a telephone or face-to-face administration format. Internet gambling was shown to have a higher rate of problem gambling in Belgium in 2006 (Druine, Delmarcelle, Dubois, Joris, and Somers, 2006); Canada in 2006/7 (Wood and Williams, 2009); Germany in 2006 (Bühringer, Kraus, Sonntag, Pfeiffer-Gerschel, and Steiner, 2007); Great Britain in 2006/7

(Wardle et al., 2007) and 2010 (Wardle et al., 2011); Iceland in 2007 (Olason and Gretarsson, 2009); Northern Ireland in 2010 (Department for Social Development, 2010); Norway in 2008 (Bakken and Weggeberg, 2008); and Sweden in 2007 (Tryggvesson, 2007) and 2008/9 (Swedish National Institute of Public Health, 2011). Several state/provincial surveys have also found Internet gambling to bear a stronger relationship to problem gambling than other forms: e.g., Australian Capital Territory in 2009 (Davidson and Rodgers, 2010); Alberta in 2008 (Williams, Belanger, and Arthur, 2011); British Columbia in 2002 (Ipsos-Reid and Gemini Research, 2003); New Brunswick in 2009 (MarketQuest Research, 2010); Newfoundland in 2009 (MarketQuest Research, 2009); Quebec in 2009 (Kairouz, Nadeau, and Paradis, 2011); California in 2005/6 (Volberg, Nysse-Carris, and Gerstein, 2006); and Maryland in 2010 (Shinogle et al., 2011).

## Is Internet gambling a cause of problem gambling or just reflective of problem gambling?

Although there is an unambiguous association between Internet and problem gambling, there are confounds that preclude causal inferences. The most important one is that very few Internet gamblers only gamble on the Internet. Rather, Internet gamblers tend to be frequent gamblers who participate in many different forms. For example, Wood and Williams (2011; and Chapter 6) found that among 1,954 international online gamblers, just 4.6 percent *only* gambled on the Internet and that the best statistical predictor of being an Internet gambler among 22 predictor variables was gambling on a large number of gambling formats (Wood and Williams, 2011; and Chapter 6). Similarly, one of the characteristic features of most problem gamblers is that they engage in many different types of gambling (e.g., Bakken and Weggeberg, 2008; Buth and Stöver, 2008; National Research Council, 1999; Sproston, Erens, and Orford, 2000; Swedish National Institute of Public Health, 2011; Wardle et al., 2007, 2011; Welte, Barnes, Wieczorek, Tidwell, and Parker, 2004; and see Chapter 6).

Thus, it is possible that involvement in Internet gambling is *reflective* of excessive gambling involvement, rather than being a cause. As evidence of this, the association between Internet gambling and problem gambling in the 2007 British Gambling Prevalence Survey becomes non-significant when controlling for number of gambling games engaged in (LaPlante, Nelson, LaBrie, and Shaffer, 2009; Vaughan Williams, Page, Parke, and Rigbye, 2008). A similar result was obtained by Halme (2011) in an analysis of the 2007 Finnish population prevalence study and by Welte, Barnes, Tidwell, and Hoffman (2009) in a sample of American youth aged 14–21.

These studies serve to remind us that multivariate approaches are far superior to univariate approaches in helping to determine a variable's unique contribution to problem gambling. They are also useful in helping correct the undue emphasis that has been placed on gambling format as a risk factor for problem gambling. Although electronic gambling machines and Internet gambling are commonly cited as 'causes' of problem gambling, Wood and Williams (2011; and Chapter 6) found that 41.7 percent of Canadian Internet problem gamblers and 46.4 percent of international Internet problem gamblers reported there was no particular form of gambling that contributed to their problems more than others.[1] Finally, these above studies are very important because they confirm that a major part of the reason for the association between problem gambling and Internet gambling has to do with the fact that they are both characterized by heavy gambling involvement.

On the other hand, it is also important to recognize that a few studies *have* found evidence that certain forms of Internet gambling pose an additive risk, even after controlling for level of gambling involvement (e.g., Internet roulette in Vaughan Williams et al., 2008; Internet casino gambling in Haß, Orth and Lang, 2012). Also, if versatile participation in a wide variety of gambling types is an important risk factor for problem gambling, then theoretically it would make sense that involvement in a wide variety of gambling locations or administration formats (i.e., online + land-based) should also be a risk factor. Indeed Internet gambling may promote greater versatility because it provides gambling via an additional new medium and because of the wide array of gambling types available at most online sites (and the accompanying free play sections where people can learn to play the different types of gambling).

The self-report of problem gamblers is also relevant. For the roughly 50+ percent of Internet problem gamblers who *do* report that certain forms of gambling have been particularly contributory, Internet gambling is one of the forms most often identified (after electronic gambling machines; Wood and Williams, 2011; and Chapter 6). One can also not ignore the increased rate with which online gambling is identified as a problematic form among people seeking treatment. For example, Internet poker was identified by only 5 percent of people calling the Swedish helpline in 2004, but became the most commonly reported problem (by 29.9 percent of callers) in 2007, one year after its legal introduction (see Chapter 7).

However, the most important caveat to the above type of cross-sectional analysis is that it does not take into account the temporal course of events that may differentiate gambling formats in their etiological relationship to problem gambling. Although gamblers will add many different forms of gambling on their path to problem gambling, the addition of certain forms (e.g., Internet gambling) may be more likely to immediately precipitate disordered gambling compared to other forms. It is also quite plausible that the online gambling may exacerbate existing problem gambling and/or hinder recovery to a greater extent than other forms of gambling because of its much greater accessibility. Longitudinal research is the only way of addressing these issues.

## Longitudinal examination of this issue

### *Bwin Division on Addiction Research Collaborative*

Researchers from the Division on Addiction at the Cambridge Health Alliance have lamented the fact that the bulk of existing Internet gambling research relies heavily on cross-sectional and retrospective self-reported data, in the absence of any examination of actual Internet gambling behaviour as it evolves over time (Shaffer, Peller, LaPlante, Nelson, and LaBrie, 2010; and see Chapter 9). These investigators have endeavoured to address this deficit in research collaboration with the European online gambling company *bwin.com.*[2] In a series of studies (partly funded by bwin.com) of the actual longitudinal gambling behaviour of 40,000+ bwin patrons, these researchers have found evidence that contradicts and challenges 'common assumptions that Internet gambling will stimulate excessive patterns of gambling' (LaPlante, Schumann, LaBrie, and Shaffer, 2008: 2412). This position is rooted in their consistent observation that the betting and gambling behaviour among most bwin customers is both moderate and adaptive (i.e., level of betting subsided over time), with the exception of the top 1–5 percent of the most heavily involved bettors (LaBrie, LaPlante, Nelson, Schumann, and Shaffer, 2007; LaBrie, Kaplan, LaPlante, Nelson, and Shaffer, 2008; LaPlante, Nelson, LaBrie, and Shaffer, 2009; and see Chapter 9). As stated by LaPlante et al. (2008) 'daily analyses of gambling activity indicated rapid adaptation to the new service, as illustrated by a short term increase in activity, peaking by the eighth day of activity and declining thereafter' (p. 2410). Moreover, the collective results of the bwin studies suggest that the net losses of the vast majority of bwin gamblers are relatively modest, with observed net losses being no larger than a median of €4 per week for the entire sample across each mode of gambling. However, for the most involved subgroups, weekly expenditure could reach on average in excess of €130 (median = €88) per week per mode of gambling (LaBrie et al., 2007; LaBrie et al., 2008; LaPlante, Kleschinsky. LaBrie, Nelson, and Shaffer, 2009).

There is no doubt that this research provides support for the previously well-established finding that only a minority of online gamblers experience problems gambling online. On the other hand, there are some important limitations in extrapolating the particularly low level of 'problematic behaviour' in the bwin studies to online gambling more generally.

First, this data is from just one of the 665 companies that currently provide online gambling. Furthermore, bwin.com is not representative of most providers. They are arguably more socially responsible than most, as illustrated by their interest in academic research collaboration, as well as the fact they are one of the small number of online companies that have sought and received certification from eCOGRA (eCommerce and Online Gaming Regulation and Assurance) as a fair and responsible gambling provider. In addition, the majority of bwin sports betting patrons have historically been German (LaBrie et al., 2007), as well as a significant minority of their casino players (30 percent from Germany and Austria; LaBrie et al., 2008). German nationals were observed to be more moderate bettors compared to people from other countries in the LaBrie et al. (2007) study, and Germany has one of the world's lowest known past-year prevalence rates of problem gambling (~0.5 percent) (Bühringer et al., 2007; Federal Center for Health Education, 2008; Williams, Volberg, and Stevens, 2012).

An additional problem with extrapolation from the bwin results is that most online gamblers patronize more than one site (see Chapters 6, 7, and 8; Wood and Williams, 2011). For example, in a sample of over 10,000 Internet casino and poker players Parke et al. (see Chapter 8) found that the typical casino player reported visiting more than six Internet casinos in the preceding three months. Jonsson (see Chapter 7) found that the typical Swedish Internet poker player patronizes two poker sites. Thus, moderate gambling behaviour at the bwin site provides no assurance that aggregated online behaviour is also moderate.

Also, as acknowledged by the bwin researchers, the moderation of gambling activity over time observed among bwin patrons could easily be explained in other ways. Bwin, like most operators, provides a monetary bonus to new customers conditional on that player depositing some of their own money and wagering this total amount several times over before making a withdrawal. This would naturally encourage a pattern of play characterized by considerable activity followed by a decline or even cessation as players move to other sites to take advantage of their bonuses. Second, driven by the perception of better value or better odds, bettors may try out different websites, and consequently play at one website for only a limited period of time.

The final problem with the bwin data is that problem gambling is not actually assessed. Although the bwin researchers decry the reliance on self-report over objective behaviour in gambling research, self-report of problems deriving from gambling is the only way to establish that problem gambling is present, as well as the actual prevalence of problem gambling among online players. Patterns of frequent gambling involvement or account closure, as used in the bwin studies, are not adequate substitutes.

### *Quinte longitudinal study*

The recently completed Quinte Longitudinal Study (QLS) (Williams et al., 2006; Williams, 2010) began in 2006, with the recruitment and assessment of 4,121 individuals, aged 17 to

89, from the Quinte region of southeastern Ontario, Canada. Individuals were recruited via random digit dialing, and were asked if they wished to participate (in exchange for a $220 honorarium) in a five-year research study about the impacts of a proposed new *racino*, which was to be built in the area. Two samples were recruited: a 'general population' sample (*n* = 3,065), and an 'at risk' sample (*n* = 1,056) selected so as to oversample people at greater risk for developing gambling problems. Participants were assessed annually using a self-administered survey instrument that was accessible online either in the research office located in Belleville, Ontario, or via their home computer. The survey took between one and two hours to complete and comprehensively assessed all variables of etiological relevance to problem gambling, including demographic characteristics; physical health; lifetime gambling behaviour; attitudes towards gambling; past-year gambling behaviour; motivation for gambling; context in which participants gambled; social exposure to gambling; availability of gambling opportunities; problem gambling status; gambling fallacies; personality; stress; current and lifetime mental health status; marital functioning; family functioning; presence of social support; community involvement and social capital; participation in recreational activity; occupational functioning; current and lifetime participation in illegal behaviour; and intelligence. Post-hoc weightings ensured that the sample closely corresponded to the age by gender distributions in the 2001 Canadian census, as well as compensating for the oversampling of people residing in single- and dual-person households. Finally, bootstrap weights (Yeo, Mantel, and Liu, 1999) were generated, in order to refine the confidence intervals when analysing data.

The retention rate of a longitudinal study is a major determinant of the validity of its results. Of the initial sample of 4,123 individuals in the QLS, a remarkable 93.4 percent completed either 4/5 or 5/5 of the annual assessments.

Although the QLS is primarily a longitudinal study of gambling, generally, it contains a small subsample of Internet gamblers that provides pertinent information about the relationship between Internet gambling and problem gambling. Among the participants, 381 people reported gambling on the Internet at least once during the five-year period of assessment. Of these, 24 became Internet gamblers in the final assessment period, and were not problem gamblers during any of the previous assessment periods, thus precluding any determination of the subsequent effect of Internet gambling on developing gambling problems. (However, for these 24 individuals, it is at least possible to confirm that problem gambling did not precede their transition to Internet gambling.) Excluding these 24 individuals from the analysis, 282 (79.0 percent) out of the 357 remaining Internet gamblers did *not* transition to problem gambling status at any point during the study, while the remaining 75 individuals (21.0 percent) *did* become past-year problem gamblers at some point during the study. Of these 75 individuals, 21 were both problem gamblers and Internet gamblers in the first assessment period, not permitting a determination of which came first. Excluding these 21 individuals from the analysis: 24 (44.4 percent) out of 54 were Internet gamblers who became problem gamblers in a subsequent assessment period; 16 (29.6 percent) out of 54 were problem gamblers who began gambling on the Internet in a subsequent assessment period; and 14 (25.9 percent) out of 54 were people who developed problem gambling and Internet gambling, apparently simultaneously, during the same assessment period (excluding assessment period 1).

These longitudinal findings yield several important conclusions. Importantly, 21 percent of people who gambled on the Internet were also problem gamblers at some point during the study. This stands in contrast to the 5.6 percent of non-Internet gamblers in the sample, who became problem gamblers at some point during the five-year study, thus confirming that

Internet gamblers as a population are characterized by much higher levels of problem gambling. It should be noted, however, that the results of the QLS study also indicate that the majority of Internet gamblers (79 percent) are able to gamble on the Internet without experiencing problems. In any event, the more crucial question, with a previously undetermined answer, concerns the temporal direction of the relationship between Internet and problem gambling. After excluding people where the temporal direction of the relationship cannot be established, three general pathways are evident: (1) 44 percent of participants initiated Internet gambling prior to experiencing gambling problems; (2) 30 percent of participants were problem gamblers who subsequently engaged in Internet gambling; and (3) 26 percent of participants developed gambling problems relatively simultaneously with their transition into Internet gambling. Thus, in answer to the oft-discussed 'chicken and egg' question about the temporal sequencing of Internet gambling versus problem gambling, the answer is that both sequences are clearly evident among the Internet gambling population. This being the case, it is also apparent that Internet gambling leading to problem gambling is a more common pathway than problem gambling leading to Internet gambling.

As far as we are aware, this is the first longitudinal study to shed light on the temporal direction of the relationship between Internet gambling and problem gambling. However, this will certainly not be the final word on this topic, as there are other longitudinal studies currently under way in Alberta (Canada), Sweden, Australia, and New Zealand that will also be able to speak to this relationship.

It is also important to realize that the QLS, while making a significant contribution to our understanding of the link between Internet gambling and problem gambling, is limited by a number of factors. For one, the causal relationship between Internet gambling and subsequent problem gambling is not unambiguously established. It is quite possible that the 44 percent of Internet gamblers who subsequently became problem gamblers may have done so even without engaging in Internet gambling (i.e., choosing to engage in Internet gambling may simply be an early sign that someone's gambling is getting out of control). A stronger case for Internet gambling being instrumental in the development of problem gambling would require a demonstration that a subsequent propensity for problem gambling was much higher when people engaged in Internet gambling for the first time, compared to other forms of gambling for the first time (an analysis that has not yet been done with this data set). A second consideration is that even though the sample is representative, it is relatively small (only 75 participants evidenced both Internet and problem gambling in a way where the general relationship could be determined). It is also limited by its inability to provide a fine-grained chronological sequencing of events in the relationship between Internet gambling and problem gambling, which could be important in identifying other variables which might be mediating this relationship. Finally, the results of the QLS study are specific to a particular jurisdiction, a particular time period, and a particular 'gambling landscape' (i.e., southern Ontario where 'legal' Internet gambling is unavailable, but with most other forms of gambling being available). This specificity of location and time, in turn, may impact which kinds of people choose to engage in Internet gambling (e.g., risk takers, who are not deterred by the legal ambiguity associated with online gambling in Canada).

## Conclusions and implications for future research

In summary, the research discussed in this chapter establishes that:

1   Most Internet gamblers do not experience gambling-related problems.

2    However, people who gamble on the Internet do have significantly higher rates of problem gambling compared to people who do not gamble on the Internet.

3    The primary reason for the strong association between Internet and problem gambling has to do with the fact that problem gamblers are versatile gamblers who tend to engage in a wide variety of gambling formats which will often include Internet gambling, whereas the prevalence rate of Internet gambling by non-problem gamblers tends to be lower.

4    However, although controlling for number of gambling formats engaged in eliminates the relationship between Internet and problem gambling in most studies, an argument can be made that the very nature of Internet gambling promotes gambling versatility. Online gambling has also been identified as a problematic form of gambling in population surveys and in some treatment settings at a rate higher than would be expected compared to population participation rates. Finally, cross-sectional analysis does not disentangle the temporal course of events that may differentiate online gambling from other forms (i.e., although gamblers add many different forms of gambling on their path to problem gambling, the addition of certain forms (e.g., Internet gambling) may be more likely to immediately precipitate disordered gambling compared to other forms). Longitudinal analysis is the only way of addressing these issues.

5    The limited existing longitudinal evidence shows that although many problem gamblers gravitate to Internet gambling, a more common pathway is for Internet gambling to precede the development of problem gambling or for it to develop simultaneously with problem gambling.

Thus, the conclusion of the present authors is that engagement in Internet gambling most likely does somewhat elevate a person's risk of developing problem gambling (although this risk level is much less than many people have presumed). Aside from the empirical evidence, this conclusion makes theoretical sense. In the substance abuse field it is well established that although drug abusers use many different substances and alcoholics consume many different beverage types, there are still certain drugs that have a greater harm potential (van Amsterdam, Best, Opperhuizen, and de Wolff, 2004; Nutt, King, Saulsbury, and Blakemore, 2007) and certain alcoholic beverages that bear a stronger relationship with whether a person becomes a heavy drinker (Jensen et al., 2002; Gronbaek, Jensen, Johansen, Sorensen, and Becker, 2004). Not all risky products are created equal. In the field of gambling, forms of gambling that should have an elevated risk profile are ones with a higher frequency of reinforcement (Parke and Griffiths, 2007; Welte, Barnes, Wieczorek, Tidwell, and Hoffman, 2007; Williams et al., 2007, 2008) and ones that are more readily available (Abbott, 2007; Meyer, Fiebig, Hafeli, and Morsen, 2011; Welte et al., 2007; Williams et al., 2007, 2008). Several forms of Internet gambling have both of these features.[3]

## Notes

1    Similarly, in the 2008 and 2009 Alberta prevalence studies 44 percent of all problem gamblers (regardless of whether they gambled on the Internet) reported there was no particular form of gambling more responsible for their problems compared to other forms (Williams, Belanger, and Arthur, 2011).

2    Known as betandwin from 1997 to 2006, bwin from 2006 to 2011, and bwin.party Digital Entertainment from March 2011 to present due to its recent merger with PartyGaming. Their initial product was sports betting, but they subsequently provided online casinos and then online poker. The headquarters are located in Gibraltar.

3   Some people have argued that the fact that problem gambling prevalence rates have stabilized and/ or decreased in recent years despite the emergence of Internet gambling is evidence that Internet gambling cannot bear a strong relationship with problem gambling. However, what this argument fails to take into account is that with Internet gambling currently only being patronized by a small minority of the population (< 5 percent in most countries), even if problem gambling rates doubled or tripled among Internet gamblers, it would not affect population-wide problem gambling prevalence rates to any significant extent.

# References

Abbott, M.W. (2007). 'Situational factors that affect gambling behavior'. In G. Smith, D. C. Hodgins, and R. J. Williams (eds), *Research and Measurement Issues in Gambling Studies* (251–78). Burlington, MA: Academic Press.

American Psychiatric Association. (2000). *DSM IV-TR: Diagnostic and Statistical Manual of Mental Disorders – Text Revision* (fourth edn). Washington, DC: American Psychiatric Association.

Azmier, J. J. (2000). *Canadian Gambling Behaviour and Attitudes: Summary Report*. Calgary, AB: Canada West Foundation.

Bakken, I. J., and Weggeberg, H. (2008). *Pengespill og pengespillproblem i Norge 2008* [Gambling Behaviour and Problem Gambling in Norway 2008]. SINTEF Rapport A8499.

Bühringer, G., Kraus, L., Sonntag, D., Pfeiffer-Gerschel, T., and Steiner, S. (2007). *Pathologisches Glücksspiel in Deutschland: Spiel-und Bevölkerungsrisiken* [Pathological gambling in Germany: Gambling and population based risks]. *Sucht, 53*(5), 296–308.

Buth, S., and Stöver, H. (2008). *Glücksspielteilnahme und Glücksspielprobleme in Deutschland: Ergebnisse einer bundesweiten Repräsentativbefragung* [Gambling and gambling problems in Germany: Results of a national survey]. *Suchttherapie, 9*, 3–11.

Davidson, T., and Rodgers, B. (2010). *2009 Survey of the Nature and Extent of Gambling, and Problem Gambling, in the Australian Capital Territory*. Report for the ACT Gambling and Racing Commission, Canberra. Retrieved from http://www.gamblingandracing.act.gov.au/Documents/ACT%20Gambling%20Prevalence%20Study.pdf

Department for Social Development (Northern Ireland). (2010). *Northern Ireland Gambling Prevalence Survey 2010*. Belfast: Author

Druine, C., Delmarcelle, C., Dubois, M., Joris, L., and Somers, W. (2006). *Etude quantitative des habitudes de Jeux de hasard pour l'offre classique et un ligne en Belgique* [Quantitative study on online and offline gambling behaviour in Belgium]. Bruxelles: Foundation Rodin.

Federal Center for Health Education (BZgA). (2008). *Glücksspielverhalten und Problematisches Glücksspielen in Deutschland 2007* [Gambling behaviour and problem gambling in Germany in 2007].

Göritz, A. S. (2007). 'Using online panels in psychological research'. In A. N. Joinson, K. McKenna, T. Postmes, and U-D. Reips (eds), *The Oxford Handbook of Internet Psychology*. Oxford University Press.

Göritz, A. S., Reinhold, N., and Batinic, B. (2002). 'Online panels'. In B. Batinic, U. D. Reips, and M. Bosnjak (eds), *Online Social Sciences* (27–47). Göttingen: Hogrefe & Huber Publishers.

Griffiths, M. (1996). 'Gambling on the Internet: A brief note'. *Journal of Gambling Studies, 12*(4), 471–3.

Griffiths, M., and Barnes, A. (2008). 'Internet gambling: An online empirical study among student gamblers'. *International Journal of Mental Health and Addiction, 6*, 194–204.

Griffiths, M., Wood, R. T. A., and Parke, J. (2006). 'A psychosocial investigation of student online poker players'. Presentation at the 13th International Conference on Gambling, Lake Tahoe, Nevada.

Gronbaek, M., Jensen, M. K., Johansen, D., Sorensen, T. I. A., and Becker, U. (2004). 'Intake of beer, wine and spirits and risk of heavy drinking and alcoholic cirrhosis'. *Biological Research, 37*, 195–200.

Halme, J. T. (2011). 'Overseas Internet poker and problem gambling in Finland 2007: A secondary data analysis of a Finnish population survey'. *Nordic Studies on Alcohol and Drugs, 28*, 51–63.

Hammer, R. D. (2001). 'Does Internet gambling strengthen the U.S. economy? Don't bet on it'. *Federal Communications Law Journal, 54*(1), 103–28.

Haß, W., Orth, B., and Lang, P. (2012). *Risk Potential of Different Gambling Activities*. Presentation at the International Gambling Conference 2012. Auckland, New Zealand.

Ipsos-Reid and Gemini Research. (2003). *British Columbia Problem Gambling Prevalence Study*. Victoria, BC: Ministry of Public Safety and Solicitor General. Retrieved from http://hdl.handle. net/1880/47569

Jensen, M. K., Andersen, A. T., Sorensen, T. I. A., Becker, U., Thorsen, T., and Gronbaek, M. (2002). 'Alcoholic beverage preference and risk of becoming a heavy drinker'. *Epidemiology, 13*(2), 127–32.

Kairouz, S., Nadeau, L., and Paradis, C. (2011). *Portrait of Gambling in Quebec: Prevalence, Incidence and Trajectories over Four Years*. Montreal, QC: Université Concordia. Retrieved from http://hdl. handle.net/1880/48548

LaBrie, R. A., Kaplan, S., LaPlante, D. A., Nelson, S. E., and Shaffer, H. J. (2008). 'Inside the virtual casino: A prospective longitudinal study of actual Internet casino gambling'. *European Journal of Public Health, 18*(4), 410–16.

LaBrie, R. A., LaPlante, D. A., Nelson, S. E., Schumann, A., and Shaffer, H. J. (2007). 'Assessing the playing field: A prospective longitudinal study of Internet sports gambling behavior'. *Journal of Gambling Studies, 23*(3), 347–62.

Ladd, G. T., and Petry, N. M. (2002). 'Disordered gambling among university-based medical and dental patients: A focus on Internet gambling'. *Psychology of Addictive Behaviors, 16*(1),76–9.

LaPlante, D. A., Kleschinsky, J. H., LaBrie, R. A., Nelson, S. E., and Shaffer, H. J. (2009). 'Sitting at the virtual poker table: A prospective epidemiological study of actual Internet poker gambling behavior'. *Computers in Human Behavior, 25*(3), 711–17.

LaPlante, D. A., Nelson, S. E., LaBrie, R. A., and Shaffer, H. J. (2009). 'Disordered gambling, type of gambling and gambling involvement in the British Gambling Prevalence Survey 2007'. *European Journal of Public Health*: Advance Access. doi:10.1093/eurpub/ckp177.

LaPlante, D. A., Schumann, A., LaBrie, R. A., and Shaffer, H. J. (2008). 'Population trends in Internet sports gambling'. *Computers in Human Behavior, 24*, 2399–414.

McBride, J., and Derevensky, J. (2009). 'Internet gambling behavior in a sample of online gamblers'. *International Journal of Mental Health and Addiction, 7*, 149–67.

MarketQuest Research (2009). *2009 Newfoundland and Labrador Gambling Prevalence Study*. Prepared for Department of Health and Community Services, Government of Newfoundland and Labrador. St. John's, NL: Department of Health and Community Services. Retrieved from http:// hdl.handle.net/1880/47656

MarketQuest Research. (2010). *2009 New Brunswick Gambling Prevalence Study*. Prepared for Department of Health and New Brunswick Lotteries and Gaming Corporation, Government of New Brunswick. Fredericton, NB. Retrieved from http://hdl.handle.net/1880/48382

Meyer, G., Fiebig, M., Hafeli, J., and Morsen, C. (2011). 'Development of an assessment tool to evaluate the risk potential of different gambling types'. *International Gambling Studies, 11*(2), 221–36.

Motivaction International. (2005). *Netherlands Participation in Paid Interactive Internet Gaming*. Retrieved August 21, 2011 from http://www.toezichtkansspelen.nl/information.html

National Research Council. (1999). *Pathological Gambling. A Critical Review.* Washington, DC: National Academy Press.

Nutt, D., King, L. A., Saulsbury, W., and Blakemore, C. 2007. 'Development of a rational scale to assess the harm of drugs of potential misuse'. *The Lancet, 369*: 1047–53.

Olason, D. T., and Gretarsson, S. J. (2009). 'Iceland'. In G. Meyer, T. Hayer, and M. Griffiths (eds), *Problem Gambling in Europe: Challenges, Prevention, and Interventions* (137–51). New York: Springer. doi:10.1007/978-0-387-09486-1.

Parke, J., and Griffiths, M. D. (2007). 'The role of structural characteristics in gambling'. In G. Smith, D. C. Hodgins, and R. J. Williams (eds), *Research and Measurement Issues in Gambling Studies* (218–49). Burlington, MA: Academic Press.

Shaffer, H. J. (1996). 'Understanding the means and objects of addiction: Technology, the Internet and gambling'. *Journal of Gambling Studies, 12*(4), 461–9.

Shaffer, H. J., Peller, A. J., LaPlante, D. A., Nelson, S. E., and LaBrie, R. A. (2010). 'Toward a paradigm shift in Internet gambling research: From opinion and self-report to actual behavior'. *Addiction Research & Theory, 18*(3), 270–83.

Shinogle, J., Volberg, R. A., Park, D., Norris, D. F., Haynes, D., and Stokan, E. (2011). *Gambling Prevalence in Maryland: A Baseline Analysis*. Baltimore, MD: Maryland Institute for Policy Analysis & Research.

Smith, G., and Wynne, H. (2002). *Measuring Problem Gambling in Alberta Using the Canadian Problem Gambling Index*. Edmonton: Alberta Gaming Research Institute.

Sproston, K., Erens, R., and Orford, J. (2000). *British Gambling Prevalence Survey 1999.* London: National Centre for Social Research.

Swedish National Institute of Public Health. (2011). *Spel om pengar och spelproblem i Sverige 2008/2009, SWELOGS, Swedish Longitudinal Gambling Study*. Report No. 3.

Tryggvesson, K. (2007) *Nätpokerspelandet i Sverige – omfattning, utveckling och karaktär 2006. SoRAD – Forskningsrapport nr 43 – 2007.* [Internet poker gaming in Sweden – scope, development and character 2006. SoRAD – Research Report no. 43 – 2007.] Stockholm: Stockholms universitet.

van Amsterdam, J. G. C., Best, W., Opperhuizen, A., and de Wolff, F. A. (2004). 'Evaluation of a procedure to assess the adverse effects of illicit drugs'. *Regulatory Toxicology and Pharmacology, 39*: 1–4.

Vaughan Williams, L., Page, L., Parke, J., and Rigbye, J. L. (2008). *British Gambling Prevalence Survey 2007: Secondary Analysis*. Gambling Commission, Great Britain. Retrieved July 20, 2011 from http://www.gamblingcommission.gov.uk/pdf/BGPS%202007%20Secondary%20analysis%20%20-%20Oct%202008.pdf

Volberg, R. A., Nysse-Carris, K. L., and Gerstein, D. R. (2006). *2006 California Problem Gambling Prevalence Survey*. Submitted to California Department of Alcohol and Drug Programs Office of Problem and Pathological Gambling. Retrieved from http://www.adp.cahwnet.gov/OPG/pdf/CA_Problem_Gambling_Prevalence_Survey-Final_Report.pdf

Wardle, H., Moody, A., Spence, S., Orford, J., Volberg, R., Jotangia, D., Griffiths, M., and Dobbie, F. (2011). *British Gambling Prevalence Survey 2010*. Prepared for The Gambling Commission. London: National Centre for Social Research. Retrieved from http://www.gamblingcommission.gov.uk/research_consultations/research/bgps/bgps_2007.aspx

Wardle, H., Sproston, K., Orford, J., Erens, B., Griffiths, M., Constantine, R., and Pigott, S. (2007). *British Gambling Prevalence Survey 2007*. London: National Centre for Social Research. Retrieved from http://www.gamblingcommission.gov.uk/research – consultations/research/bgps/bgps_2007.aspx

Welte, J. W., Barnes, G. M., Tidwell, M. O., and Hoffman, J. H. (2009). 'The association of form of gambling with problem gambling among American youth'. *Psychology of Addictive Behaviours, 23*, 105–12.

Welte, J. W., Barnes, G. M., Wieczorek, W. F., Tidwell, M. C. O., and Hoffman, J. H. (2007). 'Type of gambling and availability as risk factors for problem gambling: A tobit regression analysis by age and gender'. *International Gambling Studies, 7*(2), 183–98.

Welte, J. W., Barnes, G. M., Wieczorek, W. F., Tidwell, M. C. O., and Parker, J. C. (2004). 'Risk factors for pathological gambling'. *Addictive Behaviors, 29*(2), 323–35.

Wiebe, J., Single, E., and Falkowski-Ham, A. (2001). *Measuring Gambling and Problem Gambling in Ontario*. Ottawa: Canadian Centre on Substance Abuse.

Williams, R. J. (2010, April 10). *Quinte Longitudinal Study: Purpose, Principles and Methodological Lessons Learned*. Alberta Gaming Research Institute Annual Conference, Banff, Alberta. Retrieved from http://www.abgaminginstitute.ualberta.ca/2010_Program.cfm

Williams, R. J., and Volberg, R. A. (2011). *Population Assessment of Problem Gambling: Utility and Best Practices.* Report prepared for the Ontario Problem Gambling Research Centre and the Ontario Ministry of Health and Long-Term Care. July 22.

Williams, R. J., Belanger, Y. D., and Arthur, J. N. (2011). *Gambling in Alberta: History, Current Status, and Socioeconomic Impacts.* Final Report to the Alberta Gaming Research Institute. Edmonton, Alberta. April 2. Appendix A: 2008 and 2009 Alberta Population Surveys.

Williams, R. J., Hann, B., Schopflocher, D., Wood, R. T., Grinols, E., and McMillen, J. (2006). *The Quinte Longitudinal Study. Research project funded by the Ontario Problem Gambling Research Centre* (April 1, 2006–February 28, 2012). http://www.qeri.ca

Williams, R. J., Volberg, R. A., and Stevens, R. M. G. (2012). *Population Assessment of Problem Gambling: Methodological Influences, Standardized Rates, Jurisdictional Differences, and Worldwide Trends.* Report prepared for the Ontario Ministry of Health and Long-Term Care and the Ontario Problem Gambling Research Centre.

Williams, R. J., West, B., and Simpson, R. (2008). *Prevention of Problem Gambling: A Comprehensive Review of the Evidence 2008.* Report prepared for the Ontario Problem Gambling Research Centre, Guelph, Ontario, Canada. Retrieved Dec. 1, 2008 from http://hdl.handle.net/10133/414

— (2007). 'Prevention of problem gambling'. In G. Smith, D. Hodgins, and R. J. Williams (eds), *Research and Measurement Issues in Gambling Studies* (399–435). San Diego, CA: Elsevier. Retrieved from http://hdl.handle.net/10133/414

Wood, R. T., and Williams, R. J. (2007). 'Problem gambling on the Internet: Implications for Internet gambling policy in North America'. *New Media & Society*, 9(3), 520–42.

— (2009). *Internet Gambling: Prevalence, Patterns, Problems, and Policy Options.* Final report prepared for the Ontario Problem Gambling Research Centre.

— (2011). 'A comparative profile of the Internet gambler: Demographic characteristics, game play patterns, and problem gambling status'. *New Media & Society*. Retrieved July 27, 2011 from http://nms.sagepub.com/content/early/2011/04/29/1461444810397650.full.pdf+html.

Yeo, D., Mantel, H., and Liu, T. P. (1999). *Bootstrap variance estimation for the National Population Health Survey.* Proceedings of the Survey Research Methods Section, American Statistical Association. Retrieved from http://www.amstat.org/Sections/Srms/Proceedings/papers/1999_136.pdf

# 12 Investigating the heterogeneity of problem-gambling symptoms in Internet gamblers

*Joanne Lloyd, Helen Doll, Keith Hawton,*
*William H. Dutton, John Geddes,*
*Guy M. Goodwin, and Robert D. Rogers*

## Introduction

The rapid expansion of Internet gambling over the last decade encouraged researchers to identify features of the online gambling environment that might promote the incidence of gambling problems among users of online gambling services (Wood and Williams, 2007; Griffiths, 2003; Griffiths and Parke, 2010). However, although surveys suggest that the use of Internet gambling services among individuals recruited in student or community health samples tends to be associated with relatively high rates of gambling and problems (Griffiths and Barnes, 2008; Ladd and Petry, 2002; Wood, Griffiths, and Parke, 2007), the extant evidence about problem gambling in users of Internet gambling services remains preliminary and fragmented.

Recently, analyses of player-tracked betting patterns from a European Internet betting service have thrown more light on the way that people use the Internet to bet on sports, casino games, and poker (LaBrie and Shaffer, 2011). These investigations suggest that, while the vast majority of betting accounts involve moderate spending over time-limited intervals (LaBrie, LaPlante, Nelson, Schumann, and Shaffer, 2007; LaBrie, Kaplan, LaPlante, Nelson, and Shaffer, 2008), it is possible to identify individuals who might be at heightened risk of problematic patterns of Internet gambling, indicated for example by the use of self-limit facilities (Nelson et al., 2008) or by behavioural markers such as number, amount, or rate of bets (LaPlante, Schuman, LaBrie, and Shaffer, 2008; LaPlante, Kleschinsky, LaBrie, Nelson, and Shaffer, 2009; LaBrie and Shaffer, 2011). Recent extensions of this research, involving taxometric analysis of betting patterns, suggest that excessive online betting cannot be represented simply in categorical terms (Braverman, LaBrie, and Shaffer, 2011), highlighting the need for more information about what the clinical characteristics of gambling problems in samples of users of Internet gambling services might actually look like.

One way to learn more about the different forms gambling problems can take is to perform cluster, or latent class analysis (LCA) of the Diagnostic and Statistical Manual of Mental Disorders (DSM-IV; American Psychiatric Association, 2000) criteria items endorsed by respondents in large samples or general population surveys. This information could be useful in identifying the treatment needs of individuals whose gambling problems are manifested in different ways. Previous LCA of diagnostic criteria items in large population surveys have identified only a relatively restricted number of classes that vary, principally, in terms of the severity of gambling problems. For example, using the data from the 2007 British Gambling Prevalence Survey, McBride, Adamson, and Shevlin, (2010) identified individuals who could be characterized as 'non-problematic gamblers', 'preoccupied chasers', and 'antisocial impulsivist gamblers'. The preoccupied chasers showed a fairly high probability of reporting loss-chasing and preoccupation, but relatively low likelihood of reporting other symptoms, and most of this group scored between one and four on the DSM-IV criteria. By contrast, the antisocial impulsivists scored five or more on the DSM-IV, categorizing them as 'pathological gamblers'. They were much more likely than the other two classes to endorse each of the 10 criteria (McBride et al., 2010).

These results are broadly reflected in the findings of another LCA of the DSM-IV criteria items in a large population survey (Carragher and McWilliams, 2011). In this study, along with Xian et al.'s LCA of DSM-III criteria in middle-aged men (Xian et al., 2008) and Hong et al.'s LCA of DSM-IV criteria in older adult gamblers (Hong, Sacco, and Cunningham-Williams, 2009), the primary difference between the identified classes reflected severity (i.e. number of symptoms), and the absence of differentiated classes of problem gambler, endorsing different constellations of items, is notable. One explanation for this lack of specificity in previous LCA of DSM-IV criteria items is that they involved large-scale population surveys in which the majority of respondents did not report significant gambling participation or, if they did, they fell into the non-problem gambling class of the model. It remains possible that LCA in a sample consisting of active gamblers might reveal more latent structure. This chapter describes just such an investigation with Internet gamblers.

Here, we present an LCA of the DSM-IV pathological gambling criteria in a sample of 4,125 users of Internet gambling services recruited directly from a selection of gambling websites and assessed using a web-based questionnaire (Lloyd et al., 2010a, 2010b). Information about groups of individuals whose gambling problems are expressed in different ways across the criteria items will inform attempts to link player-tracked betting patterns to clinically significant problems (LaBrie and Shaffer, 2011). The same information could also help us assess and treat individuals whose difficulties with Internet gambling services reflect divergent underlying psychosocial profiles. Therefore, as described previously (Lloyd et al., 2010b, 2010a), we compared patterns of risk factors for psychological disorders across classes using standardized psychometric questionnaires.

## Method

The survey was conducted by the University Department of Psychiatry and Oxford Internet Institute, Oxford. It was joint-funded by the Economic and Social Research Council (RES-164-25-0008) and the Responsibility in Gambling Trust, and approved by a National Health Service Research Ethics Committee (OXREC C; 06/Q1606/151).

As described in full in Lloyd et al. (2010a, 2010b), a self-selected sample of Internet users were recruited between July and November 2007, via banners and text hyperlinks placed on gambling and gambling-related websites registered within Europe. Sampling bias towards Internet users was not problematic, as this group formed our target population.

Upon clicking a link, potential respondents entered the survey website, where they were presented with an information page. Respondents gave informed consent by clicking a button to confirm that they had read the information page and agreed to participate. Respondents provided information about their demographics and online gambling behaviour, and completed a number of validated screening questionnaires for psychological disorders. These included the 10-item criteria for DSM-IV problem gambling (American Psychiatric Association, 2000), the General Health Questionnaire (GHQ-12) (Goldberg et al., 1997), the PRIME-MD Patient Health Questionnaire (PHQ) (Spitzer et al., 1994) to screen for possible depression and panic disorder, questions modified from the Mood Disorder Questionnaire (MDQ) (Hirschfeld et al., 2000), which screen for symptoms of bipolar disorder, the CAGE alcohol screen (Ewing, 1984), and the 10-item Drug Abuse Screening Test (DAST) (Skinner, 1982). Respondents provided information about previous episodes of deliberate self-harm (DSH; intentional self-poisoning or self-injury), past-year prescription medications, and past-year illicit substances used, as well as parental gambling.

The wording and scoring criteria we used for the DSM-IV items were identical to those of the 2007 British Gambling Prevalence Survey (Wardle et al., 2007). Specifically, we used the same 10 questions to enquire about presence of each of the 10 DSM-IV criteria items surrounding gambling-related behaviour and consequences, with the four-point response scale of 'never', 'occasionally', 'fairly often', and 'very often'. Items 1–7 were scored as present with responses of 'fairly often' or 'very often', and absent for responses of 'occasionally' or 'never'. These items relate to loss-chasing; preoccupation with gambling; need to bet more and more to attain the same thrill; irritability when attempting to cut back on gambling; gambling as a means of escape; lying to others about extent of gambling; and unsuccessful attempts to cut back on gambling. The final three items: 'have you committed a crime in order to finance gambling or pay gambling debts?', 'have you risked or lost an important relationship, job, educational or work opportunity because of gambling?', and 'have you asked others to provide money to help with a desperate financial situation caused by gambling?', were scored as present for responses of 'occasionally', 'fairly often', and 'very often', and only absent if the response was 'never'. Scores of three to four were identified as 'problem gambling' cases, and five or above as 'pathological gambling' cases. Throughout, we use scores to indicate 'caseness' rather than 'disorder', because it is unreliable to make a definitive assessment of disorder without a clinical interview.

The PHQ (Spitzer et al., 1994) was scored to confirm DSM-IV criteria for subsyndromal depressive experiences: i.e. endorsement of three of nine items, including an indication of lowered mood, anhedonia, or both (Spitzer, Kroenke, and Williams, 1999). The MDQ (Hirschfeld et al., 2000) was scored as seven items or more endorsed out of 13 (Chandler, Wang, Ketter, and Goodwin, 2008). These scales were used not to identify severe cases that might satisfy diagnostic criteria for major depressive disorder or bipolar disorder as specified by DSM-IV, but rather to identify the presence of mood-related disturbances that might be expected to influence gambling behaviour.

Among other analyses (see Lloyd et al., 2010a), we conducted an LCA on responses to the 10 DSM-IV problem-gambling criteria items. We tested a series of models involving between one and seven classes, and compared models with p-values greater than 0.05 (i.e. those which accurately accounted for the data), looking at parsimony and substantive interpretation, along with additional measures of goodness-of-fit (Vermunt and Magidson, 2003). In addition to looking at $L^2$ values, we compared successive models by the Bayesian Information Criterion (BIC), the average weight of evidence criterion, and the percentage classification error. Once the best model was identified, we compared the model classes in terms of their demographics; incidence of problem gambling; incidence of substance, alcohol, and mood-related disorders; deliberate self-harm; and parental (problem) gambling. This was done using $\chi^2$ tests, followed where relevant by partitioning of the $\chi^2$ variance (Siegel, 1956) in order to determine precisely where significant between-class differences lay.

## Sample

The entire questionnaire was completed by 4,125 participants; 79.1 percent were males, and the mean age was 35.5 years (SD 11.76).

## Results

### *Latent Class Analysis (LCA)*

Of the sample, 79.5 percent scored zero to two criteria items positive on the DSM-IV, indicating no problems with their gambling; 8.7 percent scored three or four items positive, suggesting problematic gambling, and 11.8 percent scored five and above, indicating possible pathological gambling. The Cronbach's alpha reliability estimate for the DSM-IV items was good, at .87 (Nunnally, 1978).

Model fit statistics are shown in Table 12.1. Models with one to four classes did not provide an adequate fit to the data ($L^2$ p < 0.05). Models with five classes or more all provided an adequate fit ($L^2$ p > 0.05). Of these models, the five-class model provides the most parsimonious solution with the fewest parameters. The five-class solution also had the lowest classification error (i.e. it most accurately allocated the greatest proportion of cases) and the best entropy value. Entropy values approaching one indicate a clear distinction between classes (Celeux and Soromenho, 1996). The five-class model also showed the lowest (i.e. best) Bayes Information Criterion (BIC) value of all the models. BIC takes into account parsimony, and is one of the most reliable indicators of model fit (Nylund, Asparouhov, and Muthen, 2007). Taking all these into account, we considered that the five-class model was the optimal solution. Each of the 10 DSM-IV items contributed significantly towards the model's ability to discriminate between clusters, and the model explains between 40.3 percent and 56.3 percent of the variance in each of the individual DSM-IV items.

### *Description of the clusters*

Figure 12.1 provides a graphic representation of the five-class model, showing the probabilities of endorsing each DSM-IV symptom for members of each of the five classes. We term cluster one, the 'non-problem gamblers'. Over two-thirds of the sample fell into this group. They were highly unlikely to report any symptoms of problem gambling, and the minority that did report one symptom were most likely to report chasing or preoccupation.

Cluster two was the next-largest group, containing 17 percent of the sample. This group had a reasonably high chance of endorsing chasing or preoccupation, sometimes along with one other item, but there were no other strong characteristic symptoms. Following the terminology of McBride et al. (2010), we called this group 'preoccupied chasers'.

*Table 12.1* Seven candidate models following latent class analysis (LCA) of the DSM-IV criteria items for pathological gambling among 4,125 individuals recruited from Internet gambling sites

| No. classes | BIC ($L^2$) | Entropy | $L^2$ | df | p-value | Classification error |
|---|---|---|---|---|---|---|
| 1 | 2006.3087 | 1.00 | 10436.1551 | 1013 | 1.3e−1536 | 0.0000 |
| 2 | −6173.2136 | 0.90 | 2165.0945 | 1002 | 1.8e−87 | 0.0221 |
| 3 | −6956.0691 | 0.77 | 1290.7007 | 991 | 3.5e−10 | 0.0685 |
| 4 | −7087.2241 | 0.77 | 1068.0074 | 980 | 0.026 | 0.0703 |
| **5** | **−7139.0515** | **0.71** | **924.6417** | **969** | **0.84** | **0.1183** |
| 6 | −7114.1233 | 0.71 | 858.0316 | 958 | 0.99 | 0.1204 |
| 7 | −7079.2449 | 0.67 | 801.3716 | 947 | 1.00 | 0.1660 |

Notes
$L^2$ = Likelihood ratio statistic based on chi-square; BIC ($L^2$) = Bayes Information Criterion (based on the $\chi^2$). The optimal model is indicated in **bold**.

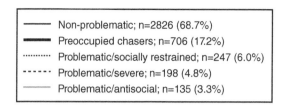

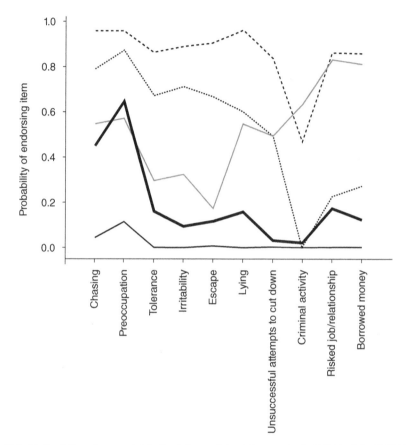

*Figure 12.1* Optimal five-class model derived from a latent class analysis (LCA) of the DSM-IV criteria items reported by 4,125 individuals recruited from Internet gambling sites. (Each class is defined in terms of the probabilities that its members will endorse each of the DSM-IV items.)

Cluster three, who were made up of 6 percent of the sample, had an even higher propensity towards chasing and preoccupation than the preoccupied chasers, but exhibited a high probability of endorsing additional items, most often tolerance, irritability, gambling for escape, lying about extent of gambling, and unsuccessful attempts to cut down. A distinctive feature of cluster three, in light of their high overall gambling involvement, is the relatively low probability of endorsing each of the final three items, i.e. crime, risking a job or relationship, and borrowing money for gambling-related issues. Because of this feature, we term cluster three the 'problematic/socially restrained' group.

Cluster four, almost 5 percent of the sample, have a high probability of endorsing all 10 items; in fact, they were the most likely of any cluster to endorse every item except for committing a crime to finance gambling. Therefore, we termed cluster four, the 'problematic/severe' group.

Finally, cluster five, who comprise just over 3 percent of the sample, were distinguished from the other problematic clusters (i.e. the problematic/socially restrained group and the problematic/severe group) by the fact that their most characteristic symptoms were the final three items, i.e. criminal activity, risking a job or relationship, and borrowing money for gambling. They were also fairly likely to report lying and unsuccessful attempts to cut down, along with chasing and preoccupation, but they are relatively low in their probability of endorsing tolerance, irritability, and gambling to escape. We termed this group the 'problematic/antisocial' group.

In the above designations, we avoid the use of the term 'pathological', in favour of the more general term 'problematic' for the latter three groups. This is because these three groups contained varying proportions of pathological/problem cases (see below).

### Distribution of gambling problems among LCA classes

Table 12.2 lists the proportion of problem and pathological gamblers (based on DSM-IV scores of three to four and five or more, respectively). $\chi^2$ tests confirmed that there was a significant difference between the classes in terms of incidence of both problem ($\chi^2 = 1110.22$, $df = 4$, $p < 0.0005$) and pathological ($\chi^2 = 3326.74$, $df = 4$, $p < 0.0005$) gambling. The highest proportion of *problem* gamblers was found among the preoccupied chasers, which was significantly greater than seen in any other group. There was no difference in the number of problem gamblers among the problematic/socially restrained and problematic/antisocial groups, but both these groups contained more cases than the non-problematic or severe/problematic groups.

By contrast, the problematic/severe class contained more pathological gamblers than any other group ($p < 0.05$), followed by the problematic/socially restrained and problematic/antisocial groups ($p < 0.05$), who did not differ from one another. The non-problematic gamblers and the preoccupied chasers contained equally low numbers of pathological gamblers, significantly fewer than all the other groups ($p < 0.05$). The distribution of symptom counts, as illustrated by Figure 12.2, highlights 'severity' differences between clusters, with the marked exception that the antisocial and socially restrained gamblers show very similar distributions. This is in line with their highly comparable proportions of problem and pathological gamblers, described above.

*Table 12.2* Percentages of non-problematic, problem, and pathological gambling cases in the five classes derived from the optimal latent class analysis (LCA) of the DSM-IV criteria items reported by 4,125 individuals recruited from Internet gambling sites

| | Non-problem gamblers (%) | Problem gamblers (3–4 DSM-IV items) (%) | Pathological gamblers (DSM-IV 5+ items) (%) |
|---|---|---|---|
| Non-problematic ($n = 2,826$) | 100 | 0 | 0 |
| Preoccupied chasers ($n = 706$) | 63 | 36 | 1 |
| Problematic/ | | | |
| socially restrained ($n = 247$) | 0 | 26.7 | 73.3 |
| severe ($n = 198$) | 0 | 0 | 100 |
| antisocial ($n = 135$) | 0 | 26.7 | 73.3 |

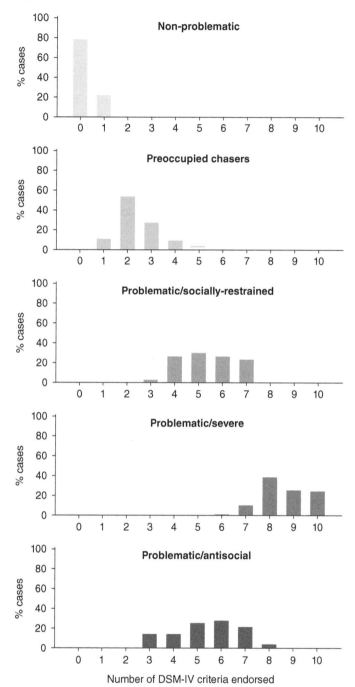

*Figure 12.2* Distribution of DSM-IV items for pathological gambling endorsed within five classes of a latent class analysis (LCA) of the items in 4,125 Internet gamblers

## *Demographic features of LCA classes*

As can be seen in Table 12.3, around one-quarter of the non-problematic cluster were female, significantly more than any other group ($p < 0.01$). This group were more likely than any other group to be married or cohabiting ($p < 0.01$), and more likely to be educated to degree level or above than any other group ($p < 0.05$), except for the preoccupied chasers. The non-problematic group were also less likely than any other group to be unemployed ($p < 0.05$), and among the least likely to be in further education, with significantly fewer numbers of students than found in the preoccupied chaser or antisocial problem gambler clusters ($p < 0.01$). The non-problematic group were also among the least likely groups to report below-average income, and significantly less likely to do so than the severe problematic or antisocial gamblers ($p < 0.05$).

The preoccupied chaser cluster had the highest ratio of males to females, and contained as high a proportion of respondents with degree-level education as the non-problematic gamblers, and a significantly higher proportion of males than the problematic/severe group or the problematic/antisocial group ($p < 0.01$). The proportion of students was also second highest in this cluster, and significantly elevated compared with non-problematic gamblers or problematic/severe gamblers ($p < 0.05$). Unemployment was higher than in the non-problematic group, but did not differ significantly from levels reported by other groups, while below-average income was less common than it was among problematic/severe or problematic/antisocial groups ($p < 0.01$).

In general, the three problematic groups had similar profiles for the majority of their demographic features. The problematic/socially restrained, problematic/severe, and problematic/antisocial groups did not differ significantly from one another in proportion of males ($p > 0.05$), people married/cohabiting ($p > 0.05$), incidence of degree-level education ($p > 0.05$), and unemployment ($p > 0.05$). The proportion of students was lower among the problematic/socially restrained groups than among the problematic/antisocial group ($p < 0.05$), and below-average income was less common among the problematic/socially restrained than the problematic/severe ($p < 0.05$) or problematic/antisocial groups (the latter narrowly missed significance; $\chi^2 = 3.61$).

## *Distribution of psychological distress across LCA classes*

The non-problematic group reported the lowest incidence of 'caseness' across all the measures, as shown in Figure 12.3. They contained fewer cases of low mood (measured with the PRIME-MD), substance abuse (measured with the DAST), mood elevation (measured

*Table 12.3* Demographics (%) of five classes derived from the optimal latent class analysis (LCA) of the DSM-IV criteria items reported by 4,125 individuals recruited from Internet gambling sites

|  | *Male (%)* | *Married or cohabiting (%)* | *Degree or above (%)* | *Unemployed (%)* | *< Avg. income (%)* |
|---|---|---|---|---|---|
| Non-problematic | 74.8 | 57.1 | 43.5 | 5.5 | 27.7 |
| Preoccupied chasers | 90.8 | 43.4 | 42.5 | 8.1 | 28.5 |
| Problematic/ |  |  |  |  |  |
| socially restrained | 85.0 | 47.4 | 36.4 | 8.9 | 30.7 |
| severe | 86.8 | 42.6 | 31.3 | 10.1 | 39.4 |
| antisocial | 85.1 | 38.8 | 28.9 | 12.6 | 40.0 |

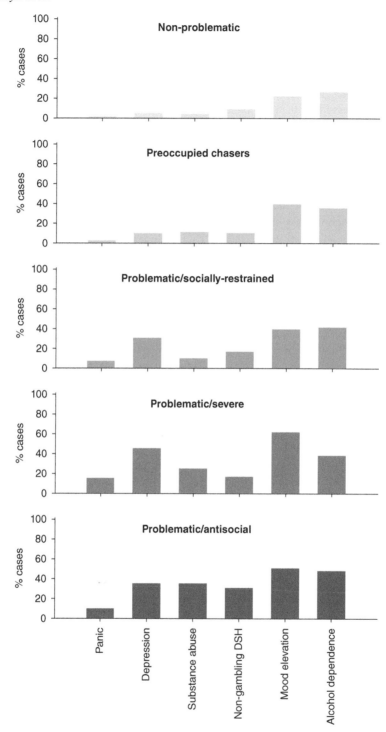

*Figure 12.3* Percentages of respondents scoring above threshold for 'caseness' for different psychological disorders in the five classes of an optimal latent class analysis (LCA) of the DSM-IV items for pathological gambling in 4,125 Internet gamblers

with the MDQ), and alcohol dependence (measured with the CAGE) than any other group in the model (see Figure 12.3). In their incidence of panic and non-gambling related DSH they were statistically comparable to the preoccupied chasers, but contained significantly fewer cases than the remainder of the groups (p < 0.05).

The preoccupied chasers, in addition to being joint lowest for panic and non-gambling-related DSH, contained fewer cases of recent low mood than any other group (p < 0.01) except for the non-problematic group. They also reported fewer cases of substance abuse and previous mood elevation experiences than the problematic/severe and problematic/antisocial groups (p < 0.01), though the number of cases were comparable with the problematic/socially restrained group (p > 0.05) (see Figure 12.3). However, alcohol dependence in this group was comparable with the problematic/severe and problematic/socially restrained groups (p > 0.05); higher than that observed in the non-problematic group (p < 0.01), but lower than in the problematic/antisocial group (p < 0.01).

Among the problematic/socially restrained respondents, the proportion of panic and low mood cases were comparable with the problematic/antisocial respondents (p > 0.05), exceeded the numbers seen among non-problematic gamblers and preoccupied chasers (p < 0.01), but fell below the numbers seen in the problematic/severe group (p < 0.01) (see Figure 12.3). There were also fewer cases of mood disturbance and substance abuse among the problematic/socially restrained group than the problematic/severe and problematic/antisocial groups (p < 0.01). On the other hand, incidence of non-gambling DSH was comparable to those of the problematic/severe group (p > 0.05), but lower than among the problematic/antisocial group (p < 0.01). Alcohol dependence among the problematic/socially restrained respondents was broadly equivalent to all the other groups, with the exception of the fewer cases of the non-problem gamblers (p < 0.01).

More of the problematic/severe respondents reported recent low mood and panic than any other group (p < 0.01) (see Figure 12.3). Reports of previous mood elevation were also significantly higher among the problematic/severe group than among any other cluster (p < 0.01) except the antisocial group. The problematic/severe group also reported higher rates of substance abuse than all other groups (p < 0.05) except the problematic/antisocial group, who were most likely to report this (p < 0.01). Alcohol dependence was also more common among the problematic/severe group than among the non-problem gamblers (p < 0.01) but less common than among the problematic/antisocial group (p < 0.05). The number of non-gambling-related DSH cases in the problematic/severe group was comparable with the problematic/socially restrained group but significantly higher than both the non-problematic gamblers and preoccupied chasers (p < 0.01) and lower than the problematic/antisocial group (p < 0.01).

Finally, the problematic/antisocial group were comparable to the problematic/socially restrained group in reports of low mood and panic, but with significantly fewer cases than in the problematic/severe group (p < 0.01). However, they were comparable to the problematic/ severe group in the number of mood disturbance cases, significantly higher than all the other groups (p < 0.01). More people within the problematic/antisocial cluster reported substance abuse (p < 0.01) and non-gambling-related DSH (p < 0.01) than in any other group (see Figure 12.3) and more alcohol-dependent cases were seen in this group than all other groups (p < 0.05) except the problematic/socially restrained groups.

## Discussion

To our knowledge, this is the first LCA of the DSM-IV criteria symptoms of a sample of gamblers recruited directly from Internet gambling sites, and the first analysis to link clusters of problem-gambling symptoms to other signs of co-occurring psychological disorders. Within our sample, we identified five classes. These comprised a non-problematic group who generally did not endorse any DSM-IV criteria items; a group of preoccupied chasers (McBride et al., 2010), the majority of whom scored below the cut-off for problem gambling, and then three problematic groups who varied in their symptom profiles. These were a problematic/severe group, who endorsed almost every DSM-IV item, a problematic/socially restrained group, and a problematic/antisocial group. Whereas the problematic/socially restrained respondents were least likely to endorse the items describing borrowing money, crime, and risking jobs and relationships because of gambling, the antisocial group showed a marked tendency to report all these items.

Of course, our survey is prone to all the usual inherent limitations of a self-selected sample, such as bias in type of respondent, multiple responses by the same individuals, limited generalizability to the wider gambling population, and inability to draw conclusions about general prevalence. It is also subject to the particular weakness of web-based survey of clinical material, i.e. an absence of interview data to determine the clinical validity of our problem-gambling cases identified through psychometric scales (Eysenbach and Wyatt, 2002). Nevertheless, the strengths of our study are in the size of the sample and the number of people endorsing several DSM-IV criteria, which allowed a fine-grained analysis of symptom profiles. This amount of data would have been extremely difficult to come by in any other way than a targeted sample of gamblers, completing self-report scales hosted remotely. Furthermore, web-based studies have been shown to be a practical method of obtaining data (Wood and Griffiths, 2007), and dovetail nicely with the growing field of web-based treatment approaches, which have begun to appear in the field of problem gambling (Monaghan and Blaszczynski, 2009).

Our data demonstrate the emergence of multiple significant differences between classes of individuals within our sample who manifest distinct DSM-IV symptom profiles. We do not claim that these classes are normative and to be found in other randomly selected samples; no doubt, these classes represent the bias inherent in the respondents obtained from the selection of gambling websites that agreed to place hyperlinks to our survey questionnaire (Lloyd et al., 2010b, 2010a). Nevertheless, our findings of distinct classes that, in part, match previous analyses of land-based gambling samples, provides some validation of the LCA (see below), implying that the clusters we have identified reflect meaningful distinctions. Our exploration of how symptom profiles relate to different demographic characteristics and health experiences may be helpful for informing regulatory policy in this area and for developing more closely targeted interventions for individuals whose Internet gambling has become problematic.

Our five-class model deviates from the three-class models identified by other LCA studies of the DSM-IV criteria (McBride et al., 2010; Carragher and McWilliams, 2011). Our non-problem gamblers, preoccupied chasers, and severe problematic group are broadly comparable with the symptom profiles seen in these other models, and are consistent with the idea that there are types of gamblers who differ from one another primarily in the severity of symptoms (Carragher and McWilliams, 2011; McBride et al., 2010; Xian et al., 2008; Hong et al., 2009). However, we also identified two other clusters (the problematic/socially restrained and the problematic/antisocial) whose members differed in their typical constellations of symptoms, even though the groups did not differ in terms of their symptom counts or in the number of problem and pathological gambling cases. This qualifies the idea that certain symptoms are simply found at the more 'severe' end of the continuum (Strong and Kahler, 2007). Our results are in general agreement with Strong and Kahler (2007), in that preoccupation and chasing occur most often among those with low overall scores on the

DSM-IV, while criminality was only frequently reported among the more severe groups with much higher scores. However, at that higher end of the 'continuum', even among equally symptomatic groups we found there to be different probabilities of endorsing the items such as criminality in these users of Internet gambling services.

There are a number of possible reasons for the greater complexity of our model. We purposively recruited our sample from Internet gambling sites, which will obviously have introduced a significant bias towards problematic gamblers. Therefore, our sample was very different from the population samples used by McBride et al. (2010) and Carragher and McWilliams (2011). Although these latter studies benefited from very large sample sizes, the low numbers of problem-gambling cases meant that neither of their final samples contained more than 80 pathological gamblers, whereas our sample contained 485 people who fell into this category. Since our sample also contained more individuals whose responses to the DSM-IV items indicated problematic gambling, the power of our LCA to detect finer-grained distinctions would have been enhanced.

Alternatively, the differences between our findings and those of earlier studies raises the possibility that users of Internet gambling services are just more diverse than users of land-based gambling services studied previously. The privacy and comfort associated with online gambling have been cited as factors likely to encourage gambling in members of the population who may not ever gamble in a traditional *offline* gambling environment (Griffiths, 2003). A broader range of people gambling online could explain different constellations of symptoms than have previously been identified. Studies applying the DSM-IV criteria to large numbers of *offline* gamblers in samples where problem and pathological gambling are as frequent as in our sample could help determine whether our findings are unique to individuals who gamble on the Internet, or whether any sample with sufficient problematic cases would yield comparable classes.

Our findings raise a number of issues relating to clinical assessment and treatment delivery, as different symptom patterns will, intuitively, make problems more or less apparent and, perhaps, require different interventions. The problematic/severe group, who report experiencing almost all DSM-IV symptoms, will need interventions covering the broad range of consequences they encounter. The particularly elevated incidence of depression, panic, and gambling-related deliberate self-harm in this group reiterates the necessity for assessment and treatment of co-morbid mood problems in severely affected individuals (Dell'Osso and Hollander, 2005, Dell'Osso, Allen, and Hollander, 2005).

By contrast, treatment of people falling into the problematic/antisocial group may be informed by this group's relative absence of 'internalized' symptoms such as tolerance, irritability when cutting down, and gambling to escape negative emotions, compared with other problem groups. Our problematic/antisocial problem gamblers share many features with a group of pathological gamblers studied by Blaszczynski, Steel and McConaghy (1997), with high impulsivity scores associated with gambling related offences, drinking problems (and drinking while gambling), and suicidal ideation. High scores on the Psychoticism subscale of the Eysenck Personality Questionnaire (EPQ) (Eysenck and Eysenck, 1975) in that study were also associated with gambling-related offences, drinking problems, and drug use (Blaszczynski et al., 1997). Our findings suggest that it is possible to identify these individuals within samples of Internet gamblers too. It may also be particularly important to consider the impact of gambling on family and friends when treating gamblers of this type (Valentine and Hughes, 2010).

The status of the preoccupied chasers remains intriguing. As in McBride et al.'s study, these individuals appear to be a relatively mildly affected group including mostly those whose

DSM-IV score is below the cut-off for risk of gambling problems (McBride et al., 2010). Whether this group is a stable 'mild' group, or whether continued Internet gambling among these individuals will facilitate transition to more problematic states is unclear. Prospective research could address this question of how distinct symptom constellations may relate to the time-course of Internet gambling, and whether remission or treatment responsiveness is influenced by initial constellations of problem-gambling symptoms.

Finally, our findings suggest that the study of Internet gambling can be enhanced by the collection of better information about the risk factors for gambling problems and psychological disorders. Information about the variety of ways in which people gamble through the Internet, and their associated health experiences (Lloyd et al., 2010b) and motivations (Lloyd et al., 2010a), could enhance behavioural approaches to identifying the risk in vulnerable individuals (LaPlante et al., 2009) by linking statistical features of betting patterns with psychological and clinical factors (Lloyd et al., 2010b).

## References

American Psychiatric Association. (2000). *DSM IV-TR: Diagnostic and statistical manual of mental disorders – Text revision* (fourth edn). Washington, DC: American Psychiatric Association.

Blaszczynski, A., Steel, Z., and McConaghy, N. (1997). Impulsivity in pathological gambling: The antisocial impulsivist. *Addiction, 92*, 75–87.

Braverman, J., LaBrie, R. A., and Shaffer, H. J. (2011). A taxometric analysis of actual Internet sports gambling behavior. *Psychological Assessment, 23*, 234–44.

Carragher, N., and McWilliams, L. A. (2011). A latent class analysis of DSM-IV criteria for pathological gambling: Results from the national epidemiologic survey on alcohol and related conditions. *Psychiatry Research, 187*, 185–92.

Celeux, G., and Soromenho, G. (1996). An entropy criterion for assessing the number of clusters in a mixture model. *Journal of Classification, 13*, 195–212.

Chandler, R. A., Wang, P. W., Ketter, T. A., and Goodwin, G. M. (2008). A new US–UK diagnostic project: Mood elevation and depression in first-year undergraduates at Oxford and Stanford universities. *Acta Psychiatrica Scandinavica, 118*, 81–5.

Dell'Osso, B., and Hollander, E. (2005). The impact of comorbidity on the management of pathological gambling. *CNS Spectrums, 10*, 619–21.

Dell'Osso, B., Allen, A., and Hollander, E. (2005). Comorbidity issues in the pharmacological treatment of pathological gambling: A critical review. *Clinical Practice and Epidemiology in Mental Health, 1*, 21.

Ewing, J. A. (1984). Detecting alcoholism: The CAGE questionaire. *Journal of the American Medical Association, 252*, 1905–7.

Eysenbach, G., and Wyatt, J. (2002). Using the Internet for surveys and health research. *Journal of Medical Internet Research, 4*, E13.

Eysenck, H. J., and Eysenck, S. B. G. (eds) (1975). *Manual of the Eysenck personality questionnaire (adult and junior)*, London: Hodder & Stoughton.

Goldberg, D. P., Gater, R., Sartorius, N., Ustun, T. B., Piccinelli, M., Gureje, O., and Rutter, C. (1997). The validity of two versions of the GHQ in the WHO study of mental illness in general health care. *Psychological Medicine, 27*, 191–7.

Griffiths, M. (2003). Internet gambling: Issues, concerns, and recommendations. *Cyberpsychology & Behavior, 6*, 557–68.

Griffiths, M., and Barnes, A. (2008). Internet gambling: An online empirical study among student gamblers. *International Journal of Mental Health and Addiction, 6*, 194–204.

Griffiths, M. D., and Parke, J. 2010. Adolescent gambling on the Internet: A review. *International Journal of Adolescent Medicine and Health, 22*, 59–75.

Hirschfeld, R. M., Williams, J. B., Spitzer, R. L., Calabrese, J. R., Flynn, L., Keck, P. E., Lewis, L., McElroy, S. L., Post, R. M., Rapport, D. J., Russell, J. M., Sachs, G. S., and Zajecka, J. (2000). Development and validation of a screening instrument for bipolar spectrum disorder: The Mood Disorder Questionnaire. *American Journal of Psychiatry, 157*, 1873–5.

Hong, S. I., Sacco, P., and Cunningham-Williams, R. M. (2009). An empirical typology of lifetime and current gambling behaviors: Association with health status of older adults. *Aging and Mental Health, 13*, 265–73.

LaBrie, R. A., and Shaffer, H. J. (2011). Identifying behavioral markers of disordered Internet sports gambling. *Addiction Research & Theory 19*, 56–65.

LaBrie, R. A., Kaplan, S. A., LaPlante, D. A., Nelson, S. E., and Shaffer, H. J. (2008). Inside the virtual casino: A prospective longitudinal study of actual Internet casino gambling. *European Journal of Public Health, 18*, 410–16.

LaBrie, R., LaPlante, D., Nelson, S., Schumann, A., and Shaffer, H. (2007). Assessing the playing field: A prospective longitudinal study of Internet sports gambling behavior. *Journal of Gambling Studies, 23*, 347–62.

Ladd, G. T., and Petry, N. M. (2002). Disordered gambling among university-based medical and dental patients: A focus on Internet gambling. *Psychology of Addictive Behaviors, 16*, 76–9.

LaPlante, D. A., Kleschinsky, J. H., LaBrie, R. A., Nelson, S. E., and Shaffer, H. J. (2009). Sitting at the virtual poker table: A prospective epidemiological study of actual Internet poker gambling behavior. *Computers in Human Behavior, 25*, 711–17.

LaPlante, D. A., Schumann, A., LaBrie, R. A., and Shaffer, H. J. (2008). Population trends in Internet sports gambling. *Computers in Human Behavior, 24*, 2399–414.

Lloyd, J., Doll, H., Hawton, K., Dutton, W. H., Geddes, J. R., Goodwin, G. M., and Rogers, R. D. (2010a). How psychological symptoms relate to different motivations for gambling: An online study of Internet gamblers. *Biological Psychiatry, 68*, 733–40.

Lloyd, J., Doll, H., Hawton, K., Dutton, W. H., Geddes, J. R., Goodwin, G. M., and Rogers, R. D. (2010b). Internet gamblers: A latent class analysis of their behaviours and health experiences. *Journal of Gambling Studies, 26*, 387–99.

McBride, O., Adamson, G., and Shevlin, M. (2010). A latent class analysis of DSM-IV pathological gambling criteria in a nationally representative British sample. *Psychiatry Research, 178*, 401–7.

Monaghan, S., and Blaszczynski, A. (2009). *Internet-based interventions for the treatment of problem gambling.* Toronto: Centre for Addiction and Mental Health.

Nelson, S. E., Laplante, D. A., Peller, A. J., Schumann, A., Labrie, R. A., and Shaffer, H. J. (2008). Real limits in the virtual world: Self-limiting behavior of Internet gamblers. *Journal of Gambling Studies, 24*, 463–77.

Nunnally, J. C. (1978) *Psychometric theory.* New York: McGraw-Hill.

Nylund, K., Asparouhov, T., and Muthen, B. (2007). Deciding on the number of latent classes in latent class analysis and growth mixture modeling: A Monte Carlo simulation study. *Structural Equation Modeling: An Interdisciplinary Journal, 14*, 353–69.

Siegel, S. (1956). *Nonparametric statistics for the behavioral sciences.* New York: McGraw Hill.

Skinner, H. A. (1982). The drug abuse screening test. *Addictive Behaviors, 7*, 363–71.

Spitzer, R. L., Kroenke, K., and Williams, J. B. (1999). Validation and utility of a self-report version of PRIME-MD: The PHQ primary care study. Primary Care Evaluation of Mental Disorders. Patient Health Questionnaire. *Journal of the American Medical Association, 282*, 1737–44.

Spitzer, R. L., Williams, J. B., Kroenke, K., Linzer, M., Degruy, F. V., 3rd, Hahn, S. R., Brody, D., and Johnson, J. G. (1994). Utility of a new procedure for diagnosing mental disorders in primary care. The PRIME-MD 1000 study. *Journal of the American Medical Association, 272*, 1749–56.

Strong, D. R., and Kahler, C. W. (2007). Evaluation of the continuum of gambling problems using the DSM-IV. *Addiction, 102*, 713–21.

Valentine, G., and Hughes, K. (2010). Ripples in a pond: The disclosure to, and management of, problem Internet gambling with/in the family. *Community, Work & Family, 13*, 273–90.

Vermunt, J. K., and Magidson, J. (2003). *Latent Gold 3.0 User's Guide.* Belmont, MA: Statistical Innovations Inc.

Wardle, H., Sproston, K., Orford, J., Erens, B., Griffiths, M., Constantine, R., and Pigott, S. (2007). *British Gambling Prevalence Survey 2007.* National Centre for Social Research.

Wood, R. T. A., and Griffiths, M. D. (2007). Online data collection from gamblers: Methodological issues. *International Journal of Mental Health and Addiction, 5,* 151–63.

Wood, R. T., and Williams, R. J. (2007). Problem gambling on the Internet: Implications for Internet gambling policy in North America. *New Media and Society, 9,* 520–42.

Wood, R. T., Griffiths, M. D., and Parke, J. (2007). Acquisition, development, and maintenance of online poker playing in a student sample. *Cyberpsychology and Behavior, 10,* 354–61.

Xian, H., Shah, K. R., Potenza, M. N., Volberg, R., Chantarujikapong, S., True, W. R., Lyons, M. J., Tsuang, M. T., and Eisen, S. A. (2008). A latent class analysis of DSM-III-R pathological gambling criteria in middle-aged men: Association with psychiatric disorders. *Journal of Addiction Medicine, 2,* 85–95.

# 13 Internet gambling, player protection, and social responsibility

*Mark D. Griffiths*

## Introduction

According to Griffiths (2001a; 2005), the underlying objective of a socially responsible gambling code of conduct is to maximize opportunity and minimize harm. This, it is argued, should also adhere to the established principle of moving forward with caution. Social responsibility and player protection should adhere to ethical principles and is becoming a regulatory requirement in an increasing number of countries. Furthermore it is expected by many customers who want to play with companies that show a high level of integrity. This is particularly relevant to online gaming where trust in the website and the operator is essential. Responsible gaming is about giving people the choice to play well-designed games in a secure and supportive environment. The long-term sustainability of gaming is dependent upon effective responsible gaming initiatives that can help gaming to develop as a low-impact mass-market form of entertainment. Therefore, responsible gaming is not just an ethical or regulatory requirement, it is also good for business, and it should also be about making a profit. After all, it would be irresponsible to be in a position where a reasonable profit could not be made as this would inevitably impact upon the quality of the service offered.

Good social responsibility practices and player protection tend to focus on three main dimensions. These are: (1) design, (2) behavioural transparency, and (3) customer support (Griffiths, Wood, Parke, and Parke, 2007; Griffiths and Wood, 2008). These three areas of social responsibility are within the wider sphere of more general corporate social responsibility that can include areas such as compliance to codes of conduct, age limits to prevent underage play, and general support for social impact initiatives. Design mainly falls into two areas for the gambling industry – design of gambling venues (e.g., environmental design of venues such as casinos, betting shops, etc.) and design of games (e.g., instant win games on the Internet, lottery product portfolios, etc.). Behavioural transparency covers those areas where the gambling industry imparts information about games to players (e.g., advertising, product purchase, staying in control), or feedback about player behaviour (e.g., behavioural monitoring). These diverse forms of information dissemination practice should be honest and imparted with integrity. Customer support relates to all those practices that either help staff understand player behaviour (e.g., ongoing staff training) or help players get any help they need in relation to their playing behaviour (e.g., staff intervention, good referral services to helping agencies). The following section highlights some of the more specific areas of social responsibility practice within these three dimensions along with some salient areas within general corporate social responsibility. Specific forms of gambling (e.g., Internet gambling) may also have additional specific social responsibility considerations and will be discussed later in this chapter.

To date, there have been a relatively small number of studies on Internet gambling and even fewer that have examined problem Internet gambling. Furthermore, there have been a variety of different studies examining different aspects of Internet gambling. These have included national studies on adult Internet gambling (e.g., Griffiths, 2001b; Gambling Commission, 2008; Griffiths, Wood, and Parke, 2009), national studies on adolescent Internet gambling (e.g., Griffiths and Wood, 2007), regional studies of Internet gamblers (e.g., Ialomiteanu and Adlaf, 2001; Wood and Williams, 2007), studies on self-selected samples of Internet gamblers (e.g., International Gaming Research Unit, 2007; Griffiths and Barnes, 2008; Wood, Griffiths, and Parke, 2007; Matthews, Farnsworth, and Griffiths, 2009), studies examining behavioural tracking data of Internet gamblers from online gaming sites (e.g., Broda et al., 2008; LaBrie, LaPlante, Nelson, Schumann, and Shaffer, 2007; LaBrie, Kaplan, LaPlante, Nelson, and Shaffer, 2008), qualitative studies of Internet gamblers (McCormack and Griffiths, 2012), Internet gambling case studies (Griffiths and Parke, 2007), studies examining very specific forms of gambling such as online poker (Wood, Griffiths, and Parke, 2007; Wood and Griffiths, 2008; Griffiths, Parke, Wood, and Rigbye, 2010), and studies examining Internet gambling and social responsibility features (Smeaton and Griffiths, 2004; Griffiths, Wood, and Parke, 2009).

Griffiths, Wardle, Orford, Sproston, and Erens (2009) provided the first ever analysis of a representative national sample of Internet gamblers. Using participant data from the 2007 British Gambling Prevalence Survey ($n = 9,003$ adults aged 16 years and over), all participants who had gambled online, bet online, and/or who had used a betting exchange in the last 12 months ($n = 476$) were compared with all other gamblers who had not gambled via the Internet. Overall, results showed a number of significant socio-demographic differences between Internet gamblers and non-Internet gamblers. When compared to non-Internet gamblers, Internet gamblers were more likely to be male, relatively young adults, single, well educated, and in professional/managerial employment.

Further analysis of the problem gambling Diagnostic and Statistical Manual of Mental Disorders (DSM-IV; American Psychiatric Association, 1994) scores showed that the problem gambling prevalence rate was significantly higher among Internet gamblers (5 percent) than non-Internet gamblers (0.5 percent). It was also found that some items on the DSM-IV were more heavily endorsed by Internet gamblers, including gambling preoccupation and gambling to escape. Griffiths, Wardle et al.'s (2009) results suggest that the medium of the Internet may be more likely to contribute to problem gambling than gambling in offline environments. More specifically, this finding suggests that for vulnerable individuals (e.g., problem gamblers), the medium of the Internet may be more problematic than offline gambling environments.

There are a number of studies that have reported exactly the same finding (i.e., that problem gamblers are more likely to be Internet gamblers than those who do not gamble via the Internet) although all these studies have either used self-selected samples, examined only one form of Internet gambling such as online poker, and/or examined particular sub-samples of the population such as students (e.g., Ladd and Petry, 2002; Wood and Williams, 2007; Griffiths and Barnes, 2008; Wood, Griffiths, and Parke, 2007). This is one reason why online gaming companies need to embed social responsibility practices throughout all of their policies and procedures.

## Internet gambling, social responsibility, and behavioural tracking tools

Over the past few years, innovative social responsibility tools that track player behaviour with the aim of preventing problem gambling have been developed, including PlayScan

– developed by the Swedish gaming company Svenska Spel – and Observer – developed by Israeli gaming company 888.com (Griffiths, Wood, Parke, and Parke, 2007; Griffiths, Wood, and Parke, 2009). These new tools are providing insights about problematic gambling behaviour that in turn may lead to new avenues for future research in the area. The companies that have developed these tools claim that they can detect problematic gambling behaviour through analysis of behavioural tracking data (Griffiths, Wood, and Parke, 2009). If problem gambling can be detected online via observational tracking data, it suggests that there are identifiable behaviours associated with online problem gambling. Given that almost all the current validated problem gambling screens diagnose problem gambling based on many of the consequences of problem gambling (e.g., compromising job, education, hobbies, and/or relationship because of gambling; committing criminal acts to fund gambling behaviour; lying to family and friends about the extent of gambling, etc.), behavioural tracking data appears to suggest that problem gambling can be identified without the need to assess the negative psychosocial consequences of problem gambling. This is because there appears to be a cluster of online behaviours that when they co-occur (discussed later in this chapter) tend to corroborate other evidence collected by the gaming operators that there is a problem (e.g., players opting for long-term self-exclusions).

Behavioural tracking tools such as PlayScan and Observer use a combination of behavioural science, psychology, mathematics, and artificial intelligence. These tools claim to detect players at risk of developing gambling problems, and offer the gamblers tools to help change their behaviour. Unlike the conventional purpose of customer databases (i.e., to increase sales), the objective of these new tools is the opposite (Griffiths and Parke, 2002; Griffiths, 2003). They are designed to detect and help those who would benefit from playing less. Such tools have been compared to a safety belt (i.e., something you use without intending to actually make use of). The use of these systems is voluntary, but the gaming operator strongly recommends its customers to use it (Griffiths, Wood, and Parke, 2009). These tools use approximately 40 parameters from the player's behaviour from the preceding year that is then matched against a model based on behavioural characteristics for problem players. If it predicts players' behaviour as risky they get an advance warning together with advice on how they can change their patterns in order to avoid future unhealthy and/or risky gambling. As these tools are based on artificial intelligence (i.e., the computer itself learns to find complex patterns in large quantities of data), it can identify behaviours showing tendencies of problem gaming even though empirical research may not yet have discovered them. Some of the implications of these insights are examined later in the chapter, specifically in relation to screening for problem gambling.

## Are online gambling companies socially responsible?

To date, only one peer-reviewed study has empirically investigated the extent to which Internet gambling companies are socially responsible. The study by Smeaton and Griffiths (2004) examined a representative selection of 30 UK-owned Internet gambling sites. Each site was examined in relation to what safeguards were in place to encourage the social responsibility of Internet gamblers. Thirteen indicators of responsible gambling were examined. The main finding on each indicator was that:

1   Half of the gaming operators asked the players to confirm if they were over the age of 18 years (15 out of 30).
2   Almost two-thirds did an age verification check of the player (19 out of 30).

3   Only a small minority did a credit check on the player (4 out of 30).

4   Most had credit limits for the players (27/30 had a maximum or minimum limit).

5   Only a small minority made reference to controlled gambling (4 out of 30).

6   Only a small minority made a link to helping organizations and/or self-help groups (4 out of 30).

7   A third showed some evidence of social responsibility practices (10 out of 30).

8   Only one operator had a facility for gamblers who wanted to exclude themselves (1 out of 30).

9   Just over one-third had a facility to instantly exit during gambling (11 out of 30).

10   One-third had a built-in pause and confirmation facility (10 out of 30).

11   Just under a half had a 'practice mode' facility (13 out of 30 all allowing any player of any age).

12   One-sixth gave no encouragement to continue gambling (5 out of 30; most on border).

13   Two-thirds gave players easy access to their account balance (20 out of 30).

Admittedly, this study is now relatively old considering the speed at which the Internet gambling industry has moved over the last few years, coupled with the fact that social responsibility has now become increasingly important for gaming companies. There is certainly anecdotal evidence that many of the most socially responsible gaming companies are engaging in high levels of social responsibility practice (Griffiths and Wood, 2008; Griffiths, 2009).

## What do online gamblers think about social responsibility tools?

This section briefly examines what online gamblers themselves think about online social responsibility tools, as this may have implications for whether gamblers will play on a particular site to begin with. However, the extent to which online gambling companies are engaging in socially responsible practices and using social responsibility tools has been little researched.

The Global Online Gambler Survey (International Gaming Research Unit, 2007) conducted for eCOGRA (eCommerce and Online Gaming Regulation and Assurance) collected data from 10,865 participants, from 96 countries, who reported that they had gambled at Internet casino sites, Internet poker sites, or both within the three months prior to the research. The survey focused on demographic variables, information on behaviour and attitudes, player protection and satisfaction, responsible gambling, and positive and negative aspects of Internet gambling. In relation to social responsibility, online gamblers were specifically asked about five particular features (i.e., self-set spending limits, self-set time limits, self-exclusion, provision of regular financial statements, and self-assessment problem gambling tests).

Although no single feature stood out as critically important, 51 to 75 percent of players (across all five social responsibility features) stated that they would consider some responsible gambling elements at least 'quite useful'. The most popular option was receiving regular financial statements, with 75 percent of respondents considering this option to be at least quite useful, and the least popular feature was self-set time limit, with 51 percent reporting this as at least quite useful. Those players who were younger, female, gambled out of boredom, and reported losing more money, were significantly more likely to consider responsible gambling features to be useful. There was a trend that if players were supportive of one type of responsible gambling feature, they would generally support the use of various consumer protection strategies. The same study also utilized a series of focus groups of regular gamblers in five countries (Canada, USA, Sweden, UK, Germany). Overall, the

*Table 13.1* Players' perception of the value of responsible gambling features (*n* = 10,865)

| Feature | Not at all useful | Not very useful | Quite useful | Very useful | Extremely useful |
|---|---|---|---|---|---|
| Self-set spending limits | 11% (962) | 18% (1,576) | 40% (3,452) | 18% (1,558) | 12% (1,046) |
| Self-set time limits | 19% (1,604) | 31% (2,614) | 32% (2,708) | 12% (989) | 7% (556) |
| Self-exclusion | 16% (1,347) | 26% (2,145) | 35% (2,857) | 13% (1,046) | 10% (813) |
| Regular financial statements | 9% (766) | 16% (1,318) | 42% (3,530) | 20% (1,700) | 13% (1,086) |
| Self-assessment test | 14% (1,186) | 23% (1,932) | 38% (3,165) | 15% (1,273) | 9% (723) |

attitudes among focus group participants were that the onus for playing responsibly should rest only with the player. Both survey and focus group data showed that players preferred informed choice options such as supplying regular financial statements to players. The majority of players were very much opposed to mandatory spend limits which they regarded as patronizing and overly restrictive.

Griffiths, Wood and Parke (2009) carried out a study for Svenska Spel examining players' attitudes and behaviour towards using social responsibility tools within PlayScan. The findings were based on a survey of 2,348 online gamblers (all clientele of Svenska Spel) who completed an online questionnaire relating to various aspects of PlayScan and online social responsibility tools.

All online gamblers were asked if they had used PlayScan. Approximately a quarter had (26 percent) compared to the three-quarters who had not (74 percent). Online gamblers who had not used PlayScan were also asked for reasons why they had not activated PlayScan. The main reason given for not using it was that they did not think they needed it (75 percent). Other lesser reasons included not knowing what PlayScan did (17.5 percent), that PlayScan was just for problem gamblers (11 percent), that they could not be bothered (7.5 percent), and/or that they did not want Svenska Spel gathering data on them (4.5 percent).

The online gamblers who had used PlayScan were asked what their reasons were for using it. The most popular reasons were players being curious about what PlayScan was (47 percent), players wanting to set time and money limits (34 percent), and players wanting to play safe (23 percent). Lesser reasons for using PlayScan included players who were concerned they were playing too much (12 percent), players wanting to better understand their playing behaviour (11 percent), and/or players wanting some help with their gambling (1 percent). A further 8 percent said they did not know the reasons why they started using PlayScan.

PlayScan users were also asked about which particular social responsibility features were of most use to them (see Table 13.2). The most useful feature was the setting of spending limits with over two-thirds of respondents (70 percent) reporting the feature to be 'quite useful' or 'very useful'. The other 'quite/very useful' endorsement ratings were being able to view their gambling profile (49 percent), performing self-diagnostic tests of gambling behaviour (46 percent), being able to self-exclude for a certain period of time (42 percent), getting information about support for gambling issues (40 percent), and getting information about predicted gambling profile (36 percent).

Respondents were also asked which features of PlayScan (if any) they had used. Over half (56 percent) had used spending limits, 40 percent had taken a self-diagnostic problem gambling test, 17 percent had used a self-exclusion feature, and 0.4 percent had contacted a gambling helpline. They were asked about which particular self-exclusion features were the most useful to them personally. The most useful self-exclusion feature was the seven-day

*Table 13.2* Useful features of PlayScan as rated by respondents (*n* = 570)

| PlayScan feature | Completely useless (%) | Quite useless (%) | Don't know (%) | Quite useful (%) | Very useful (%) |
|---|---|---|---|---|---|
| To view my current gambling profile (e.g., green, yellow, red) | 12.8 | 12.7 | 25.5 | 37.8 | 11.2 |
| Getting information about my predicted future gambling profile | 13.7 | 16.1 | 34.4 | 27.4 | 8.4 |
| Setting a spending limit | 8.2 | 10.5 | 11.2 | 33.2 | 36.8 |
| Performing a self-test of my gambling behaviour | 11.8 | 12.6 | 29.3 | 32.3 | 14.0 |
| Self-excluding myself for a specific period of time | 16.7 | 15.1 | 26.0 | 24.6 | 17.7 |
| Getting information about support for gambling issues | 17.4 | 11.8 | 31.2 | 24.0 | 15.6 |

self-exclusion, rated as 'quite/very useful' by just under half of respondents (46 percent). This was followed by one-month self-exclusion (24 percent), 24-hour self-exclusion (24 percent), and permanent self-exclusion (16 percent).

Given that PlayScan is voluntary rather than mandatory, it is hard to assess whether an uptake of a quarter of the Internet gamblers sampled is a healthy uptake or not (as there are no studies by which to make a similar comparison). Those who had not activated a PlayScan account were clearly of the view that they themselves did not need it. Some clearly had the view that initiatives such as this were really aimed at problem gamblers.

The types of self-exclusion feature varied according to the gambler's own needs. Given the (presumed) unproblematic nature of Internet gambling among respondents, it was unsurprising that only 16 percent thought permanent self-exclusion would be useful to them personally. If anything, this might appear to be a slightly higher figure than might have been predicted as it could be argued that non-problem gamblers would be unlikely to make use of a permanent self-exclusion. The seven-day exclusion period was the most useful with almost a half of PlayScan users endorsing this as their most favoured. This may have been especially useful for those who do not want to gamble for a particular period such as the week before a monthly 'pay day'. One-month and one-day self-exclusion periods were most popular for around half the PlayScan users (approximately 25 percent each). These types of self-exclusion are more likely to be associated with non-problem gamblers who may want to restrict their gambling behaviour in a very specific instance such as preceding a night of heavy drinking (e.g., 24-hour self-exclusion) or a particular time of the year like the run-up to Christmas (e.g., one-month self-exclusion). Overall, these results suggest that for PlayScan users, self-exclusion is not a tool for problem gamblers but more generally a tool for responsible gambling.

## Implications of online behavioural tracking for problem gambling screening criteria

Although obvious, it needs to be noted that problem gambling lies on a continuum of behaviour and there are always behaviours that are typically engaged in by problem gamblers that some non-problem gamblers may also engage in (Griffiths, 2009). On a diagnostic screening level, the DSM-IV criteria for pathological gambling comprise ten key indicators as to whether someone has a gambling problem (American Psychiatric Association, 1994; see Table 13.3). If a person answers positively to at least five of the following items, a diagnosis of pathological gambling would be made, whereas endorsement of three or four of the criteria would indicate a diagnosis of problem gambling. As will be argued below, only a few of these behaviours can be reliably spotted online using online behavioural tracking (the most obvious being chasing losses, salience/preoccupation, and tolerance) (Griffiths, 2009; Griffiths and Whitty, 2010). The following list highlights each of the DSM-IV questions for pathological gambling and the component of pathological gambling that each criterion is assessing. This is followed by an assessment as to what extent each criterion can be identified online (cf. Griffiths, 2009).

- **Salience/Preoccupation** (*Do you find that you are becoming preoccupied with past gambling successes or find yourself spending increasingly more time planning future gambling?*) – An online problem gambler is likely to spend a lot of time gambling online although this behaviour in itself does not necessarily indicate a problem. Anything above four hours daily play over a protracted period could be considered excessive although some forms of online gambling (e.g., online poker) may take up a lot of time and be played relatively inexpensively.
- **Tolerance** (*Do you find that you need to increase the amount of money you gamble to achieve the same enjoyment and excitement?*) – If experiencing tolerance to gambling, an online problem gambler is likely to have changed their gambling behaviour in one of two ways over time. The first example of tolerance is a gradual increase of daily play in terms of time. For instance, the gambler might start off playing 30–60 minutes a day but over the course of a few months starts to play increasing amounts of time. The second example of tolerance is the act of gambling using gradually bigger stakes over time. An online problem gambler is more likely to experience both these combined (i.e., gambling for longer and longer periods of time with bigger and bigger amounts of money).
- **Relapse** (*Have you recently tried to stop gambling but were unsuccessful?*) – Although this is difficult to detect with absolute certainty online, a typical pattern would be a gambler who gambles heavily, day-in day-out, for a period of time, and then 'disappears' for a period of time (which could be days, weeks, and sometimes even months), only to suddenly reappear and gamble heavily again.

*Table 13.3* Summary of problem gambling criteria (DSM-IV) and likelihood of identification of problem gambling behaviour online

| *DSM-IV criterion* | *Likelihood of online identification* |
| --- | --- |
| Experiencing salience/preoccupation | Very good possibility |
| Experiencing tolerance | Reasonable possibility |
| Experiencing relapse | Slight possibility |
| Experiencing withdrawal symptoms | Unlikely |
| Escaping from reality | Unlikely |
| Chasing losses | Definitely |
| Concealing involvement | Unlikely |
| Engaging in unsociable behaviour | Unlikely |
| Ruining a relationship/opportunity | Unlikely |
| Other people providing a bail-out | Slight possibility |

- **Withdrawal** (*Do you become moody or impatient when you are cutting down how much you gamble?*) – This is again difficult to detect with absolute certainty online but is most likely to surface with the use of verbally aggressive comments in those games that have chat room facilities (such as online poker).
- **Escape from reality** (*Do you ever use gambling as a way of ignoring stress in your life or even to pick you up when you feel down?*) – This is almost impossible to detect online although those players who play for long hours every day are more likely to experience escape-like feeling.
- **Chasing losses** (*Do you ever try to win back the money you lost by increasing the size or frequency of your wagers?*) – This is one of the key indicators of problem gambling and can be spotted online more easily than many other problem gambling criteria. Typical chasing patterns will include repeated 'double or quit' strategies in an effort to recoup losses. Although many gamblers use this strategy on occasion, the online problem gambler will do it repeatedly. This behaviour, above and beyond any other criteria, is most likely to signal problem gambling.
- **Conceal involvement** (*Do you ever hide how much or how often you gamble from significant others?*) – There is no way that an online gambling operator can spot this during online gambling unless such admissions are given to other players in online chat rooms.
- **Unsociable behaviour** (*Have you ever committed fraud or theft to get money to gamble with?*) – Again, there is no way that an online gambling operator can spot this during online gambling unless such admissions are given to other players in online chat rooms.
- **Ruin a relationship/opportunity** (*Has gambling ever ruined a personal relationship or an occupational or educational opportunity?*) – As with the previous two criteria, there is no way that an online gambling operator can spot this during online gambling unless such admissions are given to other players in online chat rooms.
- **Bail-out** (*Have you ever needed others to relieve a financial problem created by gambling?*) – When an online gambler has exhausted all their own funds, they will often 'beg, borrow and (eventually) steal' money to continue gambling. A player whose account is constantly 'topped up' by people other than themselves may be a problem gambler.

This brief analysis of the extent to which each DSM criterion of problem gambling can be identified online shows that only a few behaviours (chasing losses, salience/preoccupation, and tolerance) can be reliably spotted via online behavioural tracking (Griffiths, 2009; see also Table 13.3). However, the author has been informed (by various members of the online gambling industry) that problem gambling can be identified online. If this is true, it has implications for current problem gambling screening instruments. The following list contains a number of behaviours that are engaged in by online problem gamblers. This was devised by the author and based on conversations with members of the online gaming industry. These are additional to those identified above (i.e., chasing losses, spending high amounts of time and money, and increasing the amount of gambling over time). As a general 'rule of thumb', it is assumed that the more of these online behaviours that are detected, the more likely the person is to be a problem gambler.

- *Playing a variety of stakes* – This (in games like online poker) indicates poor planning and may be a cue or precursor to chasing behaviour.
- *Playing a variety of games* – Evidence from national prevalence surveys (e.g., Wardle et al., 2007) suggests that the more types of gambling engaged in, the more likely the

person is to be a problem gambler. Although this factor on its own is unlikely to indicate problem gambling, when combined with other indicators on this list it may be indicative of problem gambling.

- *Player 'reload' within gambling session* – Although any gambler can engage in such behaviour, players who deposit more money within session ('reload') are more likely to be problem gamblers. This indicates poor planning and is a cue to chasing behaviour.
- *Frequent payment method changes* – The constant changing of deposit payment methods indicates poor planning and it may be a cue to chasing behaviour. This online behaviour usually indicates shortage of funds and need to extract monies from a variety of sources. Such behaviour can also indicate bank refusal.
- *Verbal aggression* – Aggressive verbal interaction via relay chat is common among problem gamblers although losing money may cause such behaviour in any gambler. Such behaviour may be evidence of a gambler going on 'tilt' (i.e., negative cognitive and emotional reaction to losing) or withdrawal effects if out of money to gamble.
- *Constant complaints to customer services* – This is common among problem gamblers although for any gambler losing money may cause such behaviour. As with verbal aggression, such behaviour may be evidence of gamblers going on 'tilt' (i.e., negative cognitive and emotional reaction to losing).

Clearly, each of these behaviours needs to be examined in relation to at least three or four other indicative behaviours. Perhaps most importantly, and according to online gambling companies that use socially responsible behavioural tracking tools, it is a 'significant change in usual online behaviour' that is most indicative of a problem gambler. Most statistical modelling of player behaviour predicts future problematic behaviour on the basis of behavioural change over time. The behaviours highlighted in this section suggest that screening instruments in the future may be able to be developed that concentrate on the gambling behaviour itself, rather than the associated negative consequences, if it can indeed be shown that these behaviours when clustered together are highly indicative of problem gambling.

## Recommendations for a socially responsible online gaming player protection strategy

The following strategies and recommendations were developed by the author for various online gaming companies. They constitute a comprehensive set of responsible online gaming policies that include many proactive strategies. Recommendations marked with an 'E' are considered 'essential' for the online responsible gaming strategy; and those marked with a 'D' are considered to be 'desirable' for the online responsible gaming strategy.

### *Responsible gambling help and support strategies for online players*

- *Information page(s) to aid informed choice* (E) – It is essential for online gaming operators to have an information page where online clientele can get a range of information relating to gambling issues. This adheres to one of the popular underlying social responsibility philosophies (i.e., 'An informed player is a responsible player'). Potential players of Internet games should be given all the information they are likely to need to make an informed choice including (1) the chances (probability) of winning on the activity, (2) the payout ratios of the game, and (3) the prize structures of the game.

There is also an implicit assumption that all games will be fair and designed in such a way so as to protect the player. It is also important that the information page does not just contain information relating to problem gambling as this may deter some players from using the gaming site. Information should be made available in languages of the clientele.

- *Information about staying in control* (E) – Although players are clearly responsible for their own gambling, it is recommended that they should still be reminded of the need to exercise control (e.g., 'Bet with your head, not over it').
- *Mandatory information about problem gambling* (E) – At the core of exercising a duty of care is the principle of assisting players to address any concern about their gambling. For instance, it is recommended that telephone helplines and addresses of helping agencies should be displayed on web pages at the main gaming operator site. It is also recommended that online gaming companies should also have a good referral system with local and/or national helping agencies. A 'resource centre' (in the form of a frequently asked questions [FAQ] web page) could contain all the information a customer needs to learn about responsible gaming, request referral advice for a gambling problem, and undertake temporary or permanent self-exclusion, etc.
- *No encouragement to re-gamble* (E) – Providing help, information, and advice to players is to be commended. However, players should under no circumstances be encouraged to (1) increase the amount of money they have decided to gamble with, (2) enter into continuous gambling for a prolonged period of time, (3) re-gamble their winnings, or (4) chase losses.
- *Reliable payment of winnings* (E) – Given some of the socially irresponsible and fraudulent practices carried out by some gaming companies (see Griffiths [2010] for a recent overview), reliable payment options are essential for both social responsibility and gaining online trust among online players.
- *Responsible gambling message protocols immediately after initial registration* (D) – Online gaming companies should have an initiative that immediately after the registration process all players receive a 'welcome message' that includes information about responsible gambling tools and methods (the first of a number of 'reminders' about playing responsibly). Continual reminders to players that they should 'stay in control' of their gambling is another of the 'bedrocks' of a socially responsible gambling policy.
- *Use of social responsibility messages (e.g., 'health warnings' via 'pop-up' windows)* (D) – Use of non-intrusive but clear pop-up windows could be used after predetermined periods. This is useful because gambling can create dissociative states where customers can lose track of time gambling (Griffiths, Wood, Parke, and Parke, 2006). Players are responsible for their gambling, but should still be reminded of the need to exercise control. These should be 'risks of the game' and should be incorporated where they will be read by online players. These are important as most gamblers believe they can win based on faulty reasoning or belief systems (Griffiths, 1994; Parke, Griffiths, and Parke, 2007).
- *Effective online self-exclusion program* (E) – The option for online self-exclusion should be offered to any player that requests it, and is a good demonstration of an online gaming company's 'duty of care' towards its clientele. Care needs to be taken on the length of self-exclusion and the criteria for re-inclusion.
- *Short-term self-exclusion options* (D) – Research has shown that online gamblers appear to appreciate self-exclusion facilities even if they do not have a problem with gambling. Research has shown that a seven-day exclusion period appears to be the most useful to players (Griffiths, Wood, and Parke, 2009). One-month and one-day self-exclusion

periods are also popular among players. These types of self-exclusion are likely to be associated with non-problem gamblers who may want to restrict their gambling behaviour in a very specific instance such as preceding a night of heavy drinking (e.g., a 'drunk button' for 24-hour self-exclusion) or a particular time of the year like the run-up to Christmas (e.g., one-month self-exclusion). Here, self-exclusion is related to non-problem gambling (rather than problem gambling). Another short-term self-exclusion offer could include the use of a 'panic button' in online poker. For instance, some online gaming companies are considering implementing a panic button for online poker players who may go 'on tilt'. During a session on tilt, a player can spend large amounts of money. Furthermore, while chasing losses, gamblers do not think rationally about what they are doing (Griffiths, 1994; Parke, Griffiths and Parke, 2007). The panic button would therefore offer the player an instant and very easy way to immediately close their account for (say) the next 12 hours.

- *Approaching regular online players* (D) – Holland Casino has a strategy whereby they approach gamblers who visit the casino a number of times during a period, for example 15 times in a month. Online gaming companies could also consider doing this online (e.g., sending an email to a player who gambles at least four times a week). The company could focus on one of the obvious risk groups, such as young men aged between 20 and 30. Such an online approach needs to be friendly and centred around customer service rather than being accusatory. For example, a short email enquiry about their enjoyment of the website as a regular customer should be enough to identify any issues without making the player feel overly scrutinized.

- *Online support service for those players that need help* (D) – When the player takes the initial decision to self-exclude on a long-term or permanent basis, they are motivated to do something about their gambling problem. However, it can sometimes be difficult to give the self-excluded player further immediate and ongoing support. An online support service can be available via a hyperlink from the gaming website. Such a service would be regionally or nationally available and would assist players who cannot easily access self-help groups (see Griffiths and Cooper [2003] and Wood and Griffiths [2007a] for an overview of the advantages of online helping services). Such an initiative would also offer further support to a player immediately following an application for long-term or permanent self-exclusion. An online support service could include the following: (1) links to further support and help services, (2) a self-assessed diagnostic test, (3) a forum where players can talk to and support each other, (4) FAQs about problem gambling, and (5) compact 'self-help manual' for problem gamblers.

## Socially responsible restriction and control strategies for online players

In online gaming environments, many (socially responsible) restrictive practices that are commonplace in offline gaming environments are either unrealistic to initiate (e.g., not allowing people to gamble with credit cards), impossible to enforce (e.g., not allowing gambling while drinking alcohol excessively), and/or counterproductive for vulnerable players (e.g., restricting opening hours). For instance, it is unrealistic in a market where there are thousands of online gambling sites, to have limited hours of opening. In the online world, it is better to have the most socially responsible gambling sites operating alongside disreputable and/or less socially responsible gambling sites 24/7.

If the most socially responsible gambling sites were only open for 12 hours a day, players who wanted to gamble when that site was closed may be forced to gamble at a less socially responsible and/or disreputable site. Therefore, restricting the hours of operation of a socially responsible gambling website in a market where there are lots of less socially responsible gambling websites could be argued to be a socially irresponsible practice. However, there are a few restrictive practices that socially responsible gaming operators could implement online.

- *Spending limits* (E) – All online players should be allowed to voluntarily set their own spending limits (although some operators may have their own mandatory spending limit). Restricting the amount of money players can spend while gambling is viewed by authors as a good initiative in terms of social responsibility (e.g., Griffiths, 2003; Smeaton and Griffiths, 2004; Griffiths and Wood, 2008). By incorporating maximum spend limits while gambling, players can plan and pre-set their gambling behaviour.

  In relation to mandatory versus voluntary spending limits, the evidence base suggests that the most appropriate responsible gambling strategy to be implemented by online gaming operators would be for voluntary (rather than mandatory) predetermined spending limits by players. This is because individuals are likely to vary widely in the amount of disposable income they have available for leisure activities such as gambling. Therefore, a fixed mandatory spend limit will always be too little for some and too much for others. One of the more consistent research findings from the limited empirical base is that mandatory limits are unpopular with the majority of gamblers (Wood and Griffiths, 2010). This could conceivably lead to some players deciding that they would prefer to take their custom to perhaps less responsible gambling operators. Some companies also have low maximum bet sizes that will be of help to some vulnerable players but careful consideration needs to be given to the playing clientele as a whole. Many gamblers will want to play with larger amounts of money and can afford to do so. It may be the case that having a mandatory limit chosen by the players themselves is the optimal strategy in this instance.

- *Time loss limits* (D) – Again, while not radically different from general limit setting, time loss limits would be fairly easy to introduce. A few online gambling companies have introduced this as a voluntary measure and it appears to have been popular with a small base of players. This may be particularly useful for games where players may lose very little (or in fact win slightly) but who can spend inordinately long hours playing (e.g., online poker). (See Wood, Griffiths, and Parke [2007] who speculated a new type of problem gambler related to excessive poker. Here, the poker gamblers do not necessarily lose money – and may even win or break even – but can spend substantial amounts of time playing that compromises most areas of their life.)

- *Limit setting in specific games* (D) – Again, while not radically different from general limit setting, this (in relation to a specific online game) would be fairly easy to introduce to very specific forms of online gambling (e.g., maximum small blind, big blind in online poker).

- *Mandatory game breaks* (D) – It is recommended that continuous games – that is any game that can be played continually without breaks (especially the rapid, high event frequency, interactive games) – should feature a mandatory break every 60 minutes during play. Ideally this break should be for at least five minutes (if not longer). This is particularly important for those who may find it more difficult to stick to self-imposed limits. Mandatory breaks provide players with a reflective 'timeout' period to think about whether or not they wish to continue gambling. Such breaks also inhibit a player from using gambling as a way to escape from their problems by entering into a dissociative (trance-like) state through continuous gambling (Griffiths, Wood, Parke, and Parke, 2006; Wood and Griffiths, 2007b). Breaks need only last a few minutes during which time a player can 'cool off' and decide more rationally whether they should stay or go.

- *Socially responsible parameters on changing of customer spending limits* (D) – From a social responsibility perspective, players should be able to decrease their spending limits immediately. However, there should be an appreciable time period (at least 24 hours but some companies have longer periods) before being able to increase spending limits as a mechanism to overcome 'impulse' gambling.
- *Monetary game limit reminder at specific times (e.g., log in, changing game format)* (D) – Such a measure is simple, efficient, and would be fairly easy to introduce.
- *Option to set monetary game limits over different time periods for (a) all games or (b) selected games* (D) – While not radically different from general limit setting, this would be fairly easy to introduce.
- *An effective and rigorous age verification program for excluding underage players* (E) – Given that research worldwide demonstrates that children and adolescents are one of the most high-risk vulnerable groups (e.g., Griffiths, 2002; Derevensky and Gupta, 2004; Volberg, Gupta, Griffiths, Olason, and Delfabbro, 2010), it is recommended that online gaming companies use rigorous age verification measures (such as those used in the banking sector) to prevent minors from accessing its online games.
- *Restricted use of 'reload' during a gambling session* (D) – In offline gaming environments, it is recommended that automatic teller machines (ATMs or cash machines) should not be placed on the gaming floor and that there is an appreciable walk to any ATM on-site. This is so there is sufficient opportunity (like mandatory breaks) for players to take a reflective timeout period. Given that one of the common behaviours of online problem gamblers is constantly 'reloading' their play credit during a single gambling session (Griffiths, 2009; Griffiths and Whitty, 2010), it is recommended that online gaming operators restrict – where possible – within-session reloading and introduce mechanisms (such as voluntary spending limits) that allow the players to 'pre-commit' how much they are going to spend on gambling before they begin playing. In essence, restricting reloading within a gambling session is the equivalent to not allowing ATMs on the gaming floor.

### Socially responsible strategies for promoting behavioural transparency (player self-awareness of their online playing behaviour)

- *Fair site practices* (E) – There have been a number of academic writings on some of the unfair practices used by the online gaming industry including inflated chances of winning in the 'demo' and 'practice' modes, overly aggressive marketing, etc. (Smeaton and Griffiths, 2004; Sevigny, Cloutier, Pelletier, and Ladouceur, 2005; Griffiths, 2010). Therefore, all online gaming companies should include fair site practices across their whole game portfolio including the following initiatives.
- *Visible and accessible betting history* (E) – Information provided regarding the gambling behaviour of a customer is essential. An individual's betting history should detail financial outcome, profits/losses over a specified time frame as an aid to behavioural transparency. This enables gamblers to see clearly the level of involvement in gambling and the monetary outcomes of such involvement. Clear data indicating this diminishes the effect that cognitive heuristics have when discounting or ignoring incurred losses. Online gaming companies should advocate that online customers check their gambling

behaviour at least once a week. Furthermore, in the responsible gambling section, customers should be allowed to indicate that they wish to receive weekly account statements delivered to their email address. By meticulously evaluating their own gambling behaviour gamblers will be motivated to set their own parameters. It is also recommended sending an email periodically to remind customers of the importance of setting parameters. Empirical research has also shown that access to gambling history is seen as very useful by most online gamblers (International Gaming Research Unit, 2007; Griffiths, Wood, and Parke, 2009).

- *Use interactive pop-up messages about current gambling behaviour* (D) – Pop-ups about time elapsed, amount spent, profit, loss, etc. can be used to help players assess their gambling behaviour. Another socially responsible strategy might be to have pop-up windows that appear after predetermined periods. It is advisable to ask the customer if they wish to continue so that they must read and acknowledge the time and the duration of their play. Gambling can create and maintain dissociative states where customers can lose track of time and duration of gambling (Griffiths, Wood, Parke, and Parke, 2006). Therefore, actual information regarding these factors needs to be periodically recognized consciously.
- *Website clock* (E) – A website clock should always be visible and accessible. Gambling can create dissociative states where customers can lose track of time while gambling (Griffiths, Wood, Parke, and Parke, 2006).
- *Value reinforcement* (E) – An online gambling operator should emphasize the financial value of chips or online credit. This is because for most gamblers it is very likely that the psychological value of electronic cash (e-cash) will be less than 'real' cash (and similar to the use of chips or tokens in other gambling situations) (Lapuz and Griffiths, 2010). Gambling with e-cash may lead to what psychologists call a 'suspension of judgement' (Griffiths, 1993). The suspension of judgement refers to a structural characteristic that temporarily disrupts the gambler's financial value system and potentially stimulates further gambling. This is well known by both those in commerce (people typically spend more on credit and debit cards because it is easier to spend money using plastic), and by the gaming industry. In essence, e-cash 'disguises' the money's true value (i.e., decreases the psychological value of the money to be gambled). E-cash can often be re-gambled without hesitation as the psychological value is much less than the real value (Lapuz and Griffiths, 2010).
- *Utilize realistic and restrictive 'practice modes'* (E) – Any free practice mode that is offered to the customer must have an appropriate message regarding responsible gambling. The odds of winning should be the same for 'free play' modes as playing for real monies. One of the most common ways that gamblers can be facilitated to gamble online is when they try out games in the 'demo', 'practice', or free play mode. Research carried out by Sevigny, Cloutier, Pelletier, and Ladouceur (2005) showed it was significantly more commonplace to win while 'gambling' on the first few goes on a 'demo' or free play game. They also reported that it was commonplace for gamblers to have extended winning streaks during prolonged periods while playing in the demo modes. Obviously, once gamblers start to play for real with real money, the odds of winning are considerably reduced. Furthermore, access to practice modes should be prevented for those under the legal age to gamble. Giving access to such simulators could encourage someone underage to seek opportunities to gamble for real money.
- *Age verification for 'demonstration' and/or free play games* (D) – Age limit verification procedures should be required for all players – even those who are not spending money

in the free play modes. A recent British study by Ipsos MORI (2009) surveyed 8,598 schoolchildren (aged 11 to 15 years) and reported that just over a quarter of the sample had played in 'money-free mode' on Internet sites in the week preceding the survey. Further analysis of these data by Forrest, McHale, and Parke (2009) reported that gambling in money-free mode was the single most important predictor of whether the child had gambled for money, and one of the most important predictors of children's problem gambling. This finding, and other similar findings relating to youth access of free play gambling sites, has been discussed in recent comprehensive reviews of youth gambling on the Internet (see Griffiths and Parke, 2010; King, Delfabbro, and Griffiths, 2010).

- *Use of responsible gaming tools by players* (D) – It is recommended that online gaming companies voluntarily encourage players to use the responsible gaming tools (e.g., setting spend limits). Such tools are about empowering people to make their own choices, and to take personal responsibility, rather than the players being forced to do something.
- *Use socially responsible player behaviour monitoring tools such as PlayScan* (D) – Systems that track player behaviour are likely to have a significant impact on the national and international gaming markets. If a player's behaviour indicates gaming problems, it is recommended they should be deleted from the direct advertising address lists. Via such initiatives, it is also recommended that players should be offered control tools (e.g., personal gaming budgets, self-diagnostic tests of gaming habits, and the chance to self-exclude from gaming). The really innovative aspect of such technologies is that they may be able to predict the development of unhealthy gaming behaviour patterns. Furthermore, behavioural tracking tools provide many advantages for the online gaming company using them including: (1) an aid to acquiring or maintaining an operating licence, (2) compliance with law and/or organizational guidelines (e.g. World Lottery Association), (3) proactive risk management (e.g., avoidance of court cases), (4) strengthening trust mark (to increase customer base), (5) increase of customer lifetime value (to increase revenue/profit), and (6) helping customers to help themselves (customer empowerment but also reduced internal costs).

### Socially responsible marketing strategies for online gaming

- *Responsible advertising and promotion* (E) – Quite clearly it is appropriate that the online gaming industry needs to advertise and promote its facilities. In addition to conforming to each country's own advertising codes of practice, the most important recommendation would be that advertisements and promotions should not appeal to vulnerable individuals (such as minors, those with severe learning difficulties, problem gamblers, etc.) or be 'aggressive' and/or use popular celebrities. Furthermore, broadcast media advertising should be aimed at an adult audience and appear after the 9 p.m. 'watershed'. All adverts should feature the odds of winning.
- *Focus on entertainment rather than gaming in advertising and promotion* (E) – A focus on buying entertainment rather than winning money in advertising and marketing campaigns is recommended. When individuals primarily gamble to win money, and that is their only objective, that is when problems can start. That is when a proportion of vulnerable people can get into difficulty (Griffiths, 2007).
- *Limit the use of marketing promotions that reward the highest spenders* (D) – Previous writings about advertising and marketing from a social responsibility perspective have noted that it is entirely appropriate for the gaming industry to advertise and market their

products as long as it conforms to the relevant codes of compliance, is fact-based, does not oversell winning, and is not aimed at (or featuring) minors (Griffiths, 2001a). As Griffiths and Parke (2002) note, in gambling there is a fine line between customer enhancement and customer exploitation particularly when it comes to facilitating new clientele and repeat patronage. Griffiths and Parke (2003) have distinguished between two fundamentally different forms of promotional bonus – the 'general bonus' and the 'proportional bonus'. These may have different implications in terms of social responsibility. General bonuses are those offers that are provided irrespective of the type of player (e.g., an occasional gambler is as entitled to the bonus as a 'heavy' gambler). Proportional bonuses are those offers that depend on how long and/or frequently the player gambles with a particular gaming establishment. This means that 'heavy' gamblers would receive disproportionately more bonuses than an irregular player. Given that a significant proportion of the 'heaviest' gamblers (sometimes referred to as 'VIP gamblers') may be problem gamblers, it raises questions whether rewarding people the more they spend is the most socially responsible strategy.

- *Differential marketing by game type* (D) – Additionally, it would be desirable to consider marketing relating to particular types of games (such as Internet poker). For instance, some companies such as RAY (Raha-automaattiyhdistys) in Finland have introduced social responsibility policies that have been designed so that (in relation to online poker) there will be (1) no rakeback, (2) no rakeback races, (3) no VIP levels, (4) no additional prizes, (5) no sign-up bonus, (6) no bonuses for the customers, (7) no wider affiliate program, and (8) no 'refer-a-friend' functionality. RAY argues that such measures increase player protection and help inhibit problem gambling. Further empirical research is needed to assess whether this is the case.

- *Prohibition of marketing and advertising to long-term self-excluded online players* (E) – Any player who self-excludes for a significant period (three months or more) should not receive any advertising or marketing mail, email, or other messages about any form of online gambling.

- *Responsible gaming television and radio commercials* (D) – Ideally, there should also be some 'counterbalanced' radio and television adverts talking about problem gambling and its prevention. Initiatives could be actively promoted via newspaper and magazine advertisements.

## Socially responsible strategies for the design and implementation of new online games

- *Develop a protocol for the introduction of all new games* (E) – The use of guidelines by which to consider the possible impacts of a new online game is recommended. The utilization of social responsibility reports conducted by researchers and academics with expertise in responsible gaming will help ensure that up-to-date research findings are taken into account.

- *Consider using responsible gaming design tools* (D) – An objective design tool can aid in the development of socially responsible online games before they arrive at the stage where they need to be assessed through measures such as the Social Responsibility Assessment Template. Using a responsible gaming design tool such as GAM-GaRD (Wood, Griffiths, and Parke, 2007; Griffiths, Wood, and Parke, 2008) can provide another level of objective evaluation and help prevent the development of games that might then be scrapped or need drastic modification following a social responsibility assessment. GAM-GaRD can be used to identify the structural characteristics of games that present the greatest risks for excessive play. GAM-GaRD identifies which elements of a game, if any, are problematic so they can be 'adjusted' to make the game safer or can be combined with other external measures of social responsibility in an effort to reduce overall harm. GAM-GaRD was designed so that it can be used to assess any gambling-type game by anyone with a basic knowledge of the features of the game.

- *Accreditation by external organization* (D) – Before launching a new online gaming product or developing an existing one the operating company should consult, commercially in confidence, with the lead body involved with the social impact of gambling to seek external accreditation for their gaming products.

### Socially responsible staff-related strategies for online gaming

- *Dedicated responsible online gaming staff* (E) –There should be a number of staff members who are specifically trained to maintain and review the online responsible gaming initiatives outlined in the responsible gaming policy. Furthermore, they should be responsible for producing an annual social responsibility report as part of the monitoring and auditing procedures (discussed below). Using online tracking software, these staff members should also be trained to identify players who appear to be having problems and/or know how to intervene and offer support.
- *Staff training* (E) – It is recommended that online gaming companies provide relevant responsible online gaming training to relevant gaming staff. Ongoing staff training around the area of social responsibility should be given at all levels to all those working in the online gaming industry. Raising awareness of such issues is a necessity to enable staff to deal with relevant situations. It should perhaps be stated that the training is ongoing particularly because of (1) staff turnover, and (2) the development of new empirical research in the gambling studies field that continues to enhance our understanding of dealing with online problem gambling issues.
- *Auditing and testing of staff training* (E) – Staff should be regularly tested (e.g., every two years) to ensure that they fully understand the principles of the company's social responsibility policy for online gaming. In addition, it is important that the online gaming company is always fully aware of which members of staff have completed a training program and at what level. A database of staff training (of who has completed what training, and when) should be developed. Training programs should be regularly reviewed (e.g., every two years) in order to remain relevant and effective.
- *Dedicated customer support staff trained to deal with problem gamblers* (E) – It is recommended that online gaming companies educate its online customer support staff in handling enquiries regarding problem gamblers and appoint staff to monitor, enforce, and evaluate the responsible online gaming strategy. Such training should be updated every two years. Staff should also be able to identify aspects of policy and practice relative to appropriate intervention that will contribute to minimizing the harm attributable to uncontrolled online gambling. A responsible gaming manager should prepare an annual report detailing the issues relating to every aspect of the responsible online gaming policy for that year.

### Socially responsible strategies for community relations

- *The player panel: understanding the online player perspective* (D) – In order to better understand how responsible gaming impacts upon players in the online gaming environment, it is important to talk to online players and allow them the opportunity to raise their own issues from their perspective. Conducting regular focus groups with online gamblers will help ensure that the impact of the responsible online gaming policy is understood from the perspective of the player, and can identify any issues that may not be apparent from the perspective of the staff. Furthermore, regular focus groups with online players may help identify an issue quickly as they are much easier to initiate than a full-scale investigation. The player panel should comprise online players, representing different demographics, who regularly attend a meeting with responsible gaming staff. Such a panel should meet quarterly and should be compensated for their time and effort in taking part. Player panel members should be changed each year in order to gain a wide selection of individuals.

- *The stakeholder panel: liaising with support services, pressure groups, and researchers* (D) – Helpline and other support service staff and researchers in the gambling studies field usually understand a lot of the issues that relate to problem gambling and gambling environments (including online gambling). They continually hear from people with gambling problems about the factors that they find difficult to deal with in either avoiding gambling altogether, or in gambling at a more controlled level. Liaising with these stakeholders can provide a valuable insight into how the casino, or elements of it, are either helping or hindering their clients. For example, is the self-exclusion policy working in practice? Furthermore, regular meetings with stakeholders help build a relationship between the operator and the community, which is in itself a fundamental element of social responsibility. Support service staff, researchers, and other stakeholders (e.g., representatives from religious groups, pressure groups, youth workers, etc.) can be asked to attend regular (quarterly) meetings with responsible gaming staff to discuss any issues that may arise. These meetings can also be used to feedback to stakeholders how online gaming companies have initiated any new responsible gaming strategies and/or responded to concerns from previous meetings. While such meetings may at times be 'lively' they will demonstrate a commitment to community welfare and can generate insight about how that relationship can best be managed.

### Strategies that contribute to socially responsible gaming advancement

- *Support responsible gaming research in the area of online gaming* (D) – The future of responsible online gaming is dependent upon developing a better understanding of online problem gambling, 'normal' online gambling, and the development of effective responsible online gaming initiatives. Furthermore, new advances in gaming technology offer new challenges to understand the potential impact on online problem gambling levels. Supporting research into online gaming demonstrates a commitment to the core principles of responsible online gaming and a willingness to be a part of the overall solution. Money should therefore be set aside to support independent research projects.

### Evaluation and auditing of the responsible online gaming strategy

In order to examine the ongoing effectiveness of the responsible online gaming strategy, it is important that a framework for monitoring and evaluation is put in place. The following framework details how the ongoing effectiveness of the responsible online gaming strategy can be examined. There are different approaches that can be used to monitor the effectiveness of the strategy, and each has its own strengths and weaknesses. Consequently, an effective evaluation framework should attempt to triangulate data from a number of sources. Furthermore, the responsible online gaming strategy is composed of many elements and a variety of approaches will help accurately identify the effectiveness of the responsible online gaming initiatives associated with each of those elements.

- *Information audit* (E) – It is important that information about how to gamble responsibly online and how to get help for an online gambling problem is readily available for any player who requires it. Such information should be available without having to request it from a member of staff in order that customers should not feel embarrassed about seeking such information. Experience has shown that although the intentions of an online gaming operator are that such information is available and updated, sometimes this does not get translated into everyday practice. Responsible gaming staff can be instructed to carry out regular documented information audits (monthly) in order to ensure that these requirements are being met.
- *Evaluating the effectiveness of excluding underage youth using age verification* (E) – A rigorous age verification system should make excluding underage players relatively easy. However, it is important that this system is regularly tested in order to identify any problems and to demonstrate the overall effectiveness. 'Mystery shopper' operations should be conducted every six months, whereby young individuals employed by the online gaming company attempt to gamble on the gaming website.
- *Monitoring advertising* (E) – Most jurisdictions have a legal framework and/or voluntary codes of conduct within which advertising policies and guidelines are placed. Occasionally, gambling adverts are perceived by viewers to be overly aggressive, putting too much emphasis on winning, and/or targeting vulnerable groups. Focus groups can be used to gauge public opinion about particular online gaming advertising campaigns and whether any of the adverts 'cross the line'. The player panel and the stakeholder panel could also be consulted from time to time. Academic researchers can also be used to content-analyse adverts and/or advertising campaigns. Given the relatively large budgets spent on gambling (including online gambling) advertising, consumer reaction is paramount. Some companies (e.g., Svenska Spel, Loto-Quebec) have developed their own socially responsible advertising codes that rank games in terms of potential problems and have guidelines on what types of advertising can be used in what situation. Such codes need to be monitored and audited annually in the light of empirical research.
- *Evaluating the effectiveness of the online gaming self-exclusion program* (D) – Online gaming self-exclusion programs should be monitored, given that relatively little attention has been given to these programs empirically. Given the time and resources needed to implement an effective program, such initiatives should be evaluated every six months. Individuals who have accessed such programs can be asked about a variety of issues concerning the effectiveness via focus groups and/or self-report surveys. Information from the stakeholder panel should also feed into this evaluation, and may require that an evaluation is required at additional times if an issue is identified.
- *Maintain a register of problem-gambling-related incidents* (E) – This information will provide a record of how the online responsible gaming strategy is being carried out, and highlight any areas where improvements in practice are required. The register will also provide summary information for the Annual Responsible Gaming Report (see below). The Responsible Gaming Manager would be responsible for maintaining the register. Information to be recorded in the register should include:

1    identification of distressed online gamblers and the staff action taken;
2    attempts by self-excluded individuals to regain entry to the gaming website using an alternate identity;
3    self-excluded individuals who successfully regain access to the gaming website;
4    players who approach staff (online or offline) with an online gambling-related problem;
5    any incidence of aggression (verbal, written, or actual) towards a staff member or other online gambler.

•    *The Annual Responsible Gaming Report* (D) – The findings from each part of the online gaming evaluation framework should be reported in an annual social responsibility report. This document will effectively audit the overall social responsibility practices of the gaming operator's online gaming infrastructure. In addition, the report should provide an opportunity for examining any new developments in research, legislation, and technology relating to online gaming. The annual report would set the agenda for the exploration and potential implementation of any changes to the overall responsible online gaming policy. Furthermore, the report will provide documentation of the effectiveness of the strategy in providing a socially responsible environment for gambling. It will also demonstrate how the responsible online gaming strategy is both implemented and evaluated.

## Conclusions

Good social responsibility practices and player protection in online gaming tend to focus on three main dimensions (game design, behavioural transparency of products and procedures, and customer support). The strategies outlined in this chapter provide a comprehensive and integrative social responsibility infrastructure that could be used by online gaming companies to minimize harm. The social responsibility and player protection policies and initiatives that were proposed in this chapter constitute the most innovative and socially responsible practices that an online gambling operator can engage in. The responsible gaming strategy that has been developed is comprehensive, but it is acknowledged that it may not be practical for all the elements to be included in the final responsible online gaming strategy at this time. Furthermore, it must be noted that no online gaming company can totally eliminate problem gambling but robust social responsibility procedures can at least help minimize it.

From the perspective of online gaming companies, any intervention in the case of a suspected problem gambler in relation to social responsibility will be a sensitive issue. This is even more the case if the individual in question is a 'premium' customer who spends a lot of money on Internet gambling services. High-spending gambling is not (in itself) problematic, particularly if the player in question can afford it. The real issue is whether the behaviour becomes problematic. Almost all the recommendations made in this chapter are initiatives that (1) minimize harm (both time and money), and (2) highlight behavioural transparency as a way of getting the gamblers themselves to come to a decision about whether they need help for their gambling. It is only as a last resort that companies should intervene.

In working with online gaming companies, the author is well aware of the sensitivity of this particular issue. In our consultancy work with the online gaming industry, we have advised that companies email the individuals who are identified as having a possible gambling problem, informing them that as part of the company's social responsibility framework, they routinely email customers if there has been a 'significant change in their gambling behaviour' over a specified period (usually four to six weeks). The email is therefore a consequence of the policy of behavioural transparency for customers. The email does not make any reference to this being problematic per se but simply highlights that the amount of time and/or money spent has increased significantly over the specified period. The bottom of the email can include hyperlinks to such things as a self-diagnostic gambling checklist and/or gambling agencies that specialize in helping problem gamblers.

As noted above, information regarding gambling behaviour can be accessed through a 'My Account' section in the gambling website and should include a multilayer analysis of a customer's gambling behaviour on both micro- and macro-levels. A My Account page should provide a non-requested snapshot of gambling behaviour regarding profit and loss, and also financial transactions, for the last month's gambling sessions. Even customers who choose to ignore gambling expenditure will be given a true (and in some cases stark) indication of their level of gambling involvement regarding time and money usurped. Information should be readily accessible to evaluate gambling behaviour on a micro-level because the precise details of each wager (including the outcome) will be available for close inspection by the gambler.

Continual acknowledgement of actual behavioural contingencies in gambling behaviour is essential to minimize development of erroneous cognitive biases that can emerge and reduce responsible gambling behaviour. The whole process is about the 'gamblers coming to an awareness themselves' about their gambling behaviour. It is not a gaming company's job to treat problem gamblers. However, it is their job to help players analyse their own behaviour and provide a helping hand towards referral services should that be desired by the customer.

## References

American Psychiatric Association. (1994). *Diagnostic and Statistical Manual of Mental Disorders* (fourth edn). Washington, DC: American Psychiatric Association.

Broda, A., LaPlante, D. A., Nelson, S. E., LaBrie, R. A., Bosworth, L. B., and Shaffer, H. J. (2008). 'Virtual harm reduction efforts for Internet gambling: Effects of deposit limits on actual Internet sports gambling behaviour'. *Harm Reduction Journal*, 5, 27.

Derevensky, J., and Gupta, R. (2004). *Gambling Problems in Youth: Theoretical and Applied Perspectives.* New York: Kluwer Academic/Plenum Publishers.

Forrest, D. K., McHale, I., and Parke, J. (2009). 'Appendix 5: Full report of statistical regression analysis'. In Ipsos MORI, *British Survey of Children, the National Lottery and Gambling 2008–09: Report of a Quantitative Survey*. London: National Lottery Commission.

Gambling Commission (2008). *Survey Data on Remote Gambling Participation.* Birmingham: Gambling Commission.

Griffiths, M.D. (1993). 'Fruit machine gambling: The importance of structural characteristics'. *Journal of Gambling Studies*, 9, 101–20.

— (1994). 'The role of cognitive bias and skill in fruit machine gambling'. *British Journal of Psychology,* 85, 351–69.

— (2001a). 'Good practice in the gaming industry: Some thoughts and recommendations'. *Panorama (European State Lotteries and Toto Association)*, 7, 10–11.

— (2001b). 'Internet gambling: Preliminary results of the first UK prevalence study'. *Journal of Gambling Issues*, 5. Retrieved from http://www.camh.net/egambling/issue5/research/griffiths_article.html

— (2002). *Gambling and Gaming Addictions in Adolescence.* Leicester: British Psychological Society/ Blackwells.

— (2003). 'Internet gambling: Issues, concerns and recommendations'. *CyberPsychology & Behavior*, 6, 557–68.

— (2005). 'Social responsibility in lottery gambling'. *Panorama (European State Lotteries and Toto Association)*, 19, 14–16.

— (2007). 'Gambling psychology: Motivation, emotion and control'. *Casino and Gaming International*, 3(4), 71–6.

— (2009). 'Social responsibility in gambling: The implications of real-time behavioural tracking'. *Casino and Gaming International*, 5(3), 99–104.

— (2010). 'Crime and gambling: A brief overview of gambling fraud on the Internet'. *Internet Journal of Criminology*. Retrieved from http://www.Internetjournalofcriminology.com/Griffiths_%20 Gambling_Fraud_Jan_2010.pdf

Griffiths, M. D., and Barnes, A. (2008). 'Internet gambling: An online empirical study among gamblers'. *International Journal of Mental Health Addiction*, 6, 194–204.

Griffiths, M. D., and Cooper, G. (2003). 'Online therapy: Implications for problem gamblers and clinicians'. *British Journal of Guidance and Counselling*, 13, 113–35.

Griffiths, M. D., and Parke, J. (2002). 'The social impact of Internet gambling'. *Social Science Computer Review*, 20, 312–20.

Griffiths, M. D., and Parke, J. (2003). 'The environmental psychology of gambling'. In G. Reith (ed.), *Gambling: Who Wins? Who Loses?* (277–92). New York: Prometheus Books.

Griffiths, M. D., and Parke, J. (2007). 'Betting on the couch: A thematic analysis of Internet gambling using case studies'. *Social Psychological Review*, 9(2), 29–36.

Griffiths, M. D., and Parke, J. (2010). 'Adolescent gambling on the Internet: A review'. *International Journal of Adolescent Medicine and Health*, 22, 59–75.

Griffiths, M. D., and Whitty, M. W. (2010). 'Online behavioural tracking in Internet gambling research: Ethical and methodological issues'. *International Journal of Internet Research Ethics*, 3(12), 104–17.

Griffiths, M. D., and Wood, R. T. A. (2007). 'Adolescent Internet gambling: Preliminary results of a national survey'. *Education and Health*, 25, 23–7.

Griffiths, M. D., and Wood, R. T. A. (2008). 'Responsible gaming and best practice: How can academics help?' *Casino and Gaming International*, 4(1), 107–12.

Griffiths, M. D., Parke, J., Wood, R. T. A., and Rigbye, J. (2010). 'Online poker gambling in university students: Further findings from an online survey'. *International Journal of Mental Health and Addiction*, 8, 82–9.

Griffiths, M. D., Wardle, J., Orford, J., Sproston, K., and Erens, B. (2009). 'Socio-demographic correlates of Internet gambling: Findings from the 2007 British Gambling Prevalence Survey'. *CyberPsychology & Behavior*, 12, 199–202.

Griffiths, M. D., Wood, R. T. A., and Parke, J. (2008). 'Social responsibility in gambling: How to build responsibility into the programme'. *eGaming Review*, January, 43–4.

Griffiths, M. D., Wood, R. T. A., and Parke, J. (2009). 'Social responsibility tools in online gambling: A survey of attitudes and behaviour among Internet gamblers'. *CyberPsychology & Behavior*, 12, 413–21.

Griffiths, M. D., Wood, R. T. A., Parke, J., and Parke, A. (2006). 'Dissociative states in problem gambling'. In C. Allcock (ed.). *Current Issues Related to Dissociation* (27–37). Melbourne: Australian Gaming Council.

Griffiths, M. D., Wood, R. T. A., Parke, J., and Parke, A. (2007). 'Gaming research and best practice: Gaming industry, social responsibility and academia'. *Casino and Gaming International*, 3, 97–103.

Ialomiteanu, A., and Adlaf, E. (2001). 'Internet gambling among Ontario adults'. *Electronic Journal of Gambling Issues*, 5. Retrieved from http://www.camh.net/egambling/issue5/research/ialomiteanu_ adlaf_articale.html

International Gaming Research Unit (2007). 'The global online gambling report: An exploratory investigation into the attitudes and behaviours of Internet casino and poker players'. Final report prepared for eCOGRA (eCommerce and Online Gaming Regulation and Assurance).

Ipsos MORI (2009). *British Survey of Children, the National Lottery and Gambling 2008–09: Report of a Quantitative Survey*. London: National Lottery Commission.

King, D. L., Delfabbro, P. H. and Griffiths, M. D. (2010). 'The convergence of gambling and digital media: Implications for gambling in young people'. *Journal of Gambling Studies*, 26, 175–87.

LaBrie, R. A., Kaplan, S., LaPlante, D. A., Nelson, S. E., and Shaffer, H. J. (2008). 'Inside the virtual casino: A prospective longitudinal study of Internet casino gambling'. *European Journal of Public Health*. doi:10.1093/eurpub/ckn021

LaBrie, R. A., LaPlante, D. A., Nelson, S. E., Schumann, A., and Shaffer, H. J. (2007). 'Assessing the playing field: A prospective longitudinal study of Internet sports gambling behaviour'. *Journal of Gambling Studies*, 23, 347–63.

Ladd, G. T., and Petry, N. M. (2002). 'Disordered gambling among university-based medical and dental patients: A focus on Internet gambling'. *Psychology of Addictive Behaviors*, 16, 76–9.

Lapuz, J., and Griffiths, M. D. (2010). 'The role of chips in poker gambling: An empirical pilot study'. *Gambling Research*, 22(1), 34–9.

McCormack, A., and Griffiths, M. D. (2012). 'Motivating and inhibiting factors in online gambling behaviour: A grounded theory study'. *International Journal of Mental Health and Addiction*, 10, 39–53

Matthews, N., Farnsworth, W. F., and Griffiths, M. D. (2009). 'A pilot study of problem gambling among student online gamblers: Mood states as predictors of problematic behaviour'. *CyberPsychology & Behavior*, 12, 741–6.

Parke, J., Griffiths, M. D., and Parke, A. (2007). 'Positive thinking among slot machine gamblers: A case of maladaptive coping?' *International Journal of Mental Health and Addiction*, 5, 39–52.

Sevigny, S., Cloutier, M., Pelletier, M., and Ladouceur, R. (2005). 'Internet gambling: Misleading payout rates during the "demo" period'. *Computers in Human Behaviour*, 21, 153–8.

Smeaton, M., and Griffiths, M. D. (2004). 'Internet gambling and social responsibility: An exploratory study', *CyberPsychology & Behavior*, 7, 49–57.

Volberg, R., Gupta, R., Griffiths, M. D., Olason, D., and Delfabbro, P. H. (2010). 'An international perspective on youth gambling prevalence studies'. *International Journal of Adolescent Medicine and Health*, 22, 3–38.

Wardle, H., Sproston, K., Orford, J., Erens, B., Griffiths, M. D., Constantine, R., and Pigott, S. (2007). *The British Gambling Prevalence Survey 2007*. London: The Stationery Office.

Wood, R. T. A., and Griffiths, M. D. (2007a). 'Online guidance, advice, and support for problem gamblers and concerned relatives and friends: An evaluation of the *Gam-Aid* pilot service'. *British Journal of Guidance and Counselling*, 35, 373–89.

Wood, R. T. A., and Griffiths, M. D. (2007b). 'A qualitative investigation of problem gambling as an escape-based coping strategy'. *Psychology and Psychotherapy: Theory, Research and Practice*, 80, 107–25.

Wood, R. T. A., and Griffiths, M. D. (2008). 'Why Swedish people play online poker and factors that can increase or decrease trust in poker websites: A qualitative investigation'. *Journal of Gambling Issues*, 21, 80–97.

Wood, R. T. A., and Griffiths, M. D. (2010). 'Social responsibility in online gambling: The case for voluntary limit setting'. *World Online Gambling Law Report*, 9(11), 10–11.

Wood, R. T. A., and Williams, R. J. (2007). 'Problem gambling on the Internet: Implications for Internet gambling policy in North America'. *New Media and Society*, 9, 520–42.

Wood, R. T. A., Griffiths, M. D., and Parke, J. (2007). 'The acquisition, development, and maintenance of online poker playing in a student sample'. *CyberPsychology & Behavior*, 10, 354–61.

# 14 Online clinical support for people with gambling problems

*Sally Gainsbury and Richard Wood*

## Introduction

Gambling problems result in economic burden, health costs, and social strain for communities in addition to the personal and emotional distress caused to both individuals and families. The incidence and impact of gambling-related problems is increasingly recognized internationally as an important public health concern by policy makers, industry operators, treatment providers, and the community. Despite efforts taken to implement responsible gambling strategies and consumer protection policies, problem gambling still has a significant impact. For example, the Australian Productivity Commission (2010) estimated that problem gambling costs society at least A\$4.7 billion annually. Effective treatment interventions are often necessary to assist individuals to acquire the skills and knowledge necessary to control their gambling behaviour.

Although the development of gambling treatment spans decades, there is surprisingly little reliable evidence of what constitutes effective treatment for problem gambling. Less than 10 percent of problem gamblers seek formal treatment and this typically occurs following several years of gambling-related problems and only in response to a significant life crisis (Clarke, Abbott, DeSouza, and Bellringer, 2007; Ladouceur, Gosselin, Laberge, and Blaszczynski, 2001; Petry and Armentano, 1999; Productivity Commission, 2010). Attrition levels are relatively high for problem gambling treatment, ranging from 17 to 76 percent (Ladouceur, Gosselin et al., 2001; Westphal, 2006), indicating that a significant proportion of problem gamblers remain inadequately or effectively untreated. Barriers to help-seeking include feelings of shame and embarrassment, fear of stigma, difficulty attending sessions due to geographical location, transportation difficulties or work, or family commitments, misunderstandings about counselling, and a desire to solve problems unaided (Clarke et al., 2007; Evans and Delfabbro, 2005; Hodgins and el-Guebaly, 2000; Ladouceur, Blaszczynski, and Pelletier, 2004; McMillen, Marshall, Murphy, Lorenzen, and Waugh, 2004; Pulford et al., 2009; Rockloff and Schofield, 2004; Tavares, Martins, Zilberman, and el-Guebaly, 2002).

Not all problem gamblers require formal interventions, as numerous studies report that up to 60 percent of problem and pathological gamblers recover without formal treatment (Abbott, Williams, and Volberg, 2004; Hodgins, Wynne, and Makarchuk, 1999; Slutske, 2006). Problem gamblers, particularly those without severe co-morbid difficulties or complications, may benefit from brief, low-intensity interventions (Hodgins, Currie, and el-Guebaly, 2001; Hodgins, Currie, el-Guebaly, and Peden, 2004; Petry, Weinstock, Ledgerwood, and Morasco, 2008; Toneatto et al., 2008). Results from a Canadian study indicate that only 6 percent of problem and pathological gamblers seek formal help, and half of those that do prefer self-help options (Suurvali, Hodgins, Toneatto, and Cunningham,

2008). Many governments, organizations, and treatment centres recognize the limitations of existing treatment options and the capacity of any individuals with gambling-related problems to recover with brief interventions. Subsequently, it has been recommended that brief interventions be developed and implemented to assist those with gambling problems who do not desire, or are unable, to access comprehensive face-to-face treatment programs (e.g., Ontario Ministry of Health and Long-term Care, 2009; Productivity Commission, 2010).

High-speed, low-cost Internet access is widely available internationally and Internet use is increasing amongst many population groups (Miniwatts Marketing Group, 2010; Pew Internet and the American Life Project, 2011; Statistics Canada, 2010). Given its inherent features and capabilities for communication and the dissemination of information, individuals are increasingly turning to the Internet as a medium through which to obtain information and guidance in dealing with psychological problems including addictions (Pew Internet and the American Life Project, 2006). For example, reports estimate that, annually, over 10 million Americans search the Internet for information and support to quit smoking (Fox, 2005; Madden, 2006). Some population groups, including adolescents and young adults, appear to prefer to seek help online as opposed to telephone or face-to-face options (Monaghan and Wood, 2010). Accordingly, health professionals and consumers are increasingly recognizing the educational and therapeutic potential of the Internet treatment options including increased availability and ease of access and the ability to receive support and encouragement from therapists and/or peers at an interactive level.

## Internet treatment options

The Internet offers several advantages that overcome some of the barriers that prevent individuals from seeking help for mental health problems including problem gambling. Online interventions are private, potentially anonymous, convenient, and easy to access. As no face-to-face contact or appointments are required, individuals can make enquiries about and explore online treatment options at various stages of change (Prochaska and DiClemente, 1982), motivation, and readiness for treatment. This may reduce shame and embarrassment related to discussing potentially embarrassing or sensitive subjects (Griffiths and Christensen, 2006) or guilt associated with missing appointments and dropping out of treatment. Empirically supported treatments for problem gambling, including cognitive behavioural therapy (CBT) and motivational interviewing (MI) can be readily modified to be delivered through Internet interventions. Sophisticated programming can be utilized to tailor online interventions to be relevant for each unique user, based on information and responses provided during registration procedures (Etter, 2005; Etter and Perneger, 2001; Severson, Gordon, Danaher, and Akers, 2008; Strecher, Shiffman, and West, 2005; Swartz, Noell, Schroeder, and Ary, 2006). Internet interventions are cost-effective, for both providers and consumers, and can be delivered with minimal or no therapist support (Klein, Richards, and Austin, 2006; Smit, Riper, Kramer, Conijn, and Cuijpers, 2006). Subsequently, online interventions can be scaled upwards to reach a large proportion of the population, with minimal increases in costs, and can be incorporated into a stepped and shared model of treatment to fill treatment gaps (Klein et al., 2006). The benefits of online clinical support may increase treatment uptake rates and retention amongst individuals experiencing gambling-related problems.

Online clinical support includes any treatment option that engages clients through online resources, websites, and web-based methods of communication (Barak, Klein, and Proudfoot, 2009). Typically, Internet-based interventions are primarily structured self-guided programs, operated through a website, used by individuals seeking health- or mental-health-related assistance. The intervention program includes multiple components and attempts to create positive behavioural change and enhance knowledge, awareness, and understanding through the provision of educational material and interactive web-based components (Abbott, Klein, and Ciechomski, 2008). Online interventions are a relatively new form of treatment and there is currently no 'gold standard', although research is progressively leading to program refinement and increasing effectiveness. There are three main categories of online clinical interventions:

1   *Internet-based treatment interventions*: involve regular contact and interaction with a therapist throughout the treatment program, to provide support, guidance, and feedback either on a synchronous or asynchronous basis. Individuals typically complete the majority of the intervention online, by themselves, and may contact the therapist via the Internet or telephone.
2   *Internet-based self-guided interventions*: designed to promote cognitive, behavioural, and emotional changes, by instructing individuals to follow a modularized and structured evidence-based program, without direct therapist contact. These programs vary in length and level of intensity and range from a single screen with tailored automated feedback to highly structured programs with many components intended to be completed over six to twelve weeks.
3   *Internet-based peer support*: synchronous and asynchronous Internet-based communication, between registered individuals on a set topic, which may involve monitoring or participation by a moderator. Online forums, discussions boards, or organized chat groups are intended to provide emotional support, feedback, information, and assistance, in a safe and friendly manner, between a group of individuals experiencing or having experienced similar problems. This form of intervention is not intended to be a treatment program, but may be a useful adjunct or precursor to treatment.

Internet-based treatment options are not usually intended to replace traditional services, but such interventions may be an extremely useful addition for individuals who have accessed existing treatments, and for those unwilling or unable to access traditional treatment options. Online interventions may be utilized by those at various levels of risk for gambling-related problems including preventing the development of pathological gambling. These programs have the capacity to reach a large number of individuals to provide brief screening and interventions and more in-depth therapy where necessary. Despite its potential, treatment providers and regulators have legitimate concerns regarding the overall efficacy of Internet-based interventions for problem gambling, legal and ethical issues, cost and feasibility of programs, and the extent to which individuals would actually utilize technology-based services. This chapter aims to provide an overview of the use of online clinical support for individuals with gambling-related problems.

## Internet therapy

Internet therapy involves the delivery of a formal, structured, evidence-based treatment program, to individuals diagnosed with a specific disorder, utilizing Internet-based technology (Barak et al., 2009). Typical programs run over a period of six to eight weeks, and clients complete one online module per week, which includes at least one interaction with a therapist. Modules are often based on CBT, MI, and motivational enhancement therapy (MET) principles, which have empirical support as brief intervention strategies for problem gambling (Carlbring, Jonsson, Josephson, and Forsberg, 2010; Hodgins et al., 2001; Hodgins et al., 2004; Grant and Potenza, 2007; Ladouceur, Sylvain et al., 2001; Petry et al., 2006; Petry et al., 2008; Toneatto and Ladouceur, 2003). Each module may include educational materials presented using a variety of multimedia tools, interactive exercises including short answer questions, quizzes and self-assessments that provide automatic feedback, and behavioural tools, such as self-monitoring diaries, goal setting, and relapse prevention techniques. Clients typically exchange emails with their therapist once per week to discuss progress, provide feedback, answer questions, and discuss issues. Contact can also occur through live chat, video conferencing, or telephone. Following the completion of therapy, clients may be contacted for follow-up sessions to ensure the gains made in therapy are maintained.

In Internet therapy, clinician input is markedly reduced (50–80 percent less) compared to face-to-face treatment, with feedback delivered and responses and outcomes determined by an automated program (Andersson et al., 2008). For example, automatically generated tailored feedback can be given for completed online exercises and new modules may be opened, subject to completion of prior work. However, time spent on therapy by the client is not reduced (Andersson et al., 2008); in fact Internet therapy may be more time-consuming for clients than face-to-face therapy, as educational materials and practical exercises are included in homework assignments, and clients continuously report progress and obtain feedback on exercises as they are completed.

There is a growing body of evidence to support the effectiveness of Internet therapy for mental health, including addictions and problem gambling. A meta-analysis of 92 online psychotherapeutic interventions (Barak, Hen, Boniel-Nissim, and Shapira, 2008) shows an average medium effect size of 0.53 and treatment effects persist post-treatment. Direct comparison between Internet therapy and face-to-face treatment for the same problem, with random assignment to conditions, finds no statistically significant differences between treatment modalities in clinical outcome including behavioural change and client satisfaction (Barak et al., 2008; Murphy et al., 2009). These findings indicate that Internet therapy is, on average, as effective as face-to-face therapy. Further analyses suggest CBT is more effective than psychoeducational or behavioural interventions, the latter being the least suited to online treatment (Barak et al., 2008). A systematic review of Internet therapy for addictions indicates the recent development of this field, with only nine studies meeting criteria for inclusion, including one study on Internet therapy for problem gambling (Gainsbury and Blaszczynski, 2011). The review demonstrates the range of therapeutic models, treatment components, and outcome measures in use, and demonstrates the positive treatment effects reported following completion of treatment and at longer-term follow-up. The authors conclude that Internet therapy for addictions may be effective in enabling appropriate behaviour change, although further research trials are needed to explore this form of therapy (Gainsbury and Blaszczynski, 2011).

### Internet therapy programs for problem gambling

*Sweden*

Several Internet therapy programs have been established internationally for problem gambling, although few treatment outcome trials have been completed and published. A Swedish group has completed a randomized controlled trial of the Internet therapy program slutaspela.nu (Stop Playing) (Carlbring and Smit, 2008). Treatment is divided into eight modules; the first four modules involving MI techniques to assist individuals in making a decision about their gambling. These modules include asking friends and relatives for input, answering open-ended questions designed to evoke change talk, and creating a time-line to map the development of gambling-related problems. The final four modules are CBT-based, and follow a standard treatment course. Clients are instructed to complete one module each week, including reading and completing exercises, essay-style questions, and posting comments on an online bulletin board. Each week clients receive a telephone call from their therapist, who provides positive feedback and encouragement, and answers questions for approximately 15 minutes.

Results of the evaluation trial show that half the participants completed all eight modules within the specified time frame (Carlbring and Smit, 2008). After eight weeks, participants may access all modules, which appears to increase completion rates, which were found to be 68 percent at six-month follow-up. Follow-up at one month after program completion shows that gambling-related problems, anxiety, and depression were all significantly reduced in the Internet therapy group, and quality of life had increased as compared to wait-listed controls. The majority of participants were found to have made moderate or large improvements, which were maintained at 6 and 12 months following treatment. The results of this study are constrained, as individuals with severe depression were excluded, and only 66 participants were included in the trial. However, the study provides support for the use of Internet-based therapy for treating pathological gambling.

## Norway

A similar Internet therapy program for problem gambling is offered in Norway, where the geographical landscape means that many citizens live far away from treatment providers. This program, www.spillbehandling.no (Distance based therapy for problem gamblers in Norway), includes nine CBT-based weekly assignments, and all communication between therapists and clients is conducted online or via telephone (Eidem, 2008). The assignments include: motivation and goals; readiness to change; analysing gambling situations; high-risk situations and identifying automatic erroneous thoughts; self-help tools (flashcards and notebooks); financial situation and challenges; and relationships, trust, and honesty.

The site receives approximately 500 hits per month, and in the first two years of service 90 clients (86 percent male, mean age = 36 years) signed up for treatment (Eidem, 2010). A formal research trial has not been conducted, but the majority of clients who commence treatment complete the program and meet their treatment goals, including abstinence or controlled gambling (Eidem, 2010). Clients report positive feedback and satisfaction with the combination of written email assignments and telephone calls.

## Germany

Check dein Spiel (Check Your Gambling) is a personal counselling program offered in Germany which aims to help participants reach abstinence from gambling within four weeks. The program is based on the behaviour principles of self-regulation and self-control, as well as MI and solution-focused therapy. Participants have an initial chat-based conversation with a counsellor, which lasts approximately 50 minutes, during which the therapeutic relationship is established, the client is evaluated, and goals and coping strategies are developed. The clients then keep an online diary of their gambling behaviour, including related thoughts, triggers, and coping strategies while they work through several modules. The modules deal with relapse prevention, improvement of quality of life, establishing daily structure, considering advantages and disadvantages of gambling, and understanding of debt. Each week the client receives detailed feedback from the counsellor via email. After four weeks, the client has another online chat with their counsellor, which lasts approximately 30 minutes. Program participation is reviewed and discussed and relapse prevention techniques are implemented. Between September 2007 and September 2009, 197 participants registered to use the program. Of these, the majority were male (87 percent) with a mean age of 34 years (SD = 9.3), 95 percent were pathological gamblers, and 64 percent were seeking professional help for the first time. Of the 197 participants, 66 percent completed the whole four-week program. Of those who completed a follow-up questionnaire, the majority indicated that the program was significantly helpful.

## Finland

Päihdelinkki (AddictionLink) offers a full service addiction site for Finland, including peer support and discussion, self-help resources, and professional support and counselling. Founded in 1996, the site is accessed by approximately 40,000 individual visitors a month (Peltoniemi and Bothas, 2007). For example, in May 2006, 6,179 individuals took the online gambling test and 7,597 individuals used the online discussion forums. Approximately 12 percent of counselling provided by the site is for problem gambling, which includes individuals seeking help for their own gambling problems and concerned significant others seeking help relating to another's gambling.

## UK

Online gambling services in the UK are offered by GamAid and GamblingTherapy, both allowing clients to talk live with advisers online (during service hours). These services aim to assist clients in reducing their gambling behaviour but are not intended as traditional treatment services. Advisers communicate with clients to provide reassurance and give advice, rather than acting as counsellors. An evaluation study of GamAid (Wood and Griffiths, 2007) noted that the service was far more popular with women than any other comparable service, it was most popular with people who gambled online, and that users originated from many different countries.

## Australia

An Australian program, Gambling Help Online (www.gamblinghelponline.org.au), was launched in September 2009 to provide 24/7 live counselling, email support, and a range of self-help options. The program is funded by all Australian State and Territory governments, as well as the Federal government, and is run by a centre with experience in alcohol, drug, and gambling telephone and online services. Clients are instructed to complete pre-screening online, before counselling, to allow counsellors to spend less time on assessment and focus on rapport development. The treatment model for live counselling is a combination of motivational interviewing, cognitive therapy, and cognitive behavioural therapy. This model is supported by a strong internal focus on dealing with the gambling behaviour, rather than just the cause/consequences. Counsellors must be eligible for Australian Psychological Society, Australian Association for Social Workers, or Psychotherapy and Counselling

Federation of Australia membership, and have completed brief training specializing in cognitive therapy for problem gambling. Clients are offered two options:

1   Live counselling, available 24/7, providing immediate feedback. Sessions typically last 50–90 minutes and the basic structure is engagement, assessment, intervention, summary, and referral.
2   Email-based counselling, with clients offered several emails a week for approximately six weeks with a 24-hour response time.

In the first 12 months of operation, 979 live counselling contacts were made, for an average contact duration of 43 minutes (Rodda, 2010). The majority (61 percent) accessed the service anonymously, were from metropolitan areas (78 percent), and most contacts were received outside traditional business hours. Gamblers using chat were most likely to have problems with electronic gaming machines (EGMs) (70 percent), have significant gambling-related problems (99 percent), be male (58 percent), and aged under 30 (44 percent), although clients aged over 40 were significantly more likely to be female. In the same period, the online treatment service received 210 unique email requests for email support, 51 percent of which were first received during business hours. Gamblers using email were more likely to be female (53 percent) and were evenly distributed across age groups, although as with chat support, a higher proportion of males were aged under 30 and females were aged over 40. Similarly to chat clients, the majority of gamblers seeking email support had problems with EGMs and severe gambling-related problems. This program is being independently evaluated and updated based on feedback and research findings.

### Limitations

Internet therapy is not intended to be suitable for all problem and pathological gamblers or as a replacement for traditional face-to-face treatment. It is important that all clients have regular, private access to the Internet, so that they may complete all sessions and exercises, and clients are able to read, are computer literate, and can type relatively quickly. Individuals with severe gambling-related problems, or co-morbid psychological issues, may require more intensive interventions and ongoing assistance. Internet therapy programs should include motivation components, and be user-friendly, to reduce attrition and increase program completion, which is linked with treatment effectiveness. Further research is required to establish the specific components that should be included to increase treatment effectiveness and evaluate the process variables that may mediate behavioural change.

## Internet-based self-guided interventions

Internet-based self-guided interventions (referred to as Internet interventions) are programs for those who wish to deal with their gambling-related problems, without the involvement of direct therapist assistance. These programs may include single or multiple components, be highly structured and direct clients in a systematic fashion, or open access and allow clients to pick and choose the components most suitable to them. Internet interventions may have a similar modular or stage-based format to Internet therapy, but without the inclusion of therapist support (Abbott et al., 2008). Some Internet interventions include an option for participants to contact a therapist, via email or discussion forum. This option can be used if individuals have a question or need assistance. As Internet interventions do not involve ongoing therapist support, they can be scaled upwards to reach large numbers of people without significantly increasing costs, although host servers must be able to handle increases in access (Lieberman and Huang, 2008).

### Features of Internet interventions

Internet interventions often require individuals to register for, and log in to, programs with an anonymous user name or email address. This allows continuity in the use of the program, and screening questionnaires completed during the registration process may direct participants to the most suitable components, based on the information provided, or provide access to tailored content. Screening questionnaires can also provide tailored normative feedback, a technique in which an individual receives automated feedback, which compares their responses to the responses of a large normative sample of their peers (Kreuter and Wray, 2003). This personalized feedback aims to increase an individual's awareness of the extent of their gambling involvement and motivate them to make appropriate behavioural changes (Bewich et al., 2008; Cunningham, Hodgins, Toneatto, Rai, and Cordingley, 2009; Etter and Perneger, 2001). This component may be an intervention in its own right, or the first step in a larger treatment program.

As with individual therapy, online self-help interventions should be individualized to be effective (Lustria, Cortese, Noar, and Glueckauf, 2009). This is particularly important given the heterogeneity of problem gamblers, as participants may engage in various forms of gambling, differ in levels of motivation, previous treatment experience, and by age, gender, and cultural background. Pre-treatment and ongoing screening measures enable automated program customization so that individual participants are directed to the most appropriate materials (Swartz et al., 2006). For example, psychoeducation must be relevant to the most problematic form of gambling for each individual, and individuals who are seeking help for the first time are likely to require more motivational work than those who have completed face-to-face treatment and seek ongoing support. Research has found that tailored web-based programs are more efficacious than non-tailored sites (e.g., Etter, 2005; Etter and Perneger, 2001; Severson, Gordon, Danaher, and Akers, 2008; Strecher, Shiffman, and West, 2005; Swartz et al., 2006).

Internet interventions frequently utilize CBT techniques such as diaries to monitor gambling behaviours, thoughts, urges, triggers, and coping strategies. These diaries allow participants to track the patterns of behaviour and identify times and situations where they have most difficulty controlling consumption (Cunningham, 2007). Online diaries may be combined with goal-setting tools to allow an individual to monitor their behaviour and track progress towards goals. These features may provide appropriate summaries and visual reminders to assist individuals in being motivated to address gambling problems and see their progress and changes. Educational information is also provided online, as problem gambling is often associated with irrational and erroneous thoughts (Joukhador, Maccallum, and Blaszczynski, 2003; Raylu and Oei, 2002; Toneatto and Ladouceur, 2003). Online interventions can provide educative material in a variety of multimedia options including video, audio, graphics, checklists, and interactive exercises with automated feedback. Multimedia CBT programs have been shown to have better outcomes than written text (Bowers, Stuart, MacFarlane, and Gorman, 1993). Interactive exercises can include quizzes or other self-assessment features that enable users to test their knowledge of the relevant information contained within a module.

*Evidence for Internet interventions*

According to a meta-analysis that reviewed 40 well-designed outcome studies, online self-help treatments appear to be more effective than no treatment at all and just as effective in most cases as treatment administered by therapists (Scogin, Bynum, Stevens, and Calhoon, 1990). Furthermore, online interventions appear to be more effective than traditional self-help programs. Klein (2002) found that individuals spent less time in Internet-based CBT for panic disorder compared to a print-based self-help manual condition. This study also found that education levels were more likely to influence treatment outcomes of the print self-help materials compared to the Internet-based program, suggesting that Internet interventions may be more broadly used than print-based self-help programs.

Few online interventions exist for problem gambling, but some evidence supports the potential effectiveness of such programs. In a study conducted with a sample of international gamblers recruited online, participants were provided with automated personalized feedback on their gambling behaviour (Wood and Williams, 2009). The majority of participants (65 percent) reported that the interactive feedback (describing how normative their gambling behaviour was, projection of yearly expenditures, explanations of why certain beliefs held were gambling fallacies, risk of becoming a problem gambler, current score on the Problem Gambling Severity Index [PGSI], etc.) was 'somewhat' or 'very useful'. Problem gamblers were significantly more likely than non-problem gamblers to report that tailored normative feedback was useful. Furthermore, 34 percent of problem gamblers reported that they expected their gambling behaviour would decrease subsequent to receiving the feedback. This suggests that online interventions providing personalized feedback and educational information could have a potential impact on reducing problem gambling, as well as beneficial effects for non-problem gamblers (Wood and Williams, 2009).

In another personalized feedback intervention for problem gamblers, participants were mailed summaries based on a battery of assessment instruments (Cunningham et al., 2009). Participants who received feedback reported spending less money on gambling than control subjects at three-month follow-up. The feedback materials included a brief statement of the purpose of the report ('help to give you a picture of your gambling and let you know how your gambling compares with other Canadians'), and then provided a summary of gambling behaviour with a comparison of how this compared to other Canadians of their sex (Cunningham et al., 2009: 220–1). A graph was also included to visually demonstrate where their gambling fits in comparison with other Canadians. Feedback was also given on risk levels for problem gambling and a list of the actual problems the participant indicated. The next section included a description of irrational beliefs endorsed and a summary of cognitive errors. Finally, feedback included a list of techniques individuals could use to lower the risk associated with their gambling. Almost all (96 percent) recipients, who responded to the three-month follow-up survey, felt that the feedback materials should be made available to other people who wanted to modify or evaluate their gambling (Cunningham et al., 2009). The most positively endorsed element was the feedback on their risk for problem gambling, and the other elements were also positively evaluated in terms of usefulness. Although these results are from a pilot study, which limits the extent to which they can be generalized, they suggest that brief screening and feedback interventions could be very useful for gamblers and problem gamblers and suggest a full research evaluation is merited.

An online version of the tailored normative feedback intervention tested by Cunningham et al. (2009) is now available (www.CheckYourGambling.net). It offers a brief online screen in English or French that allows individuals to check how their own gambling behaviour compares to that of individuals similar to themselves. Upon completion, participants immediately receive a report that summarizes information provided and reports how their gambling behaviour and cognitions compare to their peers. Participants receive an outline of their level of risk for being a problem gambler. The report includes accurate information about irrational beliefs and behaviours and tips on how to gamble in a responsible, low-risk manner. The aim of the online screen is to assist individuals in assessing their own behaviour and being aware of whether they may need to alter their gambling or seek additional help or treatment.

### *Suitability of Internet interventions*

Internet interventions appear to be suitable for individuals at low and moderate risk of developing gambling-related problems as well as problem gamblers. Individuals with severe gambling and co-morbid problems may require more intensive interventions (Toneatto et al., 2008). As problem gambling and addiction therapy programs are traditionally dominated by men, women may feel more comfortable or find that their needs are better met by Internet interventions (Monaghan and Blaszczynski, 2009). Men also stand to benefit from Internet interventions, as they offer a more directive approach and avoid face-to-face discussions of emotions, which is preferable for men (Rochlen, Land, and Wong, 2004). Adolescents and young adults also appear to benefit from Internet interventions and prefer this format to telephone and face-to-face interventions (Monaghan and Wood, 2010). A review of online clinical support for youth shows that this form of treatment appears to be effective in assisting youth dealing with gambling problems due to their access to, and familiarity with, the media and the anonymous capabilities of this intervention (Monaghan and Wood, 2010). Internet interventions may also be tailored to be appropriate to various cultural groups. Problem gambling is a source of shame and embarrassment in certain cultural groups, and there is a reluctance to seek treatment, due to the desire to solve problems within families and misunderstanding of the nature of therapy (Oei and Raylu, 2007; Raylu and Oei, 2004). If tailored to be culturally relevant, Internet interventions may be suitable for many cultural groups to assist individuals with, and those affected by, gambling problems. Finally, Internet interventions appear to be suitable for individuals with problems related to Internet gambling. Internet gambling is cited as the main source of problems for the majority of participants of Internet therapy in Norway and Sweden and a significant proportion of clients using services in Sweden and Germany. These findings contrast with results of a study of 12,251 gamblers from 105 countries, including Internet and non-Internet gamblers, showing that non-Internet gamblers appear to be more likely to seek Internet counselling (35 percent) than Internet gamblers (30 percent; Wood and Williams, 2009). However, more Internet gamblers reported seeking help for problems (9 percent) than non-Internet gamblers (5 percent) and Internet gamblers were three to four times more likely to experience gambling problems than non-Internet gamblers (Wood and Williams, 2009). Taken together, these findings indicate that Internet interventions may provide an important source of treatment for Internet gamblers experiencing gambling-related problems.

## Peer support forums

Online peer support forums, also known as bulletin boards, exist to discuss every conceivable topic. However, there are currently very few online forums worldwide that specifically focus on issues related to gambling problems. Forums do not provide treatment, but instead offer guidance and support through engagement with an online community (Wood and Wood,

2009). Typically, forum members post written questions or statements, and other members then respond to those posts. Due to their anonymity and accessibility (usually 24-hours-per-day and seven-days-a-week), expert-moderated peer support forums can potentially provide cost-effective social support for a variety of addictive disorders (King and Moreggi, 1998).

The type of support that is received from a peer support forum is informative and practical in nature, such as strategies to avoid gambling when tempted, managing debts, and discussing a gambling problem with a family member (Wood and Wood, 2009). Support may also come in the form of encouragement from other members, for example, that dealing with a gambling problem is possible and that it does not have to be done alone (Wood and Wood, 2009). Usually online forums contain links to other support services such as crisis support, telephone helplines, self-help materials, and local treatment providers. In addition to helping people with gambling problems, forums usually offer support to friends and relatives of people with gambling problems who are looking for answers about how they can help someone else (Cooper, 2004; Wood and Wood, 2009). Whilst many users of forums may meet criteria for problem or pathological gambling, users may also have less severe gambling-related problems or have previously experienced gambling-related problems (Wood and Griffiths, 2007). The nature of forums is such that it is easy and anonymous for any person to read information posted by others, although registration is typically required to post comments in an effort to prevent spam and abuse.

Peer support forums tend to be targeted towards specific geographic populations, usually due to language limitations and/or the stipulations of the supporting funding bodies. However, forums by nature will always attract some members from other areas, unless they are deliberately excluded (Wood and Wood, 2009). It can be argued that the inclusion of members from other locations adds to the diversity of the online community, and may provide unique strategies and ideas for dealing with gambling-related problems. Furthermore, some international members are more likely to be online late at night or early in the morning, due to differences in time zones. This can help ensure that the community remains active at any time of the day or night (Wood and Wood, 2009).

### How do peer support forums work?

Forum posts (messages) are typically archived and serve as an ongoing resource that can be accessed, either by anyone who visits the forum, or by members if registration is a requirement for this resource. Joining a peer-based forum is usually free and is completed via a simple online sign-up procedure using an anonymous email address. Forums are typically moderated by an administrator and may also be moderated by certain forum members who are experienced, and trusted, in that particular online community. Moderation is usually only carried out during office hours, although moderators may (in some cases) be alerted by email notifications from other members outside these times. The role of the moderator is to facilitate civil communications between members and remove any malicious, inaccurate, or misleading posts that may contravene the rules of the forum. Members who are abusive or break other forum rules (e.g., posting spam) can be suspended or banned from the forum altogether. Removal and prevention of spam, which often links to gambling websites, is another moderator task that can take up a considerable amount of time. It is also important that the forum has good security and that member details are kept secure and to a minimum. Hackers may try to infiltrate the forum to try to gain member details (e.g., names, email addresses, etc.), and it has been known for forums to be hijacked, with demands made for money in return for allowing the forum to resume activities. Effective technical support and regular backing up of forum data are essential in order to thwart such attacks, and to guard against other technical calamities such as losing all the archived posts (Wood, 2010).

## *Effectiveness of peer-based support*

Peer support forums have been implemented with some success in other addiction fields such as problem drinking (Cunningham, van Mierlo, and Fournier, 2008) and smoking cessation (Klatt et al., 2008; Stoddard, Augustson, and Moser, 2008). For example, an evaluation of a smoking cessation website, QuitNet, found that quitting rates and continued abstinence were highly related to use of social support features, including chat rooms, forums, and internal emails (Cobb, Graham, Bock, Papandonatos, and Abrams, 2005), suggesting that online social support can act as a mechanism of change in quitting smoking. In contrast, Stoddard et al. (2008) found that the addition of a bulletin board to an online smoking cessation intervention did not have an impact on quit rates. However, as few participants (12 percent) utilized this tool, this finding may suggest that efforts to encourage the use of peer-based support may increase the effectiveness of this feature.

One major advantage of peer-based forums over other online support services is that they are easily scalable. That is, the more people who join, the more vibrant the community becomes. Having more members is likely to be beneficial to ensure that posts are responded to in a timely fashion and to reduce the likelihood of a few overriding members dominating the group (Cunningham et al., 2008; Stoddard et al., 2008). At the same time, it is not usually necessary to employ further moderators to keep up with the increased popularity of the service. By contrast, services offering one-to-one support can quickly find that they do not have the staff available to meet a growing demand (Wood, 2010).

To date, there have only been a handful of published studies that have specifically investigated the utility of online forums for helping people with gambling problems. Cooper (2004) examined the international, although predominantly North American, Gamblers Anonymous (GA) web forum. Quantitative and qualitative responses to an online survey were received from 50 people with gambling problems who used the forum. In explaining the process by which people with gambling problems discussed their issues on the forum, Cooper developed the Pathways Disclosure Model. This model suggests that the relative anonymity of peer support forums allowed members to feel more comfortable in discussing their problems compared to face-to-face or telephone support services. Lurking (i.e., visiting but not registering a presence to other users) on a peer support forum appears to make it easier for many people to consider seeking further help, including face-to-face services. This appears to be particularly true for the female clients. Furthermore, 20 percent of the sample in the study reported that they used GAweb as the exclusive means for helping them deal with their gambling problems. It is argued that for some people, online forums may be the only support they can receive because of financial, geographical, transport, and/or emotional constraints (Cooper, 2004). Given the self-selected sample included in this study, and potential bias in responses, the results have to be interpreted with caution. However, the study appears to provide some preliminary support for the usefulness of gambling support forums.

Wood and Wood (2009) examined two UK-based forums: Gambling Therapy and the GamCare forum. Both forums had been operating for several years and are run by organizations that also provide treatment services for people with gambling problems. At the time the study was conducted, there were approximately 8,000 registered members across both forums. The study involved a content analysis of 60 posts, in-depth interviews with 19 members, and a survey of 121 members. The study mapped out the type of messages posted and found that the posts examined provided advice or information to another member (38 percent), supportive messages (37 percent) aimed at either a specific individual or the community in general, stories about a member's gambling problem (25 percent), requests for help or a specific response to a request (24 percent), personal statements about gambling (10 percent), and introductions by new members (8 percent). Members reported that the forums made them feel less alone (98 percent), and that they gained insight into their problems (82 percent). Furthermore, they suggested that the forums helped remind them of how bad things could get if they gambled again (91 percent), and helped members gain better control over their gambling behaviour (72 percent). Just under half the forum members (42 percent) reported that they had never contacted another gambling support service before, and half (50 percent) reported that they felt more confident about seeking professional help after using the forums. Of those who had contacted another service, almost half (48 percent) used the forum for additional support. Similar to the study by Cooper (2004), the results from Wood and Wood (2009) are based on the responses of a small sample of self-selected participants. This limits the extent to which the results can be generalized.

GamTalk (www.GamTalk.org) is currently the only national peer-based gambling issues support forum managed in Canada for the primary benefit of Canadians. Launched in October 2008, it offers a moderated service in English and, since October 2010, in French, via its sister site ParlonsJeux (www.ParlonsJeux.org). In an ongoing study of GamTalk users, 149 respondents provided feedback about how they use the forum and the perceived benefits (Wood, 2010). Respondents were mostly female (67 percent), although as respondents were self-selecting this may not be representative of members generally. That is, more women than men may have responded to the survey request.

The most frequently reported usage of the GamTalk forum was for reading other people's posts (82 percent always or sometimes), followed by writing about their own thoughts and experiences (61 percent always or sometimes), asking questions (57 percent always or sometimes), offering advice (51 percent always or sometimes), and recording their own progress (49 percent always or sometimes). The most frequent benefit reported was being able to talk to others in similar situations (61 percent). Just under half the respondents (46 percent) suggested that anonymity was an important factor in deciding to use a forum, as was ease of access (46 percent). After using the service, two-thirds (67 percent) of respondents reported that they felt more informed about gambling issues generally, the same number (67 percent) reported that they felt more informed about other services that were available for them, and half (51 percent) suggested that they gained more insight into their own gambling behaviour.

In Sweden, the Spelinsitutet provides a free peer-based forum that is open for anyone to join (http://stodkontakten.spelinstitutet.se/). The main language is Swedish, but it is also possible to post in English. Also in Sweden, there is a closed forum that specifically supports people with gambling problems who are signed up to use a self-help manual that is also managed by the Spelinstitutet. There are currently no published findings about usage of these services.

Overall, forums appear to facilitate the contemplative stage of change in overcoming addictions (Prochaska and DiClemente, 1982). Both Cooper (2004), and Wood and Wood (2009) found that the majority of respondents, in their studies, reported that they had previously avoided seeking face-to-face support because of an unwillingness to disclose information about themselves. This appeared to relate to a perceived high level of stigma associated with having a gambling problem. Several studies have found that the issue of stigma has caused some people with gambling problems to avoid seeking treatment (Gupta and Derevensky, 2000; Hodgins and el-Guebaly, 2000; Marotta, 2000). Furthermore, Wood (2010) noted that often new members at GamTalk indicated that they had no idea of either the types of support that were available for them, or what was specifically available in their area. Wood (2010) also noted that using the forum helped them consider what to do next, by drawing upon the experiences and ideas of others.

Given that Internet gambling is the fastest growing form of gambling, online support forums may prove to be an extremely useful way of helping those who have gambling issues, either from developing a full-scale gambling problem, or for encouraging those already experiencing problems to better understand the extent of their problem and/or seek further help. Furthermore, offering peer-based support may be useful as a way of offering those who are waiting for a one-to-one session, something constructive to do while waiting to receive treatment. Similarly, forums offer something for people to do outside scheduled treatment sessions, and may even provide a diversion for clients facing the temptation to gamble online.

## Conclusions

The convenience and easy access of online clinical support offers an opportunity for many individuals to access help services who would otherwise find it difficult to receive support for gambling problems. For people in remote areas, with mobility issues, child-care considerations, or busy work schedules, online support may be their only viable option, particularly if they are not comfortable discussing such matters on the phone. Furthermore, the wide variety of services that are becoming available allows a choice of treatment from which clients can select the most suitable for their particular needs. Services range from peer-based support, which allows anyone to easily and anonymously gain information, or communicate with others in similar situations, through to complete treatment packages supported by clinicians and self-help interactive programs. Several types of online support services can be run for large numbers of clients in a very cost-effective way. However, where one-to-one clinician support is required costs begin to resemble more traditional services. It is, therefore, worth noting that not all services are scalable to meet the needs of clients on demand.

There is currently limited evidence regarding the efficacy of different types of online support services, although to date results look promising, and many traditional clinical support services also lack rigorous evaluation. Online support services may facilitate clients in seeking help by removing some of the barriers that deter some people from seeking help. In particular, the anonymity of online support appears to somewhat reduce feelings of stigma and embarrassment. There are also tentative findings suggesting that online support may have a greater appeal for women with gambling problems than comparable traditional services. However, further research is required to understand more precisely who benefits most from online support services, and in which particular circumstances. Nevertheless, online clinical support appears to have a great potential for helping a wide range of people overcome their gambling problems, either as a stand-alone treatment program or as an adjunct to other services.

## References

Abbott, J. M., Klein, B., and Ciechomski, L. (2008). 'Best practices in online therapy'. *Journal of Technology in Human Services, 26*, 360–75.

Abbott, M. W., Williams, M. M. and Volberg, R. A. (2004). 'A Prospective study of problem and regular non-problem gamblers living in the community'. *Substance Use and Misuse, 39(6)*, 855–84.

Andersson, G., Bergström, J., Buhrman, M., Carlbring, P., Holländare, F., Kaldo, V., et al. (2008). 'Development of a new approach to guided self-help via the Internet: The Swedish experience'. *Journal of Technology in Human Services, 26*, 161–81.

Barak, A., Hen, L., Boniel-Nissim, M., and Shapira, N. (2008) 'A comprehensive review and a meta-analysis of the effectiveness of Internet-based psychotherapeutic interventions'. *Journal of Technology in Human Services, 26,* 109–60.

Barak, A., Klein, B., and Proudfoot, J. G. (2009) 'Defining Internet-supported therapeutic interventions'. *Annals of Behavioural Medicine, 38*(1), 4–17.

Bewich, B. M., Trusler, K., Barkham, M., Hill, A. J., Cahill, J., and Mulherm, B. (2008). 'The effectiveness of web-based interventions designed to decrease alcohol consumption: A systematic review'. *Preventative Medicine, 47,* 17–26.

Bowers, W., Stuart, S., MacFarlane, R., and Gorman, L. (1993). 'Use of computer-administered cognitive-behavior therapy with depressed inpatients'. *Depression, 1,* 294–9.

Carlbring, P., and Smit, F. (2008). 'Randomised trial of Internet-delivered self help with telephone support for pathological gamblers'. *Journal of Consulting and Clinical Psychology, 76,* 1090–4.

Carlbring, P., Jonsson, J., Josephson, H., and Forsberg, L. (2010). 'Motivational interviewing versus cognitive behavioural group therapy in the treatment of problem and pathological gambling: A randomized controlled trial'. *Cognitive Behaviour Therapy, 39*(2), 92–103.

Clarke, D., Abbott, M., DeSouza, R., and Bellringer, M. (2007). 'An overview of help seeking by problem gamblers and their families including barriers to and relevance of services'. *International Journal of Mental Health and Addictions, 5,* 292–306.

Cobb, K. N., Graham, A. L., Bock, B. C., Papandonatos, G., and Abrams, D. B. (2005). 'Initial evaluation of a real-world Internet smoking cessation system'. *Nicotine and Tobacco Research, 7,* 207–16.

Cooper, G. (2004). 'Exploring and understanding online assistance for problem gamblers: The pathways disclosure model'. *International Journal of Mental Health and Addiction, 1,* 32–8.

Cunningham, J. (2007). 'Internet-based interventions for alcohol, tobacco and other substances of abuse'. In P. Miller, and D. Kavanagh (eds), *Translation of addictions science into practice.* New York: Elsevier-Pergamon.

Cunningham, J. A., Hodgins, D. C., Toneatto, T., Rai, A., and Cordingley, J. (2009). 'Pilot study of personalized feedback intervention for problem gamblers'. *Behavior Therapy, 40,* 219–24.

Cunningham, J. A., van Mierlo, T., and Fournier, R. (2008). 'An online support group for problem drinkers: AlcoholHelpCenter.net.' *Patient Education and Counseling, 70*(2), 193–8.

Eidem, M. (2008, June). 'Distance based therapy for problem gamblers in Norway'. Presentation at the 7th European Conference on Gambling Studies and Policy Issues. Retrieved April 27, 2009 from http://www.assissa.eu/easg/wednesday/1400-ses4/eidem_magnus.pdf

— (2010, April). 'Addressing problem gambling: Some snapshots from Norway'. Presentation at the Discovery 2010 Conference, Toronto, ON.

Etter, J. F. (2005). 'Comparing the efficacy of two Internet-based, computer-tailored smoking cessation programs: A randomized trial'. *Journal of Medical Internet Research, 7,* e2.

Etter, J. F., and Perneger, T. V. (2001). 'A comparison of cigarette smokers recruited through the Internet or by mail'. *International Journal of Epidemiology, 30,* 521–5.

Evans, L., and Delfabbro, P. H. (2005). 'Motivators for change and barriers to help-seeking in Australian problem gamblers'. *Journal of Gambling Studies, 21*(2), 133–55.

Fox, S. (2005). *Health information online.* Washington, DC: Pew Internet and American life Project. Retrieved August 19, 2009 from http://www.pewinternet.org/Reports/2005/Health-Information-Online.aspx

Gainsbury, S., and Blaszczynski, A. (2011). 'A systematic review of Internet-based therapy for the treatment of addictions', *Clinical Psychology Review, 31*(3), 490–8. doi:10.1016/j.cpr.2010.11.007

Grant, J.E., and Potenza, M. (2007). 'Treatments for pathological gambling and other impulse control disorders'. In P.E. Nathan, and J. M. Gorman (eds), *A guide to treatments that work* (3rd ed., 561–77). New York: Oxford University Press.

Griffiths, K., and Christensen, H. (2006). 'Review of randomized controlled trials of Internet interventions for mental health and related conditions'. *Clinical Psychologist, 10,* 16–29.

Gupta, R., and Derevensky, J. L. (2000). 'Adolescents with gambling problems: From research to treatment'. *Journal of Gambling Studies, 16,* 315–42.

Hodgins, D. C., and el-Guebaly, N. (2000). 'Natural and treatment-assisted recovery from gambling problems: A comparison of resolved and active gamblers'. *Addiction, 95,* 777–89.

Hodgins, D., Currie, S., and el-Guebaly, N. (2001). 'Motivational enhancement and self-help treatments for problem gambling'. *Journal of Consulting and Clinical Psychology, 69,* 50–7.

Hodgins, D., Currie, S., el-Guebaly, N., and Peden, N. (2004). 'Brief motivational treatment for problem gambling: A 24-month follow-up'. *Psychology of Addictive Behaviors, 18,* 293–396.

Hodgins, D., Wynne, H., and Makarchuk, K. (1999). 'Pathways to recovery from gambling problems: Follow-up from a general population survey'. *Journal of Gambling Studies, 15(2),* 93–104.

Joukhador, J., Maccallum, F., and Blaszczynski, A. (2003). 'Differences in cognitive distortions between problem and social gamblers'. *Psychological Reports, 92,* 1203–14.

King, S. A., and Moreggi, D. (1998). 'Internet therapy and self help groups –The pros and cons'. In J. Gackenbach (ed.), *Psychology and the Internet: Intrapersonal, interpersonal and transpersonal implications* (77–109). San Diego, CA: Academic Press.

Klatt, C., Berg, C. J., Thomas, J. L., Ehlinger, E., Ahluwalia, J. S., and An, L. C. (2008). 'The role of peer e-mail support as part of a college smoking-cessation website'. *American Journal of Preventive Medicine, 35*(6), 471–8.

Klein, B. (2002). 'A randomised controlled trial of Internet-based treatment for panic disorder'. Unpublished doctoral thesis, University of Ballarat, Victoria, Australia.

Klein, B., Richards, J. C., and Austin, D. W. (2006) 'Efficacy of Internet therapy for panic disorder'. *Journal of Behavior Therapy and Experimental Psychiatry, 37,* 213–38.

Kreuter, M. W., and Wray, R. J. (2003). 'Tailored and targeted health communication: Strategies for enhancing information relevance'. *American Journal of Health Behavior, 27,* 227–32.

Ladouceur, R., Blaszczynski, A., and Pelletier, A. (2004). 'Why adolescent problem gamblers do not seek treatment'. *Journal of Child and Adolescent Substance Abuse, 13*(4), 1–12.

Ladouceur, R., Gosselin, P., Laberge, M., and Blaszczynski, A. (2001). 'Dropouts in clinical research: Do results reported reflect clinical reality?' *Behavior Therapist,* 24, 44–6.

Ladouceur, R., Sylvain, C., Boutin, C., Lachance, S., Doucet, C., Lablond, J., and Jacques, C. (2001) 'Cognitive treatment of pathological gambling', *Journal of Nervous and Mental Disease,* 189, 774–80.

Lieberman, D. Z., and Huang, S. W. (2008). 'A technological approach to reaching a hidden population of problem drinkers'. *Psychiatric Services, 59,* 297–303.

Lustria, M. L., Cortese, J., Noar, S. M., and Glueckauf, R. L. (2009). 'Computer-tailored health interventions delivered over the web: Review and analysis of key components'. *Patient Education and Counselling, 74,* 156–73.

McMillen, J., Marshall, D., Murphy, L., Lorenzen, S., and Waugh, B. (2004). *Help seeking by problem gamblers, friends and families: A focus on gender and cultural groups.* A report to the ACT Gambling and Racing Commission. Centre for Gambling Research, Regnet, Australian National University.

Madden, M. (2006). *Internet penetration and impact.* Washington, DC: Pew Internet and American Life Project. Online. Retrieved October 4, 2009 from http://www.pewinternet.org/PPF/r/182/report_display.asp

Marotta, J. J. (2000, June). 'Recovery from gambling problems with and without treatment'. Presentation at the 11th International Conference on Gambling and Risk Taking, Las Vegas, NV.

Miniwatts Marketing Group (2010). *World internet usage and population statistics.* Retrieved October 14, 2010 from http://www.internetworldstats.com/list4.htm#high

Monaghan, S., and Blaszczynski, A (2009). *Internet-based interventions for the treatment of problem gambling.* Toronto: Centre for Addiction and Mental Health. Retrieved May 5, 2010 from http://www.problemgambling.ca

Monaghan, S. and Wood, R. T. A. (2010). 'Internet-based interventions for youth dealing with gambling problems'. *International Journal of Adolescent Health and Medicine, 22*(1), 113–28.

Murphy, L., Parnass, P., Mitchell, D. L., Hallett, R., Cayley, P., and Seagram, S. (2009). 'Client satisfaction and outcome comparisons of online and face-to-face counselling methods'. *British Journal of Social Work, 39*, 627–40.

Oei, T. P. S., and Raylu, N. (2007). *Gambling and problem gambling among the Chinese.* Queensland, Australia: University of Queensland.

Ontario Ministry of Health and Long-term Care (2009). *Every door is the right door: Towards a 10-year mental health and addictions strategy: A discussion paper.* Retrieved July 14, 2009 from http://www.health.gov.on.ca/english/public/program/mentalhealth/minister_advisgroup/pdf/discussion_paper.pdf

Peltoniemi, T., and Bothas, H. (2007, October). 'Virtual prevention and treatment in Finland: Some addictions-related examples'. Presentation at the Media Seminar, Haarlem, 4–6. Retrieved October 11, 2011 from http://www.aklinikka.fi/ajankohtaista/paihdetiedotusseminaari07/Peltoniemi%20Bothas_Virtual%20prevention%20and%20treatment%20in%20Finland.pdf

Petry, N., and Armentano, C. (1999). 'Prevalence, assessment, and treatment of pathological gambling: A review'. *Psychiatric Services, 50*, 1021–7.

Petry, N., Ammerman, Y., Bohl, J., Doersch, A., Gay, H., Kadden, R., Molina, C., and Steinberg, K. (2006). 'Cognitive-behavioral therapy for pathological gamblers'. *Journal of Consulting and Clinical Psychology, 74*, 555–67.

Petry, N. M., Weinstock, J., Ledgerwood, D., and Morasco, B. (2008). 'A randomized trial of brief interventions for problem and pathological gamblers'. *Journal of Consulting and Clinical Psychology, 76*, 318–28.

Pew Internet and the American Life Project (2006) *Online health search 2006.* Online. Retrieved October 11, 2010 from http://www.pewinternet.org/Reports/2006/Online-Health-Search-2006/01-Summary-of-Findings.aspx.

Pew Internet and the American Life Project (2011). *Daily Internet activities, 2000–2009.* Retrieved May 6, 2011 from http://www.pewinternet.org/Static-Pages/Trend-Data/Daily-Internet-Activities-20002009.aspx

Prochaska, J. O., and DiClemente, C. C. (1982). 'Transtheoretical therapy: Towards a more integrative model of change', *Psychotherapy: Therapy, Research, and Practice, 19*, 276–88.

Productivity Commission (2010). *Gambling, Final Report.* Commonwealth of Australia, Canberra.

Pulford, J., Bellringer, M., Abbott, M., Clarke, D., Hodgins, D., and Williams, J. (2009). 'Barriers to help-seeking for a gambling problem: The experiences of gamblers who have sought specialist assistance and the perceptions of those who have not'. *Journal of Gambling Studies, 25*(1), 33–48.

Raylu, N., and Oei, T. (2002). 'Pathological gambling: A comprehensive review'. *Clinical Psychology Review, 22*(7), 1009–61.

Raylu, N., and Oei, T. P. S. (2004) 'Role of culture in gambling and problem gambling'. *Clinical Psychology Review, 23*, 1087–114.

Rochlen, A. B., Land, L. N., and Wong, Y. J. (2004). 'Male restrictive emotionality and evaluations of online versus face-to-face counseling'. *Psychology of Men Masculinity, 5*, 190–200.

Rockloff, M. J., and Schofield, G. (2004). 'Factor analysis of barriers to treatment for problem gambling'. *Journal of Gambling Studies, 20*(2), 121–6.

Rodda, S. (2010, December). 'Gambling help online: Program engagement and client characteristics'. Paper presented at the 20th Conference of the National Association for Gambling Studies, Gold Coast, Australia.

Scogin, F., Bynum, J., Stevens, G., and Calhoon, S. (1990). 'Efficacy of self-administered treatment program: Meta-analytic review'. *Professional Psychology: Research and Practice, 21*, 42–7.

Severson, H. H., Gordon, J. S., Danaher, B. G., and Akers, L. (2008). 'ChewFree.com: Evaluation of a Web-based cessation program for smokeless tobacco users'. *Nicotine and Tobacco Research, 10*(2), 381–91.

Slutske, W. (2006). 'Natural recovery and treatment-seeking in pathological gamblers', *American Journal of Psychology, 163*, 297–302.

Smit, F., Riper, H., Kramer, J., Conijn, B., and Cuijpers, P. (2006, April). 'Cost-effectiveness of drinking less online'. Presentation at the International Society for Research on Internet Interventions, Stockholm, Sweden.

Statistics Canada (2010). *CANSIM individual and household Internet use*. Retrieved October 11, 2010 from http://www40.statcan.gc.ca/l01/cst01/comm32a-eng.htm.

Strecher, V. J., Shiffman, S., and West, R. (2005). 'Randomized controlled trial of a web-based computer-tailored smoking cessation program as a supplement to nicotine patch therapy'. *Addiction, 100,* 682–8.

Stoddard, J. L., Augustson, E. M., and Moser, R. P. (2008). 'Effect of adding a virtual community (bulletin board) to Smokefree.gov: Randomized controlled trial'. *Journal of Medical Internet Research, 10*(5), 53.

Suurvali, H., Hodgins, D., Toneatto, T., and Cunningham, J. (2008). 'Treatment seeking among Ontario problem gamblers: Results of a population survey'. *Psychiatric Services, 59*, 1343–6.

Swartz, H., Noell, J., Schroeder, S., and Ary, D. (2006). 'A randomised control study of a fully automated Internet based smoking cessation programme'. *Tobacco Control, 15*, 7–12.

Tavares, H., Martins, S. S., Zilberman, M. L., and el-Guebaly, N. (2002). 'Gamblers seeking treatment: Why haven't they come earlier?' *Addictive Disorders and Their Treatment, 1*(2), 65–9.

Toneatto, T., and Ladouceur, R. (2003). 'Treatment of pathological gambling: A critical review of the literature'. *Psychology of Addictive Behaviors, 17*(4), 284–92.

Toneatto, T., Cunningham, J. A., Hodgins, D., Adams, M., Turner, N., and Koski-Jannes, A. (2008) 'Recovery from problem gambling without formal treatment', *Addiction Research and Theory, 16*, 111–20.

Westphal, J. (2006, February) 'Attrition among gambling treatment patients: Clinical and research implications'. Paper presented at the International Gambling Conference, Auckland, New Zealand. Retrieved September 15, 2006 from http://www.ijma-journal.com/ppt/c05p00072.ppt#1

Wood, R. T. A. (2010, October). 'Online support for people with gambling issues'. Paper presented at the Alberta Gaming and Liquor Commission's Responsible and Problem Gambling Symposium, Edmonton, Alberta, Canada.

Wood, R. T. A., and Griffiths, M. D. (2007). 'Online guidance, advice, and support for problem gamblers and concerned relatives and friends: An evaluation of the Gam-Aid pilot service', *British Journal of Guidance and Counselling, 35*(4), 373–89.

Wood, R., and Williams, R. (2009). *Internet gambling: Prevalence, patterns, problems and policy options*. Final Report prepared for the Ontario Problem Gambling Research Centre, Guelph, Ontario.

Wood, R. T. A., and Wood, S. (2009). 'An evaluation of two UK online support forums designed to help people with gambling issues', *Journal of Gambling Issues, 23*. Retrieved May 22, 2011 from http://www.camh.net/egambling/issue23/pdfs/01wood.pdf

# Part 5

# Legal and Policy Issues

# 15  Internet gambling law

*I. Nelson Rose*

## Is Internet gambling legal?

### *Is there a prohibition in place and does it apply to this form of gaming?*

Although some state and federal law enforcement officials declare flatly, 'Yes, all online wagers are illegal,' the answer is actually complicated, depending upon such factors as where the operator and gambler are located and what form of gambling is involved.

For example, the federal government of the United States is primarily interested in organized crime, so federal laws are limited almost always to individuals involved in the business of gambling. There are no federal statutes or regulations that would apply to a casual bettor. State laws are another matter. All states outlaw operating gambling businesses for profit, with the obvious exceptions for licensed casinos, racetracks, etc. But there may be loopholes. In addition, half the states have ancient laws on the books that make it a crime even to make a bet, under some circumstances; again, with obvious and sometimes not-so-obvious exceptions.

Of course, the chances of a bettor getting into any criminal trouble, even if the law applies, are close to zero. No one has ever gone to prison for making a bet on the Internet.

Even operators face little risk, especially if they are outside the borders of the country that wants to shut them down.

Everyone in the United States and Canada is subject to at least two sets of laws, federal and state/province – and an additional set of laws if they are on tribal land. There are also laws on the city and county level, but these are usually of no consequence, except to big operators which are located and openly taking bets in that city or county.

Federal governments are not usually concerned with gambling. They may not even have power over purely local activities. The US federal government does care about organized crime. But even here, federal laws were primarily designed to help the states enforce their public policies. Most of these date from times when states completely prohibited all commercial gambling. So, federal laws usually are limited to gambling businesses using interstate commerce.

US Senator Jon Kyl (Republican, Arizona [R.-AZ]) attempted to change that with his first attempt to outlaw online gaming in the 1990s. The first draft of his Internet Gambling Prohibition Act would have made mere betting a federal crime, for the first time in American history. But the US Department of Justice, which would have had to prosecute common bettors, and remembering the bad old days when it had to enforce the earlier Prohibition on alcoholic beverages, stated publicly that it did not want to be knocking on bedroom doors to arrest $5 bettors.[1]

Internet operators, especially those which do not have licenses from foreign countries, may be violating US federal laws by taking bets online. The major statute, the Wire Act,[2] was passed by Congress 50 years ago to help the states enforce their anti-bookmaking laws. It was designed to go after 'the Wire,' i.e., the telegraph wire services illegal bookies used to get horserace results.[3] Naturally, no one thought of playing poker by phone, let alone Internet casinos. The Wire Act only applies to individuals in the business of gambling who use a wire, like a phone line, which crosses a state or national boundary.[4] Gambling businesses that conduct 100 percent of their activities inside a single state probably do not violate the Wire Act. The reason for the 'probably' is that the Justice Department under President George W. Bush said it would prosecute even pure intra-state operators, if an Internet wire crossed through a part of another state.

The federal Department of Justice believes the law covers all gambling transmitted across state lines[5]. But the words of the statute are more limited:

> Whoever being engaged in the business of betting or wagering knowingly uses a wire communication facility for the transmission in interstate or foreign commerce of bets or wagers or information assisting in the placing of bets or wagers on any sporting event or contest, or for the transmission of a wire communication which entitles the recipient to receive money or credit as a result of bets or wagers, or for information assisting in the placing of bets or wagers [is guilty of a crime].

Three United States federal courts have issued published opinions that the statute is limited to sports events and races; Internet lotteries and casinos are not banned by this particular federal law.

The cases involved suits by disgruntled gamblers, who were suing credit card companies to get their losses back, plus a lot more money, in class actions. One of the reported decisions involved class actions from around the country being heard in a federal court in New Orleans. Both that judge, and the Court of Appeals, ruled that MasterCard and Visa were not liable to the players, because the Wire Act only applies to betting on sports events and horse and dog races.[6] Federal prosecutors in the Department of Justice disagree, but it seems that online casinos, lottery, poker, and bingo would not be violating the Wire Act as it is presently worded.[7]

There are other federal anti-gambling laws. But most involve committing crimes under state laws. The Organized Crime Control Act,[8] for example, makes it a federal crime to violate state gambling laws.[9] The Travel Act[10] makes it a felony to travel or use any facility in interstate or foreign commerce to carry on 'unlawful activity,' defined as a business enterprise involving gambling 'in violation of the laws of the State in which they are committed or of the United States.'

Every state outlaws most forms of gambling, unless licensed by the state or falling under a special exception, such as charity bingo. All states make it a crime to operate an unregulated gambling game for profit. The major exceptions are social gambling, where no one makes money, other than as a winning player, and charity bingo and casino nights. Not all states allow even these exceptions, and many have tough requirements for qualifying as a charity. Commercial gambling includes, in various states, licensed pari-mutuel betting on horse and dog races and jai alai, sports betting, card rooms,[11] gaming devices, and casinos.[12] Government-run operations are limited to the State Lotteries and tribal gaming in the USA, though in Canada, the provinces often are the owners and occasionally the operators of casinos, and most of the provinces and territories are now expanding into online gaming.

Major questions remain when Internet gambling is involved and is not licensed or operated by a state or similar jurisdiction. Exactly what law is an online casino supposedly breaking? Can it even be a casino game, when there is no casino? Is a company in another state or country taking bets in that state? What if the operator is actually licensed by another government?

State laws have not been tested on online gaming, though it is likely that most courts would find that accepting bets from a resident of a state would subject even an overseas operator to that state's criminal laws. In the real world, states do not have the resources to arrest operators in other countries. The states are virtually helpless if the Internet gambling operator is licensed by another country, or is actually the foreign country itself.

State anti-gambling laws date from a century ago or even earlier. Even though gambling has become accepted by society to the point where every state, province, and territory of the USA and Canada, except Alaska and Hawaii, have legalized commercial gambling, half the US states still have laws on the books, never enforced, that expressly make it a crime to make a bet.[13]

In the United States, there are no common law crimes, meaning no activity can be punished as a crime unless there is a specific statute outlawing that activity and giving potential offenders adequate warning. Of course, some states simply have general prohibitions on all forms of gambling, such as Utah. But in most cases laws were passed over the centuries to deal with specific problems as they arose.

Laws in general and anti-gambling laws in particular are almost always reactive, not proactive. Legislators did not sit around thinking about how to handle gambling on the Internet, when the Internet had not even been invented.

Since statutes are created in a piecemeal fashion to counter a specific situation that has attracted the attention of lawmakers, the prohibitions aimed at the casual bettor are hit-and-miss in their coverage. New York has no laws against making bets. So, a person in New York City who makes a bet using the Internet with an illegal bookie in New Jersey is not breaking any federal or state law. Of course, the bookie is violating both the federal Wire Act and at least the New Jersey anti-gambling laws.

In California, there is an ancient state law that makes it a crime to accept, record, or even make a bet on a sporting event.[14] But there is no prohibition on buying lottery tickets, even illegal ones. Due to a series of bad cases and weak statutory fixes involving how the card club industry can charge their patrons, operators of licensed card clubs can 'rake the pot,' that is, take a percentage out as its revenue, no more than five times in any one poker game.[15] No one, other than card club owners, would care about this obscure law, except that another statute makes it a crime to even play in an illegal 'percentage game,' which is defined as a game where the operator rakes the pot.[16] So, even a casual player in California is unknowingly committing a misdemeanor if the operator of a poker game rakes the pot six times. And no one knows if this law applies to operators of online poker games, where the operator is not physically in California, although some players are.[17]

Internet gambling operations have attempted to get around anti-gambling laws by requiring bettors to deposit money in advance in a bank in a foreign country. Operators argue that a person in California who transfers money from a bank in Antigua to a sports book in Antigua is not actually making a bet in California. But most judges would not buy the argument.

One wild card is law enforcement on the local level. Although most gambling laws are made on the state level, there is always the remote possibility of city, county, and other local ordinances becoming involved. It is also almost, but not completely, beyond the realm of possibility that local police or district or city attorneys will try to go after online gambling that violates a local, state, or federal law.

For example, the District Attorney of Los Angeles County raided the local offices of YouBet! and seized computer information and documents. YouBet! allows punters in many states to place bets via their computers on horseraces taking place throughout the country. The bets are forwarded to tracks in states like Pennsylvania, which allows these long-distance wagers. Even though YouBet! did not take wagers from Californians, its computers were in LA County. The DA threatened to charge the company with violating the state law against 'recording' bets on horseraces outside a licensed track. Although it appeared unlikely that a modern jury would buy the idea that in 1909 the California Legislature intended to outlaw computer bets made by a bettor in Oregon with a licensed off-track betting outlet in Pennsylvania, simply because the computer was in California, YouBet! decided it was cheaper to donate a lot of money, including $200,000 to the California Council on Problem Gambling, and leave the state than pay much more in legal fees with the potential of criminal convictions. A couple of years later the State Legislature changed the law, and YouBet! returned.[18]

The situation becomes even more complex when the Internet gambling is taking place across state or national boundaries. It is relatively easy to know if an operator is violating its own local law. Most jurisdictions require licensing before a site can take bets from anyone, and spell out whether a licensed operator can accept wagers from foreign jurisdictions.

The first step in most of the cases involving cross-border gaming operators thus starts with the question of whether there is, in fact, a local law in place that restricts foreign legal gaming sites from taking bets from local residents. It is obviously often difficult to know whether there is such a prohibition, especially when the player is in a foreign country with a different legal system and language.

### Other common defenses and exceptions

Even if a law on any level can be found that might apply to online gaming, there are still the possibilities of multiple defenses. Prohibitions on foreign Internet gambling are almost always criminal, rather than civil. Criminal defendants have legal protections that do not exist in civil suits. These include requiring that the government prove its case beyond a reasonable doubt, rather than by a mere preponderance of the evidence, and requiring judges to strictly construe criminal statutes and resolve any doubts in favor of the criminal defendant. But most importantly, every element of the crime must be proved before anyone may be punished for engaging in the activity.

For example, one court ruled the Wire Act did not prohibit sending sports bets from a ship in international waters to Florida, construing the statute as requiring that there be two states or countries involved, not just one state and the high seas.[19]

Even if an activity seems to be exactly the type of action prohibited by a statute, the law has other requirements that must be met.

A government has the power to regulate activities taking place within its borders. It has the power to regulate activities involving its citizens or their property in international waters and airspace, assuming there is no conflict with the rights of other governments. But international law does not allow a state or country to regulate activity which has no impact on that sovereign or its citizens if the activity is conducted by foreign nationals in their own territory.

This has led to the creation of some legal presumptions, which have a major impact on interpreting whether a law prohibits cross-border wagering. Even though a government might have the power, there is often a strong presumption that lawmakers have not reached out beyond their jurisdictions' borders in enacting a statute.[20] Therefore, any prohibition on gambling which does expressly state that it applies to cross-border wagers may be presumed to include only activities taking place within the borders of that particular government entity.

This presumption reflects the growing recognition of international law and the impact American laws can have on the sovereignty of foreign nations. A strict drafting standard is necessary to avoid 'unintended clashes between our laws and those of other nations which could result in international discord.'[21]

There are, of course, times when it is clear that a government has acted to prohibit or regulate cross-border gambling. These are usually recently enacted statutes designed to prevent local residents from betting via the Internet, though not by punishing the bettor. The most common approach is to make it a crime to take bets online from anyone who is physically present in that jurisdiction.

A growing number of governments are passing statutes and regulations aimed at financial institutions and others who facilitate the gambling transaction. The 2006 Unlawful Internet Gambling Enforcement Act[22] makes it a crime for a gambling business anywhere in the world to accept money for a gambling transaction that violates a US federal or state law. It also calls for regulations to require financial institutions and e-wallets to identify and block money transfers for unlawful online gaming.[23]

No matter how the prohibition on cross-border gambling is set up, there are almost always express exceptions written into the statute for forms of gambling that are legal in that jurisdiction. For example, more than half the states have allowed what is called 'advanced deposit wagering' (ADW) on horseraces for years. This requires a patron to deposit money in advance, usually by credit card, with an off-track betting (OTB) operator. The punter can then make bets by phone. In December 2000 Congress amended the Interstate Horseracing Act to expressly allow ADW by computer, so long as the bet was legal in both the state where the patron was and the state where the OTB accepted the bet.[24]

### *Keeping out gambling – police power*

Assuming a government has acted to prohibit cross-border gambling the question arises whether that action was valid. In analyzing whether a jurisdiction has the power to prevent cross-border betting it is necessary to step back and analyze that government's legal relationships with other governments. Often, the state or nation has no relevant legal restrictions on its power. But increasingly governments' rights to exclude extraterritorial legal gambling are limited, due to some other, higher law. These latter include states that belong to federations and are restricted under federal laws or the federal constitutions; nations that have voluntarily, if sometimes unintentionally, agreed to let in legal gambling from other specific countries under treaties; and governments bound by the doctrine of comity, where out of courtesy and mutual respect, rather than because they are bound by a written document, states and nations recognize the laws of some other states or nations.

There seems little doubt that a government normally can exclude outside illegal gambling and even legal gambling.[25] A sovereign government by definition has power over its own territory and citizens. It is thus the inherent right of every sovereign state to protect its borders from intrusions. This right is so fundamental that it need not be spelled out explicitly in a constitution or statute.

The state's right derives not only from its right to continue to exist as an independent state, but also from the state's police power. The police power is the inherent right of a government to protect the health, safety, welfare, and morals of its citizens and residents. In the European Union (EU) it is called the 'overriding public interest,' which allows member states to take actions that would otherwise seem to violate the rights established by the treaties that created the European Common Market. In the World Trade Organization (WTO) it is called 'necessary' actions, again taken in seeming violation of the WTO treaties for reasons of necessity, such as preserving public order. The police power is most commonly connected with governmental action taken in emergency situations, especially where public health is endangered, as in a fire or an epidemic. But gambling, licensed or illegal, even legal lotteries, has always been held to fall within a state's police power.[26] For example, the US Supreme Court declared in *Edge Broadcasting*:

> While lotteries have existed in this country since its founding, States have long viewed them as a hazard to their citizens and to the public interest{...}Gambling implicates no constitutionally protected right; rather, it falls into a category of 'vice' activity that could be, and frequently has been, banned altogether.[27]

The police power has three interesting, and unusual, attributes:

1   *A government's police power is virtually unlimited.* It is the nature of government for the state to exercise power for the good of society as a whole, at the expense of individual rights. This is obvious in totalitarian and authoritarian regimes. But the same is true of democracies. Ever since Jean-Jacques Rousseau published his *Social Contract* in 1762, it has been generally accepted that a democratic state derives its sovereign power from the surrender by individuals of their natural liberties.

   Constitutional and other legal safeguards protect citizens from improper use of the government's power. But, when a jurisdiction is faced with a threat to the health, safety, and welfare of its citizens, particularly in an emergency, the police power prevails. The police power trumps constitutional and other legal rights; government has the legal right and power to do literally almost anything to anyone. At its most extreme, government can even take life without due process safeguards – the police do not conduct evidentiary hearings before shooting an Islamist terrorist who is trying to detonate a bomb.

   Because gambling is treated as a police power issue, governments can act in ways that would be unthinkable in other commercial and social settings. 'The police power of the State to suppress gambling is practically unrestrained.'[28] 'Because we are dealing with authorized gambling, the State may exercise greater control and use the police power in a more arbitrary manner.'[29]

2   *A government's police power is often tied to morality.* It used to be a given that government played an important role in upholding the moral standards of a community. But the 1970s led to a widespread belief among opinion-leaders in many countries in situational ethics, the notion that there are no absolute standards of right and wrong. By the 1980s, even anti-gambling crusaders rarely argued that gambling should be outlawed because it is immoral; they feared being viewed as right-wing religious fanatics. However, government's police powers are still aimed at morally suspect behavior, even if the justifications given are more pragmatic than religious.

   Gambling has always been inextricably linked with the morality of a society, supporting the use of the police power. The explosion of legal gambling in recent years has not weakened government's police power over gambling.

3   *Governmental police power tends to be a local issue.*[30] As the United States Supreme Court observed in upholding Puerto Rico's nearly universal ban on advertising by Puerto Rican licensed casinos, restrictions aimed at promoting the welfare, safety, and morals of the residents of a state represent a well-recognized exercise of state police power.[31] Whether the government involved is a state in a federation, like the states of Australia

and the USA, or a 'state' in a treaty organization, like the EU or WTO, it is the state that has the primary concern with police power issues. Unlike other areas of commerce, it is highly unusual for a federal government, let alone a treaty organization, to overrule police power decisions of member states.[32] Higher levels of government are not usually concerned with police power issues, unless there is a perception that a threat to society exists that is beyond the control of local government.

Police power is usually a state issue based on history and practicality. During the formative stages of modern governments the protection of citizens' health and safety was best left to authorities on the scene. Given the technology existing then, and perhaps even today, the major threats of fire and disease were not controllable from distant national capitols.[33] The very nature of the Internet has led to an unusual level of involvement by federal governments, particularly in Australia and the USA, into online gambling.

Morality also was and still is decided primarily at the state level. States tend to be small enough to appear homogeneous, or at least dominated by a single religion. Official state religions were, and are, common throughout the world.

Attitudes toward gambling are almost always written into a state's laws. As a dramatic example, feelings against gambling games ran so strong in the Massachusetts Bay Colony that the possession of cards, dice, or gaming tables, even in private homes, was outlawed.[34]

It is fair to say that governments have greater rights to decide how they want to regulate gambling than they have in almost any other area of human activity, certainly more than any other economic area.

For governments that have not voluntarily agreed to put limits on their police powers, the question of legality in the country of origin is of no particular significance. Under the police power, governments routinely exclude goods and services shipped from countries where the items are legal. Whether it is Saudi Arabia barring the importation of alcoholic beverages or the United Kingdom going after advertisements of sex tours in Thailand, the assertion that the activity is legal in the country of origin is not even made.[35] But for the states of the USA, the member states of the EU, and others who have agreed to open their borders under some circumstances, the first step must be to see if the foreign gambling is, in fact, legal under the operator's own laws.

### *Limits on police power*

Recent decisions from the United States Supreme Court, the European Court of Justice (ECJ), other trial and appellate courts in Europe and the USA, and tribunals in the WTO have shown there are often limits on a state and nation's power to keep out goods and services it finds detrimental to its citizens' welfare.

The major restrictions on a government's police power are created by the government itself: A state joined a federation and thus subjected itself to federal statutes and treaties and a federal constitution; a nation signed a bilateral treaty with another country or a multilateral treaty with possibly a large number of other nations and agreed to either allow in goods and services from its treaty partners, or at least to limit its criminal prosecutions of those partners' citizens; or a state or nation has had unwritten agreements for many years based on courtesy to respect the laws of other jurisdictions with similar legal systems, a comity of nations.

The wording of the tests may differ, but decision makers around the world have been surprisingly consistent in determining whether a government has the right to exclude cross-border betting. The basic rules can be stated easily: A government that is obligated to let in goods and services of other jurisdictions must let in outside legal gambling, unless it can show that the exclusion is to protect its residents. Laws that merely protect the local gambling operations from outside competition to maximize revenue are invalid. But even restrictions designed to limit gaming for solid reasons of protecting a society are invalid, if, in practice, they discriminate in favor of local operators.

There were only a few precedents dealing with cross-border gambling, mostly involving lottery tickets, prior to the explosion of Internet gaming. But there have always been other morally suspect industries producing goods and services that are routinely subjected to the police power of a state, such as alcoholic beverages and tobacco.

Although there has been some controversy on the issue, today there is little doubt that a government that has an absolute ban on a morally suspect commerce does not have to let it in, even if it originates in other states in its federation or treaty partners. A state or nation that makes it a crime to sell lottery tickets, with no exceptions, does not have to allow sister states or treaty partners to sell lottery tickets to is residents. This was the situation in *Schindler*,[36] Europe's first important cross-border betting case. When the United Kingdom prohibited all large-scale lotteries, the ECJ held that it could keep out advertisements for legal lotteries originating in the Federal Republic of Germany, another member of the EU.

A British law made it a crime to send tickets or advertisements of lotteries into Great Britain. The ECJ first held lotteries were a 'service' which the UK had agreed to permit;[37] but then carved out an exception, given 'the peculiar nature of lotteries':

> [Paragraph] 60: First of all, it is not possible to disregard the moral, religious or cultural aspects of lotteries, like other types of gambling, in all the Member States{...}Secondly, lotteries involve a high risk of crime or fraud, given the size of the amounts which can be staked and of the winnings which they can hold out to the players, particularly when they are operated on a large scale. Thirdly, they are an incitement to spend which may have damaging individual and social consequences. A final ground which is not without relevance, although it cannot in itself be regarded as an objective justification, is that lotteries may make a significant contribution to the financing of benevolent or public interest activities such as social works, charitable works, sport or culture.
>
> [Paragraph] 61: Those particular factors justify national authorities having a sufficient degree of latitude to determine what is required to protect the players and, more generally, in the light of the specific social and cultural features of each Member State, to maintain order in society, as regards the manner in which lotteries are operated, the size of the stakes, and the allocation of the profits they yield.

It is important again to emphasize that *Schindler* involved a government that had completely prohibited (at the time) the form of gambling under consideration. The case would be even easier if a government has outlawed all gambling. But the situation is radically different once a state or nation legalizes a form of gambling and attempts to keep out identical forms from sister states or treaty partners.

States in a federation, like the United States, are, almost by definition, not allowed to put up barriers to legal commerce from other states in the union.[38] The purpose in creating a federation is to create a single country, even if the member states retain a great amount of their original power.

The state's police power will trump the federal constitution's requirement that states must let in commerce from sister states; but, usually only if the state erecting the trade barriers has taken a strict prohibitionist stance, barring locals and foreigners alike from selling the morally suspect goods or services. States can and do raise police power concerns to justify raising barriers to outside competitors while allowing local companies, or even the state itself, to operate identical businesses. Sometimes the arguments work. But a court has to agree that not just companies in other states but those other states themselves may not be as concerned about issues like consumer health and safety. For example, there have been a few land-based casino companies that have been licensed by Nevada regulators and yet found unacceptable by New Jersey regulators.[39]

The more common situation is illustrated by an important case handed down by the Supreme Court of the United States in May 2005.[40] The states of New York and Michigan allowed their local wineries to sell wine online for delivery to local residents, but put up substantial barriers to out-of-state wineries. The Court rejected the states' police power justifications: 'keeping alcohol out of the hands of minors and facilitating tax collection.'

Justice Kennedy, writing for a 5 to 4 majority, said that the 26 states that allowed direct shipment of wine report no problem with minors. He concluded this was not surprising, since minors are more likely to consume beer, wine coolers, and hard liquor than wine; minors have more direct means of obtaining wine; and minors want instant gratification.

The ECJ has laid down standards that are very similar to those facing federated states. Protecting a local monopoly operator from competition, although a valid and entirely understandable reason, is never sufficient. The overriding reasons relating to public interests that might justify a member state of the EU excluding gambling goods and services from a provider in another member state include those listed in paragraphs 60 and 61 of the *Schindler* decision.

The WTO came to similar conclusions as to the standards to be applied when one member state claims it is excluding businesses that are legal where they originate from another member state for reasons of 'necessity.' The widely reported decision arose when Antigua filed a complaint against the United States for prohibiting cross-border betting by Antigua's licensed Internet gambling operations.

The USA asserted that its federal criminal statutes prohibiting international gambling, the Wire Act, the Travel Act, and the Illegal Gambling Business Act, were 'measures… necessary to protect public morals or to maintain public order.' Specifically, the US stated the laws were passed to address its concerns 'pertaining to money laundering, organized crime, fraud, underage gambling and pathological gambling.' In this, the first case before the WTO ever to raise the 'necessity' defense, the Appellate Body found that the USA had presented sufficient evidence to show that its concerns related to gambling, particularly remote wagering, were legitimate.[41] However, the WTO found that US federal law did discriminate against Antigua operators, because the Interstate Horseracing Act allowed state-licensed, but not foreign-licensed, cross-border wagers on horseraces.

This shows that even if a government can name significant public policy interests that it needs to protect, and convinces the court or other decision maker that the restrictions on cross-border gambling it has enacted actually do protect those interests, the restrictions will be declared invalid if they are overbroad or discriminate against foreign operators.

A statute or regulation is overbroad if there exists another way to achieve the same police power goals without infringing on fundamental rights. A ban on advertising of legal gaming would be unconstitutional or violate treaty rights if the desired goal of reducing gambling by minors could be achieved through related, but less intrusive, means, such as limiting the times and places where gaming ads may appear, or unrelated means, such as restricting hours of operation or requiring guards at the door.

The police power of a government that is part of a federation or a treaty organization is also limited by the requirement that it not discriminate against its sister sovereigns. So, the US Supreme Court struck down state laws that made it relatively easy for local wineries to take orders on the Internet and deliver wine to people's homes in the state, but difficult or impossible for wineries in other states of the union to do the same. The ECJ has repeatedly looked at whether a member state has restrictions on cross-border betting while allowing local operators to take bets from its citizens, and if so, whether the discriminatory laws can be justified on public policy grounds. And Antigua won at least part of its fight against the USA in the WTO, by showing that Congress had enacted an Interstate Horseracing Act, and not an International Horseracing Act.

### Should players care?

Taking bets online is obviously a lot more complicated and risky than merely making bets. But, even a regular bettor who has no intention of going into the business should be interested in whether the company he is dealing with is breaking the law.

Truly criminal gambling operations have historically been overwhelmingly crooked. In addition, gambling debts are difficult to enforce, even when legal. If an illegal operator refuses to pay off a winning bet, the bettor is probably out of luck, even if he can manage to serve the operator with a complaint. Of course, gambling debts work both ways. Internet gambling operators demand to have the bet deposited in advance, because they know that losers sometimes are welchers. Credit card companies have found themselves thrown out of court when they have tried to sue card owners for money advanced for gambling. And this is with legal gambling. Lenders find they have no case when they advance funds for illegal gambling.

Many online bookies and casinos claim to be licensed by foreign countries. Most sites warn potential bettors that it is up to players to determine whether their local laws make the game illegal. But the Internet has no operator. It is actually quite easy for someone to claim that he is licensed by, say, South Africa, when he is not. In fact, this actually happened. Congress created a National Gambling Impact Study Commission, chaired by the right-wing, religious Republican Kay Coles James. The Commission's Final Report claimed that South Africa had issued online gaming licenses, even though that nation was years away from even deciding whether it would allow Internet gambling.[42] Operators who claimed they were licensed by South Africa were probably not even located in that country.

How, exactly, is a player supposed to know if a game is legal? You could go to your lawyer, who should tell you he does not have the faintest idea. To know whether an Internet gambling operation is legal requires extensive legal research: (1) the lawyer analyzes the particular game or wager under all laws that might apply to both the operator and the bettor; and (2) the lawyer makes an educated guess whether laws, written before the telephone was invented, apply to twenty-first century technology.

It is easier to know when an Internet activity is illegal than when it is legal. Only a few states have passed laws which specifically mention Internet gambling. Some of the states, such as Louisiana[43] and Nevada, have enacted statutes outlawing most forms of Internet gambling. The Nevada Legislature enacted one of the clearest laws, explicitly making it a crime in Nevada for anyone anywhere in the world to take a bet online from anyone physically in Nevada and for anyone in Nevada to take a bet online from anyone anywhere in the world. Of course, Nevada's own licensed operators were exempted. So it is clear that under this state law, if an unlicensed operator in Nevada takes a wager online, that operator has committed a crime in Nevada.[44]

About the only defense would be to claim that Nevada does not have the right to outlaw activity on the Internet. This is pretty weak, but not frivolous. A federal judge in New York did rule in a pornography case that it would be too much of a burden on interstate commerce to have 50 different state laws apply to the Internet.[45]

Most states have not passed any laws explicitly dealing with Internet gambling, meaning that most Internet operations have much stronger defenses, because they do not fall neatly under any criminal statute. Discussions about online gaming usually focus on issues like sovereignty and where-does-a-bet-take-place. But, every criminal case starts with a more fundamental question: Is there a law making this particular activity illegal?

The law is so many decades behind society and technology that law enforcement officials have to make things up as they go along. This can lead to situations that would be comical, if the results were not so potentially tragic. When a prosecutor wants to go after an Internet gambling operator, he has to find an anti-gambling law, often more than 100 years old, which looks like it might fit the current facts. Like performing brain surgery with Stone Age tools, it might work, but it would be very messy.

When the Attorney General of Missouri wanted to close down an Internet casino, he had to charge the operator with setting up an illegal gambling device. The defendant pleaded guilty, so who knows if a judge would have bought the argument that the Internet turned the undercover agent's personal computer into a slot machine?

Of course, just because an online operator might not be breaking the law does not mean that betting on the Internet is safe. The argument has been made that operators will run honest games or risk losing customers. As the Mob's infiltration of Nevada casinos in the 1940s has shown, a weak regulatory system does not work in keeping out the bad guys. There is also evidence that games were often rigged to increase the house's advantage. An insider who worked for years as a casino cheat in the mid-1960s, wrote a book describing how casino personnel often cheated unsuspecting gamblers when the Mob ruled the Las Vegas Strip.[46]

Non-regulation is even worse. Observers of wide-open gambling in the nineteenth century, on riverboats and in frontier towns of the Wild West, report the anything goes policy led to widespread cheating.

What is to prevent unscrupulous operators from rigging games and refusing to pay winners, closing shop, and setting up again under another name? Is an unlicensed operator going to run an honest game? If you are a bettor, why take the chance?

## Notes

1  For more on the first Kyl bill and early attempts by states to control Internet gambling, see, I. Nelson Rose, 'America Boldly Outlaws (and Quietly Legalizes) Internet Gambling,' http://www.gamblingandthelaw.com/columns/30-amountlaw.html

2  18 U.S.C. §1084.

3  David G. Schwartz, *Cutting the Wire: Gaming Prohibition and the Internet* (Reno: University of Nevada Press, 2005).

4  I. Nelson Rose and Martin D. Owens, Jr., *Internet Gaming Law* (1st edition, Larchmont, NY: Mary Ann Liebert Publishers, 2005) at p. 148.

5  Two days before Christmas 2011, President Obama's Department of Justice issued an announcement that the Department has reversed its position, and was now reading the Wire Act as limited to sports betting.

6  *In Re MasterCard International Inc.*, 313 F.3d 257 (5th Cir. 2002), affirming 132 F.Supp.2d 468 (E.D.LA. 2001); *Jubelirer v. MasterCard International, Inc.*, 68 F.Supp.2d 1049 (W.D.Wis. 1999).

7   In an unreported decision, a federal judge in Utah did rule that poker would fall under the Wire Act. But because the decision was not officially published, it is not legal precedent and is not binding on any other court. The Court of Appeals decision, by contrast, is the final law for all federal courts in that part of the country.

8   U.S.C. §1955.

9   This federal law also requires that the illegal gambling business have at least five associates and is in business for more than 30 days or have a gross revenue of $2,000 in any single day.

10  18 U.S.C. §1952.

11  Card clubs are primarily for non-banking, also called round, games, where players bet against each other, such as poker. In California the law allows revolving deal games, like pai gow poker, where one player takes on all other players for one or two rounds. Often a group with a large fund of money acts as the dealer, or backs other players.

12  Casinos consist primarily of banking games, including table games and slot machines, where the house takes on all players. I. Nelson Rose, *Gambling and the Law* (Hollywood, California: Gambling Times, 1986) at p. 4. *Hotel Employees and Restaurant Employees Int'l. Union v. Davis*, 21 Cal.4th 585, 981 P.2d 990, 88 Cal.Rptr.2d 56 (1999).

13  I. Nelson Rose, 'The Third Wave of Legal Gambling,' http://www.gamblingandthelaw.com/articles/253-the-third-wave-of-legal-gambling.html

14  California Penal Code §337a.

15  Calif. Penal Code §337j(f).

16  Calif. Penal Code §330.

17  For more on the California card club industry, see, I. Nelson Rose, *Gambling and the Law.*

18  I. Nelson Rose, 'The Future Legal Landscape for Internet Gambling,' http://www.gamblingandthelaw.com/articles/33-antigua.html

19  *United States v. Montford*, 27 F.3d 137 (5th Cir. 1994).

20  I. Nelson Rose and Martin D. Owens, Jr., *Internet Gaming Law* (2nd edition, Larchmont, NY: Mary Ann Liebert Publishers, 2009) at pp. 235–7.

21  *E.E.O.C. v. Arabian American Oil Co.*, 499 U.S. 244, 111 S.Ct. 1227, 113 L.Ed.2d 274 (1991).

22  31 U.S.C. 5361–67.

23  For more on the Unlawful Internet Gambling Enforcement Act, often abbreviated as UIGEA, see I. Nelson Rose and Martin D. Owens, Jr., *Internet Gaming Law* (2nd edition) at pp. 124–47 and 288–306.

24  SEC. 629. Section 3(3) of the Interstate Horseracing Act of 1978 (15 U.S.C. 3002(3)) is amended by inserting 'and includes pari-mutuel wagers, where lawful in each State involved, placed or transmitted by an individual in one State via telephone or other electronic media and accepted by an off-track betting system in the same or another State, as well as the combination of any pari-mutuel wagering pools' after 'another State'.1999 CONG US HR 5548.

25  See, e.g. *People v. Milano*, Cal.App.3d 153, 152 Cal.Rptr. 318 (1979) and the cases cited therein; *Southern Bell Telephone and Telegraph Co. v. Nineteen Hundred One Collins Corp.*, 83 So.2d 865 (Fla. 1955); *Dunn v. Nevada Tax Com'n.*, 67 Nev. 173, 216 P.2d 985 (1950).

26  For a description of gambling as something akin to disease, see *Stone v. Mississippi*, 101 U.S. 814, 25 L.Ed. 1079, 1080 (1880).

27  *United States v. Edge Broadcasting Co.*, 509 U.S. 418, 113 S.Ct. 2696, 125 L.Ed.2d 345 (1993).

28  *Mills v. Agnew*, 286 F.Supp. 107 (U.S.D.C. Md.1968), citing *Ah Sin v. Wittman*, 198 U.S. 500, 25 S.Ct. 756, 49 L.Ed. 1142 (1905); *Marvin v. Trout*, 199 U.S. 212, 26 S.Ct. 31, 50 L.Ed. 157 (1905).

29  *Summersport Enterprises, Ltd. v. Pari-Mutuel Com'n.*, 493 So.2d 1085 (Fla.Ct.App. 1986), citing *Hialeah Race Course, Inc. v. Gulf Stream Park Racing Ass'n.*, 37 So.2d 692 (Fla.1948).

30  See, e.g., *Winshare Club of Canada v. Dept. of Legal Affairs*, 542 So.2d 974 (Fla. 1989).

31  *Posadas de Puerto Rico Assoc. v. Tourism Co. of Puerto Rico*, 478 U.S. 328, 341 (1986). Later limited on First Amendment grounds in *Greater New Orleans Broadcasting Association, Inc. v. United States*, 527 U.S. 173, 119 S.Ct. 1923, 144 L.Ed.2d 161 (1999).

32  '[W]e start with the assumption that the historic police powers of the States were not to be superseded by the Federal Act unless that was the clear and manifest purpose of Congress.' *Ray v. Atlantic Richfield Co.*, 435 U.S. 151, 157 (1978). This 'approach is consistent with both federalism concerns and the historic primacy of state regulation of matters of health and safety.' *Medtronic, Inc. v. Lohr*, 518 U.S. 470, 485 (1996).

33  Nations also have the inherent power to protect their borders from physical intrusion; acts of war by foreign governments obviously call for a unified federal response.

34  2 *Records of the Court Assistants of the Colony of Massachusetts Bay* 12 (1631) (1904), Law Enforcement Assistance Administration, United States Department of Justice, *The Development of the Law of Gambling: 1776–1976*, 41 (1977).

35  See., e.g., *United States v. Moncini*, 882 F.2d 401 (9th Cir. 1989) (irrelevant that child pornography mailed from Italy to the US was legal in Italy).

36  *Her Majesty's Customs and Excise v. Gerhart Schindler and Joerg Schindler, Reference for a Preliminary Ruling: High Court of Justice, Queen's Bench Division – United Kingdom*, ECJ, Case C-275/92, Doc.Num. 692J0275, Reports of Cases 1994 I-1039 (Judgment 24 March 1994).

37  Services are subject to Article 59 of the EC Treaty (now Article 49) and goods to Article 30.

38  In the United States this doctrine is known as the 'dormant Commerce Clause.' The actual Commerce Clause of the US Constitution only discusses the power of Congress to regulate interstate, international, and Indian commerce. But the courts have long accepted the idea that the states of the United States cannot, usually, keep out legal trade from other states of the union.

39  The most dramatic recent example was New Jersey declaring that MGM could not be licensed in that state unless it severed its ties with Pansy Ho, co-owner with MGM of a casino in Macau. Nevada regulators let MGM keep its gaming license, not even holding public hearings on the issue. I. Nelson Rose, 'Macau Junkets Trouble Nevada,' http://www.gamblingandthelaw.com/columns/248-macau-junkets-trouble-nevada.html

40  *Granholm v. Heald*, 125 S.Ct. 1885 (2005).

41  The WTO held the USA had not presented sufficient evidence to justify its fear of the involvement of organized crime with Internet gaming.

42  I. Nelson Rose, 'A $5,000,000 Camel,' http://www.gamblingandthelaw.com/columns/15-camel.html

43  LSA-R.S. §§14:90.3.

44  NRS §§465.091 – 465.094.

45  *American Libraries Ass'n v. Pataki*, 969 F.Supp. 160 (S.D.N.Y. 1997).

46  John Soares, *Loaded Dice: The True Story of a Casino Cheat* (Dallas, TX: Taylor Publishing, 1985).

# 16  Internet gambling policy in Europe

*George Häberling*

## Rudiments of European online gambling regulation

### A first glance at the European patchwork

A biotope for the protection of the variety of species – this is a likely picture to pop up in the mind of an observer of regulations and controls of online gambling in Europe, a young industry that emerged in 1995 when the government of Liechtenstein granted the 'International Lottery of Liechtenstein Foundation' the permit to operate certain online lottery formats.[1] Since then, no 'unité de doctrine' has developed among the roughly 40 independent countries[2] and the handful of semi-independent territories[3] deemed to constitute Europe. On the contrary, each of these jurisdictions tends to apply a rather generic model that shows little consideration of common interests and needs, but all the more of historically grown structures, typically of a monopolistic nature, that are to be protected against commercial operators acting within or across domestic borders. This pattern results in a colorful variety of sometimes odd species, of which this chapter intends to sketch some of the most interesting features.

Some years ago, the typical model applied by the majority of European countries was to (unsuccessfully) prohibit all commercial online games of chance while granting exceptions for the operation of online lotteries – and sometimes betting – to state-owned lottery companies supporting good causes. In the meantime, such a strict monopolistic approach survives in just about a handful of countries, and some of them more recently have initiated a process of liberalization. The vast majority of European countries have opted to legalize, regulate, and tax all forms of online gambling, subject to a local licensing regime with more or less stringent operational restrictions, smaller or bigger carve-outs for the lottery monopolists, and barriers against cross-border activities. And despite the EU principle of freedom to provide services, the European Court of Justice (ECJ) does not oppose a system where an online gambling operator, in order to target his products to residents of all 27 EU member states, may need 27 domestic licenses containing 27 different formats of restrictions and tax burdens.

In other words, reaction – and not proactive legislation – is the prevailing policy approach in this part of the world when it comes to online gambling. The current development of domestic regulations and controls basically was triggered by the rise of hugely successful offshore operators selling their services worldwide, often with little or no consideration for foreign restrictions. On European territory, it was the EU member state Malta[4] and the two semi-independent jurisdictions[5] Gibraltar and the Isle of Man that first granted online gambling licenses to commercial operators setting up their business infrastructure on domestic territory at the very beginning of the millennium. These initiatives were primarily motivated not by fiscal, but by economic considerations, namely the establishment of a high-tech industry providing attractive jobs. And all three pioneering jurisdictions were truly successful: the online gambling and related IT sector employs more than 3,000 people in Malta, around half that number in Gibraltar, and has become one of the pillars of the local economy in all these jurisdictions, supported by attractive fiscal incentives on corporate and gaming tax levels. In Malta, over 330 'Remote Gaming Licenses' have been issued, generating tax revenues of more than EUR 20 million per year, and around 25 licenses have been granted by Gibraltar and the Isle of Man.

However, the ECJ has ruled that other EU member states need not acknowledge Malta licenses for their own territory, so the expectation of the Malta operators to find automatic open doors throughout the EU via the Malta license was not fulfilled. Today, they basically find themselves in the same position as the other UK white-listed[6] jurisdictions, which are allowed to market their online gambling services in the UK, but need domestic licenses in each other EU member state allowing commercial gambling services and are subject there to a great and colorful variety of operational restrictions.

### The EU does not regulate online gambling

The European 'patchwork environment' is the flip side of a lack of political will to submit gambling services under sector-specific EU regulation. Instead, gambling activities are explicitly excluded from horizontal EU Acts such as the Service Directive[7] or the E-commerce Directive,[8] and therefore remain under the sovereignty of the 27 member states.[9]

However, there are some exceptions to that principle. First, gambling services are subject to a number of rules within the EU secondary legislation that are of non-industry-specific relevance. Examples of such secondary legislation include the Unfair Commercial Practice Directive,[10] the Distance Selling Directive,[11] and the Anti-Money Laundering Directive.[12]

Second, and more importantly, gambling services fall under Article 56 of the Treaty on the Functioning of the European Union (TFEU) and are thus covered by the general EU rules on the freedoms to provide services on a permanent or temporary basis. Accordingly, online gambling operators authorized in one member state may provide their services to consumers in other member states, unless those impose (even discriminatory) restrictions justified by overriding reasons in the public interest, such as consumer protection, the prevention of fraud, and incitement to squander on gambling, or the general need to preserve public order as provided for in Articles 51 and 52 TFEU and specified by the ECJ case law.

### The European Court of Justice has endorsed a wide range of protective measures

In general terms, the ECJ case law requires that member states' restrictions on online gambling be proportionate and applied in a consistent and systematic manner to all service offers in the area, no matter if provided by monopolists or commercial operators. Cross-border and other restrictions resulting from a member states' regulatory approach must bring about a genuine reduction of gambling opportunities, whereas the reduction of tax revenue following any market liberalization does not constitute a matter of overriding general interest.[13] In so far as the authorities of a member state incite and encourage consumers to participate in lotteries, betting, and other games of chance to the financial benefit of the public purse, the authorities of that state cannot invoke public order concerns relating to the need to reduce opportunities for gambling in order to justify restrictions. Restrictions must be applied without discrimination, and they must be suitable for achieving the objective which they pursue, and shall not go beyond what is necessary in order to attain it.[14] The procedure for the granting of a license must comply with the principles of equal treatment and non-discrimination and with the consequent obligation of transparency.[15]

In theory, one would expect the application of these guiding principles to set strong pillars for a reduction of national barriers against cross-border online gambling services and an opening of the EU internal market. In practical terms, however, many EU countries that have erected state-owned or other gambling monopolies tend to remain rather unimpressed and to move very slowly, thereby betting on the ECJ's tendency to undermine its own guidelines by generously granting exceptions to the principles when judging a member states' specific situation. This approach is not much of a surprise in light of the ECJ's view that, as argued by state-owned and other monopolists, online gambling bears enhanced risks of gambling addiction, fraud, and crime. Accordingly, in *Liga Portuguesa de Futebol Profissional,*[16] the ECJ has ruled that:

> The grant of exclusive rights to operate games of chance via the internet to a single operator, such as [church-owned monopolist] Santa Casa,[17] which is subject to strict control by the public authorities, may…confine the operation of gambling within controlled channels and be regarded as appropriate for the purpose of protecting consumers against fraud on the part of operators. As to whether the system in dispute…is necessary, the Portuguese Government submits that the authorities of a Member State do not, in relation to operators having their seat outside the national territory and using the internet to offer their services, have the same means of control at their disposal as those which they have in relation to an operator such as Santa Casa. In that regard, it should be noted that the sector involving games of chance offered via the internet has not been the subject of Community harmonization. A Member State is therefore entitled to take the view that the mere fact that an operator such as Bwin lawfully offers services in that sector via the internet in another Member State,[18] in which it is established and where it is in principle already subject to statutory conditions and controls on the part of the competent authorities in that State, cannot be regarded as amounting to a sufficient assurance that national consumers will be protected against the risks of fraud and crime, in the light of the difficulties likely to be encountered in such a context by the authorities of the Member State of establishment in assessing the professional qualities and integrity of operators. In addition, because of the lack of direct contact between consumer and operator, games of chance accessible via the internet involve different and more substantial risks of fraud by operators against consumers compared with the traditional markets for such games.[19]

In *Carmen Media,*[20] the ECJ has supported the German state Schleswig-Holstein's notion that online games of chance tend to be of higher risk than traditional games due to the potentially high volume and frequency of such offer in an environment which is characterized by isolation of the player, anonymity, and an absence of social control – factors, according to the Court, likely to develop gambling addiction and lead to other negative consequences. And in *de Lotto vs. Ladbrokes,*[21] the ECJ has accepted enforcement measures such as Internet protocol (IP) address blocking.

### EU authorities not amused

Naturally, the EU Commission and other EU authorities are not very pleased by the current patchwork situation. The Commission has launched a series of infringement proceedings against member states in order to verify the legality of their respective market entry barriers. Such proceedings against Italy and France in the meantime could be settled following appropriate reforms.

A few years ago, it was calculated that out of 14,823 active gambling sites accessible to European players, less than 15 percent operated with any license at all.[22] The European Commission differentiates between a 'black market' with unlicensed betting and gaming, including services provided from non-EU-countries, and 'grey' markets of operators duly licensed in one or more European Economic Area (EEA) member states, but providing gambling services to other member states without having obtained a specific authorization in those states. This unauthorized cross-border market increasingly gets under the radar of the EU Commission and is one of the reasons why the EC, in spring 2011, submitted its 'Green Paper on on-line gambling in the Internal Market' for public comment.[23] The main purpose of the paper is to launch a far-reaching public consultation on all relevant policy challenges and possible Internal Market issues resulting from the rapid development of online gambling services accessible to EU residents. The Green Paper seems to reflect that among EU authorities,[24] the view is becoming more and more widespread that liberal regimes as represented by the first-mover Malta granting 'offshore and extraterritorial licenses' do distort the mutual trust between member states by giving advantages to their licensees. There cannot be much doubt about the mid- to long-term outcome of this approach: an increasing emphasis on EU regulatory standards is to be expected.

### Some non-EU-member states add to the patchwork environment

Iceland, Liechtenstein, Norway, and Switzerland are independent countries that have chosen to remain under the auspices of the European Free Trade Association (EFTA) as their sole members, but not to join the EU. The first three, however, are part of the EU Internal Market through the Agreement on a European Economic Area (EEA) and, as a consequence, subject to an automatic adoption of all EU law, whereas Switzerland has adopted a limited number of EU rights and obligations via bilateral treaties. The EFTA Court, in cases involving Norway, has ruled twice on the legality of national gambling monopolies, thereby staying in line with ECJ judgments.[25]

In Iceland and Norway, all permitted games of chance, including online lotteries and betting,[26] are reserved for state-owned and -operated monopolies. On the other end of the scale, Liechtenstein, as from January 1, 2011, set into force one of Europe's most modern gaming acts, covering all forms of gambling and allowing for the granting of concessions and licenses to privately owned applicants for the commercial operation of casinos, lotteries, betting, games of skill, and all forms of online gaming,[27] subject to strict personal, financial, and operational criteria as known from, for example, Switzerland and Nevada. In Switzerland, the Gaming Act[28] prohibits all forms of games of chance transmitted via telecommunication. However, the two state-run lottery companies[29] and their owners, the cantons, opine to be excluded from such prohibition and have developed a wide range of online lottery and sports betting offers, including quick virtual scratch card games.[30] The Swiss Federal government has decided to end the unequal treatment of state and privately owned operators of games of chance and has tasked a working group headed by the Federal Gaming Board to draft legislation providing for a level playing field in all the areas of online gambling.

Important European online gambling hubs are the self-governing UK Crown Dependencies Alderney, Gibraltar, and the Isle of Man. None of them has a sufficient population base for commercially viable online gambling operations, and therefore they are bound to let their licensees fish in foreign waters.

## Online gambling legislation of select European jurisdictions

### *General approach to online gambling*

Broadly speaking, European countries apply one (or sometimes two) of the following three approaches to the regulation of online gambling: they (a) prohibit all or certain forms of online gambling, (b) erect state-owned or other monopolies, or (c) license, control, and tax commercial operators providing services within a more or less strictly regulated framework. Within the latter group, some small jurisdictions do not offer sufficient market potential for domestic online gambling operations and therefore allow their licensees to provide their services mainly in foreign territories.

### *Prohibition of all forms of online gambling*

A minority of EU member states traditionally prohibit all forms of online gambling, including Cyprus, Germany,[31] Greece, Lithuania, Poland, and Romania. The main political motivation behind this model is the protection of domestic monopolies on land-based games of chance against commercial operators, proudly presented to the general public as player and consumer protection. Forced to act by ECJ judgments and EC pressure, all these countries with the exclusion of Cyprus have initiated a review of their position and are in the process of searching for politically acceptable models for a cautiously balanced market opening.

In the case of federally structured Germany,[32] the ECJ ruled in September 2010 that the states' ('Bundeslaender') monopoly on lotteries and sports betting as established in the 2008 Interstate Treaty on Gambling contains unjustifiable conflicts with the freedoms granted in the European Treaties. Reluctant to allow market liberalization as always in the past, the German states now try to confine the opening of online sports betting via the introduction of 'trial period licenses', subject to a prohibitively high tax on stakes. This plan may fail before the ink on this chapter has dried. In the meantime, with the help of ineffective enforcement,[33] foreign commercial operators will continue to run betting shops in numerous cities and to offer online betting, casino, and poker games throughout Germany, thereby further reducing the monopolists' revenue streams.

### *Monopolies*

A concept adopted by quite a number of European countries is *to prohibit all commercial operators from offering online gambling services while allowing one or a small number of state-owned operators to provide lotteries and sometimes sports betting* – and in turn have such monopolists use the majority or all of their profits for public purposes or good causes including cultural, social, educational, health and similar institutions and projects as well as the sponsoring of sports clubs and sporting activities. This model can be found in EU member states such as Finland, the Netherlands,[34] Portugal, Spain,[35] and Sweden,[36] but also in the EFTA member states Norway and Switzerland. In Portugal, the exclusive holder of an online lottery and sports betting license is the religious institution Santa Casa da Misericordia de Lisboa.[37] With the exception of Norway and Sweden, all these countries currently are considering more or less far-reaching proposals for an opening up of the online casino and/or sports betting market to commercial operators. Such liberalization is driven by the bad experience that each and any of these countries became important playgrounds for thousands of foreign-based online gambling operators – many of them barely regulated and controlled on home turf – that made substantial profits by tapping the local market without paying local taxes.

Austria is the only EU member state that has opted for a *monopoly for one privately owned operator* permitted to provide all forms of commercial online gambling services.[38] Such an operator must be domiciled in Austria and is not allowed to accept bets from players residing outside Austria. In turn, it is prohibited for Austrian residents and subject to criminal sanctions to participate and purchase credits in online games of chance operated from abroad. The current holder of the exclusive online gambling concession is a privately owned joint venture between Österreichische Lotterien Gesellschaft mbH, the exclusive operator of traditional lotteries, and Casinos Austria, the exclusive operator of land-based casinos.[39]

Most of the EU member states that recently have opened their market to some degree of competition between commercial online gambling operators have retained a *mixed system* by granting licenses for *online lotteries* (and sometimes sports betting) to *monopolists* and for the *other online games including casino and poker* to *commercial operators*. This approach was first implemented in the UK when the 2005 Gambling Act made 'remote' gambling licenses available for all forms of games of chance with the only exclusion the offers of the National Lottery which is not regulated by the Act. It has since been adopted in more or less liberal formats by Belgium, Denmark,[40] France, and Italy. Other countries including Spain will soon follow.

## Competition among commercial operators

GENERAL REMARKS

In the meantime, and often only in reaction to pressure from the EU Commission and Court of Justice, the model seen most across European countries is to allow for a more or less intense competition between commercial operators of online casino games including poker and sometimes sports betting, accompanied by often stringent legal and practical entry barriers, while restricting online lotteries (and sometimes sports betting) which remain reserved for state-owned monopolies.

The original designer of this model was Italy, when, under pressure not only from EC infringement procedures attacking its heavily monopolized gaming landscape, but also from ECJ judgments[41] and huge state budget deficits, it passed emergency legislation in 2006 and 2007 allowing for the granting of online betting, betting exchange, and skill games (e.g. poker tournament) licenses. In 2009, as a measure to finance reconstruction of the city of Avila, devastated by an earthquake, online casino and poker cash games were added, but implemented only in 2011. Online lottery games including virtual scratch cards remain reserved to the lottery monopoly, which may enter sub-distribution agreements with commercial operators. Apart from computers, games can be offered via mobile phones and interactive TV. Games can only be offered to Italian residents through a gaming system using the '.it' suffix and being real-time linked to the centralized control system run by the gaming control authority AAMS via its technological partner, SOGEI, in order to record, track, and validate each wager placed by Italian residents.

RESTRICTIONS ON NUMBER OF LICENSES

An unlimited number of licenses can be granted in Alderney, Denmark, France, Gibraltar, the Isle of Man, and Malta.

In Italy and the UK, the number of sports betting licenses can be restricted. The Liechtenstein government can limit the number of licenses by way of an ordinance.

In Austria, Portugal, and Switzerland, online games of chance are authorized as an extension of the offline permits held by monopolists. Belgium applies a so-called 'license plus' system: online casino, betting, and media games licenses in a first stage are available exclusively for previously licensed operators of land-based games of chance (casino, gaming arcades, slots in bars); slow extension to other operators is planned for a second stage. The number of license holders and of (land-based) gambling establishments is restricted.

### Cross-border activities

Most gaming laws of European states[42] on the one hand foresee substantial prohibitory measures for any online gambling services not licensed by domestic authorities, regardless if provided domestically or from abroad, but on the other hand contain little or no specific provisions regarding cross-border online gambling activities.

#### 'Open border' approach

One needs only one finger to count the European jurisdictions that apply the principles of the free movement of services to the online gambling industry. Among the EU member states, the UK is the only exception committing to the European dream of cross-border service provision. UK-licensed and -domiciled operators are allowed to sell their services in other EEA and white-listed jurisdictions but not in others, while in turn all foreign operators licensed in one of these jurisdictions are allowed to cater to the UK market, advertise there, and locate some of its operation there without paying UK gaming tax. To make things worse, operators located in any other jurisdiction in the world are not hindered from servicing UK residents as long as they do not advertise. This led to a situation where only a minority of online gambling operators servicing the UK market are based there, while most have either remained in Gibraltar, Malta, or white-listed jurisdictions – or even have moved there from the UK[43] – to avoid higher UK corporate taxes, gaming tax (a 15 percent 'Remote Gaming Duty' on gross gaming revenues), and betting levy. This model was based on the UK government's bet that other European countries with important online gambling markets would follow that concept. None of them did. As a consequence, UK-based operators keep complaining about the disincentives of staying. The UK government has listened and initiated a reviewing process of the current policy regarding foreign operators which is expected to be modified. Such an overhaul of regulations was speeded up following the charges brought against Full Tilt and other online poker operators by the USA in April 2011.

The only other area where cross-border gambling came alive via consent of all states in which the services are offered is the international lottery EuroMillions. This joint venture of the lottery monopolists of ten European countries[44] was established in 2004 and allows for very attractive jackpots.[45]

#### Restrictions on cross-border activities

OPERATORS WITHOUT DOMESTIC LICENSE DEEMED ILLEGAL

This guiding principle, with the UK as the only exception, is currently applied by all European jurisdictions granting online gambling licenses to commercial operators. And there is no change of that common approach in sight.

Whoever operates games of chance without a domestic license is subject to administrative and/or criminal sanctions in the form of fines and often imprisonment. However, such sanctions typically are not enforceable when the foreign operator holds a foreign license and has no local presence.[46] This is the main reason why a number of jurisdictions have implemented IP and financial blocking measures.

RESTRICTIONS ON FOREIGN OPERATORS

Most European jurisdictions grant licenses only to operators domiciled in EEA countries. Some, including Alderney, Austria, Belgium, Gibraltar, the Isle of Man, Liechtenstein, and Malta – but not France and Italy – require domestic incorporation. In Denmark,[47] a local representative is sufficient. In addition, Denmark allows domestically licensed operators to liaise with foreign poker networks in order to access international liquidity. In France, the operator has to keep French bank accounts, must install technical infrastructure allowing the gaming authority ARJEL to monitor and audit all transactions with French players, must use the '.fr' suffix on his French platform, and in the case of a foreign headquarters must appoint a domestic tax representative and a person responsible for all legal monitoring.

SERVER HOSTING REQUIREMENTS

Alderney, Belgium, Gibraltar, Isle of Man, Liechtenstein, and Malta – but not Denmark, France, Italy, and the UK – require domestic hosting of main gaming servers. In Italy, the main server can remain in an EEA member state provided that a 24/7 remote linkup with the AAMS centralized system is guaranteed for bets validation, compliance monitoring, and tax purposes.

IP BLOCKING

Blocking measures against gambling websites without domestic license in order to build a 'ring fence' around the country seem to become more and more popular among European legislators. They typically are designed to block access from a local IP address to .com and other foreign gambling sites and often are combined with seizure of domain names.

Italy was the first European country implementing this model. In 2006, the gaming authority AAMS black-listed more than 500 gambling websites without domestic licenses, thereby forcing Italian Internet service providers (ISPs) to block access for Italian residents via domain name server (DNS) filtering and redirecting players to an AAMS site which then informs players that they were trying to gamble in prohibited territory.[48] This move resulted in a strong reduction of 'illegal' offers while almost all important operators entered into seeking (and receiving) Italian licenses, including the ones that previously were considered to be breaching domestic gaming laws. Today, the AAMS black-list contains more than 3,100 gambling websites.[49] However, quite a number of 'illegal' operators successfully play cat and mouse with AAMS by moving their Italian websites from one IP address to another.

France was next. There, specialized public servants gather evidence and identify offenders by playing under pseudonyms on unlicensed gambling sites. The gaming authority ARJEL then transmits to the operator a formal cease and desist order initiating an eight-day deadline for comment, followed by an IP and financial transactions blocking order by court that forces ISPs to take all measures[50] to stop access to the gambling services, be that via locking of the domain name, the IP address, or the Uniform Resource Locator (URL) – or via analysis of message content.[51]

Other countries with legislation allowing for IP blocking measures include Belgium, Denmark (via injunction orders against ISPs), Estonia (via blocking of specific IP addresses listed by the Tax and Customs Board; and payment service providers are obliged to freeze relevant accounts), and Germany (not enforced). Similar measures are planned in the Czech Republic and in Norway following the failure of financial blocking measures implemented in July 2010 (see below).

At this point in time, none of the jurisdictions has established a stable legal basis for forcing ISPs to block site access via Deep Packet Inspection (DPI) or similar means of message content analysis. In light of the prevailing fiscal aim of such measures, many observers believe them to be in violation of constitutional civil rights guarantees. Nevertheless, the German states' most recent draft of their new Interstate Treaty on Gambling seems to cover DPI, geotargeting, and similar obligations.

FINANCIAL BLOCKING OBLIGATIONS ON FINANCIAL SERVICE PROVIDERS

Another brick in the firewall of some European states is the general obligation of banks and other financial service providers to block transfers between players and operators without a domestic license. Such a measure is in use in Belgium, Estonia, France, and Norway. The latter limits such obligation to financial service providers with a domestic presence. As a consequence, gambling from foreign accounts or credit cards is not affected, and the decrease in use of foreign gambling websites by Norwegian players is minimal.

The legislation of Germany, Denmark,[52] and the Netherlands[53] foresees financial blocking, but implementation has not commenced due to various technical, legal, or political problems. Financial blocking is planned in Latvia.

ADVERTISING BANS ON SERVICES OF UNLICENSED OPERATORS

A number of European jurisdictions, including Cyprus, Estonia, Finland, Latvia, and Poland, ban all forms of gambling-related promotion and advertisements, no matter if gambling products are provided land based or online. Germany prohibits all gambling promotion and advertisement via TV, Internet, and other forms of electronic telecommunication. In other jurisdictions, including Austria,[54] Denmark, France, Greece, Ireland, Italy, Latvia, Liechtenstein, Malta, the Netherlands, Norway, Portugal, Romania, Slovenia, Spain, and Switzerland, the prohibition of gambling-related promotion and advertisements exclusively applies to operators not domestically licensed. This impressive list of jurisdictions mirrors the efficacy of these types of barriers. Enforcement problems typically are limited to situations where no local intermediary is needed to spread gambling promotions and advertisements, for example in the case of hypertext linking and direct mailing by foreign providers.

Sweden prohibits all forms of promotion for gambling activities operated outside the country, including all advertising via gambling websites hosted in other EU member states. In the UK, all forms, content, timing, and location of gambling advertising are subject to regulation by the Secretary of State. The unique 'white-listing' model, which most likely will be discontinued shortly, allows any online gambling operator licensed in the EEA, in Gibraltar, or in a 'white-listed' (i.e., approved) jurisdiction (currently: Alderney, Antigua and Barbuda, the Isle of Man, Tasmania) to advertise and locate some of its operation in the UK without being subject to UK licensing and gaming tax.

PROHIBITIONS IMPOSED ON PLAYERS ACCESSING FOREIGN OPERATORS' WEBSITES

Most jurisdictions do not penalize the participation of domestic players in online games of chance organized abroad, no matter if the operator holds a foreign license or not. Denmark and France expressly allow local online gambling operators to accept payments from a player's EEA-based bank account to his domestic gaming account.

Exceptions to that rule are Austria, where the player can be fined up to 7,500 euros for participating in foreign online games of chance,[55] Belgium, and Germany.[56]

### Licenses

#### Permitted games

The type of games permitted for commercial operators varies from state to state. Typically, jurisdictions that have little or no local market allow their licensees to operate all forms of games, such as casino, cash and tournament poker, betting, lotteries, and skill games. This model can be found for example in Alderney, Gibraltar, the Isle of Man, Liechtenstein,[57] and Malta.

Online lotteries throughout almost all of Europe are confined to mostly state-owned monopolists. In turn, commercial operators typically are allowed to offer some or all of casino, poker, betting, and skill games. This model we find in states including Belgium, Denmark,[58] France,[59] Italy, and the UK.[60]

#### Classes of licenses

Many jurisdictions differentiate between two or more separate classes of licenses, depending on the type of services provided, often along the following distinctions:

1  casino-type games;
2  peer-to-peer poker tournaments;
3  sports betting;
4  lotteries;
5  server hosting.

Such differentiation allows the operator to apply for those services only that are part of his individual business model; it can be found for example in Alderney,[61] Belgium, Denmark,[62] France, Liechtenstein,[63] Malta,[64] and the UK.[65] Jurisdictions with one type of license only include the Isle of Man and Italy; however, the licensing authority can exclude certain games based on an individual assessment.

### Operational restrictions

It would be a polite understatement to describe the European variety of restrictions on the operation of permitted online games of chance as *big*. In fact, the term *phenomenal* seems to be more appropriate. Even a short summary would require double the space of this chapter, and therefore, the following three areas are only briefly highlighted below: a few particularly odd regulatory features, some typical gaming tax models, and sector-specific anti-money-laundering provisions – a clearly underdeveloped element of current online gambling regulations.

When regulating online gambling, European jurisdictions have adhered to a number of commonly accepted principles. For example, commercial license applicants must prove to be fit and proper, gaming systems must adhere to technical standards set by the gaming authorities, players must not have more than one gaming account with the same operator[66] and must be identified, access to minors must be denied, cash payments and anonymous gaming accounts are prohibited, gaming transactions must be registered, and the players must be offered self-limitation and self-exclusion tools.

But: these are the exceptions, while patchwork remains the name of the rule. Quite a number of restrictions imposed on online gambling operators by European jurisdictions are quite uncommon features. A randomly generated selection might include the following examples:

* In Austria, the online gambling operator is not obliged to have its gaming system tested by independent labs, to run an IT risk management system, and to store transaction data.
* In Belgium, play is subject to loss limits, and the use of credit cards is prohibited.
* In France, online sports betting operators are prohibited from paying out prizes exceeding an average of 85 percent of all stakes wagered, the maximum amount that may be credited to a player's account is limited, and any balance exceeding that limit must automatically be transferred to the player's bank account.
* In Italy, the gambling authority AAMS has real-time access to all gambling transactions via a centralized monitoring system.
* In Malta, at intervals of one hour of play, the game must display an automatic 'reality check' suspending play until the player confirms that he has read information about time of play and financial outcome.

### Gaming tax

All European jurisdictions that license commercial online games of chance levy a separate gaming tax in addition to corporate taxes. Why? Keep in mind that such a special charge is not practiced in any other industry outside of gambling.

At first sight, the answer seems simple: states want to maximize fiscal revenues by skimming off the extraordinary profit margins of gambling operations. This model may be seen in Austria where the gaming tax is 40 percent of gross gaming revenues from online lotteries, 16 percent of the amount of prices on poker (and similar) tournaments, and 16 percent of the amount of stakes (bets) placed on all other games of chance within Austria.[67] Naturally, these tax rates are way too high to survive in a competitive environment, with jurisdictions such as Alderney, the Isle of Man, Gibraltar, Liechtenstein, and Malta charging fractions only. In other words, a set of preconditions must be fulfilled to make the Austrian gaming tax model work, namely: a 'walled garden' regime is implemented that protects a domestic monopoly from foreign competition, while the monopolist is generously endowed with freedoms to operate on a strictly commercial basis, unhindered from overregulation.

The UK has tried to maximize fiscal revenues under a different setup, namely an 'open border' approach allowing for free competition between domestically and foreign-licensed operators enjoying a wide range of operational discretion. The UK remote gaming tax is 15 percent of gross gaming revenues, increased in the case of betting by an additional 'remote betting duty'. Such a gaming tax level has proven to exceed what is sustainable in an environment of low-taxing jurisdictions: important operators such as Ladbrokes, William Hill, and Betfair removed their online business from the UK, and no major operator chose to relocate its overseas operation to Britain. As a consequence, gaming tax revenues remain much lower than expected.

Not so in Italy. There, a quick glance at a few key data shows an economically healthy combination of high online gambling turnover, strong presence of important licensees, and high gaming tax revenues. Obviously, market potential, regulatory restrictions, and gaming tax rates are well balanced. This is achieved via differentiation of tax rates based upon the specific profit margins of the different types of games. The following games are subject to a tax on turnover: lotteries 19 percent, bingo 11.5 percent, horse racing close to 10 percent, other sports betting 4.5 percent, tournament poker 3 percent.[68] All other online games, including casino and cash poker, are subject to a 20 percent gaming tax on gross profits.

France has chosen a less competitive gaming tax regime. While poker (cash games and tournaments) are moderately taxed around 2 percent of stakes, sports betting tax reaches 7.5 percent of wagers plus 1 percent levy payable to sporting organizations, resulting in much lower turnover and tax revenues than expected. This is aggravated by an additional tax disincentive directed against commercial operators: land-based monopolists have tax advantages over commercial online operators when it comes to sports betting.

Germany is another example of a state using the gaming tax regime to keep competition away from state-owned monopolists: the current draft for a new Interstate Treaty on Gambling foresees the liberalization of sports betting – but at a proposed gaming tax burden of 16 percent on turnover. This looks like a purely prohibitive measure, designed to pretend good will to the ECJ.

Under EU state aid rules,[69] the European Commission has opened two *formal investigations*: the first[70] against France to examine whether a parafiscal tax (levy) aimed at financing horse racing is in line with competition rule 41 – the Commission doubts the qualification of the mission conferred on horseracing companies as a service of general economic interest. And the second[71] against Denmark to examine whether lower taxes for online casinos (flat tax of 20 percent on the gross gambling revenue [GGR]) in comparison to a considerably higher gaming tax for land-based casinos (up to 75 percent on GGR) could procure an anti-competitive advantage for such online casinos. If this examination results in a judgment against Denmark, it would send a shockwave to all the other EEA member states applying similar distinctions based upon the higher pre-gaming-tax profitability of land-based casinos due to limitations of the number of licenses granted.

### Prevention of money laundering

In essence, anti-money laundering (AML) regulations are safeguards to keep out organized crime and other bad guys. The Internet allows for the worldwide offering of online games of chance by operators that do not hold any license at all and may not even reveal in which country their operation is located. This clearly is a problem of international dimensions (and one of the legitimate drivers towards 'walled garden' regimes). And it seems very likely that this situation, under the guidance of the Financial Action Task Force on Money Laundering (FATF),[72] will trigger the first set of truly international rules in the field of online gambling.

Land-based as well as online casinos[73] – but not lotteries – are subject to the *FATF 40 Recommendations*.[74] Since the FATF deems all forms of gambling 'at risk of being misused for money laundering or terrorist financing',[75] FATF Recommendations 5, 12, and 16 provide for a reduced transaction threshold value for casinos of USD/EUR 3,000 only. As a consequence, online (and land-based) casino operators are required to identify and verify the identity of customers when they engage in financial transactions equal to or above that threshold value. Countries must require operators to ensure that they are able to link customer due diligence information for a particular customer to the transactions conducted by that customer.

The *EU Anti-Money Laundering Directive* (AMLD)[76] applies to 'casinos', but does not explicitly reach out to (land-based) lotteries and betting or to online gambling. Most EU member states apply the AMLD to land-based as well as to online casino games.[77] On the other hand, only a small minority, including Austria, Liechtenstein, Malta, and the UK,[78] equally apply the AMLD to online lotteries and sports betting, thereby taking increased similarities between online casino and lottery games such as virtual scratch cards into account.

Most states granting online gambling licenses to commercial operators have established little or no money laundering regulations specifically designed for the online world, but work with an *analogue application* of the regulations developed for land-based casinos instead.[79] This approach obviously ignores *fundamental differences* between online and land-based casino games. Online, the operator knows and records each player's gaming history in full detail, and he links each and any gaming transaction including all cash-ins and cash-outs to the individual player (in land-based casinos, such automated data linking typically is impossible[80]). Such data processing allows the AML regulator to request automated moderators. On the other hand, in the online gambling world, the player is not physically present at the operator's premises, and therefore it becomes more difficult to verify his identity and to interview him in person when enhanced due diligence is needed.

The few jurisdictions that have implemented money laundering regulations specifically designed for the online world include Alderney and Liechtenstein, and to a much lesser degree the UK.[81] Alderney requests its licensees to incorporate 'robust client identification methods and measures in order to manage and mitigate the specific risks of non face-to-face transactions inherent in the eGambling industry'. Operators are subject to 11 pages of specific and state-of-the-art AML provisions containing obligations regarding risk assessment, normal and enhanced customer due diligence, customer identification and verification, obligations to terminate customer relationships, transaction monitoring and recording, suspicious activity reporting, employee screening and training, and record-keeping.[82] Even more elaborate and strict online-specific provisions that firmly implement the risk-based approach are foreseen in the 2010 Liechtenstein gambling act and ordinance.

The FATF, in its most recent Mutual Evaluation Reports assessing member states' compliance with the 40 Recommendations and domestic AML legislation, is increasingly reviewing the implementation of measures taken in the online gambling sector.[83] In light of FATF's policy to steadily level out regulatory weaknesses by imposing best practice models on slower moving states via repeat inspection, time will come when all jurisdictions that license online gambling operators will have to implement industry-specific AML measures similar to the Alderney and Liechtenstein models. Harmonization via international directives of a 'technical' nature – maybe the political model soon to be found throughout Europe?

## Notes

1   The permit was based on an exception from the Swiss lottery regime adopted by Liechtenstein via the so-called customs agreement with Switzerland.
2   The current 27 member states of the European Union (EU) include (in alphabetical order): Austria, Belgium, Bulgaria, Cyprus, Czech Republic, Denmark, Estonia, Finland, France, Germany, Greece, Hungary, Ireland, Italy, Latvia, Lithuania, Luxembourg, Malta, the Netherlands, Poland, Portugal, Romania, Slovakia, Slovenia, Spain, Sweden, United Kingdom. Non-EU member states

include: Albania, Andorra, Bosnia and Herzegovina, Croatia, Iceland, Liechtenstein, Macedonia, Monaco, Montenegro, Norway, San Marino, Serbia, Switzerland.
3   Including the online gambling hubs Alderney, Gibraltar, and the Isle of Man.
4   Malta is a seven-island archipelago located south of Sicily in the Mediterranean Sea, with a population of around 400,000.
5   Self-governing UK Crown Dependencies not part of the UK nor the EU.
6   That is, approved by the Secretary of State to have regulatory regimes comparable to that in the UK.
7   2006/123/EC.
8   2000/31/EC.
9   See note 2.
10   OJ L 149, 11.6.2005, p. 22.
11   OJ L 144, 4.6.1997, p. 19.
12   OJ L 309, 25.11.2005, p. 15.
13   EC Green Paper 'On on-line gambling in the Internal Market,' dated March 24, 2011, p. 7, 11, http://ec.europa.eu/internal_market/consultations/docs/2011/online_gambling/com2011_128_en.pdf
14   Case C-243/01, *Gambelli*, ECR [2003]. For example, it is not proportionate to request operators to have their seat in a particular member state.
15   EC Green Paper, p. 11.
16   Case C-42/07, ECR [2009], p. I-7633.
17   Jogos Santa Casa, set up in 2004 by the church Santa Casa da Misericordia de Lisboa.
18   Here: Malta.
19   § 67–70.
20   Case C-46/08, ECR [2010] § 103.
21   Case C-258/08 ECR [2010].
22   Cyber-criminality in Online Gaming, White Paper by Laboratoire d'Expertise en Securité Informatique, July 2006. http://www.lexsi.com/telecharger/gambling_cybercrime_2006.pdf
23   Contributions could be submitted to markt-gambling@ec.europa.eu by July 31, 2011, at the latest.
24   As seen, for example, with its current Advocate General.
25   Cases E-1/06 *(EFTA Surveillance vs. The Kingdom of Norway)* and E-3/06 *(Ladbrokes Ltd. vs. The Government of Norway)*.
26   Online casino and poker currently is prohibited.
27   The author of this chapter was mandated by the Liechtenstein government to draft the new Liechtenstein Gaming Act and all relevant ordinances.
28   Article 5.
29   Swisslos (covering the German- and Italian-speaking parts of Switzerland) and Loterie Romande (covering the French-speaking part).
30   The Swiss lottery companies' online games are of increasing importance and have reached around 6 percent of market share.
31   Online gambling licenses granted by the former German Democratic Republic are not acknowledged by the 'old' Bundeslaender.
32   Regulation of (a) slot machines in privately owned slots arcades and restaurants and (b) wagering on horse racing is with the Federal government, while all other games of chance are subject to the state's authority.
33   Many German cities are in fear of facing damage claims from betting shop owners if the ECJ overrules prohibition imposed by the Interstate Treaty.
34   de Lotto offers the online sale of lottery tickets, https://www.lotto.nl/lotto/index.html
35   In addition, a small monopoly is granted to ONCE, a non-profit organization supporting blind people, http://www.juegosonce.com
36   Monopolist Svenska Spel is also allowed to operate online poker, http://svenskaspel.se
37   https://www.jogossantacasa.pt
38   The monopoly does not include certain forms of sports betting, since the Austrian states ('Bundesländer') are permitted to grant licenses for bets covering less than 10 sports competitions (seen as games of skill).
39   Casinos Austria holds 32 percent of the capital of Österreichische Lotterien Gesellschaft mbH.

40   State-owned Danske Spil A/S online monopoly covers lottery games, but not sports betting. The company's licenses for land-based games of chance include lotteries, most forms of betting, and slot machines.

41   Including *Gambelli* and *Placanica*.

42   Including Cyprus, Finland, Germany, Greece, Hungary, Ireland, Latvia, Lithuania, Luxembourg, the Netherlands, Poland, Portugal, Slovenia, Sweden, Switzerland.

43   Prominent exits include Betfair, Bet365, Ladbroke, the Tote (a government-owned bookmaker!), and William Hill.

44   Austria, Belgium, France, Ireland, Liechtenstein (via Swisslos), Luxembourg, Portugal, Spain, Switzerland, UK.

45   Current record is 183 million euros (paid out in February 2006).

46   Due to a lack of dual criminality and/or to practical barriers of international enforcement.

47   Jointly and severally liable with license holder for payment of gaming tax.

48   Per day, 2–3 million players attempt to access sites that are blocked.

49   http://www.aams.gov.it/site.php?id=2484

50   See list of possible blocking measures and their efficacy in www.bluetouff.com/2010/08/22/arjel-meme-pas-peur-du-ridicule/

51   First applied to UK bookmaker StanJames located in Gibraltar.

52   Blocking of credit card payments via injunction orders against banks.

53   Strong opposition against governmental requests for banks and payment service providers to refrain from business with unlicensed operators persists.

54   The Ministry of Finance can approve advertising by EU-licensed operators applying high standards of player protection.

55   No known enforcement measures.

56   Criminal Act, §§ 284 and 285.

57   Traditionally, online and offline lotteries and sports betting are provided to Liechtenstein residents by Swiss co-monopolist Swisslos, under an exclusive agreement. Under the 2010 Gaming Act, the government is allowed to continue this form of cooperation.

58   With the exception of horse and greyhound racing which both remain reserved to lottery monopolist Danske Spil.

59   Poker (cash games and tournaments) and sports betting – but so far no casino or bingo.

60   The National Lottery's monopoly is restricted to big games.

61   Category 1 for business-to-customer (B2C) models; Category 2 for business-to-business (B2B) models; plus foreign gambling associate certificates.

62   In Denmark, casino-type games may include peer-to-peer (P2P) poker tournaments, sports betting, and lottery-type games.

63   The government can exclude certain games from a license granted and can foresee separate licenses for server hosting and affiliate programs.

64   Malta has four classes of license: Class 1 covers casino-type games, skill games, and online lotteries; Class 2 covers sports betting; Class 3 covers P2P, poker networks, betting exchanges, and games portals; Class 4 covers hosting and similar services.

65   The UK has 10 different types of operating licenses, restricted to certain games.

66   Exception: UK.

67   Including (prohibited!) bets placed with foreign online gambling operators.

68   Maximum buy-in was raised from 100 to 250 euros in 2011.

69   Articles 107 and 108 TFEU.

70   Case C34/2010, FR.

71   Case C35/2010, DA.

72   An inter-governmental body whose purpose is the development and promotion of national and international policies to combat money laundering and terrorist financing. The FATF currently comprises 34 member jurisdictions and 2 regional organizations, representing most major financial centres in all parts of the globe.

73   Called 'Internet casinos' by the FATF.

74   See the definition of 'designated non-financial businesses and professions', p. 12, http://www.fatf-gafi.org/dataoecd/7/40/34849567.PDF

75   Methodology, section B.20.1 (p. 29). See lottery case in: FATF, Vulnerabilities of Casinos and Gaming Sector 2009, Case 16.

76   Directive 2005/60/EC (OJ L 309, November 25, 2005, p. 15).
77   In light of a provision imposing enhanced customer due diligence measures, inter alia, when the customer has not been physically present for identification purposes, Article 13 par. 2.
78   Regarding sports betting only.
79   A typical example is Italy where online and land-based gambling operators equally must identify and verify customer identity when transactions exceed EUR 1,000, and where online-specific AML regulation is limited (see Decreto Legislativo 25 settembre 2009, n. 151, note 4 to article 13).
80   Most European casinos do not use player tracking systems.
81   Money Laundering Regulations 2007, section 10. Online casinos are required to verify and identify the customer either when he first registers for a gaming account or when he spends more than 2,000 euros in 24 hours ('threshold approach'). Operators must determine the extent of their customer due diligence measures on a risk-sensitive basis depending on the risk posed by the customer and his level of gambling.
82   Alderney e-Gambling Regulations 2009, regulation 227 and Schedule 16.
83   For example, in the February 2011 report (par. 2007), it was recommended to France to reinforce efforts to control illegal online gambling operators.

# 17 The only thing certain is uncertainty?

## Internet gambling in the United States, 1961–2011

*Bo J. Bernhard and Andrew Montgomery*

## Introduction

Early in the twentieth century, gambling was largely an illicit pastime in America. Gamblers would gauge the passion of local law enforcement when choosing to visit gambling locales like Reno, Nevada, or Long Beach, California (whose ships would head offshore into international waters so that wagers could be placed legally), or even Havana, depending upon which place was least likely to pursue criminal action against those who gambled there. These kinds of gaming jurisdictions frequently legalized and prohibited gambling, often doing both within a span of a few years. Gaming industry operators and employees, for their part, were also subject to the whims of law enforcement, uprooting operations when crusaders like California attorney general Earl Warren (later a prominent US Supreme Court justice) cracked down on gambling dens in their backyards (Moehring and Green, 2005).

Early in the twenty-first century, online gambling in the USA is following a similar trajectory, facing its own legal challenges, operational confusion, and occasional chaos as the nation decides what, exactly, to do with those who use the Internet to place wagers. Those who operate online gambling sites have found themselves under tremendous scrutiny (and even prosecution) from some of the nation's most powerful governmental agencies. For their part, America's Internet gamblers continue to chase betting spots that seem to offer a square, legal deal, not unlike their counterparts a century or so ago. As a result, and as of this writing (at the end of 2010), we might suggest that the one thing we can state with absolute certainty is that uncertainty has ruled, and the most stable space in this online sphere has been instability. Having said this, Internet gambling already has a rich and documented history in the USA, and one can certainly speculate, with some certainty, on the contours of the future for online gamblers here.

As we have learned at various points throughout this volume, the first online casinos apparently started operating in 1995, with sites that originally allowed 'free play' with imaginary money. Very quickly, however, entrepreneurs and governments alike recognized this medium's economic potential, and began to offer prizes and prize money. Almost immediately, the enterprising Caribbean nation of Antigua arrived upon the Internet gambling scene, and indeed would play the role of a major protagonist (and to the USA, an antagonist) throughout the history of Internet wagering (Schwartz, 2005).

Internet gambling was originally limited to a few games that were well suited for the format. In the beginning, sports books proved a natural fit, wedding real-time technology with a sports betting world that suddenly found itself with access to up-to-the-minute information and betting opportunities (Schwartz, 2005). Of course, ultimately the online gambling world expanded to encompass virtually every imaginable gambling activity (and a few gambling activities that had probably never been imagined by any conventional gaming industry operator). By 2001, a *New York Times* article (cleverly titled 'A Casino on the Desktop') sounded a warning that the activity had reached alarming proportions in the USA, with about one million Americans gambling online every single day (Richtel, 2001). In what would become a trend, this popularity (and scrutiny) led to increased attention from US lawmakers. After all, American players allegedly constituted a significant portion of online gambling expenditures worldwide, and in a way that was practically ungoverned (or at least untaxed and unregulated) by any US-based entity.

Today, like its parallel industry in bricks-and-mortar settings, online gaming is profoundly shaped by evolving policy, technology, and market developments. The dilemma confronting the United States is whether to pursue a strategy of prohibition (or to pursue some variant of prohibition), or to choose to legalize and regulate online gambling (or to choose some variant of legalization). This is simpler said than politically done. From 1995 to 2006, the US Department of Justice maintained the position that online gaming was an illegal enterprise; however, few attempts were made by authorities to actually combat the growing industry (Rose, 2006). Meanwhile, the number of US citizens participating in online gaming appeared to have skyrocketed during this same period (Holliday, Kelleher, Bradbury, and Crompton, 2010). Starting in 2006, a series of aggressive government moves – mostly led by conservative politicians – sought to pursue gambling operators in this sector much as Earl Warren did with gambling ships a few generations ago. Late in 2010, Capitol Hill legislators (this time led by the more liberal Harry Reid) scrambled to introduce legislation that would settle these matters 'once and for all' – only to find their efforts scuttled as the year came to a close.

Historically gambling and again online gambling in the United States seems both popular (among many gamblers) and highly unpopular (especially among powerful cultural and political conservatives). It feels inevitable, and yet it feels like it may never happen. It seems an obvious direction for one of the world's largest domestic gaming industries, and yet it seems infinitely complex for this direction to be realized. It appears that millions of Americans have voted with their (virtual) feet by participating, while it appears that the federal government, at this stage, has voted no.

These are the uncertainties of the online gambling times in America. In this chapter, we will start by examining key legislative developments associated with Internet gaming, and then we turn our attention from the government to the 'house.' Next, we engage 'the players' in America – those who gamble online (however surreptitiously or carefully). Finally we conclude with a brief discussion of what it means to write a book chapter of this sort on a topic that, by its nature, evolves constantly – thereby threatening to render attempts to capture its contours dated as soon as it is released.

## The government: what part of 'no'… ?

### The Wire Act

In the USA, it all started with the Wire Act, a law that was passed by Congress way back in 1961. Originally designed to address the growing problem of organized crime in America, the act targeted illegal bookies who took bets on sporting events via telephone (Rose, 2006).

The crux of the Wire Act is the following:

> Whoever being engaged in the business of betting or wagering knowingly uses a wire communication facility for the transmission in interstate or foreign commerce of bets or

wagers or information assisting in the placing of bets or wagers on any sporting event or contest, or for the transmission of a wire communication which entitles the recipient to receive money or credit as a result of bets or wagers, or for information assisting in the placing of bets or wagers, shall be fined under this title or imprisoned not more than two years, or both.

(Wire Act, 1961, sec. a)

Though 'wire communication' of the sort that existed in 1961 is long gone, the law's reach lives on. Recently, the United States Department of Justice (DOJ) has invoked this act to support its position that Internet wagering is illegal in the country. Critics of the position taken by the DOJ contend the old law was clearly aimed at crime organizations, and at telephone-based activity (Andrle, 2006). Further, these critics contend, the Wire Act was written and passed in 1961, long before the Internet existed, and hence it seems impossible for the law to apply in any meaningful way to the vast and various forms of Internet wagering today (Rose, 2006).

Challenges to the DOJ, however, have run into stubborn opposition. The Nevada State Legislature passed a bill in 2001 requiring the Nevada Gaming Commission to study the feasibility of online gaming in the state, including provisions that would allow the state to serve a leadership role in an increasingly global gambling landscape. Nevada Governor Kenny Guinn, eager to support the state's key industry, signed this 'server to the world' bill with this future in mind.

In response to this bill, however, the DOJ sent Nevada a stern letter, stating its opposition and reiterating its position that all forms of Internet gambling were covered by the Wire Act. In addition, the Department of Justice threatened to file charges against anyone participating in any form of online gaming, including Nevada casino operators (Rose, 2006). Known informally as the 'What Part of "No" Don't You Understand?' letter, the government's language sounded certain, and certainly sounded punitive.

These were not idle threats. In the wake of these developments came the nation's most famous prosecution of an Internet gaming operator. Jay Cohen, a partner in the Antigua-based World Sports Exchange, was found guilty of violating the Wire Act. No doubt seeking to send a message to other operators, Cohen was then sentenced to 21 months in jail. This case established a precedent that the Wire Act could be used to prosecute online sports betting operations; however, the applicability of the Wire Act to other forms of online gaming remained unclear (Kelly, 2006). For their part, online gamblers in the USA continued to play, but as we will see later, they could not be certain that they were doing so legally.

After the Cohen arrest, the Justice Department again went relatively silent on the issue, until April 15, 2011. This date, which has since become known in the online poker community as Black Friday, saw the Justice Department indict 11 executives from the three largest online poker websites in the world: Full Tilt Poker, PokerStars, and Absolute Poker. Charges against these executives included money laundering, bank fraud, and illegal gambling offenses. Most damaging were allegations that the three companies used fraudulent methods to circumvent the 2006 federal Unlawful Internet Gambling Enforcement Act (UIGEA) and receive billions of dollars from online gamblers in the United States. Often, these operators were said to be quite creative, coding online gambling expenditures as golf ball or jewelry purchases.

In addition to the indictments, the Justice Department seized the Internet addresses of the site, effectively shutting their doors. When a player attempted to access the website, an ominous message appeared: 'This domain name has been seized by the F.B.I.' This move was quite controversial, and widely seen as illegal by the online poker community, because the sites operated out of jurisdictions where online gaming is legal, such as Antigua and the Isle of Man. These actions by the Justice Department prohibited players from withdrawing deposited funds. In the ever-evolving cat-and-mouse game between the federal Justice Department and online players and operators, Black Friday was a major salvo.

### Kyl and friends: a legislative history

As Table 17.1 indicates, the past 15 years have seen a flurry of federal legislative activities in Washington DC – despite the fact that in the USA, gambling has long been viewed as a 'states' rights' issue that the federal government has little business engaging. Of course, given that the Internet by its very nature crosses state lines, this is an issue that many in the federal government believe is theirs, ultimately, to govern.

Jon Kyl, a conservative Republican senator from Arizona, was one of the first US legislators to lead the governmental charge against Internet gaming. Kyl called his first attempt the Internet Gambling Prohibition Act of 1995 (Rose, 2006). In what would become a common practice with Internet gaming, Kyl proposed this ultimately unsuccessful bill as an amendment to the Crime Prevention Act of 1995, an ostensibly noble bill that had nothing to do with online gambling activity (Rose, 2007).

*Table 17.1* Major online gambling legislation in the USA, 1995–2010

| Year introduced | Bill number | Title |
| --- | --- | --- |
| 1995 | N/A | Internet Gambling Prohibition Act |
| 1997 | S. 474 | Internet Gambling Prohibition Act of 1997 |
| 1998 | S. 2260 | Internet Gambling Prohibition Act of 1998 |
| 1998 | H.R. 4350 | Internet Gambling Prohibition Act of 1998 |
| 1998 | H.R. 4427 | Internet Gambling Prohibition Act of 1998 |
| 1999 | S. 692 | Internet Gambling Prohibition Act of 1999 |
| 2000 | H.R. 3125 | Internet Gambling Prohibition Act of 2000 |
| 2000 | H.R. 5020 | Comprehensive Internet Gambling Prohibition Act of 2000 |
| 2000 | H.R. 4419 | Unlawful Internet Gambling Funding Prohibition Act |
| 2001 | H.R. 556 | Leach–Lafalce Internet Gambling Enforcement Act |
| 2002 | S. 3006 | Comprehensive Internet Gambling Prohibition Act of 2002 |
| 2005 | H.R. 4411 | Unlawful Internet Gambling Enforcement Act (UIGEA) |
| 2006 | H.R. 4777 | Internet Gambling Prohibition Act |
| 2007 | H.R. 2046 | Internet Gambling Regulation and Enforcement Act of 2007 |
| 2007 | H.R. 2607 | Internet Gambling Regulation and Tax Enforcement Act of 2007 |
| 2009 | H.R. 2267 | Internet Gambling Regulation, Consumer Protection, and Enforcement Act |
| 2009 | H.R. 2268 | Internet Gambling Regulation and Tax Enforcement Act of 2009 |
| 2009 | S. 1597 | Internet Poker and Game of Skill Regulation, Consumer Protection, and Enforcement Act of 2009 |
| 2010 | H.R. 4976 | Internet Gambling Regulation and Tax Enforcement Act of 2010 |
| 2011 | H.R. 2366 | Internet Gambling Prohibition, Poker Consumer Protection, and Strengthening UIGEA Act of 2011 |

Three years later, the US Senate passed the latest version of Senator Kyl's bill, the Internet Gambling Prohibition Act of 1998. This time, the bill was tacked on as an amendment to The Commerce, Justice, and State Appropriations Bill. Two of Kyl's allies in the House of Representatives, Congressman Robert Goodlatte and Congressman Frank LoBiondo, both conservative Republicans, introduced a companion bill in the US House of Representatives. This bill was submitted, but was never voted on; hence, despite the Senate passing the Internet Gambling Prohibition Act, the bill never was enacted into law (Congressional Research Service, 1998).

Undaunted, Senator Kyl continued his crusade the following year in the 106th US Congress. Once again, the Senate passed the Internet Gambling Prohibition Act ('of 1999' this time). This version was less ambitious than previous bills introduced by Kyl. Specifically, it did not set out provisions for criminal punishments for individual bettors, which was an important concession to an online betting public that was largely confused and resentful about the federal government's intervention in this activity. Instead, this version sought to punish only the operators of online gaming sites (Andrle, 2006). Over in the House, Congressman Goodlatte introduced a similar bill with the same name (Congressional Research Service, 2001).

Interestingly, at this stage several Republican Congressmen broke with their party and opposed this bill. While unclear at the time to observers, a Washington DC lobbyist who would ultimately come to represent all that was nefarious about government lobbying effectively killed the bill (Schmidt and Grimaldi, 2005). During this period, the conservative lobbyist Jack Abramoff advocated on behalf of eLottery, Inc., a client that wanted to sell state lottery tickets online in the USA. Of course, if these bills prohibiting online gaming were passed, Abramoff's client would be out of business. Abramoff had notoriously close ties to top Republican Party officials: for instance, then-party leader Tom DeLay referred to Abramoff as 'one of my closest and dearest friends' (Harding, 2005). Unsurprisingly, Abramoff convinced several members of the Republican Party to oppose the online gambling prohibition legislation. Later, it emerged that Abramoff secured many of these votes with lavish trips for these same lawmakers (Schmidt and Grimaldi, 2005), and Abramoff ultimately pled guilty to corrupting public officials (Schmidt and Grimaldi, 2006). Against the backdrop of this scandal, these bills had no chance of passing, and the lifespan of this legislation was extended into middle age.

The legislative battles continued on Capitol Hill, of course. After these defeats, similar bills were introduced in the 107th and 108th Congresses, sponsored by Senator Kyl, Congressman Goodlatte, and Congressman Jim Leach, another conservative Republican. These bills all had the same intended purpose; however, they went about achieving their goals differently. Some sought to outlaw Internet gaming by making it illegal for operators to operate. Others proposed making it illegal for players to play. Some simply sought to clarify the Wire Act to include online gaming as an activity that was strictly prohibited. Finally, conservative legislators proposed attacking the issue from a financial payment angle, setting the stage for the highly influential, awkwardly acronymed Unlawful Internet Gambling Enforcement Act, or UIGEA (Congressional Research Service, 2001).

## Turn out the lights, the party's...? The Unlawful Internet Gambling Enforcement Act

Without question the nation's most far-reaching piece of legislation on online gambling passed in 2006. On October 13 of that year, President Bush signed the Security and

Accountability for Every Port Act (SAFE Port Act) into law (H.R. 4954, 2006). This bill was passed in the final minutes before Congress adjourned for the 2006 elections (Rose, 2007). Among other things, this Act required that imported containers traveling through US ports be scanned for radiation to help prevent a nightmarish terrorist attack, which was a cause that American politicians of all stripes could easily rally around (Malone, 2006).

The SAFE Port Act finds itself with a front row seat to the online gaming debates because UIGEA was attached as Title VIII. The versions of the SAFE Port Act passed by the house on May 4, 2006 (by a vote of 421–22), and the Senate on September 14, 2006 (by a vote of 98–0), contained no language related to Internet gaming. However, members of the House and Senate got together, after the initial vote, to make changes to each body's versions of the SAFE Port Act. During conference, UIGEA was added to the modified bill. The reading of the conference report was waived and the House passed the final version by a vote of 409–2 and the Senate by a unanimous consent motion (H.R. 4954). According to Senator Frank Lautenberg of New Jersey, nobody on the conference committee had read the final language. Subsequent accounts claim that many members did not know what was in the final bill (Kelly, 2009; Rose, 2007).

At this point, it is important to understand the political atmosphere that existed on Capitol Hill in the summer and fall of 2006. Republicans had controlled both houses of Congress since 1994, when the conservative party swept to victory after Bill Clinton's 1992 presidential election. By 2006, however, the party was plagued by rumors of corruption, and major news organizations and polls were reporting that the Republicans could lose their majorities in both houses of Congress (Election 2006, 2006). During this time, most of the allegations of corruption centered around one lobbyist: the now infamous Jack Abramoff. Fearing defeat, Republicans decided to campaign on social issues to energize the base of their party, unveiling what they called the American Values Agenda. This Agenda included 10 points of party values – and among them was the prohibition of Internet gaming, right alongside a ban on gay marriage and a ban on stem cell research (Preston, 2006).

Hence, the gaming industry as a whole became an unwilling poster child for the actions of Jack Abramoff (Schmidt and Grimaldi, 2005, 2006). In the summer of 2006, the Abramoff scandal was still fairly fresh in the minds of voters, and Republican lawmakers in tough re-election contests recognized the need to present an anti-corruption stance and to distance themselves from the scandal as much as possible (Weisman, 2006). Against this backdrop, it was understandable that the party decided to include the prohibition of online gaming as part of their American Values Agenda.

### *Out of my house: political responses to UIGEA*

In 2009, Congressman Barney Frank (a Democrat from Massachusetts), a politician whose liberal leanings bordered upon libertarianism (especially when it came to the government dictating what Americans could do with their free time) introduced legislation that set out to address what might be called the 'UIGEA era' in the USA. The Internet Gambling Regulation, Consumer Protection, and Enforcement Act (H.R. 2267, 2009) proposed a system to license and regulate online gaming. This was not the first time Congressman Frank had weighed in on the online gaming issue. On April 26, 2007, Frank introduced the Internet Gambling Regulation and Enforcement Act (House Financial Services Committee Press Release, 2007). This bill sought to overturn UIGEA and set up a regulatory system to license Internet gaming operators in the United States. A companion bill was sponsored by Congressman Jim McDermott, a Democrat from Washington (Cypra, 2009).

In a spirit similar to that of Australia's recent Productivity Commission recommendation that online gambling be legalized in that country, Congressman Frank's position held that prohibition was a failure. Instead, he felt the unintended victims were American consumers, who were left vulnerable to fraudulent (or at least unregulated and untaxed) business practices. For instance, safeguards to protect against underage or pathological gambling were spotty. And no tax revenues, of course, were generated from this activity despite its role as an increasing commercial giant. Finally, Frank also contended that a complete prohibition of Internet gambling represents an interference with personal liberties of American citizens, claiming that 'the existing legislation is an inappropriate interference on the personal freedom of Americans and this interference should be undone' (House Financial Services Committee Press Release, 2007: 1).

Frank's bill sought to regulate Internet gaming to address these very issues (House Financial Services Committee Press Release, 2007). Despite the defeat of this bill in committee, Congressmen Frank continued fighting to repeal UIGEA and to legalize online gaming. So, on May 6, 2009, Frank introduced the Internet Gambling Regulation, Consumer Protection, and Enforcement Act. The bill was debated and amended on July 29, 2010, in the House Financial Services Committee, which is chaired by Congressman Frank (Batt, 2010). The bill was voted favorably out of committee, by a vote of 41–22. The bill received some bipartisan support; however, the vote fell primarily along party lines with Democrats voting for the bill and Republicans opposing the bill (Batt, 2010).

At this point, once again, it is important to understand the political atmosphere on Capitol Hill during this period – in the summer and fall of 2010. Interestingly, the Democrats found themselves in exactly the same position as the Republicans did back in the summer of 2006. In 2006, polls and media reports speculated that Republicans would lose control of both houses of Congress (Election 2006, 2006); in 2010, meanwhile, polls and media reports speculated that Democrats would lose control of both houses (Newport, 2010). In 2006, Republicans faced staunch opposition from Democratic voters because of controversial policies of the Bush administration and the Republican Congress, including the wars in Iraq and Afghanistan. In 2010, Democrats faced impassioned opposition from Republican voters because of controversial policies of the Obama administration and the Democratic Congress, including the health-care reform and the stimulus bill (Gardner, Thompson, and Rucker, 2010). Ultimately, the Democrats kept control of the Senate but lost control of the House in 2010. We might say that the political atmosphere remained stable – stably divisive, and stably uncertain.

The saga that kept political pundits salivating during the 2010 election cycle was the fate of the Senate Majority Leader, Harry Reid (a Democrat). Reid happens to hail from Nevada, and was completing his fourth term as a US Senator – after a long political career that actually included stints as a state gaming regulator and as a two-term member of the US House of Representatives. As a skilled and experienced political operative, Reid rose through the ranks of his party to become the minority leader of the Senate in 2005, and then Nevada's senator took on the role of majority leader when the Democratic Party took control of the Senate in the 2006 elections.

By 2010, however, Reid was not a popular figure in his home state or on the national scene. Reid faced stiff competition from Sharron Angle, a darling of the conservative Tea Party. Angle rode the nation's anti-incumbent wave to an upset in the Republican primary, and polls showed her and Reid running in a statistical dead heat leading up to the November election. Reid enlisted the help of prominent Nevadans, including high-ranking casino executives, in his re-election bid. Many of these executives, including Jim Murren, CEO of

MGM Resorts, are registered Republicans, but supported Reid because of his powerful position in the Senate and his consequent ability to advance their interests. These endorsements by the often conservative business community were critical in Reid's re-election campaign.

Reid won the election by a narrow margin. His high-ranking supporters, including several executives from major gaming companies, supported overturning UIGEA and legalizing online gaming. It was an open secret that Reid had long opposed legalization, as he was not convinced in his regulator heart that this was an activity that could be effectively regulated. After his election, however, his position shifted, and his office began drafting a bill with the intent of legalizing and regulating online poker only. Rumors quickly spread, throughout Capitol Hill and the gaming industry, that Reid would attach an amendment to larger legislation legalizing online gaming, just as the Republicans had done in 2006 to pass UIGEA.

This bill was similar to the Frank bill in terms of intent; however, some details of the legislation were quite different. The Reid bill stipulated that only established gaming companies and race tracks could compete in the online marketplace for up to two years after the legislation was enacted. This gave current operators (including Reid supporters like MGM Resorts) a significant market advantage. Additionally, Reid's bill called for the licensing and regulating of the industry to be outsourced to certain individual states, limiting the role of the federal government – a concession to a gaming industry that wanted the US government out of its business.

Reid faced opposition from the usual Republican adversaries. Senator Kyl served notice that he would block any bill that included the online gaming attachment. Senator Mitch McConnell, the Senate Minority leader, sent a letter to Reid strongly stating his opposition to online poker legislation. Ultimately, the Republican opposition proved too formidable to overcome, and Reid was unsuccessful. The Senate adjourned, the week before Christmas 2010, without passing any legislation legalizing online gaming.

As Republican opposition appeared to doom the movement to legalize and regulate online poker, an unlikely hero emerged for proponents of the game. This unlikely hero was Rep. Joe Barton (a Republican from Texas). In June 2011 Barton introduced the Internet Gambling Prohibition, Poker Consumer Protection, and Strengthening UIGEA Act of 2011. This bill is substantively similar to the bill Senator Reid failed to get passed in December 2010. Barton, who up until this point had best been known around Capitol Hill as the Congressman who apologized to BP after the horrific 2010 Gulf of Mexico oil spill, is an unlikely, but crucial, ally for proponents of Internet poker. Barton has served in the House of Representatives since 1985 and is known on the Hill as a rank-and-file Republican.

The logical route for Barton's bill to travel would be through the House Financial Services Committee, the same committee that debated the Frank bill. As Republicans regained control of the House of Representatives in January 2011, the path to law for the Barton bill is convoluted. The House Financial Services Committee is now chaired by Rep. Spencer Bachus (a Republican from Alabama). Bachus has made his distaste for regulating online poker well known, and would not have an appetite for debating the bill in his committee. Each respective committee chairman has the absolute authority to set their committee's schedule; therefore, Bachus could simply not schedule debate on the bill, and the bill would die. Another possible committee to debate the bill is the House Judiciary Committee. This committee is chaired by Rep. Lamar Smith (a Republican from Texas). Smith's feelings on Internet poker mirror those of Rep. Bachus. Rep. Barton is the Chairman Emeritus of the House Energy and Commerce Committee. While he does not carry any official capacity to schedule a bill for mark-up, his position does curry favor with the Chairman, Rep. Fred Upton (a Republican from Michigan). Given the general Republican opposition to online poker, Barton's involvement will be crucial in moving the bill forward.

## The post-American world: the United States as (deposed and defeated?) Goliath

The twenty-first-century political landscape promises glimpses, at the very least, of what Zakaria (2008) calls a 'post-American world.' Zakaria does not argue that America is no longer a power – he simply claims this name for the chapter that comes after the 'American world' that dominated the recent international socio-political scenery. If Zakaria is right, the gaming industry is serving as a 'mirror' of sorts, reflecting American society in both its subtle and tectonic shifts.

A David-and-Goliath dispute over online gambling between the USA and Antigua illustrates this landscape well, and provides an interesting look at what the future may hold for some sectors in the US-based commercial sector. This dispute took place in the World Trade Organization (WTO), and its rulings constituted a legitimate (but ultimately ignored) defeat for US interests. Remarkably, all this happened because of online gambling.

In 2003, Antigua initiated the WTO dispute resolution process, claiming the United States violated the General Agreements on Trade in Services (GATS) by prohibiting online gaming (Faust, 2005). GATS is an international treaty to encourage WTO members to trade in things other than tangible products. Antigua claimed Internet gaming was a service; therefore, the US ban on the industry was a violation of GATS (Kelly, 2006).

The Internet, of course, has a way of transforming Davids quickly – and before the Goliaths seem to notice. The United States was, and is, one of the most powerful members of the WTO. Meanwhile, Antigua was an island nation with approximately 69,500 residents and less than 443 square miles of land (Wohl, 2009). They were, however, large enough to house a formidable Internet gaming industry, and one that led to a legitimate challenge of the world's largest economy.

In support of their claim, Antigua contended that the Wire Act, Travel Act, Anti-Gambling Business Act, and over a hundred other US federal and state measures violated GATS (Kelly, 2006). In 2004, a WTO dispute resolution panel ruled in Antigua's favor. The United States filed an appeal that claimed, among other defenses, that the country was morally opposed to online gaming. Interestingly, this moral clause was traditionally reserved for religious concerns. For instance, predominantly Muslim nations were able to forbid the free trade of alcohol. On appeal, the moral clause defense was rejected, and the original ruling was upheld (Wohl, 2009).

The WTO ruling required the United States to change its online gambling laws, so that it would not be in violation of GATS. With increasingly little appetite for international organizations like the WTO and the United Nations, however, the Bush administration did not exactly race to comply. In 2007, a WTO panel declared that the United States was not complying with the body's decision. Rather than change its laws and positions with regards to online gaming, the United States proceeded to withdraw from its commitments under GATS. Under the terms of this withdrawal, the USA was required to compensate any countries affected. Australia, Canada, Costa Rica, the European Union, India, Japan, and Macau filed claims against the USA, citing financial damage because of US withdrawal from its requirements under GATS (Wohl, 2009). The Bush administration quietly settled claims with several of these countries. Requests were made both by the press and by members of Congress for disclosure of the settlement agreements, but the Bush administration refused (Polson, 2008b). In its refusal, the administration cited 'national security,' which was a popular political trick at the time. In a letter to the administration, Congressman Frank, ever the critic of the conservatives and Bush, implied that denial of the request appeared to be a political decision, so as not to reveal information that might reflect poorly on the nation's power and might (Polson, 2008a).

## The (gambling) house: business and financial considerations

Meanwhile, US-based casino operators have observed these legislative processes with more than casual interest. From their perspective, online gaming seems an inevitability, and one that can offer these companies a lucrative opportunity to expand their offerings from the bricks-and-mortar space into a virtual one. Today, the gaming industry fears that it might suffer the same fate as the US newspaper industry. Newspapers first scoffed and dismissed the Internet's threat, and then later fought the expansion of its product into online settings – only to lose spectacularly in the end, another Goliath slain.

What kinds of financial impacts might we expect from an American legalization process? At a macro-economic level, legalization could be significant business in the USA. While online gaming revenue declined in 2007 after the passage of UIGEA (from US$6 billion in 2006 to US$4 billion in 2007), this online gambling recession was short-lived. Revenues from US customers rose in 2008 to US$5 billion, and in 2009, they rose again to US$5.1 billion. This increase took place, of course, during the Great Recession, which caused overall US gaming industry revenues to fall precipitously during this very same period (Holliday et al., 2010). In this environment, the US gaming industry is quick to note that whatever the tax rate might be for online gambling in a legalized American environment, it would yield substantial dollars. During a macro-economic time, when such funds are desperately needed, this kind of revenue could provide a tax windfall for both federal and state governments.

Given the current landscape, it is a fairly straightforward exercise to examine who the major operational players in the USA might be. These include major Las Vegas-based operators such as Las Vegas Sands, Wynn Resorts, MGM Resorts, Boyd Gaming, Station Casinos/Fertitta Gaming, and Harrah's/Caesars (the latter owns the 'World Series of Poker' brand and stands to gain from this affiliation). In addition, many companies throughout the online gaming supply chain will also find themselves with new business opportunities should the activity be legalized. For instance, online gaming operators will need to invest heavily in technological platforms that can cope with a high volume of players. Given the amount of money wagered, a reliable technology is imperative, as any system glitches have the potential to result in an enormous amount of lost revenue (and reputation).

The business costs at the outset will be weighted heavily toward marketing, in an effort to catch up with international brands that have had a head start. Given the need to rush to the market, US-based casino companies will most likely form partnerships with companies that can quickly and reliably produce the needed marketing technology. Hence, online gaming might well lead to new revenue streams for these kinds of companies as well.

Other potential partnership opportunities will arise depending on stipulations in the law. For instance, if they are allowed, a partnership between a 'name brand' US casino company and a current offshore online gaming company could benefit both parties. The offshore company would then have access to the US market and the brand recognition. For its part, the US company would be given access to the industry knowledge, experience, and technology of the offshore operator.

All this, of course, depends on whether the law and regulators will allow US companies to engage in partnerships with entities that may, in some eyes, have committed crimes of a gaming nature – the worst sin on the gaming regulatory books. Many operators have been breaking US law by offering online gaming for play in the USA, in violation of UIGEA.

Some companies have repeatedly ignored US demands that they cease and desist operations in the USA (including, most prominently, PokerStars and Full Tilt). Nor have they been punished for these acts; in fact, these companies, partly due to their open disregard for US policy, have become massively profitable industry leaders.

Other companies, most famously Party Gaming, have chosen to comply with US laws and pull out of the US market. Party Gaming did not initially withdraw from the US market, and was issued a complaint by the US Department of Justice. The complaint was settled, with Party Gaming agreeing to a $105 million settlement and agreeing to behave. This sets the table for an interesting set of dilemmas and distinctions: if the law ultimately allows for offshore partnerships, but not with companies who have broken US law, Party Gaming and other compliant companies will benefit.

Another 'winner' should legalized online gaming be realized could well be the battered US banking industry. By targeting financial transactions on online gambling sites, UIGEA scared most major US banking institutions from processing gambling payments. A newly legalized US market would presumably allow players to seamlessly transfer money from their bank accounts to online gaming companies. These transfers provide a lucrative revenue stream for banks, which will likely charge either one-time transfer fees or percentage transfer fees. Given the projections for future revenues of a legalized online gaming industry, small fees imposed by banks will result in a great deal of additional revenue for banking institutions initiating those transfers.

Finally, some of the most compelling actors on this stage come from surprising places – specifically, non-gaming companies that already have access to massive databases of Internet-based consumers. As is the case throughout the twenty-first-century economy, database management dictates the play: he who has the data, and she who manages the data well, usually 'wins.' Due to the importance of these databases, and the obvious need to design consumer-friendly websites, a number of familiar technology companies might well leap into the competitive fray.

For instance, US-based Facebook is a company that will play an important role in this industry. Facebook has immediate access to over 500 million users – a massive 'nation' of its own. Further, the company does not have to spend marketing dollars to grow that database; it does so naturally as people flock to its website. Even if Facebook does not choose to enter the online gaming market, the company would be a valuable third-party partner for any company that does compete for online gaming customers. For their part, traditional gaming operators must consider how to best compete with, or partner with companies that have had little to do with the traditional US gaming industry. The winds of uncertainty, in this case, might well make for previously inconceivable bedfellows.

## The players: social, demographic, and sociological insights on those who gamble online in the USA

In this final section, we turn our attention away from the 'law and order' side, and away from the 'house' side. Now, we will focus on the 'player' side, and seek to provide some complementary insights alongside those developed throughout the rest of this book. Unfortunately, given that relatively few scientific studies of US online gambling behavior exist, and given the uncertain statuses outlined in the rest of this chapter, the final summary statement of the American online gambler has yet to be written. However, we can examine the extant data to gain a few insights into the lives of these online players.

*US Internet gambling prevalence and demographics*

On the matter of prevalence, only a handful of studies have explored US Internet gambling rates with a representative sample. Some of these are major national studies – for instance, one was sponsored by the gaming industry's American Gaming Association (AGA, 2006), some have been carried out by major public polling firms (e.g., Taylor, Funk, and Craighill, 2006), and some have been published in the peer-reviewed literature.

The AGA's study found a past-year online gambling prevalence rate of 4 percent in 2006 – notably, just prior to the historical moment when UIGEA took effect. Meanwhile, the 2002 survey yielded a past-year rate of 0.3 percent (Welte et al., 2002). Taylor, Funk, and Craighill (2006) identified what appears to be a similar increase in online gambling: in 2006, 2 percent of Americans had placed bets on the Internet in the past year, which was up from a 1 percent figure that was recorded in 1996. Of course, methodologically speaking, Americans would have sound legal reasons to deny that they engage in online gambling, even if researchers provide assurances of confidentiality. As such, there is reason to suspect that some false negatives may emerge in this research field. Whatever the case, these figures seem low when compared with those observed in the UK, where in 2010 14 percent of citizens had placed an online wager in the past year (Wardle et al., 2011).

What do these Internet gamblers look like? Some representative surveys suggest that online gamblers appear to be younger, male, wealthier, and better educated – a finding that may not seem odd at first glance, but that places them in interesting demographic terrain (Bernhard, Lucas, and Shampaner, 2008). Specifically, these demographics place this group squarely consistent with the research literature on new technology adopters. In general, research suggests that people who adopt new technologies tend to be younger, male, more educated, and with a greater income than those who do not adopt (Danko and MacLachlan, 1983; Darian 1987; Gatignon and Robertson, 1991; Greco and Fields, 1991; Sim and Koi, 2002; Zeithaml and Gilly, 1987). Further, in looking at new technology adopters, Rogers (1983) identified five adopter categories: Innovators, Early Adopters, Early Majority, Late Majority, and Laggards. According to Rogers, Early Adopters play a key role in getting an innovation to the point of critical mass and widescale acceptance – or what Malcolm Gladwell (2000) would famously call a 'Tipping Point.'

Hence, while it certainly appears that we have not yet reached a tipping point for Internet gambling in the United States, the trends thus far definitely look familiar to those who have studied new technology adoption. This is not, as yet, a widespread recreational activity in the USA, but if history and the scientific literature are any guide, it could well be. In the future, it will be important to explore the degree to which these typologies and theories actually play out in online gambling spaces throughout the country.

*Yes we can or no we can't? Perceptions of legality in the USA*

Let us delve a bit more deeply – and differently – into the lives of these US online gamblers. Given the complexities of the legal status, and given that operators (but not gamblers) have faced scrutiny and prosecution, how do Americans interpret this landscape? Revealingly, the clear answer for most, it would seem, is that they are profoundly unclear. When asked whether online gambling was 'legal,' 'illegal,' or 'unclear,' more than half (53.7 percent) those surveyed in a recent study indicated that they were unclear on the current legal status. Meanwhile, nearly 17 percent said that they felt online gambling was legal, while 29.5 percent deemed it illegal (Bernhard, Lucas, and Shampaner, 2008). This finding underscores the fluidity and uncertainty surrounding Internet gambling in the USA today, and in itself reveals much about this chapter in the history of online gambling.

Because so many respondents seemed to be unclear on the legal status of the act, qualitative data help elaborate upon the nuances of these uncertainties (Bernhard, Lucas, and Shampaner, 2008). When probed on this topic of whether the activity was legal or illegal, Americans' responses might be characterized – to invoke the current political vocabulary in the USA – as '(Sarah) Palin-esque.' Listen as respondents hem, haw, stumble, ponder, and wonder about the status of the activity:

> 'I think it's semi-illegal.'
>
> 'It's basically – I thought (online gambling sites) were basically taken down. But there's still ways of doing it and I'm not quite sure how.'
>
> 'I think that it's – my understanding of it is that it's legal, but it's kind of like they're skirting on the illegal.'
>
> 'I think it's in kind of a gray area. It's not completely illegal because you can do the offshore thing, and there's just so many like – it's illegal this, it's illegal that.'
>
> 'It's not – it's illegal but it's also not, so that's my feeling on it, it's kind of in a gray area. It's semi-illegal, or it's semi-legal' (laughs).
>
> 'My understanding is that it's not necessarily that you can't gamble online, but the transfer of funds – the withdrawal or transfer of funds is illegal. If you can't play for money, though, what's the point? As soon as the government has a way to tax it, it'll be back up, though.'
>
> 'I'm under the impression that legal law is that you cannot gamble online, however, the enforcement of it I don't think is of interest to them right now.'
>
> 'Um, I believe that there's an unenforced law about online gambling, but I know the most recent legislation is strictly focused on the banks and money transfers.'
>
> 'Um, right now it is my understanding that any form of gambling on the Internet in the USA is illegal, I don't know if that applies to servers that are you know, located in other countries, as to the way I understand it, that's not legal now. As far as I see it, it is illegal in the country to gamble online.'
>
> 'Maybe.'
>
> 'It's a gray area.'
>
> 'It's…in transition. I would think yes, it's still illegal, but I don't think it's dead.'

Typically, qualitative data help crystallize the uncertainties of large-scale quantitative data, by providing depth and detail to one-dimensional information. However, when we listen closely to these qualitative voices, it becomes clear that things are very unclear for Americans – at least as it pertains to online gambling. And as we have seen, there is much to drive this confusion in the USA. In a country where the federal government has stayed out of the gambling debates, we have seen the feds storm actively onto the online gambling scene. American online gamblers wonder whether their wagers might be lost (even when they win), and whether often-libertarian American governmental impulses will be rejected in favor of interventionism. Once again, it would appear that uncertainty reigns for Americans, and in a manner that reflects the broader lack of clarity on this issue in the USA. Though US online gamblers continue to play with many of their domestic and international counterparts, and with many of their US dollars, their fate as legal (or illegal) animals remains murky in their own minds.

## Concluding thoughts

In closing, when conducting research on online gambling in the USA, we must remember that research is (always) conducted during moments in history, and these moments inevitably affect our findings. To be quite candid, our concern as authors is that this chapter will be dated soon after it is released. This is always the challenge when attempting to track the rapidly evolving world of twenty-first-century culture and politics. In experimental design research, this is called a 'history effect,' and it is hardly insignificant here.

Despite these challenges, we are of a mind that the future of online gambling in the USA might be clarified with a simple exercise. Imagine, for a moment, the future: 20 years from the moment of this writing. We will choose January 1, 2031 as our precise point of reference. Let us also imagine what gambling in America will look like then, given the momentum of various developments on the national gambling scene today. If we do this – if we close our eyes for a moment and think about what will certainly be a cashless world where information, technology, and recreation are all floating around us via increasingly sophisticated 'clouds' of activity – it is impossible to imagine that the Internet (or whatever the Internet 'is' in 20 years) will be less important than it is today. Similarly, it is impossible to imagine a gambling world 20 years ahead of us without the omnipresence of the Internet. Even in the face of today's uncertainties, we contend that the future is far more certain than the past has been.

## References

American Gaming Association (AGA). (2006). 'Gambling and the Internet. 2006 AGA Survey of Casino Entertainment'. Author. Retrieved from http://www.americangaming.org/newsroom/press-releases/new-aga-survey-offers-depth-profile-us-internet-gamblers

Andrle, J. (2006). 'A winning hand: A proposal for an international regulatory schema with respect to the growing online gambling dilemma in the United States'. *UNLV Gaming Research & Review Journal*, *10*(1), 59–93.

Batt, T. (2010, July 29). 'House committee votes decisively for Internet gambling'. Retrieved from http://www.gamblingcompliance.com/node/43808

Bernhard, B. J., Lucas, A. F., and Shampaner, E. (2008). 'Internet gambling in Nevada'. University of Nevada, Las Vegas International Gaming Institute.

Congressional Research Service. (1998, September 14). 'Internet gambling: A sketch of legislative proposals (with appendix)'. Washington, DC: Charles Doyle.

— (2001, January 11). 'Internet gambling: A sketch of legislative proposals in the 106th Congress'. Washington, DC: Charles Doyle.

Cypra, D. (2009, May 7). 'McDermott introduces Internet gambling tax act'. Retrieved from http://www.pokernewsdaily.com/jim-mcdermott-introduces-Internet-gambling-tax-act-2350/

Danko, W. D., and MacLachlan, J. M. (1983). 'Research to accelerate the diffusion of a new innovation: The case of personal computers'. *Journal of Advertising*, 23, 39–43.

Darian, J. C. (1987). 'In-home shopping: Are there consumer segments?' *Journal of Retailing*, 63, 163–86.

Election 2006. (2006). 'Polling Report.com'. Retrieved from http://www.pollingreport.com/2006a.htm

Faust, F. (2005). 'WTO ruling puts United States in awkward position'. *International Gaming & Wagering*, *26*(1), 18–21.

Gardner, A., Thompson, K., and Rucker, P. (2010, August 29). 'Beck, Palin tell thousands to "Restore America"'. *Washington Post*. Retrieved from http://www.washingtonpost.com/wp-dyn/content/article/2010/08/28/AR2010082801106.html

Gatignon, H., and Robertson, T. S. (1991). *Handbook of Consumer Behavior*, Englewood Cliffs, NJ: Prentice Hall.

Gladwell, M. (2000). 'The tipping point: How little things can make a big difference'. New York: Little Brown.

Greco, A. J., and Fields, D. M. (1991). 'Profiling early triers of service innovations: A look at interactive home video ordering services', *Journal of Service Marketing*, 5, 19–26.

Harding, J. (2005, April 7). 'Jack Abramoff: The friend Tom DeLay can't shake'. *Slate*. Retrieved from http://www.slate.com/id/2116389/

Holliday, S., Kelleher, G., Bradbury, M., and Crompton, J. (2010). 'United States: Regulated Internet gambling economic impact assessment'. Retrieved from H2 Gambling Capital.

House Financial Services Committee Press Release. (2007, April 26). 'Frank introduces Internet Gambling Regulation and Enforcement Act of 2007'. House Financial Services Committee.

H.R. 4954, (2006) *109 Cong., Cong. Rec. H8540–69 (2006)* (enacted).

H.R. 2267, (2009) *Internet Gambling Regulation Consumer Protection, and Enforcement Act, H.R. 2267, 111 Cong. (2009)*.

Kelly, J. (2006). 'Clash in the Caribbean: Antigua and U.S. dispute Internet gambling and GATS'. *UNLV Gaming Research & Review Journal*, 10(1), 15–19.

— (2009, November 3). 'Financial transaction providers needn't worry too much about complying with UIGEA rules'. *Gaming Law Review & Economics*, 13(3), 196–201. doi:10.1089/glre.2009.13302.

Malone, R. (2006, October 13). 'Bush signs safe port act'. *Forbes*. Retrieved from http://www.forbes.com/2006/10/13/safe-ports-act-biz-logistics-cx_rm_1013ports.html

Moehring, E., and Green, M. (2005). *Las Vegas: A Centennial History*. Reno: University of Nevada Press.

Newport, F. (2010, September 27). 'Midterm election landscape still points to republican gains'. Retrieved from http://www.gallup.com/poll/143243/Midterm-Election-Landscape-Points-Republican-Gains.aspx

Polson, S. (2008a, April 2). 'Congressmen request trade settlement details'. Retrieved from http://www.pokerlistings.com/group-sues-government-for-wto-info-27079

— (2008b, May 21). 'Group sues government for settlement info'. Retrieved from http://www.pokerlistings.com/frank-paul-request-gats-agreement-24836

Preston, M. (2006, June 28). 'House GOP promotes its "American Values Agenda"'. CNN. Retrieved from http://articles.cnn.com/2006-06-28/politics/mg.thu_1_marriage-amendment-items-expression-of-religion-act?_s = PM:POLITICS

Richtel, M. (2001, March 29). 'The casino on the desktop; bettors, veteran or novice, find the lure of online gambling hard to resist'. *New York Times*. Retrieved from http://www.nytimes.com/2001/03/29/technology/casino-desktop-bettors-veteran-novice-find-lure-online-gambling-hard-resist.html

Rogers, E. M. (1983). *Diffusions of Innovations* (3rd ed.). NY: The Free Press.

Rose, I. (2006). 'Gambling and the law: An introduction to the law of Internet gambling'. *UNLV Gaming Research & Review Journal*, 10(1), 1–14.

— (2007). 'Gambling and the law: The Unlawful Internet Gambling Enforcement Act of 2006 analyzed'. *UNLV Gaming Research & Review Journal*, 11(1), 53–6.

Schmidt, S., and Grimaldi, J. V. (2005, October 16). 'How a lobbyist stacked the deck'. *Washington Post*. Retrieved from http://www.washingtonpost.com/wp-dyn/content/article/2005/10/15/AR2005101501539.html

Schmidt, S., and Grimaldi, J. V (2006, January 4). 'Abramoff pleads guilty to 3 counts'. *Washington Post*. Retrieved from http://www.washingtonpost.com/wp-dyn/content/article/2006/01/03/AR2006010300474.html

Schwartz, D. (2005). 'Cutting the wire: Gambling prohibition and the Internet'. Reno: University of Nevada Press

Sim, L.L., and Koi, S.M. (2002). 'Singapore's Internet shoppers and their impact on traditional shopping patterns', *Journal of Retailing and Consumer Service*, 9, 115–24.

Taylor, P., Funk, C., and Craighill, P. (2006, May 23). 'Gambling: as the take rises, so does public concern'. Pew Research Center. Retrieved from http://peoplepress.org/category/publications/

Wardle, H., Moody, A., Spence, A., Orford, J., Volberg, R., Jotangia, D., et al. (2011). 'British Gambling Prevalence Survey 2010'. National Centre for Social Research. Prepared for the UK Gambling Commission.

Weisman, J. (2006, January 4). 'GOP leaders seek distance from Abramoff'. *Washington Post.* Retrieved from http://www.washingtonpost.com/wp-dyn/content/article/2006/01/03/AR2006010 301609.html

Welte, J. W., Barnes, G. M., Wieczorek, W. F., Tidwell, M. C., and Parker, J. (2002). 'Gambling participation in the U.S. – results from a national survey'. *Journal of Gambling Studies, 18*(4), 313–37. doi:10.1023/A:1021019915591

Wire Act, (1961) *18 U.S.C. § 1084* (1961).

Wohl, I. (2009, July). 'The Antigua–United States gambling dispute'. *Journal of International Commerce and Economics.*

Zakaria, F. (2008). *The Post-American World.* New York: W. W. Norton.

Zeithaml, V. A., and Gilly, M. C. (1987). 'Characteristics affecting the acceptance of retailing technologies: A comparison of elderly and nonelderly consumers'. *Journal of Retailing, 63*, 49–68.

# 18 Internet gambling and the Kahnawà:ke First Nation

*Yale D. Belanger*

## Introduction

In June 1996, the Kahnawà:ke Mohawk community south of Montreal established the Kahnawà:ke Gaming Commission (KGC) pursuant to the provisions of their Kahnawà:ke Gaming Law. The legislation dictates that Kahnawà:ke is a sovereign nation and, as such, has jurisdiction over issuing gaming licenses for lottery schemes, including online gambling sites. By January 1999, Mohawk Internet Technologies (MIT) was established as an e-gaming website to host online gambling sites on servers located on Kahnawà:ke land. Embroiled from the start in a debate regarding its operational legality, attention has in recent years shifted to the KGC's inability to provide the regulatory oversight it proudly proclaimed as its distinguishing feature. At one time the host of the largest number of international online gambling sites, Kahnawà:ke in 2011 was hosting roughly half that number, and had been the focus of two uncomplimentary reports resulting from a joint *60 Minutes–Washington Post* investigation into online cheating. Loto-Quebec's recent entry into the world of online gambling has also complicated matters, by directly pitting provincial economic interests with Kahnawà:ke's. The following chapter details these and other events that have come to embody Kahnawà:ke's rise from impoverished First Nation, clinging to historic claims of self-determination, to a leader in the ever-changing and increasingly competitive world of online gaming, that now demands both the KGC and MIT rehabilitate a sullied reputation. The first step is to elaborate the jurisdictional and legal setting from which the Kahnawà:ke online operations emerged.

## Internet gambling in Canada

Prior to 2001, foreign online casino operators seeking to expand their client base considered Canada an open jurisdiction, due to its poor legal and policy regime related to virtual gambling. Commenting in 2000, Bear Stearns, at the time one of the largest global investment banks and securities-trading and brokerage firms, criticized Canada's faulty legal scaffold: 'Because Canadian law regarding on-line gambling is as unclear as US law, groups are beginning to test authorities by setting up on both sides of the US–Canada border.' Three specific problems were identified in the company's report examining Internet gaming. First, any Canadian could potentially access gaming action over the Internet, even those sites operating outside Canada. Second, enforcement of the *Criminal Code of Canada* to censure out-of-country online gaming operations would be exceptionally difficult. Finally, upon verification of a clear connection between domestic participation in online gambling and the Internet casino operators, how the *Criminal Code* would specifically apply was far from clear (Bear Stearns, 2000).

Greater clarity followed the *Starnet* decision. A Delaware-based Internet software development company operating in Canada, Starnet Communications International, Inc. (SCI) and its various subsidiaries were incorporated in Antigua, where online gaming was legal and where SCI had an online gaming license. One subsidiary located in Vancouver, British Columbia, was responsible for website administration. Employing nearly 100 people, the Vancouver subsidiary developed the server and client software packages that permitted customer access to gaming. Suspicions that SCI was accepting online wagers led to a sting operation, during which time British Columbia's police gambled nearly $5,000 on the company's site. Charges were laid in 1999, and in 2001 the BC Supreme Court declared that Canadian-based Internet gambling sites could not legally accept bets from Canadian citizens (*R. v. Starnet Communications International Inc.*, 2001). A deal was ultimately struck: SCI pleaded guilty to one criminal gambling count under Section 202(1)(b) of the *Criminal Code of Canada*, was fined $100,000 CND, and forfeited roughly US$4 million as proceeds of crime pursuant to Section 462.37 of the *Code*. Speculation to this point suggested that, prior to establishing sufficient connection to a betting operation and Canadian jurisdiction, applying the *Criminal Code* would have been difficult (Kyer and Hough, 2003). The *Starnet* decision provided clarification: an individual or company interested in offering online gaming in Canada must minimize or eliminate all connections to Canada. Should this prove impracticable, banning Canadian access to the site appears a logical next move.

Canadian federal law has been interpreted by provincial governments as allowing them to legally operate an Internet gambling website, as long as the patronage is restricted to residents within that province. Provincially owned gambling operators in the Atlantic Provinces (Atlantic Lottery Corporation) and British Columbia (British Columbia Lottery Corporation) provide online sports betting, online 'interactive' lotteries, and the online sale of land-based lottery tickets to residents of their respective provinces. Horseracing in Canada is regulated by the Canadian Pari-Mutuel Agency under the federal Department of Agriculture. The federal agriculture minister made a rule change, in 2003, permitting horseracing bets to be placed, not just by telephone, but also by 'any telecommunication device.' As a consequence, Woodbine Entertainment, a Toronto-based horseracing track operator, began accepting online bets from across Canada in January 2004. The legality of Canadians placing non-horseracing bets with online sites outside of their province is unclear. Thus far, no Canadian resident has been prosecuted for such activity. In 2010, the Ontario, British Columbia, and Quebec governments initiated state-controlled, online gambling.

## Kahnawà:ke

Kahnawà:ke is a Mohawk community of approximately 8,000 residents, located a 15-minute drive from downtown Montreal, in the Province of Quebec. Steadfast in its claims to territorial sovereignty and internal governing authority over its 30-square kilometer land base, the Mohawk Council of Kahnawà:ke as a governing body refuses to concede to the Canadian government's claims to overarching territorial supremacy (Simpson, 2000). In the words of Grand Chief Mike Delisle Jr., 'if you go to any man, women or child in this community, no one would tell you they're Canadian' (Gordon, 2009). In addition to holding bi-yearly elections, the Council implements laws and creates institutions necessary to maintain peace, order, and good governance. Kahnawà:ke has its own police force, court, schools, hospital and fire station, and social services, all of which operate according to local laws and policy directives. Through its legislative authority, Kahnawà:ke has established various regulatory agencies that include the Kahnawà:ke Peacekeepers Ethics Committee, the Kahnawà:ke

Alcoholic Beverages Control Commission, the Kahnawà:ke Athletic Events Commission, and the Kahnawà:ke Gaming Commission (Marshall, 2010). The latter in particular challenges Quebec's claims of exclusive control over all provincial Internet gambling websites, which in turn makes Kahnawà:ke's online operations an illegal venture.

As Lazarus, Monzon and Wodnicki (2011) describe, in addition to asserting territorial sovereignty, the Kahnawà:ke Mohawks claim a constitutionally protected Aboriginal right to maintain a historic gaming and gambling tradition. The Mohawks played a wide range of games at Kahnawà:ke, including the game of *snowsnake*, with arrowheads, animal pelts, and food wagered on the matches' outcomes. *Plumstone* was another. *Hoop and javelin* was also played, whereby participants were divided among those holding hoops and others throwing sticks toward the hoops. The game the Iroquois are perhaps best known for, which was regularly played at Kahnawà:ke, is lacrosse. Dating back well before European contact (by some estimates to the 1400s), it was eagerly adopted by French and later English settlers. Gaming was an important mechanism utilized historically to resolve conflicts through peaceful means, in keeping with the Great Law of Peace, which set out the principles by which the Confederacy nations Oneida, Onondaga, Mohawks, Cayuga, and Seneca would coexist in harmony (Smith, 1975). In this regard, wagering played an integral role in Mohawk gaming practices, and became so important that games were often played for the sake of wagering rather than for simple enjoyment. Finally, regulating gaming was a fundamental facet of Kahnawà:ke culture, and included governing where and when events would be held and for what purposes. A complex array of rules and procedures encompassed everything from game rules to the types of items wagered (Morgan, 1962).

A history of internally structured gaming and wagering protocols is evident (Lazarus, Monzon, and Wodnicki, 2011). So too is a history of internal governance (i.e., self-determination) (e.g., Johnston, 1986). For much of the twentieth century, the Mohawk Council of Kahnawà:ke would govern according to historic processes (Alfred, 1995; Reid, 2004) during which time its residents participated in traditional games of chance and wagering. Local beliefs in sovereignty and the right to control gaming would, however, intersect at the end of the century, thus challenging the Quebec government's beliefs in regulatory authority over both Kahnawà:ke lands and their ability to offer and regulate online gambling.

## Implementing online gambling

A major host of online gambling sites since 1999, the Kahnawà:ke Mohawks have to date invested more than $20 million in their online operations. The KGC has granted client-provider authorizations to more than 100 gaming licensees, who have negotiated hosting agreements with MIT. Initially, a bricks-and-mortar casino was proposed in the early 1990s. However, the lingering memory of the recent civil war over gambling at the Akwesasne Mohawk reserve, located approximately 115 kilometers west of Kahnawà:ke, which resulted in several deaths, hundreds injured, and internal factionalism that to this day has not abated, provoked an extended debate concerning gambling's merits (Baron, 1998; Hornung, 1991; Johansen, 1993). In an attempt to avoid similar tumult, the issue was put to a referendum in 1994, when the community voted 724–627 against building a casino. Kahnawà:ke leaders, however, took the close vote to mean that other gaming-related strategies could be considered (Henderson, 2007). The Mohawk Council of Kahnawà:ke followed by establishing the three-member Kahnawà:ke Gaming Commission (KGC), pursuant to the provisions of the recently established Kahnawà:ke Gaming Law. The legislation dictates that, as a sovereign nation, Kahnawà:ke has jurisdiction over issuing gaming licenses for lottery schemes.

Several months of research into the benefits of hosting an Internet gambling site followed, and the results were promising. In 1998, for example, 40 international online gambling websites and 250 public and private companies operating 650 'e-gaming' web properties operated worldwide. Most importantly, an estimated $700 million in Internet gambling wagers was being spent annually (AGLC, 2004). After considered debate, the KGC quickly approved the creation of Mohawk Internet Technologies (MIT) in 1999, which the Mohawk Council financed to operate an online casino business. Intended to become a hub of a diverse assortment of e-commerce industries, MIT's focus was creating an interactive gambling industry. MIT remains a wholly owned Mohawk Council operation.

The Mohawk Council pragmatically acknowledged that Canadian law respecting Internet gaming was, at best, ambiguous. They sought to legitimize their operations in anticipation of a legal battle. In July 1999, the Mohawk Council and the KGC approached the former director of the New Jersey Division of Gaming, Frank Catania, for help with establishing a legitimate regulatory environment. With the assistance of Murray Marshall, the KGC's legal counsel, the *Interactive Gambling (Player Protection) Act, 1998*, enacted in Queensland, Australia, was used to develop a regulatory framework designed to ensure that all interactive gambling and gaming activities conducted within or from the Mohawk territory satisfied three basic principles:

1    the Commission must ensure that only suitable persons and entities are permitted to operate within Kahnawà:ke;
2    all games offered must be fair to the player; and,
3    all winners are paid.

Applicants seeking an Interactive Gaming License are required to pay an upfront $25,000 fee, which includes the estimated cost of conducting the Commission's due diligence regarding the applicant and the individuals who have provided personal information forms. Once granted a Client Provider Authorization (CPA), MIT collects a monthly fee that adds up to $10,000 annually, with no corporate or gambling taxes. The KGC is responsible for licensing the operators and ensuring regulatory compliance with rules and regulations, requiring operator transparency, and other guidelines related to issues such as audits, payouts, and underage access to gambling sites. The interactive gaming licenses are granted for two-year periods. In addition to operating a state-of-the-art server farm, MIT provides space on its servers to online casino operators that offers uncapped bandwidth and high-speed 100mps Ethernet connections. Finally, the KGC employs PriceWaterhouseCoopers to audit their operations to ensure fairness (see KGC, 2010a).

Capitalizing quickly on online gambling's increasing popularity in the early 2000s, according to Casino City, which tracks the number of online companies, by 2007 Kahnawà:ke was the world's largest host of online gambling sites (377). This was largely the result of the KGC's established presence as an Internet gambling provider, its very low fees, its possession of one of the best hosting and bandwidth capacities, and its status as the only provider physically located within the lucrative North American market. The Data Centre is manned by security guards on a 24×7 basis, and all network, electrical and mechanical systems are electronically monitored. Technical assistance is also available on a 24×7 basis. The network in particular is impressive. In addition to fast Ethernet or gigabit Ethernet connectivity, connecting to Montreal is available using multiple carriers on diverse paths. Clients have direct access to the fibre-optic backbone into the USA, and direct access to European networks via Trans-Atlantic link. Protection is in place against distributed denial-of-service (DDoS) attacks (see Continent 8, 2010).

An additional attraction of the Kahnawà:ke operation has been the belief that it is a 'safe haven' for online gambling. When US Congress passed the Unlawful Internet Gambling Enforcement Act (UIGEA), in October 2006, many Caribbean- and Central American-based sites moved their operations to the Kahnawà:ke Territory, in the belief that US officials would be less apt to prosecute individuals from this jurisdiction. The Kahnawà:ke Mohawk Council also benefited from its purchase of a 40 percent stake of Continent 8 Technologies PLC, an Isle of Man (Irish Sea) company that forged an exclusive agreement with MIT to offer its hosting services to gambling site owners. Particularly attractive was Continent 8's data centres located in the Isle of Man, Singapore, and Malta, and its private telecommunications grid, all of which ensured the infrastructure was in place to offer their international customers a global grid of computer centres to serve the gaming industry and other e-businesses (MacDonald, 2006). Expansion was contingent on revenue raised by going public, which failed in 2006. Nevertheless, Continent 8 continues to operate from Kahnawà:ke and its three offshore sites.

Little is known about how much revenue the Kahnawà:ke operation generates annually. However, in 2006, when Continent 8 issued a prospectus for potential investors in anticipation of going public, official documents indicated that MIT posted an annual net profit of US$17.4 million on revenue of $24.7 million (Moore, 2008). This occurred conspicuously at the peak of MIT's operations, suggesting that net profits have dropped in relation to Kahnawà:ke's sagging popularity. For instance, as of February 2011, Casino City reported that Kahnawà:ke is the world's fifth largest host, with 190 sites, approximately half the number of sites operating during its peak year of 2007. Kahnawà:ke is also seventh in total volume transactions. Offsetting a portion of these losses is the estimated $4 million annually in dividends it makes from its 40 percent share in Continent 8 Technologies (Moore, 2010a).

All profits are used by the Mohawk Council of Kahnawà:ke to fund local governing activities, including social services programming. The importance of this secondary-source revenue cannot be overstated. The primary source of First Nations revenue has traditionally been federal government payments through Indian and Northern Affairs Canada (INAC). The funding formula calculates individual First Nations funding levels based on populations. Kahnawà:ke leaders rationalize that these payments are monies due for their forced forfeiture of resources located in their former traditional territories. Using the one year of available data (2006–7), we are able to determine that Kahnawà:ke's net gaming revenues ($17.4 million) added 36.3 percent to its INAC disbursement for that year ($47,965,436) (INAC, 2007). These additional revenues resulted in a working budget of more than $65 million that is used to provide education, health, and other vital social programs, for which INAC funding provides a base minimum. Based on the last four year trends, these secondary-source revenues have diminished. Reports also indicate that the online operations have brought more than 200 jobs to the community, at least half of which are filled by Kahnawà:ke residents (Wright, 2008).

Implementing the online operations at Kahnawà:ke took time and a $20 million investment. It required the Mohawk Council to secure outside experts to develop a regulatory framework that was able to simultaneously satisfy customer concerns and resist Quebec's legal challenges. For a brief period the Kahnawà:ke operation hosted the most gambling sites internationally, leading to the popular belief that the community was generating considerable revenues. In fact, as site hosts that did not draw a royalty per dollar gambled, the Kahnawà:ke operations currently generate no more than $20 million annually. Recently MIT has seen its customer base substantially drop, due in part to the ubiquitous concerns about the Kahnawà:ke operation's legality, which is the focus of the following section.

## The debate over Internet gambling's legality at Kahnawà:ke

Internet gaming is in violation of Quebec's provincial gaming provisions, and the Kahnawà:ke venture is deemed an illegal operation by the Quebec government. Both the provincial and federal governments as well as the Sûreté du Québec (provincial police) have separately initiated several investigations. Then Minister of Indian and Northern Affairs Canada (INAC), Chuck Strahl, stated that the federal government had no jurisdiction regarding Mohawk activities occurring on their land, and that the gaming issue was strictly a Quebec matter (Henderson, 2007). Quebec's Minister of Public Security, Serge Menard, has gone on record as opposing the Kahnawà:ke online casinos in Quebec, on the grounds that they are illegal. However, the province as of this writing has taken no legal action to halt these activities, one reason being the still palpable tensions resulting from the Oka crisis in 1990 (Lipton, 2003).

The Province of Quebec has taken selected steps to curb illegal online gambling at Kahnawà:ke. In September 2007, Cyber World Group, which administers online casinos located on the Kahnawà:ke reserve, pleaded guilty in the Quebec Court to charges of illegal gambling and was ordered to pay a $2 million fine. As a result of this ruling, several online operators have moved their operations to other jurisdictions. The lack of provincial response to date, critics suggest, is due to officials' fears that confronting Kahnawà:ke leaders could spark an event similar to what occurred at Oka in 1990, a 79-day, $500-million clash, supported by Kahnawà:ke leaders (they blockaded a bridge linking their community with Montreal in solidarity). The Oka Standoff, as it is popularly known, occurred after Kanesetake residents (located approximately 70 kilometers to the west) asserted territorial sovereignty, in an attempt to reject the expansion of a nine-hole golf course from the Oka Township into a community burial ground shaded by sacred pine trees (Obomsawin, 2000, 1993; York and Pindera, 1991). Interestingly, a handful of warriors from Akwesasne, who were directly involved in that community's gambling-based battles, were on site at Kahnawà:ke in 1990.

To date, even though the Supreme Court of Canada has pronounced that First Nations do not possess the Aboriginal right to control and regulate casino gaming in their reserve communities, no similar case has taken aim at First Nation/Aboriginal control of online gambling. Specifically, the Supreme Court determined that on-reserve gambling facilities were not exempt from provincial legislation regulating gaming (*R. v. Pamajewon,* 1996). Although the possibility of recognizing Aboriginal rights in another case has not been exhausted, the original claim that gaming was an inherent Aboriginal right was answered for most First Nations (Belanger, 2006). No First Nation has challenged the Court to determine online gambling, and several legal scholars have effectively argued that the Mohawks of Kahnawà:ke satisfy the Supreme Court of Canada's various legal tests to rightfully claim an Aboriginal right to conduct and regulate gaming. As a historic facet of Mohawk cultural, religious, and social practices, the Mohawks of Kahnawà:ke are, accordingly, 'able to claim an Aboriginal right, under Section 35(1) of the *Canada Constitution Act, 1982,* to conduct and regulate gaming, including the online gaming activity that they are presently pursuing' (Lazarus et al., 2011). Perhaps this is in part why the Quebec legal community has never pressed to forcibly or otherwise put a halt to the online gaming operations. It needs to be briefly noted that the only way for Kahnawà:ke to prompt a Supreme Court challenge is to be charged in contravention of the *Criminal Code of Canada,* after which community leaders may initiate Aboriginal rights litigation. The federal and Quebec governments have yet to sanction either the Royal Canadian Mounted Police (RCMP) or the Sûreté du Québec to enter Kahnawà:ke and charge community leaders with a *Criminal Code* violation.

A recent Superior Court of the Province of Quebec decision (*Horne v. Kahnawà:ke Gaming Commission and Mohawk Council of Kahnawà:ke*, 2007) provides some clarity, suggesting why provincial officials have to date avoided confronting the Mohawk Council of Kahnawà:ke. On 13 February 2006, Mitchell Horne, a Kahnawà:ke community member, applied to the KGC for an Interactive Gaming License (IGL), one of two types of permits under Kahnawà:ke Gaming Law. Unlike a Client Provider Authorization (CPA), which operates gaming-related activities, the holder of an IGL must establish and maintain an infrastructure from which the CPAs operate. MIT is the holder of the sole IGL issued since 1999. After being denied an IGL permit, Horne sought an order of Mandamus, effectively asking the Superior Court to not only annul the KGC's denial of his application, and to issue the said permit upon payment of required fees, but also annulment of S. 28 of the Kahnawà:ke Gaming Commission Regulations Concerning Interactive Gaming (i.e., the regulations specifying that the KGC has the discretion to deny an application on purely policy grounds, even when the criteria for qualifying for a permit are met).

The KGC expressed its concern that the 'issuance of other IGL's is likely to significantly impact the conduct of online gaming in Kahnawà:ke from regulatory, operational and policy-making perspectives' (ibid., 3). Accordingly, Horne was informed by letter that the KGC and the Mohawk Council of Kahnawà:ke determined that, based on the best interests of the community, only one IGL should be issued. Reflecting on the previous decade's debate concerning the legality of online gambling at Kahnawà:ke, Superior Court Justice Dionysia Zerbisias found herself in an enviable position of being able to pronounce on the Kahnawà:ke online operation's legality according to Canadian law. However, she refused to address whether MIT was operating illegally. Instead, the Madame Justice provocatively concluded that the KGC is an administrative body that exercises its powers duly delegated to it by the Mohawk Council of Kahnawà:ke. It is obliged to 'administer this Mohawk law in the best interests of the Mohawks of Kahnawà:ke,' and is entrusted with the power to make all determinations related to localized gaming activities (ibid., 4). Most importantly, the centrality of the Kahnawà:ke Gaming Law to 'promote and preserve economic development, self-sufficiency and peace, order and good government within the Mohawk territories' was confirmed (ibid., 4).

This decision resonates with several federal and provincial policies aimed at augmenting First Nation's governing authority through economic development. Acknowledging that reserve-based economic ventures have rarely succeeded, and continue to 'play a minor or insignificant role as a source of personal incomes and general revenue for all but a handful of bands/tribes' (Boldt, 1993: 223; Loxley, 2010), the Canadian government announced the Inherent Rights Policy (IRP) in 1995. Specifically, this policy recognized that in matters 'internal to their communities, integral to their unique cultures, identities, traditions, languages and institutions and with respect to their special relationship to their land and their resources' the right to self-government is inherent and contained within Section 35 of the *Constitution Act* (1982) (Canada, 1998). The IRP also indicated that a First Nation's right to self-government would be recognized only after it had met the federal criteria necessary to a stable reserve economy. In its Financial Arrangements section, the IRP is clear:

> All participants in self-government negotiations must recognize that self-government arrangements will have to be affordable and consistent with the overall social and economic policies and priorities of governments, while at the same time taking into account the specific needs of Aboriginal peoples. In this regard, the fiscal and budgetary

capacity of the federal, provincial, territorial and Aboriginal governments or institutions will be a primary determinant of the financing of self-government.

(Minister of Public Works, 1995)

Similarly, a 1998 provincial policy paper entitled *Partnership, Development, Achievement* concluded that 'the major issues for the Quebec government and the aboriginal nations' are 'land and resources, economic development, self-government and self-sufficiency. These issues should be covered by negotiated settlements' (Quebec, 1998). As Marshall (2010: 333) aptly concludes, these recent federal and provincial policy statements 'have facilitated progressive discussions with indigenous communities' for the purposes of 'reaching both sectoral and comprehensive agreements on various areas of jurisdiction,' which for Kahnawà:ke includes gambling.

For the Mohawk Council of Kahnawà:ke the *Horne* decision is vital for several reasons, perhaps the most important being the Superior Court's implicit recognition of the community's internal governing and lawmaking authority, which corresponds with the Council's longstanding claims of self-determination and territorial sovereignty. It ties economic development to community well-being, while also identifying economic development as a central aspect of good governance. It also suggests that the Kahnawà:ke Gaming Law, as developed within the Mohawk territories, was an act of self-governance in an attempt to foster economic stability and, as such, Indigenous self-determination. This little-known case strengthens the argument that the choice to operate MIT, and develop internal legislation regarding local gambling matters, is indeed a by-product of Kahnawà:ke's self-determination and beyond the scope of the courts, and, more importantly, the Province of Quebec.

## The corresponding battle for legitimacy and economic sovereignty

A tension is evident, as the Mohawk Council of Kahnawà:ke attempts to balance its claims to sovereignty, with emergent international standards seeking to evolve universal compliance measures to ensure customer confidence in online gambling (see Belanger and Williams, 2011). On the one hand, the Mohawk Council of Kahnawà:ke has devised a regulatory model based on internally developed legislation, to which no additional external oversight exists. The Province of Quebec, until recently, did not offer online gambling, hence there were no provincial regulations to which to refer. Likewise, Canada has no nationwide rules in place regarding the regulation of online gambling. Therefore, while the Mohawk Council of Kahnawà:ke proclaimed strict adherence to an internally fashioned set of rules, it in many ways remains a self-regulated jurisdiction. On the other hand, by remaining independent, the Mohawk Council of Kahnawà:ke increasingly is considered a rogue state housing a diverse if not completely notable collection of online gambling companies. Kahnawà:ke leaders interestingly have never promoted their sovereignty as a 'take it or leave' proposition. Rather, it has been framed as a right to fulfill community desires for partnerships with non-Aboriginal communities and governments, which are informed by the spirit of historic and contemporary treaty relationships, and continuing group rights (e.g., Henderson, 2006; Macklem, 2001). Nevertheless, the corresponding battle for international legitimacy and economic sovereignty plays itself out daily.

Kahnawà:ke's lacklustre response to various crises has not instilled consumer confidence. In January 2008 the KGC initiated an investigation in response to player complaints that one or more people associated with Absolute Poker were winning significant jackpots, by using software that revealed opponents' hidden cards. The Commission determined that the cheating netted the culprits upwards of $700,000 over a six-week period, beginning in August 2007. Absolute Poker's management was also found to have deleted gambling logs, and refused to charge the cheaters, who were absolved of their crimes, in return for identifying how precisely they cracked the software's firewalls. Absolute Poker's parent company, Tokwiro Enterprises, was assessed a $500,000 fine. Most Kahnawà:ke residents did not realize at the time that Tokwiro Enterprises was owned by former Kahnawà:ke Grand Chief Joe Norton, the very individual instrumental in bringing online gambling to the community in the 1990s (see Hamilton, 2008). This episode undermined local attempts to display Kahnawà:ke's regulatory abilities, something industry professionals had long questioned.

Soon after the KGC announced its determination, the British Department for Culture, Media, and Sport revealed that it had refused Kahnawà:ke's application for inclusion on its 'White List' of jurisdictions permitted to advertise online gambling in the lucrative UK market. In January 2008, Kahnawà:ke Grand Chief Michael Delisle Jr. expressed his disappointment with this decision:

> Despite having been the first jurisdiction to accept and implement the world-recognized eCOGRA standard, the implementation of a mandatory continuous compliance policy, and our consistent enforcement of what may very well be the world's most stringent due diligence program, our name has not been added to the U.K.'s exclusive White List.

Hinting that Quebec officials provided an unfavourable assessment of the Kahnawà:ke's operations, he further highlighted his 'concerns regarding the process undertaken by the U.K. authority,' and that he would initiate 'inquiries to ascertain whether the application was afforded fair and objective consideration, which at this point, we do not believe was the case' (KGC, 2008).

Kahnawà:ke's leaders remain concerned with ensuring territorial integrity, as is evidenced by a key dimension of their sovereignty treatise, which is aimed at securing the right to pursue select economic development projects in their territory. In this instance, political and economic sovereignty are considered mutually inclusive concepts. Speaking in 2004, then Kahnawà:ke grand chief and MIT company chairman Joseph Norton stated, 'We have an aboriginal right to an economy and it doesn't have to be hunting trapping and gathering. We can't do that for a living any more where we live. We don't have any more natural resources.' He added that 'mainstream economic development' is the avenue to self-sufficiency (Riga, 2003). The nation-to-nation relationship, embodied in the treaties acknowledging Kahnawà:ke territorial protection, informed Delisle's contention in 2005 that 'We have always asserted that we are a sovereign people, this is our jurisdiction, this is our territory' (Hamilton, 2003). The risk, in this case, is Canada's threat to Kahnawà:ke's territorial sovereignty and governing authority.

In the spirit of nationhood, Kahnawà:ke's leaders have responded to what they perceive as additional outside threats. In 2008, for example, the Mohawk Council of Kahnawà:ke petitioned the Commonwealth of Kentucky, protesting its attempted seizure of 141 international online gambling sites. As Delisle (2009) explained, 'It's not the first time that a government has tried to prevent us from conducting business and it won't be the last. But, rest assured, we will always protect our jurisdiction and the integrity of the Kahnawà:ke Gaming Commission.' Canadian officials have publicly stated that the Kahnawà:ke people were not international political actors, but rather allies requiring protection. Kahnawà:ke leaders counter these claims citing a continuity of treaties dating back to the seventeenth century as surety of their beliefs. At times they have physically fended off federal attempts at territorial alienation, before determining in 1990 that it was time to challenge 'the Canadian government's assertion of jurisdiction [which in turn] assumes the proportion of a people struggling for their very existence' (Johnston, 1986). This resistance flared into the Oka Standoff, yet in the wake of such resistance, Canadian officials maintain that no outstanding treaty promises to economic development exist, and that the Kahnawà:ke First Nation is at present in contravention of federal statute restricting the operation of casinos or housing online casinos without provincial or federal approval.

The fight for territorial and economic sovereignty is intimately tied to Kahnawà:ke's battle for international legitimacy, the latter of which tied directly to the UK White List approval. The lack of nationhood status reaffirms Quebec assertions that Kahnawà:ke operates an illegal venture, which is potentially off-putting to many online gambling companies and potential patrons. A second segment may, however, consider the Kahnawà:ke online operations their best bet in a North American market literally void of comparable services. These and like concerns would come under public scrutiny in 2008, after another cheating scandal broke once again involving Tokwiro Enterprises.

## Anatomy of a scandal

Being left off the UK's White List was a blow to the KGC's and MIT's legitimacy. Those questioning Kahnawà:ke's ability to provide aggressive regulatory oversight had their suspicions confirmed, after a second online cheating scandal involving a poker website licensed by KGC. In January 2008, customer complaints were received about the online website operating as Ultimate Bet, that highlighted cheating incidences from June 2003 to December 2007. During this time, several users manipulated software that was placed on Ultimate Bet servers, prior to 2005, to view the normally hidden hole cards of opposing players (Gaul, 2008). The parent company Tokwira was fined (US) $1.5 million 'for its failure to implement and enforce measures to prohibit and detect fraudulent activities,' plus the costs of the Commission's investigation, which combined amounted to more than (US) $2 million. Tokwiro also refunded roughly (US) $22 million to players financially harmed by the cheating incidences. Described as the largest such reimbursement in the history of online or land-based gaming, the accounting firm KPMG oversaw the refunding process, that was calculated using a formula that gave every possible benefit of the doubt to affected players (KGC, 2009).

The KGC investigation concluded that 31 individuals were involved in the cheating, and obtained what was described as convincing evidence that former 1994 World Series of Poker champion, Russell Hamilton, headed the ring. Specifically, the vast majority of computers, associated equipment, and IP addresses used by the cheating accounts, were directly associated with Hamilton, a Las Vegas resident. Although the KGC initiated a criminal complaint against Hamilton, and continues to cooperate with law enforcement authorities, little has transpired since 2008. This incident's profile was ratcheted up following a joint *60 Minutes–Washington Post* investigation, which was critical of the KGC's response, and did nothing to satiate the fears of an increasingly suspicious customer base that was losing confidence, as evidenced by the quickly diminishing number of hosted sites.

As a KGC press release (2008) admitted, 'Unfortunately, the KGC's actions were not well communicated to the poker industry or public at large, creating an incorrect perception that the KGC was "doing nothing."' In an attempt to foster consumer confidence and improve its track record, the KGC in April 2010 revoked Maricass International Holdings Inc.'s CPA, and it took legal action to ensure Life Gaming Ltd., also known as 'betfold,' ceased displaying the KGC logo thus implying the Commission's approval and/or support. Finally, it identified a breach in the CEREUS poker network that at the time of writing had not been resolved. The KGC has provided several press releases, available on its public website, detailing the punishment meted out to Absolute Poker and Ultimate Bet, and how both companies complied with KGC directives resulting from its investigation.

## Recent developments

On 25 January 2010, the KGC launched a compliance program and appointed London-based eCOGRA (eCommerce and Online Gaming Regulation and Assurance) as a third-party inspector to provide continuing monitoring of the MIT's 55 online gambling operators. A recognized, accredited testing agency, that advises numerous jurisdictions on compliance matters, eCOGRA reviews more than 140 gaming websites and their associated software suppliers and operators, to ensure the implemented governance structures, responsibilities, processes, and approach comply with industry best practices and requirements, and recognized audit practices and principles. KGC chairman, Dean Montour, indicated that licensees expressed a strong commitment to the new compliance system that met or exceeded international best practice standards. 'The company, which is itself reviewed annually by KPMG, has the resources to assess compliance and conduct monitoring programs to ensure game fairness and adherence to key KGC objectives, and is eminently suited to the task' (KGC, 2010b). eCOGRA was appointed in 2007 by the European Gaming and Betting Association (EGBA) to implement a similar continuous compliance program for all its members. This program importantly has enabled EGBA members to demonstrate that they operate at standards that match or exceed those of European Union state gambling monopolies.

On 17 June 2010, the KGC and Financial Services Regulatory Commission for Antigua and Barbuda signed a memorandum of understanding that established an innovative regulatory relationship between the two commissions. Specifically, the pact expands on an agreement dating to 2005 that would facilitate license holders being hosted on servers in each jurisdiction. Antigua's clients will be able to access the MIT's superior bandwidth and technical services; and MIT is positioned to acquire new business. More importantly, former British colonies Antigua and Barbuda were designated White List jurisdictions in 2008, thus allowing their clients to advertise in Britain. This issue remains problematic, for several MIT clients have moved off the Kahnawà:ke server, rather than procure a separate license in a White List jurisdiction (Moore, 2010b). While the agreement indicated that Kahnawà:ke's license holders were still unable to advertise in Britain, it appears that the relationship was fostered to devise a network of related, but independent, jurisdictions, thus expanding Kahnawà:ke's reach.

Significantly challenging these efforts was Loto-Quebec's application to the provincial government for permission to offer online gambling, after a memorandum of understanding was signed in February 2010 between Loto-Quebec, the BC Lottery Corp., and the Atlantic Lottery Corp, which covers the four Atlantic Provinces (Huras, 2011). Nova Scotia, Prince Edward Island and Newfoundland and Labrador soon left the consortium, due to their concerns related to exposing their citizens to online gambling (Moore, 2010c). The partnership was required to compete with existing online sites, such as the Kahnawà:ke operation. Loto-Quebec officials expressed concern about 'illegal and unregulated gaming sites that are of dubious integrity,' and the need to 'channel the gaming offer in a controlled, safe environment with irreproachable integrity.' The KGC (2010c) struck back in a press release:

> Characterising all online gaming sites that presently offer their services in Québec as lacking in integrity is offensive, not only to gaming regulators throughout the world but

also to the many outstanding entrepeneurs [*sic*] that have built this industry and who are much better positioned to comment on its integrity than is Loto-Quebec.

As former Grand Chief Joe Norton previously noted, such assertions ring false, considering that in the late 1990s Quebec's former Native Affairs minister favoured partnering with the Kahnawà:ke Mohawks to offer online gambling. Norton explained, 'We offered both Canada and Quebec an opportunity to be a partner with us (in this venture) but they wouldn't.' He implied that issues related to revenue-sharing ultimately led provincial officials to declaim Kahnawà:ke's operations little more than an illegal venture (Moore, 2008).

Provincial cabinet approved the online gaming proposal and, on 1 December 2010, Loto-Quebec began offering eight poker games, blackjack, and roulette in an attempt to capitalize on what had grown into a $1-billion domestic industry. Once registered, only Quebec residents above 18 years of age are permitted site access, and players cannot gamble more than $10,000 per week. Loto-Quebec CEO Alain Cousineau stated that his goal was to raise an annual $50 million of the estimated $80 million spent by Quebecers (Huras, 2011). Finance Minister Raymond Bachand also indicated that the provincial cabinet approved the state-controlled alternative, in a bid 'to cannibalize illegal gambling' sites that now offer an array of gambling opportunities to Quebecers. 'I believe this to be an efficient way of fighting the underground economy' (Loto-Quebec to offer online gambling, 2010).

## Conclusion

Writing in 2006, Belanger concluded that online gambling would eventually be made legal in Quebec, but that operators such as the Kahnawà:ke would be forced 'to contend with strong opposition, ranging from anti-gambling lobbyists to public and private interests threatened by its economic potential' (p. 165). As of December 2010, Quebec has asserted its authority to offer its citizens opportunities to gamble online in an attempt to recapture $50 million of the $80 million being spent provincially. Provincial officials have embraced the spirit of the *Starnet* decision, granting itself the authority to solely offer online gambling to the exclusion of outside political agents. This could be perceived as implicit recognition of Kahnawà:ke's sovereignty, and further suggests that Kahnawà:ke, by its own admissions, is now an outside agent prohibited from doing business with Quebec citizens. Kahnawà:ke officials would likely contend that MIT itself never directly engaged Quebec citizens, rather it was the online gambling sites that MIT hosted that did. Unlike a foreign jurisdiction protected from the intrusion of outsiders in internal matters, which would for example protect Antigua from Canada's jurisdictional reach, Kahnawà:ke is 'landlocked' in Quebec and subject to Parliamentary paramountcy, and Canadian laws. And it appears that no partnership as the one proposed in the late 1990s will mature, as Quebec is now fully committed to economic competition with Kahnawà:ke.

What we have learned in recent years has shaken our societal assumptions concerning the Kahnawà:ke online operations. Prior to 2007, public perception had Kahnawà:ke's operations drawing considerable revenues. However, that year they netted $17.4 million. To put this in perspective, in 2008 Canadians gambled an estimated $675 million online (Moore, 2010c), indicating that Kahnawà:ke's net revenues would have accounted for less than 3 percent of domestic online gambling expenditures, assuming of course that only domestic wagers were accepted. As net revenues have levelled off or dropped, based on fewer host companies, international online gambling expenditures for 2010 were estimated at $24.471 billion (Canada was tabbed at $1.2 billion), signifying Kahnawà:ke's market clout is rapidly diminishing. Once touted as the globe's leading gambling site host, the KGC's poor regulatory oversight and increased global competition resulted in a near 50 percent drop in business between 2007 and 2011. The media's concentrated gaze and relentless government scrutiny have compelled the KGC to improve its oversight capacities, which has involved revoking permits and improving transparency, by placing updates and press releases on its public website and hiring eCOGRA to monitor MIT clients. The hope, one could argue, is to secure White List placement, thus legitimizing the Kahnawà:ke online operations. Additional recent agreements with Antigua, and investments, suggest that this is the end goal. Kahnawà:ke has in recent years experienced its fits and starts, while persevering to remain a crucial public symbol of the volatile nature of global online gambling.

## References

Alberta Gaming and Liquor Commission (AGLC). (2004). *Gaming policy comparisons – Key points.* Retrieved from http://www.aglc.gov.ab.ca/pdf/casino/first_nations_gaming_policy_chart.pdf

Alfred, G. R. (1995). *Heeding the voices of the ancestors: Kahnawake Mohawk politics and the rise of native nationalism.* Toronto: Oxford University Press.

Baron, E. L. (1998). 'Public participation and the choice of casinos as development strategy in Iroquois Nations'. Doctoral dissertation, Rutgers University.

Bear Stearns. (2000). *E-gaming revisited – At odds with the world.* New York: Bear Stearns.

Belanger, Y. D. (2006). *Gambling with the future: The evolution of Aboriginal gaming in Canada.* Saskatoon: Purich Publishing.

Belanger, Y. D., and Williams, R. J. (2011). 'Virtual Sovereignty: Exploring First Nations Internet gaming ventures in Canada'. In Y. D. Belanger (ed.), *First Nations gaming in Canada* (52–77). Winnipeg: University of Manitoba Press.

Boldt, M. (1993). *Surviving as Indians: The challenge of self-government.* Toronto: University of Toronto Press.

Canada. (1998). *Gathering strength: Canada's Aboriginal action plan.* Ottawa: Queen's Printer.

*Constitution Act.* (1982). *Being Schedule B to the Canada Act 1982 (UK)*, 1982, c 11.

Continent 8. (2010). *Kahnawake: E-gaming's pioneering hub.* Retrieved from http://www.continent8. com/documents/kahnawake%20ds-kw-002.pdf

Delisle, M. (2009). *Kahnawà:ke weighs in on Kentucky issue.* Retrieved February 26, 2009 from http:// www.online-casinos.com/news/news7640.asp

Gaul, G. M. (2008, November 30). 'Players gamble on honesty, security of internet betting'. *Washington Post.*

Gordon, S. (2009, December 9). 'In a town haunted by Oka, nobody is "Canadian"'. *Globe and Mail,* A3.

Hamilton, G. (2003, July 18). '"Sovereign" Reserve hits the jackpot'. *National Post,* A3.

— (2008, January 21). 'U.K. blacklists Kahnawake web gambling'. *National Post,* A2.

Henderson, H. (2007, December 12). 'The Kahnawake Gaming Commission is operating within the law in Canada'. *MajorWager.* Retrieved from www.majorwager.com/forums/mess-hall/159699-kahnawake-gaming-commission-operating-within-law-canada-hartley-henderson.html

Henderson, J. Y. (2006). *First Nations jurisprudence and Aboriginal rights: Defining the just society.* Saskatoon: Native Law Centre.

*Horne v. Kahnawà:ke Gaming Commission and Mohawk Council of Kahnawà:ke.* (2007). Retrieved from www.gamingcommission.ca/news/pr07042007a.pdf

Hornung, R. (1991). *One nation under the gun: Inside the Mohawk civil war.* Toronto: Stoddart Publishing.

Huras, A. (2011, January 15). 'New Brunswick government considering online gambling'. *Moncton Times-Transcript,* p. A12.

Indian and Northern Affairs Canada (INAC). (2007). *Auditors' report on schedule of federal government funding*. Retrieved from http://pse5-esd5.ainc-inac.gc.ca/fnp/Main/Search/DisplayBinaryData. aspx?BAND_NUMBER=70&FY=2006-2007

Johansen, B. E. (1993). *Life & death in Mohawk country*. Golden: North American Press.

Johnston, D. (1986). 'The quest of the six nations confederacy for self-determination'. *University of Toronto Law Review, 44*(1), 1–32.

Kahnawà:ke Gaming Commission (KGC). (2008). 'Mohawks respond to internet gaming decision'. Retrieved from www.gamingcommission.ca/news/pr07232008a.pdf

— (2009). 'In the matter of Tokwiro Enterprises ENRG, carrying on business as ultimate bet investigation regarding complaints of cheating'. Retrieved from http://www.gamingcommission.ca/news/pr09112009a.pdf

— (2010a) *Regulations concerning interactive gaming*. Retrieved from http://www.gamingcommission. ca/docs/RegulationsConcerningInteractiveGaming.pdf

— (2010b). 'eCOGRA appointed to test compliance of Kahnawake Gaming Commission licenses'. Retrieved from http://www.gamingcommission.ca/news.asp?ID=20

— (2010c). 'Kahnawake Gaming Commission responds to Loto-Québec comments'. Retrieved from http://www.gamingcommission.ca/news/pr02242010a.pdf

Kyer, C. I., and Hough, D. (2003). 'Is internet gaming legal in Canada: A look at Starnet'. *Canadian Journal of Law and Technology 1*(1). Retrieved November 22, 2003 from http://cjit.dal.ca

Lazarus, M. C., Monzon, E. D., and Wodnicki, R. B. (2011). 'The Mohawks of Kahnawà:ke and the case for an Aboriginal right to gaming under the Canada Constitution Act, 1982'. In Y. D. Belanger (ed.), *First Nations gaming in Canada* (35–51). Winnipeg: University of Manitoba Press.

Lipton, M. D. (2003, September). 'Internet gaming in Canada'. Presentation at Global Gaming Exposition. Las Vegas, Nevada. Retrieved from http://www.gaminglawmasters.com/jurisdictions/canada/internet.Gaming-Speech.htm. Accessed 27 March 2004. Copy of paper in author's possession.

Loto-Quebec to offer online gambling. (2010, February 3). *Montreal Gazette*.

Loxley, J. (2010). *Aboriginal, northern, and community economic development: Papers and retrospectives*. Winnipeg: Arbeiter Ring Publishing.

MacDonald, D. (2006, August 1). '"Mohawks" gamble delayed'. *Montreal Gazette*, A1.

Macklem, P. (2001). *Indigenous difference and the constitution of Canada*. Toronto: University of Toronto Press.

Marshall, M. (2010). 'Kahnawake.' In A. Cabot, and M. Balestra (eds), *Internet Gambling Report, IV* (pp. 321–34). Retrieved from http://www.gamingcommission.ca/docs/ArticleKahnawake.pdf

Minister of Public Works & Government Services. (1995). *Aboriginal self-government: The Government of Canada's approach to implementation of the inherent right & the negotiation of Aboriginal self-government*. Ottawa: Canada.

Moore, L. (2008, May 1). 'Mohawks offered governments a partnership role'. *Montreal Gazette*, B1.

— (2010a, October 30). 'Gambling deal in the cards?' *Montreal Gazette*, C1.

— (2010b, January). 'Loto-Quebec hopes online bet is winning hand'. *Montreal Gazette*, C1.

— (2010c, October 30). 'Fewer players in Loto-Quebec venture'. *Montreal Gazette*, C2.

Morgan, H. L. (1962). *League of the Iroquois, Book II: Spirit of the League*. New York: Corinth Books.

Obomsawin, A. (National Film Board of Canada). (1993). *Kahnesatake: 270 Years of Resistance*.

— (2000). *Rocks at Whiskey Trench*.

Quebec. (1998). *Partnership, development, achievement*. Gouvernement du Québec, Secrétariat aux affaires autochtones.

*R. v. Starnet Communications International Inc.*, (2001) *B.C.S.C. 125795–1*.

*R. v. Pamajewon*, (1996) *S.C.R. 821*, 22.

Reid, G. F. (2004). *Kahnawà:ke: Factionalism, traditionalism, and nationalism in a Mohawk community*. Lincoln: University of Nebraska Press.

Riga, A. (2003, June 19). 'Kahnawà:ke rakes in profit as Mohawk wins online-gambling bet'. *Montreal Gazette*, B1.

Simpson, A. (2000). 'Paths toward a Mohawk nation: Narratives of citizenship and nationhood in Kahnawake'. In D. Ivison, P. Patton, and W. Sanders (eds), *Political theory and the rights of Indigenous peoples* (113–36). Toronto: Cambridge University Press.

Smith, K. L. (1975). 'The role of games, sport, and dance in Iroquois life'. Master's thesis. University of Oregon.

Wright, L. (2008, April 19). 'Mohawk territory gambling on a risky business'. *Toronto Star,* B1.

York, G., and Pindera, L. (1991). *People of the pines: The warriors and the legacy of Oka.* Toronto: Little, Brown.

# 19 Internet gambling and online crime

*John L. McMullan and Aunshul Rege*

## Introduction

Over the past 14 years there has been a global explosion in online gambling, allowing customers to play 24 hours a day, seven days a week, from the comfort of home, work, and public places. The online industry now offers an assortment of services, such as sports betting, casino games, bingo, lotteries, blackjack, and poker. Over 650 different gambling site owners in 74 jurisdictions provide online gambling at approximately 2,350 registered sites, producing an estimated $20 billion in known revenues.

Most of these jurisdictions are located in the Netherland Antilles, Malta, the Kahnawà:ke Mohawk reserve in Canada, Gibraltar, Costa Rica, the United Kingdom, and Alderney (CasinoCity, 2010; Williams and Wood, 2007, 2009). Possible precipitating factors for this expansion include easy access, convenience and comfort of online play, legalization and cultural approval, perceived financial value to consumers, widespread advertising, celebrity endorsements and corporate sponsorships, aversion to land-based gambling clienteles and environments, preference for player-to-player competition rather than fixed-odds wagering, and likeability of the structural characteristics of online games (Williams and Wood, 2009; Wood, Williams, and Lawton, 2007; Griffiths, Parke, Wood, and Parke, 2006).

At the same time, the spread of Internet gambling has raised several issues concerning problem gambling, consumer confidence, the fairness and integrity of the games, and the security of websites (Zangeneh, Griffiths, and Parke, 2008; McMullan and Perrier, 2007). In one study of online poker players, Wood and Griffiths (2008) found that cheating was a major concern for consumers. In a second survey of Internet gamblers in 105 countries, Wood and Williams (2009) discovered that verifying the fairness of the games and identifying illegalities at gambling venues were major player concerns. Similarly, the American Gaming Association (2006) reported that about 50 percent of online casino players believed that Internet providers cheated them and 46 percent insisted that players cheated at play as well. Indeed, an international survey of over 10,000 Internet players found that about one-third of them had had disputes with gambling providers and were dissatisfied with the complaint processes (Parke et al., 2007). McMullan and Rege (2007) discovered that gambling providers were the victims of crimes such as cyberextortion, Griffiths (2010) noted that fraud at Internet sites was diverse and developing, and the Laboratoire d'Expertise en Sécurité Informatique (CERT-LEXSI, 2006) revealed that gambling companies were the perpetrators and victims of international phishing schemes, identity-theft scams, and money-laundering operations. Most recently, Giacopassi and Pitts (2009) have argued that Internet gambling is the latest victimless crime in the United States, and Ferentzy and Turner (2009) concluded that an examination of online crime and Internet gambling is an urgent research priority.

This study seeks to address this matter by investigating the types, techniques, and organizational dynamics of virtual villainy at the portals of online gambling sites. It does not examine the frequency of crime. We do not have reliable cybercrime statistics to calculate rates since 'many cybercrimes go undetected and many detected cybercrimes go unreported' (Brenner, 2007: 17). Our aim, therefore, is necessarily exploratory and qualitative in character. We ask the following questions: What types of cheats and crimes occur at online gambling sites? Who are the offenders? Who are the victims? How organized are cheating and cybercrime? Is there an organized-crime involvement in Internet gambling? How effective is legal governance in detecting, apprehending, and prosecuting cybercrime?

## Method and approach

The World Wide Web is akin to a massive library. We used the Google search engine to retrieve documents published between 2000 and 2008. It coded more pages, created larger indices, and presented the most up-to-date data when compared to other search engines. We coded for 48 combinations of keywords, such as 'cyberextortion and organized crime,' 'player collusion and gambling,' 'betting sites and fraud,' and so on. We sorted the data around four intersecting themes: online gambling; criminal techniques; the organization of cybercriminal practices; and legal control practices such as the efficacy of private cybersecurity, the quality of transborder policing, and the effectiveness of existing laws. The combination of keywords produced enormous quantities of page rankings, and we used a 10-page 100-article return process as a cut-off to obtain sample materials for each searched keyword. This criterion was a consistent means of retrieving data, and it ensured that each category was given equal weight and consideration. We retrieved 4,800 documents, but the number of articles per keyword was repetitive after the first five or six pages. This in the end narrowed our materials to about 500 documents.

Because data about cybercrimes at gambling sites were not readily available from case law or field studies, we relied on document analysis as our research method. Document analysis may be defined as a way of analysing texts in a systematic and qualitative manner for the purposes of exploring the classic questions of who said what, to whom, why, how, and with what effects (Mason, 2002; Maxfield and Babbie, 2001). While Internet documents were easy to access, use, and link and were sometimes presented in dynamic ways through threads, forums, and animations, there were some issues with quality control, accuracy of discovery, and consistency of documents over time. We dealt with these matters by relying primarily on authenticated websites such as news sites (e.g., MSNBC), security sites (e.g., McAfee), and law enforcement sites (e.g., FBI); by indexing every relevant article's uniform resource locator (URL) to create a registry of all document sources that could be checked and reexamined; and by triangulating multiple sources to verify information and look for missing data (Neuman, 2003).

We focused on the technical character of the illegal acts, the digital contexts that they occurred in, and the novel virtual socio-legal problems confronted therein. This approach stressed that, at a given point in time, certain illegal acts presented technical and social obstacles that had to be overcome for their successful completion, that we could identify and analyse the most efficient types of organization for managing these problems, and that the existence of different types of organization may be explained in terms of their technical efficiency in managing the online opportunities at hand (Best and Luckenbill, 1982; Grabosky, 2001; Brenner, 2002; Jewkes 2003, 2007; Wall, 2007). Treating the rationality of an organizational entity as a potential explanation of its existence led us to ask the following questions: Was it possible for criminals working alone to plan and execute online cheats and crimes and manage the exigencies of online security? How did this empowered loner form of cybercrime differ from digital teams that seemed able to develop collective attacks on diverse targets or from those even larger groupings that were able to establish enduring criminal networks?

## Cybernomads

### Toolkit cheats

We discovered that cybernomads tended to be solo criminal actors who stole or modified data, compromised computer systems, manipulated software for illegal purposes, or executed cyberattacks at online gambling sites. Cybernomads varied with respect to their skills and motivations, but their strength was in their software and programming expertise and in their ability to exploit sites that offered businesses or players little protection (Penenberg, 1998; Keller, 1999; Kish, 1999; Zacharias, 2004; Brenner, 2002). Toolkit cheats, for example, purchased prepackaged equipment such as scanners, sniffers, and snoopers; malware packages; password crackers; denial of service botnets; logic bombs; and algorithms that reduced their reliance on other organizational members to hack and crack gambling portals (Rogers, 2005; Gu, Liu, and Chu, 2004). SmokePoker and HoldemGenius, for example, were artificial intelligence programs, or bots, that compiled advanced mathematical algorithms and allowed cheats to see their pot-drawing-out odds and odds of winning at over 100 online poker rooms, including PokerStars, Full Tilt Poker, BoDog, Party Poker, Titan Poker, and Absolute Poker (SmokePoker, 2008; Dance, 2011). The algorithms were available from a fully functional website that also offered tutorials, customer support, and regular software upgrades to cybernomads. The latest update reviewed at the end of 2008 offered 'bug fixes' at Party Poker, Full Tilt Poker, and Absolute Poker sites; 'auto-resizing' at Titan Poker and Carbon Poker; and 'upgrade support' at two- and nine-player games at BoDog.com (HoldemGenius, 2008: 2–3). According to a bot provider spokesperson, poker bots increased their profits by '35 percent in a five-day test in January [2004] in which it was used to play 7,000 hands' (cited in Brunker, 2004: 4).

### Hackers

Other cybernomads were more advanced hackers. Some offered computer spyware, complete with service guarantees and customer support (Jellenc and Zenz, 2007; Brothersoft, 2008). Others created bot-networks using malicious codes that were covertly installed on personal or industry computers (McAfee, 2005; Symantec, 2007). These 'zombies' were then activated for simple forms of intrusive trespass or herded into armies for more adventurous criminal projects such as cyberextortion (Skoudis, 2007; McMullan and Rege, 2007). Botnet battalions were sold at various prices; 10 bots for a 24-hour 'test-drive' sold for US$5, small-scale attacks went for about US$40, and 500 bots for one month cost US$220 (Biever, 2004; Jellenc and Zenz, 2007; McAfee, 2005; Payton, 2005). Shadowcrew.com, CardersMarket. com, and CarderPlanet.com were the 'Walmarts' of the cyberunderground, where digital loot such as credit card numbers and social security data were bought and sold in bulk packages and where cybernomads schooled each other on how to upgrade malicious activities for online gambling attacks (McAfee, 2007; McMillen and Grabosky, 1998; Payton, 2005; Symantec, 2007).

Finally, cybernomads with the highest degree of technical acumen were akin to professional criminals. They executed prolonged attacks on their own and were more likely to have subcontracted their services to larger crime networks on a project-by-project basis (Rogers, 2005). One hacker, for example, targeted nine different sites for eight days, eventually closing down Full Tilt Poker for 48 hours and disrupting Titan Poker so that it only loaded for a few hours on several of the eight days (Online-Casinos, 2008: 1; Jellenc and Zenz, 2007). Other hackers stole financial information from providers and conducted clandestine transactions in the customers' names by assuming their legal identities (Cabot, 2001). Still others, like Josh 'JJProdigy' Field, used several accounts concurrently via different IP (Internet protocol, or computer) addresses and computer systems to cheat gambling providers and players. He won a $500,000 tournament but then deliberately lost the next tournament worth $140,000 to another player named ABlackCar. Party Poker later discovered that JJProdigy had operated both accounts, cheating them and their customers of nearly $200,000 (Angerman, 2008).

### Characteristics of cybernomads

Cybernomads tended to operate alone. They emerged safely from online encounters by making use of superior technical force, secrecy, impersonation, and quick attacks. They lived in the digital shadows and were prepared to take flight if necessary to evade industry, avoid victims, and escape legal agents with whom they seldom developed any stable modus vivendi. They often exaggerated their own qualities, especially when they were attacking or avenging gambling providers, which they often thought were beneath them. There were neither leader–gang relationships nor any egalitarian partnerships among cybernomads. They did, however, network with people in digital stores and websites in order to obtain supplies, gain knowledge, plan strategies, and perfect attacks. Digital loot did not have to be shared because the profits were almost always consumed by the principal actors or fixed at set commissions for services when merchandising arrangements were in force.

## Dot.cons

### Outside colluders

Cybercriminals also worked in dot.con teams that united for criminal projects that could be both occasional and ongoing. Players teamed up with other players, consultants, or website owners or managers to commit fraud, theft, and money laundering (Smed, Knuutila, and Hakonen, 2006; Yan, 2003). Most notable were the cases of ZieJustin, TheVoid, and especially Chris 'BluffMagCV' Vaughn, who was denied the $1 million prize he thought he had won because he engaged in 'seat stealing': selling his seat deep in the tournament to a more experienced associate, Sorel 'Imper1um' Mizzi, for a percentage of Mizzi's prize. Mizzi then logged on to Vaughn's account from home, and other players 'faced a completely different BluffMagCV competitor, one with a different playing style and an incredible amount of online MTT [multiple-table tournament] experience,' that opponents did not recognize and could not beat (Angerman, 2008: 2). While the gambling provider eventually tracked the account swap to Mizzi's home IP address, one security expert noted that 'if Sorel and Vaughn lived together, nobody would have known this happened.' He added, 'this [seat stealing] isn't going to stop, because it's unenforceable' (cited in World Poker Rules, 2007: 1; Angerman, 2008).

Dot.cons also exploited gambling site data packets by inserting, deleting, or modifying game events or commands (Yan and Randell, 2005; Yan, 2003). The CheckRaised Rakeback calculator application that players placed on their computers to help track commission fees taken by gambling operators was a case in point. The secret unauthorized program silently installed malware that sent customers' usernames, passwords, and account information back to teams of hackers, which used the information for blackmail and identity fraud (Naraine, 2006; Turkulainen, 2006).

### Criminal insiders

Dot.con teams also included gambling insiders, who provided and/or used privileged information for illegal purposes (Smed, Knuutila, and Hakonen, 2006). The Absolute and Ultimate Bet scandals involving Tokwiro Enterprises and the Kahnawà:ke Gaming Commission were exemplary. Suspecting unfair play, a player at Absolute Poker requested a history of the cards he was dealt during a high-stakes poker tournament. He received a detailed log of every player's hand history and IP address and discovered that at each table at which 'Potripper' played, another account, '#363,' was a 'spectator.' Indeed, once #363 entered the tournament, Potripper did not 'fold a single hand before the flop for the next 20 minutes, and then folded his hand pre-flop when another player had a pair of kings as hole cards!' (Levitt, 2007: 1). Investigations eventually linked #363's IP address to an employee of the company and the Potripper account to a former executive of the company. According to the Gaming Commission, cheating was conducted by a 'high ranking trusted consultant with access to its security systems' (Kahnawà:ke Gaming Commission [KGC], 2008a: 2). The insider consultant had real-time access to all the hole cards on all the hands and had relayed this information to his associate, Potripper. Between them, Potripper and #363 stole between $500,000 and $1 million from players over at least six weeks of undetected illegal play (Goldman, 2007; Levitt, 2007). In addition, six other superuser accounts discarded 'hands on flops despite raising preflop,' suggesting that they too were aware of their opponents' hole cards, and were part of a larger team of account deception and inside corporate collusion that was taking money from consumers, without much fear of detection or prosecution from either the company or the regulator (Casinomeister, 2005: 7; KGC, 2008a; Moses, 2008).

In the case of Ultimate Bet, 'NioNio,' won 13 of 14 sessions and banked $300,000 in profit in just 3,000 hands. This win rate was 10 standard deviations above the mean, or 'approximately equal to winning a one million dollar lottery on six consecutive occasions' (Moses, 2008: 2). Eventually it was discovered that NioNio had obtained an unfair advantage through unauthorized software code that allowed him and other perpetrators to 'obtain hole card information during live play' (KGC, 2008b: 2). The code was apparently written by individuals who worked for Excapsa Software, which had a corporate relationship with E World Holdings, a previous partner of Ultimate Bet, which then used the software to cheat the new owner (Tokwiro Enterprises) and thousands of customers of about $22 million. A total of 23 superuser accounts, involving 117 virtual personas, were deployed by several teams of industry insiders and associates to cheat consumers over 55 months of play, from June 2003 to December 2007. The vast majority of the computer devices, IP addresses, and player accounts used to obtain unauthorized information and steal money had ties to the E World Holdings Group and/or Russell Hamilton, a former World Series of Poker champion. Excapsa, which sold the faulty software to Blast Off Ltd., a company controlled by Tokwiro Enterprises, has paid out a $15-million lawsuit settlement that has been used to compensate some players for the losses that occurred before and during Tokwiro's ownership of Ultimate Bet (KGC, 2009; Hintze, 2008; KGC, 2008b; Swoboda, 2008; Polson, 2008).

Not only were corporate insiders involved in fraud, some engaged in theft by withholding winning revenues or by creating phantom sites and malware to steal from potential customers (Andrle, 2006; CERT-LEXSI, 2006; Kvarnstrom, Lundin, and Jonsson, 2000; Zacharias, 2004). Some site owners transferred potential customers' funds from their business accounts to their personal accounts and then disappeared into the ether of the Internet (Cabot, 2001; CERT-LEXSI, 2006; Penenberg, 1998; Zacharias, 2004). Others designed fake websites with fancy graphics, fraudulent licenses, and fake company phone numbers and email addresses, and stole consumers' identity data under false pretences. Still others, such as GlobalSportsNet, defrauded customers by allegedly not mailing them their winnings, while others, such as 'Fallons' and 'Bingo World,' shorted their customers on their returns (Arthur, 1997; Shaw, 2004).

Employees of gambling sites also teamed up with dot.con teams in crimes against their employers (Rogers, 2005). Employees, for example, sold company secrets, including account information, gaming software, and sophisticated algorithmic programs for deciphering random number generators, to hackers, who then cracked into gaming servers, altered their programs, and ensured that 'every roll of the dice in craps turned up doubles, and every spin on the slots generated a perfect match;...cherries across the board' (cited in Reuters, 2001: 1; Warner, 2001; McMullan and Perrier, 2003, 2007). Perhaps the best-known reported case of employee-generated crime involved Starnet Communications, where highly placed employees cheated its licensees of 85 percent of net sales. Employees created 'fake' winner accounts with modified betting histories. They changed a $20 win for a $20,000 win and deprived the licensee of $19,980. Starnet's accounting unit then paid the supposed winners out and tampered with company records to cover up their workplace crime (Gambling Magazine, 1999).

### Botnet herders and small-scale organized crime

Digital teams sometimes used bots to launder money through gambling sites. One team, for example, swamped poker rooms with inferior poker bots. Dot.con members then played against and defeated the weaker staged bots, allowing money to change hands, with team members dividing the take (OnlinePoker-News, 2007). In other instances, botnet battalions programmed to wager, pick cards, and fold were used to flood casino gaming rooms with illegal capital. Bot-herders took the last seats in the games, easily beat the zombie armies they had mustered, and cashed out the winnings as 'clean' money from the casino or poker room accounts (Sullivan, 2007). Still other dot.con teams engaged in 'chip dumping.' Proceeds from crime were deposited into fake customer accounts and deliberately 'lost' to associates at gaming tables, who then cashed the dumped winnings into a network of accounts, further smoothing the cybertrail from criminality to legality (RSeConsulting, 2006). Finally, some teams used offshore gambling sites to launder funds. From 1998 to 2005, for example, www. BetWWTS.com illegally sequestered US customers' bets, moved their illegal capital to shell corporations, and transferred the money to clandestine accounts in foreign banks in the Caribbean (Ames, 2006; Department of Justice [DOJ], 2006).

Lotteries, such as MaxLotto, were also associated with fraud involving teams of dot.cons. In 2001, it advertised that 10 percent of its worldwide $100-million lottery revenues would be donated to charities (Kelley, Todosichuk, and Azmier, 2001; PRNewsWire, 2001). By 2002, however, MaxLotto.com had disappeared from the net with its customers' capital. No prizes had been paid out and few of its listed benefactors knew of the company or had received donations from it (Bortz, 2008). Or consider the 2007 lottery fraud in India, organized by a three-handed team. The leader, Albaika, recruited Acharya online to serve as the broker for Sagwekar and other teams of agents he had commissioned to set up bogus bank accounts in Mumbai. Then Albaika sent a mass email across India, congratulating many players on winning a lottery worth millions of rupees and instructed them to deposit funds for service charges into bank accounts as a condition of receiving their jackpots. Once the money was deposited, however, Albaika used his network of agents to usurp the clients' funds, estimated to be about $8 million (*Times of India*, 2008).

### Characteristics of dot.cons

Dot.cons approached cybercrime as a working trade, and developed established routines for taking money from a large number of victims. Three circumstances favoured the establishment of this form of illegal activity. First, the dramatic expansion of Internet gambling over the last decade meant that players carried large quantities of personal e-cash in online gambling accounts. Dot.cons thrived by targeting many consumers simultaneously, by not taking too much from any one victim at any one time, and by harvesting many online personas so that consumers did not know that they were cheated or defrauded until long afterward or not at all. Second, in the digital world of multiple make-believe names and easily given trust, dot. cons were fairly safe if they could evade detection and avoid confrontations with virtual victims while they were online. Once away from cyberspace, they could melt into their own social worlds, assume their offline identities, live like other citizens, and return later to the Internet with new proxy identities (Finch, 2007). Finally, the scale and density of Internet gambling sites, activities, and users, as well as other commercial venues, meant that there were enough people on the net to form hacker undergrounds, within which techniques of crime could be developed, innovated, and passed on over time. The result of these circumstances is that dot.con teams have been able to establish a modus vivendi with industry and law enforcement such that overt conflict has so far been minimal. This has not been that difficult because crime control in virtualized worlds remains relatively underfunded, poorly resourced and organized, especially difficult to apply in shifting, borderless contexts, and lacks penalty and deterrence (Aas, 2007; Brenner, 2007; Jewkes and Andrews, 2007; McMullan and Rege, 2007).

The typical form of organization for dot.con teams has been a flexible group, consisting of two to six associates who participated in particular criminal events, in which each person had specialized roles to play in the crimes that they conducted, such as programming attack tools, creating malware, herding bots, manipulating player accounts, and laundering financial transactions. Occasionally these teams could be allied with other teams in larger groups. The most common organizational rules appeared to be that novices followed the lead of more experienced dot.cons, and that payouts were negotiated in advance of jobs and mostly honoured once criminal events were completed. As Holt (2009) observes, hackers who formed 'teams' tended to be more sophisticated, lasted for longer periods of time on the Internet, and had more developed stratification structures when compared to empowered loners.

## Assemblages

### Cyberextortion networks

Crime assemblages constituted a third type of organization related to Internet gambling, and are exemplified by the cyberextortion attacks of online sites between 2000 and 2006. The distributed denial of service (DDoS) attack was the typical technique, that began with bots that were herded into armies, weeks or months before attacks were scheduled (Paulson and Weber, 2006; Ratliff, 2005). Bots then swamped gambling providers with bogus requests that consumed all available disk space and central processing unit (CPU) time, bandwidth capability, or physical network components, and denied services to legitimate customers (McMullan and Rege, 2007; Paulson and Weber, 2006, Murphy, Pender, Reilly, and Connel, 2005). Once the sites were slowed or shut down, ransoms (US$40,000–50,000) in return for protection from further attacks were demanded: 'Dear wwts, as you can see your site is under attack. We have found a problem with your network…You will lose more than $40,000 in the next couple of hours if you do not resolve this problem,' one attacker warned in an email (cited in Karshmer, 2005: 1). If the operators did not pay up, the attacks continued and the sites suffered further disruptions and demands for tribute (Warner, 2001; Cassavoy, 2005; Germain, 2003, 2004). In 2003, BetCris was warned, 'if you choose not to pay for our help, then you will probably not be in business much longer, as you will be under attack each weekend for the next 20 weeks, or until you close your doors' (cited in Ratliff, 2005: 4). BetCris did not comply, and it took the cyberextortionists less than 20 minutes to take down the site. Hundreds of gambling sites were subjected to DDoS attacks, and cyberextortionists inflicted over $70 million in reported overall damages to British bookmakers alone in 2004 (Nuttall, 2004).

Cyberextortion networks had an elementary division of labour that included organizers, extenders, and executors (Lemieux, 2003). Organizers arranged plans for subnetwork members. They often came from legitimate activities to exploit new online opportunities in the gambling field (Gray, 2005). The mastermind in one cyberextortion ring, for example, was a 21-year-old mechanical engineering student who studied computer programming before starting to hack gambling sites for a living (Computer Crime Research Center [CCRC], 2005; McConnell International LLC, 2000). Others worked at the behest of international syndicates that provided the capital to finance attacks at online sites (Germain, 2004; Walker, 2004). Extenders were mainly recruiters who screened new members or added to the skill sets of the networks. For example, one hacker was reportedly 'contacted by a couple of different criminal organizations that offered him quite a bit of money,' and known associates of his were allegedly hired by 'various organized crime groups' (cited in Public Broadcasting Service, 2001: 3). Executors were the front-line agents, who possessed practical knowledge of reverse engineering, virus installations, and architectural vulnerabilities. They banded together to implement DDoS attacks against gambling sites from around the world. For example, three hacker rings running DDoS attacks against UK bookmakers also made 54 similar attacks, in 30 other countries, for six months, worth an estimated US$4 million (Leyden, 2006). Indeed, one cyberextortion ring had members in Moscow, St Petersburg, and Saratov who had never met face to face. As one police officer observed, this was 'not a normal organization. Everyone sat at home, and everyone had their role' (cited in Bullough, 2004: 2). This separation of tasks and personnel resulted in a remote compartmentalization structure that guaranteed a fluid, flexible, and smooth-functioning network with regenerative characteristics. So these mafias of the minute required fewer interpersonal contacts, fewer relationships based on sponsorship and discipline, and fewer hierarchical command systems to commit crimes when compared to conventional real-world organized-crime groups (Brenner, 2002; Council of Europe, 2004; McAfee, 2005; CCRC, 2005; Gray, 2005; Ferentzy and Turner, 2009).

### Phishers and identity fraud

Cyberassemblages also used gambling sites to conduct identity scams, but on a grander scale than dot.cons. One criminal network, with the help of an insider, hacked into BetOnSports' database and stole account names, addresses, phone numbers, social security numbers, and credit card and bank account numbers, which they then used for illegal purchases and identity fraud around the world (DOJ, 2007a; Mark, 2007; United States Attorney Southern District of New York [USASDNY], 2008; Caray, 2006). Another cyberassemblage combined confidence cheating with identity theft, and deployed the real addresses of the lottery Euromillion Espana to swindle consumers of an estimated \$200 million in France, Australia, the Netherlands, Britain, Romania, and East Africa (elGordo, 2008). Some network members were akin to forgers and created fake sites and administrative documents. Others posed as representatives of elGordo.com and sent convincing emails to consumers. They obtained confidential customer information through three phishing techniques: (1) the deceptive attack, where users were tricked by fraudulent messages into releasing their information through the lottery to crime groups; (2) the malware attack, where malicious code placed on customers' computers retrieved confidential user information without their consent; and (3) the Domain Name System (DNS) attack, where the IP addresses of lottery sites were altered to send victims to fraudulent servers (Emigh, 2005; CERT-LEXSI, 2006). While Spanish police eventually arrested some members, the crime network continued to function despite international court prosecutions (Queen, 2007). A third cyberassemblage involved PartyPoker.com, where phishers in a criminal enterprise designed a replica of the site and hosted it on their own illegal servers. Party Poker's customers were sent emails warning of US legislation that would affect them and were told to take remedial action by clicking a link to the cloned site's login page. Those who complied were directed to a phantom venue, where they were prompted for personal information that was then used to (1) sell legal identities for criminal use, (2) simulate real user accounts so that network members could impersonate players and gamble in their place, (3) steal playing credits from online gambling accounts, and (4) merchandise digital data such as customer account lists to competing gambling sites (CERT-LEXSI, 2006; Chen et al., 2005; Emigh, 2005; Thompson, 2007).

### Money-laundering enterprises

Criminal assemblages also operated or worked in tandem with Internet gambling sites to further other criminal pursuits. From 1997 to 2008, for example, US state and federal courts have charged and convicted gambling companies such as World Sports Exchange, World Interactive Gaming Corporation, Golden Chips Casino, Paradise Casino, Gold Medal Casino, BetCris, Dukesports, Betcorp, Betwwwts, BetonSports, Bettheduck, Sportingbet, and Safedepositsports for crimes including conspiring to violate the Wire Wager Act, tax fraud, illegal gambling, money laundering, racketeering, and enterprise corruption. While many of these prosecutions were for engaging in or enabling illegal sports betting using phone lines and computers on the Internet, several had complex structures involving formal organized-crime elements.

The Giordano money-laundering enterprise is a good case in point. Members of this network were adept at moving unlawfully earned proceeds through online casinos, shell corporations, and bank accounts to Central America, the Caribbean, Switzerland, and Hong Kong. The executors involved front companies that developed the gambling website www. playwithal.com, which enabled approximately 40,000 customers to set up accounts and place bets on football, baseball, golf, and other sports events. Giordano, the organizer, ran the strategic operation of the network; his son-in-law, the controller, oversaw the everyday operations, managed bettor information, and handled Internet accounting matters and discrepancies; and his wife and daughter, the financial officers, laundered crime proceeds to several offshore banks. Five other individuals acted as street-level clerks, runners, and enforcers, collecting bets; distributing, delivering, and transferring illegal gambling proceeds between members; and maintaining network and bettor discipline when necessary (CERT-LEXSI, 2006; North Country Gazette, 2006; Venezia, Martinez, and Livingston, 2006).

The Uvari Bookmaking network also combined an illegal gambling business with money laundering and tax evasion. They had network members and clients in New York, New Jersey, Florida, Nevada, North Dakota, New Hampshire, and Oklahoma, as well as in offshore locations, such as the Euro Off-Track in the Isle of Man and the Elite Turf Club in Curacao. The Uvari Group operated as an intermediary between gamblers and sports betting companies. They determined their 'take' based on the volume of accounts they opened at offshore sites and always returned a portion of their commissions to bettors as an incentive for them to continue using their bookmaking facilities. They created customer accounts for individual bettors, took their customers' personal information, and attached it to the social security numbers of group members, creating hundreds of dummy accounts in their own names. This permitted customers to remain anonymous and avoid paying taxes on winnings and, simultaneously, allowed the Uvari Group to launder money and claim income tax deductions by associating their customers' losses with their own accounts (CERT-LEXSI, 2006; USASDNY, 2005; DOJ, 2007b).

Finally, the Corozzo network engaged in an illegal gambling and loan-sharking enterprise that was based in the United States and Costa Rica. The network of at least 26 members relied on toll-free telephone numbers and four online betting websites to handle thousands of sport wagers each month, from November 2005 to January 2008, amounting to an estimated take of $10 million. A controller ran the operations, resolved bettor and accounting disputes, and managed account information, and three agents oversaw the offshore accounts, calibrated wins and losses, counted the weekly take, and advised the controller regarding economic matters. In addition, an onshore clerk accepted wagers over the telephone and recorded them on audiotape and on paper, six money collectors transferred gambling proceeds between members of the organization and financial institutions, and 13 runners managed bettors by accepting wagers and setting up login codes and passwords. Finally, two enforcers lent money at exorbitant interest rates to troubled bettors and instilled fear in all bettors not to miss their payments (District Attorney Queens County, 2008; North Country Gazette, 2008).

These case studies suggest that Internet gambling sites are ideal for complex fraudulent and extortionist activities that, in turn, can finance yet other crimes. Despite the strict codes for reporting financial transactions, criminal assemblages seem able to function online by manipulating accounts and aliases, making smaller cash exchanges, putting players 'on the take' on their payrolls, hiding transactions in a bewildering array of gambling and bank accounts, and mobilizing fear when necessary.

## Characteristics of criminal assemblages

Criminal assemblages were structured as ongoing projects that relied upon the time-honoured methods of long firm fraud: the willingness of a large number of victims to supply credit and information and to invest or agree to acquiesce to schemes that promised to pay well over the odds, and relatively large networks with specialized roles and authority structures. This culminated in the establishment of criminal businesses on the net, where victims were relieved of both identity and capital before bankruptcies were declared or corporations disappeared. This was especially apparent with the modus operandi of cyberextortion networks, that were remotely controlled, and that supplied contact points to assemble criminal endeavours and to develop counteractions against reluctant or resistant victims, competitors, or law enforcement agencies, after which they usually dispersed, only to resurface later (Brenner, 2002; McMullan and Rege, 2007).

However, because larger amounts of money were being appropriated in an increasingly visible way, gambling providers, regulators, police, and private security companies necessarily stepped up their efforts to prevent it. One consequence was that assemblages had to be prepared to take greater chances, including raising the risks involved in marketing their products, and using direct confrontations with their victims, while simultaneously upgrading their techniques and planning to minimize these higher risks. Assemblages upgraded the speed of operations and deployed ingenious aliases, clones, and simulations; engaged in remote planning, careful recruiting of members, and prudent online behaviour that aroused as little suspicion as possible; and communicated via screen identities that were difficult to trace. In short, speed, anonymity, synchronization, and coordination were arranged as much as possible in advance so that criminal acts appeared as 'natural' as possible and aroused few suspicions.

A second consequence was that victimized gambling sites took more precautionary licensing and registration measures, developed better internal security measures, hired private cybersecurity firms, and tried to mobilize existing law enforcement agencies to help them combat criminal networks. However, the laws governing cybercrime were and remain imprecise and confounding as to where offences occurred (i.e., whether in the country where criminal networks were based or in the jurisdiction where the crimes happened), where evidence should be collected, what laws applied and in what jurisdiction, what courts prevailed, and what sanctions were appropriate (Wall, 2007; Brenner, 2007; Jewkes and Andrews, 2007; Grabosky, 2001). Furthermore, national and transnational law enforcement agencies did not have the reach, resources, or expertise to investigate crimes that were committed from remote places in multiple sovereign jurisdictions where the offenders were not even present, which resulted in low public visibility of gambling-related crimes, few successful prosecutions, and, for the most part, paltry penalties (Nhan and Huey, 2008; Moore, 2007; McMullan and Rege, 2007; Jewkes and Andrews, 2007).

The weakness of global legal governance, not surprisingly, has encouraged multilateral policing by private-sector providers and digital security firms, and fostered self-help business solutions reliant upon authentication and encryption technologies. This has meant investing in business opportunity reduction remedies, such as detection systems, enhanced firewall protection, and patch and configuration systems to limit malware infections and software compromises, and in intelligent web-based products, such as parallel network intrusion prevention architectures and self-correcting software to identify, filter, and divert illegitimate traffic from gambling sites to improve security. But these reforms have not eliminated the problems. To start, the relations between private and public agencies have not always been workable. The case of Don Best Sports, which was extorted for $200,000, is illustrative of this problem. A computer security company tracked the cyberattacks to a chat room in Kazakhstan, but when they notified the FBI and the Secret Service, the latter 'threw up their arms because it was in Kazakhstan,' said the CEO of the private security company (cited in Ratliff, 2005: 3). Furthermore, resorting to multilateral policing and self-help solutions has been costly. Many gambling companies cannot afford the expensive investments in hardware, software, maintenance, and upgrading. The result is a global patchwork of private self-help fiefdoms, that afforded security to some, but created few industry-wide standards on safety and protection and little consensus about the best devices to stop cybercrimes early and at a distance from gambling venues. Finally, authentication and encryption technologies have created an underground cottage industry in devices and schemes to circumvent these security tools. As cybersecurity has evolved, the high-level plans of cyberthieves, cybercons, and cyberextortionists have disguised attacks, intrusions, and simulations at their point of ingress into gambling site networks; tested the guards, tech boxes, switches, and detectors for anomalies and weaknesses; and probed the new multilateral and commercial security systems for gaps, lapses, and intelligence. A never-ending cycle of enhanced detection and counterdetection measures has proliferated to rationally handle the technical problems of crime and negotiate the exigencies of legal control on the Internet, resulting in an online marketplace that remains replete with criminal potential (Jewkes, 2007; Nhan and Huey, 2008; McMullan and Rege, 2007; Wall, 2007).

## Conclusion

In sum, crime assemblages were more formal and continuous in operation when compared to the two other kinds of online criminal organization. They were more sophisticated than dot. cons or cybernomads, had the most elaborate division of labour for engaging in criminal behaviour, and lasted for an extended duration across time and space. However, despite the more complex stratification system and apparent ability to neutralize rather than evade or avoid formal law enforcement, there is no evidence that these crime networks coordinated their activities into cartels, purchased immunity from the state by bribery or influence peddling, or imposed a monopoly either by consent or coercion over cybernomads or dot. cons. There is no tendency toward a business-enterprise type of organization where the former usurps or administers the latter. More likely, there will be no sudden disappearance of cybernomads, dot.cons, or crime assemblages from Internet gambling sites in the near future. So, users, providers, and architects of online gambling sites have good reason to express concern about the protection of private information, the integrity of the games, and the security of websites because Internet gambling has been a source of crime, a vehicle for crime, and a support for crime. Like other forms of Internet commerce, it has not been immune to criminal exploitation, and what is likely is that the cases that come to the attention of the industry, regulatory authorities, consumers, and academic researchers probably represent the tip of the iceberg.

## Acknowledgment

This is an abridged version of an article that appeared in the *Journal of Gambling Issues*, no. 24, July 2010, pp. 54–85.

## References

Aas, K. F. (2007). 'Beyond "the desert of the real." Crime control in virtualized reality'. In Y. Jewkes (ed.), *Crime online*. Cullompton: Willan.

American Gaming Association. (2006). *Gambling and the Internet: The A.G.A. survey of casino entertainment*.Washington, DC: American Gaming Association.

Ames, B. (2006). 'Internet gambling operators indicted'. *PC World*. Retrieved April 2, 2008 from http://www.pcworld.com/printable/article/id,125759/printable.html.

Andrle, J. D. (2006). 'A winning hand: A proposal for an international regulatory schema with respect to the growing online gambling dilemma in the United States'. *UNLV Gaming Research & Review Journal, 10*(1), 59–93.

Angerman, A. (2008). 'Is there integrity in online poker?' *PokerPages*. Retrieved March 23, 2008 from http://www.pokerpages.com/articles/archives/angerman03.htm.

Arthur, C. (1997). 'Suckers pour cash into casino ripoffs online'. *The Independent* (London). Retrieved November 28, 2009 from http://www.independent.co.uk/news/suckers-pour-cash-into-casino-ripoffs-online-1287336.html.

Best, J., and Luckenbill, D. F. (1982). *Organizing deviance*. Englewood Cliffs, NJ: Prentice-Hall.

Biever, C. (2004). 'How zombie networks fuel cybercrime'. *NewScientist.com.* Retrieved June 5, 2005 from http://www.newscientist.com/channel/info-tech/electronic-threats/dn6616.

Bortz, B. (2008). 'LinkedIn: Bill Bortz'. Retrieved April 4, 2008, from http://www.linkedin.com/pub/4/1BB/653.

Brenner, S. W. (2002). 'Organized cybercrime? How cyberspace may affect the structure of criminal relationships'. *North Carolina Journal of Law & Technology*, 4(1), 1–41.

— (2007). 'Cybercrime: Re-thinking crime control strategies'. In Y. Jewkes (ed.), *Crime online*. Cullompton: Willan.

Brothersoft. (2008). *POD 1.1 Download*. Retrieved February 28, 2008 from http://www.brothersoft.com/pod-69549.html.

Brunker, M. (2004). 'Poker "bots" raking online pots?' *Internet roulette on msnbc.com.* Retrieved March 20, 2008 from http://www.msnbc.msn.com/id/6002298/print/1/displaymode/1098/.

Bullough, O. (2004). 'Police say Russian hackers are increasing threat'. *USA Today*. Retrieved April 5, 2008 from http://www.usatoday.com/tech/news/internetprivacy/2004-07-28-russian-hackers_x.htm.

Cabot, A. (2001). *Internet gambling report IV.* (4th edition). Las Vegas: Trace Publications.

Caray, H. (2006). 'Nigerian crooks pleaded guilty on identity theft scam with BETonSPORTS Database [online forum comment]'. Retrieved April 3, 2008 from http://www.sportshandicappingforum.com/showthread.php?t=56569.

CasinoCity. (2010). 'Casino City: Your casino directory'. Retrieved October 23, 2010, from http://www.casinocity.com/.

Casinomeister. (2005). 'Gambling federation casinos'. Retrieved April 2, 2008 from http://www.casinomeister.com/rogue/blunders/gamblingfederation.php.

Cassavoy, L. (2005). 'Web of crime: Internet gangs go global'. *PC World*. Retrieved October 25, 2005 from http://www.pcworld.com/article/122242/web_of_crime_internet_gangs_go_global.html.

Chen, Y. C., Chen, P. C., Hwang, J. J., Korba, L., Song, R., and Yee, G. (2005). 'An analysis of online gaming crime characteristics'. *Internet Research*, 15(3), 246–61.

Computer Crime Research Center (CCRC). (2005). 'U.S. cyber-crime unit focuses on Russian hackers'. Retrieved May 21, 2005 from http://crime-research.org/analytics/1226.

Computer Emergency Response Team – Laboratoire d'Expertise en Sécurité Informatique (CERT-LEXSI). (2006). *Online gaming cybercrime: CERT-LEXSI'S White Paper*, July 2006.

Council of Europe. (2004). 'Summary of the Organized Crime Situation Report 2004: Focus on the threat of cybercrime'. *Trends in Organized Crime*, 8(3), 41–50.

Dance, G. (2011). 'Poker bots invade online gambling'. Retrieved March 16, 2011 from http://www.nytimes.com/2011/03/14/science/14poker.html?partner=rss&emc=rss.

Department of Justice (DOJ). (2006). 'Money laundering indictment unsealed against major Internet gambling site operators, alleges $250 million in online wagers'. Retrieved April 2, 2008 from http://www.usdoj.gov/opa/pr/2006/May/06_crm_298.html.

— (2007a). 'Man sentenced to 34 months in prison for involvement in large identity-theft ring'. Retrieved June 1, 2010 from http://www.justice.gov/usao/nys/pressreleases/January07/elekedesentencingpr.pdf

— (2007b). 'Statement of Catherine Hanaway, United States Attorney, Eastern District of Missouri, United States Department of Justice'. Before the United States House of Representatives Committee on the Judiciary Concerning 'Internet Gambling.' Retrieved June 1, 2010 from http://judiciary.house.gov/hearings/pdf/Hanaway071114.pdf.

District Attorney Queens County. (2008). 'Twenty-six charged in $10 million dollar Gambino organized crime family gambling, loan sharking and prostitution operation'. Retrieved May 15, 2009 from http://www.queensda.org/newpressreleases/2008/february/corozzo_02_07_2008_cmp.pdf.

elGordo. (2008). 'Advice about scams'. Retrieved April 4, 2008, from http://www.elgordo.com/info/scamsen.asp.

Emigh, A. (2005). *Online identity theft: Phishing technology, chokepoints and countermeasures.* ITTC Report on Online Identity Theft Technology and Countermeasures. Retrieved March 20, 2007, from http://www.savemyos.com/organization/Additinal_PDF_files_files/Phishing-dhs-report.pdf.

Ferentzy, P., and Turner, N. (2009). 'Gambling and organized crime – A review of the literature'. *Journal of Gambling Issues*, 23, 111–55.

Finch, E. (2007). 'The problem of stolen identity and the Internet'. In Y. Jewkes (ed.), *Crime online*. Cullompton: Willan.

Gambling Magazine (1999) 'The real danger for this industry'. *Gambling Magazine*. Retrieved October 19, 2006 from http://gamblingmagazine.com/articles/starnet/starnet113.htm.

Germain, J. M. (2003). 'Computer viruses and organized crime: The inside story'. *TechNewsWorld*. Retrieved November 10, 2005 from http://www.technewsworld.com/story/31679.html.

— (2004). 'Global extortion: Online gambling and organized hacking'. *MacNewsWorld*. Retrieved May 21, 2005, from http://www.macnewsworld.com/story/33171.html.

Giacopassi, D., and Pitts, W. J. (2009). 'Internet gambling: The birth of a victimless crime'. In F. J. Schmalleger, and M. Pittaro (eds), *Crimes of the Internet*. New York: Prentice-Hall.

Goldman, R. (2007). 'Online poker players expose alleged fraud'. *ABCNews.com*. Retrieved January 29, 2008, from http://abcnews.go.com/print?id=3752500.

Grabosky, P. (2001). 'Virtual criminality: Old wine in new bottles'. *Social and Legal Studies, 10*(2), 243–9.

Gray, P. (2005). 'Hackers: The winds of change'. *Secured Newsletter*. Retrieved June 5, 2005 from http://www.iss.net/newsletters/secured/2005/mar/winds_of_change.html.

Griffiths, M. (2010). 'Crime and gambling: A brief overview of gambling fraud on the internet'. *Internet Journal of Criminology*, 1–7.

Griffiths, M. D., Parke, A., Wood, R. T. A., and Parke, J. (2006). 'Internet gambling: An overview of psychosocial impacts'. *Gaming Research and Review Journal, 27*(1), 27–39.

Gu, Q., Liu, P., and Chu, C. (2004). 'Hacking techniques in wired networks'. Retrieved March 23, 2008 from http://ist.psu.edu/s2/paper/hack-wired-network-may-04.pdf.

Hintze, H. (2008). 'Compensation resumes in UltimateBet scandal as legal agreement reached'. Retrieved November 4, 2008 from http://www.pokernews.com/news/2008/11/ultimate-bet-scandal.htm.

HoldemGenius. (2008). 'Software updates – Holdem Genius'. Retrieved April 2, 2008, from http://www.holdemgenius.com/software-updates.html.

Holt, T. J. (2009). 'Lone hackers or group crackers: Examining the social organization of computer hackers'. In F. J. Schmalleger, and M. Pittaro (eds), *Crimes of the Internet*. New York: Prentice-Hall.

Jellenc, E., and Zenz, K. (2007). 'Global threat research report: Russia'. Retrieved June 1, 2010 from http://www.verisign.com/static/042139.pdf.

Jewkes, Y. (ed.). (2003). *Dot.cons: Crime, deviance and identity on the Internet*. Cullompton: Willan.

— (ed.). (2007). *Crime online*. Cullompton: Willan.

Jewkes, Y., and Andrews, C. (2007). 'Internet child pornography: International responses'. In Y. Jewkes (ed.), *Crime online*. Cullompton: Willan.

Kahnawà:ke Gaming Commission (KGC). (2008a). *In the matter of Absolute Poker: Investigation regarding complaints of cheating (May 29)*. Kahnawà:ke Mohawk Territory.

— (2008b). *Kahnawà:ke Gaming Commission imposes sanctions on UltimateBet with regard to cheating incidents (September 29)*. Kahnawà:ke Mohawk Territory.

— (2009). *In the matter of Tokwiro Enterprises ENRG, carrying on business as UltimateBet. Investigation regarding complaints of cheating (September 11)*. Kahnawà:ke Mohawk Territory.

Karshmer, A. (2005). 'Virtual villains: Global gangsters are extorting money from online casinos with a novel threat: we'll spam you to death'. *MSNBC*. Retrieved June 1, 2010 from http://www.newsweek.com/id/54694.

Keller, B. P. (1999). 'The game's the same: Why gambling in cyberspace violates federal law'. *Yale Law Journal*, *108*(7), 1569–609.

Kelley, R., Todosichuk, P., and Azmier, J. J. (2001). *Gambling @ home: Internet gambling in Canada*. (Gambling in Canada Research Report No. 15) Calgary, AB: Canada West Foundation.

Kish, S. (1999). 'Betting on the Net: An analysis of the government's role in addressing Internet gambling'. *Federal Communications Law Journal*, *51*(2), 449–66.

Kvarnstrom, H., Lundin, E., and Jonsson, E. (2000). 'Combining fraud and intrusion detection – Meeting new requirements'. Retrieved March 10, 2007 from http://www.ce.chalmers.se/emilie/papers/Kvarnstrom_nordsec2000.pdf.

Lemieux, V. (2003). *Criminal networks*. RCMP. Retrieved June 1, 2010 from http://dsp-psd.pwgsc.gc.ca/Collection/JS62-107-2003E.pdf.

Levitt, S. D. (2007). 'The Absolute Poker cheating scandal blown wide open'. *New York Times*. Retrieved January 29, 2008, from http://freakonomics.blogs.nytimes.com/2007/10/17/the-absolute-poker-cheating-scandal-blown-wide-open/.

Leyden, J. (2006). 'Russian bookmaker hackers jailed for eight years'. *The Register*. Retrieved March 24, 2009 from http://www.theregister.co.uk/2006/10/04/russian_bookmaker_hackers_jailed/.

McAfee. (2005). 'McAfee virtual criminology report: North American study into organized crime and the Internet'. Retrieved October 20, 2005, from http://www.mcafee.com/us/local_content/misc/mcafee_na_virtual_criminology_report.pdf.

— (2007). 'McAfee North America criminology report: Organized crime and the Internet 2007'. Retrieved January 21, 2008 from http://us.mcafee.com/en-us/local/html/identity_theft/NAVirtualCriminologyReport07.pdf.

McConnell International LLC. (2000). 'Cybercrime…and punishment? Archaic laws threaten global information'. Retrieved June 1, 2010 from http://www.witsa.org/papers/McConnell-cybercrime.pdf.

McMillen, J., and Grabosky, P. (1998). 'Internet gambling'. Trends and Issues in Crime and Criminal Justice No. 88. Canberra: Australia Institute of Criminology. Retrieved December 9, 2007.

McMullan, J. L., and Perrier, D. C. (2003). 'Technologies of crime: The cyber-attacks on electronic gambling machines'. *Canadian Journal of Criminology and Criminal Justice*, *45*(2), 159–86.

McMullan, J. L., and Perrier, D. (2007). 'The security of gambling and gambling with security: Hacking, law enforcement and public policy'. *International Gambling Studies*, *7*(1), 43–58.

McMullan, J., and Rege, A. (2007). 'Cyber-extortion at online gambling sites: Criminal organization and legal challenges'. *Gaming Law Review*, *11*(6), 648–65.

Mark, R. (2007). 'BetonSports ID thief sentenced to 34 months'. Retrieved April 3, 2008 from http://www.insideid.com/print.php/3656181.

Mason, J. (2002). *Qualitative researching*. 2nd edition. London: Sage.

Maxfield, M. G., and Babbie, E. (2001). *Research methods for criminal justice and criminology*. Belmont, CA: Wadsworth.

Moore, R. (2007). 'The role of computer forensics in criminal investigations'. In Y. Jewkes (ed.), *Crime online*. Cullompton: Willan.

Moses, A. (2008). 'Aussie exposes online poker rip-off'. *Sydney Morning Herald*. Retrieved November 21, 2008 from http://www.smh.com.au/news/biztech/dogged-aussie-detective-work-reveals-10m-ripoff/2008/09/30/1222651059903.html.

Murphy, A., Pender, A., Reilly, L., and Connel, S. (2005). *Denial of service and countermeasures*. Networks and Telecommunications Research Group. Retrieved May 21, 2005 from http://ntrg.cs.tcd.ie/undergrad/4ba2.05/group2/.

Naraine, R. (2006). 'Rootkit infiltrates online poker software'. *eWeek.com*. Retrieved March 21, 2008 from http://www.eweek.com/c/a/Security/Rootkit-Infiltrates-Online-Poker-Software/.

Neuman, L. W. (2003). *Social research methods: Qualitative and quantitative approaches*. Boston, MA: Allyn & Bacon.

Nhan, J., and Huey, L. (2008). 'Policing through nodes, clusters and bandwidth'. In S. Leman-Langlois (ed.), *Techno crime: Technology, crime and social control*. Cullompton: Willan.

North Country Gazette (2006). 'Massive Internet gambling operation busted'. Retrieved March 20, 2008 from http://www.northcountrygazette.org/articles/111506InternetGambling.html.

— (2008). 'Gambino captain, others busted for sports gambling'. Retrieved May 15, 2009 from http://www.northcountrygazette.org/2008/02/07/gambino-captain-others-busted-for-sports-gambling/.

Nuttall, C. (2004). 'Hackers blackmail internet bookies: Criminals believed to be targeting Grand National'. *Financial Times*. Retrieved May 21, 2005 from http://www.toplayer.com/pdf/FinancialTimes_230204.pdf.

Online-Casinos. (2008). 'DDOS danger for online gambling sites'. Retrieved April 3, 2008 from http://www.online-casinos.com/news/news6272.asp.

OnlinePoker-News. (2007). 'Bots are used to launder money in online casinos'. Retrieved March 20, 2008 from http://www.onlinepoker-news.com/20070906/bots_are_used_to_launder_money_in_online_ich.aspx

Parke, J., Rigbye, J., Parke, A., Wood, R.T.A., Sjenitzer, J., and Vaughan Williams, L. (2007). 'The global online gambler report: An exploratory investigation into the attitudes and behaviours of internet casino and poker players'. eCommerce and Online Gaming Regulation and Assurance (eCOGRA). Retrieved November 24, 2008 from http://www.ecogra.com/Downloads/eCOGRA_Global_Online_Gambler_Report.pdf.

Paulson, R. A., and Weber, J. E. (2006). 'Cyber-extortion: An overview of distributed denial of service attacks against online gaming companies'. *Issues in Information Systems*, 7(2), 52–6.

Payton, A. (2005). 'Determining the proper response to online extortion'. Paper presented at the Information Security Curriculum Development Conference, September 23–24.

Penenberg, A. L. (1998). 'Gambler beware'. *Forbes digital tool: E-business*. Retrieved June 1, 2010 from http://www.forbes.com/1998/06/12/feat.html.

Polson, S. (2008). 'UltimateBet, Absolute owner reaches settlement'. Retrieved December 12, 2008 from http://www.pokerlistings.com/ultimatebet-absolute-owner-reaches-settlement-32573.

PRNewsWire. (2001). 'MaxLotto officially launches world's biggest continuous lottery in Britain with 69.3 million pounds sterling biweekly jackpot and 6.93 million pounds weekly jackpot'. Retrieved April 4, 2008 from http://www.prnewswire.co.uk/cgi/news/release?id=63585.

Public Broadcasting Service. (2001). 'Interview: Chris Davis'. Retrieved October 15, 2007 from http://www.pbs.org/wgbh/pages/frontline/shows/hackers/interviews/davis.html.

Queen, L. (2007). 'Smart Scarborough senior avoids lottery scam'. Retrieved June 1, 2010 from http://www.insidetoronto.com/article/46815–smart-scarborough-senior-avoids-lottery-scam.

Ratliff, E. (2005). 'The zombie hunters: On the trail of cyberextortionists'. *The New Yorker*. Retrieved June 1, 2010 from http://www.newyorker.com/archive/2005/10/10/051010fa_fact.

Reuters. (2001). 'Hackers win high stakes at gambling sites'. Retrieved June 1, 2010 from http://news.cnet.com/news/0-1005-200-7119198.html?tag = cd_mh.

Rogers, M. K. (2005). 'The development of a meaningful hacker taxonomy: A two dimensional approach'. Retrieved January 23, 2007, from https://www.cerias.purdue.edu/tools_and_resources/bibtex_archive/archive/2005–43.pdf.

RSeConsulting (2006). *A literature review and survey of statistical sources on remote gambling. Final report*. October. Retrieved August 30, 2011, from http://www.culture.gov.uk/NR/rdonlyres/89D59ABD-A1F6–4106-B922-2293997EF841/0/RemoteGamblingAppendix_RSeReport.pdf.

Shaw, C. (2004). 'Net surfing more than working? Websense cuts down on misuse'. *Investor's Business Daily*, National Edition, p. B02.

Skoudis, E. (2007). 'What are the risks of logging into a botnet control channel?' Retrieved October 31, 2007, from http://searchsecurity.techtarget.com/expert/KnowledgebaseAnswer/0,289625,sid14_gci1274217,00.html.

Smed, J., Knuutila, T., and Hakonen, H. (2006). 'Can we prevent collusion in multiplayer online games?' Retrieved January 10, 2007 from http://www.stes.fi/scai2006/proceedings/168–75.pdf.

SmokePoker. (2008). 'Free Poker Bot – Instant Download!' Retrieved March 20, 2008 from http://smokepoker.com.

Sullivan, D. (2007). 'Botnets meet Ocean's Eleven: Scamming online gambling'. Retrieved April 2, 2008, from http://www.realtime-websecurity.com/articles_and_analysis/2007/10/botnets_meet_oceans_eleven_sca.html.

Swoboda, E. D. (2008). 'Muddy waters'. Retrieved June 1, 2010 from http://www.igamingnews.com/index.cfm?page=artlisting&ContentId=189844.

Symantec. (2007). 'Symantec Internet security threat report: Trends for January – June 2007'. Retrieved October 31, 2007 from http://eval.symantec.com/mktginfo/enterprise/white_papers/ent-whitepaper_internet_security_threat_report_xii_09_2007.en-us.pdf.

Thompson, I. (2007). *Phishing attacks target PartyPoker*. Retrieved March 20, 2008, from http://www.vnunet.com/vnunet/news/2183974/phishing-attack-targets-party.

*Times of India.* (2008). 'Nigerian arrested for online fraud'. *Times of India.* Retrieved April 4, 2008 from http://timesofindia.indiatimes.com/Cities/Mumbai/Nigerian_arrested_for_online_fraud/articleshow/2714862.cms.

Turkulainen, J. (2006). 'F-Secure Trojan information pages: Small.la'. Retrieved March 21, 2008 from http://www.f-secure.com/v-descs/small_la.shtml.

United States Attorney Southern District of New York (USASDNY). (2005). 'U.S. indicts 17 in massive crackdown on multi-million dollar illegal gambling operation'. Retrieved September 24, 2007 from http://www.usdoj.gov/usao/nys/pressreleases/January05/uvarietalindictmentpr.pdf.

— (2008). 'Former Internet gambling site employee pleads guilty to stealing identities for international identity theft ring'. Retrieved June 1, 2010 from http://www.justice.gov/usao/nys/pressreleases/September08/kalonjipleapr.pdf.

Venezia, T., Martinez, E., and Livingston, I. (2006). '$3.3 Bil Casino Royale: Net Bet King of Qns. in "biggest ever" bookie bust'. *New York Post.* Retrieved April 2, 2008 from http://www.nypost.com/p/news/bust_casino_royale_net_bet_king_EIkJFy6LMixfeTga2RyxBP.

Walker, C. (2004). 'Russian Mafia extorts gambling websites'. Retrieved November 10, 2005 from http://www.americanmafia.com/Feature_Articles_270.html.

Wall, D. S. (2007). *Cybercrime: The transformation of crime in the information age.* London: Polity Press.

Warner, B. (2001). 'Hackers heaven: Online gambling'. *CBS News.* Retrieved September 14, 2005 from http://www.cbsnews.com/stories/2001/09/10/tech/main310567.shtml.

Williams, R. J., and Wood, R. T. (2007). *Internet gambling: A comprehensive review and synthesis of the literature.* Report prepared for the Ontario Problem Gambling Research Centre, Guelph, ON.

Williams, R. J., and Wood, R. T. (2009). 'Internet gambling setting the stage: History, current world wide situation, regulatory frameworks and concerns with Internet gambling'. Paper presented at Alberta Gaming Research Institute Conference, March.

Wood, R. T. A., and Griffiths, M. D. (2008). 'Why Swedish people play online poker and factors that can increase or decrease trust in poker web sites: A qualitative investigation'. *Journal of Gambling Issues, 21,* 80–97.

Wood, R. T., and Williams, R. J. (2009). *Internet gambling: Prevalence, patterns, problems and policy options.* Final report prepared for the Ontario Problem Gambling Research Centre, Guelph, ON.

Wood, R. T., Williams, R. J., and Lawton, P. (2007). 'Why do Internet gamblers prefer online versus land-based venues?' *Journal of Gambling Issues, 20,* 235–50.

World Poker Rules. (2007). 'Sorel Mizzi & Chris Vaughn: A dissenting opinion'. Retrieved March 25, 2008 from http://www.worldpokerrules.com/news.php?id=368.

Yan, J. (2003). 'Security design in online games'. Retrieved June 1, 2010 from http://www.acsac.org/2003/papers/114.pdf.

Yan, J., and Randell, B. (2005). 'A systematic classification of cheating in online games'. NetGames '05. Retrieved March 10, 2007 from http://www.research.ibm.com/netgames2005/papers/yan.pdf.

Zacharias, J. (2004). 'Internet gambling: Is it worth the risk?' Retrieved March 20, 2007 from http://www.bcresponsiblegambling.ca/other/docs/internet_gambling_jan_zacharias.pdf.

Zangeneh, M., Griffiths, M., and Parke, J. (2008). 'The marketing of gambling'. In M. Zangeneh, A. Blaszczynski, and N. Turner (eds), *In the pursuit of winning: Problem gambling theory, research and treatment* (135–53). New York: Springer.

# 20 Policy options for Internet gambling

*Robert J. Williams, Robert T. Wood,*
*and Jonathan Parke*

## Continuum of legal approaches[1]

Online gambling exists on a legal continuum. Currently, several countries prohibit most or all forms of online gambling. This includes Bermuda, Cambodia, China, Cuba, Germany, Greece, India, Malaysia, Romania, South Africa, and the Ukraine. In addition, many (predominantly Islamic) countries ban online gambling by virtue of their ban on all forms of gambling: Afghanistan, Algeria, Bangladesh, Bhutan, Indonesia, Iran, Jordan, Libya, Mali, Oman, Pakistan, Qatar, Saudi Arabia, Somalia, Sudan, Syria, United Arab Emirates, and Yemen (Online Casino Suite, 2011). At the other end are countries that have either completely legalized, or at least permit, all forms of online gambling. These include Antigua and Barbuda, Austria, Gibraltar, Liechtenstein, Netherland Antilles, Panama, the Philippines, Slovakia, and the United Kingdom. In the middle are countries that have put some legal restrictions on it. For example, many countries allow certain forms (most typically online lotteries, instant lotteries, sports betting, horse racing) and make other forms illegal (most typically, casino games). Countries with this policy include Australia, Belgium, Brazil, Canadian provinces, Chile, Czech Republic, Denmark, Finland, France, Hong Kong, Hungary, Iceland, Israel, Italy, Japan, Latvia, Lithuania, Luxembourg, Macau, the Netherlands, New Zealand, Norway, Poland, Portugal, Russia, Singapore, Slovenia, South Korea, Sweden, Switzerland, Taiwan, and the United States. Several jurisdictions allow participation in online gambling from domestic sites, but prohibit residents from accessing online gambling outside the country. Jurisdictions with this approach include Austria, Belgium, Denmark, Estonia, France, Germany, Hong Kong, Hungary, Israel, Italy, Norway, Slovenia, South Korea, and the United States. Some countries go further to restrict patronage of domestic online sites to residents only (e.g., Austria, Canadian provinces, Finland, the Philippines). Finally, a few countries permit online gambling, but prohibit their own residents from accessing these sites (e.g., Australia for online casinos, Malta, Papua New Guinea).

Because of the newness of online gambling, there are also many countries that have no specific legislation that addresses it (e.g., many Central and South American countries (Fonseca-Sarmiento, 2010) and several African and Asian countries (Online Casino Suite, 2011)). The legal approach in many countries also tends to be in flux. For example, some countries with prohibitionist stances have subsequently legalized online gambling or have indicated an intent to legalize it (e.g., Greece, Romania). Other countries that previously had legal online gambling have subsequently opted for a more prohibitionist stance (e.g., Cyprus, Germany, Poland, Russia, South Africa). Many other countries have changed their regulations regarding permissible forms, or how online gambling can be delivered. Part of this is driven by legal challenges to restrictive gambling laws that interfere with the free flow of goods and services. In particular, the European Commission has pressured several countries that provide monopolistic online gambling to open their borders to competition from other member states in the European Economic Area (see Chapter 16; Hornle and Zammit, 2010; Littler, Hoekx, Fijnaut, and Verbeke, 2011). The World Trade Organization has taken similar action against the United States.[2]

This diversity of legal approaches to Internet gambling is reflective of the lack of consensus about the appropriate legal stance that should be taken. The fact of the matter is that there are several good arguments for both prohibition and legalization of Internet gambling. The primary purpose of this chapter is to elucidate these arguments to guide policy makers in their decision making.

## Legalization versus prohibition

The main arguments for legalization are as follows:

1   It is *very difficult to effectively prohibit online gambling.* This is because of the difficulty in blocking individual players' online access to these sites, and the difficulty in prosecuting companies that legally provide these services from other countries (e.g., Andrle, 2004; Bell, 1999; Clarke and Dempsey, 2001; Crowne-Mohammed and Andreacchi, 2009; Eadington, 2004; Friedrich, 2003; Parke and Griffiths, 2004; Watson, Liddell, Moore, and Eshee, 2004).

2   It is *never a good thing to have laws that are widely disregarded as it may foster disregard for the general rule of law.* Some commentators cite the widespread societal disregard for alcohol prohibition as a model of what would happen with online gambling prohibition (e.g., Schmitt, 2007).

3   Creating domestic online gambling sites would *stem the outflow of revenue that is leaving the country and create economic benefits for the jurisdiction* (employment, increased government revenue). In addition, some of the new online gambling revenues could be used for the prevention and treatment of online problem gambling (e.g., Bell, 1999; Vandall, 2008).

4   Legally regulated sites would *better ensure player protection* (fair games, responsible gambling practices) (e.g., Parke and Griffiths, 2004; Pereira de Sena, 2008; Watson et al., 2004) and deter such things as money laundering.[3] The player protection features that currently exist on many unregulated foreign sites tend to be fairly minimal (Wiebe, 2006; and see Chapter 1). Related to this point is that online gambling offers greater potential for player protection compared to many land-based forms of gambling. This is because the player's behaviour is recorded and therefore potentially available to analysis and automatic intervention (by either the player himself/herself or by a proactive operator).

5   It should *not be the job of the state to shape people's leisure behaviour* or how they spend their money even if engagement in this behaviour does harm some people (i.e., people should have freedom of choice) (e.g., Bell, 1999).

6   Research has found that the average household income of Internet gamblers tends to be *higher* than average (Wood and Williams, 2009). Thus, *a greater portion of Internet gambling revenue likely comes from middle and higher income people* relative to what occurs for other forms of gambling.

7   *It is inevitable* that online gambling will eventually be legally available on a widespread basis. In the past 30 years, whenever a new form of gambling or regulatory practice has

been introduced in one jurisdiction, most other jurisdictions have followed suit. Expansion of gambling to the Internet is also just a natural 'evolution' that takes advantage of this important new medium for game play, communication, and financial transactions. Financial markets experienced a similar expansion to the Internet in the late 1990s. Online stock trading is now widespread.

8    Online gambling offers *better value to the consumer*. Online sites have the potential of providing better odds to the consumer because of having lower overhead costs. In addition, anything that increases competition within the market will lower the cost of the product. This has been most evident with sports betting, where online sites have effectively eroded the 'take-out' or 'hold' of bookmakers, to the benefit of consumers (see Chapter 2).

9    Even if online gambling does initially increase rates of problem gambling, the evidence from land-based gambling suggests that, *over time, populations adapt to the presence of problematic products and develop some 'inoculation' from further harm* (LaPlante and Shaffer, 2007; Shaffer, LaBrie, and LaPlante, 2004). As evidence, the rates of problem gambling in Western countries have stabilized or declined in recent years despite continuing expansion of gambling availability and increased revenues (Williams, Volberg, and Stevens, 2012). Furthermore, an argument can be made that unless the populace will *never* be exposed to this product then it may be better to develop this inoculation early on rather than later.

However, there are also many compelling arguments for prohibition of Internet gambling and counterpoints to several of these above arguments:

1    *The purpose of the law is not to conform to people's behaviour, but to (a) help shape it, and (b) codify societal values.* There are several other online activities that are very difficult to control (e.g., child pornography, sites promoting illegal behaviour, sites containing hateful content toward certain groups). There are also many laws that the general public does not strictly adhere to (e.g., illicit substance use, drinking and driving, declaring all taxable income, etc.). However, just because a law is difficult to enforce does not mean that the activity should be legalized. Rather, legal efforts to limit these activities are somewhat helpful, and certainly preferable to no action and/or legalization.

There are three primary legal approaches to limiting illegal online gambling. One is legislation that prohibits the consumer from participating in it. This can be total prohibition of participation in all forms of online gambling as is done in China, or just prohibition of participation in foreign online gambling sites, as is done in Austria, Belgium, Denmark, Estonia, France, Germany, Hong Kong, Hungary, Israel, Italy, Norway, Slovenia, South Korea, and the United States.[4] However, the deterrent effect of these laws is likely very modest, as very few of these jurisdictions actively enforce these laws.

Another approach is to legally prohibit financial institutions from processing payments to online (usually foreign) gambling sites. This approach is currently used in Belgium, Estonia, France, Hungary, Israel, Malaysia, the Netherlands, Norway, and the USA. Here again, the deterrent effect of this legal approach is likely quite modest, considering that there are many foreign financial intermediaries that provide a means to circumvent these rules (some of which have been created to meet this need) (Wood and Williams, 2009).

A final approach is to legally constrain what citizens have access to via their Internet service provider (ISP). People are often reticent about 'Internet censorship' as they associate the concept with the pervasive Internet censorship that occurs in non-Western countries such as China, Cuba, Iran, North Korea, and Saudi Arabia (OpenNet Initiative, 2011). However, as simply another form of broadcast medium it is unclear why the Internet should be treated differently from current Western laws regarding what can be legally broadcast on television, radio, or newsprint. In any case, 'Internet censorship' has actually been occurring in Western jurisdictions for many years and is becoming increasingly common. Of their own initiative, ISPs in several countries have been filtering out content/websites that involve child pornography, promote hatred or violence against certain groups, or is offensive or illegal in some manner. This currently occurs in Australia, Belgium, Canada, Czech Republic, Denmark, Finland, Iceland, the Netherlands, New Zealand, Norway, Sweden, and the United Kingdom (OpenNet Initiative, 2011). Although ISPs in these countries have done this without any legal requirement to do so, governments in most of these countries have often subsidized, encouraged, or somehow facilitated these efforts (OpenNet Initiative, 2011).

A smaller group of Western jurisdictions have gone further and have explicitly legislated ISPs to filter out material unsuitable for minors (certain Australian states), child pornography (Italy, France, South Africa), illegal copyrighted content (France), or terrorism and racial hatred (France) (OpenNet Initiative, 2011). It is fair to say that the additional desire to restrict access to *online gambling* has helped spur these legislative constraints on ISP content. In 2006 Italy became the first country to require all Italian ISPs to block local access to a 'blacklist' of foreign online gambling sites (see Chapter 16). Several other Western countries have since enacted similar legislation: Belgium, Denmark, Estonia, France, Germany, Israel, Italy, and Slovenia. Although it is not that difficult for technologically sophisticated people to circumvent ISP blocking, it is nonetheless expected that this approach has somewhat greater deterrent effect than financial blocking or laws prohibiting consumer participation.

2   *General disregard for the rule of law is more of a risk when prohibiting something the majority of people engage in (e.g., alcohol use) rather than when prohibiting something only a minority of people engage in* (e.g., Internet gambling). The prevalence of Internet gambling in most countries *that do not expressly permit it* is only in the range of 0.1–3 percent (Wood and Williams, 2009). This is roughly equivalent to the worldwide prevalence of illicit 'hard' drug use (heroin, cocaine, ecstacy, methamphetamine) (UNODC, 2010), which very few countries have contemplated legalizing. Although the prevalence of Internet gambling may continue to increase in the next few years, it is also important to recognize that its relatively low market penetration after 16 years of existence (even in countries with permissive legislation) suggests it may only ever be a small niche market.

3   *Legalization will likely increase rates of problem gambling to some extent.* There are two reasons for this. One is simply the fact that legalization of a product or service usually provides sanctioning and increased availability. This, in turn, typically results in at least a temporary increase in overall use. This is evident when legalizing new forms of gambling (e.g., Williams, Belanger, and Arthur, 2011), as well as the legalization/ decriminalization of prostitution (Jakobsson and Kotsadam, 2011; Raymond, 2003), abortion (Alan Guttmacher Institute, 2008), and cannabis (MacCoun, 2010). Worldwide, the drugs that typically cause the most problems in society are usually not the illegal ones, but rather the legal ones: i.e., alcohol, prescription drugs, tobacco.[5]

The prevalence of online gambling in each country roughly parallels its legal availability (Wood and Williams, 2009). For example, the UK has one the world's most liberal Internet gambling laws as well as the world's highest known rate (past year) of Internet gambling (14 percent in 2010,[6] NCSR, 2011). Furthermore, there is good evidence of increased Internet gambling participation subsequent to legalization or liberalization (e.g., see Chapter 7). Unfortunately, one of the basic tenets of 'single distribution theory' is that *with increased overall participation comes a reliable increase in problematic use in the general population* (Grun and McKeigue, 2000; Lund, 2008; Rose, 1985).[7] Nonetheless, it is also important to recognize that with Internet gambling currently only being patronized by a small minority of the population, even if problem gambling rates doubled or tripled among Internet gamblers it would not affect population-wide problem gambling prevalence rates to any significant extent.

The second reason that legalization will likely increase rates of problem gambling to some extent is because the nature of online gambling makes it somewhat more problematic than most other forms of gambling. This is due to its greater convenience, 24-hour access, ability to play when intoxicated, lack of player protection features, the solitary nature of the play, the fact that gamblers are playing with 'electronic' cash, the ability to play multiple sites/games simultaneously, and because it is more difficult for *Internet* problem gamblers to curb their behaviour (i.e., it is much easier to avoid land-based casinos, racetracks, and bingo halls than it is to avoid computers or the Internet) (Griffiths, 1999, 2003; Griffiths and Parke, 2002; King, 1999; King and Barak, 1999; Schull, 2005; Wood, Williams, and Lawton, 2007).

Not surprisingly, then, research has found that the prevalence of problem gambling is three to four times higher among Internet gamblers compared to non-Internet gamblers (Griffiths and Barnes, 2008; Ladd and Petry, 2002; Wood and Williams, 2007, 2009; and see Chapters 7 and 11). However, as discussed in Chapter 11, much of this association has to do with the fact that problem gamblers tend to engage in a wide variety of gambling formats that often includes Internet gambling, whereas non-problem gamblers tend to participate at lower rates. Although controlling for number of gambling formats engaged in eliminates the relationship between Internet and problem gambling in most studies, an argument can be made that the very nature of Internet gambling promotes gambling versatility (Chapter 11). Online gambling has also been identified as a problematic form of gambling in population surveys and in some treatment settings at a rate higher than would be expected compared to population participation rates (e.g., Chapter 7). Finally, cross-sectional analysis does not disentangle the temporal course of events that may differentiate online gambling from other forms. Longitudinal research in Ontario, Canada, has found that Internet gambling leading to problem gambling tends to be a more common route than problem gambling leading to Internet gambling (Chapter 11).

4   *Player protection tools are likely to have modest efficacy.* It is true that online gambling gives online operators and players better ability (compared to some land-based forms of gambling) to potentially monitor online gambling behaviour and proactively intervene (e.g., algorithms that alert the player to 'risky' gambling behaviour, players setting limits on time or money spent, or allowing the person to temporarily block all his/her activity on the site) (see Chapter 13; Williams, 2010). It is also true that there is currently considerable interest among some operators to provide these tools.

However, the problem is that the pre-commitment constraints that most online sites allow players to impose tend to be voluntary, of short duration, and sometimes revocable. Drawing upon the lessons of problem gambling prevention research (Williams, West, and Simpson, 2007, 2008) as well as the research that exists on the general effectiveness of 'pre-commitment' strategies (land-based or online), it is reasonable to surmise that these types of constraints are of primary benefit to non-problem gamblers (which may or may not translate into a decreased future incidence of problem gambling), but are unlikely to have significant benefit to the compulsive and addictive behaviour of pathological gambling (Chapter 13; Nower and Blaszczynski, 2010; Williams, 2010).[8]

However, even if mandatory, longer-term, and irrevocable constraints were available (as they will undoubtedly be on a few of the more socially responsible sites[9]), a significant disadvantage of online gambling is the ability of the player to circumvent these restrictions by directing his/her play to over 2,000 other sites (recognizing that problem gamblers are much more likely than non-problem gamblers to patronize non-domestic sites to begin with, e.g., Chapter 7). It is very unlikely that there will ever be a system whereby constraints and/or banning at one site will be universally recognized and adopted at other sites. Despite many years of ongoing efforts to create industry-wide standards, only a minority of sites and/or owners have sought and/or received eCOGRA certification (eCommerce and Online Gaming Regulation and Assurance) or membership in the Remote Gambling Association (RGA) (Chapter 1).[10] Furthermore, the online gambling industry has expressed reluctance about cross-operator application of player-imposed restrictions because of privacy issues, cost, trust, and differing technology standards (Dragicevic, 2011). The reality is that effective preclusion of 'site jumping' minimally would require legislation requiring domestic ISPs to block foreign online gambling sites and for there to be active enforcement of this legislation.

There is also a potentially important historical lesson from alcohol. The reintroduction of legal alcohol following prohibition was coincident with, and facilitated by, the simultaneous introduction of several policies that were thought to have the ability to minimize the harm of alcohol (Catlin, 1931; Fosdick and Scott, 1933). For example, it was common in several Western jurisdictions to require people to apply to the police for a permit to purchase alcohol; for there to be limits on the amount of alcohol that could be purchased by any individual in a certain period of time; and for alcohol vendors to refuse to sell alcohol and/or blacklist customers who were buying suspicious amounts of alcohol (Catlin, 1931; Fosdick and Scott, 1933). Some jurisdictions (e.g., Quebec) allowed third parties (employers, relatives, ministers/priests) to ban the sale of alcohol to individuals they deemed unable to use it responsibly. In the United States, it was illegal to sell alcohol to any Native American Indian. Finland employed a buyer surveillance system which sent social workers for a home visit to those who seemed to be purchasing too much (Järvinen, 1991). The point being made is that the introduction of these 'consumer protection' policies helped facilitate the end of alcohol prohibition and reassure everyone that alcohol could be delivered in a safe fashion. However, almost all these policies were gradually eroded away following their initial introduction (despite their utility) and are now just a distant memory.

5   *Without ISP blocking, only a portion of online gamblers will patronize a new domestic site, resulting in small or negative financial benefits to the jurisdiction and a modest increase in overall player protection.* Creating new domestic opportunities provides no assurance that people will voluntarily patronize these domestic sites so as to capture the money that is leaving. This is a fairly saturated and mature market for new online companies trying to break in. Legally sanctioned domestic sites (with better business and responsible gambling practices) will only be patronized to the extent they offer a competitive advantage to the consumer, which is often difficult to achieve. Existing 'offshore' jurisdictions will always retain a strong competitive advantage because of their longer established presence as an Internet gambling host, fewer regulations, less

stringent enforcement of these regulations, and having much lower fees and taxes (Wilson, 2006).[11] The competitive advantages that larger and better-regulated jurisdictions possess include: better player protection (fairness of games, responsible gambling practices, etc.), a more stable political environment, better capital markets, better bandwidth and hosting capabilities, and a larger pool of skilled workers (American Gaming Association, 2006; Wilson, 2006).[12] However, it is clear that there will always be many sites available and willing to accept any patron with money.

Recognizing that overall prevalence will increase with legalization, unless there is an effective way of ensuring patronization of domestic sites (i.e., rigorous enforcement of ISP filtering/blocking), legalizing online gambling and providing domestic access may actually *increase* monetary outflow, rather than retaining it.[13] For example, the introduction of a legal domestic online poker site in Sweden in 2006 produced a significant increase in the prevalence of online poker play, but only a 27.5 percent capture of the market (although another 25 percent of Swedish online poker players reported patronizing several sites that included the domestic site) (see Chapter 7). In France, it is estimated that only 43 percent of the market is currently captured by legal domestic sites (MAG, 2011). In the UK, it has been claimed that only 25 percent of the estimated 2.5 billion pounds that UK consumers currently spend on Internet gambling goes to operators licensed by the UK Gambling Commission (UK Hansard, 2011).

It is also important to recognize that the amount of online gambling revenue currently leaving most jurisdictions is usually fairly insignificant and does not currently justify creating domestic sites to try to recoup it. For example, the Minister of Finance in the province of Ontario in Canada indicated that Ontario will be introducing online gambling in 2012, primarily 'to recoup an estimated $400 million per year that is spent on offshore sites' (Artuso, 2010). However, even if this figure were true, it compares to an Ontario Gross Domestic Product of $550 billion. Thus, the loss only constitutes 0.07 percent of GDP. Most other jurisdictions have a similar very small percentage of GDP going to online gambling.

6   *A significant portion of online gambling revenue comes from problem gamblers.* Prior research has established that problem gamblers contribute approximately a third of revenue from all types of gambling (Australian Productivity Commission, 1999; Williams and Wood, 2004, 2007). In a study by Wood and Williams (2009), problem gamblers accounted for 41.3 percent of all online gambling losses in Canada, and 27.0 percent internationally. It is ethically problematic to introduce new forms of revenue generation that are known to be disproportionately derived from a vulnerable segment of the population, especially in cases where the government is the primary operator and/or beneficiary.

7   *Online stock market trading has not been beneficial.* Research has found that investors who switched from phone-based to online trading trade more actively, more speculatively, and less profitably than before (underperforming the market by around 3 percent). This appears to be due to overconfidence, augmented by self-attribution bias and the illusions of knowledge and control (Odean and Barber, 2002). Furthermore, the greater individual investor access to the stock market that has occurred with online trading has significantly exacerbated the losses that individual investors typically make relative to less active and speculative institutional traders (Barber, Lee, Liu, and Odean, 2009). Online trading has also created a large number of 'day traders', who almost always lose money in the long run (Barber, Lee, Liu, and Odean, 2004).

8   *Legalizing online gambling and redirecting some of the revenue into prevention and treatment does not offset the harm that would likely be caused.* First, educational efforts

to prevent problem gambling have fairly limited efficacy (Williams et al., 2007, 2008). Second, most of the financial, psychological, social, work/school, and legal harms associated with problem gambling cannot be undone. Once an addiction has been established, a lifelong propensity for this behaviour has been created. Treatment helps decrease risk of relapse, but does not eliminate it. Internet problem gambling is also difficult thing to treat. As mentioned earlier, people who develop addictions to land-based forms of gambling can make efforts to avoid their exposure to these forms (and/or ban themselves). However, it is much more difficult for most people to avoid the use of computers or the Internet.

## Intermediate solutions

There are several intermediate solutions that tend to be more common than either total prohibition or total legalization. For example, less problematic and contentious forms of Internet gambling could be legalized (e.g., purchase of online lottery tickets or perhaps sports betting). The main concern here is that it then becomes a 'slippery slope'. Many jurisdictions that currently allow all forms of online gambling started with the legalization of online lotteries and sports/race betting and then expanded to other forms. More generally, the initial legalization of land-based lotteries in Western countries in the 1970s was followed by the successive legalization of all other forms of gambling in subsequent decades.

Another approach is just to prohibit access to foreign online gambling sites so as to decrease monetary outflow and to better ensure patronage of domestic sites with better player protection. However, without rigorous ISP filtering/blocking this type of legislation is difficult to enforce. As stated earlier, a downside of domestic legalization is that it will likely increase overall participation in Internet gambling and, therefore, at least a temporary increase in the numbers of problem gamblers.

A third option would be only to allow *non-residents* access to domestic sites (a strategy that was historically used for land-based casinos in many countries). While there is both economic and social value in such a policy, other countries are likely to see this as a Machiavellian and predatory approach. Furthermore, this policy also provides some legitimacy and potential encouragement of online play among domestic residents.

## The best legal approach is somewhat dependent on the individual jurisdiction

Support for prohibition, legalization, or something in-between hinges on the relative importance different individuals and different societies place on each of the above arguments. Furthermore, the 'best' regulatory stance will depend somewhat on the circumstances of the individual jurisdiction:

- Jurisdictional regions (e.g., Europe) that are able to establish high-quality industry practices across all individual jurisdictions have greater potential for delivering fair games, minimization of criminal activity, capture of the domestic market, and minimization of social harm.
- Jurisdictions with highly functional/resilient populations having low rates of social problems and addictive behaviour despite widespread availability of addictive products are not likely to be as negatively impacted by Internet gambling legalization as jurisdictions with more vulnerable populations having high rates of existing social problems and addictive behaviour.

- Jurisdictions with small populations will accrue proportionally greater economic benefits with Internet gambling legalization compared to large jurisdictions, as the majority of online gambling revenue for small jurisdictions will come from outside the jurisdiction (i.e., from the USA, China, and European countries with large populations), and represent a true influx of wealth rather than just domestic money being redistributed.
- Regulatory policy needs to take public attitudes into account. There are attitudinal differences between jurisdictions concerning whether online gambling should be legalized. Wood and Williams (2009) found that roughly 65 percent of people in Caribbean countries, Europe, and the United States favoured legalization of all forms of gambling, whereas this percentage was closer to 50 percent in Canada, Asia, and South America, and less than 45 percent in Africa, Australia, and New Zealand.

## Best way of providing legal online gambling

In jurisdictions where online gambling is permitted there is wide divergence concerning how it is provided and who provides it. There are four basic approaches:

- A free-market approach that allows commercial operators from any country to provide online gambling services in a manner similar to other commercial products (although sometimes taxed at a much higher rate). This is the approach used in countries such as Alderney, Antigua and Barbuda, Australia, Cyprus, Gibraltar, Ireland, Isle of Man, Italy, Kahnawà:ke Territory, Malta, and Netherland Antilles.
- Restricting the provision of all online gambling to one or two government-owned or -controlled providers. This is the approach currently used in countries such as Brazil, Canada, Denmark, Finland, Hungary, Iceland, Israel, Luxembourg, the Netherlands, Norway, Slovenia, South Korea, Sweden, and the Ukraine.
- Restricting the provision of all online gambling to private monopolies (e.g., Austria, Hong Kong, Macau, Portugal, Singapore).
- A mixture of government-controlled monopolies (most typically providing online lotteries) and private commercial offerings (e.g., Belgium, France, Liechtenstein, Lithuania, New Zealand, the Philippines, Slovakia, United Kingdom).

Essentially, the main issues are whether online gambling (a) should be provided by the government or private commercial provider(s), and (b) whether it should be provided by a single entity (monopoly) or multiple providers. An extensive literature exists on the benefits and drawbacks of each of these approaches in the delivery of various consumer products. It is beyond the scope of this chapter to provide a review of this more generic literature. However, it is worthwhile to at least identify the main issues as they potentially relate to online gambling.

One of the arguments in favour of government delivery/control of online gambling is that it better ensures all domestic gambling revenue will be captured and stay within the jurisdiction, something that would likely occur to a lesser extent with private delivery. However, this is not a particularly strong argument, as revenue capture from private delivery could be quite high if there were high taxation rates, and private operators were also required to be locally based. Furthermore, this approach redirects money from wealth-producing sectors of the economy (i.e., private business) to sectors not known for wealth creation (i.e., government) (e.g., Gwartney, Holcombe, and Lawson, 1998). Also, monopolistic delivery (of any kind) decreases the likelihood that online gambling will be provided in the most cost-efficient and commercially appealing manner, which may result in less overall revenue to the state.

Further to this last point, it is clear that competition among multiple online gambling providers better ensures a cost-efficient and appealing consumer product compared to monopolistic delivery (see Chapter 2). However, it must also be recognized that a free market may also come at the cost of less player protection, as an open marketplace creates competitive pressure for having fewer restrictions. For example, when casino gambling was first introduced throughout the United States in the late 1980s, several player protection policies were routinely put in place (e.g., small maximum bet limits, maximum loss limits, no credit, etc.). However, to obtain a competitive advantage, casinos that opened in neighbouring states tended to be slightly less restrictive (Schwartz, 2006). Over time, a level playing field developed such that currently there are almost no casino player protection policies in place in any state.[14] (Note also the earlier point about restrictions on alcohol provision gradually being eliminated after they were initially implemented.) There is no doubt that this movement toward an unrestricted playing environment is partly driven by player preference. However, what may be preferred by most is not necessarily the best for everybody or for society more generally.[15]

A stronger argument for government control/delivery of online gambling is that it potentially provides better player protection because protection of its citizens would be of greater concern to the government than a private commercial provider (especially if it were offered in a monopolistic way where there would be less need to compete with commercial offerings). There are some important lessons from the alcohol field, where the evidence indicates that monopolistic and/or government involvement in alcohol provision is associated with less harm to the general public (Miller, Snowden, Birckmayer, and Hendrie, 2006; Popova et al., 2011; Trolldal, 2005; Wagenaar and Holder, 1996). However, the argument is sometimes made that acting in the best interests of its citizens is seriously compromised in the situation where the government also receives major financial benefits from the activity (Adams, Raeburn, and de Silva, 2009; Orford, 2009). While it is clear that prevention and treatment initiatives for problem gambling are more common in jurisdictions where government is the provider of gambling and/or receives most of the revenue (e.g., Canada, most European countries), it is also clear that most of the prevention initiatives that governments have chosen to implement have also tended to be the least effective ones that do not compromise revenue (Williams, West, and Simpson, 2007, 2008).[16]

## Notes

1   The information in this section was collected by the first author from a considerable number of sources too numerous to list. Certain online gambling portals were helpful starting points: www.casinocity.com, www.gamingzion.com, and www.onlinecasinosuite.com (World Gambling Review). Because the legal/regulatory situation is in constant flux, the information provided in this section should only be considered accurate as of July 2011.

2   In 2004 the World Trade Organization (WTO) ruled that the US prohibition of online cross-border gambling services offered by Antigua and Barbuda to US customers violated its commitment to free trade in gambling services it had made in the General Agreement on Trade in Services (GATS) (Kelly, 2006; Rose, 2007). A US appeal of this ruling in 2005 was unsuccessful. The appeal ruling noted that a legally permissible prohibition of online gambling to protect 'public morals' or 'maintain the public order' could not be used because the US legally permits telephone and online wagering on horse racing across state lines. It is important to note that the USA has not altered its prohibitionist stance toward online gambling despite these 2004 and 2005 WTO rulings.

3  This is similar to the arguments put forward for legalization of illicit drugs, prostitution, and euthanasia, and to the historical arguments for the legalization of gambling and alcohol.

4  The information in this section was collected and verified by the first author from dozens of different sources. Because the legal/regulatory situation is in constant flux, the information provided in this section should only be considered accurate as of July 2011.

5  This is not to say that the legal status of these drugs is exclusively responsible for their high rate of associated problems (i.e., alcohol would still cause problems even it is were illegal, due to its popularity).

6  Although 50 percent of this is only buying lottery tickets online.

7  This is an overall relationship that obscures differential impacts within specific subgroups.

8  Only a minority of people use player protection tools when they are voluntary, and often not the people most in need of these restraints (Williams, 2010). It is also unrealistic to expect that compulsive gamblers will be ready and able to gamble responsibly following a one-week or one-month imposed break. The primary benefit to problem gamblers who opt to use these tools is likely the ability of these tools to potentially inhibit within-session 'chasing' (at that particular site).

9  As exists in land-based gambling, there will always be a minority of jurisdictions that implement truly effective prevention techniques. However, this practice will never be widespread, partly because of the philosophical orientation of many gambling providers that the onus for responsible play lies with the player, and partly because truly effective prevention techniques compromise profits (see Point 6).

10  In August 2011, eCOGRA listed 165 approved sites, only somewhat higher than the 116 listed in August 2007. Furthermore, only 4 of the top 50 online gambling sites identified by www.online.casinocity.com currently have eCOGRA certification (i.e., Party Poker, 888 Casino, Party Casino, bwin Sportbook). The RGA only has 30 member companies, with only 12 of the top 50 site owners identified by www.online.casinocity.com as having membership.

11  For example, Kahnawà:ke only charges a $10,000 annual licensing fee, with no taxes. By comparison, the UK imposes a 15 percent tax on online gambling profits.

12  A survey of six of the world's largest online gambling operators found that their choice of jurisdiction in which to locate their operations was primarily based on the ability to repatriate funds; bandwidth and hosting capabilities; low gambling taxes; a commercial regulator; clear and comprehensive regulations; stable policy; and low corporate taxes (Mpande Advisors, 2005).

13  This is the lesson of creating domestic casinos in North America in an attempt to capture gambling dollars that were being spent in Nevada and Atlantic City. The first author (Williams) has studied this in the provinces of Ontario, British Columbia, and Alberta, and in all cases found that trips to out-of-province casinos *increased* subsequent to the creation of domestic casinos (Blue Thorn Research et al., 2007; Williams, Belanger, and Arthur, 2011). Nevada actually experienced one of its greatest periods of expansion and increased revenues coincident with the introduction of domestic casinos in Canada and the United States in the late 1980s and 1990s. One reason for this is that the creation of domestic gambling opportunities tends to increase overall participation in casino gambling, which leads to a corresponding increase in out-of-jurisdiction casino patronization. Another reason appears to be that participation in domestic casino gambling increases people's interest in visiting major international gambling destinations.

14  One of the very last player protection policies remaining was Missouri's prohibiting casino gamblers from losing more than $500 in two hours. This maximum loss policy was recently removed after several years of intensive lobbying by the Missouri casino industry to 'level the playing field' (Volkmann, 2008).

15  There are many laws that put constraints on the general public's unfettered use/ownership/provision of firearms, motor vehicles, and alcohol, even though these laws are primarily needed to deter the activities of a small minority of people who may use these things irresponsibly. Most people (not all!) accept these general restrictions, as it helps produce a healthier/safer society overall.

16  Most of these initiatives have focused on the fairly weak strategy of better education of consumers as opposed to more effective policy initiatives that constrain the availability of gambling and how it is provided. This is not the case in all jurisdictions. Some countries have enacted legislation that targets this conflict of interest and/or requires gambling providers (government or otherwise) to *effectively* mitigate the harm from the provision of gambling. This has been done to some extent in Germany, the Netherlands, and Switzerland. Germany has legislation that among other things (a)

prohibits the pay of gambling provider executives to be tied to gambling revenue; (b) requires that the monitoring of compliance with gambling regulations be done by authorities not connected to the fiscal interests of the state; (c) requires all new gambling products to be reviewed by an advisory board of gambling addiction experts prior to their introduction; (d) requires gambling providers to detect and exclude problem gamblers from gambling venues (Meyer, Hayer, and Griffiths, 2009). The Netherlands prohibits gambling providers from making a personal profit. All games are either for 'good causes' or taxes; the one exception is slot machines outside of casinos.

# References

Adams, P. J., Raeburn, J., and de Silva, K. (2009). 'A question of balance: Prioritizing public health responses to harm from gambling'. *Addiction, 104,* 688–91.

Alan Guttmacher Institute (2008). *Facts on Induced Abortion in the United States.* GuttmacherInstitute, on line http://www.guttmacher.org/pubs/fb_induced_abortion.html

American Gaming Association (2006). 'An analysis of Internet gambling and its policy implications'. AGA 10th Anniversary White Paper Series. http://www.americangaming.org/assets/files/studies/wpaper_internet_0531.pdf

Andrle, J. D. (2004). 'A winning hand: A proposal for an international regulatory schema with respect to the growing online gambling dilemma in the United States'. *Vanderbilt Journal of Transnational Law, 37,* 1389–422.

Artuso, A. (2010, August 10). 'Ontario wagers online gambling a winner'. *Ottawa Sun.* Retrieved from http://www.ottawasun.com/news/canada/2010/08/10/14981586.html

Australian Productivity Commission (1999). *Australia's Gambling Industries* (Report No. 10). Canberra: AusInfo.

Barber, B. M., Lee, Y-T., Liu, Y-J., and Odean, T. (2004). 'Do individual day traders make money?' Evidence from Taiwan [Working Paper]. Retrieved from http://faculty.haas.berkeley.edu/odean/papers/Day%20Traders/Day%20Trade%20040330.pdf

Barber, B. M., Lee, Y-T., Liu, Y-J., and Odean, T. (2009). 'Just how much do individual investors lose by trading?' *Review of Financial Studies, 21,* 785–818.

Bell, T. (1999, March 8). *Internet Gambling: Popular, Inexorable and (Eventually) Legal* (PolicyAnalysis no. 336.) Retrieved from http://www.cato.org/pubs/pas/pa336.pdf

Blue Thorn Research, Population Health Promotion Associates, PFIA Corporation, and Williams, R. J. (2007). *Socioeconomic Impacts of New Gaming Venues in Four British Columbia Lower Mainland Communities: Final Report.* Submitted to the Gaming Policy and Enforcement Branch, Ministry of Public Safety & Solicitor General, Government of British Columbia. Retrieved from http://www.pssg.gov.bc.ca/gaming/reports/docs/rpt-rg-impact-study-final.pdf

Catlin, G. E. G. (1931) *Liquor Control.* New York: Henry Holt; London: Thornton Butterworth.

Clarke, R., and Dempsey, G. (2001). 'The feasibility of regulating gambling on the Internet'. *Managerial and Decision Economics, 22*(1–3), 125–32.

Crowne-Mohammed, E. A., and Andreacchi, R. (2009). 'The unavailability of common law remedies for victims of online gambling fraud'. *Gaming Law Review and Economics, 13*(4), 304–9.

Dragicevic, S. (2011). 'Time for change: The industry's approach to self-exclusion'. *World Online Gambling Law Report, 10*(7), 06–08.

Eadington, W. R. (2004). 'The future of online gambling in the United States and elsewhere'. *Journal of Public Policy and Marketing, 23,* 214–19.

Fonseca-Sarmiento, C. (2010). '10 considerations for implementing Internet gambling in Latin America'. *Gaming Law Review and Economics, 14*(2), 75–9.

Fosdick, R. B., and Scott, A. L. (1933). *Toward Liquor Control.* New York & London: Harper & Brothers.

Friedrich, T. J. (2003). 'Internet casino gambling: The nightmare of lawmaking, jurisdiction, enforcement, and the dangers of prohibition'. *Common Law Conspectus, 11*(2), 369–88.

Griffiths, M. D. (1999). 'Gambling technologies: Prospects for problem gambling'. *Journal of Gambling Studies, 15*(3), 265–83.

— (2003). 'Internet gambling: Issues, concerns, and recommendations'.*CyberPsychology & Behavior, 6*(6), 557–68.

Griffiths, M. D., and Barnes, A. (2008). 'Internet gambling: An online empirical study among student gamblers'. *International Journal of Mental Health and Addiction, 6,* 194–204.

Griffiths, M. D., and Parke, J. (2002). 'The social impact of Internet gambling'. *Social Science Computer Review, 20*(3), 312–20.

Grun, L., and McKeigue, P. (2000). 'Prevalence of excessive gambling before and after introduction of a national lottery in the United Kingdom: Another example of the single distribution theory'. *Addiction, 95*(6), 959–66.

Gwartney, J., Holcombe, R., and Lawson, R. (1998). 'The scope of government and the wealth of nations'. *Cato Journal, 18*(2), 163–90.

Hornle, J., and Zammit, B. (2010). *Cross-Border Online Gambling Law and Policy.* Cheltenham, UK: Edward Elgar.

Jakobsson, N., and Kotsadam, A. (2011). 'The law and economics of international sex slavery: Prostitution laws and trafficking for sexual exploitation'. *European Journal of Law and Economics.* Advance online publication. doi: 10.1007/s10657-011-9232-0.

Järvinen, M. (1991) 'Controlled controllers: Women, men and alcohol'. *Contemporary Drug Problems 18,* 389–406.

Kelly, J. M. (2006). 'Clash in the Caribbean: Antigua and U.S. dispute Internet gambling and GATS'. *UNLV Gaming Research and Review Journal, 10*(1), 15–19.

King, S. A. (1999). 'Internet gambling and pornography: Illustrative examples of the psychological consequences of communication anarchy'. *CyberPsychology and Behavior, 2*(3), 175–93.

King, S. A., and Barak, A. (1999). 'Compulsive Internet gambling: A new form of an old clinical pathology'. *CyberPsychology & Behavior, 2*(5), 441–56.

Ladd, G. T., and Petry, N. M. (2002). 'Disordered gambling among university-based medical and dental patients: A focus on Internet gambling'. *Psychology of Addictive Behaviors, 16(1*), 76–9.

LaPlante, D. A., and Shaffer, H. J. (2007). 'Understanding the influence of gambling opportunities: Expanding exposure models to include adaptation'. *American Journal of Orthopsychiatry, 77,* 616–23.

Littler, A., Hoekx, N., Fijnaut, C., and Verbeke, A-L. (2011). *In the Shadow of Luxembourg: EU and National Developments in the Regulation of Gambling.* Netherlands: Martinus Nijhoff.

Lund, I. (2008). 'The population mean and the proportion of frequent gamblers: Is the theory of total consumption valid for gambling?' *Journal of Gambling Studies, 24*(2), 247–56.

MacCoun, R. J. (2010). *Estimating the Non-Price Effects of Legalization on Cannabis Consumption* [Working Paper]. Rand Drug Policy Research Center. Retrieved from http://www.rand.org/content/dam/rand/pubs/working_papers/2010/RAND_WR767.pdf

MAG (2011, February 3). *'Jeux en ligne' in the French Market: Key Features, Strengths and Weaknesses of the French Legal Gaming Offer.* Retrieved from http://www.mag-ca.it/Download_k_files/%22Jeux%20en%20ligne%E2%80%9D%20in%20the%20French%20Market_2011.pdf

Meyer, G., Hayer, T. and Griffiths, M. (2009). *Problem gambling in Europe: Challenges, prevention, and interventions.* New York: Springer.

Miller, T., Snowden, C., Birckmayer, J., Hendrie, D. (2006). 'Retail alcohol monopolies, underage drinking, and youth impaired driving deaths'. *Accident Analysis & Prevention, 38*(6), 1162–7.

Mpande Advisors (2005, October). *Report on the Regulation of Interactive Gambling.* Pretoria, South Africa: National Gambling Board. Retrieved from http://www.ngb.org.za/uploads/reportOnTheRegulationOfInteractiveGambling1.pdf

National Centre for Social Research (NCSR) (2011). *British Gambling Prevalence Survey 2010.* Report prepared for the UK Gambling Commission. Retrieved from http://www.gamblingcommission.gov.uk/PDF/British Gambling Prevalence Survey 2010.pdf

Nower, L., and Blaszczynski, A. (2010). 'Gambling motivations, money-limiting strategies, and precommitment preferences of problem versus non-problem gamblers'. *Journal of Gambling Studies, 26,* 361–72.

Odean, T., and Barber, B. M. (2002). 'Online investors: Do the slow die first?' *Review of Financial Studies, 15*(2), 455–87.

Online Casino Suite (2011). 'Worldwide gambling: International betting laws by country'. Retrieved from http://onlinecasinosuite.com/website/

OpenNet Initiative (2011). *Country Profiles* [an updated online source of information concerning current Internet censorship policies and practices in each country]. Retrieved from http://opennet. net/research/profiles

Orford, J. (2009). 'Governments as promoters of dangerous consumptions'. *Addiction, 104,* 693–5.

Parke, A. J., and Griffiths, M. (2004). 'Why Internet gambling prohibition will ultimately fail'. *Gaming Law Review, 8*(4), 295–9.

Pereira de Sena, P. (2008). 'Internet gambling prohibition in Hong Kong: Law and policy'. *Hong Kong Law Journal, 38*(2), 453–92.

Popova, S., Patra, J., Sarnocinska-Hart, A., Gnam, W. H., Giesbrecht, N., and Rehm, J. (2011). 'Cost of privatization versus government alcohol retailing systems: Canadian example'. *Drug and Alcohol Review.* doi:10.1111/j.1465–3362.2010.00276.x.

Raymond, J. G. (2003). 'Ten reasons for not legalizing prostitution'. In M. Farley (ed.), *Prostitution, Trafficking and Traumatic Stress* (315–32). New York: Haworth Press.

Rose, G. (1985). 'Sick individuals and sick populations'. *International Journal of Epidemiology, 14,* 32–8.

Rose, I. N. (2007). 'Gambling and the Law: The U.S. fails again (and again and again) in the WTO'. *Gaming Law Review, 11*(3), 185–8.

Schmitt, M. D. (2007). 'Prohibition reincarnated – the uncertain future of online gambling following the Unlawful Internet Gambling Enforcement Act of 2006'. *Southern California Interdisciplinary Law Journal, 17,* 381–404.

Schull, N. D. (2005). 'Digital gambling: The coincidence of desire and design'. *Annals of the American Academy of Political and Social Science, 597*(1), 65–81.

Schwartz, D. G. (2006). *Roll the Bones: The History of Gambling.* New York: Gotham Books.

Shaffer, H. J., LaBrie, R. A., and LaPlante, D. (2004). 'Laying the foundation for quantifying regional exposure to social phenomena: Considering the case of legalized gambling as a public health toxin'. *Psychology of Addictive Behaviors, 18*(1), 40–8.

Trolldal, B. (2005). 'An investigation of the effect of privatization of retail sales of alcohol on consumption and traffic accidents in Alberta, Canada'. *Addiction, 100*(5), 662–71.

UK Hansard (2011, January 20). *UK House of Commons Daily Hansard.* Column 1036. Retrieved from http://www.publications.parliament.uk/pa/cm201011/cmhansrd/cm110120/debtext/110120–0002. htm

United Nations Office on Drugs and Crime (UNODC) (2010). *World Drug Report 2010.* United Nations Publications: New York. Retrieved from http://www.unodc.org/unodc/en/data-and-analysis/WDR-2010.html

Vandall, F. (2008). 'Why we are outraged: An economic analysis of Internet gambling'. *Richmond Journal of Global Law and Business, 7*(3), 291–6.

Volkmann, K. (2008, November 5). 'Casinos prepare to stop limiting losses'. *www.BizJournals.com.* Retrieved from http://www.bizjournals.com/stlouis/stories/2008/11/03/daily34.html?b=122568840 0%5E1728146&brthrs=1

Wagenaar, A. C., and Holder, H. D. (1996). 'The scientific process works: Seven replications now show significant wine sales increases after privatization'. *Journal of Studies on Alcohol, 57*(5), 575–6.

Wardle, H., Sproston, K., Orford, J., Erens, B., Griffiths, M., Constantine, R., and Pigott, S. (2007). *British Gambling Prevalence Survey 2007.* London: National Centre for Social Research. Retrieved from   http://www.gamblingcommission.gov.uk/research_consultations/research/bgps/bgps_2007. aspx

Watson, S., Liddell, P., Moore, R. S., and Eshee, W. D. (2004). 'The legalization of Internet gambling: A consumer protection perspective'. *Journal of Public Policy & Marketing, 23*(2), 209–13.

Wiebe, J. (2006). 'Internet gambling safeguards: What are online gaming sites doing to protect customers?' *Newslink*, Fall/Winter, 4–6. Published by the Responsible Gambling Council. Retrieved July 12, 2007 from http://www.responsiblegambling.org/articles/NewslinkFallWinter2006.pdf

Williams, R. J. (2010). *Pre-Commitment as a Strategy for Minimizing Gambling-Related Harm.* White Paper prepared for Unisys Australia Pty Limited and Responsible Gaming Networks (Victoria, Australia). July 8. Submission to Parliament of Australia Inquiry into Pre-Commitment Systems. http://hdl.handle.net/10133/1287

Williams, R. J., and Wood, R. T. (2004). 'The proportion of gaming revenues derived from problem gamblers: Examining the issues in a Canadian context'. *Analysis of Social Problems and Public Policy, 4*(1), 1–13.

Williams, R. J., and Wood, R. T. (2007). 'The proportion of Ontario gambling revenue derived from problem gamblers'. *Canadian Public Policy, 33*(3), 367–88.

Williams, R. J., Belanger, Y. D., and Arthur, J. N. (2011). *Gambling in Alberta: History, Current Status, and Socioeconomic Impacts.* Final Report prepared for the Alberta Gaming Research Institute. April 2, 2011. Retrieved from http://hdl.handle.net/1880/48495

Williams, R. J., Volberg, R. A., and Stevens, R. M. G. (2012). *Population Assessment of Problem Gambling: Methodological Influences, Standardized Rates, Jurisdictional Differences, and Worldwide Trends*. Report prepared for the Ontario Ministry of Health and Long-Term Care and the Ontario Problem Gambling Research Centre.

Williams, R. J., West, B. L., and Simpson, R. I. (2007). 'Prevention of problem gambling'. In G. Smith, D. C. Hodgins, and R. J. Williams (eds), *Research and Measurement Issues in Gambling Studies* (399–435). Burlington, MA: Elsevier.

Williams, R. J., West, B. L., and Simpson, R. I. (2008). *Prevention of Problem/PathologicalGambling: A Comprehensive Review of the Evidence.* Report prepared for the Ontario Problem Gambling Research Centre. Guelph, Ontario, CANADA. Retrieved from http://hdl.handle.net/10133/414

Wilson, P. (2006, August). 'Remote gambling and the 2005 Act – Is a UK license worth the trouble?' Presentation at the Global Remote and E-Gambling Research Institute Conference. Amsterdam, Netherlands. Retrieved July 12, 2007 from http://www.gregri.org/files/conference/Peter_Wilson.pdf

Wood, R. T., and Williams, R. J. (2007). 'Problem gambling on the Internet: Implications for Internet gambling policy in North America'. *New Media & Society, 9*(3), 520–42.

Wood, R. T. and Williams, R. J. (2009). *Internet Gambling: Prevalence, Patterns, Problems, and Policy Options.* Final Report prepared for the Ontario Problem Gambling Research Centre, Guelph, Ontario. Retrieved from http://hdl.handle.net/10133/693

Wood, R. T., Williams, R. J., and Lawton, P. (2007). 'Why do Internet gamblers prefer online versus land-based venues?' *Journal of Gambling Issues, 20* (June), 235–50. Retrieved from http://hdl.handle.net/10133/375

# Index